"Today, the promises and pitfalls of multiculturalism, internationalism and globalization fill our headlines and our daily lives. As a result, there is an increasingly urgent need for peacemakers who can bring sensitivity, insight, evidence and skill to helping us navigate cultural differences, particularly those that are deep, invisible and sacred. This extraordinary book—*The Routledge Handbook of Intercultural Mediation*—is the most current and comprehensive resource for those intrepid mediators who serve as our guides in these tumultuous times. It will serve as the canon for this work, and a treasured resource for decades to come."

Peter T. Coleman, *Professor of Psychology and Education, Director of the Morton Deutsch International Center for Cooperation and Conflict Resolution at Columbia University, USA*

"I cannot think of a better volume to help us make sense of the avalanche of intercultural 'nightmares' that we have been facing since early 2020—and before that! Dominic Busch has managed to put together a stimulating interdisciplinary and visionary compendium around intercultural mediation. Together with the authors they remind us that mediation does not just matter in times of emergencies but that it is pivotal to the very notion of interculturality at all times. The handbook retells the past of intercultural mediation, keeps us up to date with today's research and inspires us for the future. It should be on everyone's must-read list."

Fred Dervin, *Professor of Multicultural Education, University of Helsinki, Finland*

"The ideas and practices of intercultural mediation draw (or at least, should draw) from a wide variety of subject matter, fields and research traditions. A thorough academic treatment that crosses all these 'silos' is overdue, and *The Routledge Handbook of Intercultural Mediation* addresses this gap in style. Its array of authors shows not only the expected level of expertise as well as the range of cultures and nations for such a work, but also a creative selection of fields and backgrounds. A list of the wide variety of research settings in this book might begin with the sciences, business, law, engineering, health care and linguistics, but it won't end there. This is an essential resource for anyone who is trying to understand what mediators can do, and how they can improve, in the complex interactions that make up intercultural work."

Christopher Honeyman, *Managing Partner at Convenor Conflict Management, Washington, DC, USA*

"A global pandemic, geopolitical ructions, social and economic inequality, and the rise of artificial intelligence provide stark reminders as to why intercultural mediation continues to matter. Learning to live well together is an enduring project of humanity, and understanding how to achieve this remains at the core of the concept and practices of intercultural mediation. This volume traces the evolution of this term and its various manifestations across diverse disciplines, paradigms and cultural worldviews. It represents a comprehensive, rich and compelling account of why intercultural mediation remains crucial for reciprocal engagement, justice and peace that must occur if we are to come together to face the great challenges that lie ahead."

Michelle Kohler, *Senior Research Fellow, Research Centre for Languages and Cultures, UniSA: Justice and Society, University of South Australia, Australia*

"This collection is particularly broad, being interdisciplinary and international as well as intercultural, including the topics covered, disciplines represented, and chapter authors, and thus should be relevant to an uncommonly large group of researchers, practitioners, and students."

Wendy Leeds-Hurwitz, *Director of the Center for Intercultural Dialogue and Professor Emerita at the University of Wisconsin-Parkside, USA*

"The new handbook weaves together interdisciplinary insights into the role of intercultural mediation in situations of conflict, dialogue, and more inclusive forms of community-building across varied cultural and organizational contexts. As well as contributing to debates about the meanings of culture and interculturality, the book provides a nuanced view of the field, laying out theoretical achievements and gaps and identifying promising practices."

Kirstie McAllum, *Department of Communication, Université de Montréal, Canada*

"A unique and stimulating collection of perspectives and insights on the interplay between mediation and culture. The authors come from a wide array of disciplines and cultures and explore a variety of situations at different levels of abstraction. This book can enrich anyone's ability to recognize, understand, and deal wisely with cultural influences in mediation—and other situations."

Leonard L. Riskin, *Visiting Professor, Northwestern University Pritzker School of Law, USA*

"Given the numerous wars between nations and violent conflicts within nations in today's world, it's obvious that neutral third parties trained in intercultural mediators are needed to help resolve such conflicts. In light of this, *The Handbook of Intercultural Mediation* should be required reading for this important group of professional mediators."

Joseph A. Scimecca, *Professor of Sociology, George Mason University, USA*

"*The Routledge Handbook of Intercultural Mediation* is a *tour de force*. This work is a dazzling achievement written with great skill by a global community of scholars, and whose usefulness will have a long life. This book makes a significant contribution toward nonviolent social change, especially when placed against the backdrop of the current urgencies of global pandemic and the horrors of war. Beginning with an initial review of the literature, the stage is set for current and future researchers and practitioners to reexamine how they (we) have thought about culture, conflict, and community. As the reader is invited to assume roles of observer and participant, an impressive gathering of international contributors explores diverse aspects of intercultural mediation as a process of dispute resolution, a byproduct of translation and pedagogy, and as a communicative or socio-political aspiration. These authors present a wide range of approaches, disciplines, voices, and perspectives that highlight, yet bring cohesion to disparate epistemological and methodological tensions."

Mary Adams Trujillo, *Professor Emerita of Communication Arts and Conflict Transformation, North Park University, USA*

"Full of innovative approaches and observations, including alternatives to and critiques of a Western-only approach to mediation, this *Handbook of Intercultural Mediation* is a treatment of mediation that examines interculturality as it should be done- comprehensively, globally, and respectfully. This volume, appearing as the world struggles with the global impact of both epidemic and war, could hardly be more timely. It is unique in bringing both depth and breadth to the topic of intercultural mediation. Especially remarkable for the range of scales represented, from analyses of language to international politics, the volume is destined to be a touchstone for work in mediation, and for intercultural studies generally, for years to come."

Geoffrey White, *Professor Emeritus, Department of Anthropology, University of Hawai'i, USA*

THE ROUTLEDGE HANDBOOK OF INTERCULTURAL MEDIATION

Offering unique coverage of an emerging, interdisciplinary area, this comprehensive handbook examines the theoretical underpinnings and emergent conceptions of intercultural mediation in related fields of study.

Authored by global experts in fields from intercultural communication and conflict resolution to translation studies, literature, political science, and foreign language teaching, chapters trace the history, development, and present state of approaches to intercultural mediation. The sections in this volume show how the concept of intercultural mediation has been constructed among different fields and shaped by its specific applications in an open cycle of influence. This book parses different philosophical conceptions as well as pragmatic approaches, providing ample grounding in the key perspectives on this growing field of discourse.

The Routledge Handbook of Intercultural Mediation is a valuable reference for graduate and postgraduate students studying mediation, conflict resolution, intercultural communication, translation, and psychology, as well as for practitioners and researchers in those fields and beyond.

Dominic Busch is a full professor of intercultural communication and conflict research at the faculty of human sciences, University of the Bundeswehr Munich, Germany.

ROUTLEDGE HANDBOOKS IN COMMUNICATION STUDIES

The Routledge Handbook of Strategic Communication
Edited By Derina Holtzhausen and Ansgar Zerfass

The Routledge Handbook of Digital Writing and Rhetoric
Edited by Jonathan Alexander and Jacqueline Rhodes

The Routledge Handbook of Positive Communication
Edited by José Antonio Muñiz Velázquez and Cristina M. Pulido

The Routledge Handbook of Mass Media Ethics
Edited by Lee Wilkins and Clifford G. Christians

The Routledge Handbook of Comparative World Rhetorics: Studies in the History, Application, and Teaching of Rhetoric Beyond Traditional Greco-Roman Contexts
Edited by Keith Lloyd

The Routledge Handbook of Media Use and Well-Being: International Perspectives on Theory and Research on Positive Media Effects
Edited by Leonard Reinecke and Mary Beth Oliver

The Routledge Handbook of Queer Rhetoric
Edited by Jonathan Alexander and Jacqueline Rhodes

The Routledge Handbook of Nonprofit Communication
Edited by Gisela Gonçalves and Evandro Oliveira

The Routledge Handbook of Intercultural Mediation
Edited by Dominic Busch

The Routledge Handbook of Corporate Social Responsibility Communication
Edited by Amy O'Connor

For a full list of titles in this series, please visit www.routledge.com/series/RHCS

THE ROUTLEDGE HANDBOOK OF INTERCULTURAL MEDIATION

Edited by Dominic Busch

NEW YORK AND LONDON

Designed cover image: © monaMonash / Getty

First published 2023
by Routledge
605 Third Avenue, New York, NY 10158

and by Routledge
4 Park Square, Milton Park, Abingdon, Oxon, OX14 4RN

Routledge is an imprint of the Taylor & Francis Group, an informa business

© 2023 selection and editorial matter, Dominic Busch; individual chapters, the contributors

The right of Dominic Busch to be identified as the author of the editorial material, and of the authors for their individual chapters, has been asserted in accordance with sections 77 and 78 of the Copyright, Designs and Patents Act 1988.

All rights reserved. No part of this book may be reprinted or reproduced or utilised in any form or by any electronic, mechanical, or other means, now known or hereafter invented, including photocopying and recording, or in any information storage or retrieval system, without permission in writing from the publishers.

Trademark notice: Product or corporate names may be trademarks or registered trademarks, and are used only for identification and explanation without intent to infringe.

Library of Congress Cataloguing-in-Publication Data
Names: Busch, Dominic, 1976–editor.
Title: The Routledge handbook of intercultural mediation / edited by Dominic Busch.
Description: New York, NY : Routledge, 2023. | Includes bibliographical references and index. |
Identifiers: LCCN 2022020757 (print) | LCCN 2022020758 (ebook) |
ISBN 9781032129747 (hardback) | ISBN 9781032130606 (paperback) |
ISBN 9781003227441 (ebook)
Subjects: LCSH: Intercultural communication. | Cross-cultural studies. |
Communication and culture.
Classification: LCC HM1211 .R68 2023 (print) | LCC HM1211 (ebook) | DDC
303.48/2--dc23/eng/20220518
LC record available at https://lccn.loc.gov/2022020757
LC ebook record available at https://lccn.loc.gov/2022020758

ISBN: 978-1-032-12974-7 (hbk)
ISBN: 978-1-032-13060-6 (pbk)
ISBN: 978-1-003-22744-1 (ebk)

DOI: 10.4324/9781003227441

Typeset in Bembo
by MPS Limited, Dehradun

CONTENTS

List of figures	*xii*
List of tables	*xiii*
Notes on contributors	*xiv*
Preface by Dominic Busch	*xxvi*

Introduction: The interdisciplinary vision of intercultural mediation 1
Dominic Busch

PART I
Professional intercultural dispute mediation **21**

1 Culture and mediation: A 2020s perspective on early criticism of Western
  paradigms 23
  Greg Bond

2 Cross-cultural disputes and mediator strategies 30
  Carrie Menkel-Meadow

3 De-essentializing notions of self and identity in mediation 43
  Ida Helene Asmussen

4 Cultural humility in intercultural mediation 51
  Shino Yokotsuka

5 Intercultural mediation training 59
  Claude-Hélène Mayer

vii

Contents

6 Interculturality in Online Dispute Resolution (ODR) 67
Dorcas Quek Anderson

7 Policing and intercultural mediation: Forms of triadic conflict management 77
Catharina Vogt and Stefanie Giljohann

8 Putting culture into a perspective in intercultural mediation 85
Katharina Kriegel-Schmidt

PART II
Intercultural mediation in international politics 93

9 Interculturality in the concept of peace mediation 95
Anne Holper

10 Hybrid peace mediation in the age of pandemics 104
Anine Hagemann and Isabel Bramsen

11 The political dimensions of culture and religion in mediation 111
Mohammed Abu-Nimer and Timothy Seidel

12 Third parties' involvement in contexts of political conflict and power imbalances 119
Helena Desivilya Syna

13 Seeing people in interactive peacemaking through a consciousness lens 128
Susan H. Allen

14 The past is the past—or is it? Considering the role of the past in intercultural mediation 136
Barbara Tint, Minji Cho, and Martha Doyle

15 The politics of intercultural space: Inclusive, unobtrusive, and failed mediation 145
Haynes Collins

PART III
De-centering Alternative Dispute Resolution (ADR) 153

16 Imagining a racially diverse and inclusive mediation field: Uncovering the structural hurdles 155
Maria R. Volpe and Marvin E. Johnson

Contents

17	Intercultural mediation from a European perspective *Agostino Portera*	163
18	Islamic forms of intercultural mediation *Akram Abdul Cader*	172
19	Transforming conflict cultures through mediation *Kenneth Cloke*	180
20	Indigenous conflict management strategies beyond the ADR paradigm *Hamdesa Tuso*	189

PART IV
De-essentializing culture in intercultural mediation   **199**

21	The discourse of thirdness in intercultural mediation *Malcolm N. MacDonald*	201
22	The triadic character of intercultural learning: Insights from edusemiotics *Juming Shen and Ying Zhou*	210
23	The bridge metaphor in intercultural mediation *John Corbett*	220
24	Using creative non-fiction to pinpoint moments of deCentering in intercultural mediation *Adrian Holliday*	229
25	Emic and etic perspectives on culture in mediation *Alena L. Vasilyeva*	237
26	Professional dispute mediators' notions of culture *Dominic Busch, Emilian Franco, and Andrea Hartmann-Piraudeau*	245
27	Design thinking and design communication for intercultural conflict management *Patrice M. Buzzanell, Sean Eddington, Evgeniya Pyatovskaya, and* *Aliah Mestrovich Seay*	253

PART V
Theorizing intercultural mediation   **263**

28	Theorizing mediation from the perspective of legal anthropology *Marc Simon Thomas*	265

29 Anthropological approaches to culture in conflict mediation 275
Rebecca Golbert

30 Anthropology and mediation in an environmental conflict: Worldview
translation as synthesis 284
Brenda J. Fitzpatrick

31 Weaving together three strands of research: Culture, communication, and
conflict 292
Deborah A. Cai and Edward L. Fink

32 Intercultural mediation as intercultural competence 301
Jan D. ten Thije

33 It takes three to tango. A sociological triadology 310
Ulrich Bröckling

34 A framework for understanding intercultural mediation from the
standpoint of a systemic theory of communication 320
Claudio Baraldi

PART VI
Linguistic explorations of intercultural mediation 329

35 Research from conversation analysis on intercultural mediation 331
Angela Cora Garcia

36 Managing culturality in mediation sessions: Insights from membership
categorization analysis and discursive psychology 340
Siobhan Brownlie

37 Intercultural mediation from the perspective of linguistic pragmatics 349
Anthony J. Liddicoat

38 Storytelling, culture, and identity in mediation 358
Brian L. Heisterkamp

PART VII
Psychological tools for analyzing intercultural mediation 367

39 Cultural intelligence in intercultural mediation 369
Gabriela Gonçalves and Cátia Sousa

Contents

40 Research from psychology on intercultural mediation: Cultural values and emotional intelligence 378
Marjaana Gunkel, Christopher Schlägel, and Vas Taras

41 Measuring intercultural mediation in the context of intergroup conflict: Classical and modern test theory approaches to scale assessment 387
Sara Rubenfeld and Richard Clément

PART VIII
Translation research and intercultural mediation **397**

42 Intercultural mediation in translation and interpreting studies 399
Mustapha Taibi

43 Translation as intercultural mediation—The evolution of a paradigm 408
Cinzia Spinzi

44 The mediating role of empathy in community interpreting 416
Leticia Santamaría Ciordia

45 Exacerbating cultural differences in translation/interpreting as intercultural mediation 423
Jiayi Wang

PART IX
Intercultural mediation in foreign language education and the arts **433**

46 The intercultural speaker as an intercultural mediator 435
Melina Porto and Manuela Wagner

47 Intercultural mediation in contexts of translanguaging 445
Keiko Tsuchiya

48 Children as intercultural mediators 455
Zhiyan Guo

49 Intercultural mediation in the world language classroom 464
Christelle Palpacuer Lee

Index 472

FIGURES

6.1	The impact of culture on communication within mediation	69
6.2	The impact of the fourth-party culture on mediation	70
6.3	Interaction between individual cultures and fourth-party culture in mediation	73
12.1	Implementation of third-party involvement in Jewish-Arab environmental partnership	123
15.1	Bramley Baths 1903. Photo courtesy of Bramley Baths	147
22.1	Model of Peirce's trichotomy	211
22.2	Semiotic model of an intercultural communication process	212
22.3	Semiosis and the expansion of the semiosphere	213
22.4	Intercultural learning: Modification of Peirce's trichotomy	217
24.1	Grammar of culture	235
32.1	Interrelations of five approaches to intercultural communications (ten Thije 2020a, 7)	302
33.1	Types of triads (Caplow 1956, 491)	315
33.2	Playing field three-sided football	318
40.1	Summary of results for meta-analytic structural equation modeling	383
41.1	Test information curve—Anglophone	393
41.2	Test information curve—Francophone	394
45.1	A conceptual model of T/I's intercultural mediation	425
45.2	The main causes of IM failure in translation/interpreting	430
46.1	Students mediating for third parties by distributing leaflets	441
47.1	Phases and practices of mediation with translanguaging	452

TABLES

4.1	Differences between cultural humility and cultural competence (Lee, Wong, and Alvarez 2009)	55
10.1	Advantages and disadvantages of virtual diplomacy	105
23.1	CEFR achievement scales for 'overall mediation' (North, Goodier, and Piccardo, 2018: 105)	225
32.1	Transcript of mediation by a non-professional interpreter (ten Thije 2020a, 19)	303
40.1	Meta-analytic correlation matrix	382
41.1	Intercorrelations among cultural mediation items for the Francophone group, including perpetrator (above diagonal) and victim (below diagonal) scenarios	390
41.2	Intercorrelations among cultural mediation items for the Anglophone group, including perpetrator (above diagonal) and victim (below diagonal) scenarios	390
41.3	Fit indices of one and two factor models	390
41.4	IRT results of discrimination (α) and difficulty (β) for involved and avoidant factors for Francophone group	392
41.5	IRT results of discrimination (α) and difficulty (β) for involved and avoidant factors for Anglophone group	392
44.1	Elements of quality assessment in community interpreting	417
45.1	Major reasons for IM failure in translation/interpreting	425

CONTRIBUTORS

Akram Abdul Cader is the head of education for San Mateo County Health Department's Medical Center and Clinics located in San Mateo, California. Akram's research interests revolve around the Islamic influences of business practices, motivation, mediation, marketing, and human resources. His teaching interests span a variety of subjects in strategy, management, cultural competence, and Islamic studies. Akram also consults in the field of Islamic manuscript study and Islamic history.

Mohammed Abu-Nimer is a professor of international peace and conflict resolution, American University. He is the founder of the Salam Institute for Peace and Justice, and co-founder of the *Journal of Peacebuilding and Development*. He is also senior advisor to the KAICIID Interreligious and Intercultural Dialogue Center. He has worked for over three decades in a number of conflict areas, including the Middle East, Chad, Niger, Mindanao, Sri Lanka, etc. on issues related to conflict resolution, Islamic models of peacebuilding, inter-religious dialogue, civic education, forgiveness and reconciliation, and the evaluation of peacebuilding programs. He has published many scholarly books and articles, and his most recent is *Making Peace with Faith: The Challenges of Religion and Peacebuilding* (2018), edited with Michelle Garred.

Susan H. Allen is an associate professor and director of the Center for Peacemaking Practice at the Jimmy and Rosalynn Carter School for Peace and Conflict Resolution at George Mason University. She holds an M.S. and Ph.D. from the same institution. She previously taught at American University and previously worked with President Jimmy Carter at the Carter Center in Atlanta, Georgia, U.S. She has extensive experience with peacemaking processes in the South Caucasus as a practitioner as well as theorist. She is the author of *Interactive Peacemaking: A People-Centered Approach* (Routledge, 2022).

Ida Helene Asmussen, Ph.D., associate professor at the University of Copenhagen, has taken a particular interest in the cultural norms embedded in restorative justice practices, and has given several talks and released numerous publications within the field of mediation. She is also a practicing mediator in victim-offender mediation (VOM) in Denmark.

Claudio Baraldi is a professor of sociology of cultural and communicative processes at the University of Modena and Reggio Emilia, Department of Studies on Language and Culture, where he teaches sociology of communication and theory and methods of dialogue and mediation. His research concerns communication systems and forms of communication. His most important interest is in the analysis of methods and techniques for dialogic facilitation of participation and mediation in education and health care. He has written several papers in international books and journals and has published, edited, and co-edited several international volumes, for Bloomsbury, John Benjamins, Palgrave, Routledge, Springer, and Sage.

Greg Bond lectures in mediation and communication at Technical University of Applied Sciences Wildau, Germany. He is a practicing workplace mediator and facilitator and a mediation trainer and has conducted mediation training around the world. He is a member of a number of advisory boards for mediation organizations, including for the master's program in Mediation and Conflict Management at European University Viadrina, Frankfurt (Oder), Germany. He has a PhD in German literature from the University of Nottingham, UK, and a master's in mediation from European University Viadrina. He has published widely on mediation, intercultural mediation, and German literature.

Isabel Bramsen (PhD) is vice director of peace and conflict studies and associate senior lecturer at Lund University, Department of Political Science. In her research, she applies a micro-sociological framework to study diverse phenomena from diplomacy, peace processes, and dialogue to nonviolent resistance and violence in a variety of contexts in the Middle East, Europe, South America, and Asia. She has published widely, e.g., in *International Affairs*, *Review of International Studies* and *Third World Quarterly*. She is the co-author of *International Konfliktløsning* (Samfundslitteratur 2016) and co-editor of the anthology *Addressing International Conflict: Dynamics of Escalation, Continuation and Transformation* (Routledge 2019).

Ulrich Bröckling is professor of cultural sociology at the Albert Ludwigs University of Freiburg. After studying sociology, modern history, and philosophy, he received his doctorate in 1996. From 1991 to 1999, he worked as a publishing editor. Academic stations led him to the universities of Constance, Leipzig, and Halle-Wittenberg. His main research interests are studies of governmentality, technologies of the self, and contemporary social theory. Selected publications in English language: *The Entrepreneurial Self. Fabricating a New Type of Subject*, London/New York: Sage 2016; *Governmentality. Current Issues and Future Challenges*, New York/London: Routledge 2011 (co-editor with Susanne Krasmann and Thomas Lemke).

Siobhan Brownlie is an Honorary Research Fellow in the Centre for Translation and Intercultural Studies at the University of Manchester, UK, and she teaches at Le Mans Université, France. Siobhan undertakes research in the field of intercultural communication, and has published articles that approach mediation from an intercultural communication perspective. Her interest in mediation is both theoretical and practical, since she was trained and acted as a volunteer workplace mediator at the University of Manchester.

Dominic Busch is a professor of intercultural communication and conflict research at Universität der Bundeswehr München, faculty of human sciences. In 2004, he completed his doctorate on the subject of intercultural mediation at European University Viadrina Frankfurt (Oder). There, he was a junior professor for intercultural communication from 2006 to 2011. In his research, Dominic takes a discourse-analytical view on the contents of academic discourses. His research focuses on how societies project ethical aspirations into the way they deal with interculturality (https://doi.org/g625) and how notions of culture are used in mediation research to create different understandings of intercultural mediation (https://doi.org/hgsk).

Notes on contributors

Patrice M. Buzzanell (Ph.D., Purdue) is a professor in the Department of Communication at the University of South Florida. Her research coalesces around career, work-life policy, resilience, gender, and engineering design in micro-macro contexts. Her NSF funding focuses on engineering ethics scales and everyday ethical processes as well as design thinking for the professional formation of engineers. Her awards include: ICA 2021 Chaffee Career Achievement and 2016 Fisher Mentorship Awards; NCA 2021 Becker Distinguished Service Award and 2015 Distinguished Scholar; and Purdue's 2014 Provost Outstanding Mentor Award and 2015 Distinguished University Professor. Fellow and past president of ICA, she also has served as president of the Council of Communication Associations and the Organization for the Study of Communication, Language and Gender.

Deborah A. Cai (Ph.D., Michigan State University) is professor and senior associate dean in the Klein College of Media and Communication at Temple University, and she is a faculty member in the Media and Communication doctoral program. Deborah is an international researcher with expertise in intercultural communication, persuasion, and negotiation and conflict management. Deborah is a Fellow in the International Academy of Intercultural Researchers and past president of the International Association for Conflict Management. She served as editor of the journal *Negotiation and Conflict Management Research* and is editor of the four-volume collection of research *Intercultural Communication* (Sage, Benchmark in Communication).

Minji Cho is a doctoral student in Toulan School of Urban Studies and Planning at Portland State University. Minji's research interests include planning theory, conflict transformation, cultural diversity, and social justice. Specifically, she focuses on the impact of cultural differences in communication styles and approaches for conflict transformation on the planning process and outcomes. Prior to coming to Portland State University, she received her bachelor's and master's degree in urban planning and engineering at Yonsei University, Seoul, South Korea.

Richard Clément is emeritus professor of psychology at the University of Ottawa. His current research interests include issues related to bilingualism, second-language acquisition, and identity change and adjustment in the acculturative process, topics on which he has published extensively in both French and English, in America, Asia and Europe. He is an elected Fellow of both the Canadian and the American Psychological Associations and the Royal Society of Canada. As well, he has recently been made a Knight of the Order of the Academic Palms by the Republic of France.

Kenneth Cloke is a mediator, arbitrator, coach, consultant, and trainer specializing in resolving complex multi-party disputes, including transnational, marital, divorce, family, grievance and workplace disputes, organizational, public policy, and school conflicts, and designing preventative conflict resolution systems. He has worked in over 25 countries and is the founder and first president of Mediators Beyond Borders. He has published 20 books on conflict resolution, recently *The Crossroads of Conflict* and *Politics, Dialogue, and the Evolution of Democracy*.

Haynes Collins is director of intercultural studies in the School of Languages, Cultures and Societies at the University of Leeds. His research falls broadly into the category of intercultural communication/studies and he is specifically interested in how institutional and media discourses mobilise the concept of culture and interculturality to serve ideological agendas. His research interests also include ethnographic exploration of small culture formation in unique environments such as swimming pools. He teaches intercultural communication at undergraduate and postgraduate level and is the program manager for the MA in Professional Languages and Intercultural Studies (MAPLIS).

Notes on contributors

John Corbett is a professor of English at BNU-HKBU United International College in China. He is the author of numerous books and articles, including *An Intercultural Approach to English Language Teaching* (2nd edition, 2022), *English in Medical Education: An Intercultural Approach to Teaching Language and Values* (with Peih-ying Lu, 2012), and *Intercultural Language Activities* (2010). He has also published widely on corpus linguistics, translation studies, and Scottish literature and language. He is an honorary professor at the University of Glasgow and has been a visiting professor at the University of Sao Paulo.

Helena Desivilya Syna holds a PhD in psychology and a minor in program evaluation from the State University of New York at Buffalo. She is a full professor of social/organizational psychology and diversity/conflict management. She currently serves as the chair of Department of Sociology and Anthropology and the head of the Center for Diversity and Intergroup Conflicts Studies at the Max Stern Yezreel Valley College. Professor Desivilya Syna is the editor-in-chief of *Conflict Resolution Quarterly*. She is also an associate at the Taos Institute. Her publications include: a book entitled *Managing Diversity in Places and Times of Political Tensions: Engaging Inter-group Relations in a Conflict-Ridden Society*, published by Palgrave Macmillan/Springer; over 40 articles in international peer-reviewed journals; 25 book chapters; and 2 books she edited—*A paradox in partnerships: the role of conflict in partnership building* and *Women's Voices in Management: Identifying Innovative and Responsible Solutions*.

Martha Doyle leads product management within the healthcare industry, focused on payor-transformation and access to person-centered care. She is a postgraduate student at Portland State University, studying collaborative governance with an interest in intercultural relations. Martha received her bachelor's degree at Portland State University in political science and criminology and criminal justice. Martha is active with the American Heart Association and was named a 2022 AHA Woman of Impact for her contributions. She resides in Portland, Oregon.

Sean Eddington (Ph.D., Purdue University) is an assistant professor of communication studies at Kansas State University and an organizational communication researcher with primary interests in career communication, new media, resilience, and gendered organizing. Regarding career communication, Dr. Eddington's work has examined change efforts in higher education using design thinking approaches. Specifically, his work has examined (1) the on-boarding experiences of new engineering faculty and (2) educational cultures that impact the professional formation of engineers (funded by the National Science Foundation). Eddington's research on new media, gender, and organizing explores the intersections of gender organizing online and communicative construction of resilience vis-à-vis Reddit communities.

Edward L. Fink (A.B., Columbia University; M.S., Ph.D., University of Wisconsin-Madison) is Laura H. Carnell Professor of Media and Communication at Temple University. He studies attitude change and research methods. He has received the 2020 Randall Harrison Outstanding Article Award from ICA's Information Systems Division and the 2018 Outstanding Contribution to Communication Science Award from ICA's Communication Science and Biology Interest Group. He is an ICA Fellow and a Fellow of Sigma Xi, The Scientific Research Honor Society. He has received ICA's B. Aubrey Fisher Mentorship Award and has been editor of *Human Communication Research*. He is from the Bronx.

Brenda J. Fitzpatrick has a PhD in anthropology from the University of British Columbia and an MA in Peace and Conflict Studies from the Joan B. Kroc Institute at the University of Notre Dame. She was the recipient of a Vanier Canada Graduate Scholarship and a Mackenzie King Travelling

Notes on contributors

Scholarship. Her doctoral research, an ethnography of the conflict over a hydroelectric dam in northeastern BC, investigated the intersections between anthropology and conflict transformation. Prior to beginning her PhD, she worked in international relief, development, and peacebuilding in Kenya, South Sudan, the Philippines, and Indonesia.

Emilian Franco is a research associate at the professorship for intercultural communication and conflict research at Universität der Bundeswehr München, faculty of human sciences. Emilian holds a BA in drama and media studies as well as political sciences from Nürnberg University, and he holds an MA in intercultural communication from Ludwig-Maximilians-Universität München, where he is currently a PhD student. Emilian is currently doing international ethnographic fieldwork in software start-up firms, which places his research in the field of science and technology studies (STS).

Angela Cora Garcia is a professor in the Department of Natural and Applied Sciences at Bentley University in Waltham, Massachusetts. Her main areas of research are conversation analytic studies of mediation sessions, emergency phone calls to the police, air traffic communications, and political speeches and interviews. She is the author of a textbook on conversation analysis, *An Introduction to Interaction: Understanding Talk in Formal and Informal Settings* (Bloomsbury Academic Press, 2013), and a conversation analytic study of mediation, *How Mediation Works: Resolving Conflict through Talk* (Cambridge University Press, 2019).

Stefanie Giljohann has dedicated herself to research in police and forensic psychology since 2005. As a psychologist, she is particularly interested in practice-oriented research, such as change processes in police forces, prevention and intercultural credibility assessment. She has been part in numerous research projects, as for example in the EU-funded projects COMPOSITE and IMPRODOVA. Science communication for research, practice, and the public is another important field, which connects her research with her work in continuing education at the Technical University of Berlin.

Rebecca Golbert has been the executive director of the Helen Diller Institute for Jewish Law and Israel Studies at UC Berkeley since 2013. She oversees the Institute's academic programming, manages its visiting faculty program and teaching curriculum, and supports its broader work engaging students and faculty. She received her DPhil in social anthropology from the University of Oxford and a master of dispute resolution degree from the Straus Institute for Dispute Resolution at Pepperdine University School of Law. Her scholarly work reflects overlapping interests in Jewish and Holocaust studies, anthropology and ethnography, and conflict resolution and mediation. She has published articles on Ukrainian Jewish community and identity, Holocaust memory and memorialization in Ukraine, and culture and mediation.

Gabriela Gonçalves, graduated in psychology, social and organizational area and PhD in psychology (UCL, Louvain-la-Neuve, Belgium) and is an assistant professor in the Department of Psychology and Educational Sciences. She is a member of the Centre for Research in Psychology (CIP/UAL) & University of Algarve, Portugal.

Marjaana Gunkel is a professor of organization and human resource management at the Free University of Bozen-Bolzano in Italy. Her research interests lay in the fields of international human resource management and international organizational behavior. Her research has a high relevance to practice. The results of her studies have been published in various international journals including *Journal of World Business*, *Journal of International Management*, *International Business Review*, and *International Journal of Human Resource Management*.

Notes on contributors

Zhiyan Guo, PhD. is an associate professor of Chinese, University of Warwick; Senior Fellow, Higher Education Academy, UK; Fellow of Warwick International Higher Education Academy (2019–22); and chair (2016–18) of the British Chinese Language Teaching Society (https://www.bclts.org.uk/). Her research interests are in intercultural communication, language acquisition, Chinese characters and reading, and language teaching and technology. She has published articles in these areas and edited books on Chinese pedagogy and been review editor of journals. She is the author of the monograph *Young Children as Intercultural Mediators: A Study of Mandarin-Speaking Chinese Families in Britain* published by Multilingual Matters.

Anine Hagemann is acting director of the Center for Resolution of International Conflicts (CRIC) and a postdoctoral fellow at the Department of Political Science at the University of Copenhagen. Her research focuses on diplomacy, peacebuilding and protection. Dr. Hagemann has published a handful of articles and reports and has worked as a career diplomat both for the United Nations Department of Peacekeeping and Danish Ministry of Foreign Affairs, from which she is currently on sabbatical.

Andrea Hartmann-Piraudeau is an internationally certified mediator and the managing director and founder of a mediation institutes in Germany (www.consensus-group.de) that conduct mediations and also local and international trainings to become a mediator (www.im-campus.com). In the course of her work as a trainer, researcher, and mediator, Andrea has created numerous trainings and curriculums. Both nationally and internationally. Andrea holds a Ph.D. Her research and publications areas are emotions in conflicts and the effects of mediator's inventions on the outcome of mediations and negotiations, intercultural mediation. She holds a master's degree in communication-science, sociology, and linguistics and a master's in mediation.

Brian L. Heisterkamp, Ph.D. is a professor of communication studies at California State University, San Bernardino. His teaching and research are focused on mediation, conflict management, interpersonal communication, family communication, and LGBTQ families.

Adrian Holliday is a professor of applied linguistics and intercultural education at Canterbury Christ Church University, UK, where he supervises research in the sociology and politics of the intercultural and English employing critical qualitative methods, and headed PhD research across the university until 2017. In the 1970s and 1980s he worked as an English teacher and university curriculum developer in Iran, Syria, and Egypt. His publications deal with native-speakerism, the Western ideologies that marginalize other cultural realities, and qualitative research methodology.

Anne Holper, co-director of the Center for Peace Mediation, European University Viadrina, Frankfurt (Oder), Germany, is a scholar of applied peace and conflict studies, mediator and coach, with a PhD in applied ethics/political philosophy on intercultural procedural ethics in Europe-China. She specialized her research, teaching, consultancy, and facilitation work on improving methods of mediation, dialogue, and dilemma management in peace processes and polarized societies. She leads the Tough Choices Research Cluster of Viadrina, ETH Zurich, swisspeace, Kiev Mohyla Academy; consults the German Foreign Office in the Viadrina Mediation Hub; and coaches various actors in the field, e.g., in Ukraine.

Marvin E. Johnson, J.D. is a nationally recognized mediator, arbitrator, and trainer. He has worked for numerous federal agencies; the National Football League Players' Association; and was a professor of labor relations, law, and dispute resolution. Mr. Johnson has been recognized by three presidents of the United States, a secretary of the U.S. Department of State, a governor of Maryland,

Notes on contributors

a chief judge of the Maryland Court of Appeals, and a county executive for Prince George's County for his dispute resolution expertise. He provides diversity and dispute resolution training and lectures extensively on the subject of conflict management. Mr. Johnson has written widely on dispute resolution and diversity.

Katharina Kriegel-Schmidt holds a full professorship of social work at the European University of Applied Sciences in Hamburg, Germany. After having completed her doctorate at Friedrich-Schiller-University Jena in 2012 (*Intercultural Mediation: The Argument for a Perspective-Relative Model*), she has since been working on a theoretical framework of intercultural mediation. In 2017, Katharina Kriegel-Schmidt founded the School of Intercultural Mediators (SIM) based in London and Berlin. She is head of the Intercultural-Mediation-Training Course (interculture) in Berlin and co-head of the German National Research Group on Mediation (ForMed). Katharina Kriegel-Schmidt lives together with husband and son in Berlin.

Anthony J. Liddicoat is a professor in the Department of Applied Linguistics at the University of Warwick and Adjunct Professor in Justice and Society at the University of South Australia. His research interests include language and intercultural issues in education, discourse analysis, and language policy and planning. He is currently co-convenor of the AILA Research Network Intercultural mediation in language and culture teaching and learning/La médiation interculturelle en didactique des langues et des cultures and Executive Editor of *Current Issues in Language Planning* and Co-editor of the book series *Language and Intercultural Communication in Education* (Multilingual Matters).

Malcolm N. MacDonald is editor of *Language and Intercultural Communication* (LAIC); and a committee member of IALIC. After teaching in the Seychelles NYS, University of Kuwait and NTU Singapore, Malcolm lectured at the universities of Stirling, UTM Malaysia, St Andrews, Exeter and Warwick, where he is currently based as researcher and editor. Malcolm's principal interests are: intercultural ethics and literature; and the discourses of security and medicine. Malcolm has published extensively in journals ranging from *Educational Philosophy and Theory* to *Discourse and Society*. His monograph with Duncan Hunter is entitled *The Discourse of Security: Language, Illiberalism and Governmentality*.

Claude-Hélène Mayer is a full professor in industrial and organizational psychology at the Department of Industrial Psychology and People Management, University of Johannesburg, Johannesburg, South Africa. She holds PhDs in psychology, management, and political sciences from Germany and South Africa and master degrees from Germany and the United Kingdom. Her research areas are transcultural mental health and well-being, intercultural mediation and conflict management, transforming shame, psychobiography, and women in leadership. She also works as an intercultural consultant, mediator, and systemic therapist.

Carrie Menkel-Meadow is a distinguished professor of law (and political science), University of California, Irvine and Chettle Professor of Law, Dispute Resolution and Civil Procedure, Emerita at Georgetown University Law Center. She is the author of over 25 books and 200 articles on dispute resolution, legal feminism, socio-legal studies, legal ethics, and law and culture; most recently *Very Short Introduction to Negotiation* (Oxford University Press 2022) and (with Lela Love and Andrea Schneider) *Mediation: Practice, Policy and Ethics*, 3rd ed. (Wolters Kluwer 2020). She has taught mediation and dispute resolution in 25 countries. She is the recipient of many honorary doctorates and awards in the United States and Europe for her work in international and domestic dispute resolution. She has consulted on dispute resolution for the United Nations, the World Bank, the

Notes on contributors

Federal Judicial Center, and many public and private institutions. She has been a mediator for over 30 years in both public and private disputes.

Aliah Mestrovich Seay, LCMFT #855, is an extension specialist for the Department of 4-H Youth Development at Kansas State University and a licensed clinical marriage and family therapist. She holds a B.S. degree in clinical psychology in French (Université de Caen, Basse-Normandie, France) and a M.A. degree in counseling psychology (Argosy University). She is currently a doctoral student in Leadership Communication at the K-State Staley School of Leadership Studies. With over 20 years of experience in higher education and the not-for-profit sectors, Aliah's research interests involve intercultural communication, critical whiteness studies, critical empathy, and intercultural listening for racial healing and reconciliation.

Christelle Palpacuer Lee (Ed.D) is an associate teaching professor in language education at the Rutgers Graduate School of Education, Rutgers The State University of New Jersey, USA. Her work addresses interculturality, multiple literacies, and educational action for justice, equity, and solidarity in language teacher education and across sites of practice.

Agostino Portera is a professor of intercultural education, head of the Centre for Intercultural Studies, and director of the Master 'Intercultural Competences and Management' at the University of Verona. He studied psychology in Rome, has a Ph.D. in intercultural education in Freiburg (Germany), and was visiting professor at the Universities of Würzburg, London, UCLA Los Angeles, OISE-Toronto, and Wellington. He has published several books and articles on identity, intercultural education, intercultural competence, and intercultural counseling, including *Education and Intercultural Identity* (with Z. Bauman). Routledge, 2021; *Intercultural Mediation, Counselling and Psychotherapy in Europe*, Cambridge Scholars, 2020 (with R. Moodley and M. Milani); and *Intercultural and Multicultural Education,* Routledge 2011 (with C.A. Grant).

Melina Porto holds an MA ELT (Essex University), a PhD in sciences of education (Universidad Nacional de La Plata -UNLP-, Argentina), and a postdoctoral degree in humanities and social sciences (Universidad de Buenos Aires, Argentina). She is a researcher at the National Research Council (CONICET), professor at UNLP and honorary research fellow at the University of East Anglia (2019–2024). Her research interests include intercultural language education, intercultural citizenship, pedagogies of discomfort, service learning, and ethics, among others.

Evgeniya Pyatovskaya is a doctoral student at the University of South Florida. Her research interests are in organizational, intercultural communication, and feminist perspectives on communication and organizational leadership and resilience. Evgeniya is a Fulbright FLTA and Atlas Corps alumna with an extensive international work experience that she builds on in her scholarly work. One of her most recent projects looks at feminist narratives of resilience in the context of the pandemic and how culture-specific notion of agency influences what resilience looks like and what its long-term consequences can be.

Dorcas Quek Anderson is an assistant professor of Law in the Singapore Management University's Yong Pung How School of Law. As a practicing mediator and a former district judge, Dorcas' research is drawn from her experience and explores the interaction between dispute resolution developments and access to justice. Her research has been published in international journals including the *Civil Justice Quarterly* and the *Harvard Negotiation Law Review*. Dorcas is also a fellow of the National Centre for Technology and Dispute Resolution which engages in research on online dispute resolution.

Notes on contributors

Sara Rubenfeld is a defense scientist in Director General Military Personnel Research and Analysis in Canada's Department of National Defence, where she is the section head for the Leadership, Culture and Ethics team. She completed her PhD in social-cultural psychology at the University of Ottawa. Her research interests include second-language learning, intergroup dynamics, sexual misconduct, and bystander intervention.

Leticia Santamaría Ciordia holds a PhD in translation and intercultural communication from the University of Valladolid (Spain) and a Certificate of Advanced Studies in interpreter training and pedagogical innovation from the University of Geneva (Switzerland). She has been teaching conference interpreting (French-Spanish) since 2006 at the Faculty of Translation and Interpreting in Soria. She is a freelance interpreter for the private market and public services in courtroom and healthcare settings since 2007. Their working languages are Spanish, Polish, French, and English. Her main research interests include ethics and decision making in interpreting, sociolinguistics, and intercultural communication.

Christopher Schlägel is a professor of behavioral international management at the Otto von Guericke University Magdeburg, Germany. His current research focuses on various topics international management and international/comparative entrepreneurship as well as the critical assessment of research methodology in international management/international business research. The results of his research have been published in various international journals, e.g., *Entrepreneurship Theory and Practice, Journal of World Business, International Business Review, Journal of International Management*, and *Management International Review*.

Timothy Seidel is an associate professor of peacebuilding, development, and global studies. He is the director of the Center for Interfaith Engagement at Eastern Mennonite University in Harrisonburg, VA. He holds a PhD from the School of International Service at American University in Washington, DC.

Juming Shen received his PhD in higher educational studies from Queensland University of Technology in 2013. He is currently an assistant professor and head of the Learning Institute for Future Excellence at the Academy of Future Education, Xi'an Jiaotong Liverpool University. He is the director of the Chinese Association for Language and Semiotic Studies, the co-editor of *Language and Semiotic Studies*, and editorial member of *Language and Sign*. Dr. Shen's research interest is focused on intercultural communication studies, educational policy studies, and semiotics.

Marc Simon Thomas is a legal anthropologist, trained in law and in cultural anthropology, and has specialized in empirical research on dispute settlement. He is appointed as associate professor in sociology of law at Utrecht University. Besides teaching, he is a researcher within the Montaigne Centre for Rule of Law and Judicial Administration at the same university. His research interests concern empirical, qualitative socio-legal research on mediation and responsive justice in the Netherlands.

Cátia Sousa graduated in human resource management (Universidade Lusíada do Porto), master's in work sciences and labor relations (ISCTE-IUL), and PhD in psychology (Faculty of Human and Socials Sciences, University of Algarve, Portugal). Sousa is a guest adjunct professor in the School of Management, Hospitality and Tourism/University of the Algarve and member of the Centre for Research in Psychology (CIP/UAL) & University of Algarve, Portugal.

Notes on contributors

Cinzia Spinzi is an associate professor at the University of Bergamo. She holds a PhD in English for Specific Purposes, an MA in translation studies from the University of Birmingham, and a research fellowship from the City University of London. She is co-editor of *Cultus: The Journal of Intercultural Mediation and Communication*. Her research interests include language/cultural mediation and translation, corpus linguistics, and functional grammar applied to the study of ideology and metaphors in specialized communication, with a particular focus on political and tourism discourses.

Mustapha Taibi is an associate professor in interpreting and translation at Western Sydney University, and editor of *Translation & Interpreting: The International Journal of Translation and Interpreting Research*. Among the books he has published: *Community Translation* (2016); *New Insights into Arabic Translation and Interpreting* (2016); *Translating for the Community* (2018); *Multicultural Health Translation, Interpreting and Communication* (with Meng Ji and Ineke Crezee, 2019); and *Translating Cultures: An Introduction for Translators, Interpreters and Mediators* (with David Katan, 2021).

Vas Taras is an associate professor of international business at the University of North Carolina at Greensboro. He received his PhD in international human resources and organizational dynamics from the University of Calgary, Canada. He is the founder of the X-Culture Project (www.X-Culture.org). His research and work revolve around cross-cultural and global virtual teams and experiential approaches to international business education and development. He is an associate editor of the *Journal of International Management*, the *International Journal of Cross-Cultural Management*, and *Cross-Cultural Strategic Management*.

Jan D. ten Thije is a professor intercultural communication at the Utrecht Institute for Linguistics and at the Department of Languages, Literature and Communication. He previously was an associated professor at Utrecht University (2002–2019) and previously Hochschuldozent at the Department for Intercultural Communication at Chemnitz University of Technology (1996–2002), visiting professor at the Department for Applied Linguistics at Vienna University (2001), and lecturer and researcher at the Department for General Linguistics (University of Amsterdam) (1994–1996). He studied general linguistics and Dutch language and culture in Amsterdam (University of Amsterdam) and received his PhD at Utrecht University (1994) with research focusing intercultural discourse in advisory institutes. His main fields of research concern institutional discourse in multicultural and international settings, lingua receptiva/receptive multilingualism, intercultural training, language education, and functional pragmatics.

Barbara Tint is a professor of conflict resolution at Portland State University, a peace psychologist and a global facilitator, trainer, and mediator. Her work has focused largely on the psychological dynamics involved in the causes, prevention and intervention within international, social, and community conflict. Her areas of specialization include dialogue, power, gender, culture, and resilience. She has lived and worked on every continent (ok, not Antarctica) and has published on a wide range of topics including her ongoing work in collective memory, dialogue in intergroup conflict, peace education and culture, and the processes involved in the creation of reconciliation processes for diaspora communities. Barbara is also a trained improviser and an award-winning storyteller and brings these methods into her work.

Keiko Tsuchiya is an associate professor at the School of International Liberal Arts, Yokohama City University, Japan, where she teaches graduate/undergraduate modules of English philology, applied linguistics, and English language teaching. She received an MA in English language teaching from Nottingham Trent University (UK) and a PhD in applied linguistics from Nottingham University (UK). Her research involves multimodal analysis of multiparty interaction, healthcare communication, CLIL (Content and Language Integrated Learning), and ELF (English as a Lingua Franca) in Japanese contexts.

Hamdesa Tuso was born and raised in Oromia (Ethiopia). He studied at Avondale College (NSW), Australia and completed his PhD at Michigan State University (USA). Over the last three decades, he has taught in the field of peace and conflict studies at five universities in North America (United States and Canada). Areas of his specialization for teaching and research include: (1) indigenous process of peacemaking; (2) nationalism; (3) intergroup conflict; and (4) human rights. He has widely published in the areas of ethnic conflict and indigenous process of peacemaking. He is the lead-editor of the book *Creating the Third Force: Indigenous Processes of Peacemaking* (2016).

Alena L. Vasilyeva received her PhD from the School of Communication and Information, Rutgers, the State University of New Jersey, USA, in 2010 and her Candidate of Science (Kandidat Nauk) from Minsk State Linguistic University, Belarus in 2002. She is currently an associate professor at the Department of Communication, University of Massachusetts Amherst. Her general research interests include culture, deliberation, disagreement management, social identity, and the coordination of actions in personal and public contexts.

Catharina Vogt (née Decker) has been working since 2008 as a researcher and consultant in the field of service interactions, leadership, and conflict management. She is part of the Hamburg-based think tank RespectResearchGroup where she completed her PhD on respectful leadership. As a psychologist by training, she coordinated the EU-funded projects COREPOL, on police's intercultural conflict resolution, and IMPRODOVA, on frontline responder interaction in cases of domestic abuse, at the German University of the Police (DHPol) in Münster. Her research has been published in various outlets.

Maria R. Volpe, Ph.D. is a professor of sociology at the John Jay College of Criminal Justice—City University of New York and director of the CUNY Dispute Resolution Center. An internationally known scholar, Dr. Volpe has lectured, researched, and written extensively about dispute resolution processes, particularly mediation, administers grant-funded projects, and has been widely recognized for her distinguished career in the field of dispute resolution. Her research has focused on police use of mediation, conflict resolution in higher education, dispute resolution responses to disasters and crises since 9/11, and the roots of diversity and barriers to minority participation in dispute resolution.

Manuela Wagner is a professor of language education at the University of Connecticut, Storrs, USA. She is particularly interested in the interplay of theory and practice of intercultural citizenship and has co-edited *Teaching Intercultural Competence Across the Age Range: From Theory to Practice* (2018) and *Education for Intercultural Citizenship: Principles in Practice* (2017), and co-authored *Teaching Intercultural Citizenship Across the Curriculum: The Role of Language Education* (2019). Other research interests include conviction in education humor research in a variety of contexts, and first language acquisition (pragmatic development in infants and children and language development in children with autism spectrum disorder).

Jiayi Wang, an associate professor at De Montfort University, UK, has conducted research on pragmatics, intercultural communication, and translation/interpreting. Her recent publications include the article *Culture, context, and concerns about face: Synergistic insights from pragmatics and social psychology* (with Spencer-Oatey 2020) and a forthcoming co-edited volume on English language learning with Cambridge University Press. Jiayi obtained her PhD in applied linguistics from the

University of Warwick, specialising in professional intercultural communication. She served as an international project manager at the Ministry of Justice and as a high-level conference interpreter/translator for such organizations as the Supreme Court, *Fortune Magazine*, and AstraZeneca.

Shino Yokotsuka is a doctoral student in the Department of Global Governance, Human Security, and Conflict Resolution at the University of Massachusetts, Boston. After completing basic mediation training at Massachusetts district courts, Shino has worked as a graduate research assistant for the Massachusetts Office of Public Collaboration, the statutory state office of dispute resolution established to broaden state-wide access to community mediation. She has been assisting with the PSG Diversity Project designed to diversify a mediation field through cultural humility approach, collaborating with nine community mediation centers located in Massachusetts.

Ying Zhou is the English for Academic Purposes (EAP) language lecturer and Year 1 Core EAP Deputy Head of Division at the School of Languages of Xi'an Jiaotong Liverpool University. She has been teaching English language in higher education institutions for over eight years and is currently a doctor of education candidate at the University of Bath. Her publications and research interests lie in areas of English-medium instruction, learner strategy, and intercultural communication. She is also a reviewer on the editorial board of the *International Journal of English Language Teaching*.

PREFACE

Intercultural mediation, by the very existence of the term, goes on and on as an idea, as a vision, and as a hope—to resolve problems in constructive ways on an individual and a global level. This applies above all to dealing with interculturality, an area the research community itself had long considered only as a problem, although it harbors opportunities as well. Intercultural mediation is a vision. It comes in many variations, and this book aims to bring them together. This diversity is productive, not least because it involves having a positive vision in the first place, reflecting on it, and sharing ideas about it on a global level. There have always been many various thoughts on intercultural mediation, including institutionalized mediation: For improving foreign language teaching, empowering migrants and refugees, and, last but not least, containing large-scale crises. Third-party help may be the last resort, which becomes clear time and again in particularly challenging situations. As this handbook was being prepared, in the spring of 2022, horrific devastation took place in Ukraine; for many Western observers, it was unexpected, and it seemed unstoppable. In such situations, intercultural mediation also needs to foster intercultural sustainability (Busch 2016): For lasting intercultural relationships that cannot be easily undermined or misused.

Moreover, this handbook was written and prepared during the global crisis of the COVID-19 outbreak. Many authors worldwide have experienced this as a time of radical and unprecedented change. Often, they had to work on their contributions under challenging conditions. Work on this book also often had to pause and adjust to local crises and challenging situations. We communicated via videoconference and thus worked together on a global project. I want to thank all the authors at this point for this excellent, incredibly committed, and always very close cooperation. They will carry on the idea of the potential of intercultural mediation to the next generations. I would also like to thank Gil Dominik Keller for his advice, thoughtfulness, editing, and all-around support. Also, thanks to Emilian Franco for his critical reading of the final manuscript and Christina Strauß for proofreading specific sections. I want to thank Felisa Salvago-Keyes, Sean Daly, and Grant Schatzman from Routledge/Taylor & Francis Books for their always friendly and highly dedicated support at every stage of the book project.

Reference

Busch, Dominic. 2016. "What Is Intercultural Sustainability? A First Exploration of Linkages Between Culture and Sustainability in Intercultural Research." *Journal of Sustainable Development* 9 (1): 63. 10.5539/jsd.v9n1p63

INTRODUCTION: THE INTERDISCIPLINARY VISION OF INTERCULTURAL MEDIATION

Dominic Busch

Intercultural mediation refers to situations and contexts with triadic communication constellations seen as intercultural—by the participants, observers, or both. From this triad, it is hoped—by whomever—that there will be a constructive effect of whatever form on the communication event and outcome. This idea first emerged in applied research on conflict resolution, especially in practical conflict mediations in intercultural contexts. However, many other social science disciplines have also taken up the idea, such as research on intercultural communication, translation studies, foreign language teaching and learning, psychology, and political science. Methodological approaches also come from ethnology, cultural anthropology, and qualitative social research in general.

What is unique about the career of the term intercultural mediation is that only these various adaptations can explain its increased ascribed appeal in so many different disciplines. The ascribed attractiveness increases within each discipline due to interdisciplinary glimpses into the respective neighboring disciplines. Conversely, this interdisciplinary affinity often obscures the view that the individual disciplines may have very different ideas about intercultural mediation based on their paradigms and fields of study. In this constellation, this handbook aims to increase interdisciplinary transparency and trace the discursive career of the term, its different interpretations, and theoretical groundings. This handbook aims to identify the limits of the explanatory power of the term due to paradigmatic (non-)fits or paradigm shifts in individual disciplines and the future potentials of the term thanks to its interdisciplinarity.

Therefore, of what is discussed here as intercultural mediation, the practical and applied area of Western-style conflict resolution is only a small part. Partly, however, it is also the starting point of a long journey through disciplines and fields of application. This journey intentionally and purposefully expands the notion of intercultural mediation in a far-reaching manner. The idea of intercultural mediation is thus understood and explored in a comprehensive and holistic sense.

A generic definition of intercultural mediation

Intercultural mediation generally refers to a situation where a third or further person, group, or entity intervenes in previously dyadic interactions. In this line of thinking, this new triad promises to modify the situation so that those involved may experience it as constructive. Intercultural mediation as a term evokes the very idea of a chance for intercultural understanding and positive co-existence in many people's minds. The adjective intercultural additionally suggests modifying the given situation in some way, adding more complexity, modifying the constellation of roles, adding

DOI: 10.4324/9781003227441-1

challenges or even opportunities. This vision of intercultural mediation draws its appeal from the idea that a generally considered challenging situation can resolve by a fundamental transformation (turning the dyad into a triad).

The term *interculturality* here serves as a black box standing for these very different challenges. The mere idea that there could be a solution to these challenges sounds attractive to many. Moreover, this idea is so general that it holds across many academic paradigms. Conversely, such an idea of intercultural mediation is enhanced and sustained precisely because many different scholarly perspectives support this view.

Visions like these are the central drivers for progress, development, and change in research and societies. Therefore, these visions should be taken seriously and form the main basis for further research. Similarly, for the idea of intercultural mediation, an interest in the construct has evolved in various academic disciplines and social fields of action.

Not surprisingly, this gives rise to very different understandings of what intercultural mediation is supposed to be. It should also be borne in mind that initial enthusiasm for the idea of intercultural mediation using this very term has been evident in research and practice in Western societies since about the 1980s. Since then, many of the relevant disciplines and fields have undergone significant paradigm shifts, requiring a review of whether and how ideas of intercultural mediation continue to be appropriate here or have adapted to these new paradigms.

Given this tradition, the authors in this handbook are a second and new generation of researchers on intercultural mediation. They are surveying and reflecting on a long preceding epoch and often distance themselves from the founding fathers' ideas, discuss them, and develop them further. This shows that the research field on intercultural mediation is full of life more than ever. It provides essential impulses across paradigms and continues to advance interdisciplinary research and networking.

It should be noted from the outset that the concept of intercultural mediation carries a wide variety of meanings, not only in academia. It is also unclear in everyday social practice and can be understood to mean completely different things. Pokorn and Mikolič Južnič (2020) have shown that the perspectives of national languages beyond English ascribe different connotations to the term intercultural mediation. Alternatively, the term is not only imported but indeed translated into another language and filled with new connotations. In our world's cultural and linguistic diversity, intercultural mediation is a term that crosses borders, but at the same time, it permanently sparks different interpretations. To be able to explore this interdisciplinary interplay at least somewhat in a systematic way, the following sections will first take the route via the disciplines.

Intercultural mediation in conflict and dispute resolution

Although formal and informal conflict mediation is undoubtedly a social phenomenon, for many publications in the field, the concept of culture or interculturality remains insignificant until today. Thus, when we speak of intercultural mediation here, we are not speaking about a mainstream orientation of the field. However, we are still dealing with a topic that, at best, continues to be assigned its niche category. Nevertheless, the literature in this area is very up to date. This introduction cannot review this literature exhaustively here; instead, it will mention only a few recent works by way of example.

In her *Mediation Handbook*, Alexia Georgakopoulos (2017, 3) features mediation as a culture-universal tool thanks to its enormous flexibility. Just because mediation is undoubtedly also based on culture-specific groundings and origins, it will be able to quickly adapt to other cultural contexts and transform itself if necessary. Jennifer L. Schulz (2020) has recently underlined this deep cultural embeddedness of notions of mediation has recently in her study on *Mediation and Popular Culture*. Mediation or specific aspects of it are also echoed in fictional genres in television shows and movies—not only in an explicit form taking the example of professional mediators, as in the United States show *Fairly Legal* but also in a more implicit form of social roles, as in the example of the protagonist in the motion picture *The Fabulous Destiny of Amélie Poulain*. What is at stake is that conflict resolution is a ritual and an object of culture and culturality.

Intercultural mediation vs. rationalistic negotiation research

Kevin Avruch (2003, 352) sees the main reason for the lack of more enthusiasm for culture in conflict resolution and its development out of negotiation research and game-theoretical, rational-choice-based approaches, which did not leave any room for culture (itself). Druckman and Wall's (2017) review and synopsis of 60 years of publications in the *Journal of Conflict Resolution* confirm this view. Indeed, Druckman and Wall (2017, 1910) distinguish mediation as a particular case from negotiation and consider the former much more complex: Mediation is typically fraught with tons of principles that *de facto* chase mediation of negotiation theory's rational negotiation theory choice scheme.

The rationality-based negotiation scheme peaked in popularity beyond the discipline with Ury and Fisher's (1981) *Getting to Yes* manual. Nevertheless, the arrival of culture into the reception of conflict and negotiation research had not been unrehearsed. This disposition has been dormant for a long time and takes the form of the distinction between conflicts of interest and conflicts of values. According to Druckman and Wall (2017, 1905), Aubert (1963) was the first to introduce values as a factor in 1963. The idea of value conflicts allows relatively easy conclusions about underlying cultures and cultural differences. At the same time, however, this new cultural paradigm in conflict resolution research confines the whole new approach to one specific, etic-essentialist notion of culture. What is undoubtedly new and challenging for negotiation-oriented mediation research up to this point is the assumption here that value-based conflicts cannot usually resolve through negotiation.

The search for forms of mediation in other cultures

Another approach to the field in the literature is searching for forms of mediation in other cultures. Again, James A. Wall, for example, very early, has published several studies on mediation in societies in the so-called Far East (e.g., Wall 1990; but see also Wall's excellent systematic overview in Wall and Dunne 2012). Also, his more recent article with Daniel Druckman portrays, for example, China as a mediation-friendly culture because of its collectivist character. This is also one reason why mediation in China has the form of an institution to quite an extent, the authors argue. From a Western perspective, mediation in China is also an instrument for educating the population: Mediators remind their parties of their social virtues. Parties here should comply and behave like 'good citizens' (Druckman and Wall 2017, 1913).

Cultural differences in disputing behavior

Other earlier ways of addressing the issue of intercultural mediation build on the assumption that people in different cultures dispute in different ways. For example, Tricia Jones (2006) in Margaret Herrmann's (2006) *Blackwell Handbook of Mediation* discusses cross-cultural differences in how emotions are experienced and expressed. Emotions are perceived, communicated, and performed with different rituals in different cultures, affecting how mediators and their parties should deal with them in mediation. To put this difference to work, Lewicki, Saunders, and Barry (2010, 234) draw on Jeswald W. Salacuse's (1988) distinction between deductive and inductive cultures: Some cultures focus more on relationships, they say, others focus more on the issue. Negotiators should choose their strategies based on how familiar or unfamiliar they are with each other's cultures. For the latter case, the authors recommend consulting a mediator who may also provide translation services (Lewicki, Saunders, and Barry 2010, 246).

Given this somewhat stagnant incorporation of cultural concepts into mediation practice and mediation research, it is perfectly reasonable to ask who wanted, and for what reasons, to bring the two concepts of mediation and culture so close to each other in the first place. Regarding the field of mediation practice, the literature today is replete with countless retrospective reconstructions of the origins, the roots, and the genesis of this phenomenon, itself nowadays so diversified and barely identifiable in a uniform manner. The self-conception of Western professional conflict mediators sees their shared roots mainly in the *Alternative Dispute Resolution* movement that emerged in the United States in the second half of the 20th century. From an analytical perspective, in his contribution to this volume, Simon Thomas goes back even further. The norms and expectations now applied to mediation had been prepared much longer before in legal anthropology. Pruitt and Kressel (1989, 2) see the origins and the initial spark of interest in mediation as being in its use in international conflicts. This perspective often motivates authors toward a more abstract understanding of the concept of mediation and towards finding a definition that is as generic and broad as possible. Pruitt and Kressel, for example, define mediation with this in mind as

> third-party assistance to people who are trying to reach agreement in a controversy. There are hundreds of things a mediator can do to help, ranging from simply being present at a joint discussion to thinking up new ideas and arguing for them vigorously.
>
> *(Pruitt and Kressel 1989, 1)*

A definition like this may appear empty at first sight, yet its primary purpose is to express the authors' awareness of the tremendous cultural boundedness of concrete forms of mediation. This shows just how much the notion of mediation emerges among the various conflict management techniques. It distinguishes itself precisely by its immense grounding in cultural values and from which it also draws its strengths in the end. In the light of this cultural awareness, Kevin Avruch (2003, 351) also opts for an umbrella definition of intercultural mediators as "practitioners functioning as third parties and intervenors in intercultural and interethnic conflicts and disputes." This new awareness recommends intercultural mediators be sensitive to the various influences of culture on all levels, including the mediation process (Turk and Ungerleider 2017, 288).

There has always been a plethora of publications accompanying the practice of mediation attempting to teach how to do good mediation properly (notice Pruitt and Kressel 1989, 2 as well). In this tradition, literature for intercultural mediators is also often devoted to advising imaginary practitioners. Avruch (2003), for instance, summarizes that there are two distinct paths that intercultural mediators will need to consider given the multiple influences and understandings of culture. On the one hand, mediators should know how to adequately analyze their situation with a view of the real cultural differences. On the other hand, mediators must also keep in mind that actors also often use cultural identities as a tool and often construct them in the first place, just to underpin their positions. Mediators will need to respond in two different ways—by pointing out cultural differences on the one hand and by deconstructing them on the other. It can be challenging for mediators to decide which of the two situations they are dealing with. Within this complex field, Bowland, Batts, Roy, and Trujillo (2022) argue for a re-centering of (intercultural) mediation research around the mediating persons.

This diversity in the roles, functions, and definitions of culture challenges the many approaches to the practice of mediation. Therefore, authors here tend to make their paradigms as flexible and as hybrid as possible, as in the case of Michelle LeBaron's (2003) concept of cultural fluency, for example. Beyond that, the idea that mediation serves a transformative functional role for civil societies has also been explored repeatedly for intercultural mediation. For example, mediatory work may serve as an access-to-justice project in assisting and integrating migrants and refugees

Introduction

(for a validating case study report from Catalonia, cf. Agustí-Panareda 2006; and for a power-critical assessment from northern Italy, cf. Baraldi 2009).

However, the question as to whether a social transformation is possible does not even arise since problems and challenges emerge simply from the actual situation. For example, Valero-Garcés (2007) portrays the activities of migration helpers, who often end up as translators, cultural mediators, and mediators all in one person, and out of necessity, must perform on an instead lay autodidactic basis. Helakorpi, Lappalainen, and Sahlström (2019) record a similar scenario of community mediators, as social workers, supporting disadvantaged and marginalized groups, in this case, the Roma.

Intercultural mediation in research on interculturality

Research on intercultural communication, too, seems to be curious about the phenomenon of intercultural mediation. On the one hand, this is from a completely different angle than the field of conflict resolution. While conflict resolution centers around conflict, intercultural research focuses on culture and interculturality. Nevertheless, in part, both disciplines share a few parallels in their paradigmatic and ethical background assumptions. The relatively new theme of intercultural mediation appears natural to both sides. However, there are also some discrepancies, which sometimes go unseen in the euphoria of interdisciplinary research. This handbook aims to shed more light on precisely this arena of the in-between.

Research on interculturality has been conducted with various close-by terms and labels, such as intercultural communication, cross-cultural communication, interethnic communication, amongst many others. Such conceptual definitions often almost combine without a second thought with considerations of what is to be understood by intercultural competence based on these definitions. However, many scholars simultaneously commit to rigorous conceptual distinctions around interculturality according to their research interests. Nevertheless, Alvino Fantini (2009, 457) invites us to admit that these terms have been used with the same meaning and in an interchangeable way throughout the last decades. Hence, the subject area cannot be understood in an adequate and comprehensive frame of reference unless all these terms—and sub-terminologies—are considered equally in the research process. According to John Condon (2015, 451),

> *intercultural communication* refers to what transpires when people engage in communication with others whose experiences, assumptions, sense making, and behaviors are different. The emphasis in this field is not on *objective culture,* including *material culture,* much of which is popularly identified as the whole of culture, such as art, literature, food, architecture, and recorded histories. [...] Intercultural communication concerns the *process* through which shared meanings are *co-created* through engagement. These shared meanings are also directly affected by *subjective culture*—cultural assumptions, expectations, and behaviors so deeply learned that they are easily imagined to be human nature. Individuals may even assume that culturally influenced ways of thinking, which have been learned from and shared with their communities of origin, are a matter of *common sense.*

In contrast, Anthony Liddicoat (2015) narrows *interculturality* as a term to refer only to intercultural contact situations where culturality does matter to the interaction between the participants. Furthermore, Adrian Holliday joins this attitude specifying:

> My emerging definition of the intercultural is therefore whenever and wherever we en-counter cultural practices and values that cause us to position and reposition ourselves.
>
> *(Holliday 2022, 7)*

Even more specifically, Manuela Guilherme (2015) uses the notion of critical interculturality, deriving this critical approach from the paradigm of critical pedagogy. Culturality here links with conflicts and power imbalances on micro and macro levels. Critical interculturality seeks to increase people's awareness of this interlinkage in society. This also entails an ethical call to action: People are invited to act to transform their contexts, as well as those of society as a whole, to make them more just and sustainable (Guilherme and Dietz 2015, 7). Gunther Dietz (2018) finally advances *interculturality* as a generic umbrella term. It should embrace earlier, rather static and essentialist conceptions of intercultural communication, more recent, dynamic, and liquid notions, and an awareness of their ethical implications.

In research on interculturality, attention to power-critical perspectives has emerged as a core part of the paradigm. Part of this entails the assumption that the way people deal with interculturality and their understanding of it results from underlying ideologies. As Adrian Holliday (2011, 1) puts it, both the social and the scientific concern with intercultural communication always serve people to "to construct ideological imaginations both of themselves and others." To this, Fred Dervin (2016, 82) further adds that presuming interculturality to be an ideological construct is itself, of course, an ideology in turn.

Intercultural mediation in translation research

In translation studies, the terms *mediation* and *mediating* also often serve as synonyms for translation, but with the connotation of translations always involving culture and language (an overall impression quite apparent even when reviewing Malmkjaer's 2017 *Handbook of Translation Studies and Linguistics*). Kramsch (1999) has explored the notion of *thirdness* in this field very early. Currently, John Corbett, in this volume, discusses the metaphorical use of the term mediation in the translation community as building bridges. Valdéon (2021) had previously explored the metaphor of the translator as a gatekeeper—and in that sense, a mediator.

Moreover, scholars from translation research and foreign language didactics have unlinked the idea of mediation from the imperative of a third person. Insights through triadic thinking should, at best, already emerge in the minds of individuals, as Liddicoat points out in this volume. Also, in this volume, MacDonald explains that a triad is already inherent in the semiotic character of communication. Eichinger (2003, 96) had developed the idea of intrapersonal mediation because the narrow legal view of mediation did not suit the intercultural field. People achieve intercultural mediation in that sense in their everyday lives. These efforts of cultural translation find an extensively explored field of application in medicine and medical consultation. Here, cultural mediators assist in various ways in counseling and communicating with migrants and refugees. In this context, Kirmayer, Guzder, and Rousseau (2014) speak of "cultural consultation," while Miklavcic and LeBlanc (2014) explore the role of "cultural brokers."

Intercultural mediation in foreign language teaching

In foreign language didactics, Wierlacher (2003) re-interprets the teacher as a (cultural) mediator. As he (2003, 332) puts it, the term "mediating cultures" was first introduced by Norbert Platz (1991) into a German-speaking field—and maybe the international hype starts all the more as a result. Mediation here means a cultural transfer. However, the objectives had also shifted. Eichinger's (2003, 96) teaching concepts still align with the sub-discipline of *xenology*, a branch for exploring how people can understand otherness and foreignness.

Subsequent studies, instead, focus more on creating a sense of community that resolves all other problems. Wierlacher here had launched a new discipline called Intercultural German Studies, which Allison Phipps (1999) criticized for its ethnocentric starting point and its ignorance of power imbalances. According to Alred and Byram (2002), the concept of the *intercultural speaker* takes the mediator figure in foreign language didactics a decisive step forward.

Indeed, foreign language teachers are always intercultural mediators, write Keating Marshall and Bokhorst-Heng (2018). However, sometimes they are unaware of this and, accordingly, would need the appropriate training. Both the mediation and the mediator metaphors received an enormous boost in prominence in foreign language didactics when the term was made central to the *Common European Framework of Reference for Languages (CEFR)*. This scheme aimed at assessing foreign language proficiency, as devised by the Council of Europe around the turn of the millennium (Pym and Ayvazyan 2017, 402). Mediating here becomes a central competence of what a learner is supposed to master when studying a foreign language. In this book, John Corbett, Christelle Palpacuer Lee, Melina Porto, and Manuela Wagner, as well as Sara Rubenfeld and Richard Clément address the CEFR in their chapters.

Intercultural mediation in cultural anthropology

Also, anthropology and later cultural anthropology both had a long-standing interest in observing how people deal with conflict. Edward Tylor (1896, v) termed *anthropology* "the sciences of Man and Civilization," and in similar veins, Franz Boas (1940, v) resumed that anthropology always was about learning from the history of humankind about today. In the present, anthropology is turning more strongly to questions that are also considered socially relevant and pressing. Coleman, Hyatt, and Kingsolver (2017, 12) define the goals of contemporary anthropology as "coming to terms with finding new ways to understand the axes of difference, conflict and division at the forefront of national discussions all over the world." And similarly, Basu (2017, 130) summarizes that "we have seen an increasing tendency for the ethnographic gaze to be turned on such contemporary contexts as bioethics, climate change, conflict resolution, corporate social responsibility, environmentalism, human rights, international development, and labor migration."

Moreover, although anthropology is interested in studying human conflict, its exploration starts more or less from scratch because there is no such thing as one conflict theory. According to Rössel (2013), the notion of conflict in the social sciences played a prominent role in analyzing macro-social contexts. The primary focus of the social sciences has been to understand how societies cohere, yet some authors have also addressed disruptive forces. Scholars such as Weber, Marx, and Simmel studied colliding interest groups within societies and their role in society. Power-critical approaches in the social sciences, which are always theories of conflict, emerged from this thinking. On the other hand, interpersonal disputes between individuals have received less attention in theory building so far. This area receives attention only with the development of neoliberal tendencies in society, where individuals are made responsible for good community coexistence.

Of course, in cultural anthropology, personalities such as Clifford Geertz (1960) have always been interested in forms of conflict, not least in his famous study on cockfights in Bali (Geertz 1973). Later on, a sometimes comparative, sometimes emic exploratory approach to procedures similar to mediation emerged and helped put the cultural reach of Western mediation practices into perspective. Peter Black and Kevin Avruch (1989) were the leading theoreticians in this field. Traditionally, authors have attempted to map the enormous variety of forms found by publishing collections of case studies in anthologies. Avruch, Black, and Scimecca (1991) presented groundbreaking work in their volume on *Conflict Resolution: Cross-Cultural Perspectives*. Watson-Gegeo and White's (1990) anthology on *The Discourse of Disentangling: Conflict, Person and Emotion in the Pacific*, released the year before, is in that tradition, as is later Fry and Björkqvist's (1997) *Cultural Variation in Conflict Resolution*, and also Aureli and de Waal's *Natural Conflict Resolution* (2000). D'Estrée and Parsons' (2018a) *Cultural Encounters and Emergent Practices in Conflict Resolution Capacity-Building* brings a new theory-building impetus to the field, further developing Avruch's thinking. Bramsen,

Poder, and Wæver's (2019) edited volume on *Resolving International Conflict* hosts case studies through the lens of political science. Moscati, Palmer, and Roberts' (2020) *Comparative Dispute Resolution* is another impressive collection. Part of the volume deals with Gulliver's (1979) early study of *Disputes and Negotiations: A Cross-Cultural Perspective*, where Gulliver had sought cultural universals in conflict management as a basis for his approach.

While most of these studies take emic approaches, the fact that they are brought together in one book suggests that comparisons will produce more insights. As a rule for comparative studies in cultural research, Doris Bachmann-Medick (2016, 192) warns against assuming that there will also be a proper *tertium comparationis* for such comparisons without question. In their volume, Koch and Sunde (2020) take an optimistic stance in searching for commonalities in legal culture. In contrast, Bachmann-Medick assumes that more cultural relativist approaches may have their doubts in this respect. Moreover, this research field's orientation often implies that normative and descriptive approaches interweave: What do we study conflict management procedures for? Apart from pure anthropological curiosity, visions for constructive social transformations are always at stake here as well.

Mediation—more than just a temporary craze in intercultural research?

As discussed in the above paragraphs, a brief comparison of both areas of conflict resolution and intercultural research on mediation does not only disclose differences in their respective understandings of the subject matter. The common pleas can indicate that two concepts might indeed be a good fit for each other. The idea of mediation in intercultural research often serves more like an image that would not be much more than a metaphor from the point of view of conflict research. Metaphors such as these can be found in exchange research frequently, for example (Jackson 2018). Already, Gullahorn and Gullahorn (1960), for instance, are writing about Fullbright scholars going overseas as visiting professors and there taking on roles of cross-cultural mediators.

German-language discourses on intercultural communication at the turn of the millennium illustrate these pleas for intercultural mediation. Here, Jürgen Bolten (2001, 924) argues in favor of intercultural mediation referring to recent introductions to mediation as an emerging new concept at that time (Altmann, Fiebiger, and Müller 1999; Haumersen and Liebe 1998; Heimannsberg and Schmidt-Lellek 2000). Bernd Müller-Jacquier and Jan ten Thije (2000, 42) maintain that intercultural mediators should be communicative experts on the cultures from which participants in mediation come. As third parties, they foremost are expected in the position to recognize intercultural misunderstandings and to point them out to the parties. Menno-Arend Herlyn (2001) evidences an in-depth study of conflict resolution literature, also drawing on international sources such as Lederach (1995) as well as Fisher and Ury (1981). Jacob Bercovitch's (e.g., 1989) œuvre bridges the interdisciplinary gaps between intercultural relations and conflict studies, as does Stella Ting-Toomey (e.g., 1985), who is likewise at home in both intercultural and conflict research. Very early on, Stephen Bochner (1973) has explored the figure of the mediating man between cultures. Much of the early works, particularly psychology, recur to culture shock theory (Oberg 1958), stating that people experience psychological and physical distress from their exposure to otherness. These scenarios compose a well-fitting situation, making it seem plausible that people in intercultural contact need help they cannot cope with themselves without (Gullahorn and Gullahorn 1963). By extending the discipline into linguistic pragmatics, linguistic research on intercultural communication showed that linguistic events, such as misunderstandings, go hand in hand with human emotions (Jaszczolt 1996), which created a bridge to the risk of conflict escalation. Juliane House (2003) confirms that linguistics' notion of the figure of misunderstanding attached to intercultural communication attracts the idea of the need for third-party clarification assistance.

Introduction

A rapprochement of intercultural research and conflict research at the turn of the millennium

Busch (2005) elaborated that around the turn of the millennium, both subjects of intercultural communication and conflict research had been gradually converging about their underlying ideas and presumptions to a point, making a reciprocal exchange of concepts reasonable. This rapprochement and a gradual unfolding of analogies in both fields appeared in a series of various features coinciding at a similar time. That period saw significant advances in mediation research and a shift away from the past rationalist negotiation paradigm. While this is undoubtedly a longer-term and more widespread development, there are some prominent articulations, as in the *transformative mediation* approach advocated by Bush and Folger (1994) and the *narrative mediation* model proposed by Winslade and Monk (2000). Intercultural research also shifted its attention from its earlier concern with the problem of understanding the other toward interactional and constructivist approaches to identity.

Shared insight: The importance of interpersonal recognition

For instance, Folger and Bush's key concept of *recognition* comes quite close to considerations from linguistic research on the role of politeness in intercultural contact. The notion of recognition was likewise part of the descriptive approach to positive and negative linguistic politeness strategies. Brown and Levinson (1987, 4:70) had borrowed and advanced Erving Goffman's (1955) facework theories for tracing language politeness expressions in linguistics. Stella Ting-Toomey (1988) later adopted the same approach to describing the perils of misunderstanding in intercultural contact situations (Busch 2005, 139–40). Moreover, even later, she applied her approach to mediation practice (Ting-Toomey 2012) where facework theory had found its place, too (Littlejohn and Domenici 2006).

Shared insight: New attention to the macro level

Bush and Folger also envision their transformative approach to mediation as an endeavor to transform society. Through experiencing transformative mediations, individuals in a society should become more conflict-competent about future issues. Mediation discourse with this leaves the micro-level of analysis and discussion, traditionally centered on the situation-based mediation talk among a few people. Mediation has instead become embedded in the overall societal context. Menkel-Meadow (1995, 217) confirms that the question of to what extent mediation can change society is of great interest in that epoch in general. To change society, Menkel-Meadow writes, is a "common vision" (1995, 218). These ideologies are obscure, she says, and need further exploration. Similarly, research on intercultural communication at the turn of the millennium shifted its focus from the mere micro-situation of the interpersonal encounter to addressing broader societal scenarios (Busch 2005, 141–42). Holliday (2016, 18) says that our view is always ideological, and O'Regan and MacDonald (2007) further specify that this also applies to our ideas of interculturality and how we deal with it.

Shared insight: Slow down and reflect more when interacting

Reflexivity has undoubtedly been a central theme since the Enlightenment. Yet, Byrd Clark (2020, 92–4) in intercultural research reveals the central role of reflexivity as we move from positivist paradigms toward interpretive approaches. In general, reflexivity denotes a slowing down of decision making, whereby people refrain from believing that they can arrive at hasty insights and possibilities for action. Reflexivity emerges in mediation practice for similar reasons (Rothman 2014) and slowing down allows for reflection. Moreover, mediators intervening as third parties in dyadic interaction can often achieve deceleration.

Shared insight: The potentials of re-framings and third spaces

Both areas discovered an attraction to the very idea of overcoming challenging issues by placing them in a new framing (Busch 2005, 147–48). Intercultural research thrilled to the concept of the *third space*, believing it to be a viable solution—a subtle and harmony-focused re-interpretation of Homi Bhabha's (1988) metaphor that he had used to describe social conflict, as MacDonald (2019) reveals. In an alternative interpretation, Xu (2021) posits third spaces themselves as mediators. Like the protected space of mediation, foreign language didactics also envisions learning a foreign language in a self-determined way in a protected space. It is about "speaking under reserve" as Eichinger (2003, 100) points out. As for mediation, Pereira (2019) explores the parallels of the concept with that of the third space, and Hunter (2008) explores the potential of the concept by applying Lederach's (1995) concept on peacebuilding measures through theater projects. Both fields build on the assumption that everybody perceives reality in their specific construction. To allow interaction, a minimum of overlap is needed between these realities (Busch 2005, 150–1).

Shared insights: The potentials of communicative re-phrasing and paraphrasing

Even verbal communication strategies to ensure mutual understanding exist in similar forms in intercultural research and conflict resolution literature. In intercultural research, reformulations and paraphrasing may help ensure understanding and intelligibility (Chiang and Mi 2011). This technique is even similar to translating between languages. Mediation scholars likewise endorse various techniques of reformulation in conversation. For example, Friedman and Himmelstein (2008, 65) use the term *loop of understanding*, whereby the continued reformulation of what is understood serves as a circular movement to ensure mutual understanding.

Shared insights: Responsibility as a key

Both research on conflict resolution and interculturality identify concepts of mutual responsibility as central to an ethics of interculturality and, therefore, intercultural mediation. Ferri (2018) pleads for a concept building on Levinas' notion of responsibility in research on interculturality. In conflict resolution research, Wilson (2010) argues in favor of an ethics of caring conversation and care. Furthermore, Harvey (2002, 523) sees everyone as responsible for his/her fellow humans at any time, so what Ferri and Wilson claim should go without saying. Harvey derives a responsibility for active intervention, i.e., in mediation, from this insight. In the light of an ethics of discourse, Harvey adds that any actor either as a member of a majority or of a minority will always have the right of and be in charge of justifying their attitude.

Emerging promises for reciprocal enhancement

Just as some parallels between intercultural research and mediation research surfaced on an explicit or implicit level around the turn of the millennium, there were also several gaps on one of the sides that the other side could very well address. One key issue here is whether the field's particular problems also have solutions: While intercultural research saw many problems, it did not have any precise solutions. Mediation research, to put it simply, had precisely the opposite. Here, mediation scores with its easy-to-understand phase models designed to be understood by almost everyone and, at best, even replicated (for a discussion of phase models in mediation, cf.

Introduction

Herrman, Hollett, and Gale (2006, 61–2) stating that the idea had been imported from negotiation research and practice as discussed in Holmes (1992) as well as their references to Weitzman and Weitzman (2000, 187); Johnson and Johnson (1989); and Felstiner, Abel, and Sarat (1980). These phase models also appeared in popular guidebooks, leading to a broader reception of the concept beyond academia—and even into neighboring disciplines such as intercultural research.

This straightforward approach of the phase model coincides with intercultural research and its new weariness against the previous focus on problems. There was a recent enthusiasm for a more in-depth look at successful intercultural communication (Koole and ten Thije 2001, 584). Therefore, in intercultural research, authors would certainly welcome practical and effective methods, which is where the phase model comes in. One factor that links intercultural research and mediation research at the turn of the millennium is mediation's momentum for expansion in times of a broader euphoria about the method.

Mediation is repeatedly seen as something that can be transferred to other fields of action (for example political mediation in Touval and Zartman 1985; academia as mediation in Mecea 2016; the mass media as mediators in Gilboa 2000 and many more) and even to other cultures (as examples, cf. Wildau, Moore, and Mayer 1993; Brubaker and Verdonk 1999; and for a critical view cf. Honeyman and Cheldelin 2002). So the very likelihood of transferability is already in the air (Busch 2005, 160). It may also be the end of the Cold War with its dualism and the subsequent search for new orientations (Fukuyama 1992) and/or awareness about the old dualism not transforming itself into a more constructive arrangement (Huntington 1993) that triggered the enthusiasm for mediation at that time.

Intercultural communication as a neoliberal project

Western societies expect their individuals to manage interculturality constructively. This is a *de facto* neoliberal project inherent in almost the whole discourse on intercultural competence (Kubota 2016; Hua, Handford, and Young 2017; Gray, O'Regan, and Wallace 2018). Institutions only rarely intervene, for example, in managing migration, immigration, or flight. Moreover, institutions generally do not take a moral stance but instead deal with legal issues formally, such as issuing residence permits and distinguishing legal statuses (Vertovec 2007). Mediation can be understood here as a communitarian project that restores and empowers the level of civil society (Wieviorka 2003).

Deductive vs. inductive conceptions of intercultural mediation

Busch (2005, 165–84) had shown with a discourse analysis how concepts of mediation in research on intercultural communication were primarily imports from conflict research. Moreover, tacitly, this easy adoption without significant changes had even been celebrated. As Busch pointed out, such an approach limits itself in terms of the additional revenue it is expected to deliver compared to traditional intercultural research. Most importantly, this transfer did no longer even check whether its imports from conflict resolution practice matched the problems identified as characteristic of intercultural communication. The imports may undoubtedly address some of the problems associated with interculturality. However, the new tool will not even be able to address another part (hidden and unnoticed misunderstandings)—and this non-coverage, or mismatch, will not even be noticed.

Busch (2005, 265) terms this transfer of the pre-existing concept of intercultural mediation to a new field a *deductive concept of intercultural mediation*. Against this, Busch (2005, 185–7) proposes a new, *inductive* path to conceptions of intercultural mediation. This is where scholars are encouraged to unlearn their normative precepts of mediation altogether to explore in a freer and more far-reaching approach precisely those triadic interventions that will be most appropriate when dealing precisely with those issues central to intercultural communication. Busch (2005, 187–93) calls for considering spontaneous intercultural lay mediation *to explore intercultural mediation* in full. After all, people who will witness difficulties in intercultural contact and who may be able to provide help as third parties will very likely be less professional than conflict mediators, but instead, much more frequently, people in their everyday situations. An understanding of this kind far exceeds the common distinction between formal and informal mediation. It is precisely this kind of perspective with a broad view that is also proposed for this handbook. For instance, in this volume, Tsuchiya empirically explores the potential of lay third persons in everyday situations.

Intercultural mediation in the light of paradigm shifts in cultural theory

Social theory and many of its sub-disciplines have undergone various paradigm shifts over the past few decades. This means that applied disciplines, or disciplines that center around a theme or an object, will see their themes and objects from possibly very different lights. Given paradigm shifts, objects and topics may suddenly seem irrelevant or disappear altogether. Accordingly, the idea of intercultural mediation has persisted, requiring research on how respective concepts change in the light of these paradigm changes. Even more precise findings would be needed on the directions of influences. To what extent do paradigms determine ideas about intercultural mediation? To what extent do ideas about intercultural mediation influence paradigmatic and ethical approaches to research and theory building? Practically all the disciplines involved here have produced reflections on such paradigm shifts, and often these also have similarities and parallels across disciplines. Here, a brief example of intercultural research and conflict research will illustrate this point. For instance, Hua Zhu, in her introduction (Zhu 2016a) to her anthology *Research Methods in Intercultural Communication* (Zhu 2016b), elaborated on how research on intercultural communication has gone through four paradigms in a sequential manner. Zhu lists the *positivist*, the *interpretive*, the *critical*, and the *constructivist* paradigm (Zhu 2016a, 6–13). Each paradigm entails its epistemological assumptions as to how and in what ways scholars can enter the field and what they will see. This also goes in hand with varying ethical beliefs about what researchers and practitioners should do in relevant situations.

Maria Dasli (2011) earlier had focused even more specifically on this different normative-ideological load and research orientation associated with the different paradigms when she spoke of different *moments* in intercultural research. Dasli's concept is of particular interest to this issue, not least because after a "cultural awareness" moment, Dasli had spoken of a subsequent "cross-cultural mediation" moment, upon which she suggested a "critical intercultural language pedagogy" moment (Dasli 2011, 23–33). Dasli finds the idea of mediation most plausible as long an interpretative paradigm is assumed in which the actors build their constructions of reality. Further research will be needed to determine whether mediation also makes sense in the other paradigms and moments.

Conflict research follows similar paradigmatic trends, with Kevin Avruch (2007, 14) even recommending a closer alignment with cultural anthropology. With a few exceptions, such as Laura Nader's work (cf. even more clearly in their later publication in Mattei and Nader 2008), he complains that this discipline is still far behind. That is the only way to make underlying ideologies, such as the constant harmony orientation in the ADR movement, apparent and allow for reflection (Avruch 2007, 13). That said, a variety of hidden paradigms do exist, as Barbara Wilson (2010), for instance, reveals through her reading of seminal monographs on mediation research. Accordingly, Fisher and Ury's (1981) *Getting to Yes*, follows utilitarian ethics; Bush and Folger's (1994) *The Promise of Mediation*, in contrast, mirrors communitarian ethics. Winslade and Monk's (2000) *Narrative Mediation* builds upon Habermas' discourse ethics, and Bowling and Hoffman's (2003) *Bringing Peace into the Room* displays ethics of virtue.

LeBaron, McCandless, and Garon (1998, 1–3) review the literature on culture and conflict between 1992 and 1998, noticing an opening of the research field from culture-essentialist to including culture-constructivist approaches and a high increase in in-depth cultural research as well as

Introduction

a growing variety of theories, models, and practice tools, respectively. Challenging the politics of multiculturalism with its blindness to power structures and identity constructions is the primary ethical driver that LeBaron et al. see in research on conflict and culture at that epoch.

Busch (2016), recurring with Heinemann and Zurth (2013), resumes that authors in mediation have very different understandings of what makes a mediation intercultural. These understandings may be

(1) 'Intercultural mediation' means that participants to a mediation originate from different (national) cultures. (2) 'Intercultural mediation' means that a mediator originates from another culture than do his clients. (3) 'Intercultural mediation' deals with conflicts arising from cultural differences. (4) 'Intercultural mediation' embraces any ways of triadic conflict management beyond jurisdiction that do not recur to the Western model of Alternative Dispute Resolution (ADR). (5) 'Intercultural mediation' includes any attempts of applying forms of ADR to intercultural settings. (6) 'Intercultural mediation' means that forms of ADR are applied to Non-Western cultural contexts.

Busch (2016, 187–8) reveals that authors from these fields tend to choose those models of culture that best support their initial assumptions about intercultural mediation.

D'Estrée and Parsons (2018b, 3) identify four "developmental waves over the last approximately 30 years in the transfer of neutrality-based 'institutional' or 'formal models' of mediation to many developing counties (sic) with highly diverse cultures" (d'Estrée and Parsons 2018b, 3). Starting from a first wave of transferring Western mediation models to other cultures without any changes in the 1980s, a second wave brought attention to the effects of culture in the discipline. Etic analyses of cultural differences in conflict management highlighted general dimensions of cultural variation (d'Estrée and Parsons 2018b, 10–1). A third wave called for closer looks at particular cultural contexts, where ethnographic and emic approaches produced detailed descriptions of conflict management habits in singled-out cultures. D'Estrée and Parsons argue that today's world needs a new, fourth wave acknowledging that in times of globalization, cultures and cultural conflict resolution styles influence each other and merge. Cultural hybridity is an everyday matter of fact. So conflict resolution practices should be analyzed and described in their culture-hybrid and context-based genesis (d'Estrée and Parsons 2018b, 11–2).

Quek Anderson (2019, 123) proposes a perspective on intercultural conflict resolution that, from a critical cosmopolitan standpoint, may eventually add another fifth wave to d'Estrée and Parsons' (2018b) four waves model.

Every person in our increasingly globalised world is exposed to a multiplicity of places. This reality makes for rather complex analysis of the nexus between a particular place and human behaviour. Singapore, a cosmopolitan society, has considerable diversity in race, age groups and worldviews. Within this society, each person will have a unique conceptualisation of a given place, depending on the exposure to different influences.

(Quek Anderson 2019, 123)

Consequently, adequate analyses of intercultural conflict mediations will need to consider each individual's particular construction of their intercultural lifeworlds.

A ride through the handbook sections and how to understand their order

This interdisciplinary and highly diverse approach to the subject of intercultural mediation is the reason for its emergence. An unusual arrangement attempts to consider this diversity and mutual interconnectedness in this handbook. It is undoubtedly an implicit narrative underlying this order, and the discourse around intercultural mediation may also evolve in an almost stereotypical way here. Still, a first step into the field might be to study the approaches and (intercultural) challenges of professional conflict mediation in the Western tradition.

This is where the book starts with the contributions in *Part I: Professional intercultural dispute mediation*. While this part focuses on interpersonal contexts, *Part II: Intercultural mediation in international politics* addresses formal constellations at macro levels in society, where the transformative potential of mediation will also be discussed. The following three parts discuss theoretical problems that arise in the interplay of reflecting on relationships between culture and conflict transformation, focusing primarily on new and current challenges brought about by recent paradigms in cultural theory. Correspondingly, *Part III: De-centering Alternative Dispute Resolution (ADR)* addresses various challenges of de-ethnocentering and de-centering intercultural mediation. *Part IV: De-essentializing culture in intercultural mediation* looks at challenges arising from the ever-present threat of essentializing culture—notably in applied disciplines. *Part V: Theorizing intercultural mediation* collects approaches striving for theorizing the phenomenon of intercultural mediation. Many of these approaches originate in the fields of anthropology and cultural anthropology.

This orientation following traditional academic disciplines continues over the next four sections. *Part VI: Linguistic explorations of intercultural mediation* focuses primarily on conversation analytic methods to uncover the communicative management of situations of intercultural mediation. Here, language-based culturalizations play an essential role. Therefore, the conversation analytic approach is especially suitable for analyzing micro contexts in everyday life. *Part VII: Psychological tools for analyzing intercultural mediation* brings together contributions to the study of phenomena of intercultural mediation from the field of psychology. Above all, aspects of human conflict behavior come into view, whereby the chances and limits of constructive interaction between individuals will always depend on their willingness to do so. *Part VIII: Translation research and intercultural mediation* explores the vast field and seminal contributions from translation research, seeing intercultural mediation as an internal state of mind alongside the more traditional interpersonal construct. *Part IX: Intercultural mediation in foreign language education and the arts* follows directly and deals with various educational contexts, which have always fundamentally relied on ideas of mediation and where approaches to intercultural mediation are also being actively developed. Consequently, the order of contributions presented here cannot be understood as a series but rather as a circular layout of all sections. All areas contribute to an overall picture of intercultural mediation.

References

Agustí-Panareda, J. 2006. "Cross-Cultural Brokering in the Legal, Institutional and Normative Domains: Intercultural Mediators Managing Immigration in Catalonia." *Social and Legal Studies* 15 (3): 409–33. 10.1177/0964663906066618.

Alred, Geof, and Mike Byram. 2002. "Becoming an Intercultural Mediator: A Longitudinal Study of Residence Abroad." *Journal of Multilingual and Multicultural Development* 23 (5): 339–52. 10.1080/01434630208666473.

Altmann, Gerhard, Heinrich Fiebiger, and Rolf Müller. 1999. *Mediation. Konfliktmanagement für Moderne Unternehmen*. Weinheim, Basel: Beltz.

Aubert, Vilhelm. 1963. "Competition and Dissensus: Two Types of Conflict and of Conflict Resolution." *Journal of Conflict Resolution* 7 (1): 26–42. 10.1177/002200276300700105.

Aureli, Filippo, and Frans B. M. de Waal, eds. 2000. *Natural Conflict Resolution*. Berkeley: University of California Press.

Avruch, Kevin. 2003. "Type I and Type II Errors in Culturally Sensitive Conflict Resolution Practice." *Conflict Resolution Quarterly* 20 (3): 351–71. 10.1002/crq.29.

Avruch, Kevin. 2007. "A Historical Overview of Anthropology and Conflict Resolution." *Anthropology News* 48 (6): 13–4. 10.1525/an.2007.48.6.13.

Avruch, Kevin, Peter W. Black, and Joseph A. Scimecca, eds. 1991. *Conflict Resolution. Cross-Cultural Perspectives*. New York/Westport/London: Greenwood.

Introduction

Bachmann-Medick, Doris. 2016. *Cultural Turns: New Orientations in the Study of Culture*. Berlin: De Gruyter.

Baraldi, Claudio. 2009. "Forms of Mediation: The Case of Interpreter-Mediated Interactions in Medical Systems." *Language and Intercultural Communication* 9 (2): 120–37. 10.1080/14708470802588393.

Basu, Paul. 2017. "Communicating Anthropology. Writing, Screening, and Exhibiting Culture." In *The Routledge Companion to Contemporary Anthropology*, edited by Simon Coleman, Susan Brin Hyatt, and Ann E. Kingsolver, 124–43. London, New York, NY: Routledge.

Bercovitch, Jacob. 1989. "International Dispute Mediation: A Comparative Empirical Analysis." In *Mediation Research: The Process and Effectiveness of Third-Party Intervention*, edited by Kenneth Kressel and Dean G. Pruitt, 284–99. San Francisco, CA: Jossey Bass.

Bhabha, Homi K. 1988. "The Commitment to Theory." *New Formations* 5: 5–23.

Black, Peter W., and Kevin Avruch. 1989. "Some Issues in Thinking About Culture and the Resolution of Conflict." *Humanity & Society* 13 (2): 187–94. 10.1177/016059768901300207.

Boas, Franz. 1940. *Race, Language and Culture*. New York: Macmillan.

Bochner, Stephen. 1973. *The Mediating Man: Cultural Interchange and Transnational Education*. Honolulu, HI: East-West Center.

Bolten, Jürgen. 2001. "Interkulturelles Coaching, Mediation, Training und Consulting als Aufgaben des Personalmanagements internationaler Unternehmen." In *Strategisches Personalmanagement in globalen Unternehmen*, edited by Alois Clermont, Wilhelm Schmeisser, and Dieter Krimphove, 909–26. München: Vahlen.

Bowland, S. Y., Hasshan Batts, Beth Roy, and Mary Adams Trujillo, eds. 2022. *Beyond Equity and Inclusion in Conflict Resolution: Recentering the Profession*. The ACR Practitioner's Guide Series. Lanham: Rowman & Littlefield.

Bowling, Daniel, and David A. Hoffman. 2003. *Bringing Peace Into the Room*. San Francisco, CA.: Jossey-Bass.

Bramsen, Isabel, Poul Poder, and Ole Wæver, eds. 2019. *Resolving International Conflict*. Abingdon, Oxon, New York: Routledge. 10.4324/9781315102009.

Brown, Penelope, and Stephen C. Levinson. 1987. *Politeness. Some Universals in Language Usage*. Cambridge: Cambridge University Press.

Brubaker, David, and Tara Verdonk. 1999. "Conflict Transformation Training in Another Culture: A Case Study from Angola." *Mediation Quarterly* 16 (3): 303–19. 10.1002/crq.3890160308.

Busch, Dominic. 2005. *Interkulturelle Mediation. Eine theoretische Grundlegung triadischer Konfliktbearbeitung in interkulturell bedingten Kontexten.* [Intercultural Mediation. A Theoretical Foundation of Triadic Conflict Management in Contexts Affected from Interculturality]. Frankfurt am Main: Peter Lang.

Busch, Dominic. 2016. "Does Conflict Mediation Research Keep Track with Cultural Theory?" *European Journal of Applied Linguistics* 4 (2): 181–206. 10.1515/eujal-2015-0037.

Bush, Robert A. Baruch, and Joseph P. Folger. 1994. *The Promise of Mediation: Responding to Conflict Through Empowerment and Recognition*. San Francisco: Jossey Bass.

Byrd Clark, Julie S. 2020. "Reflexivity and Criticality for Language and Intercultural Communication Research and Practice." In *The Routledge Handbook of Language and Intercultural Communication*, edited by Jane Jackson, 2nd edition, 86–106. Routledge. 10.4324/9781003036210-7.

Chiang, Shiao-Yun, and Han-Fu Mi. 2011. "Reformulation: A Verbal Display of Interlanguage Awareness in Instructional Interactions." *Language Awareness* 20 (2): 135–49. 10.1080/09658416.2011.559243.

Coleman, Simon, Susan Brin Hyatt, and Ann E. Kingsolver. 2017. "Introduction to an Engaging Discipline. The Challenge of Creating a Companion to Contemporary Anthropology." In *The Routledge Companion to Contemporary Anthropology*, edited by Simon Coleman, Susan Brin Hyatt, and Ann E. Kingsolver, 3–23. London, New York: Routledge.

Condon, John C. 2015. "Intercultural Communication, Definition Of." In *The Sage Encyclopedia of Intercultural Competence*, edited by Janet Marie Bennett, 451–3. Thousand Oaks: Sage. 10.4135/9781483346267.n151.

Dasli, Maria. 2011. "Reviving the 'Moments': From Cultural Awareness and Cross-cultural Mediation to Critical Intercultural Language Pedagogy." *Pedagogy, Culture & Society* 19 (1): 21–39. 10.1080/14681366. 2011.527118.

Dervin, Fred. 2016. *Interculturality in Education: A Theoretical and Methodological Toolbox*. London: Palgrave Macmillan.

Dietz, Gunther. 2018. "Interculturality." In *The International Encyclopedia of Anthropology*, edited by Hilary Callan, 23: 1–19. Oxford, U.K.: Wiley. 10.1002/9781118924396.wbiea1629.

Druckman, Daniel, and James A. Wall. 2017. "A Treasure Trove of Insights." *Journal of Conflict Resolution* 61 (9): 1898–1924. 10.1177/0022002717721388.

Eichinger, Ludwig M. 2003. "Mediation und Vermittlung. Verstehen erzeugen und Verständnis wecken." In *Mediation und Vermittlung*, edited by Alois Wierlacher, 95–106. Jahrbuch Deutsch Als Fremdsprache 29. München: iudicium.

d'Estrée, Tamra Pearson, and Ruth J. Parsons, eds. 2018a. *Cultural Encounters and Emergent Practices in Conflict Resolution Capacity-Building*. Cham: Springer International Publishing. 10.1007/978-3-319-71102-7.

d'Estrée, Tamra Pearson, and Ruth J. Parsons. 2018b. "The State of the Art and the Need for Context-Grounded Practice in Conflict Resolution." In *Cultural Encounters and Emergent Practices in Conflict Resolution Capacity-Building*, edited by Tamra Pearson d'Estrée and Ruth J. Parsons, 1–29. Cham: Springer International. 10.1007/978-3-319-71102-7_1.

Fantini, Alvino E. 2009. "Assessing Intercultural Competence. Issues and Tools." In *The Sage Handbook of Intercultural Competence*, edited by Darla K. Deardorff, 456–76. Thousand Oaks, London, New Delhi, Singapore: Sage.

Felstiner, William L.F., Richard L. Abel, and Austin Sarat. 1980. "The Emergence and Transformation of Disputes: Naming, Blaming, Claiming." *Law and Society Review* 15 (3–4): 631–54.

Ferri, Giuliana. 2018. *Intercultural Communication—Critical Approaches and Future Challenges*. Cham, CH: Palgrave Macmillan.

Fisher, Roger, and William Ury. 1981. *Getting to Yes: Negotiating Agreement without Giving In*. Boston: Houghton Mifflin.

Friedman, Gary J., and Jack Himmelstein. 2008. *Challenging Conflict: Mediation through Understanding*. Chicago, IL: American Bar Association.

Fry, Douglas P., and Kaj Björkqvist, eds. 1997. *Cultural Variation in Conflict Resolution: Alternatives to Violence*. Mahwah, N.J.: Lawrence Erlbaum.

Fukuyama, Francis. 1992. *The End of History and the Last Man*. New York, Toronto, New York: Free Press, Maxwell Macmillan Canada.

Geertz, Clifford. 1960. "The Javanese Kijaji: The Changing Role of a Cultural Broker." *Comparative Studies in Society and History* 2 (2): 228–49. 10.1017/S0010417500000670.

Geertz, Clifford. 1973. "Deep Play: Notes on the Balinese Cockfight." In *The Interpretation of Cultures*, edited by Clifford Geertz, 412–53. New York: Basic Books.

Georgakopoulos, Alexia. 2017. "Introduction: Revealing the World of Mediation." In *The Mediation Handbook: Research, Theory, and Practice*, edited by Alexia Georgakopoulos, 1–6. New York: Routledge.

Gilboa, Eytan. 2000. "Mass Communication and Diplomacy: A Theoretical Framework." *Communication Theory* 10 (3): 275–309. 10.1111/j.1468-2885.2000.tb00193.x.

Goffman, Erving. 1955. "On Facework: An Analysis of Ritual Elements in Social Interaction." *Psychiatry* 18: 213–31.

Gray, John, John P. O'Regan, and Catherine Wallace. 2018. "Education and the Discourse of Global Neoliberalism." *Language and Intercultural Communication* 18 (5): 471–7. 10.1080/14708477.2018.1501842.

Guilherme, Manuela. 2015. "Critical Pedagogy." In *The Sage Encyclopedia of Intercultural Competence*, edited by Janet Marie Bennett, 139–42. Thousand Oaks: Sage. 10.4135/9781483346267.n54.

Guilherme, Manuela, and Gunther Dietz. 2015. "Difference in Diversity: Multiple Perspectives on Multicultural, Intercultural, and Transcultural Conceptual Complexities." *Journal of Multicultural Discourses* 10 (1): 1–21. 10.1080/17447143.2015.1015539.

Gullahorn, John T., and Jeanne E. Gullahorn. 1960. "The Role of the Academic Man as a Cross-Cultural Mediator." *American Sociological Review* 25 (3): 414–17.

Gullahorn, John T., and Jeanne E. Gullahorn. 1963. "An Extension of the U-Curve Hypothesis." *Journal of Social Issues* 19 (3): 33–47. 10.1111/j.1540-4560.1963.tb00447.x.

Gulliver, Philip Hugh. 1979. *Disputes and Negotiations: A Cross-Cultural Perspective*. Studies on Law and Social Control. New York: Academic Press.

Harvey, Jesamine. 2002. "Stereotypes and Moral Oversight in Conflict Resolution: What Are We Teaching?" *Journal of Philosophy of Education* 36 (4): 513–27. 10.1111/1467-9752.00292.

Haumersen, Petra, and Frank Liebe. 1998. "Interkulturelle Mediation. Empirisch-analytische Annäherung an die Bedeutung von kulturellen Unterschieden." In *Migration, Konflikt und Mediation. Zum interkulturellen Diskurs in der Jugendarbeit*, edited by Lothar Breidenstein, Doron Kiesel, and Jörg Walther, 135–55. Frankfurt/Main: Haag und Herchen.

Heimannsberg, Barbara, and C. J. Schmidt-Lellek, eds. 2000. *Interkulturelle Beratung und Mediation. Konzepte, Erfahrungen, Perspektiven*. Köln: EHP, Organisation.

Heinemann, Franziska, and Erik Zurth. 2013. *Welche Rolle spielt Das Verständnis von Kultur in Konzepten interkultureller Mediation im Rahmen der Mediations- und Konfliktforschung?* [What Role Do Notions of Culture Play in Concepts of Intercultural Mediation Within Research on Mediation and Conflict?]. Neubiberg: Universität der Bundeswehr München, Faculty of Human Sciences: Unpublished seminar paper.

Helakorpi, Jenni, Sirpa Lappalainen, and Fritjof Sahlström. 2019. "Becoming Tolerable: Subject Constitution of Roma Mediators in Finnish Schools." *Intercultural Education* 30 (1): 51–67. 10.1080/14675986.2018.1537671.

Herlyn, Menno-Arend. 2001. "International Business Mediation. 'The Art of Being Unconditionally Constructive.'" *Global Player. International Management & Business Culture* 3: 32–3.

Herrman, Margaret S., Nancy Hollett, and Jerry Gale. 2006. "Mediation from Beginning to End: A Testable Model." In *The Blackwell Handbook of Mediation. Bridging Theory, Research, and Practice*, edited by Margaret Herrmann, 19–78. Malden MA, Oxford, Victoria: Blackwell.

Herrmann, Margaret, ed. 2006. *The Blackwell Handbook of Mediation. Bridging Theory, Research, and Practice*. Malden MA, Oxford, Victoria: Blackwell.

Holliday, Adrian. 2011. *Intercultural Communication and Ideology*. Los Angeles, London, New Delhi, Singapore, Washington DC: Sage. 10.4135/9781446269107.

Holliday, Adrian. 2016. *Doing & Writing Qualitative Research*. 3rd edition. Los Angeles: Sage.

Holliday, Adrian. 2022. "Searching for a Third-Space Methodology to Contest Essentialist Large-Culture Blocks." *Language and Intercultural Communication* 22 (3): 367–380. 10.1080/14708477.2022.2036180.

Holmes, Michael. 1992. "Phase Structures in Negotiation." In *Communication and Negotiation*, edited by Linda Putnam and Michael Roloff, 83–106. Thousand Oaks, CA: Sage. 10.4135/9781483325880.n5.

Honeyman, Christopher, and Sandra I. Cheldelin. 2002. "Have Gavel, Will Travel: Dispute Resolution's Innocents Abroad." *Conflict Resolution Quarterly* 19 (3): 363–72. 10.1002/crq.3890190308.

House, Juliane. 2003. "Misunderstanding in Intercultural University Encounters." In *Misunderstanding in Social Life. Discourse Approaches to Problematic Talk*, edited by Juliane House, Gabriele Kasper, and Steven Ross, 22–56. Harlow: Pearson.

Hua, Zhu, Michael Handford, and Tony Johnstone Young. 2017. "Framing Interculturality: A Corpus-Based Analysis of Online Promotional Discourse of Higher Education Intercultural Communication Courses." *Journal of Multilingual and Multicultural Development* 38: 283–300. 10.1080/01434632.2015.1134555.

Hunter, Mary Ann. 2008. "Cultivating the Art of Safe Space." *Research in Drama Education: The Journal of Applied Theatre and Performance* 13 (1): 5–21. 10.1080/13569780701825195.

Huntington, Samuel P. 1993. "The Clash of Civilizations?" *Foreign Affairs* 72: 22–49.

Jackson, Jane. 2018. *Interculturality in International Education*. New York: Routledge. 10.4324/9780429490026.

Jaszczolt, Katarzyna. 1996. "Relevance and Infinity: Implications for Discourse Interpretation." *Journal of Pragmatics* 25: 703–22.

Johnson, David W., and Roger T. Johnson. 1989. *Cooperation and Competition: Theory and Research*. Edina, NM: Interaction Books.

Jones, Tricia. 2006. "Emotion in Mediation: Implications, Applications, Opportunities, and Challenges." In *The Blackwell Handbook of Mediation. Bridging Theory, Research, and Practice*, edited by Margaret Herrmann, 277–305. Malden MA, Oxford, Victoria: Blackwell.

Keating Marshall, Kelle, and Wendy D. Bokhorst-Heng. 2018. "'I Wouldn't Want to Impose!' Intercultural Mediation in French Immersion." *Foreign Language Annals* 51 (2): 290–312. 10.1111/flan.12340.

Kirmayer, Laurence J., Jaswant Guzder, and Cécile Rousseau, eds. 2014. *Cultural Consultation*. International and Cultural Psychology. New York: Springer. 10.1007/978-1-4614-7615-3.

Koch, Sören, and Jørn Øyrehagen Sunde, eds. 2020. *Comparing Legal Cultures*. Revised and Extended edition. Bergen: Fagbokforlaget.

Koole, Tom, and Jan D. ten Thije. 2001. "The Reconstruction of Intercultural Discourse: Methodological Considerations." *Journal of Pragmatics* 33 (4): 571–87. 10.1016/S0378-2166(00)00035-7.

Kramsch, Claire. 1999. "Thirdness: The Intercultural Stance." In *Language, Culture and Identity*, edited by Torben Vestergaard, 41–58. Aalborg: Aalborg University Press.

Kubota, R. 2016. "The Social Imaginary of Study Abroad: Complexities and Contradictions." *Language Learning Journal* 44: 347–57. 10.1080/09571736.2016.1198098.

LeBaron, M. 2003. *Bridging Cultural Conflicts. A New Approach for a Changing World*. London: Jossey-Bass.

LeBaron, Michelle, Erin McCandless, and Stephen Garon. 1998. *Conflict and Culture. A Literature Review and Bibliography. 1992–1998 Update*. Fairfax VA: George Mason University, Institute for Conflict Analysis and Resolution.

Lederach, John Paul. 1995. *Preparing for Peace. Conflict Transformation Across Cultures*. Syracuse: Syracuse University Press.

Lewicki, Roy J., David M. Saunders, and Bruce Barry. 2010. *Essentials of Negotiation*. 5th edition. New York, NY: McGraw-Hill/Irwin.

Liddicoat, Anthony J. 2015. "Interculturality." In *The International Encyclopedia of Language and Social Interaction*, edited by Cornelia Ilie, Todd L. Sandel, and Karen Tracy, 1–5. Chichester, UK; Malden, MA, USA: Wiley Blackwell. 10.1002/9781118611463.wbielsi048.

Littlejohn, Stephen, and Kathy Domenici. 2006. "A Facework Frame for Mediation." In *The Blackwell Handbook of Mediation. Bridging Theory, Research, and Practice*, edited by Margaret Herrmann, 228–46. Malden MA, Oxford, Victoria: Blackwell.

MacDonald, Malcolm N. 2019. "The Discourse of 'Thirdness' in Intercultural Studies." *Language and Intercultural Communication* 19 (1): 93–109. 10.1080/14708477.2019.1544788.

Malmkjaer, Kirsten, ed. 2017. *The Routledge Handbook of Translation Studies and Linguistics.* London: Routledge. 10.4324/9781315692845.

Mattei, Ugo, and Laura Nader. 2008. *Plunder: When the Rule of Law Is Illegal.* Malden, MA: Blackwell.

Mecea, Mihaela. 2016. "Training in Intercultural Mediation in a Multicultural University: Contributions for Fostering International Stability." *AI & Society* 31 (3, S.I.): 393–9. 10.1007/s00146-015-0602-y.

Menkel-Meadow, Carrie. 1995. "Book Review." *Negotiation Journal* 11 (3): 217–42. 10.1007/BF02187218.

Miklavcic, Alessandra, and Marie Nathalie LeBlanc. 2014. "Culture Brokers, Clinically Applied Ethnography, and Cultural Mediation." In *Cultural Consultation*, edited by Laurence J. Kirmayer, Jaswant Guzder, and Cécile Rousseau, 115–37. New York: Springer. 10.1007/978-1-4614-7615-3_6.

Moscati, Maria, Michael Palmer, and Marian Roberts, eds. 2020. *Comparative Dispute Resolution.* Cheltenham, UK; Northampton, MA: Edward Elgar. 10.4337/9781786433039.

Müller-Jacquier, Bernd, and Jan D. ten Thije. 2000. "Interkulturelle Kommunikation: Interkulturelles Training und Mediation." In *Linguistische Berufe. Ein Ratgeber zu aktuellen linguistischen Berufsfeldern*, edited by Michael Becker-Mrotzek, Gisela Brünner, and Hermann Cölfen, 39–59. Frankfurt am Main: Lang.

Oberg, Kalervo. 1958. *Culture Shock and the Problem of Adjustment to New Cultural Environments.* Washington, DC: Department of State, Foreign Service Institute.

O'Regan, John P., and Malcolm N. MacDonald. 2007. "Cultural Relativism and the Discourse of Intercultural Communication: Aporias of Praxis in the Intercultural Public Sphere." *Language and Intercultural Communication* 7 (4): 267–78. 10.2167/laic287.0.

Pereira, Fatima. 2019. "Teacher Education, Teachers' Work, and Justice in Education: Third Space and Mediation Epistemology." *Australian Journal of Teacher Education* 44 (3): 77–92. 10.14221/ajte.2018v44n3.5.

Phipps, Alison. 1999. "Intercultural Germanistics." In *Schwellen. Germanistische Erkundungen einer* Metapher, edited by Nicholas Saul, 289–303. Würzburg: Königshausen & Neumann.

Platz, Norbert, ed. 1991. *Mediating Cultures. Probleme des Kulturtransfers. Perspektiven für Forschung und Lehre.* Essen: Verlag Die Blaue Eule.

Pokorn, Nike K., and Tamara Mikolič Južnič. 2020. "Community Interpreters versus Intercultural Mediators: Is It Really All about Ethics?" *Translation and Interpreting Studies* 15 (1): 80–107. 10.1075/tis.20027.koc.

Pruitt, Dean G., and Kenneth Kressel. 1989. "Introduction: An Overview of Mediation Research." In *Mediation Research: The Process and Effectiveness of Third-Party Intervention*, edited by Kenneth Kressel and Dean G. Pruitt, 1–8. San Francisco, CA: Jossey Bass.

Pym, Anthony, and Nune Ayvazyan. 2017. "Linguistics, Translation and Interpreting in Foreign Language Teaching Contexts." In *The Routledge Handbook of Translation Studies and Linguistics*, edited by Kirsten Malmkjaer, 393–407. London: Routledge.

Quek Anderson, Dorcas. 2019. "Court-Annexed Mediations within Singapore: A Complex Interface between Individual Place and the Court Environment." In *The Nexus among Place, Conflict and Communication in a Globalising World*, edited by Pauline Collins, Victor Igreja, and Patrick Alan Danaher, 20: 121–44. Singapore: Springer. 10.1007/978-981-13-5925-5_7.

Rössel, Jörg. 2013. "Conflict Theory." In *Oxford Bibliographies in Sociology*, edited by Lynette Spillman. New York; Oxford, UK: Oxford University Press. 10.1093/OBO/9780199756384-0035.

Rothman, Jay. 2014. "The Reflexive Mediator." *Negotiation Journal* 30 (4): 441–53. 10.1111/nejo.12070.

Salacuse, Jeswald W. 1988. "Making Deals in Strange Places: A Beginner's Guide to International Business Negotiations." *Negotiation Journal* 4 (1): 5–13. 10.1111/j.1571-9979.1988.tb00441.x.

Schulz, Jennifer L. 2020. *Mediation & Popular Culture.* London: Routledge. 10.4324/9780429059551.

Ting-Toomey, Stella. 1985. "Toward a Theory of Conflict and Culture." In *Communication, Culture and Organizational Processes*, edited by William B. Gudykunst, Lea Stewart, and Stella Ting-Toomey, 71–86. Beverly Hills, CA: Sage.

Ting-Toomey, Stella. 1988. "Intercultural Conflict Styles: A Face-Negotiation Theory." In *Theories in Intercultural Communication*, edited by Young Yun Kim and William B. Gudykunst, 213–35. Newbury Park, CA: Sage.

Ting-Toomey, Stella. 2012. "Understanding Intercultural Conflict Competence. Multiple Theoretical Insights." In *The Routledge Handbook of Language and Intercultural Communication*, edited by Jane Jackson, 279–95. Oxon, New York: Routledge.

Touval, Saadia, and I. William Zartman. 1985. *International Mediation in Theory and Practice.* Boulder Washington, D.C.: Westview Press.

Turk, A. Marco, and John Ungerleider. 2017. "Experiential Activities in Mediation-Based Training: Cyprus, 1997–2013." *Conflict Resolution Quarterly* 34 (3): 281–300. 10.1002/crq.21183.

Tylor, Edward B. 1896. *Anthropology. An Introduction to the Study of Man and Civilization.* New York: D. Appleton.

Valdeón, Roberto A. 2021. "Translation: From Mediation to Gatekeeping and Agenda-Setting." *Language and Intercultural Communication* 21 (1): 24–36. 10.1080/14708477.2020.1833903.

Valero-Garcés, C. 2007. "Challenges in Multilingual Societies. The Myth of the Invisible Interpreter and Translator." *Across Languages and Cultures* 8: 81–101. 10.1556/Acr.8.2007.1.5.

Vertovec, Steven. 2007. "Super-Diversity and Its Implications." *Ethnic and Racial Studies* 30 (6): 1024–54. 10.1080/01419870701599465.

Wall, James A. 1990. "Mediation in the People's Republic of China." In *Theory and Research in Conflict Management*, edited by Afzalur M. Rahim, 109–19. New York: Praeger.

Wall, James A., and Timothy C. Dunne. 2012. "Mediation Research: A Current Review." *Negotiation Journal* 28 (2): 217–44. 10.1111/j.1571-9979.2012.00336.x.

Watson-Gegeo, Karen Ann, and Geoffrey M. White, eds. 1990. *The Discourse of Disentangling: Conflict, Person and Emotion in the Pacific.* Stanford, CA: Stanford University Press.

Weitzman, Eben A., and Patricia Flynn Weitzman. 2000. "Problem Solving and Decision Making in Conflict Resolution." In *The Handbook of Conflict Resolution: Theory and Practice*, edited by Morton Deutsch and Peter T. Coleman, 185–209. Hoboken, NJ: Jossey-Bass/Wiley.

Wierlacher, Alois. 2003. "Vermittlung." In *Handbuch Interkulturelle Germanistik*, edited by Alois Wierlacher and Andrea Bogner, 330–7. Stuttgart: J.B. Metzler.

Wieviorka, Michel. 2003. *Mediation: A European Comparison.* Paris: Centre for Sociological Analysis and Intervention.

Wildau, Susan T., Christopher W. Moore, and Bernard S. Mayer. 1993. "Developing Democratic Decision-Making and Dispute Resolution Procedures Abroad." *Mediation Quarterly* 10 (3): 303–20. 10.1002/crq.3900100309.

Wilson, Barbara. 2010. "Mediation Ethics: An Exploration of Four Seminal Texts." *Journal of Conflict Resolution* 12 (1): 119–42. 10.1002/crq.118/pdf.

Winslade, John, and Gerald Monk. 2000. *Narrative Mediation.* San Francisco: Jossey-Bass.

Xu, Yujun. 2021. "All At-Sea with Learning Spaces, Interculturality and Yin-Yang." *Language and Intercultural Communication*, 1–19. 10.1080/14708477.2020.1869247.

Zhu, Hua. 2016a. "Identifying Research Paradigms." In *Research Methods in Intercultural Communication: A Practical Guide*, edited by Hua Zhu, 3–22. Chichester: Wiley Blackwell. 10.1002/9781119166283.

Zhu, Hua, ed. 2016b. *Research Methods in Intercultural Communication: A Practical Guide.* Chichester: Wiley Blackwell.

PART I

Professional intercultural dispute mediation

1

CULTURE AND MEDIATION: A 2020S PERSPECTIVE ON EARLY CRITICISM OF WESTERN PARADIGMS

Greg Bond

When looking for early publications that consider the role of culture in mediation, then it will come as no surprise that these were written and published in the USA. The modern mediation movement, as it is often called, began in the USA, and so did first attempts to question some of its assumptions and challenge its implicit claims to universality from different cultural perspectives.

In their seminal book on negotiation, *Getting to Yes*, Roger Fisher and William Ury do not focus in any way on mediation, but nonetheless their theory remains a foundation for mediation practice to this day, with the linear phase model and many underlying principles of mediation embodied in their steps in negotiation theory and practice, from *separate the people from the problem*, to *focus on interests not positions*, to dev*elop options for mutual gain*. Culture did not figure at all in this book (Fisher and Ury 1981), though it was included briefly in newer editions from 1991 onward in the additional questions asked and answered section, as an answer to the question: "How should I adjust my negotiating approach to account for differences of personality, gender, culture, and so on?" (Fisher, Ury, and Patton 2007, 173), where the answers are pragmatic pieces of advice with no reflection on any need to question or alter any of the fundamentals of principled negotiation. But nor does *Getting to Yes* need to address culture—Fisher and Ury were writing from the perspective of the USA of their time, and yet their book also has a timeless quality, having weathered the decades astoundingly well. The fact that the principled negotiation model developed in *Getting to Yes* is still taught all over the world would suggest either that it crosses cultures well or that the (hegemonial) dissemination and marketing of the model and its underlying cultural assumptions have been incredibly successful. This is probably not a simple either/or, but a both/and. And there is no way of really knowing to what degree the model of principled negotiation is adapted when taught in different contexts.

Three books stand out when looking for early attempts to situate dispute resolution and mediation within culturally different practices, and to thereby challenge hitherto unreflected assumptions. These are David Augsburger's *Conflict Mediation across Cultures: Pathways and Patterns* (1992), Kevin Avruch's *Culture and Conflict Resolution* (1998), and John Paul Lederach's *Preparing for Peace: Conflict Transformation Across Cultures* (1995). I will begin by addressing each of them in turn.

To provide a grounding for the idea that the Western approach might be culturally relative, Augsburger draws on two prominent models used in early cross-cultural studies at the time—Edward T. Hall's high and low context theory and Stella Ting-Toomey's face theory. When it addresses cultural difference, his book focuses on contrasting community-based forms of dispute

DOI: 10.4324/9781003227441-3

resolution in traditional (ethnic, indigenous) settings, where a trusted and known third party is an intermediary and often has decision-making authority, and the commercialized lawyer-based Western model of mediation, in which the intermediary is a detached professional. At the time he wrote *Conflict Mediation across Cultures* Augsburger was a Christian theologian and pastor (and still is at the time of writing this chapter), and he has written widely on peace-making, forgiveness, and pastoral care. In this book he takes a broad and non-academic anthropological approach to conflict from various perspectives, presenting anecdotes, folk tales, proverbs, and wisdoms taken from indigenous cultures around the world. The book contains one chapter devoted to mediation, in which Augsburger becomes most specific in a critique of the 'key Western assumptions' in negotiation theory and their post-colonial dissemination, drawing on Fisher and Ury as a model. He names eight points of difference, referring to the 'Western' values as 'conflict myths':

> To illustrate, several key Western assumptions—conflict myths—are explored in the following paragraphs, and their inadequacies in intercultural settings are noted.
>
> First, people and problems can be separated cleanly; interests and positions can be distinguished sharply. Negotiation can focus on problems and interests without becoming person- and people-oriented. However, in most cultures in the world, equal attention must be given to both person and problem, to relationship and goals.
>
> *(Augsburger 1992, 206)*

> Second, open self-disclosure is a positive value in negotiations.
>
> *(Augsburger 1992, 207)*

> Third, ownership is a crucial value in negotiations. [...] In some cultures only the person or persons at the top of the hierarchy make the decision.
>
> *(Augsburger 1992, 208)*

> Fourth, immediacy, directness, decisiveness, and haste are preferred strategies in timing. [...] Many cultures find that the best way to reach an agreement is to give the matter sufficient time to allow adjustments to be made, accommodations to emerge, and acceptance to evolve and emerge.
>
> *(Augsburger 1992, 208)*

> Fifth, proportionate requests, negotiable terms, minimal expectations, and bottom-line positions should be offered as the starting point in negotiation. [...] Some cultures are more visibly conflictual than others; [...]. Flexibility in negotiating styles and a willingness to respect and participate in each other's patterns of conflict resolution are necessary.
>
> *(Augsburger 1992, 208)*

> Sixth, language employed should be reasonable, rational, and responsible. In some cultures, depreciative language, extreme accusations, and vitriolic expressions are used as a negotiating power tactic.
>
> *(Augsburger 1992, 208)*

> Seventh, no is no and yes is yes [...]. In some cultures, one does not say no to an offer; requests are not phrased to elicit negations; when an offer is affirmed, the real meanings are weighed and assessed carefully.
>
> *(Augsburger 1992, 209)*

Eighth, when an agreement is reached, implementation will take care of itself as a legal consequence.

(Augsburger 1992, 209)

This list sets out much of what later writers on mediation and culture identify when they attempt to define difference, frequently going back to a critique of interests-based negotiation and mediation, in which an autonomous individual knows and advocates their own underlying interests in the course of a mediation process. The first point of critique, based on the assumption that negotiations can focus on problems and interests without becoming person- and people-oriented, may certainly reflect practice in some contexts all over the (Western) world today—wherever mediators strive to get work on the substantive issues and merits rather than emotions. Yet here there is a misreading of Fisher and Ury that has turned out to be remarkably persistent. When they proposed separating the people from the problem, Fisher and Ury did not mean that negotiation should not be people-oriented. Quite the contrary: if the people's emotions and perceptions matter, these should be heard and understood, if necessary at length. They should not, however lead to a neglect of the merits (the substantive material or legal standards) of whatever is at stake. A more thorough and differentiated discussion of this paradigm in terms of culture would still be highly desirable today.

Another early author who takes issue with Fisher and Ury is Kevin Avruch, an anthropologist and sociologist. His book, *Culture and Conflict Resolution*, also takes a broad approach to defining culture and conflict cultures, while in a chapter on 'Discourses of Culture in Conflict Resolution' it becomes more specific in its critique of the rational-choice thinking that arguably underpinned the field of conflict resolution theory and practice in the USA at the time. Avruch notes that culture is a blind spot in Fisher and Ury (Avruch 1998, 77–8) and criticizes their underlying focus on game theory and utility (74–6). He explicitly names the context from which all the theory and practice derives: "for conflict resolution, as for some other expert domains, the practice overwhelmingly has been culturally situated within a North American, male, white, and middle-class world" (78), and: "Fisher and Ury's theory corresponds deeply to the idealized Anglo middle-class model of what negotiation looks like" (79). This rings true, of course, but the argument lacks evidence, and Avruch, like Augsburger, simplifies matters when he gets into the detail, here again on the concept of separating the people from the problem: "But can we imagine a world where emotions and disputes are parsed differently, where separating the people from the problem, which in effect means separating the person from his or her emotions, is not conceivable?" (78). It is my contention that this oversimplifies Fisher and Ury.

Avruch takes issue with the person of the mediator too, arguing that a cultural perspective challenges the "American cultural presupposition […] that the best mediator is completely impartial and unbiased, ideally unconnected, in fact, to the parties or their concerns" (83–4), which derives from the neutrality of the courts in the justice system and the idea of the mediator as a middle-class professional. "The ethnographic record in general does not support the existence of the uninvolved third party as either the norm or the ideal" (84), Avruch writes, without, however, providing much empirical evidence. This lack of empirical study runs through all the literature on intercultural mediation, and indeed literature on mediation in general—it is, after all, a confidential or discreet process, even where it is not based on allegedly Western concepts of professional non-disclosure—so that while challenges to cultural assumptions frequently seem to make sense, there is often no way of knowing beyond readers weighing up what they read with own experience.

Avruch mentions two further paradigms that later authors develop. Firstly, he criticizes the 'problem-solving workshop' and thus the rational problem-solving approach in mediation, with its analytical methods and focus on material costs and benefits (91–4). Secondly, he posits the idea of 'a culture genesis'—a hybrid or third way that develops when cultures meet in mediation and negotiation: "The new culture is a metaculture of shared schemas and ideational encodements, of understandings and symbols, by means of which the parties achieve a new image of their world" (99). The idea is not particularly illustrated with examples.

The third groundbreaking work on mediation and culture is *Preparing for Peace: Conflict Transformation Across Cultures* by John Paul Lederach, like Augsburger a Mennonite Christian, and a sociologist and professor in peacebuilding—all three authors of these early books asking as to the culture of dispute resolution come from professional and academic cultures outside of the legal profession and the law schools where negotiation theory and mediation were developing at the time. Lederach's book focuses on training, and he takes a critical look at the practice of training and the export of training from the USA around the world—a critique that certainly remains relevant today, as this export has burgeoned. Lederach notes that conflict is a social construct that will differ culturally, and he sees culture as social knowledge and experience that we can understand through processes of engagement, but not as a set of techniques that can be taught and learned. This conclusion bears weight still today, for, although the field of theory has developed, much practical training is still based on the idea of culture as a set of techniques and knowledge about local behaviors that be acquired from experts.

Lederach addresses the expert-driven 'prescriptive transfer of knowledge' (Lederach 1995, 32) and explores the difference between 'prescriptive' and 'elicitive' training, whereby the latter uses 'implicit indigenous knowledge' (56), with the trainer no longer in the position of being the expert but rather in a position of ignorance. Lederach remains vague when it comes to defining what this indigenous knowledge might be, so that for a work of a practitioner his book remains very much a theoretical contribution. There is the thought that the paraphrasing method that mediators use widely may not gel well when a given setting might be more accustomed to silence (52–3). His critique of the Western model is that it is based on assumptions that communication is rational and direct, and on disclosure (104), so that it is to be assumed that the indigenous forms of communication a trainer elicits are less direct—here too there are echoes of Edward T. Hall. And Lederach astutely notes that the elicitive approach is not always going to be satisfying to participants in training, as they will also expect to 'move beyond current practices' (67), so that a careful balance between the elicitive and the prescriptive will be required. Here, Lederach implicitly favors the elicitive: "we should not operate on the supposed, self-evident basis that conflict resolution, as we understand it in North America, is a good thing worthy of wide dissemination" (119). This warning has been repeated since, for example by Nadja Alexander, who notes that "the forces of globalization—and some would argue, Americanization—have seen the facilitative model of mediation exported worldwide by first-world consultants, training institutions, and universities" (Alexander 2009, 512–3).

In summary, the critiques offered by Augsburger, Avruch, and Lederach focus firstly on underlying principles of mediation and negotiation relating to their heuristics (focus on the individual, interests-based, separate the people from the problem), secondly on their cultural origins (educated Western white middle-class male; in the paradigmatic case with a background in law), and thirdly on their dissemination as a post-colonial act. All three of these themes have been further developed, generally from within the system that produces them, so that the potential other voices they identify uncannily remain quiet or silent.

The self-critical tone persists as the field develops, with authors such as Joseph Folger and Robert Bush adding a further nuance in their critique of the 'problem-solving orientation' that is "closely aligned with an individualistic ideology that is central to the mainstream culture of the United States" (Folger and Bush 1994: 13). Folger and Bush argue that collaborative problem-solving in mediation is based on an ideology that "conflicts represent problems faced by autonomous individuals in achieving mutual needs satisfaction. Further, it reflects the view that conflict resolution can and should involve finding solutions that maximize the satisfaction of every individual involved" (13). This can again be read as a critique of the Harvard school's (Fisher and Ury and their followers) negotiation theory grounded in rational choice. Leo Montada takes a similar view of the 'standard model' of mediation, highly influenced by conceptions of human actors pursuing rational economic benefit. For Montada, this standard model is individualistic in cultural terms, and among its features he includes: direct and adversarial confrontation of issues and differences between the parties; voluntary participation; separation of factual or substantial issues from emotional issues; the use of neutral third-party mediators; and the autonomy of the parties in making decisions (Montada 2009). In a response to Montada, Alexander added the principle of confidentiality to the list of relative values that will not easily transfer across cultures (Alexander 2009).

Further fundamental critique of a standard Western model and its transfer across cultures focuses on the historical paradigm of Western colonialism, although this tends to be done without making use of the discipline of narrative history to give the argument substance. Instead the theme is addressed as theory. Nonetheless, the introduction of the concept of (political) power into the literature adds to the critiques provided by earlier contributors. David Kahane (2004) argues that interests-based mediation is rooted in Western liberalism, which historically excluded large parts of the world from its definitions of civilized humanity as well as from access to justice. Notions of neutral adjudication and impartiality are relative and linked to historical constellations of power that pertain to this day. Interests-based negotiation has its historical and cultural roots within a hegemonic and imperialist Western tradition of values and institutions, and to endeavor to implement this model across the world is an ethnocentric continuation of Western hegemony. Kahane is another author who sees the template of Western negotiation theory exemplified by *Getting to Yes*, which "is presented as universally applicable" but is instead "culturally laden, presupposing a social ontology that regards us as individual bearers of interests and maximizers of utility for us or our group" (Kahane 2004: 33). Today, these arguments seem to me on the one hand to be as relevant as they ever were, while they lack the force that would be brought to them by specific historical or present-day case studies of the practical consequences of this use of Western power. On the other hand, the concept of interests that underlies principled negotiation, once expanded beyond a focus on material or substantive gain, is arguably well equipped to cross cultures—there may be relationship interests, community interests, personal (face-saving and many other) interests, spiritual interests, interests based on health and well-being, participation and involvement interests, identity-based interests, restorative interests, process interests, and many more. These may also be seen as needs of course, but the term used (interests, needs, concerns) is less significant than the question as to whether, once this basic tool in mediation is taken beyond monetary or material gain, the concept can then work across cultures, meaning that the critique of the Western model would require some rethinking. The critical discourse focusing on negotiation and mediation that takes Fisher and Ury to task fails to address the flexibility of this concept.

Probably the most far-reaching and challenging critique of the Western hegemony over conflict resolution theory is Morgan Brigg's book *The New Politics of Conflict Resolution* (2008). Brigg argued that Western conflict resolution arises within the norms of power of the rational liberal order. Brigg asks how conflict resolution across cultures encounters and deals with 'difference,' and hereby draws on postcolonial and postmodern social theory and philosophy. 'Rational individualism' not only disavows the other person's differences, it also disavows the difference within oneself (Brigg 2008: 160). Brigg's contribution represents a less common in-depth application of a critical identity theory to conflict resolution.

The critiques of a dominant individualistic Western approach to conflict resolution could be complemented by looking at work on other or different conflict resolution and mediation cultures, in which the Western model that the above commentators have sought to question is not seen as the dominant mode. Nabil N. Antaki (2006) writes about 'Cultural Diversity and ADR Practices in the World,' and discusses a number of informal alternative dispute resolution practices in Muslim communities, China, Japan, and Africa, all of which offer alternative value sets to the interests-based model of the West. The main distinction that Antaki has focused on is that between 'communitarian' and 'individualistic' societies—with communitarian describing more traditional indigenous practices across the world that have significantly different expectations about how mediators and disputants might behave. And in their book on mediation in Asia, Lee and Hwee (2009) asked as to the appropriateness of direct, individualistic, interests-based conflict communication within cultures in which 'connectedness,' 'face,' 'relationships,' 'harmony,' and the 'authority' of leaders (in the case of mediation within these cultures, mediators could be seen as leaders) are prime cultural paradigms. Here again, the work of Edward Hall can be seen between the lines.[1]

Research and theory on mediation and culture, with their attempts to critically identify cultural differences that can have crucial impacts on conflict resolution, argue against any universally valid model—interests-based negotiation or any other. But most of the argument is highly abstract, with no examples from practice and without any refined sense of context. These contexts may be manifold: from commercial mediation under the shadow of the law, to international peace mediation, which would be expected to be a field that would offer plenty of specific insight but is remarkably understudied and under-referenced in literature on mediation and culture, to family mediation, to community dispute resolution, to legal and administrative frameworks for dispute resolution and conflict management, to models used in training and teaching, or to work on what it means that the majority of international transfer in dispute resolution training and practice takes place through the medium of English. The early literature operates largely void of contexts, while drawing again and again on the same theory (principled negotiation, face theory, high- and low-context theory), and it lacks specificity on a number of levels. It fails to ask what the (individualistic, rational, interests-based, problem-solving) Western model has achieved in terms of cultural transformation and paradigm shifts within its own contexts (the West). It fails to ask to what extent a concept such as 'Western' is helpful and useful as knowledge and practice cross into other contexts, offering little reflection on the questionable value of thinking in terms of us and them or the West and the rest (for a critical view of this see Appiah 2006). It does not sufficiently ask what it means to talk about peace from a position of power. It fails to give a voice to whatever practices it is (allegedly) blind and deaf to, in that it does not provide a narrative for the repressed—whatever the Western model overwrites, writes out, or eradicates, both in discourse and in practice. I contend that these gaps remain with us in theory and practice to this day. Nonetheless, these critical approaches to Western theory and practice are important and the major question they ask repeatedly matters: Are our concepts of conflict and mediation suited to the diverse world of resolution in practice, or are we engaging in a post-colonial discourse and practice when we take our negotiation and dispute resolution models around the world, or even when we make other cultures the objects of our cross-cultural studies?

In her poem 'Conflict Resolution for Holy Beings,' which I recommend reading in full, Joy Harjo uses commonplace ideas from contemporary (Western, white, middle class, and male) dispute resolution theory as headings to each section, contrasting them with a poetic voice that articulates a specific historical experience of conflict and its resolution. The critique is radical, exposing the tenets of the conflict resolvers as an ideology of power used in the name of a practice of elimination. Is this where we must be looking now, in the 2020s, as we consider dispute resolution and culture in the context of growing awareness that culture cannot be seen in isolation from the politics of power?

1. SET CONFLICT RESOLUTION GROUND RULES:
Recognize whose lands these are on which we stand.
Ask the deer, turtle, and the crane.
Make sure the spirits of these lands are respected and treated with goodwill.
The land is a being who remembers everything.

(Harjo 2015)

Note

1 Some of the above literature review draws on an earlier article in *Negotiation Journal* (Bond 2013).

References

Alexander, Nadja. 2009. "Mediation and the Myth of Universality." *Erwägen Wissen Ethik* 4: 512–13.

Antaki, Nabil N. 2006. "Cultural Diversity and ADR Practices in the World." In *ADR in Business. Practice and Issues across Countries and Cultures*, edited by Jean-Claude Goldsmith, Arnold Ingen-Housz, and Gerald. H. Pointon, 265–303. Alphen aan den Rijn: Kluwer Law International.

Appiah, Kwame Anthony. 2006. *Cosmopolitanism: Ethics in a World of Strangers*. New York: W.W. Norton.

Augsburger, David. W. 1992. *Conflict Mediation across Cultures: Pathways and Patterns*. Louisville, KY: Westminster/John Knox Press.

Avruch, Kevin. 1998. *Culture and Conflict Resolution*. Washington: United States Institute of Peace Press.

Bond, Greg. 2013. "Mediation and Culture: The Example of the ICC International Commercial Mediation Competition: Mediation and Culture." *Negotiation Journal* 29 (3): 315–28. 10.1111/nejo.12027

Brigg, Morgan. 2008. *The New Politics of Conflict Resolution: Responding to Difference*. Basingstoke, UK: Palgrave Macmillan.

Fisher, Roger, and William Ury. 1981. *Getting to Yes: How to Reach Agreement without Giving in*. Boston: Houghton Mifflin.

Fisher, Roger, William Ury and Bruce Patton. 2007. *Getting to Yes: How to Reach Agreement without Giving in*. London: Random House Business Books.

Folger, Joseph P., and Robert A. Baruch Bush. 1994. "Ideology, Orientations to Conflict, and Mediation Discourse." In *New Directions in Mediation: Communication Research and Perspectives*, edited by Joseph P. Folger and Tricia S. Jones, 3–25. Thousand Oaks: Sage.

Harjo, Joy, 2015. *Conflict Resolution for Holy Beings*. New York and London: W.W. Norton.

Kahane, David. 2004. "What is Culture? Generalizing about Aboriginal and Newcomer Perspectives." In *Intercultural Dispute Resolution in Aboriginal Contexts*, edited by Catherine Bell and David Kahane, 28–56. Vancouver: University of British Columbia Press.

Lederach, John Paul. 1995. *Preparing for Peace: Conflict Transformation Across Cultures*. New York: Syracuse University Press.

Lee, Joel, and Teh Hwee Hwee, eds. 2009. *An Asian Perspective on Mediation*. Singapore: Academy Publishing.

Montada, Leo. 2009. "Mediation – Pfade zum Frieden." *Erwägen Wissen Ethik* 4: 501–11.

2
CROSS-CULTURAL DISPUTES AND MEDIATOR STRATEGIES

Carrie Menkel-Meadow

What is culture?

It is said about culture that as we are the fishes who swim in it, it is like the water we swim in—it is all around us; it governs how we breathe, eat, interact with others, communicate, and live. While 'in' it and 'of' it, we are hardly aware of it, it is so much a part of our environment, beliefs, and actions. But we are humans, not fishes (though like fish we come in many different kinds of groups or 'schools'), and we do observe others and ourselves, communicate with each other, most often to survive and flourish together, but sometimes producing disputes and conflicts, as we often process the world through our own cultural lenses. This chapter outlines some of the issues that emerge in mediation when disputants are of different cultures and so have what we have come to call 'inter-cultural conflicts' (Chew 2001; Ross 1997; Avruch and Black 1993; Avruch 1998).

Culture is a product of 'groupness' including practices, beliefs, norms, rules, behaviors, and customs which are often further identified with race, nationality, ethnicity, religion, gender, and social groups (e.g., self-identifying non-binary, LGBTQ+) and even voluntary associations and affiliations (e.g., political parties, gangs) and 'status' cultures (e.g., student, academic, legal, professional, 'business' capitalist culture, working class). Culture affects the way we see and process the world, with language, images, assumptions, norms, and the choices we see as acceptable and viable in particular situations.

However, most of us belong to several 'cultures' (Sen 2006; Crenshaw 1989), some by ascription (assignment by birth, assumptions of others, laws or rules) and some by choice, affiliation, or achievement (e.g., professional license, education, training, and attainment). How 'we' look to others and how we 'see' ourselves may be quite different things. Though culture is assumed to be practiced in, and often 'policed' by groups (social norms, religious rules, laws) it is enacted by individuals (and also by group leaders or political officials representing nations, companies, or interest groups).

Thus, 'intercultural conflict' occurs as individuals, groups, and even nations enact behaviors that cause misunderstandings, competitions, disputes, conflicts, and sometimes violence. Some conflicts are 'veridical' (real disputes over scarce or limited resources, e.g., land or water, a job); others are attitudinal (different values or belief systems), pretextual (the stated conflict actually masks a deeper or different conflict), identity based (conflict based on perceived differences of persons, not ne-cessarily related to concrete dispute), latent (under the surface and unexpressed but important), and others are socially constructed (meaning possibly changeable or re-characterizable as conditions or perceptions change). What a conflict is, is itself a cultural construct and the parties to any conflict may define and see a conflict in very different ways. As the marriage counselor John Gottman

30

DOI: 10.4324/9781003227441-4

(Gottman and Gottman 2018) has noted, it is not the amount of conflict in a marriage that will predict its success or failure, but how the parties process their conflict (e.g., respectfully, rather than dismissively) and as all relationships have some conflict, some reciprocity and joint decision making may be more important than the quantity (or even intensity) of the conflict. As many famous peacemakers have said, conflicts are made by humans, they can also be unmade (managed or resolved) by humans.

Scholars in many different fields (anthropology, sociology, psychology, and political science), in studying the many ways in which culture is expressed have developed many controversial taxonomies of culture. Samuel Huntington famously claimed a 'clash of cultures' was politically imminent (before 9/11) among and between Western 'developed' democracies, Japanese culture (separate from), Asian (Confucian), Latin American, Islamic, and sub-Saharan African cultures because of different value systems and preferences which created institutions of different political, religious, and economic goals, some of which were inherently incompatible with others (Huntington 2011). Other commentators more optimistically hoped that with the end of the Cold War and the fall of the Berlin Wall, with the end of most colonization (1989) we would begin a new era of 'cosmopolitanism' and peace (Ignatieff 1993) or as Francis Fukuyama put it "the End of History" (1992). This has not happened, either in international politics or at the group-ethnic-political sub-national levels, as, in fact, we are now in a period of increased polarization in much of the world (Menkel-Meadow 2018a).

Anthropologists, sociologists, and social psychologists have also developed a taxonomy of cultural communication patterns, derived from national and religious cultural values that suggest that there is a continuum of human behaviors (which can be predicted from membership in a particular culture) on the following dimensions (Hofstede et al. 2010 (original publication of research from IBM, Hofstede 1980)), later supplemented by others:

- individualism-collectivism,
- uncertainty avoidance (risk preferences),
- power distance (role of hierarchy or equality in culture and decision making),
- long vs. short term orientation,
- masculinity-femininity,
- emotional expressiveness (Hammer 2005),
- direct (literal) vs. indirect (euphemisms, assumed similar cultural norms) communication,
- high (assumption of homogeneity in cultural expectations) vs. low (heterogeneity) context cultures (Hall 1959; 1976),
- physical distance in communication,
- time/deadline/punctuality sensitivity.

These characterizations of basic values and human communication (derived from surveys of first IBM, then other multi-national corporation, employees) have been used in countless studies to verify or test whether these categories comport with particular national (or professional) cultures in business dealings, negotiation, management, and general cross-cultural communications and decision making (see e.g., Brett 2014), often employing stereotypic or patterned characterizations of particular cultural practices in business dealings or dispute resolution (see Acuff 2008). As some (problematic to this author) conclusions suggest, in high power distance cultures (Latin America, Asia) deference will be paid to higher status, older, male superiors in both organizational and national hierarchies. Cultures with less social equality will be distrustful of younger, 'minority,' and female participants. Low power distance (more 'equality' focused) cultures will enjoy greater flexibility, creativity, and likely more direct communication and participation in the processes of mediation and decision making.

This literature and the lucrative business and dispute resolution cultural consulting apparatus (see e.g., Schuler 2016), including even the International Mediation Institute's (2022a; 2022b) *Cultural Competency Certification* process, which attempts to teach about these cultural differences and then 'certify' those who are interculturally competent (including language, residency, and knowledge of different legal and social systems) is also widely criticized, on both academic and practical grounds. 'Intercultural training' often presumes the 'otherness' of some who are not at the center or core of the activity, e.g., common or civil law business contracting, employment in multi-national (and increasingly diverse) companies, operating around the world (with whose rules, languages, and work cultures as the norms?). One could ask—how much intermediation of these more diverse relationships is 'inter-cultural' (assuming some equality of communication, practices, and decisions/resolutions) and how much is expected 'assimilation' to the dominant culture by learned manipulation of cultural 'differences'? As John Barkai has put it—the "Popeye Problem" ("I am what I am and that's all that I am"), seeing the world from within one's own cultural assumptions (Barkai 2008). For a few examples of sensitivity to more 'integrative' or culturally specific and context specific mediation models see Ting-Toomey (1994) (for Asian or more 'collectivist' cultures) and Smolyaninova and Popova (2019) for a more 'integrative' model of mediation in migrant, culturally diverse educational environments in Russia and Europe.

Anthropologists, such as Kevin Avruch, working in the conflict resolution field note that culture is not a 'thing' (monolithic, unchanging, homogeneous, or uniform within any grouping) and that any particular individual may have memberships in several cultural groups so that which 'culture' will be salient in any particular conflict may not be so easily determined. With the advent of international mediation, negotiation, and dispute resolution (and business management) education and training, a more professional culture of a transnational nature (e.g., all those who have studied at Harvard's Program on Negotiation or the UK's CEDR mediation training) may share a more cosmopolitan culture of 'canons' of dispute resolution (including language, interventions and structures) which may be more salient than other social, national, ethnic or gendered identities (Rubin and Sander 1991; Menkel-Meadow 2003). On the other hand (see below), the assumptions of the universality of such canons as *Getting to Yes* (Fisher, Ury, and Patton 1991: focus on interests, not positions, invent options for mutual gain, separate the people from the problem, and use objective criteria) are increasingly challenged as culturally ethnocentric (assuming rationality, pragmatic problem solving, and excluding other processes and measures of agreement, focus on feelings, relationship, community, and morality and ethical factors: Menkel-Meadow (2016)).

What is mediation culture?

Does mediation have a culture all its own? Mediation is derived historically from the Bible (it was Solomon who was going to cut the baby in half to resolve a dispute between two mothers mediating or arbitrating when the 'real' mother said "give it her, rather than cut it in half"?), Confucian 'harmony' culture (Lee and Hwee 2009; Chew and Lim 2006), sulha (peace or 'resolution') in Islamic and Middle Eastern cultures (Abu-Nimer 1996), and various forms of African community dispute resolution processes ("it takes a village"; Ubuntu (Akinola and Uzodike 2018), gacaca).

Mediation as a conflict resolution process actually has several cultures—is it its goal to produce a settlement (a 'task' focus), to encourage understanding and recognition and improve the relations of the parties (Bush and Folger 2005) or to preserve harmony and peace for the larger community, in addition to resolving the particular disputes of the parties? Mediation has been successfully used to create new norms and provide communities (e.g., gay, migrants, religious groups) with little to no access to conventional courts a dispute resolution process of their own (Freshman 1997; Waldman 1997). These days, mediation processes are being used to clear dockets (mandatory court mediation programs) or increase access to justice (the argument now being made for online mediation). Is mediation a new 'lingua franca' or Esperanto language of common or more 'universal' customs or practices of dispute resolution to be used in cross-border international disputes, where both different languages and different legal systems may make traditional court-based dispute resolution more difficult (Menkel-Meadow 2018b; 2015a; 2016). Does mediation require compromise, the seeking of 'joint gain,' and creative tailored solutions of substance while focusing on mutual understanding, empathy, party participation, self-determination, dialogue, and consent in process, to distinguish it from more rule and command based processes of adjudication and arbitration?

Different goals and purposes of mediative processes in turn affect the techniques, tools, and interventions particular mediators might use—e.g., facilitative, or evaluative (Riskin 2003), transformative and communication enhancing (Bush and Folger 2005; Friedman and Himmelstein 2008), or decisional and arbitration-like for political purposes (Fu and Palmer 2017; Lubman 1997; Cohen 1966). Each mediation process or system may use different kinds of mediators—volunteers from a community, law trained lawyers or judges, sitting judges, or other judicial officers, 'wise elders' in religious or other communities, experts in highly technical mediations (e.g., patent or tax disputes), psychologists, architects, engineers, accountants, family members, or totally 'lay' mediators. As the song says, "different strokes for different folks" (Stewart 1969)—different purposes and goals and different kinds of mediators will approach mediation processes differently—what I call 'process pluralism' in choices about forms of decision making (2016).

Yet modern mediation and the standard form of mediation training occurring in courts and private organizations today is likely to use a relatively common format and template for behaviors—one that I (1995) and others (Gunning 1995; Press and Deason 2021) have called an overly 'Westernized' (and White) assumption of a 'neutral' third party (mediator) presiding over or facilitating an individualized 'talking cure' with protocols of story/claim narration, agenda creation, and managed into 're-framed' solvable issues, facilitated brainstormed negotiated agreements, and a pragmatic sense of problem solving and future oriented solutions. This ideology and practice of mediation can be both highly effective, but also culturally very specific, all while generating a variety of critiques for 'privatizing' justice (removing disputes from the transparency of public court settings for accountability) or ignoring past injustices (Gunning 1995; Izumi 2010; Menkel-Meadow 2004).

As one of the founders of the modern *Alternative, Appropriate, Accessible, Aspirational* dispute resolution movement I was asked to begin to train mediators in many other countries, beginning in the early 1980s. I turned down requests to train (others accepted) in such places as the former Soviet Union and Haiti in the early years either because I felt I did not know enough about the relevant (legal) culture (Russia) or because I feared corruption (Haiti) in both the legal and alternative dispute resolution systems. In my view, the quality of mediation does depend on the quality of the legal system which either supports or supplements mediation (and may have to be used to enforce mediation agreements). In the late 1980s, at the request of a colleague with whom I had taught before, I went to Norway to teach mediation to law students, lawyers, government officials, and some diplomats (what chutzpah—Norwegian diplomats are masters of mediation—see *Oslo Accords*!). I assumed that as the daughter of a German-born engineer, I knew enough about ('rational') Northern European culture (growing up in a multi-cultural European-American home with multiple languages) to teach others how to use this form of legal and social problem solving. To my then (1988) surprise and intercultural education I saw that despite cultural dimension indices of many analysts and stereotypic assumptions, the Norwegians I encountered were as 'high context' (indirect, reticent, hierarchical, and tradition based) as any measure of assumed 'Asian' (I do not approve of 'pan' continental categories such as Asian or African or Latin American, where there are so many differences within such categories) traditional high context harmony culture. At that time the Norwegians I encountered (highly educated and of several generations) were not taken with American 'talking cures' in settings that were too informal for significant legal matters (which would eventually require notarization and other legal formalities). This is not to say the Norwegians did not use therapy and meditation (and lots of drinking!) to explore and express feelings in other (non-legal contexts), but the Americanized 'talking cure' did not then catch on in Norwegian legal circles. Some of that has changed now (Sperr 2013), but it is important to note that much of the motivation for the development of mediation in many societies has been due to docket-clearing where there are long queues for court proceedings (Ali 2018)—that was not true in Norway at the time. So, motivations to mediate can come from very different sources (legal reform, social and political problem solving, transnational dispute resolution (European Directive 2008/52/EC 2008), community, family, and psychological relationship issues). Many countries came to mediation first through labor conciliation (a different, often government-managed process) with includes more active intervention (and solution suggestions or commands).

About a decade later (late 1990s) I was asked to train and teach mediation in Paraguay, Argentina, Brazil, and later Chile. After learning enough Spanish to understand and to do some teaching (always with both language translators and co-teachers from the countries in which I was working) I saw cultural differences not quite measured by the anthropologists and sociologists studying intercultural negotiations and mediations. The Argentines took to mediation like fish to water. Not only had some of their judges (former Appellate Judge Gladys Alverez) done some training in the United States, but Buenos Aires had the highest per capita ratio of therapists and psychologists to population of almost any nation (due to many factors, including immigration pre- and post-WWII from Freudians and others from the European continent). The café society, then examining its political transition from dictatorship to democracy and exploring some forms of human rights restitution and restorative justice, was verbal, voluble, and wanting to talk about problems—both national and personal. In Chile, mediation came not as fast—a more reticent culture, still reeling from some 'social amnesia' about the Pinochet dictatorship (Menkel-Meadow 2015b) and also generally more formal took somewhat to mediation, but more slowly and more motivated by legal system reforms in both civil and criminal law. Chile, however, had very successful labor conciliation programs and a unique mediation program for the settlement of indigenous land claims, using very different methods and techniques in different settings.

The country of my parents' birth, Germany, eventually has also taken to mediation—both to deal more honestly and directly with its Nazi past and to formalize reforms to the legal system to encourage, if not require, mediation prior to litigation (Hess and Pelzer 2013). Over the last 20 years I have worked with mediation promoters/trainers/teachers in Germany, Belgium, France, the Netherlands, Ireland, Italy, Spain, the UK, Switzerland, Israel, Singapore, China, Hong Kong, Australia, Chile, Argentina, Nicaragua, Costa Rico, Paraguay, Brazil, Mexico, Canada, and Russia. Italy tried to mandate mediation in all civil cases (de Palo and Oleson 2013), which then was ruled unconstitutional by the Italian Cour di Cassione but now requires parties to attend informational meetings about mediation in all civil cases.

As I have written elsewhere (Menkel-Meadow 2015a), the uptake of various forms of mediation in different countries may depend on varied legal cultures. Some legal cultures are not unitary. The United States, the UK, Australia, Canada and Israel, for example, have highly adversarial legal cultures with a great deal of litigation. At the same time, legal reformers, social workers, psychologists and others have developed very effective mediation programs—some mandatory, some supplementary to more contested legal processes (Alexander 2009; Steffek et al. 2013). Other legal cultures direct parties to more conciliatory processes as a condition precedent to other forms of dispute resolution (China, Japan) some of which is now mirrored in international treaties requiring parties to climb a ladder of tiered dispute resolution processes (e.g., Law of the Sea) and the three regional human rights courts of the world (African, European, and Inter-American) all provide for some form of amiable settlements achieved through mediatory or conciliatory processes. These are settings in particular where intercultural mediation is a necessity as parties will frequently be of different national, social, and legal cultures. Newer nation states (coming out of colonialism or from transitions from dictatorships or civil wars) are creating newer, more hybrid systems of dispute resolution and, in including such processes as Truth and Reconciliation Commissions (e.g., South Africa, Liberia, Bolivia) may provide more hybrid dispute resolution systems internally to create more mediation like processes for dispute resolution within different groups of the population. Intercultural mediation is just as important in domestic disputes as in the international disputing of nations or transnational commercial and familial dealings.

What strategies, techniques, and tools for mediation are in intercultural settings?

There is no shortage of scholarship, training manuals, and advice from professionals on how to conduct intercultural mediations, both in obviously international contexts, but also in domestic inter- or multi-cultural settings (e.g., Barkai 2008; Gunning 1995; Press and Deason 2021; Izumi 2010; LeBaron and Pillay 2006; International Mediation Institute 2022a; 2022b). This section highlights some of the strategies, interventions, techniques, tools, skills, and interpersonal accountability devices presented in the literature, followed by a brief review of some of the current critiques of standard mediation practices and schemas.

To begin, every mediation that has an intercultural element (isn't that all mediations where parties have some dispute and see the world and their particular situation differently?) needs to begin with a serious intercultural *analysis* (Avruch and Black 1993). Who are the parties? *How many* of them are there? From *where* do they come? *What is the dispute* about (it's 'res')? How might each of the parties *see or interpret the dispute differently*? How might *context and type of dispute* matter? Commercial, employment, family, identity, education, health, housing, injury, personal, or community? What is the *desired outcome* of the parties? Peace treaty, contract, settlement of a lawsuit or dispute, making a new relationship, forging a new country, family, setting borders and boundaries? All of these are variations on what kinds of disputes might require different sets of interventions or choices of behaviors. Then, in multi-cultural settings, the preparation must also include as much learning as possible about both the particular 'cultures' involved (which may include not only nationality, ethnicity, race, gender, political, but profession, class, education, and other 'cross-cutting' statuses and identities) and the subject matter of the dispute. Mediators of intercultural disputes must develop 'meta' preparation as well—standing outside of the dispute, what processes, techniques, tools, and interventions may be more appropriate for particular problems. Thus, there are at least three layers to prepare for—process, substantive matter, and the intermediation of 'differences' however they are perceived, constructed, and enacted at individual, organizational, and even national levels.

Self-assessment

Any mediator beginning a multi- or intercultural mediation session of any kind should ask, "Am I the right person for this job"? What competence do I have to offer the parties? Language, familiarity with the culture, substantive expertise? Should I get a co-mediator to add diversity, knowledge, assistance, ability to do several caucuses or separate meetings at the same time, aid with process management? How was I invited into this process? By the parties themselves, by some authority or mandated scheme (e.g., court mandated mediation), by the request of another third party or institution? Should there be 'matching' of mediator(s) to nationalities, race, ethnicity, or gender of the parties (see e.g., LaFree and Rack 1996; Charkoudian and Wayne 2010, 2009; Press and Deason 2021)? What is my stance with respect to the parties—can I really be 'neutral' (can anyone?) or 'unbiased' or 'without bias or prejudice'? As human beings we are all likely to have predispositions and our own cultural identities in any dispute. How should these be described, disclosed, and monitored? Are there any conflicts of interest—personal, professional? Am I aware of my own implicit/unconscious biases and any cultural (White, Western, Northern, male?) characteristics that assume I (or the methods I use) am the 'norm' by which the mediation will be conducted (Izumi 2010; Press and Deason 2021; Gunning 1995, Menkel-Meadow 1995)?

Case assessment

How might case type affect the kind of mediation which is offered: International crisis diplomats (see the different approaches and styles of George Mitchell in Northern Ireland, contrasted to Richard Holbrooke in Bosnia, Curran, Sebenius, and Watkins 2004), back-channel mediators, complex business deals, family disputes, employment disputes, educational disputes. How many parties are involved? Are all the stakeholders at the table—should others be invited? Consider such issues as future generations in environmental disputes or children in divorce disputes, or insurers in construction disputes. Are there serious power imbalances between or among the parties? How might that affect who should be invited, how mediation is conducted (separate sessions, joint sessions) and how decisions will be made about what is agreed to. Are the parties pro se (alone) or represented by lawyers or other helpers? Are the parties from the same spoken language or will they need translators? Do the parties share culture(s) (religion, workplace, nationality, ethnicity, race, gender) or are the parties demographically or culturally from 'different' situations or understandings? Are the parties of close to equal statuses-titles, educational achievement, economic class, business partners—or will the 'power' or class or race or ethnicity or gender or economic differences manifest in power and communication differentials? Will the parties identify their own 'differences' or will mediators be sensitive or oblivious to more subtle racial, class, gender, ethnic issues, and ways of communicating (see Gadlin 1994; Ting-Toomey et al. 2000)?

Preparation and ground rules

Before any meeting of the parties, it is always advisable to consider what the parties' expectations are likely to be—is this a first encounter, with other parties, with mediation itself? Many suggest the use of pre-meetings (done separately, either in person or on phone or video chat) to learn about parties and their expectations, to develop trust, to answer questions and to begin to understand what is important to the parties. Many mediators use pre-mediation written submissions but note this too could be a cultural issue—is writing a favored form of communication, does a written document of any sort make positions in a mediation more rigid, less flexible, advantage those with sophisticated professional helpers? How should the physical space be structured (e.g., sitting on the floor or chairs, with a table or not, in a circle or rectangular conference table)? How much physical/social distance between parties and with the mediator(s)? How shall the parties be addressed (formally, or first names)? What food or drink should be served (Liebman 2000)? What ground rules of engagement should be set in advance—is confidentiality a need, can it be guaranteed, who will parties share information with? Complex international business disputes will have to provide for some mediation of shared procedural rules (as international arbitrations do in *Terms of Reference* meetings (see Menkel-Meadow 2008))—whose evidence rules will prevail (discovery of documents, expert witnesses, privilege, all of which vary by legal (common law, civil law, or mixed system) culture. Do ground rules of no interruptions, 'tone control,' and etiquette policing 'privilege' certain cultural communication practices?

Mediator role(s)

Mediators have different approaches—facilitative, evaluative, narrative, transformative, and hybrid combinations of all these. In situations where parties may not all share understandings of what mediators do, it is especially important for mediators to describe what they do and where appropriate to negotiate particular roles with the parties. While the American conception of a 'third-party neutral' became an expected norm in many kinds of mediations, many parties now choose 'expert' mediators (as in intellectual property or high-tech disputes) who may know the parties and operate more like the 'wise elders' (in suggesting possible solutions and outcomes) that looks more like traditional mediation in Asian or African practices. Community mediation and various forms of indigenous and religious mediation have panels of 'elders' or facilitators (often too patriarchal in some contexts) or more 'inclusive' participation by whole communities in facilitating dispute processes (see e.g., Harmon-Darrow et al. 2020).

Communication/facilitation

In intercultural disputes, mediators are likely best advised to use more elicitive (asking questions and drawing out from the parties) approaches than more directive statements to encourage parties to express what is important to them on their own terms. It is especially important to consider the order of talk—who goes first often sets the terms and terrain (primacy and controlling the narrative, Gunning 1995). A skilled mediator should be able to sensitively 'reframe' issues and create agendas that do not privilege or give primacy to particular parties. Active listening, restating, and confirming what is being said is always important, but is especially important in settings where the parties may need not only language translations, but conceptual and interest translations. For some parties, decision making will be 'rational' and 'principled,' for others emotions, religious, or ethical commitments will be most salient, and others may simply want to accomplish what is most 'practical' (what I call the *head, heart, and stomach discourses of dispute resolution*, Menkel-Meadow 2018a). Caucuses are likely to be needed, especially in situations of different expectations of privacy, decision making, and information sharing. One of the great ironies of intercultural mediation is often that where mediators might prefer 'face to face' dialogues and empathic communication to encourage mutual understanding, the need for 'face saving' is often best achieved through the use of caucus meetings where the parties are not face to face and mediators can more 'neutrally' present proposals and reduce the reactive devaluation that occurs when parties devalue what is offered by their adversaries. When communication patterns (direct vs indirect modes of communication) are not 'matched' by the parties, mediators can literally either 'sit in the middle' of communications, help to interpret meanings or offer proposals, whether in separate rooms or in joint sessions. Consider how many international crises and peace agreements have been accomplished by shuttle diplomacy and 'go-betweens' without the principal parties being in the same room at the same time (e.g., Viet Nam Paris Agreement, U.S.-Iranian hostage crisis 'resolution,' Oslo Accords, Dayton Accords).

Bargaining/problem solving

Modern (Western) approaches to mediation prefer to facilitate party agency and autonomy by using such specific techniques as brainstorming, storyboarding, nominal voting procedures, and exercises to create joint gain and shared solutions to problems. In some settings this pressure to 'create' and openly share is just the opposite of what some parties will want (closer to an evaluative, command idea coming from a wise elder). Some parties in mediation (whether from individual preferences or cultural expectations) will be collaborative, active, and keen to resolve problems—others will be adversarial, seeking to 'win' even in what is supposed to be a consensual setting. A culturally sensitive mediator has to be able to navigate different negotiation styles, again often by using questions—"what would happen if […]," "If you don't like X, what would you propose instead?," "Who else do you need to consult to see if Y will be acceptable?" Where the parties come from different negotiation traditions and practices, interventions (e.g., power balancing) and mediator suggestions or proposals are tools that can move things forward. Modern critiques of the mediator's 'neutral' stance (see below) suggest mediators may need to take responsibility for and 'call out' improper behavior or unfair proposals (Menkel-Meadow and Wheeler 2011). For many mediators the challenge is to 'mediate' the different discourses of reason/principle, political, ethical, and religious commitments, as well as practical deal making and necessary compromise (Menkel-Meadow 2017) for mediation to function as a process that produces some improved conditions for the parties.

Reaching agreements

There are often different understandings of the appropriate time for reaching agreements. In complex international settings, time for relationship building, socializing, gift giving, rituals and ceremonies, or banquets may be expected. Task-oriented Americans often want to conclude deals quickly and see the transaction as more important than the relationship. A culturally skilled mediator needs to conduct, orchestrate, and manage the timing of negotiations and deal making, and to confirm in many different ways that agreements (and the procedures for their realization and execution are clear—'reality testing') are understood by all parties (and committed to writing, if culturally or legally mandated) and approved by those with authority to do so. 'The devil is often in the details' as we say and the mediator of a dispute with parties who don't always share world views will have to work doubly hard to be sure there actually is a mediated outcome that will be complied with. Good agreements may have contingent provisions for adaptation to new conditions, new evidence or data (consider environmental and economic disputes) or re-evaluation of terms (consider agreements made in restorative justice or transitional justice settings.) Good mediators plan ahead with the parties to craft dispute resolution provisions for any issues that may arise from a mediation agreement.

Evaluation, feedback, and assessment

No mediation is complete until the parties and mediators assess what they have done and engage in any mutually agreed to feedback process. The best mediators are self-reflecting (and reflexive) and seek to de-brief, not only particular interventions (with co-mediators and participants where possible) they have engaged in, but consideration of 'what went well,' 'what might have been done differently,' and what other possible options were available for substantive solutions. Where parties agree, mediators might meet again after the mediation is concluded to learn about implementation and reactions to the process. A learning model would allow the parties to consult with others to assess what they have accomplished. Perhaps a mediator will learn s/he/they need some further training in diversity, equity, and cultural inclusion sensitivity and methods or to be updated on substantive matters, law or uses of technology. A spirited debate in the largely unregulated field of mediation is the extent to which mediators should be 'accountable' for the agreements they facilitate. For many mediators the accountability is in the parties' consent and agreement to whatever outcome is reached (Mayer, Stulberg, Susskind, and Lande 2012) as a core value of 'self-determination.' For others, mediators have a responsibility to ensure that agreements reached with their assistance should not be unjust, unfair, unenforceable, or unlawful (Menkel-Meadow and Wheeler 2011). In many jurisdictions around the world, some case law and court decisions now adjudicate some claims of unfair influence, coercion, or defective contracting as some check on mediation processes (Coben and Thompson 2006).

Critiques of the 'standard' mediation templates

In recent years, much of the 'standard' template of mediation has been criticized from a number of quarters. As mediation began to gain currency in both court and legal settings, as well as private commercial settings, it moved out from its initial sources in community and indigenous models and practices of dispute resolution. Some were concerned about the privatization of justice, with processes and agreements occurring in secret without transparency or the application of the rule of law, often used in settings where the parties in dispute were of unequal 'arms' (economic status, access to lawyers and legal advice, race, gender, ethnicity, immigration status, etc., Delgado et al. 1985; Grillo 1991). From the beginning, there was criticism of specific tools, techniques, and strategies that were considered derived only from Western-Northern cultures (e.g., the notion of a 'neutral' third party, the requirement to talk directly in narrative form, to search for future-oriented pragmatic solutions and relinquish the 'past' and claims of hurt, harm, or anger "for the good of the [...] future" (children, company, country, community)). There have been specific charges of some mediation as being manipulative (Greatbatch and Dingwall 1989) as mediators use 'selective facilitation' techniques to move parties toward the mediator's desired outcomes. More recently, some have claimed that mediation is not only Western or 'northern' but White (Press and Deason 2021), not permitting voice for subordinate groups, particularly Blacks in cultures (like the United States) with systemic racism. Others see the potential promise of mediation for interpersonal communication and understanding and practical business agreements, as well as international law disputes between countries in some cases, but express concerns that mediative approaches to highly polarized societies cannot be so easily 'scaled up' to whole societies, even with many groups organizing town halls, living room conversations, and other deliberative democracy events that use mediative tools for facilitating dialogue in search of mutual understanding.

At an institutional level, truth and reconciliation processes have used mediative techniques of narrative, apologies, requests for forgiveness, and amnesty even when reparations and restitution (as in smaller scale restorative justice (Menkel-Meadow 2007) victim-offender settings have worked) are rare.

Most mediators of cross-cultural disputes are optimists (and realists!). Where some see intractable differences between and among people of different faiths, political systems, races, genders, and ethnicities, most of us see hope in the curiosity that we feel about different approaches to the problems that humans must confront. A well-conducted intercultural mediation is one committed to learning, curiosity, empathy, some creativity, and some forms of human communication. Intercultural mediation is talk in service to human understanding and peaceful co-existence and hopefully, human flourishing. Mediation is a sensibility to approach others with whom one is in conflict to understand them (and ourselves) better and to seek a better situation than one was in before the mediation (and with solutions that may be specifically tailored to parties' needs and interests). We try to make lemonade or lemon pie out of lemons. (Or think of all the uses of lemons in different cultures!!) It is not simple or easy in many cases, but without it we may be doomed. As one who grew up in the shadows of the United Nations, I still harbor a belief that we have more similarities as humans than differences—at least enough to try to resolve our many disputes without unnecessary harm or violence.

References

Abu-Nimer, Mohammed. 1996. "Conflict Resolution Approaches.: Western and Middle Eastern Lessons and Possibilities." *American Journal of Economics and Sociology* 55 (1): 35–52. 10.1111/j.1536-7150.1996.tb02706.x

Acuff, Frank L. 2008. *How to Negotiate Anything with Anyone Anywhere around the World.* 3rd ed. New York: AMACOM/American Management Association.

Akinola, Adeoye O., and Ufo Okeke Uzodike. 2018. "*Ubuntu* and the Quest for Conflict Resolution in Africa." *Journal of Black Studies* 49 (2): 91–113. 10.1177/0021934717736186

Alexander, Nadja Marie. 2009. *International Comparative Mediation: Legal Perspectives. Global Trends in Dispute Resolution.* Austin, Frederick, MD: Wolters Kluwer Law & Business.

Ali, Shahla F. 2018. *Court Mediation Reform: Efficiency, Confidence and Perceptions of Justice*. Cheltenham, UK: Edward Elgar.

Avruch, Kevin. 1998. *Culture and Conflict Resolution*. Washington, DC: United States Institute of Peace Press.

Avruch, Kevin, and Peter W. Black. 1993. "Conflict Resolution in Intercultural Settings: Problems and Prospects." In *Conflict Resolution Theory and Practice: Integration and Application*, edited by Dennis J. D. Sandole and Hugo van der Merwe, 131–45. Manchester, UK: Manchester University Press.

Barkai, John. 2008. "What's a Cross-Cultural Mediator to Do? A Low-Context Solution for a High-Context Problem." *Cadorzo Journal of Conflict Resolution* 10 (1): 43–89.

Brett, Jeanne M. 2014. *Negotiating Globally: How to Negotiate Deals, Resolve Disputes, and Make Decisions across Cultural Boundaries*. Third edition. San Francisco, CA: Jossey-Bass.

Bush, Robert A. Baruch, and Joseph P. Folger. 2005. *The Promise of Mediation: The Transformative Approach to Conflict*. Rev. ed. San Francisco: Jossey-Bass.

Charkoudian, Lorig, and Ellen Kabcenell Wayne. 2009. "Does It Matter If My Mediator Looks like Me? The Impact of Racially Matching Participants and Mediators." *Dispute Resolution Magazine*, Spring 2009: 22–4.

Charkoudian, Lorig, and Ellen Kabcenell Wayne. 2010. "Fairness, Understanding, and Satisfaction: Impact of Mediator and Participant Race and Gender on Participants' Perception of Mediation." *Conflict Resolution Quarterly* 28 (1): 23–52. 10.1002/crq.20011

Chew, Irene K. H., and Christopher Lim. 2006. "A Confucian Perspective on Conflict Resolution." *The International Journal of Human Resource Management* 6 (1): 143–57. 10.1080/09585199500000007

Chew, Pat K., ed. 2001. *The Conflict and Culture Reader*. New York: New York University Press.

Coben, James Richard, and Peter N. Thompson. 2006. "Disputing Irony: A Systematic Look at Litigation About Mediation." *Harvard Negotiation Law Review* 11: 43–146.

Cohen, Jerome Alan. 1966. "Chinese Mediation on the Eve of Modernization." *California Law Review* 54 (3): 1201–26. 10.15779/Z38MR10

Crenshaw, Kimberle. 1989. "Demarginalizing the Intersection of Race and Sex: A Black Feminist Critique of Antidiscrimination Doctrine, Feminist Theory and Antiracist Politics." *University of Chicago Legal Forum* 1: 139–67.

Curran, Daniel, James K. Sebenius, and Michael Watkins. 2004. "Two Paths to Peace: Contrasting George Mitchell in Northern Ireland with Richard Holbrooke in Bosnia-Herzegovina." *Negotiation Journal* 20 (4): 513–37. 10.1111/j.1571-9979.2004.00041.x

Delgado, Richard, Chris Dunn, Pamela Brown, Helena Lee, and David Hubbert. 1985. "Fairness and Formality: Minimizing the Risk of Prejudice in Alternative Dispute Resolution." *Wisconsin Law Review* (1985): 1359–404. https://scholarship.law.ua.edu/fac_articles/584

De Palo, Giuseppe, and Ashley E. Oleson. 2013. "Regulation of Dispute Resolution in Italy: The Bumps in the Road to Successful ADR." In *Regulating Dispute Resolution: ADR and Access to Justice at the Crossroads*, edited by Felix Steffek, Hannes Unberath, Hazel Glenn, Reinhard Greger, and Carrie Menkel-Meadow, 239–68. Oxford: Hart Bloomsbury. 10.5040/9781474200219.ch-010

European Directive 2008/52/EC (2008). Directive of the European Parliament on Certain Aspects of Mediation in Civil and Commercial Matters (with European Code of Conduct for Mediators, May 21, 2008).

Fisher, Roger, William Ury, and Bruce Patton. 1991. *Getting to Yes: Negotiating Agreement Without Giving In*. 2nd edition. Boston: Houghton Mifflin.

Freshman, Clark. 1997. "Privatizing Same-Sex 'marriage' through Alternative Dispute Resolution: Community-Enhancing versus Community-Enabling Mediation." *UCLA Law Review* 44: 1687–771.

Friedman, Gary J., and Jack Himmelstein. 2008. *Challenging Conflict: Mediation through Understanding*. Chicago, IL: American Bar Association.

Fu, Hualing, and Michael Palmer. 2017. *Mediation in Contemporary China Continuity and Change*. London: Wildy, Simmonds and Hill.

Fukuyama, Francis. 1992. *The End of History and the Last Man*. New York: Free Press.

Gadlin, Howard. 1994. "Conflict Resolution, Cultural Differences, and the Culture of Racism." *Negotiation Journal* 10 (1): 33–47. 10.1111/j.1571-9979.1994.tb00004.x

Gottman, John Mordechai, and Julie Schwartz Gottman. 2018. *The Science of Couples and Family Therapy: Behind the Scenes at the "Love Lab."* New York: W. W Norton.

Greatbatch, David, and Robert Dingwall. 1989. "Selective Facilitation: Some Preliminary Observations on a Strategy Used by Divorce Mediators." *Law & Society Review* 23 (4): 613–42.

Grillo, Trina. 1991. "The Mediation Alternative: Process Dangers for Women." *The Yale Law Journal* 100: 1545–610.

Gunning, Isabelle R. 1995. "Diversity Issues in Mediation: Controlling Negative Cultural Myths." *Journal of Dispute Resolution* 1: 55–93.

Hall, Edward Twitchell. 1959. *The Silent Language. Garden City*. NY.: Doubleday.

Hall, Edward Twitchell. 1976. *Beyond Culture*. New York: Anchor Books.

Hammer, Mitchell R. 2005. "The Intercultural Conflict Style Inventory: A Conceptual Framework and Measure of Intercultural Conflict Resolution Approaches." *International Journal of Intercultural Relations* 29 (6): 675–95. 10.1016/j.ijintrel.2005.08.010

Harmon-Darrow, Caroline, Lorig Charkoudian, Tracee Ford, Michele Ennis, and Erricka Bridgeford. 2020. "Defining Inclusive Mediation: Theory, Practice, and Research." *Conflict Resolution Quarterly* 37 (4): 305–24. 10.1002/crq.21279

Hess, Brukhard, and Nils Pelzer. 2013. "Regulation of Dispute Resolution in Germany: Cautious Steps towards the Construction of an ADR System." In *Regulating Dispute Resolution: ADR and Access to Justice at the Crossroads*, edited by Felix Steffek, Hannes Unberath, Hazel Glenn, Reinhard Greger, and Carrie Menkel-Meadow, 209–38. Oxford: Hart Bloomsbury. 10.5040/9781474200219.ch-009

Hofstede, Geert. 1980. *Culture's Consequences: International Differences in Work-Related Values*. Beverly Hills, CA.: Sage.

Hofstede, Geert H., Gert Jan Hofstede, and Michael Minkov. 2010. *Cultures and Organizations: Software of the Mind: Intercultural Cooperation and Its Importance for Survival*. 3rd edtion. New York: McGraw-Hill.

Huntington, Samuel P. 2011. *The Clash of Civilizations and the Remaking of World Order*. New York: Simon & Schuster.

Ignatieff, Michael. 1993. *Blood and Belonging: Journeys into the New Nationalism*. New York: Farrar, Straus, and Giroux.

International Mediation Institute (2022a). Criteria for QAP Intercultural Competence, available at https://imimediation.org/orgs/cag-icc/

International Mediation Institute (2022b). Criteria for Approving Programs to Qualify Members for IMI Intercultural Certification, available at ISC.Chair@IMImediation.org

Izumi, Carol. 2010. "Implicit Bias and the Illusion of Mediator Neutrality." *Washington University Journal of Law & Policy* 34 (1): 71–155.

LaFree, Gary, and Christine Rack. 1996. "The Effects of Participants' Ethnicity and Gender on Monetary Outcomes in Mediated and Adjudicated Civil Cases." *Law & Society Review* 30 (4): 767–798.

LeBaron, Michelle, and Venashri Pillay, eds. 2006. *Conflict across Cultures: A Unique Experience of Bridging Differences*. Boston: Intercultural Press.

Lee, Joel, and Hwee Hwee Teh, eds. 2009. *An Asian Perspective on Mediation*. Singapore: Academy Pub.

Liebman, Carol B. 2000. "Mediation as Parallel Seminars: Lessons from the Student Takeover of Columbia University's Hamilton Hall." *Negotiation Journal* 16 (2): 157–182. 10.1111/j.1571-9979.2000.tb00211.x

Lubman, Stanley B. 1997. "Dispute Resolution in China after Deng Xiaoping: Mao and Mediation Revisited." *Columbia Journal of Asian Law* 11 (1): 229–391.

Mayer, Bernard, Joseph B. Stulberg, Lawrence Susskind, and John Lande. 2012. "Panel Discussion—Core Values of Dispute Resolution: Is Neutrality Necessary?" *Marquette Law Review* 95 (3): 805–828.

Menkel-Meadow, Carrie. 1995. "Book Review: The Many Ways of Mediation: The Transformation of Traditions, Ideologies, Paradigms, and Practices." *Negotiation Journal* 11 (3): 217–42. 10.1111/j.1571-9979.1995.tb00065.x

Menkel-Meadow, Carrie. 2003. "Correspondences and Ontradictions in International and Domestic Conflict Resolution: Lessons From General Theory and Varied Contexts." *Journal of Dispute Resolution* 2 (2003): 319–352.

Menkel-Meadow, Carrie. 2004. "Remembrance of Things Past? The Relationship of Past to Future in Pursuing Justice in Mediation." *Cadorzo Journal of Conflict Resolution* 5 (2): 97–115.

Menkel-Meadow, Carrie. 2007. "Restorative Justice: What Is It and Does It Work?" *Annual Review of Law and Social Science* 3 (1): 161–87. 10.1146/annurev.lawsocsci.2.081805.110005

Menkel-Meadow, Carrie. 2008. "Are Cross-Cultural Ethics Standards Possible or Desirable in International Arbitration?" In *Mélanges en l'honneur de Pierre Tercier*, edited by Peter Gauch, Franz Werro, and Pascal Pichonnaz, 883–904. Genève, Zurich, Bâle: Schulthess Médias Juridiques.

Menkel-Meadow, Carrie. 2011. "Mediating Multiculturally: Culture and the Ethical Mediator." In *Mediation Ethics: Cases and Commentaries*, edited by Ellen Waldman, 305–37. San Francisco, CA: Jossey-Bass.

Menkel-Meadow, Carrie. 2015a. "Variations in the Uptake of and Resistance to Mediation Outside of the United States." In *Contemporary Issues in International Arbitration and Mediation: The Fordham Papers 2014*, edited by Arthur W. Rovine, 189–221. Leiden: Nijhoff.

Menkel-Meadow, Carrie. 2015b. "Process Pluralism in Transitional-Restorative Justice. Lessons from Dispute Resolution for Cultural Variations in Goals beyond Rule of Law and Democracy Development (Argentina and Chile)." *International Journal of Conflict Engagement and Resolution* 3 (1): 3–32.

Menkel-Meadow, Carrie. 2016. *Mediation and Its Applications for Good Decision Making and Dispute Resolution*. Cambridge, UK: Intersentia. 10.1017/9781780687568

Menkel-Meadow, Carrie. 2017. "The Morality of Compromise." In *The Negotiator's Desk Reference. Vol. 2*, edited by Christopher Honeyman and Andrea Kupfer Schneider, 13–22. Saint Paul, MN: DRI Press.

Menkel-Meadow, Carrie. 2018a. "Why We Can't 'Just All Get Along': Dysfunction in the Polity and Conflict Resolution and What We Might Do About It." *Journal of Dispute Resolution* 18 (1): 5–25.

Menkel-Meadow, Carrie. 2018b. "Mediation 3.0: Merging the Old and the New." *Asian Journal on Mediation* 1 (2018): 1–20: https://ssrn.com/abstract=3312971

Menkel-Meadow, Carrie J., and Michael Wheeler. 2011. *What's Fair: Ethics for Negotiators*. San Francisco, CA: Jossey-Bass.

Press, Sharon, and Ellen E. Deason. 2021. "Mediation: Embedded Assumptions of Whiteness?" *Cadorzo Journal of Conflict Resolution* 22 (1): 453–98.

Riskin, Leonard L. 2003. "Decisionmaking in Mediation: The New Old Grid and the New New Grid System." *Notre Dame Law Review* 79 (1): 1–53.

Ross, Marc Howard. 1997. "The Relevance of Culture for the Study of Political Psychology and Ethnic Conflict." *Political Psychology* 18 (2): 299–326. 10.1111/0162-895X.00059

Rubin, Jeffrey Z., and Frank E. A. Sander. 1991. "Culture, Negotiation, and the Eye of the Beholder." *Negotiation Journal* 7 (3): 249–54. 10.1111/j.1571-9979.1991.tb00620.x

Sen, Amartya. 2006. *Identity and Violence: The Illusion of Destiny*. New York, NY: Norton.

Schuler, Susanne (2016). *Intercultural Mediation at Work*. Available at bookboon.com

Smolyaninova, Olga G., and Julia V. Popova. 2019. "Specific Issues of Training Intercultural Mediators for Education in Europe and Russia." *Journal of Siberian Federal University. Humanities & Social Sciences* 12 (2): 247–60. 10.17516/1997-1370-0392

Sperr, Anneken Kari. 2013. "Regulation of Dispute Resolution in Norway. Vertical and Horizontal Regulatory Strategies." In *Regulating Dispute Resolution: ADR and Access to Justice at the Crossroads*, edited by Felix Steffek, Hannes Unberath, Hazel Glenn, Reinhard Greger, and Carrie Menkel-Meadow, 329–62. Oxford: Hart Bloomsbury. 10.5040/9781474200219.ch-013

Steffek, Felix, Hannes Unberath, Hazel Glenn, Reinhard Greger, and Carrie Menkel-Meadow, eds. 2013. *Regulating Dispute Resolution: ADR and Access to Justice at the Crossroads*. Oxford: Hart Bloomsbury. 10.5040/9781474200219

Stewart, Sylvester (Sly and the Family Stone). 1969. "Everyday People." *Stand!* New York: Epic.

Ting-Toomey, Stella. 1994. "Managing Intercultural Conflicts Effectively." In *Intercultural Communication: A Reader*, edited by Larry A. Samovar and Richard E. Porter, 7th edition, 360–71. Belmont, CA: Wadsworth.

Ting-Toomey, Stella, Kimberlie K. Yee-Jung, Robin B. Shapiro, Wintilo Garcia, Trina J. Wright, and John G. Oetzel. 2000. "Ethnic/Cultural Identity Salience and Conflict Styles in Four US Ethnic Groups." *International Journal of Intercultural Relations* 24 (1): 47–81. 10.1016/S0147-1767(99)00023-1

Waldman, Ellen A. 1997. "Identifying the Role of Social Norms in Mediation: A Multiple Model Approach." *Hastings Law Journal* 48 (4): 703–69.

3
DE-ESSENTIALIZING NOTIONS OF SELF AND IDENTITY IN MEDIATION

Ida Helene Asmussen

Introduction

The following chapter is an exploration of how the social constructivist self-identity concept still has an undeveloped potential to challenge and inform the field of mediation. Although the social constructivist understanding of self has dominated scientifically across disciplines over the last 30 years, it does not correlate with core assumptions within theory and practice in the very common, internationally-used interest-based approach of mediation. A shift from an individual, essentialist self-identity to a relational, contextual self-identity would provide more scientific grounding and consistence, as well as potentially improving the prospect of achieving dispute resolution between parties, including in intercultural conflict situations.

Before the classic approaches such as phenomenology and hermeneutics were challenged by a social constructivist idea of truth, human expressions were understood as representing authentic, essentialist self-identity. On this basis, mediation becomes a process of 'opening' the parties up in order for them to uncover and articulate authentic needs and interests—inspired by negotiation theory (Fisher and Ury 1981; Lax and Sebenius 2006). With a social constructivist approach, there is no 'essence' as such to unveil. What is done and said by the parties is primarily seen as an expression of the here-and-now-context, and to that end it doesn't really make sense to think of the mediation process as a way to uncover stable, inherent truths about the hidden interests and needs of the parties. This has, to a large extent, been embraced by narrative mediation (Winslade and Monk 2008) and Winslade addressed this same challenge in a 2006 publication, but most mediation theory and practice still implies a phenomenological and hermeneutic approach to self-identity (Richbell 2015; Vindeløv 2012; Adrian 2012; Kovach 2004; Moore 2003).

First, this chapter will explore the social constructivist self-identity concept proposed in the works of Erving Goffman. Goffman was among the first theorists to formulate the notion that human behavior and interaction depend on the norms and expectations of a given context, and—though somewhat overlapping—introduced the most acknowledged and thorough theory on the face-to-face meeting, which encapsulates the core significance of mediation quite precisely. Accordingly, Goffman's flexible and heuristic development of practice-applicable concepts for the face-to-face-meeting are transferable to the mediation situation (Jarrett 2013; Asmussen 2017).

In order to ground the theoretical concepts and exemplify how the social constructivist view on self-identity brings new perspectives on what occurs in a mediation session, this chapter will go on to present the conclusions of a research study by the author which uses a framework based on Goffman's

DOI: 10.4324/9781003227441-5

work as its foundation. The social constructivist self-identity concept will thus be discussed in relation to its main task of uncovering interests and needs in the prevailing interest-based approach to mediation. Finally, the research study sheds light on the cultural aspect of mediation through a reflection on intercultural mediation. This chapter builds on the author's previous extensive research, as documented in more detail in Asmussen 2014, 2015, 2017, and 2018.

The contextual, negotiable self

The background to Goffman's focus on face-to-face meetings is his thesis that the moment "an individual enters the presence of others" (Goffman 1959, 13) a set of projective and interactive processes are initiated which establish the framework for human expression, the understanding of self and that of the surrounding world. These processes guide the individual in knowing what is expected from them and outline the self that they perform in a given situation. In other words, the way one presents oneself is always situated and relationally contingent on how 'the other' is perceived. A particular definition is "in charge of the situation," as Goffman puts it (1961, 133) in terms of the interpretation references that the immediate situation gives rise to. As the participants' positions are assigned on the basis of the definition of the situation, participants in mediation (as in other situations) are striving to find out, and from time to time fight about, the "definition of the situation" (Goffman 1967). It is through this interpretation process that an individual adapts a situation-appropriate 'face.' Referencing his studies from the Shetland Islands, Goffman reports how some islanders amused themselves by actually observing this face-shift. The Shetland Islands are flat, there are no physical obstructions to most sightlines, and in the 1960s people only tended to use dim lights indoors. That made it possible to amuse oneself by observing a visitor (who didn't know they were being observed), drop whatever expression they were manifesting, and replace it with a sociable one just before reaching the door to a cottage. Guests who knew they were being observed, for their part, would adopt a social face a long distance from the house, "thus ensuring the projection of a constant image" (Goffman 1959, 8).

Goffman's context concept is an expansion of the Conversation Analysis terminology's construction of identity as doing-being (Sacks 1984) to underline that being is to be defined by what people 'do' as opposed to the essentialist idea of 'who they are.' For instance, doing-tired by yawning or doing-happy by smiling does not necessarily imply that the person who yawns or smiles is, in fact, tired or happy as the expressions are responses in a given context. Consequently, a social constructionist would not even use the term 'identity,' but rather 'self-representation' or 'self-performance.'

In Goffman's later work, *Frame Analysis* (1974), he brings attention to—what would translate into a mediation situation as—what the participants bring to the mediation interaction. He uses the frame metaphor to define the notion that we organize our experience of normative principles in a specific context-related way, that makes the participants simultaneously producers and products of the framing (Goffman 1974; Branaman 1997; Asmussen 2017).

A limited number of newer, empirical qualitative studies of mediation sessions that borrow from Goffman are available (Bruce 2013; Rossner 2011; 2013; Dignan et al. 2007; Heisterkamp 2006). The following section presents the main conclusions from a qualitative research study that consequently employed Goffman's aforementioned concepts of contextual self-identity (Asmussen 2015) and serves the perspective about intercultural mediation.

Confessional framing in mediation

The research study presented in the following is an analysis of positions created in Victim Offender Mediations (VOM). Today the term *position* is more precise in regard to catch the flexible and changing positioning in the interaction, while 'role' in traditional social psychology and sociological role theory refers to a more determinant and stable character. The study is based on empirical data from observations of VOM in Denmark and interviews with the participants (offenders, victims, mediators, and supporters). The research on face-to-face-interaction as the most concise research object of analyzing social construction characterizes the interactionist theory axis used in the study, drawing in particular on Goffman's role theory, conversation analysis, positioning theory, and discursive psychology. This interactionist take on the production of self is combined with the Chicago School's empirical, micro-sociological approach to interaction (Asmussen 2015).

As the study found a pattern of repeated positions among the participants referring to an overall cultural framing (more follows), the term *line* is used (Goffman 1982, 5). Two main lines were found, respectively, among those who were identified as perpetrators and those who were deemed victims. Among the perpetrators, the main line is called the exemplary perpetrator, demonstrating the characteristics of an ideal sinner. They were generally regretful and repenting, expressing concern for the victim, and assuring the other participants of plans to lead a non-sinful life. On the other hand, the main line among victims was found to be the so-called altruistic victim. This line expressed charity and forgiveness by downplaying the crime and focusing on the perpetrator's rehabilitation. Against this backdrop, the study showed how the lines were structured by an unspoken cultural frame referring to Christian absolution as the overarching, powerful narrative (Asmussen 2015). The term *Christian* refers to the common worldview from the New Testament, that holds both Catholic and Protestant references.

To exemplify this framing, one of the perpetrators ascribing to the exemplary perpetrator line spoke in an interview about the benefits of participating in a mediation:

> I'm at peace, there are so many stupid thoughts that I can let go, a relief of some kind, calm. [… .] I mean, she (the victim) has seen me with tears in my eyes now, and I think that's also what's brilliant about this.
>
> *(Asmussen 2015, 31)*

As expressed here, the 'sinner' is comforted by showing the victim regret and remorse, and the victim is afforded some satisfaction by witnessing the perpetrator's remorse: "I think it was good talking to him, right, and finding out how bad he felt about it and that it had really made him think, right? That maybe he'll take a different road, right?" (ibid.). The underlying logic is that the sinner's acknowledgement of wrongful acts, their remorse and regret, generate a feeling of liberation and redemption for the perpetrator and satisfaction for the victim (Foucault 1978, 62; Asmussen 2015, 31). This conclusion actualizes essential parts of Foucault's thinking. Foucault states that the pastors' imperative for confession did not cease with the church's loss of formal significance. It has continued its influence through the notion of confession as a means of liberation in terms of the unspoken perception and practice of Christian logics in modern society—albeit handed down and reproduced in more opaque and subtle forms. The study therefore suggested that VOM practice could be seen as a 'modern absolution practice.'

Foucault describes how the 4th to 6th century Christian literature elaborated on the role of the shepherd and how that rationalized mundane pastoral leadership. This new leadership meant that the pastor became accountable for the sins of the individuals in his congregation on Judgement Day (Foucault 2000). The pastor was hence dependent on the individuals allowing him admittance to their inner life of their own accord, e.g., relating their sins:

> He must know what is going on, what each of them does—his public sins. Last, but not least, he must know what goes on in the soul of each one, that is his secret sins, his progress on the road to sanctity.
>
> *(Foucault 2000, 309–10)*

Against this backdrop, a logic developed that each individual was obliged to confess their sins to God and submit to related practices, including the absolution. Seen from this perspective, mediation is based on the idea of liberation through the articulation and externalization of an inner truth (Asmussen 2018, 140).

The presence of the absolution frame was also discernible when participants refused to accept the premise of the session. Among the victims, this took the form of a discredited line, named the uncompromising victim. This line was structured around a resistance toward entering the defined, cultural script and the corresponding positions (Asmussen 2015): "There is no power without potential refusal or revolt" (Foucault 2013 [1979], 152). For these victims, the mediation session became a struggle to redefine and negotiate the position that was assigned for them according to the altruistic expectations concerning their behavior. The following is an example of this struggle, as described in an interview. During a meeting, a participant apparently found himself provoked by the altruistic line shown by the other victims present in the meeting who had shown care toward the person participating as a perpetrator, e.g., by asking whether he had someone to be with on Christmas Eve:

> We are the aggrieved party, right, maybe we should have sat in a long row and he would have been made to sit up front with his caseworkers, like, this is us and that's him, well, now we know who he is, but actually, when you are sitting in a circle, who is who?

The quote shows the struggle to reverse the definition of the situation by use of the framing of the well-known space for handling criminal offences, the courtroom, defined by its separation and differentiation between the parties—and particularly as the place where victims are given preferential treatment and perpetrators are put on display (see findings of similar position in Swedish VOMs: Jacobsson, Wahlin, and Andersson 2012, 243). The majority, though, found a way to align with the 'available' positions in VOM, outlined by the cultural-Christian framing (Asmussen 2014; 2015).

The study also showed how the mediator's position of power is conferred by the setting itself. "The mediator encourages the participants to display emotions, and express a sense of responsibility, conscience, empathy and reconciliation. This is achieved by establishing a number of therapeutic techniques such as recapitulation, summarization and certain types of questioning" (Asmussen 2015, 38; Zernova 2008; Pavlich 2013).

To support the study's conclusion about the confessional ethos framing in Danish VOMs, the Norwegian conferencing script for criminal cases was studied. *Conferencing* is an approach to alternative conflict resolution engaging both family and local community (Dale 2006, 44). Conferencing programs have been developed in Australia, the USA, Canada, Great Britain, Northern Ireland, Belgium, and Norway, and other countries are providing similar programs (Zinnstag, Teukens, and Pali 2011, 18). In the beginning of the 1990s a systematic model including a *script* was developed (Walker 2002, 3). The script for this model has formed the foundation for several conferencing programs in western countries, including the Norwegian conferencing script. The script is a written guide including lines and questions for the facilitators. An analysis of this script, again, demonstrates the Christian absolution figure. The script is as such an institutionalization of the practice of modern Christian absolution, or in other words the Christian reference framing might be a more general framing within restorative justice (ADR in criminal cases).

Revealing interests and needs

It is a common core task for the mediator to encourage the parties to reveal their needs and interests in relation to the conflict. This builds on an assumption of the self that differs from the contextual self-identity, as the parties are seen as 'carriers' of essential, authentic interests and needs to be uncovered through the mediation process. Winslade, who has criticized the essential links of "interests" and "needs" because of the implied notion of "individual ownership or biological imperative" (2006, 509), suggests the use of the term *entitlement* instead:

> the idea of entitlement can give us leverage in the context of a dispute and therefore open up more options for forward movement. There is something about the dominant idea of 'interests' that makes them nonnegotiable and accords them 'taken-for-granted' status. Interests are understood to preexist and their legitimacy to be scarcely open to examination. Entitlements, on the other hand, lend themselves more easily to close scrutiny, debate and challenge. (ibid., 509–10)

The self-evident, 'taken-for-granted' status described here might reflect the fact that mediators are understood to lack an articulated, scholarly theoretical framework as a base for their practice (Coleman et al. 2015; De Girolamo 2013, 46; Susskind and Susskind 2008, 201), which could result in them creating their own "lay theories" (Della Noce, Bush and Folger 2002).

Furthermore, this way to define the mediation session takes the focus away from the notion of context as producing and reproducing the interests and needs expressed by the parties. As the study presented above showed, a cultural, context-related definition of the situation seems to have the power to shape specific lines and positions among the participants.

If the expressions are solely interpreted as voicing the participants inner selves, the mediation might bypass the possibility of helping the parties to recognize a counterproductive framing of the conflict, that might be key in the constructive changing of the conflict. This also multiplies the "opportunities for norm-clarification" (Christie 1977). Christie's citation refers to the opportunity that lay people have in forums of alternative settlement to discuss the degree of convergence between their moral opinion and the materialized letter of law. An expanded version of this line of thought is that, when unfolding the cultural narratives, the participants have an opportunity to broaden the understanding of their own and other cultures, as well as deepening the understanding of how culture shapes their own view of the conflict, themselves and the other party.

This perspective might, furthermore, make it easier for people to make changes. If a person presumes that a conflict is bound to issues that they can to some extent choose to frame and label according to their preferences, it might actually be easier to change the view of the conflict and the other party.

Other elements connected to the essentialist thinking and accordingly in line with disclosure of interests and needs are similarly challenged in the social constructivist perspective—such as the 'neutrality' of the mediator, and the distinction between process and content or outcome (more about these issues in Garcia 2019; Izumi 2010; Douglas 2008; Heisterkamp 2006).

The social constructivist view on identity could also be embodied in other versions, including post-structuralism, e.g., Latour and Fairclough; structuralist constructivists, e.g., Bourdieu; and classic American constructivists, e.g., Berger and Luckmann. Social constructivism, as such, covers a row of self-identity-definitions and part of this row is the interactionist view of self as a product of a social and contextual situation—here presented in the form of Goffman's role theory as the point of departure. Moreover, it might be necessary to underline that Goffmanian self-identity has been laid out as both a 'pure' social product (Manning 2000) and possessing agency of strategic and manipulating interaction (Branaman 1997). As mentioned, in this context, he is used with an interactionist view to maintain the dynamic challenge and negotiation of positions in the mediation sessions.

There is at least one mediation model, though, that draws on social constructivism. Narrative mediation finds its basis in narrative therapy (Winslade, Monk, and Cotte 1998; Alexander 2008, 116) and, as the name indicates, this approach assumes that people's 'reality' is primarily constructed by story lines. Hence, narrative mediation focuses on listening and understanding the stories of the participants as this is seen as the key to improving the relationship and resolving the conflict (Garcia 2019; Winslade and Monk 2008; LeBaron 2002). By discovering and deconstructing the stories related to the conflict at stake, the mediator creates a basis for new and more constructive stories going forward. It is worth noting that stories within the narrative mediation model are culturally and not individually based, which leads up to the final perspective on intercultural mediation that sums up this chapter.

Conclusion and the perspective of intercultural mediation

Intercultural mediation is defined here as the way in which more than one (national) culture is represented in the mediation, because of the character of the conflict, the approach taken or the participants themselves, including the mediator (covering all the definitions in Heinemann and Zurth 2013 in Busch 2016, 187–88). According to Goffman, our self-representations are continuously shaped by attempts to adapt to societal norms and values—this is obviously part of our culture. Individuals are culturally molded each in their unique way, while simultaneously being molded in a number of similar ways, as illustrated in the research featured above. It goes without saying that the higher the degree of cultural diversity, the more likely cultural differences are to play a role in the conflict. When this is the case, it seems even more important to externalize, understand, deconstruct, and potentially change the culturally influenced narratives, positions, discourses, and framing in a mediation session. With this approach, participants are also given a tool to critically reflect on self-understandings and truth-telling that might be implied by the mediator and facilitating institution in the conflict interaction. Narrative mediation has shown a way to go, and although it is certainly affordable it is not easy to translate into practice. Increasing globalization and development in the field of intercultural mediation though make it seem more urgent than ever to create convergence between the social constructivist identity-concept and mediation theory and practice. This alignment is particularly important in light of identity politics that might make people reluctant to take recourse to intercultural mediation because it necessarily implies the establishment of some kind of criteria—reinforcing problematic 'identity markers'—for defining the status of a differing culture.[1]

Note

1 With thanks to my colleague, associate professor Lin Adrian, who has been an invaluable discussant during the work on this text.

References

Adrian, Lin. 2012. *Mellem retssag og rundbordssamtale. Retsmægling i teori og praksis.* København: Djøf Forlag.
Alexander, Nadja. 2008. "The Mediation Metamodel: Understanding Practice." *Conflict Resolution Quarterly* 26 (1): 97–123. 10.1002/crq.225.
Asmussen, Ida Helene. 2014. *Fra retsstat til omsorgsstat—om syndsforladelse i konfliktråd.* København: Djøf Forlag.
Asmussen, Ida Helene. 2015. "Performing Absolution Narratives in Restorative Justice." *Restorative Justice* 3 (1): 28–48. 10.1080/20504721.2015.1049870.
Asmussen, Ida Helene. 2017. "Old Goffman as a New Research Strategy in Restorative Justice." In *Critical Restorative Justice*, edited by Ivo Aertsen and Brunilda Pali, 143–58. Oxford, Portland: Hart Publishing. 10.5 040/9781509906659.ch-009.
Asmussen, Ida Helene. 2018. "Mediation in Light of Modern Identity." In *Nordic Mediation Research*, edited by Anna Nylund, Kaijus Ervasti, and Lin Adrian, 133–43. Cham: Springer International. 10.1007/978-3-319-73019-6_8.
Branaman, Ann. 1997. "Goffman's Social Theory." In *The Goffman Reader*, edited by Charles C. Lemert and Ann Branaman, xlv–lxxxii. Cambridge, MA: Blackwell.
Bruce, Jasmine. 2013. "Understanding 'Back Stage' and 'Front Stage' Work in Restorative Justice Conferences: The Benefits of Using Ethnographic Techniques." *Current Issues in Criminal Justice* 25 (1): 517–26. 10.1080/10345329.2013.12035978.

Busch, Dominic. 2016. "Does Conflict Mediation Research Keep Track with Cultural Theory?" *European Journal of Applied Linguistics* 4 (2): 181–206. 10.1515/eujal-2015-0037.

Christie, Nils. 1977. "Conflicts as Property." *The British Journal of Criminology* 17 (1): 1–15. 10.1093/oxfordjournals.bjc.a046783.

Coleman, Peter T., Katharina G. Kugler, Kyong Mazzaro, Christianna Gozzi, Nora El Zokm, and Kenneth Kressel. 2015. "Putting the Peaces Together: A Situated Model of Mediation." *International Journal of Conflict Management* 26 (2): 145–71. 10.1108/IJCMA-02-2014-0012.

Dale, Geir. 2006. *Fra konflikt til samarbeid grunnbok i konfliktarbeid med ungdom.* Oslo: Cappelen akademisk.

De Girolamo, Debbie. 2013. "Mediation: Exploring the Prism." In *The Fugitive Identity of Commercial Mediation: Negotiations, Shift Changes and Allusionary Action*, edited by Debbie De Girolamo, 45–71. London, New York: Routledge.

Della Noce, Dorothy J., Robert A. Baruch Bush, and Joseph P. Folger. 2002. "Clarifying the Theoretical Underpinnings of Mediation: Implications for Practice and Policy." *Pepperdine Dispute Resolution Law Journal* 3 (1): 39–65.

Dignan, James, Anne Atkinson, Helen Atkinson, Marie Howes, Jennifer Johnstone, Gwen Robinson, Joanna Shapland, and Angela Sorsby. 2007. "Staging Restorative Justice Encounters against a Criminal Justice Backdrop: A Dramaturgical Analysis." *Criminology & Criminal Justice* 7 (1): 5–32. 10.1177/1748895807072474.

Douglas, Susan. 2008. "Neutrality in Mediation: A Study of Mediator Perceptions." *QUT Law Review* 8 (1): 139–57. 10.5204/qutlr.v8i1.88.

Fisher, Roger, and William Ury. 1981. *Getting to Yes: Negotiating Agreement without Giving In.* Boston: Houghton Mifflin.

Foucault, Michel. 1978. *The History of Sexuality.* New York: Pantheon Books.

Foucault, Michel. 2000. "'Omnes et Singulatim': Toward a Critique of Political Reason." In *Power. Essential Works of Foucault 1954-1984, Vol. 3.*, edited by James D. Faubion, 298–325. New York: New Press.

Foucault, Michel. 2013 [1979]. "Pastoral Power and Political Reason." In *Religion and Culture*, edited by Jeremy Carrette, 135–52. New York: Routledge.

Garcia, Angela Cora. 2019. *How Mediation Works: Resolving Conflict Through Talk.* Cambridge: Cambridge University Press. 10.1017/9781139162548.

Goffman, Erving. 1959. *The Presentation of Self in Everyday Life.* Garden City, NY: Doubleday.

Goffman, Erving. 1961. "Role Distance." In *Encounters. Two Studies in the Sociology of Interaction*, edited by Erving Goffman, 73–134. Harmondsworth, UK: Penguin University Books.

Goffman, Erving. 1967. *Interaction Ritual. Essays on Face-to-Face Behavior.* New York: Pantheon Books.

Goffman, Erving. 1974. *Frame Analysis: An Essay on the Organization of Experience.* New York: Harper & Row.

Goffman, Erving. 1982. *Interaction Ritual. Essays on Face-to-Face Behavior.* New York: Pantheon.

Heinemann, Franziska, and Erik Zurth. 2013. Welche Rolle spielt das Verständnis von Kultur in Konzepten interkultureller Mediation im Rahmen der Mediations- und Konfliktforschung? [What Role Do Notions of Culture Play in Concepts of Intercultural Mediation Within Research on Mediation and Conflict?]. Neubiberg: Universität der Bundeswehr München, Faculty of Human Sciences: Unpublished seminar paper.

Heisterkamp, Brian L. 2006. "Taking the Footing of a Neutral Mediator." *Conflict Resolution Quarterly* 23 (3): 301–15. 10.1002/crq.139.

Izumi, Carol. 2010. "Implicit Bias and the Illusion of Mediator Neutrality." *Washington University Journal of Law and Policy* 34 (2010): 71–155.

Jacobsson, Maritha, Lottie Wahlin, and Tommy Andersson. 2012. "Victim–offender Mediation in Sweden: Is the Victim Better Off?" *International Review of Victimology* 18 (3): 229–49. 10.1177/0269758012446985.

Jarrett, Brian. 2013. "Making Mediation Work: A Sociological View of Human Conflict." In *40th Anniversary of Studies in Symbolic Interaction (Studies in Symbolic Interaction, Vol. 40)*, edited by Norman K. Denzin, 40: 395–421. Bingley, UK: Emerald. 10.1108/S0163-2396(2013)0000040020.

Kovach, Kimberlee K. 2004. *Mediation: Principles and Practice.* 3rd edition. St. Paul, MN: Thomson/West.

Lax, David A., and James K. Sebenius. 2006. *3-D Negotiation: Powerful Tools to Change the Game in Your Most Important Deals.* Boston, MA: Harvard Business School Press.

LeBaron, Michelle. 2002. *Bridging Troubled Waters: Conflict Resolution from the Heart.* San Francisco: Jossey-Bass.

Manning, Philip. 2000. "Credibility, Agency, and the Interaction Order." *Symbolic Interaction* 23 (3): 283–97. 10.1525/si.2000.23.3.283.

Moore, Christopher W. 2003. *The Mediation Process.* San Francisco: Jossey-Bass.

Pavlich, George. 2013. *Governing Paradoxes of Restorative Justice.* London: Routledge-Cavendish. 10.4324/9780203065952.

Richbell, David. 2015. *How to Master Commercial Mediation: An Essential Three-Part Manual for Business Mediators.* London: Bloomsbury Professional.

Rossner, M. 2011. "Emotions and Interaction Ritual: A Micro Analysis of Restorative Justice." *British Journal of Criminology* 51 (1): 95–119. 10.1093/bjc/azq075.

Rossner, Meredith. 2013. *Just Emotions: Rituals of Restorative Justice*. Oxford: Oxford University Press. 10.1093/acprof:oso/9780199655045.001.0001.

Sacks, Harvey. 1984. "Notes on Methodology." In *Structures of Social Action: Studies in Conversation Analysis*, edited by Maxwell J. Atkinson and John Heritage, 21–7. Cambridge: Cambridge University Press.

Susskind, Noah, and Lawrence Susskind. 2008. "Connecting Theory and Practice." *Negotiation Journal* 24 (2): 201–9. 10.1111/j.1571-9979.2008.00178.x.

Vindeløv, Vibeke. 2012. *Reflexive Mediation: With a Sustainable Perspective*. Copenhagen: DJØF.

Walker, Lorenn. 2002. "Conferencing: A New Approach for Juvenile Justice in Honolulu." *Federal Probation Journal* 66 (1): 1–7.

Winslade, John. 2006. "Mediation with a Focus on Discursive Positioning." *Conflict Resolution Quarterly* 23 (4): 501–15. 10.1002/crq.152.

Winslade, John, and Gerald Monk. 2008. *Practicing Narrative Mediation: Loosening the Grip of Conflict*. San Francisco: Jossey-Bass.

Winslade, John, Gerald Monk, and Alison Cotte. 1998. "A Narrative Approach to the Practice of Mediation." *Negotiation Journal* 14 (1): 21–41. 10.1111/j.1571-9979.1998.tb00146.x.

Zernova, Margarita. 2008. *Restorative Justice. Ideals and Realities*. London: Routledge. 10.4324/9781315264875.

Zinnstag, Estelle, Marlies Teunkens, and Brunhilda Pali. 2011. *Conferencing: a way forward for restorative justice*, European Forum for Restorative Justice. https://www.euforumrj.org/sites/default/files/2019-11/final_report_conferencing_revised_version_june_2012_0.pdf.

4
CULTURAL HUMILITY IN INTERCULTURAL MEDIATION

Shino Yokotsuka

Introduction

In an increasingly globalized world today, communities face a growing need for intercultural mediation. In the workplace, school, family, and local community, people have no other choice but to be exposed and to interact with others of diverse cultural backgrounds. While such exposures have the potential of helping people to exchange new ideas, develop critical thinking, awareness, and cross-cultural communication skills, the exposure also involves certain risks, such as those of causing misunderstandings, developing stereotypes, and elevating hostility against culturally different others, resulting in an escalation of cultural conflicts in their communities. Even though intercultural mediation has the huge potential for mitigating such cultural misunderstanding and tensions, there is a huge gap between intercultural mediation's potential for constructively resolving such conflicts and the reality of how it has been practiced and utilized. This chapter addresses the existing limitations and challenges of intercultural mediation in the contexts of community mediation service in the United States, with a particular focus on cultural humility. In order to make community mediation truly inclusive, intercultural mediation needs to play a key role. However, intercultural mediation is often understood in terms of cultural competency that could oppress some communities' voices, especially those of traditionally marginalized communities. This chapter suggests that there is a need for intercultural mediators becoming culturally humble to make community mediation accessible to those with diverse backgrounds.

This chapter proceeds as follows. The beginning part of this chapter explains the existing problem of racial and cultural homogeneity in the community mediation field in the United States and why it is problematic from the perspective of intercultural mediation. The second part touches on the cultural competency approach and its limitations, explaining why this approach cannot be a long-term solution to develop intercultural mediation skills and to increase accessibility to community mediation for all. The latter part addresses the importance and the potential of cultural humility approach in advancing intercultural mediation to the next level of embracing cultural differences. After briefly introducing a few examples of utilizing the cultural humility approach in practice, this chapter concludes by suggesting the importance of intercultural mediation practitioners to continue learning humbly from the populations/communities that they serve.

DOI: 10.4324/9781003227441-6

The problem of community mediation: The field remains culturally homogeneous

Community mediation is defined by the National Association for Community Mediation (NAFCM) as constructive processes to "preserve individual interests while strengthening relationships and building connections between people and the groups, and to re-create systems that make communities work for ALL of us." Yet, in reality, the door to mediation has not been opened to all. The mediation field remains not only racially and culturally homogenous, but also unused by the traditionally marginalized populations such as People of Color (Smith 2000). Even though there exists no concrete and systemic statistical demographic data, the mediator demographics are considered to be very similar to that of lawyers in the United States.

According to the American Bar Association 2020 Report: Lawyer demographics, 63.2% of lawyers are male and 36.8% are female. In addition, 85.9% of lawyers are Caucasian/White, followed by 4.7% African Americans, 4.6% Hispanic, 2.1% Asian, 1.9% Multiracial, 0.4% Hawaiian/Pacific Islander and Native Americans respectively (American Bar Association 2020). Zippia, the U.S.-based career website, analyzes the data of registered people's resumes as mediators. According to Zippia's data, the most common race/ethnicity among mediators is White, which is approximately 79%; followed by Hispanic or Latino, 7.1%; Black or African American, 5.6%; Asian, 5.6%; and Native 0.2% (Zippia 2021).

People of Color are often excluded from community mediation. For example, the data suggests that there exists only 3.8% or 122 People of Color among 3,200 Supreme Court Certified Circuit Civil Mediators in Florida (Gordon 2020). This is a very common trend across the United States. This lack of diversity also exists within the organizational structures of community mediation centers. Even though not enough data exists, it is widely recognized that a lack of diversity within community mediation centers' governing/advisory boards across the country is a huge problem. NAFCM's nine-point model for community mediation was designed to address the issue of diversity, stating that community mediation should be "a private non-profit or public agency or program with mediators, staff and governing/advisory board who are representative of the diversity of the community served."

Thus, a huge division exists between people/organizations who provide community mediation services and people who need them the most. While many people who provide community mediation services are racially and culturally homogenous, people who are in need of the services are diverse marginalized people, including racial and ethnic minorities and the economically disadvantaged. In general, People of Color and undocumented immigrants are cautious of using formal legal services, such as going to court or the police, due to their fear of deportation, arrest, and police brutality (Provine and Sanchez 2011). From their perspectives, the system unfairly allocates suspicion on them and is not designed to bring justice for all.

The concept of community mediation emerged in the wake of the civil rights movement in the 1960s–1970s (Hedeen 2004). The origin of community mediation is to empower such marginalized and oppressed individuals and communities and to "take back control over their lives from a government institution that was seen as not only inefficient, but also oppressive and unfair" (American Bar Association Section of Dispute Resolution 2007). Although community mediation services are a potential alternative for resolving disputes for marginalized populations, the community mediation field has not yet been fully ready to embrace racial, ethnic, and cultural diversities.

Community mediation should serve all community members equally and inclusively. In other words, community mediation should have more representations of people with diverse racial, ethnic, and cultural backgrounds in terms of both its organizational structure and the populations that community mediation serves (Smith 2000; Massachusetts Office of Public Collaboration 2020). Yet, there is a huge disparity between such hope and reality. Hence, a question arises: 'What are the barriers preventing the informal justice system, namely, mediation from being accessible to all?'

Barriers of preventing community mediation from being accessible for all

Generally, trained volunteer mediators play a significant role in community mediation within the United States. Community mediation centers are characterized by "the use of trained community volunteers as the primary providers of mediation services" (National Association for Community Mediation 2021). According to the data, there are about 600 community mediation programs and more than 25,000 active volunteer community mediators across the country (Jacobs 2010). Many community mediation centers face financial difficulties, and due to these financial limitations along with the economic downturn in the wake of the pandemic, volunteer mediators have become more important than ever (Jacobs 2010).

While NAFCM and many community mediation centers acknowledge the necessity of diversifying mediator rosters, there exists a huge social and structural barrier. A conversation between Roberto Chené of New Mexico, the co-chair of the National Conference on Peacemaking and Conflict Resolution and Janice Tudy-Jackson, former director of Victim Services in New York City addresses that:

> Those who have been and continue to be available to mediate during the day at our downtown centers are primarily people who are retired, or professionals with flexible work schedules, or people who do not have to work for a living. However, in the communities served by some of our community-based mediation centers, a large number of people in these communities have more than one job and would find volunteering a hardship.
>
> *(Smith 2000)*

As stated earlier, the mediation field remains racially and culturally homogenous. Many volunteer mediators are people of prestige, such as lawyers who can make their living by practicing law and retirees who have enough time and money. Traditionally marginalized populations such as People of Color and ethnic and cultural minorities do not have enough time and money which would enable them to become involved in community mediation (United States Census Bureau 2020). Their priority is to work hard to feed their family so that they can sustain their living.

Structural social injustice is one of the predominant factors of keeping community mediation racially and culturally homogenous. In other words, community mediation has been embedded in traditional White values (Press and Deason 2021). Here the necessity of intercultural mediation skills becomes apparent. Although instituting fundamental social and structural change is extremely challenging, mediators should be able to be equipped with intercultural communication skills and understandings. However, another question arises: What would be the best way to develop such intercultural mediation skills?

The limitations of the cultural competency approach

The concept of culture is extremely complex. The British cultural theorist Raymond Williams famously stated that "culture is one of the two or three most complicated words in the English language." More than over a half century ago, two American anthropologists, Alfred Louis Kroeber and Clyde Kluckhohn conducted their research on definitions of culture, resulting in discovering more than 150 definitions for the concept (Kroeber and Kluckhohn 1952). Another American anthropologist, Kevin Avruch (1998), addressed six inadequate assumptions about culture that would diminish the utility of the cultural concept as an analytical tool for understanding conflict and conflict resolution: Culture is homogeneous; culture is a thing that can act almost independently of human actors; culture is uniformly distributed among members of a group; an individual possesses but a single culture, thus culture is synonymous with group identity; culture is custom, holding the idea that culture is structurally undifferentiated; culture is timeless, assuming a changeless quality of culture. In other words, culture has diversities even within the same cultural group. For example, Hispanic culture is often perceived to be homogeneous. However, not all Hispanic people share the same cultural traditions, interpret their cultures in the exact same way, and come from the same countries or same regions. Also, culture is fluid rather than static. Culture is constantly changing, adopting itself to new interpretations, environments, and challenges.

Even though culture is far more complex than one can imagine, the mediation field has a tendency of oversimplifying it. Today, a cultural competence approach instead of cultural humility has been a very popular strategy in the conflict resolution field to handle cultural diversity and inclusiveness. Cultural competence is defined as being capable of functioning effectively in the context of cultural difference (Flaskerud 2007). That is to say, developing cultural competency means to cultivate an ability to understand, communicate with, and effectively interact with people across cultures (Martin and Vaughn 2010). While the cultural competency approach has the positive intention of deepening intercultural understanding, the problematic aspects of cultural competency are its lack of awareness of multidimensional identities/cultures and the existing power imbalances. The most serious concern of the cultural competency approach is that it assumes that cultural knowledge or skill is something people can 'master' (Fisher-Borne, Cain, and Martin 2015).

The limitation of the cultural competence approach is well-illustrated by the example of the following African American nurse and Latino physician (Chavez 2012). There was an African American nurse who took care of a middle-aged Latino patient, and this patient had undergone surgery several hours ago. A Latino physician on a consult service approached this patient's bedside and commented to the nurse, saying that this patient seemed to have been in a great deal of postoperative pain. The nurse immediately responded to the physician and dismissed his/her comment, saying that the nurse took a cross-cultural medicine class in her nursing school and learned that Hispanic patients over-express pain that they are feeling, and therefore, there is no need to take it seriously. This Latino physician had a difficult time helping this nurse to see this from a different perspective from the one she already had through her education because the nurse was excessively focused on her self-proclaimed cultural expertise.

While this Latino physician could have been a great resource for the nurse in that moment, the nurse felt that she did not need it because of her notion of cultural competence. This similar tendency can be observed in the community mediation field. Board members as well as mediation practitioners are often highly educated and middle-class people in a society. People, especially those who are providers of the services and are trained in academia, assume that they know 'everything.' This notion makes marginalized populations feel that their voices are not heard (Tervalon and Murray-García 1998). Hence, another question arises: Considering all such limitations of the conventional approach to cultural differences, how should intercultural mediation be improved to better serve the needs of people of diverse cultural backgrounds?

The potential of cultural humility in intercultural mediation

Based on these facts, one can argue that the conversation surrounding intercultural mediation has not devoted sufficient efforts toward including culturally, ethnically, or racially distinct minority groups. A traditional approach taken by community mediation centers to approach such under-represented communities/populations was that community mediation centers have simply explained about their services and missions to these populations/communities and have invited them to use the services (Yokotsuka, Palihapitiya, and Ho 2021). Some community mediation centers have promoted diversity and cultural competency training or encouraged their mediators or staff to take intercultural mediation courses offered by external training institutions (Warren 2009). The cultural competency approach places more emphasis on self-proclaimed cultural expertise. Again, such approaches do not entail community mediation centers' and practitioners' efforts to deeply and humbly understand culturally different underrepresented populations' needs and challenges, possibly preventing them from utilizing the services.

Hence, there is a clear need for listening to and empowering those often-silenced communities so that intercultural mediation can be developed in a truly inclusive way. In this vein, intercultural mediation should incorporate the concept of cultural humility. For the reader's convenience, the fundamental differences between them are visually displayed in Table 4.1. We should note the three core elements of cultural humility here. The first core element is "Lifelong learning and critical self-reflection"; then, "recognize and mitigate power imbalances"; and lastly, "institutional account-ability" (Tervalon and Murray-García 1998). In the process of learning culture and of developing intercultural mediation skills, there are no such achievable goals. As stated previously, culture is far more complex than one can imagine. Culture has not only been constantly changing, but it also has tremendous diversities within the same or different cultures (Avruch 1998). Rather than assuming that cultural knowledge is something one can 'master,' individual limitations in knowledge should be acknowledged with humility (Derr 2020).

Table 4.1 Differences between cultural humility and cultural competence (Lee, Wong, and Alvarez 2009)

	Cultural Competence	Cultural Humility
Perspectives on culture	Acknowledges cultural differences and own worldviews	Acknowledges the multidimensional cultural identities and backgrounds
	Acknowledges challenges such as unconscious biases and stereotypes	Recognizes that working with cultural differences is a lifelong and ongoing process
	Acknowledges that differences exist in the context of systemic discriminations	Emphasizing not only understanding the 'other' but the importance of critical reflection of 'self'
	Assumes that culture is uniformly distributed among groups and has a changeless quality, in comparison with cultural humility	
Assumptions	Assumes the problem is a lack of knowledge, awareness, and skills to work across lines of difference	Assumes that in order to understand clients, we must also understand our communities and ourselves
	Mediation practitioners and organizations can develop and master knowledge and skills to work across lines of cultural difference and communicate between different cultures	Requires humility and recognition of power imbalances that exist in client-mediator relationships, community mediation center-community relationships, and in societal structure.
Components	Knowledge	Challenging power imbalances
	Skills	Institutional accountability
		Ongoing self-reflection
Stakeholders	Mediation practitioners	Community/population
		Client of various cultural backgrounds especially those who have been underrepresented throughout
		Practitioner
		Institution/organization, including community mediation centers
Critiques	Focus on knowledge acquisition	Lack of empirical data
	Lead to stereotyping the other based on their 'mastered' knowledge and skills	Lack of conceptual framework
	Suggests an endpoint—achievable goals	

In addition, the existing power dynamics have a huge impact on cultural understandings. Although we all have unconscious assumptions and biases, many taken-for-granted social norms have been influencing people's belief, behaviors, and attitudes towards the so-called *other* cultures. Such taken-for-granted social norms are often intertwined with power. Those who are in power tend to create those social norms to maintain and protect their value systems (Evans, Avery, and Pederson 2000). As stated previously, community mediation in U.S. contexts has been predominantly influenced by racially homogeneous and Western-centric values. Mediation practitioners have risks of unconsciously applying their biases and taken-for-granted norms into their mediation practices, possibly silencing the voices of those who do not share the mainstream cultural backgrounds.

For example, Asian American people's voices are often overlooked in the United States because of the taken-for-granted idea in conflict resolution that people need to speak up and directly confront each other in order to receive the assistance they need. In many Asian cultures, conflicts are perceived negatively. Many Asian Americans tend to avoid direct confrontation because they see conflicts as negative and place an importance on relations and social harmony (Kim et al. 2007; Morris et al. 1998; Hofstede 2011). Consequently, they tend not to raise their voices in a direct and explicit manner as many Westerners do, and perhaps this is one of the reasons they are largely overlooked. Many articles point out how Asians are often forgotten and are treated as if they are model citizens who have no need to receive assistance (Wong and Halgin 2006; Lee, Wong, and Alvarez 2008). Similarly, even trained intercultural mediators could overlook Asian Americans' needs because of how Asian Americans perceive conflicts and the way they communicate. Mediators' unconscious bias could silence culturally different others' voices. In addition, while many people believe that "culture is uniformly distributed among members of a group" (Avruch 1998), this belief has risks of overlooking the rich dimensions of diversity contained within the same culture. For example, research found that three East Asian countries, namely, China, Korea, and Japan, have different conflict management styles (Kim et al. 2007). Additionally, Chinese, Korean, and Japanese cultures are also not homogenous, having diversities within. This explains the importance of treating the process of developing intercultural mediation skills as a life-learning and critical self-reflection process rather than achievable knowledge. It is almost impossible to master such knowledge (Fisher-Borne, Cain, and Martin 2015), and therefore, community mediation centers as well as mediation practitioners, need to continue humbly learning from community members because the community knows best. That is to say, they are the experts of themselves.

Community mediation centers' efforts to learn through cultural humility

Some community mediation centers and practitioners have started advocating for the importance of cultural humility in intercultural mediation. For example, the Conflict Resolution Consultant Agency HumanKind Workshop facilitates their workshops for mediation practitioners, 'Cultural Humility and Mediation,' focusing on self-reflection and mindfulness by learning to "get out of the way of the parties through achieving an awareness of our own power imbalances or cultural constraints" (HumanKind Workshop 2020). Their workshop on cultural humility was implemented by the well-known nonprofit conflict resolution organization, the Association for Conflict Resolution in 2017 at the Association for Conflict Resolution of Greater New York's 16th Annual Conference: Strengthening Our Resolve (Association for Conflict Resolution Greater New York Chapter 2017).

In 2020, the Massachusetts Office of Public Collaboration (MOPC) launched the *Public Service Grant Diversity Project* to assist the nine community mediation centers in Massachusetts with identifying marginalized populations, their outreach processes and trust building, and organizing listening sessions in order to humbly learn from the target marginalized populations and to increase access to justice particularly for those underrepresented populations/communities. With respect to the cultural humility approach to this project, MOPC and collaborating community mediation centers held listening sessions with such underrepresented populations, including Brazilian, Cambodian, Latinx, and African American communities (Yokotsuka, Palihapitiya, and Ho 2021). The primary purpose of the listening sessions was to listen carefully and humbly to the traditionally marginalized populations/communities because they are the experts who know about their communities' needs and barriers more than anyone else.

By humbly learning from the community members who are the experts of their lives, MOPC and collaborating community mediation centers are aiming to align the institutional bottom-line with the needs of traditionally underserved populations so that community mediation centers can better serve them. While the PSG diversity project is still ongoing, there are some important preliminary findings such as language barriers, lack of trust and awareness issues, and cultural norms. The purpose of the project is to open the door of community mediation for all, but not just for those who can only speak English. However, in reality, there is a shortage of bilingual mediators and community mediation centers' websites as well as their materials, are mostly written in English only. Many immigrant communities, especially undocumented immigrants, are extra cautious of trusting and establishing relationships with *outsiders*, including community mediation centers. For the populations/communities of high-context cultures, unknown neutral third party's interventions are quite challenging because they value relationships and trust. In that context, family members, respected elders, or religious/community leaders' interventions are perceived to be more natural (Yokotsuka, Palihapitiya, and Ho 2021). These findings would lead to the next step, which is how community mediation centers can overcome such limitations and challenges to increase access to justice for all.

Conclusion

Although this chapter refers to community mediation in U.S. contexts, the importance of cultural humility would be significant in many different mediation contexts. The cultural shift from competency to the humility approach has just started. In order to develop and practice truly inclusive intercultural mediation, mediation practitioners and organizations must continue learning humbly from the populations/communities that they serve. These new efforts could possibly expand the concept of intercultural mediation and increase intercultural mediation's accessibility for all.

References

American Bar Association. 2020. *ABA Profile of the Legal Profession 2020.* https://www.americanbar.org/content/dam/aba/administrative/news/2020/07/potlp2020.pdf

American Bar Association Section of Dispute Resolution. 2007. *A Manual for Legal Services and Pro Bono Mediation Programs.* Washington, DC: American Bar Association: https://s3.amazonaws.com/aboutrsi/59316376f8851827014cb4de/pro_bono_manual_final.authcheckdam.pdf

Association for Conflict Resolution Greater New York Chapter. 2017. *ACR-GNY Strengthening Our Resolve 2017 Annual Conference Agenda.* https://www.acrgny.org/event-2506926

Avruch, Kevin. 1998. *Culture & Conflict Resolution.* Washington, DC: US Institute of Peace Press.

Chavez, Vivian. 2012. *Cultural Humility: People, Principles and Practices.* San Francisco, CA: San Francisco State University.

Derr, Lisa. 2020. "Mediating with Cultural Competence." Mediate.Com. https://www.mediate.com/articles/derr-cultural.cfm

Evans, Ronald W., Patricia G. Avery, and Patricia Velde Pederson. 2000. "Taboo Topics: Cultural Restraint on Teaching Social Issues." *The Clearing House: A Journal of Educational Strategies, Issues and Ideas* 73 (5): 295–302. 10.1080/00098650009600973

Fisher-Borne, Marcie, Jessie Montana Cain, and Suzanne L. Martin. 2015. "From Mastery to Accountability: Cultural Humility as an Alternative to Cultural Competence." *Social Work Education* 34 (2): 165–81. 10.1080/02615479.2014.977244

Flaskerud, Jacquelyn H. 2007. "Cultural Competence: What Is It?" *Issues in Mental Health Nursing* 28 (1): 121–3. 10.1080/01612840600998154

Gordon, David. 2020. "ADR in Florida, the Severe Lack of Diversity." https://www.palmbeachbar.org/adr-in-florida-the-severe-lack-of-diversity/

Hedeen, Timothy. 2004. "The Evolution and Evaluation of Community Mediation: Limited Research Suggests Unlimited Progress." *Conflict Resolution Quarterly* 22 (1–2): 101–33. 10.1002/crq.94

Hofstede, Geert. 2011. "Dimensionalizing Cultures: The Hofstede Model in Context." *Online Readings in Psychology and Culture* 2 (1): 1–26. 10.9707/2307-0919.1014

HumanKind Workshop. 2020. "Who We Are." https://www.humankindworkshop.com/who-we-are

Jacobs, Becky L. 2010. "Volunteers: The Power of Community Mediation." *Nevada Law Journal* 11 (2): 481–501.

Kim, Tae-Yeol, Chongwei Wang, Mari Kondo, and Tae-Hyun Kim. 2007. "Conflict Management Styles: The Differences among the Chinese, Japanese, and Koreans." *International Journal of Conflict Management* 18 (1): 23–41. 10.1108/10444060710759309

Kroeber, Alfred Louis, and Clyde Kluckhohn. 1952. *Culture: A Critical Review of Concepts and Definitions.* Cambridge, M.A.: Peabody Museums.

Lee, Stacey J., Nga-Wing Anjela Wong, and Alvin N. Alvarez. 2008. "The Model Minority and the Perpetual Foreigner: Stereotypes of Asian Americans." In *Asian American Psychology*, edited by Nita Tewari and Alvin N. Alvarez, 69–84. Psychology Press. 10.4324/9780203809839

Martin, Mercedes, and Billy Vaughn. 2010. "Cultural Competence: The Nuts & Bolts of Diversity & Inclusion." *Diversity Officer Magazine*. October 25, 2010. https://diversityofficermagazine.com/cultural-competence/cultural-competence-diversity-inclusion/

Massachusetts Office of Public Collaboration. 2020. "Massachusetts Community Mediation Center Grant Program: Fiscal Year 2020 Report & Evaluation." *University of Massachusetts Boston ScholarWorks* 12. https://scholarworks.umb.edu/cgi/viewcontent.cgi?article=1029&context=mopc_pubs

Morris, Michael W., Katherine Y. Williams, Kwok Leung, Richard Larrick, M. Teresa Mendoza, Deepti Bhatnagar, Jianfeng Li, Mari Kondo, Jin-lian Luo, and Jun-chen Hu. 1998. "Conflict Management Style: Accounting for Cross-National Differences." *Journal of International Business Studies* 29 (4): 729–47. 10.1057/palgrave.jibs.8490050

National Association for Community Mediation. 2021. "Community Mediation within the United States." https://www.nafcm.org/page/field

Press, Sharon, and Ellen E. Deason. 2021. "Mediation: Embedded Assumptions of Whiteness?" *Cardozo Journal of Conflict Resolution* 22, 453–98. https://papers.ssrn.com/abstract=3869110

Provine, Doris Marie, and Gabriella Sanchez. 2011. "Suspecting Immigrants: Exploring Links between Racialised Anxieties and Expanded Police Powers in Arizona." *Policing and Society* 21 (4): 468–79. 10.1080/10439463.2011.614098

Smith, Melinda. 2000. "Diversity in Community Mediation: A Conversation with Janice Tudy-Jackson and Roberto Chené." *Mediation Quarterly* 17 (4): 369–76. 10.1002/crq.3890170408

Tervalon, Melanie, and Jann Murray-García. 1998. "Cultural Humility Versus Cultural Competence: A Critical Distinction in Defining Physician Training Outcomes in Multicultural Education." *Journal of Health Care for the Poor and Underserved* 9 (2): 117–25. 10.1353/hpu.2010.0233

United States Census Bureau. 2020. "Poverty Thresholds by Size of Family and Number of Children." https://www.census.gov/data/tables/time-series/demo/income-poverty/historical-poverty-thresholds.html

Warren, Naomi. 2009. "An Analysis of Diversity Trainings in United States Community Mediation Centers." *RSI Resolution Systems Institute.* https://www.aboutrsi.org/library/an-analysis-of-diversity-trainings-in-united-states-community-mediation-centers

Wong, Frieda, and Richard Halgin. 2006. "The 'Model Minority': Bane or Blessing for Asian Americans?" *Journal of Multicultural Counseling and Development* 34 (1): 38–49. 10.1002/j.2161-1912.2006.tb00025.x

Yokotsuka, Shino, Madhawa Palihapitiya, and Jarling Ho. 2021. "Increasing Access to Justice: Engaging Marginalized Populations through the PSG Diversity Project to Diversify the Homogeneous Mediation Field." In *Association for Conflict Resolution 2021 Conference.* https://cdn.ymaws.com/acrnet.org/resource/resmgr/conference/2021_conf/acr_2021_conf_program.pdf

Zippia. 2021. "Mediator Demographics in the US: Mediator Statistics by Race." https://www.zippia.com/mediator-jobs/demographics/

5

INTERCULTURAL MEDIATION TRAINING

Claude-Hélène Mayer

Introduction

Mediation is a very old human practice to resolve human conflict all over the world (Wall, Stark, and Standifer 2001). It is described as a very flexible and adaptable practice of mediation and negotiation which makes it suitable as a constructive practice which can be implemented in various cultural settings (Busch and Mayer 2017).

During the past decades, intercultural mediation has been defined in various ways and it has been referred to as a conflict intervention practice in which the conflict parties (Mayer 2019, 2021; Bierbrauer 2009) or the mediator share different cultural backgrounds (Irving, Benjamin, and San-Pedro 1999). Intercultural mediation is understood as a conflict intervention practice that combines different cultural approaches to managing conflicts through third-party interventions based on culture-specific approaches (Mayer, Boness, and Kussaga 2010; Ting-Toomey 2010).

Who can become an intercultural mediator and how one can methodically acquire the skills to become an intercultural mediator differs across cultures (Mayer 2021). Mediation practices can be found globally, across spatial and time zones, various religious and spiritual practices. How individuals prepare to mediate across cultures differs: in some cultures, intercultural mediators are identified due to their personal skills, their charisma, and their abilities to communicate and negotiate across cultural divides. In other cultures, they are being trained in specific mediation skills which are often defined and standardized by a national/regional mediation association and/or laws.

This chapter investigates the state of the art in research and practice in intercultural mediation training and explores how individuals can and should be trained in intercultural mediation to resolve conflicts in an interculturally competent, peaceful, sustainable and effective way. Previous literature on mediation training defines mediation as a communication practice as a flexible, innovative, and creative means, but fails to define mediation training (e.g., Raines, Hedeen, and Barton 2010). Training is here defined as the systematic development of knowledge, skills, and attitudes required by an individual to perform adequately a given task or job (Armstrong 1988). Intercultural training focuses on training intercultural skills and competences (Flechsig 1996). Mediation training relates to a systematic development of cognitive, affective, and behavioral abilities to perform in mediation.

State of the art: Intercultural mediation training

The question how mediation can be trained, especially when it comes to different cultural contexts, is a complex question due to the fact that mediation as a culture-specific concept and training

DOI: 10.4324/9781003227441-7

(methodologies) towards becoming an intercultural mediator varies across social and cultural context (Busch, Mayer, and Boness 2010; Mayer and Vanderheiden 2016). Intercultural mediation training needs to address the process of mediation, the roles of the mediator and the conflict parties defined, the expectations, the aims, and the underlying values different across cultures (Lindemann, Mayer, and Osterfeld 2018, Mayer 2021). Training methodologies need to adjust didactically according to the specific training context to be effective (Flechsig 2001). Mediators can be trained in formal educational settings (off-the-job) or in applied private, professional, and work-related settings (on-the-job). Individuals who become intercultural mediators often have a specific interest in working across cultures and within ethnically diverse contexts (Leanza et al. 2020). Intercultural mediation training addresses the development of different skills, such as basic and advanced mediation and communication skills, intercultural awareness and competence, self-reflective and critical thinking skills, growth and self-development skills, as well as systems thinking skills.

Mediation skills

Mediation skills include basic techniques of communication and conflict management which need to be trained. They include practices, such as mirroring, active listening, paraphrasing, visualization, I-messages, non-violent communication, but also the application of certain questioning techniques (Lindemann, Mayer, and Osterfeld 2018). Mediators need to know how to collect and structure new information and how to address conflictual patterns and visualize information through techniques such as mindmapping, sociogramming, and flowcharting. Mediators need to be trained in the process of mediation (Lindemann, Mayer, and Osterfeld 2018), exploring expectations and aims while considering differences and similarities in values and conflict mediation practices (Mayer 2017a). The process includes training in introduction, conflict presentation, the deeper exploration of the conflict, the solution-finding process, the definition of an agreement, and contract.

Intercultural mediation training further teaches awareness of culture-specific mediation processes (Mayer 2021) and creates conscious approaches to deal with other intersectionalities, such as gender, diversity elements, age, (dis-)abilities, educational background, and different socio-cultural strata (Mayer 2017b). Besides the skills and behavioral training aspects, intercultural mediators are also trained in attitude adjustment and affective aspects to be open-minded, positive, growth-oriented, constructive, self-reflective and self-critical, open to cultural differences, and ambiguities as well as working across potential language barriers (Mayer 2021).

Lindemann, Mayer, and Osterfeld (2018) highlight that mediation (skills) can be learned through theory and practice. Intercultural mediation training therefore includes different didactical approaches and methodologies, including, for example, theoretical knowledge as well as practical approaches, such as case studies work, simulations, role-plays, reflections, and discussions to address challenges. In intercultural mediation, training tools need to be adjusted according to the cultural complexities to understand conflicts and their dynamics in their culture-specific ways and find solutions across cultures (Mayer 2013a, b). Intercultural mediation trainings therefore need to include ethnological and ethnographic knowledge that can support the success of intercultural mediation on cognitive, affective, and behavioral levels (Mayer 2013c).

Intercultural competence and communication skills

Culture is viewed as learnable, dynamic and changeable (Mayer 2021). It is defined as a general, complex system that has an impact on the perceptions, thoughts, feelings, and actions of human beings (Bhugra and Becker 2005) and builds an underlying framework for evaluating (systemic) relationships, value concepts, and the positioning of the self in the context of a group (Mayer and Viviers 2014). It determines a kind of social and cultural order within a system (Durant 1981).

Culture relates to constructing a pattern of meaning and systems which is drawn from ideologies, religion, sciences, and arts to provide orientation to individuals within broader systems, such as groups, organizations, or society (Geertz 1973). However, Welsch (2011) emphasizes that culture is a construction of the interplay of individual, social and societal concepts, thoughts, perceptions, meaning-making, emotions, and worldviews (Eckersley 2007). Culture is seen as contributing to the acceleration, simplification, and improvement of transcultural competence and learning within social groups or societies (Herbrand 2002). Therefore, intercultural competences and diversity management need to be part of intercultural mediation training (Ramos 2016; Brownlie 2017).

The degree of mediators' and conflict parties' own intercultural competences plays a major role in mediation (Mayer 2021): Mediators need to develop their culture-specific knowledge competence, emotional flexibility, and behavior based on developing their knowledge of foreign cultures, ability to change perspectives, as well as the construction of an intercultural mediation culture (Liebe, and Gilbert 1996), culture-sensitive communication practices (Mayer 2021), and intercultural communicative competence (Mignosi 2019).

There are five intercultural principles which are needed to create an operational intercultural mediation space of mutual understanding, empathy, and collaborative ethos, using culturally appropriate behaviors (Townsend 2002). They include flexibility, tolerance, hope, respect and reciprocity, and inquisitiveness to learning and the need to initiate a reciprocal and reflective mediation space to be reflected (Townsend 2002). Bolten (2007) combines different everyday competences such as expertise, strategic, individual and social competences, and then links these to the component of the description and the ability of cultural processes. Training of mediators need to include developing their professional knowledge, their skills to organize the mediations and lead them to solutions, their empathy and their social skills, as well as their own personal and individual motivations, role definitions, and self-critical considerations.

Smolyaninova and Popova (2019) have described that training intercultural mediators for educational contexts in Europe and Russia is a challenge due to the complexity of the subject in terms of mediation, intercultural communication and competence to harmonizing intercultural and international relations, challenges in language skills and interpretation deficits in specific cultural situations (Radeva and Saržoska-Georgievska 2018). Therefore, intercultural mediators need to be trained in intercultural communication and translation as well (Liddicoat 2016). In Russian contexts, mediation training is extremely important due to the multi-ethnic and multi-religious context in which in particular migrant children suffer due to strong ethnic and religious tension and a Russian language deficit (Radeva and Saržoska-Georgievska 2018). Teachers need to be trained here to become intercultural mediators and intercultural mediation training is supposed to be part of the teacher training curriculum.

Intercultural mediation training is also an important tool in the Belgic health care system to mediate access and improved quality of treatment for minority members, such as members of Turkish, Morrocan, and Italian clients (Nierkens, Krumeich, de Ridder, and van Dongen 2002). Through the training, the ability to create intercultural dialogue and harmonious interethnic relations to improve the understanding as well as the knowledge of 'the other' are fostered (Smolyaninova 1991, 1).

Training intercultural mediators needs to include emotional competence training and trauma management (Raga, Sales and Sánchez 2020), but also training how to understand and deal with social justice approaches (Brownlie 2017). Others have pointed out that non-verbal aspects need to be part of intercultural mediation training not to miss out on non-verbal clues in conflict mediation (Mignosi 2019).

Self-reflection and critical thinking skills

Intercultural mediation training needs to address a self-reflective attitude and critical thinking skills, to foster a self-definition of being an agent of change, aiming at self-transformation and transformation of others (Avanitis and Kameas 2014). Ethical aspects of intercultural mediation need to be taken into consideration in intercultural mediation training (Pokorn and Južnič 2020). Values, ethics and norms are negotiated in intercultural mediation and mediators need to be prepared to deal with the different cultural approaches to ethics and moral behavior (Mayer 2021). Mayer (2021) emphasizes that training needs to include the clarification of human values, the different types, styles, causes, and forms of conflict (Moore 2014). Reflection on identities also needs to be conducted in intercultural mediation training since they are often part of intercultural conflict (Mayer 2008, 2021) taking perceptions, interpretations, intentions, and expressions into consideration.

Systemic thinking skills

In intercultural mediation, the competence to see and observe systems' dynamics is extremely important since conflict partners are usually bound to certain systems and systemic dynamics (Lindemann, Mayer, and Osterfeld 2018). Systemic thinking processes in intercultural mediation include, for example, the understanding of the interconnectedness of the relations of elements, subsystems and processes which impact on the conflict and its dynamics in terms of manifestation and solution. In systemic thinking processes, it is assumed that the whole is greater than the sum of its parts and that holistic processes are needed to construct sustainable adequate solutions (Mayer and Viviers 2016). In intercultural mediation training, it is required to recognize how the different elements of the systems interact and communicate with each other and how they make sense and build a purposeful unit within the conflict scenario (Meer 2008). The communication within a system's dynamic aims at reducing complexities within the systems' context (Luhmann and Bednarz, 2005) and the intercultural mediator needs to develop the communicative skills to reduce complexity and create mutual understanding. The culture of systemic thinking within an intercultural mediation process helps the mediator to understand how the conflict parties create their conflict realities (Ludewig 2005). By training systemic thinking approaches, mediators are trained to accentuating the focus of a problem in a new way and by seeing it from a solution-oriented perspective (de Shazer 2004).

Ruesch and Bateson (1995, 305) view the acting individual as an element of the system: The social system is built out of 'participating individuals' who negotiate the system's reality. However, according to Ruesch and Bateson (1995), communication happens on four different layers: on the intrapersonal level (what is going on within one person), the interpersonal level (what is going on between two or more persons), the level of group processes (interactions between many people) and the level of cultural processes (interactions between large groups, cultural groups, and/or in society as a whole). According to Bateson (1980), it is the "difference that makes a difference," whereby the difference is part of the observer's construction of reality and not an objective fact. That means that within the system, the processes observed are always a construction of the person who interacts and the person who observes. Von Foerster (1995) who advises that actions should always aim at increasing the quantum of possibilities, points out that actions are defined as meaningful if they expand the possibilities of choice within a system.

The "rationality of arbitrariness" (March and Olsen 1976), such as circularity, solution-orientation (Bamberger 2001; de Shazer 2004), resource-orientation, and growth-orientation to explore the system's complexity, without preferring a certain way of addressing themes and topics in systemic intercultural mediation, need to be trained in intercultural mediation training.

In systemic thinking, circularity is one of the main concepts used, based on the assumption that human behaviour, feelings and thoughts are part of a socially and psychologically constructed reality. Generally, systemic thinking is founded on a solution-focused approach, considering the assumption that "Problem talk creates problems, solution talk creates solutions" (von Schlippe and Schweitzer 2003, 35). The focus on solutions and how solutions can be supported (Bamberger 2001) leads to more solutions, whilst the focus on problems can easily lead to a problem trance and an increase in problems. Scheinecker (2007) indicates that solutions are stimulated through the analysis and perception of differences, the search for resources, future-orientation, acknowledgment and respect, as well as cooperative actions and the retention of respect towards the mediator. In intercultural mediation training, systemic approaches need to be trained to ensure a complex view on the conflict and mediation situation, the complexity of the cultural context, and a solution-oriented view. Specific systemic communication techniques are usually trained through exercises and role plays, simulation situations, analyzing video material, and practice of systemic questioning.

Intercultural mediation training methods

Usually, training material in intercultural mediation training is supplied by the trainers of intercultural mediators who are in many countries certified as trainers by national or regional mediation associations. In the practical-oriented formal learning approaches in intercultural mediation training, learning can happen in a safe space and individuals, becoming mediators, can explore their own abilities, emotions, and attitudes and discuss and integrate them on cognitive, affective, and behavioral levels. The learning in intercultural mediation trainings usually happens on cognitive levels through exploring theoretical concepts which include learnings about conflict, mediation, culture, intercultural theories, and communication and mediation theories and techniques and specific concepts, such as ethics in mediation, non-violent communication or mediation in specific contexts, such as schools or organizations. The theoretical trainings are then applied in practical learning sessions, mediation simulation, and role-plays. These are prepared through exercises, plenum and peer group discussions, case studies which are dealt with either individually or in teamwork.

On the affective levels, individuals learn in the intercultural mediation training to reflect on their own emotions, create emotional intelligence, and empathy. Mediators learn to reflect, discuss, and express their feelings in specific and non-violent ways. Further, mediators also learn how to recognize, interpret, and decode emotions and emotional expressions across cultures.

Finally, on behavioral levels, they learn various ways to address the conflict parties in a culturally acceptable way. Mediators learn how to reflect on their culture-specific behaviors and they learn how to use different interpretation techniques to interpret the behavior of the conflict parties. The aim in behavior aspects is to explore what the personal preferences are and how to react stress-free in uncommon or different cultural situations.

Conclusions and recommendations

In this chapter, intercultural mediation training is defined and skills, emotions, and attitudes are presented that need to be addressed in these trainings. Particularly in Western contexts, it is assumed that intercultural mediation should be trained in formal intercultural mediation training sessions and through applying different learning methodologies, such as simulations, exercises, case studies, role-plays, etc. to learn practical intercultural mediation skills and an open and interculturally competent attitude.

In the future, more research is needed with regard to intercultural mediation training and the effectiveness of the application of the trained skills on cognitive, affective, and behavioral levels during the application of the skills in real intercultural mediation scenarios. This kind of research should be conducted in different sociocultural contexts with regard to the different areas in which intercultural mediation is applied. Further, there is a void in empirical research from transcultural and transdisciplinary perspectives which needs to be addressed with regard to developing intercultural mediation training sessions in different cultural contexts. Intercultural mediation training material needs to still be developed further and evaluated through empirical research.

In terms of intercultural mediation training practice, standards could be developed on national, international, and global levels. These standards could support the development of effective, combined universal and culture-specific training units and materials for a standardized intercultural mediation training practice. Practitioners from different cultural backgrounds should, however, get together and share their values, practices, ethics, and experiences in training. This could support intercultural mediation trainers in different culture-specific settings to reflect also upon their different cultural biases and these biases on their intercultural mediation training.

References

Armstrong, Michael. 1988. *Handbook of Human Resource Management*. New York NY: Nicholas Publishing.

Avanitis, Eugenia, and Achilles Kameas, eds. 2014. *Intercultural Mediation in Europe: Narratives of Professional Transformation*. Champaign, IL: Common Ground.

Bamberger, Günter. 2001. *Lösungsorientierte Beratung*. Weinheim: Beltz.

Bateson, Gregory. 1980. *Mind and Nature: A Necessary Unity*. Toronto: Bantam Books.

Bierbrauer, Günter. 2009. "Interkulturelles Verhandeln." In *Handbuch Mediation*, edited by Fritjof Haft and Katharina Gräfin von Schlieffen, 2nd edition, 433–53. München: Beck.

Bhugra, Dinesh, and Matthew A. Becker. 2005. "Migration, cultural bereavement and cultural identity." *World Psychiatry*, 4 (1): 18–24.

Bolten, Jürgen. 2007. *Interkulturelle Kompetenz*. Erfurt: Landeszentrale für politische Bildung Thüringen. http://nbn-resolving.de/urn:nbn:de:gbv:27-20100511-134918-7.

Brownlie, Siobhan. 2017. "Mediation Through an Intercultural Communication Lens." *Mediation Theory and Practice* 2 (1): 34–53. 10.1558/mtp.32579.

Busch, Dominic, and Claude-Hélène Mayer. 2017. "Interkulturelle Mediation. Forschungsstand und offene Fragestellungen innerhalb einer Mediationswissenschaft." In *Mediation als Wissenschaftszweig. Im Spannungsfeld von Fachexpertise und Interdisziplinarität*, edited by Katharina Kriegel-Schmidt, 177–88. Wiesbaden: Springer VS.

Busch, Dominic, Claude-Hélène Mayer, and Christian M. Boness, eds. 2010. *International and Regional Perspectives on Cross-Cultural Mediation*. Frankfurt am Main: Peter Lang.

de Shazer, Steve. 2004. *Der Dreh. Überraschende Wendungen und Lösungen in der Kurzzeittherapie*. Heidelberg: Carl Auer.

Durant, Will. 1981. *Kulturgeschichte der Menschheit*. Frankfurt am Main: Ullstein.

Eckersley, Richard M. 2007. "Culture, Spirituality, Religion and Health: Looking at the Big Picture." *The Medical Journal of Australia* 186 (S10): S54–S56. 10.5694/j.1326-5377.2007.tb01042.x.

Flechsig, Karl-Heinz. 1996. *Einführung in die interkulturelle Didaktik*. Internal Working Paper. Göttingen: Institut für Interkulturelle Didaktik.

Flechsig, Karl-Heinz. 2001. *Beiträge zum interkulturellen Training*. Internal Working Paper. Göttingen: Institut für Interkulturelle Didaktik.

Geertz, Clifford J. 1973. *The Interpretation of Cultures*. New York: Basic Books.

Herbrand, Frank. 2002. *Fit für fremde Kulturen: Interkulturelles Training für Führungskräfte*. Bern: Haupt Verlag.

Irving, Howard H., Michael Benjamin, and Jose San-Pedro. 1999. "Family Mediation and Cultural Diversity: Mediating with Latino Families." *Mediation Quarterly* 16 (4): 325–39. 10.1002/crq.3900160403.

Leanza, Yvan, Rebecca Angele, François René de Cotret, Serge Bouznah, and Stéphanie Larchanché. 2020. "Former au travail avec interprète de service public et à la médiation interculturelle." *L'Autre* 21 (1): 73. 10.3917/lautr.061.0073.

Liddicoat, Anthony J. 2016. "Intercultural Mediation, Intercultural Communication and Translation." *Perspectives—Studies in Translatology* 24 (3): 354–64. 10.1080/0907676X.2014.980279.

Liebe, Frank, and Nadja Gilbert. 1996. *Interkulturelle Mediation—eine schwierige Vermittlung. Eine empirischanalytische Annäherung zur Bedeutung von kulturellen Unterschieden*. Berlin: Berghof Forschungszentrum für konstruktive Konfliktbearbeitung.

Lindemann, Holger, Claude-Hélène Mayer, and Ilse Osterfeld. 2018. *Systemisch-lösungsorientierte Mediation und Konfliktklärung. Ein Lehr-, Lern- und Arbeitsbuch für Ausbildung und Praxis*. 2nd edition. Göttingen: Vandenhoeck & Ruprecht.

Ludewig, Kurt. 2005. *Einführung in die theoretischen Grundlagen der systemischen Therapie*. Heidelberg: Carl Auer.

Luhmann, Niklas, and John Bednarz. 2005. *Social Systems*. Stanford, CA: Stanford Univ. Press.

March, James G., and Johan P. Olsen. 1976. *Ambiguity and Choice in Organizations*. Bergen: Universitetsforlaget.

Mayer, Claude-Hélène. 2008. *Managing Conflict Across Cultures, Values and Identities*. Marburg: Tectum.

Mayer, Claude-Hélène. 2013a. "Tanz der Kulturen. Mediationstools in transkulturellen Settings sorgsam und wirksam einsetzen." In *Konfliktlösungs-Tools. Klärende und deeskalierende Methoden für die Mediations- und Konfliktmanagement-Praxis in Teams und Gruppen*, edited by Peter Knapp, 84–9. Bonn: managerSeminar.

Mayer, Claude-Hélène. 2013b. "Komplexität auf einen Blick. Erfolgreich mit Genogramm, Organigramm und Systemaufstellungen arbeiten." In *Konfliktlösungs-Tools. Klärende und deeskalierende Methoden für die Mediations- und Konfliktmanagement-Praxis im Business*, edited by Peter Knapp, 124–9. Bonn: managerSeminar.

Mayer, Claude-Hélène. 2013c. "Kulturpsychologische und ethnologische Einsichten: Transkulturelle Mediation." In *Mediation und Konfliktmanagement*, edited by Thomas Trenczek, Detlev Berning, and Cristina Lenz, 86–91. Baden-Baden: Nomos.

Mayer, Claude-Hélène. 2017a. "Transkulturelle Mediation aus interdisziplinären Perspektiven." In *Mediation und Konfliktmanagement*, edited by Thomas Trenczek, Detlev Berning, Cristina Lenz, and Hans-Dieter Will, 2nd edition, 128–33. Baden-Baden: Nomos.

Mayer, Claude-Hélène. 2017b. "Diversität und Intersektionen als vielfältige Herausforderungen in Konflikt und Mediation: Gender—Kultur—Differenz." In *Mediation und Konfliktmanagement*, edited by Thomas Trenczek, Detlev Berning, Cristina Lenz, and Hans-Dieter Will, 2nd edition, 134–8. Baden-Baden: Nomos.

Mayer, Claude-Hélène. 2019. *Trainingshandbuch Interkulturelle Mediation und Konfliktlösung. Didaktische Materialien zum Kompetenzerwerb.* 3rd edition. Münster: Waxmann.

Mayer, Claude-Hélène. 2021. *Intercultural Mediation and Conflict Management Training. A Guide for Professionals and Academics.* Cham: Springer International. 10.1007/978-3-030-51765-6.

Mayer, Claude-Hélène, and Elisabeth Vanderheiden, eds. 2016. *Mediation in Wandelzeiten. Kreative Zugänge zur interkulturellen Konfliktbearbeitung.* Frankfurt am Main: Peter Lang.

Mayer, Claude-Hélène, and Rian Viviers. 2014. "'Following the word of God': Empirical insights into managerial perceptions on spirituality, culture and health." *International Review of Psychiatry* 26 (3): 302–14. 10.3109/09540261.2014.914473.

Mayer, Claude-Hélène, and Rian Viviers. 2016. "Systemic thinking and transcultural approaches in coaching psychology: Introducing a new coaching framework." In *Coaching Psychology: Meta-Theoretical Perspectives and Applications in Multicultural Contexts*, edited by Llewellyn E. van Zyl, Marius W. Stander, and Aletta Odendaal, 205–30. Cham: Springer International Publishing. 10.1007/978-3-319-31012-1_10.

Mayer, Claude-Hélène, Christian M. Boness, and Samuel T. Kussaga. 2010. "Usuluhishi. Terms and concepts of intercultural mediation and conflict management from Tanzanian perspectives." In *International and Regional Perspectives on Cross-Cultural Mediation*, edited by Dominic Busch, Claude-Hélène Mayer, and Christian M. Boness, 53–80. Frankfurt am Main: Peter Lang.

Meer, Andreas. 2008. Informatikprojekte in komplexen Systemen. Retrieved from http://www.ehealthsummit.ch/downloads/2008_referate/Meer_Andreas_SEHS2008.pdf.

Mignosi, Elena. 2019. "Bridges between people: Nonverbal mediation in an intercultural perspective and training proposals." *Studi sulla Formazione/Open Journal of Education*, 22 (1): 265–81. 10.13128/Studi_Formaz-25569.

Moore, Christopher W. 2014. *The Mediation Process. Practical Strategies for Resolving Conflict.* 4th edition. San Francisco: Jossey-Bass.

Nierkens, Vera, Anja Krumeich, Ri de Ridder, and Martien van Dongen. 2002. "The future of intercultural mediation in Belgium." *Patient Education and Counseling* 46 (4): 253–9. 10.1016/S0738-3991(01)00161-6.

Pokorn, Nike K., and Tamara Mikolič Južnič. 2020. "Community interpreters versus intercultural mediators: Is it really all about ethics?" *Translation and Interpreting Studies* 15 (1): 80–107. 10.1075/tis.20027.koc.

Radeva, Biljana, and Emilija Saržoska-Georgievska. 2018. "Interpreter training: Taking account of intercultural communication." *Journal of Contemporary Philology* 1 (1): 33–46. 10.37834/JCP1810033r.

Raines, Susan, Timothy Hedeen, and Ansley Boyd Barton. 2010. "Besr practices for mediation training and regulation: Preliminary findings." *Family Court Review* 48 (3): 541–54. 10.1111/j.1744-1617.2010.01328.x.

Raga, Francisco, Dora Sales, and Marta Sánchez. 2020. Interlinguistic and intercultural mediation in psychological care interviews with asylum seekers and refugees: Handling emotions in the narration of traumatic experience. *Cultus: The Intercultural Journal of Mediation and Communication*, 13: 94–122.

Ramos, Nuno Vladimiro Pereira. 2016. Intercultural Competence in Conflict Mediation: A Mixed-Methods Approach on Training Design and Outcome Assessment. Doctoral Thesis. Lisbon. Retrieved from http://hdl.handle.net/10071/14589.

Ruesch, Jürgen, and Gregory Bateson. 1995. *Kommunikation: die soziale Matrix der Psychiatrie.* Heidelberg: Carl Auer Systeme.

Ting-Toomey, Stella. 2010. "Intercultural mediation: Asian and Western conflict lens." In *International and Regional Perspectives on Cross-Cultural Mediation*, edited byDominic Busch, Claude-Hélène Mayer, and Christian M. Boness, 79–98. Frankfurt am Main: Peter Lang.

Scheinecker, Martina. 2007. Lösungsfokussierte Beratung bei Konflikten in Unternehmen. In *Organisationsentwicklung und Konfliktmanagement. Innovative Konzepte und Methoden*, edited by Rudi Ballreich, Marlies Fröse, and Hannes Piber, 345–59. Zürich: Haupt.

Smolyaninova, Olga G. 1991. Training model of school intercultural mediators master program at Siberian Federal University. Proceedings of INTED2019 Conference 11–13 March 2019 Valencia, Spain.

Smolyaninova, Olga G., and Julia V. Popova. 2019. "Specific issues of training intercultural mediators for education in Europe And Russia." *Journal of Siberian Federal University. Humanities & Social Sciences* 12 (2): 247–60. 10.17516/1997-1370-0392.

Townsend, Jon. 2002. The Intercultural Mediator: The nexus of practice and theory. Retrieved from http://www.agreementswork.com/TheInterculturalMediator.php.

von Foerster, Heinz. 1995. *Wissen und Gewissen. Versuch einer Brücke.* Frankfurt: Suhrkamp.

Schlippe, Arist von, and Jochen Schweitzer. 2003. *Lehrbuch der systemischen Therapie und Beratung.* Göttingen: Vandenhoeck & Ruprecht.

Wall, James A., John B. Stark, and Rhetta L. Standifer. 2001. "Mediation." *Journal of Conflict Resolution* 45 (3): 370–91. 10.1177/0022002701045003006.

Welsch, Wolfgang. 2011. "Kultur aus transkultureller Perspektive." In *Lehrbuch Kultur. Lehr- und Lernmaterialien zur Vermittlung kultureller Kompetenzen*, edited by Dietmar Treichel, and Claude-Hélène Mayer, 149–57. Münster: Waxmann.

6

INTERCULTURALITY IN ONLINE DISPUTE RESOLUTION (ODR)[1]

Dorcas Quek Anderson

Introduction

Culture has been perceived as influencing a dispute in multiple ways, depending on the exact definition of culture and the relevant lens in analyzing disputes. Culture could be seen as a shared meaning system (Triandis 2002, 16). Disputes arise from the collision of differing perceptions of reality (Mayer 2020, 8). Culture may also be understood as constituting norms and beliefs used to process disputes (Avruch 2003, 354). Under this conceptualization, cultural differences influence views on how the conflict should be managed (Avruch 2003, 354).

In addition, culture could be analyzed in relation to perceptual orientations towards aspects including time or power. Different orientations will affect the effectiveness of communication amongst disputants and the mediator (Avruch 2003, 4). In this regard, a large proportion of intercultural dispute resolution research has examined mediator skills required to handle different cultural styles. Notably, the International Mediation Institution's (2011) inter-cultural certification criteria emphasize the mediator's awareness of cultural focus areas related to Hofstede's (2011) and Hall's (1976) cultural dimensions.

Regardless of the lens used to elucidate the impact of culture on disputes, the existing research implicitly presumes the use of face-to-face mediation. For instance, scholarship on nonverbal cues have focused on cultural differences in physical reactions to body movements such as sitting positions (Matsumoto and Hwang 2013), as well as cultural variance in physical space (Hall 1976). Intercultural mediation research has largely been premised on the physical environment.

The advent of online dispute resolution

Amidst these developments, the mediation process has been rapidly evolving to adapt to the virtual environment. As early as the 1990s, new dispute resolution systems were created to handle a burgeoning volume of disputes arising from internet transactions, including eBay's online negotiation and mediation services for e-commerce disputes (Katsh 2021, 7–9). Rapid developments of such systems led to the creation of the term *online dispute resolution (ODR)*, referring to online dispute resolution systems that included the elements of efficiency, expertise, and trust (Katsh and Rifkin 2001, 73–92). The early ODR systems simply replicated the physical mediation process (Katsh and Rabinovich-Einy 2017, 33). By the turn of the 21st century, ODR systems increasingly diverged from in-person dispute resolution processes. The eBay and Paypal ODR systems featured sophisticated tiered systems for users to resolve

DOI: 10.4324/9781003227441-8

their disputes through online negotiation, and if negotiation failed, there would be online mediation, followed by virtual adjudication. Many judiciaries also introduced ODR systems—including British Columbia's Civil Resolution Tribunal—providing tiered online processes including problem diagnosis, negotiation, and mediation (Katsh and Rabinovich-Einy 2017, 33 and 151). At the same time, mediation practitioners conducted mediation using technological tools, with the Zoom videoconferencing app being the recently favored tool.

After several decades of evolution, the current ODR systems do not necessarily resemble the conventional mediation process which typically entails a neutral mediator facilitating the negotiations of two or more disputants. Unlike this triadic process, ODR has been described as involving technology as the 'fourth party' (Katsh and Rifkin 2001). This metaphor conveys the assistance that technology provides to the human dispute resolution practitioner including enabling virtual communication, providing negotiation support to disputants, and diagnosing legal problems (Katsh 2021, 15). In some ODR systems, the fourth party displaces the human third party (Rabinovich-Einy and Katsh 2021, 63). Apart from introducing the fourth party's impact, ODR systems differ from mediation because of the potential inclusion of diverse dispute resolution processes. A case in point is the Civil Resolution Tribunal, an end-to-end system providing negotiation, mediation, early neutral evaluation, and adjudication (Salter 2017, 120). By comparison, other ODR online platforms such as CREK have been designed to facilitate the mediation process through the provision of a common platform to exchange documents and secured communication channels for the mediator to communicate with the parties (Rabinovich-Einy and Katsh 2021, 51). In short, ODR has diverged from the conventional mediation process.

Because of the marked differences between ODR and mediation, the analysis of cultural influences on ODR necessarily differs from intercultural mediation. Rainey and Jadallah (2021, 238–40) highlighted that technology is both a participant and a channel in the ODR process. This reality results in three broad cultural influences on ODR: The culture of the mediator, the culture of the disputing parties, and the culture of technology as the fourth party. The mediator culture refers to the assumptions, values, and expectation the mediator brings to the table as a result of his or her training with a body of like-minded professionals. The ODR process is also infused with the disputants' particular worldviews. Furthermore, a fourth-party culture may arise from cultural preferences of designers of ODR systems, or a virtual culture with its own norms that may alter pre-existing cultural identities (Rainey and Jadallah 2021, 241). The interface of multiple sources of culture, coupled with the wide scope of ODR systems and tools, results in challenges in delineating the precise influence of culture on ODR. Unlike intercultural mediation, the scholarship in this multi-disciplinary area is still at a nascent stage. Nevertheless, its insights on the interface between culture and computer-mediated communication are beneficial for dispute resolution practitioners navigating the ODR environment. This chapter will, therefore, draw from this field to examine the impact of culture on ODR.

Cultural variations affecting communication within the mediation process

Before examining the intercultural aspects of ODR, it is crucial to understand the existing intercultural mediation research premised on face-to-face interactions. As illustrated in Figure 6.1, a mediator in an in-person mediation has to manage two streams of communication: Interaction between the disputants, and mediator-disputant communication.

Busch has observed that the intercultural mediation literature has largely adopted an essentialist approach that perceives culture from the standpoint of the 'norm' (Busch 2016, 190–91). By contrast, a constructivist paradigm perceives culture as shaping individuals and constantly responsive to environmental exigencies (Avruch 2003, 368). The essentialist approach usually emerges in conjunction with an *etic* perspective that tends to form universal categories to compare Western with non-Western practices. By comparison, an *emic* paradigm construes a conflict as a unique event to be understood within its own context (Busch 2016, 186). This author has previously argued for a

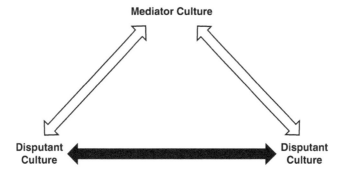

Figure 6.1 The impact of culture on communication within mediation

constructivist-emic approach to intercultural mediation that seeks to understand each individual's unique preferences (Quek Anderson and Knight 2017, 91). Nevertheless, it is helpful when understanding individual preferences to refer to essentialist categories such as individualist tendencies as a starting point, while also avoid forming generalizations about individuals holding cultural preferences corresponding to their group's general traits.

The plethora of theories on intercultural communication could be subsumed within two broad clusters. The first group relates to communication styles. Hall's (1976) conceptualization of low context as opposed to high-context communication systems has been most influential in this regard. A high-context communication style implicitly conveys the intended meaning through multilayered contexts and nonverbal channels, resulting in indirect verbal communication patterns (Ting-Toomey 1999). The second set of theories are associated with management of relationships. One widely examined aspect is the extent of self-disclosure. A study of American college students' intercultural friendships found that individualism correlated positively with the depth and honesty of self-disclosure (Chen and Nakazawa 2009). Individualists were also more likely than collectivists to seek emotional support in times of need (Feng 2015). Another unique concept affecting relationships is *face*, referring to how a person wants others to perceive them and how the person treats others according to their self-conception expectations (Ting-Toomey 2005). Individualistic and independent persons appear to have more self-face concern and less other-face concerns than collectivists (Oetzel, Garcia, and Ting-Toomey 2008).

The impact of the fourth-party culture on intercultural communication

The fundamental question is whether intercultural differences in communication styles remain when the mediation process is shifted from the physical to the virtual environment. There is yet to be consensus on this issue, especially when mediators and parties' expectations have drastically evolved to embrace online processes since the COVID pandemic struck in 2020. Rainey and Jadallah (2021, 240–41) suggested that online communication has created a third path into which disputants from divergent cultures may enter when working together online. Consequently, the intercultural differences in in-person communication may not necessarily be replicated in the virtual environment. Research on computer-mediated communication has similarly shown that communication using technological tools is greatly influenced by the pervasiveness of the relevant technology (Mason and Hacker 2003). Hence, the existing research coheres well with the ODR metaphor depicting technology as a fourth party, akin to humans, that exerts a discernible influence on the mediator and disputants. As shown in Figure 6.2, technological communication tools have effectively introduced a fourth-party culture with its own norms that interact with the parties' pre-existing cultural differences.

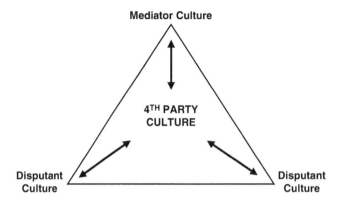

Figure 6.2 The impact of the fourth-party culture on mediation

The interface of the fourth-party culture with the mediator's and disputants' cultures results in considerable complexity. This section will first highlight the prominent theories explaining how technological communication tools influence the communication process, before discussing the impact of culture on online communication.

The fourth-party culture

One group of *cues-filtered-out theories* (Culnan and Markus 1987) focuses on the lack of nonverbal cues in computer-mediated communication (CMC) modes. Media richness theory (Daft and Lengel 1986) and social presence theory (Short, Williams, and Christie 1976) were conceptualized in relation to early communication modes such as email. The former concept differentiated between communication media in terms of the number of cue systems provided and the immediacy of feedback. The latter concentrates on a medium's capacity to convey individuals' presence. Technological tools with low media richness and low social presence may result in lower levels of trust amongst negotiators and more impersonal interaction (Naquin and Paulson 2003).

In reaction to the cues-filtered-out theories' assumption that communication media have fixed properties, the second cluster of theories posit ways in which *users adapt their behavior* to newer forms of online communication. The social information processing (SIP) theory suggests that individuals are able to adjust to the lack of nonverbal cues over time and change their behavior such as engaging in more elaborate exchanges (Walther, Anderson, and Park 1994). They may also exchange more relational information than they would normally share face to face (Walther and Burgoon 1992). The level of self-disclosure was shown to be higher in text-based CMC compared to face-to-face interaction (Tidwell and Walther 2002). The SIP model was further developed into the more elaborate hyperpersonal model, which uses several components of the communication process to propose how CMC may encourage greater self-disclosure (Walther 1996).

The above sample of theories attests to the uncertainty concerning how individuals adjust their communication and negotiation behavior in response to the fourth party. There could either be more trust-breaking behavior, or greater self-disclosure and building of intimate relationships. It remains to be seen whether a consistent fourth-party communication culture has emerged despite the growing ubiquity of online communications.

The interface of the fourth-party culture with the mediator's and disputants' culture

The consideration of the impact of cultural preferences adds even greater complexity to this analysis. A growing body of studies have asserted that the existing CMC theories failed to consider the impact of cultural differences. Some studies have suggested that the degree of disclosure varies according to the individualism-collectivism dimension. Yum and Hara (2006) found differences in online self-disclosure behaviors of college students from the United States, Japan, and Korea. Notably, there was a positive relationship between self-disclosure and trust-building for the American students, which substantiates the SIDE (*social identity model of deindividuation effects*; Lea and Spears 1992) and SIP theories proposing the use of greater self-disclosure to overcome the lack of cues in online communication. In stark contrast, a greater level of self-disclosure exchange for Korean students led to greater distrust and did not have any impact on trust for the Japanese students. In another study of college students, collectivism was associated with fewer self-disclosures in online relationships than in face-to-face relationships (Tokunaga 2009). Furthermore, the differences in self-disclosure behavior in face-to-face and online relationships were more pronounced amongst individuals with high collectivist preferences than those high in individualism. Tokunga suggested that individuals with stronger collectivist orientations may choose not to self-disclose in online communications because the lack of nonverbal cues hampers their understanding of the counterparty's motives and their perception of the repercussions of self-disclosure. Furthermore, the concern of negative perceptions may be more salient for persons with collectivist tendencies and high face concerns (Ting-Toomey 2005). Hence, if the online environment obscures motives underlying self-disclosure, such individuals would want to avoid self-disclosure to avoid conflict. In sum, these studies strongly indicate that theories such as SIP have to be adjusted to account for cultural differences (Yum and Hara 2006).

Other scholars have argued that Hall's theory of contextuality affects the level of self-disclosure in online communication. Identity is essential for high-context individuals to know how to interact in a given context. The lack of identity-based contextual cues in the virtual environment hampers them from determining acceptable behavior and may result in these individuals choosing to say as little as possible (St.Amant 2002, 201). One study validated this hypothesis by showing that the Indian respondents disclosed less private information in internet forum discussions than the German counterparts, a result running counter to the SIDE theory that visual anonymity encouraged greater self-disclosure (Pflug 2011, 134). The Indian participants also used more emoticons, showing that individuals from high-context cultures place great importance on nonverbal cues and thus rely more heavily on emoticons to convey additional information.

Apart from affecting self-disclosure, a high or low-context culture could affect communication behavior across different types of technological modes. Setlock, Fussell, and Neuwirth (2004) examined Chinese and American dyads' negotiation behavior using both instant messaging and in-person interaction. Text messaging, being a lean medium under media richness theory, had no impact on the duration of communication required for the American dyads. In contrast, the Chinese dyads talked much longer in the face-to-face setting. Greater richness could have encouraged these individuals from high context cultures to spend time on politeness and relationship-building activities. A subsequent follow-up study suggested that the auditory feature of the communication medium was most important for high-context cultures (Setlock, Quinones, and Fussell 2007).

Does the existing research provide mediators with greater certainty on the disputants' likely online behavior based on their cultural preferences? In line with a constructivist-emic approach to understanding culture, there appears to be no formulae indicating how individuals with differing cultural preferences will behave in the virtual environment. Nevertheless, there could be a principled framework to guide our analysis.

Understand the features of the relevant ODR system

It is first important to recognize the multiple variations across different communication media in terms of the availability of visual or audio channels, immediacy of feedback, and the degree of social presence. Technological media such as text messaging lack visual cues compared to videoconferencing.

However, the rapid emergence of sophisticated technological tools with multiple features such as avatars, videos, and graphics requires mediators to be flexible in their analysis of the relevant media.

Be aware of individuals' likely response to the fourth party

Some research suggests that deficits in media richness and social presence could generally breed greater distrust, encourage trust-breaking behavior, and hamper collaborative behavior in negotiations. For example, videoconferencing has been shown to support higher levels of inter-party trust than text-based communication (Kurtzberg et al. 2017). While negotiation through videoconferencing has not been found to result in lower levels of trust compared to face-to-face negotiations, it has been stressed that many of its features—including Zoom fatigue—suggest a negative impact on trust (Ebner 2021, 100). At the same time, other research has posited that less media-rich technological tools will not necessarily lead to difficulties in relationship-building because individuals are able to adapt their behavior, including increasing the level of self-disclosure, to overcome inherent limitations within the media. According to theories such as SIP, as individuals get more accustomed to using platforms such as Zoom for mediation and negotiation, they may rapidly adjust their negotiation behavior. Conclusions from earlier research about reduced trust in less media-rich modes may then be inapplicable.

Consider how cultural preferences may affect individuals' responses to the fourth party

Under the constructivist-emic perspective, it is difficult to discern individuals' cultural preferences as a person may not readily share the cultural dimensions associated with their group. A Chinese disputant may not necessarily have the same collectivist preferences as his or her peers. Nevertheless, culture is a major variable affecting individuals' adaptation of their behavior to the online environment. In this regard, intercultural new media studies have shown multiple ways in which cultural preferences could influence disputants' responses to deficiencies in channels or social presence. High collectivist and face concerns may result in limited self-disclosure and sharing, leading in turn to greater distrust amongst disputants. On the other hand, persons placing a high value on relationship-building or have a preference for high-context communication could adapt to the lack of cues by conveying emotions in other ways such as emoticons, or spending more time in rapport building before proceeding to the negotiation proper. The existing research has yet to establish clear trends on how cultural preferences will impact individual communication behavior between disputants. In short, the jury is still out as to whether the conventional intercultural differences in physical communications will continue to be manifested in the online setting.

Implications on mediation and ODR practice

The online mediator

ODR systems vary in terms of technological sophistication. Nevertheless, even the most basic form of ODR, such as Zoom mediation, could be impacted by intercultural responses to technology and present unprecedented obstacles to the human mediator. Figure 6.1 and its accompanying text set out the two sets of interactions that a mediator has to manage. A mediator using an online communication tool must be cognizant of how both streams of communications could be altered by each person's culturally specific response to the online environment, as illustrated in Figure 6.3.

Videoconferencing could provide a false sense of security because it appears closest to face-to-face interaction (Park and Whiting 2020). Yet this mode still obscures nonverbal cues and reduces social presence. The mediator cannot assume that the disputants will display their cultural preferences in

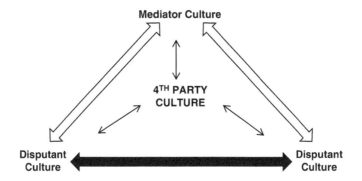

Figure 6.3 Interaction between individual cultures and fourth-party culture in mediation

the same way as they would in-person. Neither is it helpful to generalize on how all disputants will behave in the online setting. Instead, the mediator has to observe the disputants' communication patterns in terms of how much is shared and signs of potential distrust or disengagement. On the other hand, a disputant may also show signs of oversharing of information and emotions, in a way that is not characteristic of their usual behavior. These signs offer the mediator the opportunity to explore each disputant's perceptions and conclusions, and to address any misconceptions promptly.

A culturally sensitive online mediator could intentionally create substitutes to the nonverbal cues for disputants, particular those who have high-context preferences, to make up for the loss of nonverbal contexts and cues. For instance, mediator Lee Jay Berman shared that he would verbally articulate some of the cues or body language that are missing from videoconferencing, such as expressing how he wished he was sitting next to the party to offer a tissue to someone who is crying (Roberts and Berman 2020, 12:54). In the same vein, a mediator who senses an individual's high need for rapport-building and emotional connection could offer time for informal conversation within the mediation. The mediator could also model self-disclosure in the early part of the mediation to signal that candid disclosure is the norm and is to be encouraged within online mediation.

The design of ODR systems

More sophisticated ODR systems will also benefit from greater awareness of cultural variations in online behavior. It has been commonly assumed that electronic negotiations may be more effective than offline ones because of reduced time and social pressure (Köszegi and Kersten 2003). Indeed, many well-known ODR systems feature the use of asynchronous negotiation (such as using text messaging) as a first step. While this feature may save costs by requiring less human intervention, designers of systems should consider the likely implications on the disputants' relationship. Some commentators suggest that text-based communication could reduce confrontational dynamics and emotive communication (Ebner et al. 2009). However, the lack of visual and other nonverbal cues may also encourage more uninhibited behavior, which could translate into contentious exchanges that exacerbate existing distrust. It is also conceivable how cultural preferences could further accentuate contentious and or unproductive negotiation behavior. A party who views the other party's self-disclosure with distrust may respond negatively to offers made or be disengaged in the negotiations, causing further frustration to the counterparty. Hence, the implicit assumptions and goals underlying the design of ODR systems have to be articulated. If efficiency is the overriding concern, other important outcomes such as rapport-building could be neglected when designers do not give serious thought to the likely human response to the ODR system.

Conclusion

The development of ODR has underscored the many assumptions underlying general virtual behavior as well as intercultural differences in dealing with disputes. While technology as the fourth party could have created a common space that could reduce in-person cultural differences, the fourth-party culture also has interacted with each person's cultural tendencies, resulting in unprecedented complexity in communication behavior in ODR processes. While the ensuing complexity poses challenges to ODR practitioners and ODR system designers, it provides an excellent opportunity to suspend pre-existing assumptions concerning intercultural mediation and to carefully observe and adapt to disputants' unique responses to the virtual environment.

Note

1 This research/project is supported by the National Research Foundation, Singapore under its Emerging Areas Research Projects (EARP) Funding Initiative. Any opinions, findings, and conclusions or recommendations expressed in this material are those of the author(s) and do not reflect the views of National Research Foundation, Singapore.

References

Avruch, Kevin. 2003. "Type I and Type II Errors in Culturally Sensitive Conflict Resolution Practice." *Conflict Resolution Quarterly* 20 (3): 351–71. 10.1002/crq.29

Busch, Dominic. 2016. "Does Conflict Mediation Research Keep Track with Cultural Theory?" *European Journal of Applied Linguistics* 4 (2): 181–206. 10.1515/eujal-2015-0037

Chen, Yea-Wen, and Masato Nakazawa. 2009. "Influences of Culture on Self-Disclosure as Relationally Situated in Intercultural and Interracial Friendships from a Social Penetration Perspective." *Journal of Intercultural Communication Research* 38 (2): 77–98. 10.1080/17475750903395408

Culnan, Mary J., and M. Lynne Markus. 1987. "Information Technologies." In *Handbook of Organizational Communication: An Interdisciplinary Perspective*, edited by Frederic M. Jablin, Linda L. Putnam, Karlene H. Roberts, and Lyman W. Porter, 420–43. Thousand Oaks, CA: Sage.

Daft, Richard L., and Robert H. Lengel. 1986. "Organizational Information Requirements, Media Richness and Structural Design." *Management Science* 32 (5): 554–71. 10.1287/mnsc.32.5.554

Ebner, Noam. 2021. "The Human Touch in ODR: Trust, Empathy and Social Intuition in Online Negotiation and Mediation." In *Online Dispute Resolution: Theory and Practice: A Treatise on Technology and Dispute Resolution*, edited by Mohamed S. Abdel Wahab, M. Ethan Katsh, and Daniel Rainey, 73–136. The Hague: Eleven International Pub.

Ebner, Noam, Anita D. Bhappu, Jennifer Gerarda Brown, Kimberlee K. Kovach, and Andrea Kupfer Schneider. 2009. "You've Got Agreement: Negoti@ting via Email." In *Rethinking Negotiation Teaching: Innovations for Context and Culture*, edited by Christopher Honeyman, James Coben, and Giuseppe De Palo, 89–114. St. Paul, MN: DRI Press.

Feng, Hairong. 2015. "Embracing Cultural Similarities and Bridging Differences in Supportive Communication." *Journal of Asian Pacific Communication* 25 (1): 22–41. 10.1075/japc.25.1.02fen

Hall, Edward Twitchell. 1976. *Beyond Culture*. New York: Anchor Books.

Hofstede, Geert. 2011. "Dimensionalizing Cultures: The Hofstede Model in Context." *Online Readings in Psychology and Culture* 2 (1): 1–26. 10.9707/2307-0919.1014

International Mediation Institution. 2011. "Criteria for Qualifying Assessment Program Intercultural Competence." https://imimediation.org/orgs/cag-icc/

Katsh, M. Ethan. 2021. "Online Dispute Resolution (ODR): A Look at History." In *Online Dispute Resolution: Theory and Practice: A Treatise on Technology and Dispute Resolution*, edited by Mohamed S. Abdel Wahab, M. Ethan Katsh, and Daniel Rainey, 1–18. The Hague: Eleven.

Katsh, Ethan, and Orna Rabinovich-Einy. 2017. *Digital Justice: Technology and the Internet of Disputes*. New York: Oxford University Press. 10.1093/acprof:oso/9780190464585.001.0001

Katsh, M. Ethan, and Janet Rifkin. 2001. *Online Dispute Resolution: Resolving Conflicts in Cyberspace*. San Francisco: Jossey-Bass.

Köszegi, Sabine, and Gregory Kersten. 2003. "On-Line/Off-Line: Joint Negotiation Teaching in Montreal and Vienna." *Group Decision and Negotiation* 12 (4): 337–45. 10.1023/A:1024879603397

Kurtzberg, Terri R., Sang Hoon Kang, and Charles E. Naquin. 2017. "The Effect of Screen Size and E-Communication Richness on Negotiation Performance." *Academy of Management Proceedings* 2017 (1): 11980. 10.5465/AMBPP.2017.11980abstract

Lea, Martin, and Russell Spears. 1992. "Paralanguage and Social Perception in Computer-mediated Communication." *Journal of Organizational Computing* 2 (3–4): 321–41. 10.1080/10919399209540190

Mason, Shana M., and Kenneth L. Hacker. 2003. "Applying Communication Theory to Digital Divide Research." *IT and Society* 1 (5): 40–55.

Matsumoto, David, and Hyisung C. Hwang. 2013. "Cultural Similarities and Differences in Emblematic Gestures." *Journal of Nonverbal Behavior* 37 (1): 1–27. 10.1007/s10919-012-0143-8

Mayer, Claude-Hélène. 2020. *Intercultural Mediation and Conflict Management Training: A Guide for Professionals and Academics*. Cham: Springer. 10.1007/978-3-030-51765-6

Naquin, Charles E., and Gaylen D. Paulson. 2003. "Online Bargaining and Interpersonal Trust." *Journal of Applied Psychology* 88 (1): 113–20. 10.1037/0021-9010.88.1.113

Oetzel, John, Adolfo J. Garcia, and Stella Ting-Toomey. 2008. "An Analysis of the Relationships among Face Concerns and Facework Behaviors in Perceived Conflict Situations: A Four-culture Investigation." *International Journal of Conflict Management* 19 (4): 382–403. 10.1108/10444060810909310

Park, So Yeon, and Mark Whiting. 2020. "Beyond Zooming There: Understanding Nonverbal Interaction Online." *Microsoft New Future of Work 2020* https://www.microsoft.com/en-us/research/publication/beyond-zooming-there-understanding-nonverbal-interaction-online/

Pflug, Jan. 2011. "Contextuality and Computer-Mediated Communication: A Cross Cultural Comparison." *Computers in Human Behavior* 27 (1): 131–7. 10.1016/j.chb.2009.10.008

Quek Anderson, Dorcas, and Diana Knight. 2017. "Managing the Inter-Cultural Dimensions of a Mediation Effectively—A Proposed Pre-Mediation Intake Instrument." *Australasian Dispute Resolution Journal* 89: 89–97.

Rabinovich-Einy, Orna, and M. Ethan Katsh. 2021. "Lessons from Online Dispute Resolution for Dispute System Design." In *Online Dispute Resolution: Theory and Practice: A Treatise on Technology and Dispute Resolution*, edited by Mohamed S. Abdel Wahab, M. Ethan Katsh, and Daniel Rainey, 49–72. The Hague: Eleven.

Rainey, Daniel, and Alma Abdul-Hadi Jadallah. 2021. "ODR and Cultural Components of Dispute Engagement." In *Online Dispute Resolution: Theory and Practice: A Treatise on Technology and Dispute Resolution*, edited by Mohamed S. Abdel Wahab, M. Ethan Katsh, and Daniel Rainey, 229–48. The Hague: Eleven.

Roberts, Gene and Lee Jay Berman. 2020. "The Soft Underbelly of Online Mediation." https://www.youtube.com/watch?v=0869CwCBCGU

Salter, Shannon. 2017. "Online Dispute Resolution and Justice System Integration: British Columbia's Civil Resolution Tribunal." *Windsor Yearbook of Access to Justice* 34 (1): 112–29. 10.22329/wyaj.v34i1.5008

Setlock, Leslie, Pablo-Alejandro Quinones, and Susan Fussell. 2007. "Does Culture Interact with Media Richness? The Effects of Audio vs. Video Conferencing on Chinese and American Dyads." In *2007 40th Annual Hawaii International Conference on System Sciences (HICSS'07)*, 13–23. Waikoloa, HI: IEEE. 10.1109/HICSS.2007.182

Setlock, Leslie D., Susan R. Fussell, and Christine Neuwirth. 2004. "Taking It out of Context: Collaborating within and across Cultures in Face-to-Face Settings and via Instant Messaging." In *Proceedings of the 2004 ACM Conference on Computer Supported Cooperative Work—CSCW '04*, 604. Chicago, IL: ACM Press. 10.1145/1031607.1031712

Short, John, Ederyn Williams, and Bruce Christie. 1976. *The Social Psychology of Telecommunications*. London, New York: Wiley.

St. Amant, Kirk. 2002. "When Cultures and Computers Collide: Rethinking Computer-Mediated Communication According to International and Intercultural Communication Expectations." *Journal of Business and Technical Communication* 16 (2): 196–214. 10.1177/1050651902016002003

Tidwell, Lisa Collins, and Joseph B. Walther. 2002. "Computer-Mediated Communication Effects on Disclosure, Impressions, and Interpersonal Evaluations: Getting to Know One Another a Bit at a Time." *Human Communication Research* 28 (3): 317–48. 10.1111/j.1468-2958.2002.tb00811.x

Ting-Toomey, Stella. 1999. *Communicating Across Cultures*. New York: Guilford Press.

Ting-Toomey, Stella. 2005. "The Matrix of Face: An Updated Face-Negotiation Theory." In *Theorizing About Intercultural Communication*, edited by William B. Gudykunst, 71–92. Thousand Oaks, CA: Sage.

Tokunaga, Robert S. 2009. "High-Speed Internet Access to the Other: The Influence of Cultural Orientations on Self-Disclosures in Offline and Online Relationships." *Journal of Intercultural Communication Research* 38 (3): 133–47. 10.1080/17475759.2009.505058

Triandis, Harry C. 2002. "Generic Individualism and Collectivism." In *The Blackwell Handbook of Cross-Cultural Management*, edited by Martin Gannon and Karen Newman, 16–45. Oxford: Blackwell.

Walther, Joseph B. 1996. "Computer-Mediated Communication: Impersonal, Interpersonal, and Hyperpersonal Interaction." *Communication Research* 23 (1): 3–43. 10.1177/009365096023001001

Walther, Joseph B., Jeffrey F. Anderson, and David W. Park. 1994. "Interpersonal Effects in Computer-Mediated Interaction: A Meta-Analysis of Social and Antisocial Communication." *Communication Research* 21 (4): 460–87. 10.1177/009365094021004002

Walther, Joseph B., and Judee K. Burgoon. 1992. "Relational Communication in Computer-Mediated Interaction." *Human Communication Research* 19 (1): 50–88. 10.1111/j.1468-2958.1992.tb00295.x

Yum, Young-ok, and Kazuya Hara. 2006. "Computer-Mediated Relationship Development: A Cross-Cultural Comparison." *Journal of Computer-Mediated Communication* 11 (1): 133–52. 10.1111/j.1083-6101. 2006.tb00307.x

7

POLICING AND INTERCULTURAL MEDIATION: FORMS OF TRIADIC CONFLICT MANAGEMENT

Catharina Vogt and Stefanie Giljohann

Introduction

In the context of policing, intercultural mediation involves two conflicting sides and a neutral mediator, in line with classical mediation models. However, the mediator can be part of the police force, as can the conflict partner, so long as the mediator's neutrality and consistency of the process with the goals and essential prerequisites of mediation are maintained. The overarching goal is to increase the satisfaction of those in conflict by enhancing mutual understanding and knowledge (Walker, Archbold and Herbst 2002). By introducing mediating procedures, police forces have opened up an additional path in executing their duty to ensure justice and security. Instead of focusing on evidence, guilt, and punishment, intercultural mediation fosters constructive dialogues, sustainable understanding, and peaceful relations.

The insights presented in this chapter show a general picture. Nationally and regionally, laws, policing, and mediation practices can differ as they adapt to the society in which they are embedded.

Policing

To understand how intercultural mediation consolidates and transforms policing, we will first provide a brief overview of police work and culture fundamentals.

Police work

In democratic societies, police must respond neutrally and promptly, treating everyone with equal respect (Carty 2008). Police work consists of service functions to execute the law and maintain public order and safety. Although often mistaken for mere fighters of crime, police spend much of their time acting as public information bureaus and pacifying family conflicts (Westley 2005). Bayley (2005) argues that the police's primary function is to deal with and settle potential or ongoing conflicts. Everyday situations apart from family conflicts are interventions due to noise disturbance and conflicts between neighbors, other parties, or the police in response to controls or any other of their legal obligations. Police work is defined by laws that naturally cannot wholly prescribe police action and often give leeway on how to assess and handle a specific situation. Within their discretion, police officers can enforce the law with varying degrees of leniency, which may cause conflicts if their actions are perceived as overly strict. Accordingly, police are usually experienced in attentive listening,

DOI: 10.4324/9781003227441-9

de-escalation, and conflict resolution; thus incorporating highly relevant competencies for mediation. Nonetheless, their involvement in conflict resolution is not always welcome, and their presence may even constitute an escalating factor due to their roles (Decker and Kersten 2015).

Police culture

Policing comes with a culture that is shaped by the role of being the state's executive force and its traditionally (albeit slowly changing) masculine norms. Above all, law enforcement officers must act lawfully, but also police officers can fail or misbehave (Miller 2004). Second, being the state's executive goes hand in hand with the claim that police win conflicts to maintain their credibility in the eyes of the state and the public. This entails creating win-lose outcomes in favor of the police even in situations where win-win would be preferable to de-escalate and gain trust in the long run. As a result, police are perceived by the public and internally as powerful and intimidating. Research has further shown that the so-called 'cop culture' leads to an imbalanced error culture, a failure to acknowledge wrongdoing, and many losses in lawsuits against the police in court (e.g., Porter and Prenzler 2016). All in all, Reiner (2002) describes cop culture as having five elements: Machismo, mission-action-cynicism-pessimism, suspicion, isolation/solidarity, and conservatism. Accordingly, police officers might be characterized by and act according to these norms of their professional culture during conflicts and intercultural mediation (Carrillo 2021).

Policing in multicultural societies

Policing in multicultural societies is strongly influenced by the opinions and experiences of police and communities, as we will outline in the following sections. Ways of addressing conflict differ for these two parties.

Police interacting with citizens in intercultural contexts

Although the police deal with all groups of society, they interact with members of the marginalized groups more often—both as victims and suspects of 'non-white collar' offenses and crimes. In many countries, marginalized groups live in low socioeconomic status, have low education, poor health conditions, and an unstable social environment that often comes with a history of displacement, migration, and discrimination (Viruell-Fuentes 2007). Crime reports usually do not cover perpetrators' living conditions. However, groups with a migration background tend to be overrepresented as suspects of crime (Adamson 2020). It is to be clarified that despite this, most citizens with a multicultural background are not involved in criminal offenses. As to the reasons for their over-representation in crimes, the causes are multifaceted; precarious living conditions, crime-trivializing cultural values, or discrimination by the legal sector play a role, for example. Interactions with members of minorities can be influenced by the knowledge of the general statistics or the subjective impression of the overrepresentation of minorities in crimes. Further, briefings, the police officers' prior negative experiences, biases, and stereotypes shape these interactions (Kahn and Davies 2017).

On the other hand, citizens' cultural lenses are also shaded by beliefs and expectations about the police. Some members of minorities hold a positive image of the police, regarding them as necessary to take care of law and order—others fear the police and expect that they are prejudiced against them. Their view (or stereotype) of a biased, antagonistic, or even brutal police force can stem from storytelling and media coverage but may also be grounded on painful personal experiences in their social network.

Perception of subjective safety is tied to the citizens' view of and contact with police, and in the intercultural context, both too little and too much police presence can cause concern (Decker, Kersten, and Kunz 2014). An apparent multicultural background and/or a perceived minority status is related to a perception of increased sensitivity to offense or lack of respect. On this basis, Decker and Kersten (2015) assume that intercultural conflicts between citizens and police ignite and escalate faster.

Intercultural conflicts between police and citizens

There are different reasons why police and citizens with multicultural backgrounds come into conflict. Police complain about citizens from migrant communities who provoke conflict by reacting highly emotionally, pretending to lack language skills, accusing police of racism, shouting at and insulting police officers, disrespecting female police officers, and by trying to keep and conceal police-relevant conflicts within the community (Decker et al. 2014; Frankus and Mayrhofer 2014; Hera and Arnold 2014). On the other hand, citizens with a multicultural background complain about police officers who yell at or mock them; who do not communicate enough or who communicate in a manner that is overly complicated, informal, or humiliating; who conduct physical checks of the opposite gender; conduct identity checks perceived as racial profiling; give preferential treatment to the majority ethnic group; use physical violence; or give unreasonably high fines (ibid.).

Suppose police perceive a conflict with a citizen after their operation is finished. In that case, they are more likely to leave the situation or cope with it by discussing it with colleagues, supervisors, friends, or family. Therefore, non-criminal behavior by citizens, even if perceived as unfair, usually remains unaddressed; after all, there exists no complaints office for this. On the other hand, a citizen's official complaint also allows police officers to explain their point of view and engage in a dialogue.

If citizens perceive a conflict after interaction with the police, they have several options to deal with this, partly depending on the local infrastructure. Apart from applying individual coping strategies or addressing the police (online) complaint management service, they can complain at the police station or to an ombudsperson, NGO, other impartial commission of inquiry, or even court. However, citizens with a multicultural or migration background, in particular, have a high threshold before making a complaint. Kunz et al. (2016) report that multicultural citizens often do not consider their complaints to hold much chance of success due to the expectation of the 'blue wall of silence' within the police and the prevailing view of the judiciary that the police are more trustworthy than the citizenry. Also, complainants are under high psychological strain during the process, especially if they lack knowledge of national avenues for conflict resolution and the law, have heard about adverse outcomes of previous cases, and fear secondary victimization or countersuits. Although the police's (excessive) use of force is a typical reason for citizens to complain in court, reasons are more manifold (Decker and Kersten 2015), the lowest common denominator being all forms of disrespect. Predominantly, police complaints do not concern very severe conflicts (Riley, Prenzler, and McKillop 2020). Motives behind the complaint are more often the desire for an explanation or apology or the prevention of further misconduct towards others, rather than the desire to punish the police officer. Based on their literature analysis, Riley, Prenzler, and McKillop (2020) conclude that a large proportion of complainants are willing to participate in mediation and that police officers and citizens who have experienced mediation expressed a high level of satisfaction.

Triadic intercultural mediation between citizens and police

While some policing approaches aim at enhancing the relationship between police and minorities through 'informal ways of mediation,' others include 'state-of-the-art mediation.' Before elaborating on this continuum, we will first address the general prerequisites of these approaches.

Prerequisites of intercultural mediation between citizens and police

The more elusive shades of disrespectful treatment lend themselves very well to mediation. In contrast, the boundary of mediation must be drawn where potentially criminally relevant behavior, such as evident forms of severe racism or assault, occurs. Additionally, mediation should not be initiated when the history of complaints against a police officer suggests that systematic misconduct has occurred or could be solely an attempt to avoid disciplinary sanctions. Another prerequisite is that no parallel legal or other proceedings deal with the same conflict, ensuring data protection. Whether or not police officers may attend external mediation depends on police regulations.

Voluntary participation is another essential prerequisite. It can be argued that police officers agree to mediation as the professional consequences of non-compliance would be distressing (Volpe 2014). On the other hand, the fact that any conflict partners can end mediation is evidence of the voluntary nature of the process. The ability to end the process also deflates the concerns of critics of intercultural mediation in the police context, who fear that mediation cannot balance out systemic organizational discrimination and power asymmetry but rather perpetuates these. If that should eventuate, legal options remain. Moreover, if police officers fail in attempting fair, informal mediation in the field, citizens can approach the police complaints system later.

In most cases, the standard requirement of free choice of a mediator will not be given, as mediation structures are generally insufficiently developed. This makes all the more critical the prerequisite that the mediator upholds the principle of neutrality. It is the mediator's responsibility to establish an atmosphere of equality, mutual respect, and trust in the mediation process, which is not to be predetermined. The possibility of members of minorities bringing a representative of an NGO to balance any perceived power asymmetry should not be ruled out. In this particular police context of intercultural mediation, mediators must have special training for the mediation process. Background knowledge of police work and the culture of the conflict parties, or at least the particularities of intercultural settings, can ensure that mediators can explain and moderate the process without any ambiguities.

Police officers with multicultural backgrounds

In line with representative bureaucracy theory (Groeneveld and Van de Walle 2010), recruitment for diversity within the police is widely seen as a promising approach to enhance the trust of minorities and reduce intercultural misunderstandings and conflict. Accordingly, the High Commissioner on National Minorities of the Organization for Security and Co-operation in Europe (OSCE, High Commissioner on National Minorities 2006) gave the following recommendation:

> The composition of the police—at local, regional and national levels and including senior as well as junior ranks, and also civilian personnel—should reflect the diversity of the population. The public image of the police as an ethnically representative body needs to be actively promoted.

Police initiatives of the recruitment of underrepresented minorities can be noted worldwide (van Ewijk 2012), increasing the ratio (Home Office 2021; Hyland and Davis 2021). However, with very few exceptions, the racial gap remains prominent worldwide (ibid., see Leatherby and Opple 2020).

Runde and Flanagan (2010) argue that minority police officers can foster reflective thinking, the adoption of other perspectives, and mutual understanding, which are important steps in intercultural mediation. Decker and Kersten (2015) initially examined the benefits and costs of multicultural police officers dealing with intercultural conflicts, concluding that police officers with a migrant background frequently improve outcomes in conflict resolution. In their interview study, police officers with migrant backgrounds are described in numerous examples of triadic interactions as "(…) 'solving,' 'regulating,' 'de-escalating,' or 'mediating' (…)" (Decker and Kersten 2015, 473). We understand the triadic conflict resolution attempts of officers of migrant backgrounds as intercultural mediation in the broadest sense. It is preventive ad hoc or informal mediation: The conflict is already resolved on-site, rendering a subsequent complaint and mediation unnecessary. Police officers with a migration background can create the necessary environment for a constructive dialogue and solution process: Firstly, they often act as language mediators. One German-Turkish police officer in Decker and Kersten's study (2015, 472) stated: "When I came there and spoke Turkish with them, they, […] regardless if young or old, they relaxed." Secondly, they can reduce the distance between the fronts and facilitate the exchange of perspectives by acting as cultural mediators. They have a good understanding of each side's motives and logic of action. They are regarded as trustworthy by both parties, as another quote of this study shows (ibid., 469):

> … And they shouted at each other and my colleague went there and then […] called for reinforcements and then I said: 'Stay calm, they only argue.' For him, it was too stressful, and he probably thought: 'We cannot manage this situation by ourselves, we need reinforcement.'

Lastly, the state executive and the cultural minority belong to both sides, but not taking either side and staying impartial, they act as conflict mediators. This impartiality has to be proved consistently, as the following statement shows (Decker and Kersten 2015, 475):

> Our migrant colleagues say: 'No matter who is with me, I talk half a minute then translate for the colleague who is with me […]. Also, your counterpart shall see that it is important for you to take along your German colleague.'

Otherwise, the trust and respect of the conflicting parties will be lost.

Community policing with an intercultural focus

Community policing is widely used in police forces, under slightly varying terminology, and with an immense range in terms of the actual scope of community involvement. We align with the understanding of Abanades (2019), who defines it as a "police service that is designed and trained to listen to the parties, analyze the problems, propose solutions and evaluate the results of those solutions with the participation of society" (Abanades 2019). The assumption that a lack of mutual understanding and knowledge is at the root of a conflict leads to engaging in a direct dialogue to bridge this gap. This makes community policing a highly effective approach to managing intercultural conflict (ibid.). By involving community representatives in the design and implementation of policing and, especially in cases where professional mediators or specially trained police officers are involved, this approach is a transition from the traditional, rather supervisory executive policing model to a participatory, more conflict resolution-oriented and preventive one. The involvement of professional external mediators or the training of police officers by these is anchored in numerous models of community policing, for example, multicultural outreach and engagement programs (e.g., Police Executive Research Forum 2018), workshops (e.g., "Police and Immigrants in Open Discussion," Hassel 2016) or associations (e.g., "Fair and Sensitive," Frankus and Mayrhofer 2016). All of these connect police and members of minorities to become familiar with each other, reduce prejudices, and deal with actual or simulated conflicts with the help of mediators. Training is essential for the successful implementation of community policing in this context. For example, the Lisbon Municipal Police's training strategy was awarded a prize by the Council of Europe for its effectiveness, sustainability, and applicability to other regions and countries (Mayr et al. 2015). It provides a model for programs in which community mediators train police officers. Another award-winning mediation approach illustrates the positive effects that community policing can achieve through mediation (Dehbi 2019). The police of the Finnish city of Forssa used mediation to reduce violent crime between locals and residents of a reception center. This project was continuously evaluated positively in terms of developing its collaborative structures, the quality of the cooperation and dialogue within them, and the progress in conflict resolution. The program achieved the intended prevention of further polarization and the reduction of conflicts and tensions. Positive side effects were the liberation of police resources and an increased sense of community and belonging.

Police complaint management in multicultural contexts

Complaint and discipline systems are crucial to police accountability, providing citizens with the means to appeal to any perceived injustice, including racial discrimination and misconduct of individual officers or police practices such as racial profiling. It was common practice to evaluate complaints internally throughout the world, generally following formal, ideally transparent procedures. However, complaint systems tended to be rather document- than dialogue-oriented. There was also growing dissatisfaction and distrust of what were perceived to be 'biased' complaint procedures and low success rates of complaints (Walker, Archbold and Herbst 2002). For this reason, police forces have increasingly opened up to dialogue with citizens in the spirit of mediation, contributing to an exchange of perspectives and interactive conflict resolution. At a low threshold, a relatively informal level, complaints may result in the leadership stepping in to apologize and restore positive contact with the citizen. Some police forces or departments have specialized designees who get involved with the citizens. Some even have specialized designees or units for complaints with intercultural references. Some complaint management approaches are already very similar to classical mediation in terms of objectives and implementation, as can be derived from anecdotal reports on the websites of police complaint offices or case studies. Ernst (2016) presents an exemplary case of such intercultural mediation, in which representatives of the police are both conflict partners and mediators. This case of assumed racial profiling and discrimination by the police during the religious celebration of a Jewish family in Germany illustrates how both conflict parties gain mutual respect for their different feelings and viewpoints and finally appreciate each other through mediation.

Mediation of intercultural conflicts between police and citizens can also occur outside police forces. One characteristic of democratic structures is that independent commissions of inquiry control police work. Such an investigative body shall review cases of racial discrimination by the police and help "promote friendly settlement of disputes," as recommended by the European Committee against Racism and Intolerance (European Commission Against Racism and Intolerance ECRI 2007, 15). This can be achieved, for example, by a national institution, a specialized (police) ombudsperson, or a civilian oversight commission. Furthermore, NGOs specializing in the legal support of ethnic minorities offer mediation in a form that does not differ from mediation in a non-police context. Often, these NGOs have collaborated with the police before and established mutual trust and respect (Frankus and Mayrhofer 2014). They also empower citizens with multicultural backgrounds to complain at police stations and to suggest mediation as means of conflict resolution.

Conclusion

Resolving conflicts is part of the fundamental concept of policing, while triadic intercultural mediation in the sense of 'traditional mediation' clashes with several values of the police organizational structure and culture and the societal belief system. It will be challenging but crucial for police to continually assess and adapt their conflict management approaches within this continuum. After all, intercultural mediation is a promising approach to enhance organizational learning within police forces, trigger positive changes in police culture, and apply more compatible perspectives on policing in contrast to the traditional, rather adversary-oriented approach. A more diverse and representative police force, which courageously applies community policing and incorporates a fair and transparent complaints system, including the possibility of mediation, can reduce the power asymmetry and discrimination perceived by members of minorities. Consequently, intercultural mediation can promote trust in the government and its legal authorities and increase security.

References

Abanades, David M. 2019. "Intercultural Cities—Manual on community policing". Council of Europe. https://rm.coe.int/intercultural-cities-manual-on-community-policing/16809390a5

Adamson, Göran. 2020. "Migrants and Crime in Sweden in the Twenty-First Century." *Society* 57 (1): 9–21. 10.1007/s12115-019-00436-8

Bayley, David H. 2005. "What do the Police do?" In *Policing: Key Readings*, edited by Tim Newburn, 141–9. Cullompton: Willan Publishing.

Carrillo, Deisy. 2021. "Police Culture and Gender: An Evaluation of Police Officers' Practices and Responses to Domestic Abuse." *Journal of Global Faultlines* 8 (1): 69–80. 10.13169/jglobfaul.8.1.0069

Carty, Kevin. 2008. *Guidebook on Democratic Policing by the Senior Police Adviser to the OSCE Secretary General.* Vienna: OSCE. https://www.tandis.odihr.pl/handle/20.500.12389/19832

Decker, Catharina, and Joachim Kersten. 2015. "Minority Police Officers' Contribution to Police-Ethnic Minority Conflict Management." *European Journal of Policing Studies* 2 (4): 461–81.

Decker, Catharina, Joachim Kersten, and Navina Kunz. 2014. "Challenging Integration and Police Presence: Determinants of Subjective Safety for Persons with a Turkish Migration Background." *Archiwum Kryminologii*, no. XXXVI (January): 325–340. 10.7420/AK2014K

Decker, Catharina, Navina Kunz, Ansgar Burchard, and Joachim Kersten. 2014. "Turkish Migrants in Conflict with the Police in Germany: Conflict Analysis and Recommendations for Conflict Resolution." In *Police—Minority Relations: Policing—Ethnic Minorities* edited by Andrea Kozary, 11–28. Budapest: L'Harmattan.

Dehbi, Chadia. 2019. "CommunityOriented Policing in the European Union Today—Toolbox." European Crime Prevention Network. https://eucpn.org/sites/default/files/document/files/Toolbox14_EN_LR.pdf

Ernst, Melanie. 2016. "The Internal Audit Section of the Berlin Police." In *Strengthening Democratic Processes: Police Oversight through Restorative Justice in Austria, Hungary and Germany* edited by Catharina Vogt and Joachim Kersten, 109–15. Frankfurt a. M.: Verlag für Polizeiwissenschaft.

European Commission Against Racism and Intolerance (ECRI). 2007. *General Policy Recommendation no. 11: On Combating Racism and Racial Discrimination in Policing.* https://www.coe.int/en/web/european-commission-against-racism-and-intolerance/recommendation-no.11

Frankus, Elisabeth, and Hemma Mayrhofer. 2014. "Conflicts and Conflict Resolution between Police and African Minority in Austria." In *Police—Minority Relations: Policing—Ethnic Minorities*, edited by Andrea Kozary, 29–52. Budapest: L'Harmattan.

Frankus, Elisabeth, and Hemma Mayrhofer. 2016. "Restorative Justice Approaches for Dealing with Conflicts between the African Minority and the Police in Austria." In *Strengthening Democratic Processes: Police Oversight through Restorative Justice in Austria, Hungary and Germany*, edited by Catharina Vogt and Joachim Kersten, 35–50. Frankfurt a. M.: Verlag für Polizeiwissenschaft.

Groeneveld, Sandra, and Steven Van de Walle. 2010. "A Contingency Approach to Representative Bureaucracy: Power, Equal Opportunities and Diversity." *International Review of Administrative Sciences* 76 (2): 239–58. 10.1177/0020852309365670

Hassel, Heidrun. 2016. "Cooperation for Public Safety—Police and Immigrants in Open Discussion." In *Strengthening Democratic Processes: Police Oversight through Restorative Justice in Austria, Hungary and Germany*, edited by Catharina Vogt and Joachim Kersten, 101–8. Frankfurt a. M.: Verlag für Polizeiwissenschaft.

Hera, Gabor, and Petra Arnold. 2014. "Roma-Police Relationship from a Roma Perspective." In *Police—Minority Relations: Policing—Ethnic Minorities*, edited by Andrea Kozary, 53–60. Budapest: L'Harmattan.

Home Office. 2021. *Police Workforce. Ethnicity Facts and Figures.* https://www.ethnicity-facts-figures.service.gov.uk/workforce-and-business/workforce-diversity/police-workforce/latest

Hyland, Shelley S., and Elizabeth Davis. 2021. *Local Police Departments, 2016: Personnel.* Washington, DC: US Department of Justice, Office of Justice Programs, Bureau of Justice Statistics. https://bjs.ojp.gov/content/pub/pdf/lpd16p.pdf

Kahn, Kimberly Barsamian, and Paul G. Davies. 2017. "What Influences Shooter Bias? The Effects of Suspect Race, Neighborhood, and Clothing on Decisions to Shoot: Suspect Race, Neighborhood, and Clothing on Decisions to Shoot." *Journal of Social Issues* 73 (4): 723–43. 10.1111/josi.12245

Kunz, Navina, Catharina Vogt, Joachim Kersten, and Ansgar Burchard. 2016. "Complaint Procedures and Restorative Justice Solutions for Conflicts between Police and Turkish minority People." In *Strengthening Democratic Processes: Police Oversight through Restorative Justice in Austria, Hungary and Germany*, edited by Catharina Vogt and Joachim Kersten, 65–82. Frankfurt a. M.: Verlag für Polizeiwissenschaft.

Leatherby, Lauren and Richard A. Opple Jr. 2020. "Which Police Departments Are as Diverse as Their Communities?" *The New York Times*. https://www.nytimes.com/interactive/2020/09/23/us/bureau-justice-statistics-race.html

Mayr, S., Grazyna Wittgen, A. Theodosiou, M. Aspioti, I. Coune, Hans Verrept, Cláudia Santa Cruz, M. Diniz, Akrivi-Irene Panagiotopoulou, M. T. Papagiannopoulou, L. Bianconi, C. Raguso and D. Kaczmarczyk. 2015. "Description of 10 Good Practices in Intercultural Mediation for Immigrants (IMfI) throughout Europe and Suggestions for Transfer." http://www.mediation-time.eu/images/O2_English.pdf

Miller, Laurence. 2004. "Good Cop—Bad Cop: Problem Officers, Law Enforcement Culture, and Strategies for Success." *Journal of Police and Criminal Psychology* 19 (2): 30–48. 10.1007/BF02813871

OSCE, High Commissioner on National Minorities. 2006. *Recommendations on Policing in Multi-Ethnic Societies.* Vienna: Organization for Security and Co-operation in Europe (OSCE). https://www.osce.org/hcnm/policing-recommendations

Police Executive Research Forum. 2018. *Strengthening Relationships between Police and Immigrant Communities in a Complex Political Environment: Multicultural Outreach and Engagement Programs for Police Agencies.* https://www.policeforum.org/assets/PoliceImmigrantCommunities.pdf

Porter, Louise E., and Tim Prenzler. 2016. "The Code of Silence and Ethical Perceptions: Exploring Police Officer Unwillingness to Report Misconduct." *Policing: An International Journal of Police Strategies & Management* 39 (2): 370–86. 10.1108/PIJPSM-10-2015-0108

Reiner, Robert. 2002. "Cop Culture." In *Criminology: A Reader*, edited by Yvonne Jewkes and Gayle Letherby, 276–87. London: Sage.

Riley, Mary, Tim Prenzler, and Nadine McKillop. 2020. "Alternative Dispute Resolution and Mediation of Complaints against Police in Australia and New Zealand." *Police Practice and Research* 21 (1): 3–17. 10.1080/15614263.2018.1500284

Runde, Craig. E., and Tim A. Flanagan. 2010. *Developing your Conflict Competence*. San Francisco: Wiley.

van Ewijk, A. R. 2012. "Diversity within Police Forces in Europe: A Case for the Comprehensive View." *Policing* 6 (1): 76–92. 10.1093/police/par048

Viruell-Fuentes, Edna A. 2007. "Beyond Acculturation: Immigration, Discrimination, and Health Research among Mexicans in the United States." *Social Science & Medicine* 65 (7): 1524–35. 10.1016/j.socscimed.2007.05.010

Volpe, Maria R. 2014. "Police and Mediation: Natural, Unimaginable or Both." In *Moving Toward a Just Peace: The Mediation Continuum*, edited by Jan Marie Fritz, 91–105. Dordrecht: Springer.

Walker, Samuel, Carol Archbold, and Leigh Herbst. 2002. *Mediating Citizen Complaints Against Police Officers: A Guide for Police and Community Leaders*. Washington, DC: Government Printing Office. https://cops.usdoj.gov/RIC/Publications/cops-w0725-pub.pdf

Westley, William. 2005. "Responsibilities of the Police." In *Policing: Key Readings*, edited by Tim Newburn, 137–40. Cullompton: Willan Publishing.

8
PUTTING CULTURE INTO A PERSPECTIVE IN INTERCULTURAL MEDIATION

Katharina Kriegel-Schmidt

Putting culture into a perspective in order to conceptualize intercultural mediation

If we follow Cassirer's concept of culture, oriented on *meaning*, humans create their world in cultural activity (Cassirer 1923/2020). To interact, people must rely not only on behavior but also on anticipating the other person's expectations (Mead 1934). Routine anticipation of another person's expectations is thriving because people can access common meanings and do not have first to develop this knowledge in a personal encounter. When thus perspectivized as cultural beings, humans are *social* beings in the first place. One of the most important messages is that the individual's interpretations do not occur in isolation: Instead, the individual's activity closely connects to collectives. Therefore, cultural approaches in sociology conceive of individuals as *subjects* (Wiede 2020, 3). Culture always creates familiar diversity of meaning between subjects and subject cultures (within national boundaries, for example). Mediators are aware of this diversity, and if the differences are familiar, they typically do not lead to blocked actions.

Intercultural mediation—as understood by this chapter—focuses not only on any conflict that mediation deals with in a methodical, systematic manner but also on precisely this human particularity: The power of interpretation and its relation to collectivity. Intercultural mediation concentrates on escalating a crisis. Efforts for reciprocity are more difficult during a conflict, as interpretations and efforts to interact with one another remain fruitless. Complications multiply under conditions of *unfamiliar diversity*, which can arise even if the people involved have been interacting with one another for many years. A bicultural couple, a heterogeneous team, or a family can discover the foreignness of the Other in mediation. Following the founder of *Objective Hermeneutics*, Ulrich Oevermann, (Teller-Report 2021), interpretations, also and especially in a crisis, typically occur unconsciously and routinely: Instead of producing interpretations, the subject is occupied primarily with reproducing them. However, conscious, intentional reflection is also possible (Oevermann 2001, 46). Moreover, this is where intercultural mediation finds its place: In conflicts, it intends to overcome those problems that arise from conflicting, collectively created interpretations and claims to interpretation.

Perspectivity? A fruitful response to the problem of action

A cultural-theoretical approach to mediation processes helps to focus on numerous phenomena. By their very nature, intercultural situations are also characterized by openness and variety. However, in

DOI: 10.4324/9781003227441-10

mediation, this is not an advantage. The helper routine provided for mediators by their concept of action (Kriegel-Schmidt 2012, 215) threatens to be overwhelmed when a construct as complex as culture is included. Inspired by one of Pierre Bourdieu's suggestions, the *idea of perspectivity* that is to be introduced here aims first to consider how much of a person's view of the object can be traced back to the perspective from which it is seen (Kriegel-Schmidt 2021, 6).

Secondly, a perspective always requires an abstraction: We reduce what we see to a particular approach, suggesting a specific interpretation. This awareness of the mediators' perspectivity is the primary mode of intercultural mediation discussed in this chapter and thus corresponds to a constructivist approach. Praxis research discusses the pressure to make quick decisions (Oevermann, Allert, Konau, and Krambeck 1987, 439). Even without a cultural focus, mediators often have difficulty keeping an eye on all essential aspects while remaining capable of acting. Establishing various cultural-theoretical perspectives undertakes a necessary selection of empirical observations. This process leads to two areas of cultural activity. They highlight the *triadic structure of mediation*. The intention is to respond to the difficulties in remaining able to act even in the face of overcomplexity, which necessarily results from cultural perspectives. To achieve this aim, the theory-based perspectives model presented here has been adapted to a didactic approach in intercultural mediation training (Kriegel-Schmidt, Zwania-Rößler, and Schmidt 2019). Using cultural perspectives in mediation processes can enable questions related to these aspects. In line with arguments from cultural sociology, the (self-) reflection of the parties and mediators is to be increased. These questions can be raised in the follow-up and preparation for the mediation process. If the questions are related to mediation occasions, they will be part of the mediation process itself.

There seems to be a widespread uneasiness in the German-language mediation discourse about designating a mediation process as intercultural mediation. An overview and explanation of ten existing definitions for intercultural mediation in German-language discourse can be found in Kriegel-Schmidt (2012, 136). It is also difficult to say when mediation can be viewed as intercultural mediation based on methodological aspects. Mayer (2020) has made such attempts, although the focus is less on observation tools and more on modeling mediation as a process principle. In the perspectives model, the indication for whether a mediation process is an intercultural mediation or not comes from the professional's view of the mediation situation. A mediation process is considered intercultural if the mediator uses a cultural lens (based on methodological approaches). Culture thus becomes a *category of observation*.

As described previously, culture is about collective interpretations and mechanisms of interpretation that people use to explain their world and subjugate it, but they also use to explain themselves and to which they are subjugated. In terms of cultural and educational theory, the focus is on people's dependencies and their possibilities for emancipation. In cultural processes of interpretation, mediation deals with the pre-reflexive dimensions of culture that are not easily accessible by the conscious and dimensions that the conscious can more easily access. It is about knowledge—viewing culture as knowledge is an approach suited to working with conflicts and is offered by the German sociologist Andreas Reckwitz (2017, 2020a, 2020b). Reckwitz uses studies from post-structuralist social sciences, including Bourdieu's concept of habitus and Foucault's concept of technologies of the self. His theory of culture provides several advantages for working with conflicts:

1   Reckwitz understands culture primarily as a collective form taken on by subjects. Subjects experience themselves as competent, attractive, healthy, and normal. This form bundles specific characteristics, abilities, and risks. Subjects appear as a "bundle of dispositions" (Reckwitz 2020a, 51) that they obtain in their affinity groups and cannot exchange.
2   Culture can depict the multicultural reality within societies. Cultures are collective knowledge orders that, on the one hand, can be linked by language and that arise within national

boundaries. On the other hand, however, there are various cultures within the same space, as different subject forms exist parallel. For Christmas, for example, members of the same family gather, but they still belong to different subject cultures.

3   Cultures (within societies) are in conflict with one another. From the subject's perspective, the normality of a subject form seems not only desirable but also expected, healthy, and right.

4   At all times, every society produces a dominant subject form that precludes other subject forms from existing in the same place contemporaneously. Cultural dominance is not always accepted without question. Various protest formats like populism and Trumpism can thus be interpreted as a critique of elites (Reckwitz 2020a, 16–7).

Objects of observation

The scaffold of cultural sociology can be used to describe and understand cultural phenomena in mediation. Likewise, statements can be made about the culturality of interventions and tools.

Interactions among all participants

The perspectives model places its focus on the triadic interaction in mediation. It considers all actors to be involved in the communication process. If we assume both activated and dormant dyadic relations in the classic mediation triad, this includes:

*   the dyad of the conflict parties,
*   the conflict party/mediator dyads,
*   the (possible) dyad of the mediators in a co-mediation setting.

Mediation process and mediators' actions

Mediation should be understood as a concept of action to clarify the (cultural) link between mediation principles, methods, techniques, and other elements (Kriegel-Schmidt 2012, 212–302). People who apply this concept of action *are* acting. From a cultural-theoretical point of view, that is very important to note: Mediators are not neutral in the process that justifies their actions, and they take the side of their tool (Montada and Kals 2013, 64). At all times, the mediators act intending to guide the dissent into a particular form. This active construction of dissent is carried out according to the concepts of the culture that was hegemonious: Mediators and mediation "singularize" (Reckwitz 2020b, 28) the dissent and the conflict parties. Following current contributions in German cultural sociology, mediation is a "subjectivizing agency" (Kriegel-Schmidt 2012, 453) and consolidates the hegemony (Bröckling 2017). As the basis for action in intercultural mediation, the perspectives model assumes that mediation is a tool that has become cultural and has cultural effects: Mediation corresponds to the "imaginary of communication" (Schmidt 2016, 212). As shown above, the model also assumes that the actor using this cultural tool is a cultural actor. In this regard, mediation proves a powerful, hegemonious concept of action.

Working with four perspectives in intercultural mediation: The perspectives model

The perspectives model of intercultural mediation allows us to generate hypotheses based on cultural-theoretical concepts regarding incomprehensibility and escalating dynamics, than can arise at all times and among all participants in a mediation (Kriegel-Schmidt, Zwania-Rößler, and Schmidt 2019). Mediators can use the perspectives model in the context of their everyday actions. The concept of action for mediation remains the same: It offers the mediator the typical and thus secure basis for actions. It is assumed that the mediation process meets a demand, regardless of whether it was already adapted to specific challenges in advance, e.g., by combining culturally appropriate methods or setting up mediator tandems in international contexts (Kiesewetter and Paul 2011).

The perspectives model sets four axes along which the mediators can orient themselves to develop intervention possibilities flexibly from case to case. Each of these four perspectives provides different requirements for action. For practical work with conflicts, the perspectives offer simplified constructs: They separate phenomena that, in reality, often occur in a mixed form. Focusing on a didactic approach, the careful, analytical separation of the four perspectives is necessary for depicting, practicing, and habituating the perspectives model. The starting points for working with this model could be explicit assumptions and perceived preconceptions from the mediator(s), the conflict parties remarking on or addressing relevant issues, hesitations in acting, or incomprehensibilities experienced in the dyads. In the following sections, the theoretical foundations of each perspective will be outlined. In mediation training, they lead to the testing of various intervention strategies (Kriegel-Schmidt, Zwania-Rößler, and Schmidt 2019).

The perspective of the cultural knowledge of action of all mediation subjects

Any knowledge that tells us what we should do in a given situation is action-oriented. In this type of knowledge, two forms can be differentiated:

> When asked, the subjects can easily communicate part of this knowledge: This is known as *"explicit* knowledge." However, this knowledge is incomplete without a second type of knowledge, *"tacit* knowledge" (Loenhoff 2011, 58). Tacit knowledge—physical knowledge—allows the subject to perform all executions routinely. The other person can easily interpret the behavior and integrate it into their behavior—for the most part, without any incomprehensibilities. Tacit knowledge is knowledge about how a person must make a declaration of love, for example, and which emotions need to be mobilized in the act.
>
> *(Reckwitz 2016)*

Various concepts that hold central importance in one culture may only have marginal importance or none in another context. Armin Nassehi, a German sociologist with Iranian parentage, gives an exciting insight into the term *Heimat* (Krämer 2018). A plurality of perspectives is the norm in modern societies (Nassehi 2011). Beyond this familiar diversity, however, a joint effort is needed to grasp unfamiliar contexts of meaning that only become relevant in a conflict or are never questioned. Intercultural mediation makes implicit knowledge explicit by using detailed, specific questions, thereby making this kind of knowledge visible.

The collective orientation for behavior is not tangible until it can be expressed verbally. Finding a verbal form in which everyone can understand the content is the task of intercultural mediation. In this case, together with the effort of all the participants, it makes the cultural differences explicit through means of intersubjective *translation*. An approach that should be avoided is trying to lecture about cultural spaces of meaning. Mediators cannot act as experts on understanding self and the world; instead, they can only guide others to an understanding of self and others through forms of "reflective showing" (Glenewinkel and Kraft 2017, 521).

The perspective of communicative action of all mediation subjects

In the perspective of communicative action, opportunities for observing arise from linguistic and conversation-analytical studies on mediation (Pick 2017). Perspectives 1 and 2 are closely related:

The analytical axes for action orientation and linguistic-communicative phenomena border and even overlap. Thus, the areas depicted as separate phenomena here are separate only in the observational tools (perspectives) for the observations, not in reality. In the second perspective, mediators are also interested in cultural knowledge. The focus is mainly on implicit (tacit) knowledge, so a linguistic rule cannot necessarily be named even if people follow it. As soon as a subject exists, permanent reception processes begin. Behavior is interpreted, and this interpretation may require comparing what is meant and what is understood.

For the mediation process, it is helpful to establish that each communicative act is made up of one verbal and three non-verbal components (Watzlawick, Beavin, and Jackson 2011). A speaker familiar with the rules will ensure that they fit together without dissonance. Dissonant communication, in which the messages on various levels contradict one another, creates incomprehensibilities that can seem extraordinarily uncomfortable—or can be used intentionally to create a humorous effect. What behavior fits which situation can be reconstructed as communication rules that are culturally embedded and imbued with meaning (Straub, and Weidemann 2006).

The incomprehensibility that arises when faced with unknown rules is understood as a problem with the other person. In this context, Müller-Jacquier complains that "many current approaches psychologise intercultural communication" (Müller-Jacquier 2003, 51). People who misunderstand an action tend to judge the other person's invisible *characteristics* such as attitudes, intentions, and values. This means a false conclusion is drawn with negative consequences for the rest of the communicative process. As Busch (2019) emphasizes, mediation does not primarily target this form of misunderstandings and subtle incomprehensibilities that are at the heart of intercultural communication research. With the second perspective, mediators can practice on this additional conflict level.

The perspective of the cultural constructions of all mediation subjects

If others question our knowledge of action, then cultural, group-specific constructions gain importance to one another. Perspective 3 emphasizes the link between these possible constructions with the emotions of those who are constructing. Individuals are passionately connected to their habitus: "We like what we have and would not have it otherwise" (O'Connor 2006, 62). With a "passionate attachment" (Butler 1997, 7), we are bound to our subjectivity and develop the desire to protect and care for it. These behaviors are familiar when we talk about acting like a *real* boy or girl or, on the other side of the coin, contradicting gender expectations in the *right* way. According to Bourdieu's thinking, subjects must create their anti-subject: "Positive subject models depend on a demarcation vis-à-vis a negative subject model. The subject positions this anti-subject using processes of exclusion regarding undesirable characteristics" (Reckwitz 2020a, 57–8). Identification and differentiation (including extreme varieties) are a normal part of cultural activity in which no one is excluded (Straub 2021, 91).

However, this function might turn communication efforts in mediation down when the ostensible culture or individuality of the Other is being abjected. 'Abjection' underscores the negative feelings that go along with rejection: The critical point of this psychoanalytical concept by Julia Kristeva (1982) relates to the nearly unlimited destructive consequences of the abjected: From condescending ridiculing and stigmatizing to the exclusion from sympathy or even eradication. "Abjection is a psychological process, a defense mechanism with direct social consequences that cause the abjected Other to suffer and can cause serious damage" (Straub 2021, 89).

In contrast to the construction of Others, *self*-constructions are the reversed case of cultural expressions in mediation. They are equally important and not to be ignored as they can be understood as an essential expression of doing identity (Kaufmann 2014). Various forms of connections to an imagined collective are becoming ever more critical for intercultural mediation (Anderson 1983/2006), and this collective can appear as more or less new ideological self-labeling. The mindset linked with self-labeling makes it more difficult to live together in a community, sometimes extremely difficult, and often leads the subjects into conflicts that are not seemingly possible to be solved with consensus but only through subjection. Conflicts that come to mediation from this area can question the mediation process itself, as the conflict parties demand special treatment depending on their race, sex, and/or gender (Fourest 2020). How can the third perspective of the model serve intercultural mediation processes? According to culture-psychological research (Thomas 2010), with the help of this perspective, mediators can encourage to humanize the caricature or concept of an enemy. To this end, they should not attempt to individualize any attempt at categorization (e.g., cultural), which might be assumed from mediation techniques. Instead, mediators should take up this categorization and help formulate questions.

The perspective of power disparities among all mediation subjects

Cultural dispositions are an essential source of power disparities, including the context of mediation. While subjects of a particular collective have specific knowledge and practices, these play no role in other collectives or are only very subordinate. Some can and want to speak about what is going on inside themselves, use facilitating concepts, and are familiar with supportive practices. Others have nowhere near these kinds of resources. However, in the same society, people with varying dispositions are placed before the same tasks. Different dispositions, therefore, lead to inequalities. The possibilities to make decisions about others and oneself are fundamentally unequally distributed. Mediation deals with this by supporting personalized interpersonal interactions and inter-individual dialogues in a separate space. Using the fourth perspective encourages mediators to perceive inequalities that arise due to superiority regarding possibilities for action. A confrontation between the power perspective and culture theory in the perspectives model of intercultural mediation leads to the following theses:

1   Individual encounters in mediation also involve a meeting of social positions.
2   Having your autonomy limited by another person is not specific to a particular class. Anyone can have the experience of being a victim and present themselves as being one because a public discourse has developed around this topic.
3   The attention to power inequalities is not universal but part of specific cultural knowledge.

The perspective of power disparities has an inherent skepticism of the idea that in communicative situations that are characterized by cultural heterogeneity, the participants are different but have equally accessible opportunities of acting and living: On equal footing, of equal value, with equal rights. This perspective says that this idea is an illusion (Bourdieu 1980, 32). Suppose an inequality perspective was argued primarily based on class and social strata before 2000. In that case, there seem to be more people in all classes and strata who experience negative consequences from power imbalances with which they are confronted. The change is proven by those affected by the abuse of power, who, e.g., in the case of sexual abuse, say that until recently, they "didn't even have the language to talk about misconduct of this nature. We feel like we have only been able to name it […] in the first place since Weinstein and #MeToo" (Heidmann 2020). It can also make sense to consider the inequality topics as an expression of cultural change (Reckwitz 2017). Cultural change is characterized by new discourses embedded deeply in some collectives and not at all in others.

Singularization discourses typically come from the university-educated middle class and are usually led by people with financial resources and social influence (e.g., artists, journalists, teachers, students, and politicians). However, the milieu that is closely linked to singularization corresponds only to around 30% of the population in Germany (Reckwitz 2020b). Within its individualization discourses, there is a discourse on inequality and discrimination that can also be classified as an expression of humanism (De Singly 2005): It is directed against stereotyping, norming, restrictions, degradations, and violence and argues for equal opportunities, development opportunities, fulfilling of needs, participation, and co-determination. This is all done in the name of the singular individual. These individuals do not characterize themselves through categories by others or memberships but their uniqueness.

Attempts to assert new norms that promote individualism with the corresponding cultural knowledge and establish new cultural practices can, however, be experienced as oppression. This is particularly the case if it is a minority that makes this assertion and if this minority does not make up even one-third of the total population and yet has the means to assert its goals (Reckwitz 2020b). People, thus, fight for "cultural hegemony" (Reckwitz 2020a, 81). Applied to mediation, every situation can also be influenced by power, power discourses, and mutual accusations of discrimination. The fourth perspective is meant to assist intercultural mediation in differentiating between an *objective* and a *subjective* dimension of power: On the one hand, we find fundamental power inequalities (objective dimension) that are not always immediately apparent in personal interactions because discrimination is implicitly anchored in the structures, routines, and discourses of everyday life (El-Mafaalani 2021). On the other hand, we find the subjective dimension: Experiences of disadvantage and discrimination that are equally important. These experiences can be interpreted as failed respect or maladjusted self-regard. Both the objective and subjective dimensions of power produce different problems for conflict management. An intercultural mediation process that takes on the perspective of power inequalities starts with the assumption that accusations and excuses do not show all the information that could contribute to resolving the situation.

Big guns like racism, Othering, and discrimination are essential to identities, and in part, they are linked to strong emotions while silencing the other person. That is why they should be questioned in mediation such that the individual biographical backgrounds behind them are understood, but the aggression they contain is lessened. In a successful case, with the help of this and the other three perspectives of the perspectives model, all mediation subjects can understand more about one another by learning to *read* the other person in (also) culturally more complex ways.

References

Anderson, Benedict. 1983/2006. *Imagined Communities: Reflections on the Origin and Spread of Nationalism.* London, New York: Verso.

Bourdieu, Pierre. 1980. *Questions de Sociologie. Documents.* Paris: Minuit.

Bröckling, Ulrich. 2017. *Gute Hirten führen sanft. Über Menschenregierungskünste.* Berlin: Suhrkamp.

Busch, Dominic. 2019. "Intercultural Conflict Mediation." In *Oxford Bibliographies in Communication*, edited by Patricia Moy. Oxford University Press. 10.1093/obo/9780199756841-0229

Butler, Judith. 1997. *The Psychic Life of Power: Theories in Subjection.* Stanford: Stanford University Press. 10.1515/9781503616295

Cassirer, Ernst. 1923/2020. *The Philosophy of Symbolic Forms.* Three Volume Set. London: Routledge.

De Singly, François. 2005. *L'individualisme est un humanisme.* Paris: Puf.

El-Mafaalani, Aladin. 2021. *What's the Point of Racism? From the Invention of Human Races to Anti-Racist Resistance.* Köln: Kiepenheuer & Witsch.

Fourest, Caroline. 2020. *Génération Offensée: De la police de la culture à la police de la pensée.* Paris: Bernard Grasset.

Glenewinkel, Werner, and Volker Kraft. 2017. "Zum Verhältnis von Mediation und Beratung." In *Mediation als Wissenschaftszweig*, edited by Katharina Kriegel-Schmidt, 499–523. Wiesbaden: Springer Fachmedien Wiesbaden. 10.1007/978-3-658-18257-1_40

Heidmann, Patrick. 2020, 12. November. Vorurteile machen mich wütend. *TAZ.* https://taz.de/MeToo-Spielfilm-The-Assistant-auf-DVD/!5723816/

Kaufmann, Jean-Claude. 2014. *Identités: la bombe à retardement.* Paris: éditions Textuel.

Kiesewetter, Sybille, and Christoph C. Paul, eds. 2011. *Cross-Border Family Mediation: International Parental Child Abduction, Custody and Access Cases.* Frankfurt am M: Metzner.

Krämer, Klaus. 2018: "Patriotic term 'Heimat' driving new German 'identity politics'—An interview with Armin Nassehi", *Deutsche Welle.* https://p.dw.com/p/2v3KH

Kriegel-Schmidt, Katharina. 2012. *Interkulturelle Mediation: Plädoyer für ein Perspektiven-reflexives Modell*. Berlin, Münster: LIT.

Kriegel-Schmidt, Katharina. 2021. "(Multi-)Perspektivisches Sehen." *Konfliktdynamik* 10 (1): 6–7. 10.5771/21 93-0147-2021-1-6

Kriegel-Schmidt, Katharina, Isabell Zwania-Rößler, and Klaus Schmidt. 2019. "Neuer Umgang mit Vielfalt: Kulturelle Schweisen für Mediatoren mit dem Perspektiven-Modell." In *Praxishandbuch Professionelle Mediation*, edited by Stefan Kracht, Andre Niedostadek, and Patrick Sensburg, 1–22. Berlin, Heidelberg: Springer. 10.1007/978-3-662-49657-2_58-1

Kristeva, Julia. 1982. *Powers of Horror: An Essay on Abjection. European Perspectives*. New York: Columbia University Press.

Loenhoff, Jens. 2011. "Tacit Knowledge in Intercultural Communication." *Intercultural Communication Studies* 20 (1): 57–64.

Mayer, Claude-Hélène. 2020. *Intercultural Mediation and Conflict Management Training: A Guide for Professionals and Academics*. Cham: Springer. 10.1007/978-3-030-51765-6

Mead, George Herbert. 1934. *Self, Mind and Society*. Chicago: Charles W. Morris.

Montada, Leo, and Elisabeth Kals. 2013. *Mediation: Psychologische Grundlagen und Perspektiven*. Weinheim: Beltz.

Müller-Jacquier, Bernd. 2003. "Linguistic Awareness of Cultures: Principles of a Training Module." In *From International Exchanges to Intercultural Communication: Combining Theory and Practice*, edited by Peter Kistler and Sini Konivuori, 50–90. Jyväskylä: EMICC Programme & University of Jyväskylä.

Nassehi, Armin. 2011. *Gesellschaft der Gegenwarten. Studien zur Theorie der modernen Gesellschaft II*. Berlin: Suhrkamp.

O'Connor, Justin. 2006. "Art, Popular Culture and Cultural Policy: Variations on a Theme of John Carey." *Critical Quarterly* 48 (4): 49–104. 10.1111/j.1467-8705.2006.00735.x

Oevermann, Ulrich. 2001. "Die Struktur sozialer Deutungsmuster—Versuch einer Aktualisierung." *Sozialer Sinn* 2 (1): 35–81.

Oevermann, Ulrich, Tilman Allert, Elisabeth Konau, and Jürgen Krambeck. 1987. "Structures of meaning and objective Hermeneutics." In *Modern German Sociology*, edited by Meja Volker, Dieter Misgeld, and Nico Stehr, 436–47. New York: Columbia University Press.

Pick, Ina. 2017. "Der Beitrag der (angewandten) Gesprächslinguistik zur Erforschung von Mediation." In *Mediation als Wissenschaftszweig*, edited by Katharina Kriegel-Schmidt, 109–19. Wiesbaden: Springer. 10. 1007/978-3-658-18257-1_9

Reckwitz, Andreas. 2016. "Praktiken und ihre Affekte." In *Praxistheorie*, edited by Hilmar Schäfer, 163–80. transcript Verlag. 10.1515/9783839424049-008

Reckwitz, Andreas. 2017. *The Invention of Creativity: Modern Society and the Culture of the New*. Malden, MA: Polity.

Reckwitz, Andreas. 2020a. *Das hybride Subjekt. Eine Theorie der Subjektkulturen von der bürgerlichen Moderne zur Postmoderne*. Weilerswist: Velbrück Wiss.

Reckwitz, Andreas. 2020b. *The Society of Singularities*. Cambridge: Polity Press.

Schmidt, Klaus. 2016. "Die Entstehung und Bearbeitung von Konflikten." In *Handbuch Mediation. Methoden und Technik, Rechtsgrundlagen, Einsatzgebiete*, edited by Fritjof Haft and Katharina Gräfin von Schlieffen, 209–24. München: C.H. Beck.

Straub, Jürgen. 2021. "Welterschließende Affekte und das explanative Potenzial eines psychoanalytischen Konzepts für die Kulturpsychologie: Abjektion." *Cultura & psyché* 2 (1): 83–97. 10.1007/s43638-021-00024-w

Straub, Jürgen, and Doris Weidemann. 2006. "Psychology, Culture, and the Pursuit of Meaning: An Introduction." In *Pursuit of Meaning*, edited by Jürgen Straub, Doris Weidemann, Carlos Kölbl, and Barbara Zielke, 11–20. transcript Verlag. 10.1515/9783839402344-intro

Teller-Report. 2021: "On the death of Ulrich Oevermann: Experiencing reality from four-year-olds." *Teller-Report. Now You Can See Non-English News* (11.10.2021). https://www.tellerreport.com/news/2021-10-11-on-the-death-of-ulrich-oevermann--experiencing-reality-from-four-year-olds.HybSIDWMSY.html

Thomas, Alexander. 2010. "The Self, The Other, The Intercultural." In *Handbook of Intercultural Communication and Cooperation: Basics and Areas of Application*, edited by Eva-Ulrike Kinast, Sylvia Schroll-Machl, and Alexander Thomas, 2nd edition, 39–52. Göttingen: Vandenhoeck & Ruprecht. 10.13109/9783666403279.39

Watzlawick, Paul, Janet Beavin, and Don Jackson. 2011. *Pragmatics of Human Communication: A Study of Interactional Patterns, Pathologies and Paradoxes*. New York: WW Norton & Co.

Wiede, Wiebke. 2020. "Subjectification, the Subject, and the Self. Version: 3.0." *Docupedia-Zeitgeschichte* 21.12.2020: 1–38. 10.14765/ZZF.DOK-2076

PART II

Intercultural mediation in international politics

9

INTERCULTURALITY IN THE CONCEPT OF PEACE MEDIATION

Anne Holper

Introduction[1]

In the field of peace mediation, a subfield of international politics, interculturality (as culture itself) is not one of the predominant buzzwords. The semantic ground, which in other fields is designated by the terminology of culture, here is marked by terms such as identity, values or belief systems and diversity, but also inclusivity, the local and insider mediation (see, for example, Rothman 1997; Arnauld 2014; Roepstorff and Bernhard 2013; Hirblinger and Landau 2020). However, unlike other mediation fields more influenced by anthropological and cultural studies, in the peace mediation con-text there is no commonly established conceptual and methodological approach for dealing with those issues.

At the same time, both scholars and practitioners point to the critical relevance of interculturality for the dynamics of inter-state/international and intra-state/intrasocietal conflict, not least regarding the increasingly conflictual intra-societal tensions: "Societies across the world are becoming more polarized and divisive politics feeds on people's underlying fears. Culture is often invisible to conflict parties who can only view the world with their own lens, thus value clashes can seem unsurmountable" (Abatis 2021, 10; see also Brandsma 2016; Moghaddam 2018; Tajfel and Turner 2004; Cuhadar 2020).

This relevance applies to substantive conflict issues such as human rights violations, which often have a cultural dimension in addition to their political and normative ones; to process questions, as mediators can face considerable difficulties if the involved actors' ingrained procedural cultures, including those of the mediators, how one should behave in and handle conflict are incompatible (Kraus ([now Holper]) 2011; Londoño Lázaro 2003, 323); but it also applies to peace interventions as a whole, whose value-laden cultural premises and quasi-colonial patterns have been hotly debated in terms of the "liberal peace" paradigm (Finlay 2015; de Coning and Gray 2018; Tanabe 2019).

Terms and concepts

Interculturality

This chapter follows the understanding of intercultural mediation as a mediation between people of different identities and under consideration of various diversity categories that the introduction to this book registers for the field of applied conflict mediation. The underlying understanding of culture is that of a system of contingent patterns of meaning-making and interaction that define the

DOI: 10.4324/9781003227441-12

affiliations of individuals to identity groups and organize their interaction. According to the basic semiotic rule "to be identifiable as A, A needs to be different from B" (following Saussure 1993 [1916]), it is the difference from other groups' orientations, attitudes, behaviors, thinking, and worldview that actually creates 'identity.'

This understanding of culture has three critical implications for interculturality in conflict and peace mediation:

> First, the shared understanding among members of a group regarding how to deal with each other (following the anthropological definitions of culture, see Kroeber and Kluckhohn 2016 [1952]) serves as a *rule system for collective coordination and individual social recognition*. This implies that conflict parties from different cultures may not only fail to decipher each other's idiomatic rules but will also tend to reject the other's rules, as following them might imply a loss of recognition and effective collective action in their own social environment.

Second, as its shared beliefs, values, customs, and behaviors provide strategies to cope with needs, problems, and losses (Boeijen 2020, 18, referring to the definition of Plog and Bates 1976), culture can have *existential sense-making, stabilizing and orienting functions*. These functions can make "culturally based conflicts … the most difficult to mediate because they tend to implicate sacred values that appear nonnegotiable" (Shapiro 2021, 8). If such non-negotiable values are under perceived or actual threat (see, as an example, the effects of identity politics in Ukraine, Zhurzhenko 2014), intercultural difference can form the seemingly natural dividing line for in-group/out-group cleavages, de-humanization and group-related misanthropy and violence (Tajfel and Turner 2004; Demmers 2016, 52–6).

Third, pointing precisely in the opposite direction—as culture is seen as an evolutionary response to the ambiguity and variability of changing circumstances (Boeijen 2020, 11)—it is understood as a *contingent, diverse, and constantly shifting adaptation* process (Sen 2007) that includes the ability to unlearn—and relearn another—culture (Meyer-Drawe 2010).

All of this confirms the importance of a clear conceptual and methodological approach to dealing with interculturality in peace mediation.

Peace mediation

The term *peace mediation* has been used since the early 2000s—initially in Switzerland and Germany, then internationally—to describe the increasing activities of mediation in the context of violent conflict, crisis diplomacy, and peace processes (Hellmüller, Palmiano Federer, and Zeller 2015; Holper and Kirchhoff 2021; Federal Foreign Office, and Initiative Mediation Support Germany 2017; Kirchhoff and Kraus (now Holper) 2017). The term includes facilitated negotiations and mediation activities in all process stages, from pre-talks to ceasefire negotiations and peace agreement implementation, covering mediation, mediation support, and dialogue (Federal Foreign Office, and Initiative Mediation Support Germany 2017, 1).

The term established and professionalized a specific type, a subcategory of mediation that explicitly aims at making peace between warring parties and within war-torn societies. It thereby regrouped and redefined a type of activity in the intersection of three existing fields that in part dealt with violent intra- or interstate conflict: International/political mediation and crisis diplomacy (political sector), conflict transformation (development, social sector), and conflict resolution (organizational, societal sector) (Bercovitch and Gartner 2009; Greig and Diehl 2012; Kleiboer 1996). With the compositum 'peace,' the term at the same time introduced a new distinction to forms of political mediation and crisis diplomacy that focus primarily on violence containment and political stability, and less on the conditions for sustained peace.

The new terminological framing also may have contributed to the last decade's rise of mediation in the context of peace processes; within in a couple of years international and regional organizations such as the UN, the EU, the OSCE, the African Union as well as many states recognized and institutionalized mediation as a viable means for ending violent conflicts and pursuing foreign policies. Today, the peace mediation field is a full branch with its own departments and networks, methods, norms and policies, conferences and trainings, and full-scale projects based on considerable donor budgets.

In 2012, the 'UN Guidelines for Effective Mediation' put together what can be understood as the policy concept of peace mediation (United Nations 2012) and which is widely accepted as the basic reference framework for the field. Remarkably, it does not use the compositum 'peace,' arguably to include as many mediation activities in the field of crisis diplomacy and political mediation as possible. It defines mediation of a "process whereby a third party assists two or more parties, with their consent, to prevent, manage or resolve a conflict by helping them to develop mutually acceptable agreements" (United Nations 2012, 1).

There is a growing body of scholarly work, but no consolidated scientific concept of peace mediation yet (see Holper and Kirchhoff 2021, 193–219). Most scholarly concepts see "consent of conflict parties," "nonviolence," and "nonbinding involvement of third party" as the conditions for calling moderated negotiations a mediation (Goertz, Diehl, and Balas 2016, 155). More practical and realist concepts differentiate between different types of mediation regarding the use of power, pressure and coercion (Mason 2021, 32–4), e.g., between "pure" and "power" mediation, "capability" and "credibility" leverages, which are clearly complementary in strengths and weaknesses (Fisher 2001, 11; Svensson 2007; Reid 2017). The most debated boundary to neighboring approaches (for an overview see Fisher 2001, 11) is that between peace mediation and diplomacy: "Diplomacy predominantly focuses on a country's own foreign policy goals and interests, whereas mediation is a consensus-based method to further all parties' interests. This leads to differing concepts of the roles of diplomats and mediators and, consequently, different approaches" (Federal Foreign Office, and Initiative Mediation Support Germany 2017, 1).

The multiplicity of actors involved in peace mediation processes is reflected in the multi-track approach (Palmiano Federer et al. 2019; Crocker, Hampson, and Aall 1999) and in the proliferation of and competition between mediation actors (Lanz and Gasser 2013; Lanz 2021). On the part of the conflict parties, top leaderships of governments and armed non-state actors, elites and decision-makers from civil society, religious groups, business corporations as well as grassroots actors are in-volved (so called Tracks 1 to 3). On the side of the third parties are representatives of intergovernmental and regional organizations (UN, EU, OSCE, AU, etc.) as well as states (e.g., United States, Norway, Switzerland, South Africa, China, Russia, Germany), local and international NGOs (e.g., St. Egidio, HD Centre, Crisis Management Initiative, Carter Center), as well as eminent persons and religious leaders engage as mediators.

The high complexity of today's violent conflicts (not only multiplicity actors but also multi-layered causes, self-perpetuating violence, a multiplicity of armed, often extremist groups, interplay of geo-politics and local interests, economies materially benefitting from war) means that mediation efforts in this context always work on the edge of the impossible. And it also means that they are only partial, often invisible, multi-sequenced measures within larger and longer-term crisis containment or peace processes, with many unavoidable setbacks (Lanz 2021, 41).

Mediation efforts in South Sudan help illustrate the aforementioned aspects: After a bloody conflict had spread across the country, mediation efforts led by the International Intergovernmental Authority on Development (IGAD), pushed representatives of the two main parties (government of Republic of South Sudan, Sudan People's Liberation Movement-in-Opposition (SPLM/SPLA-IO)) to the table in 2013. Later, other relevant actors participated in the talks, such as former SPLM prisoners, civil society representatives, faith-based leaders, other political parties, and representatives of women's organizations (USIP n.d.). The first mediated Agreement on the Resolution of the Conflict in South Sudan (ARCSS) of 2015 was not implemented; new mediation efforts began in 2017, reaching the Revitalized Agreement in 2018 (IGAD 2018) including provisions for power-sharing, a durable ceasefire and security in the country, access to humanitarian assistance, management of financial and economic re-sources, as well as an outline on transitional justice and accountability (Tombe 2019).

The role and relevance of interculturality in peace mediation

If we look at (e.g., anthropological) research on the whole peace sector, there is broad agreement that interveners, conflict parties, and populations regularly belong to different national, regional, professional, organizational, social, ethnic, and religious communities with specific cultural frameworks that shape their interpretation of constraints, interests, and contexts (Autesserre 2011, 3). This implies that the success or failure of peace interventions depends strongly on the handling of intercultural questions.

However, this common sense is only shared by a handful of scholars in the peace mediation field itself (see Duursma 2020; Lücke and Rigaut 2002). The only four references in the UN Guidance for Effective Mediation show that interculturality clearly plays a subordinate role in the mainstream concept: "Preparedness" lists "cultural sensitivity for the specific conflict situation" as the last of four criteria for a competent mediator, after experience, skills, and knowledge (United Nations 2012, 7). "National ownership" refers to "local cultures and norms" and "specific cultural approaches to negotiation and communication" that mediation processes need to adapt to (United Nations 2012, 14, 15). Finally, mediation actors' different "political cultures" will make "coherence, coordination and complementarity" of multi-mediator engagements "difficult" (United Nations 2012, 18). Looking at the whole field, there is a general tendency to disregard culture in peace mediation—similarly to what Avruch describes for the conflict resolution and ADR field—ranging from "benign neglect" to "active resistance to incorporating culture to theory and practice" (Avruch 2003, 252).

This might be explained with (at least) five factors:

> First and very pragmatically, in the *context of violent conflicts*, where power diplomacy, sanctions, and the militarization of conflict are the alternative means in the arsenal with which to compete, mediation is under constant pressure to defend its own "soft" approach. This is likely to reduce the inclination of mediation actors to engage with other soft factors such as interculturality.

Second and related to the first point, it is the *positivist tradition* of politics and diplomacy as well as political science and international law that inform the concepts and frameworks of peace mediation itself. This tradition presumes the "universality of rational choice theory and economistic behaviorism as templates for panhuman cognition and social relations" (Avruch 2003, 352), clearly opposed to the idea of culture that assumes the cultural variability of cognition and social relations. Others might just consider culture too abstract a factor to become operationally relevant (Londono Lazaro 2003, 340).

Third, the *methodological approach* of peace mediation is a descendant from the Harvard Negotiation Project's 'Getting to Yes' paradigm, which is explicitly oriented toward concrete individuals or defined groups and their positions, interests, needs, and values (Federal Foreign Office, and Initiative Mediation Support Germany 2016, 5), rather than toward more collective, less tangible cultures: "Conventional mediation training and literature often focus heavily on issues and relationships, but sometimes neglect the cultural context in which conflicts arise" (Abatis 2021, 12).

Fourth, there is also some *conceptual skepticism* about whether the use of culture as a reference factor in peacemaking does not inevitably provide new projection surfaces for divisive, pejorative narratives (one culture supposedly being more peaceful than the other, along with their respective representatives), neglecting the dynamics of othering and cultural racism (Holper and Kyselova 2021). As an example, 'multicultural' peace policies can fail because they often paradoxically reproduce the very exclusionary ingroup/outgroup patterns they are meant to remove, e.g., by classifying less liberal cultures as not reconcilable with their own paradigm (Nadarajah and Rampton 2015, 50). In communal dialogues in Ukraine, for instance, it is likely that one-sided pro-Russian views of participants tend to change into 'multicultural' views, so that pro-Russian political and social perspectives continue to be absent from Ukrainian peace discourses (A. Holper and Kyselova 2021, 7–8).

Fifth and very generally, it seems to be a question of *proportionality*: Although its overall relative importance may be underestimated, culture is in fact only one of many relevant contextual factors (economic, environmental, political, security, etc.) that need to be considered in complex peace mediation processes.

For the above reasons, engaging in discussions about the general relevance of interculturality in the peace mediation field seems not to be useful. But there is actually a potential for improvement in determining the relevance of interculturality in each individual conflict and peace mediation process, which seems to vary greatly due to contextual factors: "Over-emphasis can lead to a disconnect from tangible conflict issues (e.g., economic situation, human rights, legal-institutional set-up), while under-emphasis can lead to a lack of understanding of how actors give meaning to such tangible conflict issues" (Aroua, Bitter, and Mason 2021, 1).

Different types of responses to intercultural issues in peace mediation

Reflecting the varying relevance of interculturality in peace mediation contexts, there are significant differences in the default responses of the more classical (interest- and identity-based) and novel (hybrid-adaptive and agonistic) approaches in peace mediation.

Interest based mediation: Tracing culture back to interests

The interest-based school in the peace mediation field tends to support the underlying assumption that 'cultural differences' or 'intercultural misunderstandings' might conceal conflicts of interest and power, or, in the worst case, even be used to justify acts of discrimination and violence (e.g., in the case of human rights violations or genocide). The argument of culture ('sacred, non-negotiable values') is potentially suspected of forcing recognition of political (not cultural) positions. In other words, the rhetoric of culture is often suspected of being a strategic means to another end, which prevents engagement with culture as a dimension in its own right. The response following from this perspective is that intercultural issues should be de-culturalized and traced back to the actual conflicts of interests to minimize the number of non-negotiable claims.

Identity-based mediation: Bridging the non-negotiables

A second type of response, which enters peace mediation from social psychology, points in an almost opposite direction: It says that in an 'emotionally charged conflict' that triggers the 'tribes' effect, it is essential to respect non-negotiable sacred elements in order to build new joint identities that bridge the divides and reorganize the relationships (Rothman 2014; Shapiro 2017; Korostelina 2007). Thus, when conflicts involve the identity level, interculturality is considered an irreducible dimension in conflict and mediation processes. However, cultures are seen as complex systems with both non-negotiable and formable areas that can and need to be addressed with different objectives and approaches.

Hybrid, adaptive mediation: Balancing the differences

A third type of response translates the ideas of identity-based mediation to the structural anatomy of peace processes: The hybrid peace concept aims to merge internationally supported peace operations and local approaches to balance the 'compliance' and 'incentivizing powers of liberal peace actors' with the 'ability of local actors to resist, ignore or adapt liberal peace interventions' and to 'present and maintain alternative forms of peacemaking' (Mac Ginty 2010). Adaptive mediation aims to identify and quickly respond adequately to important changes in volatile processes (Coleman, Kugler, and Chatman 2017), recognizing that uncertainty is an intrinsic quality of complex social systems and employing tools that cope with complexity, setbacks, and shocks (de Coning and Gray 2018). Here, culture is one factor that calls for tailoring mediation processes to given cultural contingencies in order to ensure the contextual acceptability and effectiveness of peace interventions.

Agonistic dialogue: Abandoning the consensus

Agonism, a concept from political philosophy (Mouffe and Wagner 2013), now applied to the field of peacebuilding and dialogue (Rumelili and Strömbom 2021; Aggestam, Cristiano, and Strömbom 2015; Nagle 2014; Brandsma 2016; Ramsbotham 2010), contends that consensus-driven peace interventions can fail to serve their purpose in highly divisive conflicts: When views are irre-concilable, pushing toward consensus can question self-/group-stabilizing ways of thinking and thereby create a sense of threat against the group and a need for defense, and thus pushbacks toward even more antagonistic relationships and identities. Agonism instead means normalizing differences through disaggregated recognition: People agree to disagree, no longer trying to understand but accepting the other's perspective, and focusing on pragmatic regulations for peaceful coexistence, often with the trade-off of a constant struggle over small issues (Aggestam, Cristiano, and Strömbom 2015; Maddison 2015; Strömbom 2020; Hirblinger and Landau 2020; Rothman 1997). In this theory, the endurance of non-reconcilability between different cultural views enables the nego-tiation of functional issues and non-violent co-existence, rather than the futile attempt to build bridges.

Conclusion: Existing building blocks and gaps to be filled

Currently there is no consistent approach to interculturality in peace mediation. A basic conceptual reference frame would be valuable, in order to assess the relevance of culture in concrete peace mediation processes and target relevant intercultural aspects in a suitable manner.

The following conceptual and methodical building blocks that draw on the field's own ap-proaches could be integrated into such a conceptual frame:

- First, *what differences must be tolerated*? Recognizing where intercultural understanding, consensus and cooperation does not work might open new space for what does work.
- Second, *what incidents can be used as entry points*? Intercultural misunderstandings, mistrust, and perceived and real attacks on identity can be traced back to divergent but logically compre-hensive perspectives, concerns, and intentions, even if behaviors and actions are rejected.
- Third, *how can symbolic elements of involved cultures be used to build bridges*? The parts of cultural identity that are not sacred but of symbolic value can be used as starting points for building joint meta-cultures that offer the frame, the basis or even the glue for difficult negotiation processes.
- Fourth, *what do the parties to the conflict actually want*? 'Intercultural issues,' too, are driven by concrete interests of individual or collective actors. Their cultural nature cannot legitimize them, but neither can the instrumentalization of culture delegitimize those interests.

Nevertheless, the general question of whether and when culture and mediation as such do (not) go together remains partly unanswered. The rational choice approach, which underlies the political sphere, is however not the worst one when it comes to culture, because its assumption of a universal human rationality protects against imputing a 'lower rationality' to the 'others.' Conversely, it is precisely such presumed universalist assumptions that might limit peace mediation activities to adherents of a specific cultural system. Perhaps this circular problem can be opened in confronting the new interculturalities at home: In many countries now, the nexus between radical disagreement, polarization and intercultural difference in our own societies also must be illuminated.

Note

1 The author would like to express her thanks to Anna Dick for her background support, to Lars Kirchhoff for the joint ideas that went into this article, and to Dominic Busch for his valuable feedback.

References

Abatis, Katrina. 2021. "Inviting the Elephant into the Room: Culturally Oriented Mediation and Peace Practice." *ETH Zurich*. 10.3929/ETHZ-B-000494207

Aggestam, Karin, Fabio Cristiano, and Lisa Strömbom. 2015. "Towards Agonistic Peace-building? Exploring the Antagonism–Agonism Nexus in the Middle East Peace Process." *Third World Quarterly* 36 (9): 1736–53. 10.1080/01436597.2015.1044961

Arnauld, Jean. 2014. "Legitimacy and Peace Processes: International Norms and Local Realities." In *Legitimacy and Peace Processes: From Coercion to Consent*, edited by Alexander Ramsbotham, Achim Wennmann, and Conciliation Resources, 21–7. London: Conciliation Resources.

Aroua, Abbas, Jean Nicolas Bitter, and Simon J. A. Mason. 2021. "The Role of Value Systems in Conflict Resolution." *Policy Perspectives* 9 (9): 1–4. 10.3929/ethz-b-000514318

Autesserre, Severine. 2011. "Constructing Peace: Collective Understandings of Peace, Peacemaking, Peacekeeping, and Peacebuilding." *Critique Internationale* 51 (2): 153–67. 10.3917/crii.051.0153

Avruch, Kevin. 2003. "Type I and Type II Errors in Culturally Sensitive Conflict Resolution Practice." *Conflict Resolution Quarterly* 20 (3): 351–71. 10.1002/crq.29

Bercovitch, Jacob, and Scott Sigmund Gartner, eds. 2009. *International Conflict Mediation: New Approaches and Findings*. London: Routledge. 10.4324/9780203885130

Boeijen, Annemiek van. 2020. *Culture Sensitive Design: A Guide to Culture in Practice*. Amsterdam: BIS publishers.

Brandsma, Bart. 2016. *Polarisation: Understanding the Dynamics of Us versus Them*. Culemborg: BB in Media, Studio Bassa.

Coleman, Peter T., Katharina G. Kugler, and Ljubica Chatman. 2017. "Adaptive Mediation: An Evidence-Based Contingency Approach to Mediating Conflict." *International Journal of Conflict Management* 28 (3): 383–406. 10.1108/IJCMA-11-2016-0090

de Coning, Cedric, and Stephen Gray. 2018. "Adaptive Mediation." Conflict Trends, no. 2. https://www.accord.org.za/conflict-trends/adaptive-mediation/

Crocker, Chester A., Fen Osler Hampson, and Pamela R. Aall, eds. 1999. *Herding Cats: Multiparty Mediation in a Complex World*. Washington, D.C: United States Institute of Peace Press.

Cuhadar, Esra. 2020. *Understanding Resistance to Inclusive Peace Processes*. Peaceworks vol. 159. Washington, DC: United States Institute of Peace. https://www.usip.org/sites/default/files/2020-03/pw_159-understanding_resistance_to_inclusive_peace_processes-pw.pdf

Demmers, Jolle. 2016 (was 2017). *Theories of Violent Conflict. An Introduction*. London: Routledge. 10.4324/9781315715025

Duursma, Allard. 2020. "African Mediators Outperform Their Non-African Counterparts - Here Is Why." *Political Violence at a Glance. Expert Analysis on Violence and Its Alterna-tives* (blog). April 30, 2020. https://politicalviolenceataglance.org/2020/04/30/why-african-mediators-outperform-their-foreign-counterparts/

Federal Foreign Office, and Initiative Mediation Support Germany. 2016. "Conflict Analysis and Mediation Entry Points." Fact Sheet Series Peace Mediation and Peace Media-tion Support.

Federal Foreign Office, and Initiative Mediation Support Germany. 2017. "Basics of Media-tion. Concepts and Definitions." Fact Sheet Series Peace Mediation and Peace Mediation Support.

Finlay, Andrew. 2015. "Liberal Intervention, Anthropology and the Ethnicity Machine." *Peacebuilding* 3 (3): 224–37. 10.1080/21647259.2015.1081123

Fisher, Roger. 2001. *Methods of Third-Party Intervention*. Berlin: Berghof Foundation.

Goertz, Gary, Paul Francis Diehl, and Alexandru Balas. 2016. *The Puzzle of Peace: The Evolution of Peace in the International System*. Oxford University Press. 10.1093/acprof:oso/9780199301027.001.0001

Greig, J. Michael, and Paul F. Diehl. 2012. *International Mediation*. Cambridge, UK; Malden, MA: Polity.

Hellmüller, Sara, Julia Palmiano Federer, and Matthias Zeller. 2015. *The Role of Norms in Internation-al Peace Mediation*. Bern: swisspeace.

Hirblinger, Andreas T., and Dana M. Landau. 2020. "Daring to Differ? Strategies of Inclusion in Peacemaking." *Security Dialogue* 51 (4): 305–22. 10.1177/0967010619893227

Holper, Anne, and Lars Kirchhoff, eds. 2021. *Peace Mediation in Germany's Foreign Policy: Uniting Method, Power and Politics. Interdisziplinäre Studien zu Mediation und Konfliktmanagement*. Baden-Baden: Nomos.

Holper, Anne, and Tetiana Kyselova. 2021 (was 2020). "Inclusion Dilemmas in Peacebuilding and Dialogues in Ukraine." *Peace and Conflict: Journal of Peace Psychology* 27 (3): 475–85. 10.1037/pac0000524

IGAD. 2018. "Signed Revitalized Agreement on the Resolution of the Conflict in South Sudan." 2018. https://igad.int/programs/115-south-sudan-office/1950-signed-revitalized-agreement-on-the-resolution-of-the-conflict-in-south-sudan

Kirchhoff, Lars, and Anne Isabel Kraus (now Holper). 2017. "Mediation in Internationalen Konflikten Und Friedensprozessen." In *Mediation und Konfliktmanagement. 2. Überarbeitete Auflage*, edited by Thomas Trenczek, Detlef Berning, and Christina Lenz, 640–46. Baden-Baden: Nomos.

Kleiboer, Marieke. 1996. "Understanding Success and Failure of International Mediation." *Journal of Conflict Resolution* 40 (2): 360–89. 10.1177/0022002796040002007

Korostelina, Karina V. 2007. "Identity and Conflict: Implications for Identity Conflict Man-agement." In *Social Identity and Conflict: Structures, Dynamics, and Implications*, edited by Karina V. Korostelina, 201–38. New York: Palgrave Macmillan US. 10.1057/9780230605671_10

Kraus (now Holper), Anne Isabel. 2011. "Culture-Sensitive Process Design: Overcoming Ethical and Methodological Dilemmas." *Politorbis* 52 (2): 35–48.

Kroeber, Alfred, and Clyde Kluckhohn. 2016 [1952]. *Culture: A Critical Review of Concepts and Definitions.* . London: Forgotten Books.

Lanz, David. 2021. "Peace Mediation in the International Political Context: Challenges and Niches for Germany." In *Peace Mediation in Germany's Foreign Policy: Uniting Method, Power and Politics*, edited by Anne Holper and Lars Kirchhoff, 39–47. Baden-Baden: Nomos.

Lanz, David, and Rachel Gasser. 2013. "A Crowded Field: Competition and Coordination in International Peace Mediation." *Mediation Arguments* 22: 1–20.

Londoño Lázaro, María Carmelina. 2003. "The Effectives of International Mediation. The Current Debate." *International Law. Revista Colombiana de Derecho Internacional* 2 (December): 319–41.

Lücke, Kai, and Aloys Rigaut. 2002. "Cultural Issues in International Mediation." In *EU as Mediator*, 45. University of Nottingham. https://www.nottingham.ac.uk/research/groups/ctccs/projects/translating-cultures/documents/journals/cultural-issues-mediation.pdf

Mac Ginty, Roger. 2010. "Hybrid Peace: The Interaction Between Top-Down and Bottom-Up Peace." *Security Dialogue* 41 (4): 391–412. 10.1177/0967010610374312

Maddison, Sarah. 2015. "Relational Transformation and Agonistic Dialogue in Divided Societies." *Political Studies* 63 (5): 1014–30. 10.1111/1467-9248.12149

Mason, Simon J. A. 2021. "Developing a State's Mediation Profile: Core Dimensions and Key Questions." In *Peace Mediation in Germany's Foreign Policy: Uniting Method, Power and Politics*, edited by Anne Isabel Holper and Lars Kirchhoff, 2–38. Baden-Baden: Nomos.

Meyer-Drawe, K. 2010. "Zur Erfahrung des Lernens. Eine phänomenologische Skizze." *Santalka* 18 (3): 6–17. 10.3846/coactivity.2010.22

Moghaddam, Fathali M. 2018. *Mutual Radicalization: How Groups and Nations Drive Each Other to Extremes*. Washington, DC: American Psychological Association.

Mouffe, Chantal, and Elke Wagner. 2013. *Agonistics: Thinking the World Politically*. London, New York: Verso.

Nadarajah, Suthaharan, and David Rampton. 2015. "The Limits of Hybridity and the Crisis of Liberal Peace." *Review of International Studies* 41 (1): 49–72. 10.1017/S0260210514000060

Nagle, John. 2014. "From the Politics of Antagonistic Recognition to Agonistic Peace Building: An Exploration of Symbols and Rituals in Divided Societies." *Peace & Change* 39 (4): 468–94. 10.1111/pech.12090

Palmiano Federer, Julia, Julia Pickhardt, Philipp Lustenberger, Christian Altpeter, and Katri-na Abatis. 2019. Beyond the Tracks? Reflections on Multitrack Approaches to Peace Pro-cesses. Report of Centre for Humanitarian Dialogue, Center for Security Studies ETH Zurich, Folke Bernadotte Academy, swisspeace. https://www.hdcentre.org/wp-content/uploads/2020/01/Beyond-the-Tracks-Reflections-on-Multitrack-Approaches-to-Peace-Processes.pdf

Plog, Fred, and Daniel G. Bates. 1976. *Cultural Anthropology*. 1st ed. New York: Knopf.

Ramsbotham, Oliver. 2010. *Transforming Violent Conflict. Radical Disagreement, Dialogue and Survival*. London: Routledge. 10.4324/9780203859674

Reid, Lindsay. 2017. "Finding a Peace That Lasts: Mediator Leverage and the Durable Resolution of Civil Wars." *Journal of Conflict Resolution* 61 (7): 1401–31. 10.1177/0022002715611231

Roepstorff, Kristina, and Anna Bernhard. 2013. "Insider Mediation in Peace Processes: An Untapped Resource?" *Sicherheit & Frieden* 31 (3): 163–9. 10.5771/0175-274x-2013-3-163

Rothman, Jay. 1997. *Resolving Identity-Based Conflict in Nations, Organizations, and Com-munities*. San Francisco, CA: Jossey-Bass.

Rothman, Jay. 2014. *From Identity-Based Conflict to Identity-Based Cooperation. The ARIA Approach in Theory and Practice*. New York: Springer.

Rumelili, Bahar, and Lisa Strömbom. 2021. "Agonistic Recognition as a Remedy for Identity Backlash: Insights from Israel and Turkey." *Third World Quarterly, August*, 1–19. 10.1080/01436597.2021.1951607

Saussure, Ferdinand de. 1993 [1916]. *Course in General Linguistics*, edited by Charles Bally and Roy Harris. London: Duckworth.

Sen, Amartya. 2007. *Identity and Violence: The Illusion of Destiny*. New York, NY: Norton.

Shapiro, Daniel. 2017. *Negotiating the Nonnegotiable: How to Resolve Your Most Emotionally Charged Conflicts*. New York: Penguin Books.

Shapiro, Daniel. 2021. "Mediating the Depths of Human Experience." In *Inviting the Elephant into the Room: Culturally Oriented Mediation and Peace Practice*, edited by Katrina Abatis, 7–9. Zürich: ETH Zürich.

Strömbom, Lisa. 2020. "Exploring Analytical Avenues for Agonistic Peace." *Journal of International Relations and Development* 23 (4): 1–23. 10.1057/s41268-019-00176-6

Svensson, Isak. 2007. "Mediation with Muscles or Minds? Exploring Power Mediators and Pure Mediators in Civil Wars." *International Negotiation* 12 (2): 229–48. 10.1163/138234007X223294

Tajfel, Henri, and John C. Turner. 2004. "The Social Identity Theory of Intergroup Behavior." In *Political Psychology*, edited by John T. Jost and Jim Sidanius, 276–93. 10.4324/9780203505984-16

Tanabe, Juichiro. 2019. "Beyond Liberal Peace: Critique of Liberal Peacebuilding and Ex-ploring a Post-Liberal Hybrid Model of Peacebuilding for a More Humane World." *Social Ethics Society Journal of Applied Philosophy* 5 (1): 19–42. 10.17265/2328-2134/2017.08.001

Tombe, Sandra. 2019. "Revitalising the Peace in South Sudan. Assessing the State of the Pre-Transitional Phase." *ACCORD Conflict Trends* 2019 (1). https://www.accord.org.za/conflict-trends/revitalising-the-peace-in-south-sudan/

United Nations. 2012. "Guidance for Effective Mediation." https://peacemaker.un.org/guidance-effective-mediation

USIP. n.d. "South Sudan Peace Process: Key Facts." United States Institute of Peace. Accessed February 26, 2022. https://www.usip.org/south-sudan-peace-process-key-facts

Zhurzhenko, Tatiana. 2014. "A Divided Nation? Reconsidering the Role of Identity Politics in the Ukraine Crisis." *Die Friedens-Warte* 89 (1–2): 249–67.

10
HYBRID PEACE MEDIATION IN THE AGE OF PANDEMICS

Anine Hagemann and Isabel Bramsen

Introduction

When the world began locking down in the early spring of 2020 due to the spread of COVID-19, all diplomatic engagement, including peace diplomatic efforts at all levels, were forced to stop or transition to online communication (Balakrishnan 2020). While some transitions where relatively unproblematic, the turn to virtual forms of communicating is particularly precarious in peace diplomatic efforts, as international peace mediation processes are a particularly fragile part of international diplomacy, characterized by navigating in and trying to improve conditions of low degrees of trust, understanding and cooperation between conflicting parties. How could fragile political processes of peacemaking continue during these new conditions? What were the pros and cons of transitioning to virtual solutions? And how did this leave ways of working changed after the world started opening up again? In this chapter we explore questions about peace mediation and its transition to virtual and hybrid forms.

The arrival of a new era of digital diplomacy has been pronounced a number of times (The Economist 2021) yet prior to 2020 there was a reluctance in the field of international peace mediation to take mediation efforts online (USIP 2020, 3). However, in the spring of 2020, when COVID lockdowns were introduced rapidly in many parts of the world, it resulted in an intensified virtualization representing a dramatic change in international peace mediation, described by a senior UN mediator as a "huge seismic change to the way we do business" (The Economist 2021). The abrupt change in practices of peace diplomacy during the COVID lockdown almost presented a natural experiment that enabled researchers to investigate how peace diplomacy works when you take out a central ingredient, namely the physical, face-to-face meeting (Bramsen and Hagemann 2021, Eggeling and Adler-Nissen 2021, Naylor 2020).

While the possibilities of virtual peace diplomacy have been heralded as a great opportunity for inclusion (USIP 2020), many professionals are also acutely aware of the limitations to international mediation. As one expert put it: "Let's be honest. Peace processes are suffering" (Author interview, 29 June 2020). This chapter presents an account of some of the possibilities and challenges of international peace mediation in the age of pandemics. It does so by defining international peace mediation, explaining the opportunities and challenges of virtual and face-to-face peace mediation and lastly discusses strategies of mediators as well as facets of complementarity in new hybrid ways of mediation.

104

DOI: 10.4324/9781003227441-13

International peace mediation

International peace mediation can be conducted between leaders of conflicting parties at the highest levels, such as political ministers (track one), but also between actors at other levels such as lower-ranking officials, civil society leaders, or religious leaders (track two) or at the grassroots level (track three). Third-party mediators most often facilitate dialogue at the higher levels, while mediation on other tracks can be more diffuse and can be facilitated by third parties or by parties or interest groups themselves. This chapter mainly focuses on the upper tiers of mediation, i.e., track one and two.

It is important to note that while this chapter focuses on the micro-dynamics of interaction in peace diplomacy, any mediation process and the possible related resolution or transformation of a conflicts is subject to the influence of a number of outside and contextual factors, including battlefield realities, geopolitics, Great Power politics, resources, and inequalities, all of which have significant impact on mediation efforts.

The goal of peace diplomacy is what we, at the micro-level, conceptualize as diplomatic *approachment*; the process of coming closer to each other little by little, in terms of breaking down mistrust and understanding each other's preferences and red lines, perhaps even softening up positions or generating fragile social bonds. Whereas the concept 'rapprochement' is accepted language in diplomacy to denote the "establishment of or state of having cordial relations" (Merriam Webster), the idea of *approachment* refers to frail beginnings at the micro-level of perhaps an emerging process of rapprochement (Bramsen and Hagemann 2021).

Effects of virtualizing meetings

Whereas technology can facilitate certain parts of interaction, it can hamper others. In a study of virtual mediation where we interviewed 20 participants in mediation efforts in Yemen and Syria, we found several advantages and disadvantages related to virtualizing peace mediation (Bramsen and Hagemann 2021). The general sentiment among participants in peace diplomatic efforts was that virtual diplomacy could never substitute physical meetings, as too many things were lost, what we refer to as a *difficulty in generating approachment*. Likewise, there were important disadvantages related to *confidentiality and disrupted interaction*. Despite the experience among all informants that virtual meetings where difficult for conducting dialogue they also pointed towards a number of surprising advantages of virtual communication relating to *accessibility, frequency,* and *equalized interaction* (Table 10.1).

Advantages of virtual diplomacy

Looking first at the advantages of virtual meetings, the COVID shutdowns and the resulting rapid transition of many discussions online enabled a higher degree of *accessibility* for many participants involved in or around peace diplomacy. This included groups such as refugees and women who were not able or funded to travel could participate virtually. Important fora such as the UN Security Council introduced online briefings from the field more regularly and have since continued to do so. Accessibility by conflict parties to high level players, such as Ambassadors and Special Envoys,

Table 10.1 Advantages and disadvantages of virtual diplomacy

Advantages	Disadvantages
Accessibility	Confidentiality
Frequency	Disrupted interaction
Equalized interaction	Difficult to generate approachment

who were not busy traveling, also increased. But also, the accessibility to conflict parties by mediators and internationals was in some cases heightened. This was because entry costs to meetings were lowered—both practically and culturally; it was not expected on either side that people would travel to meet, rather it became normalized to meet virtually, whereas in many settings the culture had been that to meet and discuss at a higher political level, meeting physically was a requirement. In these ways the virtual space in conflict contexts plays an especially important role for actors to transcend the boundaries of physical space. The increased accessibility was limited to a group of people with access to technology and those in the immediate periphery of peace processes. A large majority of people in conflict affected countries did not gain greater access to peace diplomacy because of limited access to technology.

Interestingly, an advantage of virtualizing communication that was emphasized by several informants, was its ability to *equalize interaction*. In physical meetings, there are several ways in which you can dominate the room through the way you enter the room, the way you shake hands, position yourself in the room, sit on the chair, etc. In virtual meetings this ability to reinforce and exercise power is limited (Bramsen and Hagemann 2021). Women in particular in some cases benefited from the diminished importance of body language and assertiveness as a component in the interaction and found virtualization could *level the playing field* for them, also because in virtual meetings it became more apparent who had most speaking-time. This finding echoes research in other areas, such as studies of education and communication, where women and girls also experienced that virtual space can have equalizing potential for their participation.

Another constructive feature of the online transition of peace processes was that it was possible to have more *frequent* meetings. When it came to internal meetings within conflicting parties or amongst third-party actors, the ability to have more frequent meetings significantly improved the collaboration. Many things could be discussed along the way, and quick meetings could be squeezed into a day with back-to-back meetings, as they were short, efficient, and did not require travel. Also, across large special differences for example amongst Syrian diaspora or third-party actors operating from different countries, this was highly useful.

Disadvantages of virtual diplomacy

A continued and heightened concern for conflict parties in sensitive dialogue processes in the virtual realm was *confidentiality* and the risk of surveillance. Confidentiality is crucial for parties to feel that they can express themselves freely in a safe space without things being leaked, recorded, or used against them. Although fear of confidentiality being compromised is a general risk in peace diplomacy, the virtual realm further exacerbated this danger, making it especially difficult—or impossible—for the virtual realm to be a trust-building space. This has severe consequences for the potential output of peace diplomatic efforts and the possibilities to counter dynamics of fear, mistrust, and insecurity.

The nature of interaction itself was also sometimes affected in the virtual meeting space, where communication would not be a dynamic back-and-forth process between people face-to-face in a physical room together. Because the virtual space stalled responses, *interaction would often become disrupted* if it was too rapid, entailing the need for formalized steering of virtual meetings, inhibiting any natural flow or rhythm to emerge between people. Whereas rhythmic, focused, and engaged interaction has the potential to generate social bonds (Bramsen and Poder 2018, Holmes and Wheeler 2020), an interaction where people interrupt each other or take long breaks, as is the case in much virtual communication, diminishes the potential for a sense of shared space, connection or understanding between people. On the other hand, this also lowered the potential for conflicts to escalate in virtual situations. Also, for parties who refuse to be in a room together, virtual space, with more formalized facilitation and the distance which comes with that might be a way to meet without really meeting and a step in a process towards meeting physically.

The most devastating disadvantage of virtual meetings in the context of peace diplomacy is the *difficulty in generating approachment* via virtual platforms. Whereas peace processes often involve meetings over many consecutive days over several weeks, virtual peace diplomacy has the same limitations as all other online meetings—it is not possible to keep focus and energy for many hours in an online discussion. Rather the meetings which were held were much shorter—typically between one and two hours. The inability to meet over longer periods of time online makes it more difficult to approach an opponent little by little and generate approachment. This is also related to the fact that the *informal space and time*, which is automatically generated during physical retreats for consecutive hours, days, and even weeks of peace negotiations is also removed in virtual settings. Any orchestrated or organically arising possibilities to meet and interact with each other in meetings breaks, in the hallways and even in the bathroom, and the informal conversations which happen over coffee, a cigarette, or shared meals is completely lost in non-physical meetings. This more informal interaction is critical for generating approachment as parties come to see each other in other settings, and the forms of interaction possible in in-formal encounters are more likely to generate social bonds (Bramsen and Hagemann 2021; Hagemann and Bramsen 2019). Hence, virtual peace diplomacy is highly disadvantaged in that regard, although there do exist ways of circumventing this to some extent, as we describe in the following.

Emerging virtual mediation strategies

A large part of navigating digital tools in mediation is about understanding the limitations and the potential of the technology at hand and using this knowledge to work with it and adapt it to contextual circumstances. As the previous sections outlined, working to cultivate trust, understanding, and togetherness is at the heart of any mediation process. These can all contribute to approachment, the micro-level process of parties coming slightly closer to each other.

Mediators have already begun working on how they can best use virtual platforms. International organizations such as the United Nations have worked to enhance understanding and advance new technologies in general to support their mediation efforts (United Nations 2020a) including guidance on social media as well as using AI to conduct consultations with much broader bases of stakeholders simultaneously than is normally possible in mediation and consultation processes. More precisely, the UN has conducted two AI-powered consultation processes in relation to peace mediation efforts recently (United Nations 2020b; Brown 2021), one in summer 2020 in Yemen, where the United Nations was able to survey more than 500 people and get their assessment of the most pressing issues, bringing this back to parties at the table; another in Libya where UN Mission held several digital dialogue sessions, each attracting more than 1000 people. These sessions included both survey elements and sections where constituents were able to ask questions and political candidates had to respond directly to these questions, increasing transparency and accountability.

This section outlines some of the emerging new strategies, which have been identified to us by mediators as they began to transition to virtual mediation. First, mediators explained that they spend a great deal of time on *bilateral consultations* with parties, sometimes called *shuttle diplomacy*, where they oscillate back and forth between each party, feeling out positions and trying to understand priorities, red lines, and internal dynamics at a level of detail that would not have been the case for mediators working at a distance before. Whereas in physical meetings, mediators could check in, sense the room, and make adjustments along the way, this process is harder in the virtual realm and thus requires more fine-tuning in advance. Second, and related to the above, mediators found it necessary to devote *more preparation time* prior to meetings. Because virtual meetings have to cover a lot of ground in a short amount of time and there are not the same possibilities of reading the room, detailed legwork in advance including a clearly defined agenda, acceptable language, and an in-depth understanding of the parties' opinions on items ahead of time was necessary. Third, the use of *several facilitators* in online mediation has become common practice. This allows for one person to chair the meeting and guide the overall conversation, while others can chat with participants individually or in groups and support the lead mediator in understanding how sentiments are developing as a meeting progresses. The facilitators working in the background can both observe what is going on in terms of facial expressions and what is being said and can also actively follow up bilaterally with individuals to understand whether some people are uncomfortable or dissatisfied, or to explain, if things seem to be unclear to participants. Much of this information will then ideally be fed back into the main mediation process between the mediators.

In general, when virtual solutions are invoked, mediators have to take on a very active and involved role. The fact that agendas and meeting content are more tightly controlled and prepared than before also means that mediators are playing a greater role in setting agendas and formulating possible solutions; thus virtualization potentially confers great power but also great responsibility on mediation teams, with the related responsibility to work harder to ensure ownership of the process among the parties. Mediation actors also describe how the inclusion of virtual space demands a lot of time and around-the-clock engagement because of having the possibility and therefore the obligation to maintain in contact with parties constantly and continually—the role of mediating peace has perhaps become even more demanding than previously.

The future is hybrid

While the COVID lockdowns accelerated and mainstreamed the use of digital technologies in diplomacy and peace mediation, they also shed light on boundaries and limitations of virtual mediation. In the new age of pandemics, digital tools in mediation are here to stay and are constantly being improved. At the same time, the power of face-to-face meetings, not least in the fragile area of peace mediation, has also been clearly demonstrated. What does a hybrid model for mediation in pandemic times look like? This section argues that peace mediation efforts will most likely use a mixture of face-to-face and virtual tools going forward. We point to three aspects of hybridity or complementarity of the two, which are emerging as virtual tools have become normalized and international travel has allowed for a reopening of societies and renewed possibilities of conducting face-to-face meetings.

First, there is complementarity in maintaining *momentum and approachment*: Some peace talks (for example the 2012–2016 talks on Colombia) happen with 2–3 week intervals, while others (such as the 2016–2017 on the Philippines) have months in-between every physical meeting. While face-to-face meetings are often very intense while they happen, momentum can be lost during the time between meetings. Even more problematically for peace processes, approachment may also be lost in-between meetings. For example, a participant described how the parties to the conflict in Yemen would approach each other during physical peace talks, both when it came to softening up positions and trusting the adversaries, but then when they returned to the context of war and fighting on the ground, these sentiments would relatively quickly dissolve. Here, virtual meetings and social media such as chat groups can be a tool for keeping momentum in the time between physical meetings. Several UN peace processes enhanced their communication with parties over social media in 2020. For example, in the Libyan context, UN officials maintained momentum of negotiations during the first COVID-lockdown in 2020 by meeting bilaterally online with a number of different military factions.

Second, digital technologies can be used to enhance *collaboration and coordination* between third-party actors, especially at the level of track two diplomacy. It is a well-known challenge, that (too) many track two mediation processes or actors in a conflict can be problematic, as they may compete to solve the same conflicts or at least that a better coordination between such organizations can enhance their effectiveness and impact in the conflict setting. Wallensteen and Svensson (2014, 322) ask "How are conflicts between the mediators mediated?" and here virtual meetings may provide part of the answer. Finally, ensuring broad inclusion and consultation at the track one and a half and track two levels is key to ensuring broad political buy-in, legitimacy, and ownership. In the Syrian context, Syrian civil society groups reported meeting much more regularly as the world went into lockdown in 2020, allowing them to coordinate their positions, draft position papers, and develop politically as a movement. In Myanmar in 2020, different women's groups across the Rakhine state were able to meet with the UN Special Envoy because the meeting was online, offering them a chance to hear from each other and find common ground—a change from each group having separate meetings with the Envoy, which was the practice prior to COVID lockdown precautions. Virtual, internal communication amongst third-party organizations and within parties to the conflict may well be continued after the pandemic with potentially very positive impacts on the coherence and coordination of peace diplomatic efforts.

Third, there is a complementarity in the *perceived formality, symbolism, and gravitas* when it comes to the two formats. In many conflicts, mediators and conflict parties concluded that it was virtually impossible to start up new processes or continue fragile ones in the virtual space. Many peace processes grounded to a halt in the spring of 2020. This is an indicator of the symbolism and importance of face-to-face meetings. They can be especially important in the beginning of new negotiations to whittle away initial misunderstandings and mistrust and generate initial approachment. Once a process is more progressed, it is in many cases easier to maintain a dialogue which involved both face-to-face and virtual meetings. However, there are also examples of processes, where the format of the virtual meeting was used as an *icebreaker* because of the lower degree of symbolism of an online meeting as opposed to being in the same room physically. While the online meeting then might not be used to take the same kinds of decisions, in some contexts this can be an advantage in terms of getting parties to the table. An example of this the resumption of talks between the federal government of Somalia and the federal member states dialogue in Somalia. A virtual meeting that was held between leaders in these fora in June 2021 served as an icebreaker and after a first online meeting, a face-to-face meeting followed. This suggests that in some cases online meetings can serve as *proximity talks*, bringing parties together online as an interim step towards meeting physically.

Conclusion

International mediation efforts during the COVID-19 lockdowns intensified an already ongoing virtualization process of international peace diplomacy. While virtual meetings in some cases allow for increased accessibility, equalize interaction, and enable more frequent meetings, the interaction they create are often disrupted and there are challenges to confidentiality. The biggest drawback of mediation in virtual settings is the loss of a range of physical registry of sensibilities, which face-to-face meetings can uniquely provide, and which can be a key tool in breaking cycles of mistrust, misunderstanding, and distance.

In addition, local contexts play a very important role in determining the applicability and relevance of digital tools. In one setting the step of meeting at all is too fraught to move online and in other contexts, it is exactly the decrease in symbolism of the virtual meeting, which makes it possible to start meeting. More generally, whereas in some countries there is wide access to digital tools and the internet, other contexts have severe inequalities when it comes to access, and it is mainly elites and youth who can access digital tools. In-depth understanding and analysis of local contexts as well as how they play into hybridity remains key for mediators and other actors engaged in conflict resolution and mediation.

While virtual meetings cannot replace physical meetings, they can serve as a useful and complementary tool for mediators. In the current age of pandemics, hybrid models of mediation will likely be the way forward. The complementarity between physical and virtual meetings can take at least three specific forms, including in their timing, maintaining momentum of a mediation process, enhancing collaboration and coordination between third-party mediation actors and taking advantage of virtual meetings' perceived formality, symbolism, and gravitas vis-à-vis physical meetings. Mediators have already begun developing strategies for improving virtual mediation, including intensifying bilateral consultations and devoting more time for rigorous preparation of meetings, as wells as using multiple mediators and multiple channels of communication as part of facilitating dialogue. Continued experimentation with the complementarity of new and old tools is likely to continue in this new phase of hybridity in peace diplomacy.

References

Balakrishnan, Vivian. 2020. "Diplomacy in a Post-Covid-19 World." *The Straits Times*, June 25, 2020. https://www.straitstimes.com/opinion/diplomacy-in-a-post-covid-19-world

Bramsen, Isabel, and Anine Hagemann. 2021. "The Missing Sense of Peace: Diplomatic Approachment and Virtualization during the COVID-19 Lockdown." *International Affairs* 97 (2): 539–60. 10.1093/ia/iiaa229

Bramsen, Isabel, and Poul Poder. 2018. *Emotional Dynamics in Conflict and Conflict Transformation*. Berlin: Berghof Foundation. https://berghof-foundation.org/files/publications/bramsen_poder_handbook.pdf

Brown, Dalvin. 2021. "The United Nations Is Turning to Artificial Intelligence in Search for Peace in War Zones." *Washington Post*, April 23, 2021. https://www.washingtonpost.com/technology/2021/04/23/ai-un-peacekeeping/

Eggeling, Kristin Anabel, and Rebecca Adler-Nissen. 2021. "The Synthetic Situation in Diplomacy: Scopic Media and the Digital Mediation of Estrangement." *Global Studies Quarterly* 1 (2): ksab005. 10.1093/isagsq/ksab005

Hagemann, Anine, and Isabel Bramsen. 2019. *New Nordic Peace: Nordic Peace and Conflict Resolution Efforts*. Copenhagen: Nordic Council of Ministers. 10.6027/TN2019-524

Holmes, Marcus, and Nicholas J. Wheeler. 2020. "Social Bonding in Diplomacy." *International Theory* 12 (1): 133–61. 10.1017/S1752971919000162

Naylor, Tristen. 2020. "All That's Lost: The Hollowing of Summit Diplomacy in a Socially Distanced World." *The Hague Journal of Diplomacy* 15 (4): 583–98. 10.1163/1871191X-BJA10041

The Economist. 2021. "Diplomacy Has Changed More than Most Professions during the Pandemic," April 29, 2021. https://www.economist.com/international/2021/04/29/diplomacy-has-changed-more-than-most-professions-during-the-pandemic

United Nations. 2020a. *Digital Mediation Toolkit*. https://peacemaker.un.org/digitaltoolkit

United Nations. 2020b. "Cutting-Edge Tech in the Service of Inclusive Peace in Yemen - Yemen." *ReliefWeb*. https://reliefweb.int/report/yemen/cutting-edge-tech-service-inclusive-peace-yemen

Wallensteen, Peter, and Isak Svensson. 2014. "Talking Peace: International Mediation in Armed Conflicts." *Journal of Peace Research* 51 (2): 315–27. 10.1177/0022343313512223

11

THE POLITICAL DIMENSIONS OF CULTURE AND RELIGION IN MEDIATION

Mohammed Abu-Nimer and Timothy Seidel

Introduction: Mediation across boundaries

Mediation is about relationships, movement, and crossing boundaries. Mediation implies that there has been some movement through distance and across difference in order to see and hear another. This boundary-crossing is always mediated through historical experiences of culture, religion, and power. An effective mediator attends to these experiences as influential factors in a conflict. The mediator can do this in less invasive ways by serving to facilitate interactions between parties as they figure out how to resolve and transform conflict. Or the mediator might bring significant power and agenda to the situation that shapes the outcome, thereby impacting the situation in a manner more imposing than facilitating.

The term *multi-track diplomacy* is often used where mediation occurs outside of political diplomatic society. It is in this sector where the political dimensions of culture and religion become salient in mediation. Civil society actors such as religious leaders and religious organizations play a critical role in mediating conflicts in ways that state actors—whether because of access or power or history—are not able to. Cultural and religious mediators are an integral part of the social fabric of many societies. Their role varies from stabilizing and restoring a status quo to shifting power relations after a violent crisis affects the existing social order. For example, religious and traditional leaders are often called upon to mediate conflict in tribal and rural communities, especially when state authorities and the rule of law appear weak.

Culture and religion shape how conflict is understood and experienced and so are already present in mediation and conflict resolution practices. Relegating them to the periphery is inadequate and ineffective—especially if we are to uncover and understand the often Eurocentric character of mediation models. Particularly in international contexts, these models might ignore the power dynamics introduced by third parties intervening in conflict situations and underestimate the effect of cultural norms and values in the mediation process. With this in mind, mediation as a form of *intervention* in conflict contexts is an inherently political act. Attention to culture and religion is critical to understanding the power dynamics of conflict contexts by both interrogating the claims to neutrality of third parties and underscoring the importance of relationships to mediation. For example, the selection of a secular mediator to handle a conflict situation in Palestine-Israel when the issue is related to the Al Aqsa Mosque in Jerusalem certainly reduces the mediator's or third party's capacity to connect with Jewish and Muslim religious parties too.

DOI: 10.4324/9781003227441-14

In this chapter, we explore *how* culture and religion are meaningful and meaning-making elements to conflict and mediation, *why* this is important to understanding power and empowerment, and the ways that interfaith engagement offers *lessons* to mediators. We conclude by discussing several principles, processes, and biases for the mediator to consider when accounting for these dynamics.

Culture and religion as *meaningful* and *meaning-making* in conflict resolution

Attending to the role of culture and religion in mediation is a matter of crossing boundaries—whether in terms of individual, communal, social, or national identities—both for parties to a conflict as well as for the mediator. However, this notion of crossing boundaries in ways impacted by culture and religion has not always received proper attention, and when it has it is not always in a way that attends to the role of the mediator in the process (Abu-Nimer 1996).

Often culture and religion are seen as irrelevant, or worse an obstruction, to an effective resolution of conflict. This approach is not unrelated to the perspective that the modern state requires relegating culture and religion to the periphery where politics does not really happen. And yet many individuals, communities, and organizations are motivated by their faith. According to the Pew Research Center 84% of the world's population holds some form of religious affiliation and is increasing as a share of the world's population (Pew Research Center 2015). This is significant not only because of the ways religion and faith matter to the majority of the people in the world but also because of the ways political actors manipulate or exploit religious identity to consolidate power. We better understand violence and conflict when religion and faith are not simply reduced to a private, personal sphere but are integral to the lived experiences of people who may not always separate out religion. Here we see religion and faith, along with race, gender, and class, as both *meaningful* in terms of social identity and difference and *meaning-making* in terms of the stories and the everyday worlds people inhabit. Accessing the religious narratives of parties in a mediation or peace process is essential, especially when politicians and religious leaders have manipulated those narratives to justify violence.

Some conflict resolution and peacebuilding theory and practice have developed an appreciation for this. For example, faith-based organizations (FBOs) have emerged highlighting the importance of "making peace with faith" (Garred and Abu-Nimer 2018). These groups make the case that the sacred and spiritual elements present in religious identity are an asset for peacebuilding and inclusion, as opposed to violence and exclusion, and cannot simply be dismissed as politically irrelevant in the resolution of conflict.

Discussions on the role of culture and religion in conflict resolution is quite diverse. This ranges from viewing culture and religion as irrelevant or even obstructive to conflict resolution, to seeing its relevance but only in instrumental terms (with homogenized and static definitions of people and groups), to viewing cultural variation and religious difference as fundamentally significant to the narration and analysis of conflict and its subsequent resolution, especially when emphasizing particularity, local knowledge, and power relations (Cohen 1997 [1991]; Lederach 1995; Avruch 1998; Trujillo et al. 2008). This can include explorations of the role of religion and religious symbols in the analysis of conflict—how conflict is expressed in religious terms—and the role of religion in the resolution of conflict—attending to religion and religious identity amongst conflicting parties as well as with the identity of the mediator and appealing to religion for transformative moments in conflict (Abu-Nimer 2003; Omer, Appleby, and Little 2015).

It also matters *how* we consider culture and religion. In our discussions and conceptions of mediation, how do binaries such as religion/secular present themselves? And how do they contribute to our ability to imagine and (de)legitimize new possibilities? For example, the tendency to cast the religious (as irrational) against the secular (as rational) can be observed in the work of many

American and European government organizations and agencies. Those self-described 'secular' organizations often define themselves in opposition to religious groups and religious parties. When coupled with political power, this grants secular institutions the power to name and (de)legitimize religious organizations (Seidel 2012).

When acknowledging religious and cultural identities and experiences as not peripheral but central—as *meaningful* and *meaning-making*—conflict resolution and peacebuilding models will be constructed and practiced more from within and less from above and outside of the parties involved and most impacted in conflict (Abu-Nimer 2001; Abu-Nimer and Seidel 2017).

Politics, power, and empowerment

The political dimensions of culture and religion in mediation have to do with how power is configured, consolidated, and challenged. One way to consider the political dimensions is to focus primarily on the state as the primary political actor and state activity, whether policy- or war-making, as primary political action. However, this would be a limiting focus that confines culture, religion, and faith to a private matter of individual preference. Instead, a focus on politics that is not only about electoral politics or parliamentary politics, but extra-parliamentary politics or contentious politics (Tilly and Tarrow 2015), brings civil society into view, where a whole landscape of actors and activities can be seen and considered that do not take the state as the point of departure for social life.

We have seen this taking place in the past two decades with intergovernmental and governmental agencies realizing the need to engage religious actors in peace processes and especially in responding to violent extremism. However, this engagement in many cases remains symbolic and fairly limited. Many of these agencies do not invest resources or build internal capacity for enhancing engagement with religious actors. For example, the European Union, United Nations, African Union, and ASEAN structures have limited focal points on such topics and so it does not make it on to their global, national, or regional agenda.

Implicit in this approach is an understanding of culture and religion mindful of the pitfalls of reification and homogenization. A more critical posture considers the dynamics of power, where culture is seen as a site of struggle and a place where multiple interpretations come together, but where there is always a dominant force. For this reason, we highlight the role of power and power analysis to not only account for the cultural constitution of needs and claims but also power differentials that may exist between conflicting parties (VeneKlasen and Miller 2002). This includes analyzing the different forms power may take, the different spaces it is acted out, and the different levels it is expressed (Gaventa 2006).

This analysis also explores the kinds of power present (and available) in a conflict situation, for example power *over*, power *to*, power *with*, and power *within* (often linked to culture, religion, or other aspects of identity). Attention to culture and religion can allow mediators to navigate these forms of power from within while outside mediators who often lack the inner worldview of the parties tend to import or utilize their own external lenses of power analysis.

This attention to power can also help parties re-narrate the constructive role conflict can play. Roberto Chene argues that a "dominance paradigm" often operates in a way that translates difference into conflictual, unhealthy, and unimprovable human relationships. Getting beyond "pretend diversity," he says, requires recognizing that social contexts need to be restructured and power relations reconfigured. Mediation with an approach that includes creative conflict resolution and creative discomfort "can help others acquire a spirit of embracing, not avoiding, conflict. Framed and creatively mediated and facilitated properly, our conflicts are simply grand opportunities to learn and be transformed" (2008, 36).

Dismissal of power from the equation reinforces a status quo that maintains dominant power relations and precludes any opportunity for 'empowerment' and transformation. Deploying cultural and religious mediators does not necessarily prevent this disempowerment or support of status quo, on the contrary traditional mediators can be manipulated for such outcome (Abu-Nimer 2003). This only underscores the importance of attending to power and political dynamics when considering culture and religion in mediation.

Interfaith and intrafaith engagement in mediation

More than maintaining a certain level of religious literacy in designing and implementing third-party interventions, developing the skills and sensibilities for interfaith engagement is important for the mediator. One of the ways we understand this is by working to create religiously pluralistic and inclusive spaces where conflicting parties can move through distance and across difference in order to see and hear another. For example, UN special envoys to Libya and the process they initiate for mediation has to include the various Islamic spiritual and religious ways of practicing. Emphasizing the pluralistic nature of local Islamic groups in such a context can assist in countering the *realpolitik* dynamics often imposed by the international diplomatic culture. However, an engagement process of religious and cultural diversity needs to be an integral part of the entire process and not an add-on (symbolic) at the end or beginning.

Whereas cultural and religious diversity simply describes the presence of difference (e.g., the variety of racial, ethnic, and religious identities in a community), pluralism, and inclusion describe the ways a community actively includes and accommodates and are shaped into a new community through those differences. This could include accommodating dietary needs, providing prayer spaces, learning about and celebrating each other's cultural and religious traditions. Thus, mediation processes, setup, formation of agenda, location, etc. have to reflect participant beliefs in religiously diverse spaces and communities.

Interfaith engagement offers an alternative to 'political and diplomatic secularism.' This is not secular as a kind of identity or orientation, but secularism as a norm and dominant ethic (and political doctrine) that requires things like *disintegration* (so that we cannot bring our whole selves to what we do) and *denial* of our own particularity (whether as individuals or as an institution with particular histories), which is to also say an *erasure* of cultural difference, faith, or otherwise.

Moving beyond a focus on diversity recognizes that it is not enough, for example, to simply bring Muslims and Christians together. Too often the language of faith is absent from these meetings, and the space constructed by the practitioners or the convening agency is often framed as a place for learning technical skills and for the individual to become an agent of change divorced from their spirituality.

The skills and sensibilities needed for interfaith engagement assume a grounded identity, especially for the mediator—a particular cultural and religious identity from which to relate across difference. Building the capacities for interfaith engagement is integral to removing barriers to full participation and a sense of equity and inclusion to participants.

This includes paying attention to the ways that religion and faith is always racialized and gendered. That is to say, this includes exploring the racialized histories of colonialism that constitute our understandings of religion and conflict. A more deliberate complexification of dominant understandings of the religious and the secular aids in centering voices and experiences often marginalized in conflict resolution and peacebuilding theory and practice, and offering a more radical challenge to the logic of international relations—a logic that turns on the secular-religious binary and reproduces a 'secular bias.'

Acknowledging and dealing with these biases in mediation processes, especially in interreligious and religious contexts, is a crucial step for any third-party intervention. Much of these biases can be implicit and unconsciously influence the verbal and nonverbal behaviors and attitudes of the third party. Obviously, a Sri Lankan Buddhist monk or Muslim leader will be easily able to identify and sense the cultural and religious bias of a Christian diplomat who just arrived to the northeast region in Sri Lanka to carry on one of his missions to assess the situation in preparation for another round of negotiation between the various political parties. Some of the following principles might help such outside mediators to better relate to such stakeholders as an outsider.

Principles, processes, and biases

There are several elements and conditions to consider when attending to these dynamics that we will frame in terms of *principles*, *processes*, and *biases*.

Principles

First among the principles we highlight is *self-reflexivity*. This is related to our discussion above on understanding power. The role and impact of the mediator must be accounted for including their cultural, religious, and political identity or location. This speaks to a sort of reflexivity and humility a mediator needs to recognize their (in)ability to fully understand and comprehend the cultural and religious codes and discourses, acknowledge biases, and monitor effects. The mediator as reflective practitioner attends to these insider-outsider dynamics. And while we do not explore this at length here, the role of gender and race as well as faith and in terms of the identity of the mediator is an important consideration. Especially in intercultural and interreligious settings, they need to engage in self-reflexive exercises to realize where they stand on the question of the role of faith in the specific conflict. Such a question should accompany the whole process of intervention and not only at one stage, simply reading an article on the topic.

It is simply a matter of mediator capacity and competency but mediator impact. 'Do no harm' is a well-known principle both in the fields of medicine and in humanitarian intervention that applies to mediation (Anderson 1999; Kadayifci-Orellana and Maassarani 2021). This principle recognizes that any third-party intervention will have an impact and even change the landscape of the conflict situation. Traditional dispute resolution has not always addressed these issues, but the entry of the mediator or mediation team can not only significantly affect the power relations in the dynamics of the mediation but, indeed, becomes a part of the conflict itself. Again, it is a question of the role and the social location of the mediator that can either normalize certain social realities or problematize them by identifying their political and structural elements. No matter how thoughtful the design, how rigorous the approach, power is at work in mediation, making self-awareness and reflexivity on the part of the mediator critical. For example, deploying an American Christian evangelical as a special envoy to Israel-Palestine influences the perceptions of power relations in of all the parties involved.

It is critical to pay attention to the *motivation* of the parties. Many participants take part in conflict resolution and peacebuilding interventions because of their faith, religious affiliation, and belief systems. For example, for a Muslim, the act of participation may be described as a duty to Allah and Allah's commandment to do peace. However, this does not mean that participants during an intervention will only focus on their faith or belief system; on the contrary, even though faith and religion is present in a mediation, most peacebuilding interventions are focused on non-theological issues, that all community members have in common such as health, climate, governance, or security. How participants understand religion and faith will be deeply connected to the ways in which they chose to express their faith while discussing daily issues and challenges faced by their communities. In addition, it is often the case that participants frame their perception of the conflict based on the obstructions they experience in practicing their faith in their daily lives and in shared common spaces.

Finally, it is important to recognize and acknowledge *cultural and religious differences* among conflicting parties. Such differences should be assessed as to their potential impact on the communication process generally or how it invokes the framing of needs, values, and identities in a given conflict situation. This requires the sort of faith and interfaith engagement we have been describing that avoids a simple, instrumentalized role for religion. This also requires a mediation process and design to be more complex and less simply facilitative in nature or free of religious discourse, a discussion we now turn to.

Processes

There are several implications to be drawn from this discussion as it relates to designing, monitoring, and evaluation processes. Critical to the design stage is considering culture and religion in the *conflict analysis* as well as the *power analysis* we described above. This would include attention to key questions like: Who? (e.g., actors, organizations, and institutions); Where? (e.g., context, levels, and spaces); What? (e.g., sectors, issues, and power); Why? (e.g., motivations); How? (e.g., strategies, methods, and models).

Intentionally *integrating faith into the design, monitoring, and evaluation* of the intervention will ensure it is shaped and influenced by the religious identity or the participants' affiliations. Thus, the preparation, delivery, and follow-up of the intervention will be rooted and affected by the faith of the participants. Even in the analysis stage, mediators need to think about possible responses to questions around the causes of the conflict (e.g., 'God caused it'). In addition, in many cases there are participants who perceive the roles of conflict structures and systems (economic, political, social, etc.) as 'secondary' or 'earthly,' as opposed to the primary cause of divine intervention (Garred and Abu-Nimer 2018).

The design should also consider the intercultural and interreligious dynamics of the conflict. For example, when designing an interfaith dialogue or mediation process between Muslims and Jews in Europe and focusing on their common issues as religious and ethnic minorities in that context, it is essential in the preparation stage that the intervention considers how each of the participants theologically perceives members of the other community. This relates to the discussion above on interfaith engagement. Similarly, when Hindu, Muslim, and Christian groups meet to discuss their common concerns in northern Sri Lanka, their religious identity should not be seen as an obstacle to confronting their common concerns. On the contrary, it should be viewed as an asset that will facilitate the creation of their common bond.

'Secular bias'

A focus on bias is important when considering culture and religion in mediation, both because of the emphasis we place on self-reflexivity and because of the bias toward secularism in many approaches to conflict resolution. There are times when a third party who conducts the intervention is afraid of introducing and addressing various aspects of the faith and religious identities of the participants. Thus, the mediator avoids any mention of faith, values, identity, and affiliation of the parties despite the fact that participants might have no resistance to such an approach. Indeed, in many communities around the world, participants often expect to and they themselves frame conflict issues in religious terms.

For example, in Sierra Leone when an international agency conducted a workshop between Muslim and Christians to address the common concern of post-war integration of child soldiers into their communities, the third party avoided any conversation on how Islam and Christianity deal with this issue. At some point during the intervention, the participants themselves asked each other: how does your faith instruct you to deal with this issue? Such a question can be intentionally integrated into the process by the mediator.

Another way the secular bias manifests is in the state-centric approaches that persist in international conflict resolution. The persistence of a realpolitik that maintains a state-to-state focus falls short because of its neglect of civil society actors and activities that then ignore issues regarding culture and religion. To address these dynamics, third-party interventions should intentionally create space for faith and religious identities to be expressed and practiced to serve the purpose of peacebuilding. In fact, faith and spirituality should be considered an essential component of the intervention, with activities built into the design such as prayer, mediation, fasting, singing, or other rituals (Garred and Abu-Nimer 2018; Olupayimo 2018).

A 'postsecular' approach probes these biases, and foregrounds the lived experiences, the everyday, of people who do not always separate out religion but recognize its co-constitution with the various social, political, and economic elements of their lives. Expecting participants in a mediation process to separate their faith identity from their issues or daily concerns is another form of disempowerment and can be experienced as an imposition from an external and alienating secular agency on their local cultural and religious context.

This also matters at the conceptual level, re-narrating the pedagogies, tools, and skills introduced and utilized in the intervention in ways that are rooted in faith traditions. Attention to secular biases can prevent recycling abstract conflict resolution including mediation tools and approaches divorced from social and historical context. For example, when conducting capacity building workshops and trainings on mediation in Jewish, Christian, or Muslim settings, the design of the initiative and the third parties involved could integrate questions such as: 'How did the Prophets mediate and arbitrate conflicts?' 'What does your faith say about mediation?' 'What does it mean to listen in your faith?' In this way, training cannot be simply reduced to question of how 'expert' diplomats, United Nations, or other political or civil society leaders deliver mediation—often Eurocentric notions of expertise dismissive of religion and faith.

Conclusion

Paying attention to the political dynamics of culture and religion in mediation opens up new perspectives for third-party interventions, highlighting both possibilities and limitations. Indeed, mediation itself cannot address all the root causes of complex social conflict where power is expressed in varying forms at multiple levels. As Abu-Nimer (1996) highlighted in comparing Western and non-Western mediation processes, the different power dynamics, expected outcomes, signature of agreements, etc., must be taken into consideration since they affect the sustainability of agreements and settlements. Also, more recently, as Kadayifci-Orellana and Maassarani remind us, mediation "must be part of a comprehensive and strategic approach to peacebuilding if a just and sustainable peace is to be reached" (2021, 53) that might include nonviolent campaigns and movements to shift power, reconciliation and reparation efforts to address past harms, and legal and political advocacy to push for more just and equitable policies.

This underscores the approach we have discussed in this chapter that does not confine culture and religion to one piece of the peace—an instrumentalized variable in a conflict resolution equation—but as a *meaningful* and *meaning-making* element in people's lives and communities.

References

Abu-Nimer, Mohammed. 1996. "Conflict Resolution Approaches. Western and Middle Eastern Lessons and Possibilities." *American Journal of Economics and Sociology* 55 (1): 35–52. 10.1111/j.1536-7150.1996.tb02706.x

Abu-Nimer, Mohammed. 2001. "Conflict Resolution, Culture, and Religion: Toward a Training Model of Interreligious Peacebuilding." *Journal of Peace Research* 38 (6): 685–704. 10.1177/0022343301038006003

Abu-Nimer, Mohammed. 2003. *Nonviolence and Peacebuilding in Islam: Theory and Practice.* Gainesville, FL: University Press of Florida.

Abu-Nimer, Mohammed, and Timothy Seidel. 2017. "Culture, Religion, and Politics in International Mediation." In *The Handbook of Mediation: Theory, Research and Practice*, edited by Alexia Georgakopoulos, 324–33. London: Routledge.

Anderson, Mary B. 1999. *Do No Harm: How Aid Can Support Peace—Or War*. Boulder, London: Lynne Rienner Publishers.

Avruch, Kevin. 1998. *Culture and Conflict Resolution*. Washington, DC: United States Institute of Peace.

Chené, Roberto M. 2008. "Beyond Mediation—Reconciling an Intercultural World: A New Role for Conflict Resolution." In *Re-Centering Culture and Knowledge in Conflict Resolution Practice*, edited by Mary A. Trujillo, Sandra Y. Bowland, Linda J. Myers, Phillip M. Richards, and Beth Roy, 32–6. New York: Syracuse University Press.

Cohen, Robert. 1997 [1991]. *Negotiating across Cultures: International Communication in an Interdependent World*. Washington, D.C.: United States Institute of Peace.

Garred, Michelle, and Mohammed Abu-Nimer, eds. 2018. *Making Peace with Faith: The Challenges of Religion and Peacebuilding*. Lanham, MD: Rowman and Littlefield.

Gaventa, John. 2006. "Finding the Spaces for Change: A Power Analysis." *IDS Bulletin* 37 (6): 23–33. 10.1111/j.1759-5436.2006.tb00320.x

Kadayifci-Orellana, S. Ayse and Tarek Maassarani. 2021. *Religion and Mediation Action Guide*. Washington, DC: United States Institute of Peace.

Lederach, John P. 1995. *Preparing for Peace: Conflict Transformation across Cultures*. Syracuse, NY: Syracuse University.

Olupayimo, Dolapo Z. 2018. "Religious Songs in Conflict Situations: An Interrogation of Selected Yoruba Coded Church Songs." In *Atone: Religion, Conflict, and Reconciliation*, edited by Akanmu G. Adebayo, Brandon D. Lundy, and Sherrill W. Hayes, 217–28. Lanham, Boulder, New York, London: Lexington Books.

Omer, Atalia, R. Scott Appleby, and David Little. 2015. *The Oxford Handbook of Religion, Conflict, and Peacebuilding*. Oxford University Press. 10.1093/oxfordhb/9780199731640.001.0001

Pew Research Center. 2015. *The Future of World Religions: Population Growth Projections, 2010–2050*. Washington, D.C.: Pew Research Center's Forum on Religion & Public Life.

Seidel, Timothy. 2012. "Development, Religion, and Modernity in Palestine-Israel." *CrossCurrents* 62 (4): 424–41. 10.1111/cros.12001

Tilly, Charles, and Sidney G. Tarrow. 2015. *Contentious Politics*. 2nd edition. New York, NY: Oxford Univ. Press.

Trujillo, Mary Adams, Sandra Y. Bowland, Linda James Myers, Phillip M. Richards, and Beth Roy, eds. 2008. *Re-Centering Culture and Knowledge in Conflict Resolution Practice*. New York: Syracuse University Press.

VeneKlasen, Lisa, and Valerie Miller. 2002. *A New Weave of Power, People & Politics: The Action Guide for Advocacy and Citizen Participation*. Oklahoma City: World Neighbors.

12

THIRD PARTIES' INVOLVEMENT IN CONTEXTS OF POLITICAL CONFLICT AND POWER IMBALANCES

Helena Desivilya Syna

Global trends and third-party involvement in intricate contexts

The current era has featured intricate human existence abound with significant challenges owing to profound changes in social, economic, political, technological, and environmental domains, exacerbated by the COVID-19 global crisis. Amidst a wide variety of transformations, the flight of refugees from warfare zones in Africa and Asia and their attempts of immigration into Europe, the political tensions within Europe, clashes in South and Central America, discords and tensions in the United States, and active political conflicts in the Middle East have all enhanced social divisions and magnified protracted intergroup conflicts (Desivilya Syna 2020; Dhanani, Beus, and Joseph 2018).

Recent decades have also presented deterioration of democratic processes in reputable Western democracies (Kashima 2019; Müller 2016). Such negative developments interfere with active participation of citizens in decision and policy making, processes deemed crucial for constructive conflict engagement (Kristeva 1991; Lederman 2019; Follett 1918).

Profound technological progress has boosted the pervasiveness of encounters among diverse social groups. However, interactions with the 'other' in workplaces, neighborhoods, and educational institutions have often stemmed from necessity rather than deliberate and free choice. Importantly, these encounters among diverse individuals and groups have often evolved in the context of political conflicts and power imbalance, such as between national majorities and national or ethnic minorities, in some cases the latter also constituting immigrants.

This chapter focuses on the intricate contexts of protracted political conflicts, exploring the queries: What is the nature of involvement of third parties in such conflicts—mediation, building consensus, intergroup facilitation, social advocacy? What mechanisms underlie third parties' actions?

The chapter title intentionally purports to third-party involvement in political and asymmetric conflicts rather than embracing the originally designated term 'intercultural mediation' by the book editor. The modification stems from both the epistemological as well as ontological orientation underlying this work on conflict engagement and diversity management in deeply divided societies, entrenched in protracted intergroup discord.

Notwithstanding vast research on mediation and consensus building in communities and organizations (Adrian and Fjell 2021; Charkoudian, Eisenberg, and Walter 2019; Wall and Kressel 2017), our grasp regarding third-party involvement in profoundly divided societies, plagued by protracted

DOI: 10.4324/9781003227441-15

asymmetric intergroup conflicts, remains limited (Desivilya Syna 2020). This chapter sheds light on this lacuna.

The chapter presents the underlying theoretical perspectives, frames and unpacks the key concepts. It provides an illustration of third-party involvement in Jewish-Arab partnership in Israel and culminates with insights regarding third parties' involvement in contexts of political conflicts.

Third party acts in the context of intergroup asymmetric political conflicts

Studying precarious contexts compelled integrating the social-psychological essentialist perspective with the critical sociological approach and embracing corresponding methodologies: Quantitative and qualitative, including program evaluation research (Desivilya Syna 2020). The research also draws on performative inquiry—emphasis on the living experiences of the 'rivals' thereby allowing not only to unravel their unique subjective perspectives but also to highlight the interface of theory and praxis (Shotter and Tsoukas 2014).

Juxtaposing and linking the essentialist perspective with the critical orientation allows gaining a deeper grasp of the paradoxical mission of coping with intergroup conflicts in contexts immersed in prolonged political conflicts.

The essentialist approach underscores universal individual and group-level limitations in processing the social world, manifested at the different modalities of human experience: Individual motivations, perceptions, emotions, behaviors, and intragroup dynamics as they unravel in the relationships between the adversary groups. These elements encompass shrinking motivation for contact, mounting intransigence of each party, biased and self-serving perceptions, growing distrust and de-legitimization of the adversary, increasingly negative affect, difficulties in communicating with the other party, and a growing tendency for violent behaviors (Bar-Tal 2011; Desivilya Syna 2020; Syna Desivilya 2004). The impediments on the individual level are accompanied by adverse phenomena on the group level such as in-group favoritism—a tendency for overly positive evaluation and support of the in-group while disparaging outgroups—mounting internal conformity and sanctioning of dissent, leading to enhanced polarization between diverse groups (Syna Desivilya 2004; Tajfel & Turner 1986).

The critical approach illuminates the contextual issues, particularly the role of dominant social institutions in shaping the imbalanced power relations between the privileged and their disadvantaged counterparts (Dhanani et al. 2018; Foucault 1994; Müller 2016; Zanoni et al. 2010). Such social construction engenders an overarching antagonistic atmosphere impeding social justice, equality, mutual respect, and legitimacy, instead fostering exclusion and separation. These destructive developments discourage building genuine partnership and collaboration between diverse groups (Maoz 2011; Syna Desivilya 2004).

Framing divided society, negotiation, and third-party intervention

Definition of the key concepts is vital to the analysis of third-party involvement and acts in everyday, real-life discords in the context of political asymmetric conflict.

Divided society denotes profound societal rifts, featuring groups with opposing, mutually exclusive, national, ethnic and cultural identities, nourished and reaffirmed by subduing rival identities. Such invidious framing of competing identities significantly undermines the odds of identifying common needs and interests by diverse groups (Hargie, Dickson, and Nelson 2003; Schaap 2006). Protracted political conflicts form an extreme instance of a divided society, manifesting several prominent characteristics: Perpetuation, obstinacy, inevitability of discords, jeopardized existential needs, and a sense that the frictions are insolvable (Bar-Tal 2011). Protracted intergroup conflicts tend to intensify, frequently bursting into aggression and violence, producing cumulative injurious multifaceted (motivational, emotional, cognitive, and behavioral) and multi-dimensional (individual, group, and overall community level) residues labeled as conflict escalation (Coleman 2004; Desivilya Syna 2020; Syna Desivilya 2004). The incremental negative legacies evolve in the context of social construction where social elites implant agendas designed to preserve power asymmetries: Maintaining the power positions of dominant groups while undermining, delegitimizing, and marginalizing other groups.

How does third-party involvement in tensions among diverse parties in the precarious contexts of political conflicts and power asymmetries evolve?

Tackling the query requires unpacking the terms 'negotiation' and 'third-party' intervention in conflict.

This work builds on pooled definitions, relying on the essentialist and the critical schools of thought as regards the terms 'negotiation' and 'third party,' yet drawing more heavily on the latter due to the strong political overtones and power-related issues embedded in divided societies, the target of this chapter.

Social psychologists define negotiation as a process designed to resolve differences by means of give-and-take or a process whereby the parties seek consensus and attempt to coordinate their perceptions and actions (Glenn and Susskind 2010; Pruitt and Carnevale 1993). Scholars of organizational behavior introduced the term 'negotiating reality,' that is the parties' joint attempts to develop mutual understanding regarding the rules underlying their relationships (Eden and Huxham 2001; Friedman and Antal 2005; Putnam 2010). Collier (2009) has embraced a similar framing of the term 'negotiation,' defining it as a process of building identities and constructing reciprocal terms of engagement.

Scholars advocating the critical perspective as regards social conflict, frame negotiation as a vital component of social activism process aiming to transform power relations, manifested by battles against institutional oppression and quest for of social justice (Hansen 2008).

Pooling together the social psychological, organizational, and critical orientation definitions, negotiation is construed as informal communication processes between the parties aimed at coordinating and synchronizing individual or group understanding concerning the principles governing their bonds, while underscoring their power relations. As portrayed earlier, collaboration between adversaries in the context of divided societies, engulfed in protracted and escalated political conflicts, tends to deteriorate, in turn impeding the odds of direct coordination of the rules of engagement. To allow daily constructive interactions in common spaces of encounters—at work, communities, and educational institutions—interventions of third parties deem vital.

Akin to the integrated definition of the term 'negotiation,' third-party intervention also reflects an attempt to pool together the essentialist and critical perspectives towards social conflict. Thus, it draws on the interest-based approach, propagated by the Alternative Dispute Resolution (ADR) scholars (Goldberg et al. 2020) and interface it with the approach embraced by proponents of transformative and narrative mediation, peace activists, and advocates of critical approaches to social conflict (Bush and Folger 2005; Collier 2009; Mayer 2004; Siira 2012; Winslade and Monk 2000).

According to the ADR approach, third-party intervention is designed to provide alternatives to power-based (contention) and rights-based (adjudication) conflict management, focusing on interest-based patterns of dispute resolution (Goldberg et al. 2020). Mediation has become the prevailing application of the interest-based third-party intervention, implemented in a variety of contexts and geographical locations, such as court-referred civil cases, communities (neighborhoods), family (notably divorce), and work organizations (Adrian and Fjell 2021; Charkoudian et al. 2019; Wall and Kressel 2017). The main principles of mediation entail voluntary participation by the parties in a process facilitated by impartial (neutral) and by and large external mediator(s). Third-party intervention aims at assisting the adversaries to attain a mutually crafted and accepted agreement that promotes their joint interests. Mediators encourage dialogic communication between the parties, attempting to foster a common definition of the problem, subsequently promote exchanging information on needs and interests and search for mutually beneficial solutions (Wall and Kressel 2017).

Recent research points at the limitations of mediation in addressing the structural aspects of the parties' relationships, reflecting power asymmetries between social groups. Thus, the mediators' efforts tend to focus on the interpersonal dimension of the adversaries' bonds, accordingly resolving the specific conflict helping them to reach mutually acceptable agreements (Adrian and Fjell 2021).

These findings resonate with Mayer's (2004) fundamental critique concerning conflict experts' practices, notably methods derived from ADR, calling for tailor-made implementation of third parties' involvement and actions in a wide range of disputes. The scholar urges developing intervention practices adapted to the nature of the conflict and its context, the parties' characteristics, and feasibility of implementation.

Consequently, Mayer challenges the concept of neutrality, questioning the capacity of third parties to maintain impartiality, as such a seemingly neutral stance may violate moral obligations, human rights, value, and identity-oriented foundations, especially when engaging with conflicts rooted in asymmetric power relations between collectives, manifested in political protracted conflicts. In the latter case, a third party can rarely act as a neutral, often resorting to advocacy of the marginalized or silenced party and employs a rights-based approach rather than interest-based mediation.

Another aspect of Mayer's critique pertains to practical elements of implementation: The necessity of prolonged involvement throughout all phases of the conflict. This may entail intervention at the early stages, attempts to prevent escalation, a preliminary decision on which parties should be involved, helping to build organized groups and establish consensual platforms, allowing to implement dialogic communication at later stages of conflict engagement.

As the author's work has revolved around contexts of asymmetric political conflict, she draws on Mayer's arguments and builds on the construal of the term negotiation portrayed earlier. Hence, third-party intervention is framed as a series of facilitation processes whereby conflict scholars' and practitioners' endeavor to embolden the parties' attempts to negotiate reality in natural spaces of encounter such as workplaces, communities, and educational institutions (Desivilya Syna 2020; Eden and Huxham 2001; Friedman and Antal 2005; Putnam 2010). This construal of third-party involvement ties it to the concept of conflict engagement considered by conflict scholars as a relationship-building process, allowing diverse protagonists to gain mutual understanding of the structure and dynamic facets of the conflict (Desivilya Syna 2020; Hansen 2008). The informal process of relationship development fosters genuine partnership built on the foundation of mutual trust (Syna Desivilya and Palgi 2012).

This conception of third-party intervention tilts towards the critical perspective to social conflict, accentuating the political and power aspects that nurture intergroup relations in precarious settings. Accordingly, third parties' acts aim to expand and improve the protagonists' conflict engagement capabilities while confronting political tensions in their daily life. Third-party acts include raising awareness of the protagonists concerning the paradoxical features of real-life intergroup encounters in active and post-conflict societies, that is, the need to cooperate with the 'enemy,' and encouraging them to acknowledge the intricacy. This goes far beyond dealing with intercultural differences; it requires introspecting and reflecting upon deeply laden legacies of protracted conflict (Desivilya Syna 2020). Third parties also explore jointly with the protagonists' ways of transforming the power relations in the direction of just, equal, and inclusive relations in natural spaces of encounter.

Fostering constructive and significant metamorphosis of relations between 'adversaries' given the profound residues of protracted political discord, warrant collaboration among all the stakeholders. Such cooperative stance allows to direct the intervention at multiple levels and modalities of human experience (Bekerman 2018; Desivilya Syna 2020; Dixon et al. 2012; Syna Desivilya 2004; Raz Rotem, Arieli, and Desivilya Syna 2021). Hence, third parties are not sole experts, but they join forces with the parties and other partners from the public, private, third and fourth sector, and the civil society at large in building sustainable partnerships.

Third parties' involvement

The underlying mechanisms of third-party involvement mentioned above lean on the principles of recognition and empowerment—the pillars of transformative mediation—on the search for shared meaning and joint narratives, which is rudimentary in narrative mediation but also on social advocacy, which is inherent in peace and social activists' work (Bush and Folger 2005; Collier 2009; Siira 2012; Winslade and Monk 2000).

Notwithstanding the emphasis on the critical perspective, third-party involvement in contexts of asymmetric political conflicts may incorporate elements of building consensus among the protagonists and the dialogic aspects of interest-based mediation, yet cannot pledge neutrality (Glenn and Susskind 2010; Mayer 2004; Wall and Kressel 2017).

Figure 12.1 summarizes the impetus (Why?), actions (What? How?), and the anticipated outcomes of third-party interventions in daily discords between diverse protagonists in natural spaces of encounter, foreshadowed by protracted and asymmetric political conflicts. The next section provides an illustration of the model's implementation.

Third-party actions in the context of Israel's asymmetric political conflict: An illustration

Israeli society comprises a national majority of Jewish immigrants and their descendants and a minority of Palestinians, who stayed in Israel after 1948, and their descendants. The Jewish majority manifests internal rifts: Religious-secular, Ashkenazi (European)-Sephardic (Asian-African), veterans-newcomers, and doves (political left)-hawks (political right). The Arab minority also includes several subcategories: Sunni Muslims, various Christian groups, Druze, and Bedouin. All of the latter minority groups grapple with inequality, but they also present internal status variance and diverse identities, periodically displayed in internal discords and open clashes.

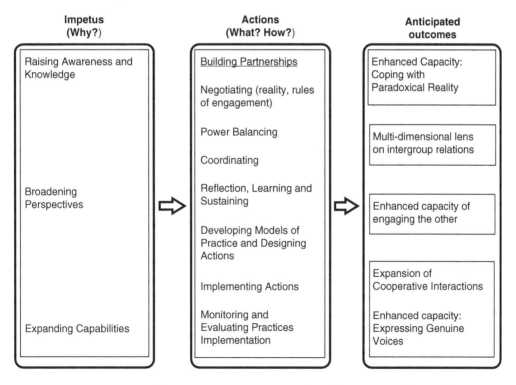

Figure 12.1 Implementation of third-party involvement in Jewish-Arab environmental partnership

Due to multiple divisions, encounters between diverse social groups and subgroups in Israeli society have periodically engendered intergroup tensions. However, the Jewish-Palestinian split has been the most pronounced as a consequence of the protracted Israeli-Palestinian asymmetric political conflict, often exacerbated by tensions with the Hamas, the Palestinian authority, and the overall complexity of regional Middle Eastern political conflicts.

The main goal of this illustration is to illuminate the need to consider the diverse needs of minority in contrast with the majority group members, while building intergroup partnerships in the context of protracted asymmetric political conflicts. The authors (Desivilya Syna and Rottman 2012) coined the term 'power asymmetry sensitivity (PAS)' in order to show that in settings of power imbalance this kind of sensitivity appears crucial at the structural and the processes facets of the partnership.

The concept and the related model of practice has developed amidst evaluation research, following a partnership project between a Jewish nation-wide environmental NGO and an Arab planning NGO in Israel. These organizations collaborated in an attempt to foster legal and planning solutions to environmental problems in Arab communities.

The authors drew on Fuller's assertion (2011) that change in power dynamics necessitates active third-party involvement. Reconciling disparities entails valuing the parties' standpoints and their diverse practices, such as the strategies embraced by each side in processing and documenting. The facilitation role of an external third party becomes significant due to awareness concerning power asymmetries, capacity to assist in surfacing hidden agendas, promoting confrontation of the hidden issues and alongside establishing the platforms allowing to engage them, consequently fostering transformation in power relations.

In the given case, the evaluation research team has evolved as the third party, practically acting at two phases: First, holding personal meetings with the leaders of the two organizations to learn about their perceptions about the partnership and subsequently conducting joint meetings in a format of focus groups, facilitating the discussion by the parties of common concern issues. In the individual meetings, the third party gained awareness concerning the controversial issues and frictions between the partners and solicited information with regard to the desired agenda items to be raised and discussed in the joint meetings. Thus, in the joint meetings, it was possible to assist the parties to voice their specific concerns and thoroughly discuss them.

The main hidden issue was budget administration, manifesting the sensitivity of power relations in the Jewish-Arab partnership and the significant role of a third party in facilitating engagement with this intricacy. It was clearly revealed in the separate meeting with the leaders of the Arab organization, pointing at their lack of involvement in financial matters seemingly due to random division of tasks between the partners. The Jewish partner assumed the responsibility for budget administration. Superficially, the role of the Jewish partner had no bearing on the dynamics of the partnership development and was actually not discussed at the initial stages of the project. As the partners have been contemplating possible expansion of the partnership, the Arab leaders voiced their reservation at the separate meetings with regard to their continued exclusion from financial management and consequently their willingness to sustain the partnership.

The leaders of both organizations discussed the latter issue at the joint meeting. The process, facilitated by the research team, aimed at coordinating and integrating the needs and concerns of both partners and developing knowledge synergistically as befit building trust-based rather than power-based partnership (Syna Desivilya and Palgi 2012).

Aside to the crucial role of the third party in surfacing the latent issues, the case also highlights the importance of PAS concept to the characteristics of a third party, notably its composition. The involvement of a minority member facilitator appeared crucial in dispelling the false harmony within the minority-majority partnership (Syna Desivilya and Palgi 2012). Such a deceptive atmosphere has evolved as a result of the majority partner recurring patronizing attempts to 'compensate' the minority counterpart for its inferior standing.

Accordingly, the separate meetings with the Jewish partner were facilitated by the two Jewish researchers, whereas third-party composition in the separate meetings with the Arab partner included the Jewish researchers and an Arab facilitator. The Arab facilitator was highly active in the joint meetings, steering the discussion on issues related to the potential expansion of the project, such as developing a proposal, especially its financial components. He deliberately pushed this hidden issue from behind the curtain to the front stage, encouraging direct engagement of the partners with their differences, hitherto evaded by both parties. Presumably, avoidance of a confrontation with the controversial issues by the partners stemmed from power imbalance, consequently a tendency to adopt accommodation tactics in order to preserve harmony.

The active stance of the Arab facilitator has altered the process of negotiating the rules of engagement by the partners, allowing both parties to voice their concerns vis-à-vis the other (Desivilya Syna 2020).

In sum, the specific case highlights the essence of third parties' involvement in daily tensions between parties at work, embedded in the context of protracted political and asymmetric conflict. It demonstrates the main elements of the model presented in Figure 12.1:

- Sensitivity and raising awareness concerning both the explicit and the implicit facets of power relations between the minority and majority parties.
- Direct engagement with controversial issues by means of negotiating reality and rules of engagement and moving conflicts from the hidden into the visible sphere. The latter aspect is deemed vitally important due to the dominant proclivity to maintain ambiguity as a means of preserving harmony between the parties.
- Joint planning of coordination forums and sustaining of parties' relations through ongoing reflection and learning with regard to the partnership's processes and structure.
- The need to involve a third party, representing both majority and minority parties as a means to foster and maintain genuine partnership.

The case clearly demonstrated that implementation of third-party involvement in contexts foreshadowed by asymmetric political conflict is highly challenging even in partnerships evincing at least at the face value cooperative relationships between the minority and majority partners.

Conclusions: Insights and further queries

Implementing third-party intervention in precarious settings of protracted political conflicts and power imbalance evince marked challenges, particularly in building genuine partnerships based on trust and engaging with the intricate role and complex, multiple identities of the third party—as entrepreneur (project initiator), leader, facilitator, and social advocate (Desivilya Syna 2020). Another difficulty entails challenging the mainstream, as manifested in the complicated negotiation with formal authorities, while trying to mobilize their support for the projects (Kristeva 1991; Siira 2012).

An active third-party role is vital in uncovering the parties' implicit difficulties in dealing with the 'enemy' in organizations engulfed by deeply ingrained intergroup rifts, especially the residues of protracted and asymmetric political conflicts. Such activities of third parties include raising awareness regarding the manifestations of exclusion, marginalization, silencing, delegitimization, and explicit discrimination. Third-party involvement also comprises developing a critical consciousness and learning how to negotiate the terms of engagement—negotiating power-relations (Desivilya Syna and Rottman 2012; Eden and Huxham 2001; Foucault 1994; Hansen 2008).

The challenge of third parties in natural spaces of encounter revolves around counteracting the dominant proclivity of scholars and practitioners in the fields of social conflict to craft clear-cut solutions, namely, resolving conflicts rather than helping the protagonists to express their distinct voices and expand their capabilities to engage with the multifaceted and often paradoxical aspects underlying their relationships.

Third parties' involvement, aimed at broadening and deepening joint spaces for encounters among diverse parties, which are founded on dignity, respect, equality, and inclusion, despite protracted political tensions and power imbalance, requires courageous, innovative, and vanguard orientations, reaching far beyond intercultural mediation. The author and associates have attempted to follow this kind of approach. Yet, they are still grappling with the intricacies and queries, such as longitudinal follow-up of the joint encounters in real-life settings and deciphering the long-term gains of third parties' involvement. Are their efforts fruitful in enhancing the protagonists' capacities to engage the paradoxical reality, developing multifocal lens on intergroup relations, expanding their capabilities to collaborate with the adversary despite of the macro-level impediments and foster the capacity of the parties to express genuine voices? We shall continue collaborating with the protagonists and stakeholders, jointly conducting future research at natural spaces of encounter to shed light on these hitherto ambiguous issues.

References

Adrian, Lin, and Solfrid Mykland Fjell. 2021. "Coexisting When Living next Door: The Agreements Neighbors Make in Mediation." *Conflict Resolution Quarterly* 38 (3): 157–74. 10.1002/crq.21297

Bar-Tal, Daniel, ed. 2011. *Intergroup Conflicts and Their Resolution*. New York: Psychology Press. 10.4324/9780203834091

Bekerman, Zvi. 2018. "Working towards Peace through Education: The Case of Israeli Jews and Palestinians." *Asian Journal of Peacebuilding* 6 (1): 75–98. 10.18588/201805.00a046

Bush, Robert A. Baruch, and Joseph P. Folger. 2005. *The Promise of Mediation: The Transformative Approach to Conflict*. Rev. ed. San Francisco: Jossey-Bass.

Charkoudian, Lorig, Deborah T. Eisenberg, and Jamie L. Walter. 2019. "What Works in Alternative Dispute Resolution? The Impact of Third-party Neutral Strategies in Small Claims Cases." *Conflict Resolution Quarterly* 37 (2): 101–21. 10.1002/crq.21264

Coleman, Peter T. 2004. "Paradigmatic Framing of Protracted, Intractable Conflict: Toward the Development of a Meta-Framework-II." *Peace and Conflict: Journal of Peace Psychology* 10 (3): 197–235. 10.1207/s153279 49pac1003_1

Collier, Mary Jane. 2009. "Negotiating Intercommunity and Community Group Identity Positions: Summary Discourses from Two Northern Ireland Intercommunity Groups." *Negotiation and Conflict Management Research* 2 (3): 285–306. 10.1111/j.1750-4716.2009.00041.x

Desivilya Syna, Helena. 2020. *Diversity Management in Places and Times of Tensions: Engaging Inter-Group Relations in a Conflict-Ridden Society*. Cham: Springer International. 10.1007/978-3-030-37723-6

Desivilya Syna, Helena, and Amit Rottman. 2012. "Role of Power Asymmetry Sensitivity in Jewish-Arab Partnerships." *Conflict Resolution Quarterly* 30 (2): 219–41. 10.1002/crq.21058

Dhanani, Lindsay Y., Jeremy M. Beus, and Dana L. Joseph. 2018. "Workplace Discrimination: A Meta-Analytic Extension, Critique, and Future Research Agenda." *Personnel Psychology* 71 (2): 147–79. 10.1111/peps.12254

Dixon, John, Mark Levine, Steve Reicher, and Kevin Durrheim. 2012. "Beyond Prejudice: Relational Inequality, Collective Action, and Social Change Revisited." *Behavioral and Brain Sciences* 35 (6): 451–66. 10.1017/S0140525X12001550

Eden, Colin, and Chris Huxham. 2001. "The Negotiation of Purpose in Multi-Organizational Collaborative Groups." *Journal of Management Studies* 38 (3): 373–91. 10.1111/1467-6486.00241

Follett, Mary Parker. 1918. *The New State-Group Organization, the Solution of Popular Government*. New York: Longmans, Green and Co.

Foucault, Michel. 1994. *The Order of Things: An Archaeology of Human Sciences*. New York: Penguin Random House.

Friedman, Victor J., and Ariane Berthoin Antal. 2005. "Negotiating Reality: A Theory of Action Approach to Intercultural Competence." *Management Learning* 36 (1): 69–86. 10.1177/1350507605049904

Fuller, Boyd. 2011. "Power, Adaptive Preferences, and Negotiation: Process Specifics Matters." *Planning Theory & Practice* 12 (3): 455–61. 10.1080/14649357.2011.617502

Glenn, Phillip, and Lawrence Susskind. 2010. "How Talk Works: Studying Negotiation Interaction." *Negotiation Journal* 26 (2): 117–23. 10.1111/j.1571-9979.2010.00260.x

Third parties' involvement

Goldberg, Stephen B., Frank E. A. Sander, Nancy H. Rogers, and Sarah R. Cole. 2020. *Dispute Resolution: Negotiation, Mediation, Arbitration, and Other Processes*. Seventh edition. New York: Wolters Kluwer.

Hansen, Toran. 2008. "Critical Conflict Resolution Theory and Practice." *Conflict Resolution Quarterly* 25 (4): 403–27. 10.1002/crq.215

Hargie, Owen, David Dickson, and Seanenne Nelson. 2003. "Working Together in a Divided Society: A Study of Intergroup Communication in the Northern Ireland Workplace." *Journal of Business and Technical Communication* 17 (3): 285–318. 10.1177/1050651903017003002

Kashima, Yoshihisa. 2019. "Neoliberalism and Its Discontents: Commentary on Social Psychology of Neoliberalism." *Journal of Social Issues* 75 (1): 350–55. 10.1111/josi.12314

Kristeva, Julia. 1991. *Strangers to Ourselves?* New York: Columbia University Press.

Lederman, Shmuel. 2019. *Hannah Arendt and Participatory Democracy: A People's Utopia*. Cham: Springer International. 10.1007/978-3-030-11692-7

Maoz, Ifat. 2011. "Does Contact Work in Protracted Asymmetrical Conflict? Appraising 20 Years of Reconciliation-Aimed Encounters between Israeli Jews and Palestinians." *Journal of Peace Research* 48 (1): 115–25. 10.1177/0022343310389506

Mayer, Bernard S. 2004. *Beyond Neutrality: Confronting the Crisis in Conflict Resolution*. San Francisco, CA: Jossey-Bass.

Müller, Jan-Werner. 2016. *What Is Populism?* Philadelphia: University of Pennsylvania Press.

Pruitt, Dean G., and Peter J. Carnevale. 1993. *Negotiation in Social Conflict*. Pacific Grove, CA: Brooks/Cole.

Putnam, Linda L. 2010. "Negotiation and Discourse Analysis." *Negotiation Journal* 26 (2): 145–54. 10.1111/j.1571-9979.2010.00262.x

Raz Rotem, Michal, Daniella Arieli, and Helena Desivilya Syna. 2021. "Engaging Complex Diversity in Academic Institution: The Case of 'Triple Periphery' in a Context of a Divided Society." *Conflict Resolution Quarterly* 38 (4): 303–21. 10.1002/crq.21305

Schaap, Andrew. 2006. "Agonism in Divided Societies." *Philosophy & Social Criticism* 32 (2): 255–77. 10.1177/0191453706061095

Shotter, John, and Haridimos Tsoukas. 2014. "Performing Phronesis: On the Way to Engaged Judgment." *Management Learning* 45 (4): 377–96. 10.1177/1350507614541196

Siira, Kalle. 2012. "Conceptualizing Managerial Influence in Organizational Conflict-A Qualitative Examination: Conflict Influence." *Negotiation and Conflict Management Research* 5 (2): 182–209. 10.1111/j.1750-4716.2012.00096.x

Syna Desivilya, Helena. 2004. "Promoting Coexistence by Means of Conflict Education: The MACBE Model." *Journal of Social Issues* 60 (2): 339–55. 10.1111/j.0022-4537.2004.00115.x

Syna Desivilya, Helena, and Michal Palgi. 2012. "Building Academics-Practitioners Partnership as Means for Generating Usable Knowledge." In *The Paradox In Partnership: The Role of Conflict in Partnership Building*, edited by Helena Syna Desivilya and Michal Palgi, 64–78. Sharjah: Bentham Science. 10.2174/97816080521101110101010064

Tajfel, Henri, and John C. Turner. 1986. "The Social Identity Theory of Intergroup Behavior." In *Psychology of Intergroup Relations*, edited by William G. Austin and Stephen Worchel, 2nd edition, 7–24. Chicago: Nelson-Hall.

Wall, James A., and Kenneth Kressel. 2017. "Mediator Thinking in Civil Cases: Mediator." *Conflict Resolution Quarterly* 34 (3): 331–67. 10.1002/crq.21185

Winslade, John, and Gerald Monk. 2000. *Narrative Mediation. A New Approach to Conflict Resolution*. San Francisco: Jossey-Bass.

Zanoni, Patrizia, Maddy Janssens, Yvonne Benschop, and Stella Nkomo. 2010. "Guest Editorial: Unpacking Diversity, Grasping Inequality: Rethinking Difference Through Critical Perspectives." *Organization* 17 (1): 9–29. 10.1177/1350508409350344

13

SEEING PEOPLE IN INTERACTIVE PEACEMAKING THROUGH A CONSCIOUSNESS LENS

Susan H. Allen

Introduction to interactive peacemaking

Interactive peacemaking (Allen 2022) refers to the peacemaking part of the larger set of interactive conflict resolution approaches. Interactive conflict resolution (Fisher 1997; 2005; 2016) includes Burton's controlled communication or Analytic Problem Solving (Mitchell and Banks 1996); Doob's Human Relations Workshops (Doob and Foltz 1973); Kelman's Interactive Problem Solving (Kelman 2000); Volkan's psychodynamic approach (Volkan 1994); Hal Saunders' Sustained Dialogue (Saunders 2003); and other related approaches. These approaches share in common the interaction of people in facilitated processes designed to support constructive engagement contributing to conflict resolution.

Interactive conflict resolution can be active in the early stages of conflict before a war seems likely, where efforts focus on addressing polarization and divergent interests and needs. Interactive conflict resolution during conflict escalation can be aimed at addressing the underlying issues in conflict in order to prevent the outbreak of violence. Interactive conflict resolution during periods of violence will seek both to consider the underlying issues and also ways to end the violence. Interactive conflict resolution after violence may focus on addressing issues that will allow avoidance of further violence or may focus on longer term reconciliation. The interactive peacemaking approach emphasizes the phase of conflict just before, during, or after war, and focuses on preventing or ending war.

Galtung identified "Three Approaches to Peace: Peacekeeping, Peacemaking, and Peacebuilding" (Galtung 1976) and then-UN Secretary General Boutros Boutros-Ghali identified three other approaches, Preventive Diplomacy, Peacemaking, and Peacekeeping (Gali 1992). In Galtung's conception of peacekeeping, the parties are kept away from each other by a physical force that separates them and that threatens retaliatory action if either party encroaches on the other. Peacemaking focuses on addressing the sources of the tensions between the parties. And peacebuilding focuses on building structures conducive to long term peace. In Ghali's conception, preventive diplomacy focuses on stopping escalation or spread of conflict. Peacemaking focuses on bringing parties to agreement. And peacekeeping (in Ghali's context) is the deployment of UN Peacekeeping troops. Both of these understandings of peacemaking focus on addressing areas of disagreement and building agreement.

Thus, interactive peacemaking refers to peace efforts that involve the interaction of people aimed at addressing tensions or disagreements to build agreement and avoid or stop war. Mediation and peacemaking are intertwined, as some mediation is peacemaking, aimed at stopping or preventing war. Much mediation is interactive peacemaking, when the mediation involves interaction of the

128   DOI: 10.4324/9781003227441-16

parties to a conflict that may escalate to war or has already done so. Some mediation is conducted with very limited interaction such as through shuttle diplomacy; such efforts are not particularly 'interactive.' The focus here with interactive peacemaking is on the direct interaction of parties in a conflict in facilitated processes aiming at addressing issues in conflict so that war is stopped or avoided or does not recur.

Having defined the term 'interactive peacemaking' and contextualized it with the concepts of mediation and interactive conflict resolution, we now turn to considering the theory and practice of interactive peacemaking, with an emphasis on intercultural and consciousness dynamics. We look at the approach that develops when we refocus to see people as central in peacemaking. Next, we turn to considering how we learn and further develop the theory and practice of peacemaking. This leads us to some elemental rules for research and practice in interactive peacemaking. With people at the center, we turn to consciousness dynamics in interactive peacemaking. Finally, we consider some areas for further development of approaches to interactive peacemaking, such as ways of supporting those involved in making peace with offering useful knowledge of other cases and other peace process dynamics.

A people-centered approach

Interactive peacemaking is a people-centered approach (Allen 2022) in that it engages people directly in interactions aimed at peacemaking, and it focuses on addressing conflict issues and building towards agreement, including on issues that directly affect people living in the conflict context. By addressing needs such as access to healthcare, food, livelihoods, education, etc., interactive peacemaking addresses people's needs, not only political status issues. Working on such issues can improve the lives of conflict-affected populations and also build trust and working relationships to allow the parties to gradually take on more and more sensitive issues. For example, access to health care may be considered a universal human right and can sometimes be addressed without taking on political status or other more controversial issues. When parties cooperate through interactive peacemaking to improve access to health care, for example, they learn to work together to address issues. This practice paves the way for working on more complex topics.

Fisher (2005) documents such "paving the way" in his book of that title: *Paving the Way: Contributions of Interactive Conflict Resolution to Peacemaking*. The nine cases examined present variations on a theme: Interactive peacemaking processes contribute to overall peace. Facilitated interactions amongst influential people from conflict areas lead to improved understanding, improved relationships, innovations in the official peace process, and related 'transfer effects' from unofficial to official peacemaking. These processes are particularly useful as pre-negotiation processes or in parallel with ongoing negotiations; the unofficial processes serve to generate and assess ideas that then feed into the official negotiations after unofficial consideration.

The global context of conflicts changes, and the practice of interactive peacemaking continues to evolve. The field gives rise to emergent practices (d'Estrée and Parsons 2018). Thus, the best practices in interactive peacemaking are therefor also evolving (Allen 2020). While early innovators of interactive peacemaking emphasized impartial outsiders as key facilitators (Mitchell and Banks 1996), practice often includes local insider-partial (Lederach 1997) peacemakers, too. Insider-partials bring significant strengths to their peacemaking. These strengths include local knowledge including cultural and linguistic fluency and deep contacts; life-long commitment to the region; abilities to convey ideas from the interactive process to the political leadership; and of course, local peacemakers engaged in long-term peacemaking develop their own facilitation skills and their own reputations as trustworthy peacemakers in their community and beyond (Allen 2022, 87). The cultural fluency of local peacemakers is a highly significant strength. Outsiders can miss so much, even after decades working in one culture.

Learning and knowledge in people-centered engagement

We peacemakers learn these emergent practices, note the evolving practices, and share our insights through reflective practice and related ways of knowing. The knowledge central to such people-centered engagement is known as *phronesis* (Aristotle 2011), a practical knowledge gained through experience. Reflective practice emphasizes learning *with* more than learning *about* or doing research *with* rather than doing research *on*. In addition to learning about these people-centered approaches as outside analysts, we learn significantly by learning with people together in these people-centered processes. Reflective practice (Argyris and Schon 1974) allows peacemakers, both locally and globally based, to learn through their experience. Inspired by Freire's *Pedagogy of the Oppressed*, peacemakers work together to innovate, figuring out constructive approaches for their own contexts, learning by doing, and also learning from other contexts, too. As practices develop, theory in this field does, too.

There is something in common across so many conflicts globally: People living in conflict know their own conflict is unique. And, amongst all these unique conflicts, peacemakers can find it helpful to consider what worked in one conflict and ask if that approach, or a locally meaningful variation, might be helpful in the conflict they are now working on. People working locally in their own conflicts can be hungry for stories of what has worked elsewhere and can appreciate questions that emerge from other contexts. Such forms of knowledge respect the local culture and the agency of local peacemakers to craft their own peace processes.

Interactive peacemaking practice builds knowledge, or practice builds theory (Allen 2022, 18) both through induction from experience and also through deduction, drawing on theories. Woven together, these complementary approaches form an abduction (Peirce 2010, 45) approach. Lehti describes this knowledge creation amongst mediators:

> the abduction is the phenomenon-centric approach based on the hermeneutic circle in which collected empirical observations complement but also revisit the original conceptualization of a particular phenomenon, which in this particular case is peace mediation.
>
> *(Lehti 2019, 8)*

This hybrid approach to knowledge, combining both the case specific and the generalizable, both the induction and deduction, and both the practice and theory, resonates with the hybrid approach to peacemaking: Engaging both the local and the global, both general Western models and specific local approaches. Hybridity has emerged in the conflict resolution field after (first) a period in which much attention was focused on dominant Western models, then (second) a period of simplifying cultural differences to consider several characteristics of conflict resolution cultures, then (third) a pivot of focus on indigenous approaches to conflict resolution, and finally (fourth) a hybrid intermingling of Western and local approaches (d'Estrée and Parsons 2018, 10–7).

The conflict resolution field has experienced a turn to the local (Mac Ginty and Richmond 2013), and now is in a fourth wave of conflict resolution practice that blends together local and global strengths meaningfully (Avruch 2018; d'Estrée and Parsons 2018). In this context of interactive peacemaking, culture matters, local agency matters, and also external models matter, too. Our conflicts and their resolution are complexly shaped by multiple factors.

With the turn towards complexity-informed approaches to peace and conflicts, the field has come to embrace: Both the connectedness of local and global conflicts, and of local and global peacemaking; both the agency of an individual actor potentially making a difference in a complex system and the forces of systems maintenance that tend towards ongoing conflict dynamics; and both the uncertainties that are inherent in predicting complex conflict dynamics, and also the roles observers play in affecting conflict dynamics. As a field, conflict resolvers are learning to see the 'both and' in approaching conflicts. Both local and global matter. Both individual actions and also social-political-economic forces matter. And observation is both useful and at the same time not able to predict linear change. Conflict dynamics do not predictably shift through simple causation, but rather change non-linearly, multiple shifts contribute to change.

Learning from peacemaking experience has shifted the theories informing our approaches to peacemaking towards people-centered, hybridity, and complexity. With that, we have developed new understandings of terminology in the field. Once, we saw track one diplomacy, the official diplomacy between states. Then, we began to recognize in practice a phenomenon that came to be labeled track two diplomacy, the unofficial engagement by unofficial people bridging conflict divides (Montville 1987; 1991). Soon, we saw also multi-track diplomacy, including bridging roles played by unofficial people in business, journalism, education, religion, the arts, and more (Diamond 1991). And, continuing to learn from practice, we recognized that sometimes unofficial processes involved official people, blending track one and track two into track one and a half (Nan 1999; 2004; 2005; Nan, Druckman, and Horr 2009). As the practice of peacemaking has developed over time, the theory has, too, as it describes and explains the evolving practices.

In teaching research methods to doctoral students in conflict resolution at the Carter School for Peace and Conflict Resolution at George Mason University recently, I recalled a book from my coming-of-age time in the 1980s entitled *Everything I Really Need to Know, I Learned in Kindergarten* (Fulghum 2004). The first essay, which gave the book its title, made the point that we can find life guidance in the elemental lessons we share with young children as these resonate throughout all stages of life. These lessons include:

> Share everything. Play fair. Don't hit people. Put things back where you found them. Clean up your own mess. Don't take things that aren't yours. Say you're sorry when you hurt somebody. Wash your hands before you eat … .
>
> *(Fulghum 2004, 2)*

Recalling the model of that essay, I proposed to the class that, in some sense, 'Everything I really need to know about research, I learned through practice.' In other words, conflict resolution practice has much to teach conflict resolution researchers.

Rules of peacemaking practice that apply also to conflict resolution research include:

- Listen. Listen carefully. Listen deeply. Listen with openness to really hear.
- Learn. Be open to learning new knowledge and new perspectives.
- Be aware of your own positionality.
- Be clear about your roles.
- Be aware of power dynamics.
- Be aware of culture and context.
- Be aware of process.
- Ask how you can partner supportively. Ask the people most involved how you can help.
- Reflect.
- Learn from experience.
- Adapt.
- Respect incremental development as well as radical transformation.
- Do no harm.
- Be ethical.
- Be collaborative. Engage a broader network where appropriate.
- Treat people as human beings with agency.
- Let go of control.
- Do what is possible.

- See your engagement as only a contribution.
- Balance 'both … and.' Consider both the specific and the general, the individual and the group, the local and the global, the short and the long term.

Most of these suggestions should be self-explanatory, as the kindergarten lessons were. But perhaps several call for further clarifications, beyond the short form listed. For example, why respect incremental development as well as radical transformation? In practice, peacemaking engages both gradual trust building, working step by step on low-hanging fruit, and incrementally building towards potential radical shifts such as comprehensive peace settlements. In research, there are insights built by chipping away at the gaps in our knowledge, gradually building insights from studies that take on one slightly new perspective and then another. These can add up to a knowledge that eventually leads to a radical paradigm shift (Kuhn 1970).

It also may not be immediately obvious why both practitioners and researchers would need to be collaborative and work in concert with larger networks. For practitioners, collaboration increases coordination and complementarity in peace processes that are inherently complex with multiple actors contributing to shifting peace dynamics. If an individual were to attempt to help in a peace process without any awareness of all the other parts of the peace process, that person's actions might be counterproductive, setting up forum-shopping amongst parties that might derail a productive process. The reality of today's peace processes is that no one person can claim credit for making peace. It takes two at least to make a conflict, and more than that to make peace. So many people have to choose peace for peace to emerge and be lasting in contexts where conflict has broken out. All of those people deserve credit for the choices they make. Similarly, for researchers, any research into peacemaking is built on many other related inquiries that have laid the groundwork for new research. Acknowledging this history places current research in context, making its meaning clear. Just as in practice, it would be nonsensical to present any conflict resolution research as entirely original with no connection to research and practice that has come before.

And why treat people as human beings with agency? Why let go of control? Practitioners in peacemaking may invite people to come to dialogues or other interactive spaces, and they may ask people to engage constructively. But peacemaking is a voluntary activity. No one can be compelled to participate, nor to do so constructively. The facilitator can shape the process but cannot control the choices people make during or after a discussion. Similarly, in research, the researcher can shape the research process, framing questions precisely to elicit helpful knowledge, but the researcher cannot control what they will find. The research results are to be determined. In meaningful research, the outcomes are not known ahead of time. People are in some ways unpredictable.

Much of the development in learning, research, and theory-building related to peacemaking in the recent decades can be linked directly to practice and practice-based insights. In the conflict resolution sphere, the means of research and the means of practice are connected. Research is a form of conflict resolution practice, as observations impact the observed, and as scholars impact conflict narratives and options considered by conflict parties.

Consciousness in intercultural interactive peacemaking

As long as conflicts have divided different cultural groups, peacemaking has been practiced interculturally, and much of this peacemaking has been highly interactive.

In previous work, I identified five ways considering consciousness helps us understand intercultural conflict resolution:

1. Increasing awareness allows greater freedom to act constructively in conflict and conflict resolution. 2. Much conflict resolution practice can be seen as supporting shifts in

Interactive peacemaking

consciousness. 3. Transitional space allows shifts in consciousness supportive of constructive engagement in conflict and conflict resolution. 4. Embodied engagement can support individual shifts. 5. Improve conflict resolution practice to better support shifts in consciousness.

(Nan 2011)

These insights can be considered also specifically in relation to intercultural interactive peacemaking as a particular approach within the broader conflict resolution field. We consider each in turn, adapted for specific relevance to intercultural interactive peacemaking, below.

First, *increasing awareness* supports increasing opportunities for constructive engagement in intercultural interactive peacemaking. In interactive peacemaking processes, participants learn about each other's perspectives and see their own perspectives in new light. They may realize what is most important to them and realize areas where they can be more flexible. All of this increased awareness gives people more choices. They can choose with awareness that allows them to see their own actions in a clearer context.

Second, significant intercultural interactive peacemaking approaches support *shifts in consciousness*. Significant breakthroughs in peacemaking happen when the people involved change how they think. For example, rather than simply gaining new knowledge, they may see themselves and the conflict in a new way.

Third, intercultural interactive peacemaking may engage *transitional space* in support of shifts in consciousness. When two cultural groups come together in an interactive peacemaking context, they may create a third culture as a sort of transitional space that opens up the possibility of letting go of the future they were set on and allowing envisioning of a new future.

Fourth, intercultural interactive peacemaking may be strengthened through *embodied engagement*. Embodied ways of knowing can offer people a literally solid sense of self that allows openness to new knowledge, new perspectives, and new insight. Breaking bread together is a time-honored way of coming together with the body involved. Even a coffee break with pastries can serve those purposes of bringing people together with their full bodies, stomachs included. By getting out of our heads, at least to bring awareness of our stomachs, we bring more of our whole selves into peacemaking. Our hearts and souls must be part of holistic peacemaking.

And fifth, we can *innovate* intercultural interactive peacemaking to better support shifts in consciousness. Practice continues to evolve as conflicts change. Faced with the pandemic and travel restrictions, many peacemaking efforts moved online. Such innovations can be structured in ways that consider how to further promote shifts in consciousness. For example, I have scheduled Zoom sessions amongst parties in a conflict context that do not focus on a substantive conversation, but rather allow some sharing of personal stories and catching up as old friends. That rehumanizing relational engagement seems to help participants be creative about what new possibilities may emerge.

In addition to these insights, drawn from reflective practice of conflict resolution more broadly as well as specific intercultural interactive peacemaking experience, we can also consider insights on peacemaking that emerge from taking a people-centered approach to peacemaking practice.

People-centered approach: Towards further evolution of intercultural interactive peacemaking

Putting people at the center of both peacemaking practice and peacemaking research opens up questions that require further exploration as we develop both theory and practice further. With people primary, we maintain awareness of institutions, and social and economic and political forces, but we also acknowledge the individual choices that people make that contribute to war and peace. With this focus, we can ask, what can we do to support people in making constructive choices that support peace?

One area of rapid development recently has been the availability of open access or otherwise accessible evidence that can inform current peace practice. For example, at George Mason University, the Better Evidence Project offers a curated set of research, case studies, and other resources that offer guidance to those facing current challenges in peacemaking. The long-standing Peace Agreements Database at the University of Edinburgh offers the texts of all known peace agreements from 1990 to June 2021. The United Nations Peacemaker site offers general and also tailored guidance on mediation. And the Beyond Intractability database offers various articles, interviews, and other forms of knowledge related to conflict resolution in an open access format. Such efforts are based upon the idea that knowledge, such as access to previous case studies or access to previous peace agreements, can support people who are facing peacemaking challenges today. To improve upon the usefulness of this growing body of online information, we must learn what kinds of guidance is most useful and how it can be most expeditiously accessed. This would be one area for further development as we continue innovating in support of people-centered peacemaking practice.

References

Allen, Susan H. 2020. "Evolving Best Practices: Engaging the Strengths of Both External and Local Peacebuilders in Track Two Dialogues through Local Ownership." *International Negotiation* 26 (1): 67–84. 10.1163/15718069-BJA10006

Allen, Susan H. 2022. *Interactive Peacemaking: A People-Centered Approach*. London: Routledge. 10.4324/9781 003189008

Argyris, Chris, and Donald Schon. 1974. *Theory in Practice: Increasing Professional Effectiveness*. San Francisco: Jossey Bass.

Aristotle. 2011. *Aristotle's Nicomachean Ethics*. Chicago: University of Chicago Press.

Avruch, Kevin. 2018. "Towards the Fourth Wave of Conflict Resolution Practice." In *Cultural Encounters and Emergent Practice in Conflict Resolution Capacity-Building*, edited by Tamra Pearson d'Estree and Ruth J. Parsons, 387–401. London, England: Palgrave Macmillan.

Diamond, Louise. 1991. *Multi-Track Diplomacy: A Systems Guide and Analysis*. Grinnell, IA: Iowa Peace Institute.

Doob, Leonard W., and William J. Foltz. 1973. "The Belfast Workshop: An Application of Group Techniques To a Destructive Conflict." *Journal of Conflict Resolution* 17 (3): 489–512. 10.1177/002200277301700305

Estrée, Tamra Pearson d', and Ruth J. Parsons. 2018. *Cultural Encounters and Emergent Practices in Conflict Resolution Capacity-Building. Rethinking Peace and Conflict Studies*. Cham: Palgrave Macmillan. 10.1007/ 978-3-319-71102-7

Fisher, Ronald J. 1997. *Interactive Conflict Resolution*. Syracuse, NY: Syracuse University Press.

Fisher, Ronald J., ed. 2005. *Contributions of Interactive Conflict Resolution to Peacemaking*. Lanham, MD: Lexington Books.

Fisher, Ronald J. 2016. *Ronald J. Fisher: A North American Pioneer in Interactive Conflict Resolution*. Cham: Springer. 10.1007/978-3-319-39038-3

Fulghum, Robert. 2004. *All I Really Need to Know I Learned in Kindergarten: Uncommon Thoughts on Common Things*. 15th Anniversary edition. Ballantine Books.

Gali, Boutros Boutros. 1992. "An Agenda for Peace: Preventive Diplomacy, Peacemaking, and Peace-Keeping." United Nations. https://www.un.org/ruleoflaw/files/A_47_277.pdf

Galtung, Johan. 1976. "Three Approaches to Peace: Peacekeeping, Peacemaking, and Peacebuilding." *Impact of Science on Society* 1 (2): 282–304.

Kelman, Herbert C. 2000. "The Role of the Scholar-Practitioner in International Conflict Resolution." *International Studies Perspectives* 1 (3): 273. 10.1111/1528-3577.00027

Kuhn, Thomas S. 1970. *The Structure of Scientific Revolutions*. 2nd edition. Chicago: University of Chicago Press.

Lederach, John Paul. 1997. *Building Peace: Sustainable Reconciliation in Divided Societies*. Washington, D.C.: United States Institute of Peace Press.

Lehti, Marko. 2019. *The Era of Private Peacemakers: A New Dialogic Approach to Mediation. Rethinking Peace and Conflict Studies*. Cham, Switzerland: Palgrave Macmillan. 10.1007/978-3-319-91201-1

Mac Ginty, Roger, and Oliver P. Richmond. 2013. "The Local Turn in Peace Building: A Critical Agenda for Peace." *Third World Quarterly* 34 (5): 763–83. 10.1080/01436597.2013.800750

Mitchell, Christopher, and Michael Banks. 1996. *Handbook of Conflict Resolution: The Analytical Problem Solving Approach*. New York: Pinter.

Montville, Joseph. 1987. "The Arrow and the Oliver Branch: The Case for Track Two Diplomacy." In *Conflict Resolution: Track Two Diplomacy*, edited by John McDonald and Diane B. Bendahman, 5–20. Washington, D.C.: Foreign Service Institute, State Department.

Montville, Joseph. 1991. "Transnationalism and the Role of Track Two Diplomacy." In *Approaches to Peace: An Intellectual Map*, edited by Scott Thompson and Kenneth Jensen, 254–69. Washington, D.C.: United States Institute of Peace Press.

Nan, Susan Allen. 1999. "Complementarity and Coordination of Conflict Resolution Efforts in the Conflicts over Abkhazia, South Ossetia, and Transdniestria." Fairfax, Virginia: George Mason University.

Nan, Susan Allen. 2004. "Track One and a Half Diplomacy: Searching for Political Agreement in the Caucasus." In *NGOs at the Table: Strategies for Influencing Policies in Areas of Conflict*, edited by Mari Fitzduff and Cheyanne Church, 57–75. Lanham, MD: Rowman & Littlefield.

Nan, Susan Allen. 2005. "Track One-and-a-Half Diplomacy: Contributions to Georgian-South Ossetian Peacemaking." In *Paving the Way: Contributions of Interactive Conflict Resolution in Peacemaking*, 161–73. Lanham, MD: Lexington Books.

Nan, Susan Allen. 2011. "Consciousness in Culture-based Conflict and Conflict Resolution." *Conflict Resolution Quarterly* 28 (3): 239–62. 10.1002/crq.20022

Nan, Susan Allen, Daniel Druckman, and Jana El Horr. 2009. "Unofficial International Conflict Resolution: Is There a Track 1½? Are There Best Practices?" *Conflict Resolution Quarterly* 27 (1): 65–82. 10.1002/crq.248

Peirce, Charles S. 2010. *Philosophy of Mathematics: Selected Writings*, edited by Matthew Moore. Bloomington: Indiana University Press.

Saunders, Harold H. 2003. "Sustained Dialogue in Managing Intractable Conflict." *Negotiation Journal* 19 (1): 85–95. 10.1111/j.1571-9979.2003.tb00282.x

Volkan, Vamik. 1994. Psycho-dynamic approaches to conflict resolution Interview by Susan Allen.

14

THE PAST IS THE PAST—OR IS IT? CONSIDERING THE ROLE OF THE PAST IN INTERCULTURAL MEDIATION

Barbara Tint, Minji Cho, and Martha Doyle

Introduction

The Mediterranean air blew gently by as I sat on the Tel Aviv balcony of my colleague, an Israeli peace educator who had devoted his life to using his academic and civil society platforms to address the narratives and structures informing the Israeli/Palestinian conflict. The year was 2000 and I was conducting research on collective memory and conflict resolution (Tint 2010a, 2010b). I wanted to understand more about how our understanding and integration of the past impacted our perception of current conflicts and, ultimately, our ability—and will—to resolve them. It was two months before what would become known as the second Intifada that was about to break out in the region, as the cycles of conflict and violence were reaching a crescendo. We felt the tensions, knowing they could either be dissipated or inflamed by the current attempts to resolve the conflict. We pondered so many questions: How could these societies move forward into a peaceful future with so much conflict and violence embedded in their past? How could they integrate what had happened into what might be possible? How could they reconcile their different perceptions of the story? My colleague leaned over the breakfast table and replayed the scenes he had witnessed many times in his inter-group work: "You want to know about the past? I'll tell you something. EVERYONE wants to talk about the past. But they want to talk about *their* past."

And so begins our exploration of the role of the past in intercultural mediation. George Santayana is famed for having said "Those who cannot remember the past are condemned to repeat it" (1953). But in considering the role of the past in conflict, it seems equally possible that the opposite could be true—that those who remember their past (and remember it in particular ways) can remain stuck in cycles of conflict that last long into the future. And while there may be some universal truths in both of these perspectives, the phenomenon of engaging with the past is also deeply personal and cultural. Any interculturalist will focus on the myriad ways in which cultural differences inform almost everything about a person or group's engagement with the world. Addressing the past is no different. As culture can be defined either broadly or specifically, the term 'intercultural' becomes a slippery slope of the intersectionality of group identities, individual un-iqueness, and social milieus. In many ways, the notion that every interaction is, in some ways, an intercultural interaction (Singer 1987) is the base from which we work. This allows for the com-plexities of our intersectionalities, reducing the propensity for blanket assumptions about group

136

DOI: 10.4324/9781003227441-17

differences while simultaneously understanding group norms, values, and patterns that inform how people engage within their social contexts.

This is important as we explore how different cultural milieus orient toward the past and the impact this *may* have on interpersonal and intergroup conflict and its mediation. We encourage all mediators and conflict interventionists to lead with what we call *informed curiosity*. Being knowledgeable about patterns must inform our interventions, but not define them. Ideally, they will inform the questions we ask of ourselves and the conflict parties with whom we work, supporting skillful interventions based on inquiry and not assumption. With this lens in mind, this chapter examines shared and differing cultural orientations to the past, explores the impact of these orientations on conflict engagement, and recommends effective mediation strategies for addressing these dynamics in conflict resolution and mediation processes.

What is the past? History, memory, individual, and collective remembrance

Before we dive into the relationship between conflict and the past, it is important to understand what we mean by 'the past.' While it may be interpreted as anything that has happened prior to this point, how we understand the past is part of our cultural conditioning AND part of what keeps it tangled so deeply with conflict. How those in conflict engage with the past has been a source of significant research and exploration (Arai 2015; Bar-Tal, Halperin, and de Rivera 2007; Cairns and Roe 2003; de le Fuente et al. 2014; Ferraro 1994; Ji et al. 2009; Li and Cao 2018; Nicholson 2016; Peetz and Wohl 2019; Tint 2010a, 2010b). Once something has happened, it is subject to interpretation, revision, denial, forgetting, minimization, amplification, selectivity, and manipulation for a variety of purposes.

The distinction between history and memory must be acknowledged as they are often confused with one another and require different responses in conflict mediation. History is seen or understood as a factual accounting of what has happened. Memory is seen as constructed, where reality is subjective, fluid, and purposeful and cannot be separated from the beliefs and goals of those who create it. This happens on both conscious and unconscious levels. In social or political conflicts, while there are records, media reports, accounts in history books, we have seen, over and over, the erasure of certain histories, revisionist accounts of events, and historical retelling that serves particular political agendas. Who tells the historical stories and how they are told impacts the passing down of history in myriad ways. In interpersonal conflicts, where there is typically no 'record' of events, history and memory are more fluidly merged as people come with differing realities with no 'objective' accounting of events. In both social/political and interpersonal conflicts, people's different accounting of events and inability to reconcile them is a frequent cause and perpetrator of conflict. In all scenarios, we must toggle between acknowledging the subjectivity and validity of differing perceptions in conflict and acknowledging real harms and factual events. The proliferation of subjective perceptions or differing historical narratives that deny real events can cause great harm and perpetuate injustice. As mediators and conflict interventionists, we need to have our eye on this very delicate balance.

In exploring the past, we must also consider the concept of collective memory—memory held by social groups—as a significant dimension of how people engage with conflict. Each individual is part of a social collective that has its own narratives informing how those individuals engage with the world (Connerton 1989; Fentress and Wickham 1992; Halbwachs 1992; Hutton 1993; Kappmeier et al. 2019; LeGoff 1992; Middleton and Edwards 1990; Nicholson 2016; Pennebaker, Páez, and Rimé 1997; Tint 2010a, 2010b). Within this discourse, neither individual nor group memory can exist independently from the social domains in which people live; the process of remembering is contextual and occurs within the collective dimension of lived experiences. While considering memory as a collective rather than an individual phenomenon, we must also understand that the many collective memories in any society are as numerous as the groups or cultures within it and they often conflict with one another. It is through this multiplicity of memories that we see the emerging relationship between memory and conflict. While collective memory addresses this phenomenon within social groups, we must also consider any individual as carrying those collective thoughts, memories, emotions, stories, and narratives within them.

Before we move into our exploration of particular cultural orientations to the past, we note what we consider to be these universal truths across all cultures knowing that they will play out differently: History is remembered subjectively. It is carried at both the individual and collective levels. Memory is an active process, calling for its participants to engage selectively with the objects and experiences of the past. It is the existence of multiple and often conflicting memories combined with this subjectivity and furthering of personal or political agendas that makes how we engage with the past a significant dimension of conflict. Different cultures engage with the past in different ways.

Differing cultural orientations to the past

We now turn our attention to exploring differing cultural orientations to the past and their potential impact on conflict and mediation processes. In considering how different cultures engage with and make meaning of the past, our analysis focuses on three areas: 1) temporal orientation, 2) immediate vs. long-term relationship to time, and 3) collective vs. individual impact.

Temporal orientation

Temporal orientation refers to beliefs about time and is an important dynamic that is influenced by our cultural environments. Research suggests that significant differences exist between cultural mindsets around time, and particularly, the past. Understanding these temporal perspectives across cultures can help establish a basis of understanding for how each person's unique cultural identity contributes to their relationship to past events and how this is showing up in the present. This is critical to understanding the layered dynamics of how conflicting parties process conflict as they spar over events that occurred one day, one year, or one generation ago. Present-oriented cultures tend to believe that the future cannot be known because it has not yet come, and the past also cannot be known because people's memories are partial and selective. They think that the past is mostly a present reflection of historical occurrences (Hampden-Turner and Trompenaars 2010). Other cultures place more value on the past as significant in its own right. People whose temporal orientation is past-focused are more influenced by the past and how it is prioritized or valued within their culture (de le Fuente et al. 2014; Li and Cao 2018; Ji et al. 2009; Robinson et al. 2015).

There are various examples of this. Buddhists conceptualize the past in front of them, and often look to the past when considering how to solve current problems, believing it holds valuable lessons; a belief in karma asserts that the future is directly linked to the past. In contrast, Taoists, who conceptualize the future in front and the past behind them, believe in immortality and the pursuit of eternal life (Li and Cao 2018). Though Buddhists and Taoists in China may diverge, the Chinese more generally have been shown to focus on the past more than dominant culture U.S. and Canadian North Americans. While North Americans view a linear trajectory of events, the Chinese hold beliefs that time is cyclical and that the events of history repeat themselves (Ji et al. 2009). Malagasy people conceptualize the past visibly in front of them, with the future flowing through them from behind as it is yet known. The Madagascar population often consults their ancestors and views the past as dynamic; it is something to be learned from and enjoyed (Lewis 2014). Moroccan Arabs typically place the past in front, while Spaniards map it behind (de la Fuente et al. 2014). Culturally specific temporal-orientation also appears to extend even to subgroups such as political affiliations and sports fan groups (Peetz and Wohl 2019; Robinson et al. 2015).

Understanding monochronic and polychronic time perspectives is also critical in understanding how cultures vary in their thinking regarding the passage of time (Brislin and Kim 2003; Ferraro 1994; Hall 1983; Lewis 2014; Meyer 2014; Nishishiba 2017). Monochronic time, often observed in cultures such as the urban white United States, Australian, and Northern European contexts, typically view time as a limited but valuable resource; like currency, it can be spent, saved, invested, and wasted. Appointments generally focus on tasks, one purpose at a time with a clear beginning and end. Polychronic time, often observed in cultures such as Mexico, U.S. Indigenous communities, and Northern African contexts, is more fluid. Agendas are focused more on relationships than tasks, and there is an understanding that things begin and end more organically. These differences in time orientation can often be a source of conflict and can also play out attempts to resolve it.

A seminal example that demonstrates the intersection of cross-cultural time perspectives and temporal-orientation is illustrated in a story of the Hopi tribe and the attempt by the U.S. Commission on Indian Affairs to provide infrastructure improvements on the reservation and surrounding areas while stimulating the economy by hiring Hopi workers (Hall 1983). The Hopi, followers of a ceremonial calendar and intensely focused on farming their land, were outraged to be accused of poor workmanship as they clashed with the government on labor timelines and shift scheduling to complete the improvement project. On its face, this could be seen as a simple example of monochronic vs. polychronic timekeeping cultures colliding. However, there are deeper issues connected to power, history, and trauma. The Hopi had a long memory of and still lived the impacts of the brutal colonialism they had experienced at the hands of the bureaucrats' European settler ancestors. For the Hopi, the past was firmly with them and in front of them and there was little interest in adjusting their lives to adapt to the schedule of the U.S. government. Representatives of the government, oriented to the present tasks at hand, had not properly accounted for the impact of the past and cultural differences in their planning efforts.

Immediate vs. long-term relationship to time

A short-term and long-term orientation to time also influences cultural differences in considering the value of the past. Hofstede, Hofstede, and Minkov (2010) explain that a society with a short-term orientation tends to make an effort to solve the immediate problems they face and place more value on results for the immediate future. In these cultures, there is a high value on respect and preservation of traditions and ancient norms rather than worrying about or planning for the future. A long-term orientation society, on the other hand, focuses more on sustained efforts toward longer-term future rewards. A long-term orientation typically has a holistic view of time, valuing the past, present, and future rather than focusing only on short-term impacts of actions (Bearden 2006; Nevins, Bearden, and Money 2007). People from a future-oriented perspective tend to be less interested in solely keeping traditional thoughts, values, and norms because they believe that the importance of values and information from the past can change with the times. In other words, factors that were valuable in the past may be considered worthless in the present, and vice versa (Hofstede, Hofstede, and Minkov 2010; Nishishiba 2017; Samovar et al. 2016). The Haudenosaunee (Iroquois), a long-term orientation society, lives by the Seventh Generation Principle, which highlights that the decisions we make now should be considered as to how they will impact seven generations forward to build sustainability into the future (PBS 2021).

Collective vs. individual impact

Studies on cultural differences also demonstrate that different ways of thinking between individualist and collectivist societies can impact the valuing of past events and behaviors surrounding them. Specifically, collective societies are more likely to place an emphasis on the connection between past, present, and future than individualist societies. Indeed, most East Asian countries, which have more collectivist ways of thinking, tend to have a holistic view of the universe, which emphasizes societal harmony and dialectical relations because they assume the interconnectedness of the whole of the universe. This mode of thinking emphasizes the importance of understanding multi-causality and the ripple effects of the actions that are relatively far away from the focal events. People from Western countries tend to see society as less complicated and believe that people can understand the world with fewer factors typically applying mono-causality and direct and immediate attributions (Chen and Starosta 2003; Maddux and Yuki 2006; Nisbett 2004; Shi-xu 2009). Ji et al. (2009) demonstrate that since the Chinese tend to display a greater ability to recollect the past and feel the temporal distance between past events and the present more closely than European North Americans, past information and collective memory have a huge influence on their decision-making. Collective societies are more deeply steeped in a worldview that what happens to some, happens to all. Therefore, past events are more likely to be carried in the stories of individuals who may not have been directly involved in the events in question.

Addressing the past in mediation

When it comes to practice, there are specific intervention strategies that can (and should) be in the mediator's toolbox. All of these tools will need to be nuanced by the knowledge, skill and the experience of any mediator involved. While staying away from formulaic approaches to mediation, we will present these elements that are important to consider in both interpersonal conflict as well as social community conflict. We embrace Lederach's (1995, 1997) paradox of having to focus on both the past and the future, and this will always be the mediator's balancing act. But what is clear is that if the past is not addressed adequately, particularly from the perspective of those most injured by it, conflict will not likely be resolved for a healed future to emerge.

Exploration

At the root of any mediated engagement, there needs to be an intentional exploration of the past. This includes inviting all parties to share what has happened, what is important to them, what feels unresolved to them, and which part of history is still in the room. Because of differing temporal orientations, some parties might feel the need to reference longer term issues, while others may be more focused on those most recent. Because parties from different cultural backgrounds are likely to have a differing emphasis on the past, and may have different communication styles, it can be useful to explore the power and the meaning of the past both directly and indirectly, through metaphor and story (Rafferty 2017). It can also be very important for parties to understand each other's orientation in this area. It is helpful to acknowledge the general notion that different people or different cultures may be more or less focused on the past and its ancestral role in the current reality. This can become a very tricky dimension of a mediated process, partly because a party's orientation to the past may or may not be in their awareness. While it might create additional frustration for parties to navigate a different temporal orientation, increased understanding and normalization can help mitigate this frustration.

Differing histories

As we have articulated, differing versions of the past are often part of what brings people to mediation and often what interferes with its success. A mediator must make space for all versions of history to come into the room while attempting to create a more integrated shared narrative. As differing narratives emerge, we can invite a shared walk through history (Montville 2001).

The mediator's job is to reflect back on what they hear as well as to have parties do that for each other to the best of their ability. It is important, at this point, for a mediator to acknowledge that differing historical narratives are a common phenomenon in conflict so as to normalize this and work with the parties is to try to find mutual understanding for each other's stories. There is a fine balance here, between acknowledging the subjectivity of perception and memory while not denying real hurts or injustices that have happened (Nicholson 2016). Focusing on experience rather than 'facts' can be an important dimension of increased mutual understanding. From this, it is more likely possible to navigate a new, shared narrative about both the past and the future.

Acknowledgment

One of the most important dimensions of exploring the past is acknowledging it. A mediator may first need to model or open the door to acknowledging the historical harm that either or both of the parties may have experienced. However, it is ultimately acknowledgment of historical harm from a perpetrator to a victim that is a critical dimension to successfully resolving conflict (Bar-Tal, Halperin, and de Rivera 2007; Kelman 2004; Lederach 1997; Tint 2010a, 2010b). This becomes tricky because in many conflicts, all parties may feel like the victim; a competition of victimhood (De Guissmé and Licata 2017; Montville 2001; Noor et al. 2012) is often at play in small- and large-scale conflicts. Mutual acknowledgment is key when there is real harm on all sides; however, mediators must be careful not to equalize a legitimately imbalanced historical story. The mediator's task is to find ways for parties to acknowledge the harm experienced by the other party while balancing the weight of historical harms. Ideally, that acknowledgment comes with a certain level of taking responsibility. This is more difficult if people are in defense or denial of their role in the historical harm. While not wanting to reinforce this competition of victimhood, a mediator must evaluate if the relative historical harms are being addressed proportionately in a mediation process. Again, the temporal orientation is critical here; how far back are different parties focused in their need for acknowledgment? Is there tension in the desire for accountability and acknowledgment around things that the other party considers 'old history'? The mediator can effectively support different parties to get what they need around their temporal orientation to the past, underscoring the difference in past focused dimensions.

Apology

Genuine apology for past harm—intentional or unintentional—is a critical factor in releasing the power of the past in current day realities (Augsburger 1992; Kelman 2004; Lederach 1997; Mellor, Bretherton, and Firth 2007; Tint 2009). Sincere apology is also connected to parties' temporal orientation and may be related to immediate or long-term historical events which can become a sticking point between parties. Apology is necessary, but not typically sufficient. It is a critical building block in resolving past harms, but it does not stand alone. Ideally it is joined with future behavior change, reparations of sort and continued proactive efforts to prevent similar harms from happening again. This is true in both small-scale and large-scale conflicts. Mediators must have their eyes on all aspects of this and the potentially differing orientations of the parties.

Conflict roles

Where someone is situated in a conflict will have a great deal to do with how much they want to excavate the past. As the Angolan proverb warns, *The one who throws the stone forgets; the one who is hit remembers forever*. If those harmed do not feel that their injuries have been adequately acknowledged, they are likely to continue driving that point and may be seen as 'stuck in the past.' Those who have perpetrated wrongdoing are more likely to want to look forward: 'the past is the past' we often hear. Furthermore, who has power and what kinds of power is a critical dimension to who is supported by focusing on either the past, present or future. Often, revisiting past events and fully exploring the range of immediate or long-term past injuries, can be challenging and uncomfortable for those in power who may be more resistant because of fear of accountability and loss of power that may occur. Whether it is an issue of systemic power such as race or individual power such as hierarchical rank in an organization, those with less power may be more motivated to explore the past but also more fearful because of potential consequences for doing so. Here, a mediator must work to create the safety for lower powered parties to express their truth.

Mediator orientation

Mediators have a critical role here in determining how much time is allocated to the past. In any choice, we must be conscious as to whom it may favor or disfavor. As with all aspects of a mediator's choices, our own cultural and professional biases are useful to understand. In Fisher and Ury's initial text (1981), they say "look forward not back." This highly Western approach to conflict is one that often exists in boardrooms and policy negotiations. If a mediator favors looking to the future, they may inadvertently perpetuate harm by not allowing for a full excavation of the past. If a mediator focuses on the recent past while not considering the generational and ancestral implications important to some parties, they deny the differing cultural forces that may impact resolution. Therefore, in all mediation processes, it is important that a mediator 1) understands their orientation to the past, 2) is able to be flexible in working with the temporal orientations of others, 3) integrates these issues into their interventions, and 4) considers the power of their interventions and how they may impact parties from different conflict roles and temporal orientations.

Conclusion

The past is with us. It cannot be undone. Its impact is very much in the present and here to stay. And here to stay in different ways depending on people's cultural orientation to their story. It will always be a delicate balance focusing between past, present, and future. Even distinguishing them from one another may be a fallacy; Albert Einstein said: *The distinction between the past, present and the future is only a stubbornly persistent illusion.* In our work as mediators, we encourage the goals of flexible, compassionate, and co-partial engagement with all parties' relationship with the past. And hopefully we can impart that to parties in conflict so that they can focus, not only on their own past, but on the past of others as well. This gives us hope for a shared future.

References

Arai, Tatsushi. 2015. "Engaging Conflict History: Toward an Integrated Method of Conflict Resolution Dialogue and Capacity Building." *Conflict Resolution Quarterly* 32 (3): 277–98. 10.1002/crq.21113

Augsburger, David W. 1992. *Conflict Mediation Across Cultures: Pathways and Patterns.* London: Westminster John Knox Press.

Bar-Tal, Daniel, Eran Halperin, and Joseph de Rivera. 2007. "Collective Emotions in Conflict Situations: Societal Implications." *Journal of Social Issues* 63 (2): 441–60. 10.1111/j.1540-4560.2007.00518.x

Bearden, W. O. 2006. "A Measure of Long-Term Orientation: Development and Validation." *Journal of the Academy of Marketing Science* 34 (3): 456–67. 10.1177/0092070306286706

Brislin, Richard W., and Eugene S. Kim. 2003. "Cultural Diversity in People's Understanding and Uses of Time." *Applied Psychology* 52 (3): 363–82. 10.1111/1464-0597.00140

Cairns, Ed, and Michael Roe. 2003. *The Role of Memory in Ethnic Conflict.* New York: Palgrave Macmillan.

Chen, Guo-Ming, and William J. Starosta. 2003. "Asian Approaches to Human Communication: A Dialogue." *Intercultural Communication Studies* 12 (4): 1–15.

Connerton, Paul. 1989. *How Societies Remember*. Cambridge, UK: Cambridge University Press.

De Guissmé, Laura, and Laurent Licata. 2017. "Competition over Collective Victimhood Recognition: When Perceived Lack of Recognition for Past Victimization Is Associated with Negative Attitudes towards Another Victimized Group: Competition over Collective Victimhood Recognition." *European Journal of Social Psychology* 47 (2): 148–66. 10.1002/ejsp.2244

Fentress, James, and Christopher Wickham. 1992. *Social Memory*. Oxford: Blackwell Press.

Ferraro, Gary P. 1994. *The Cultural Dimension of International Business*. New Jersey: Prentice Hall.

Fisher, Roger, William L. Ury, and Bruce Patton. 1981. *Getting to Yes: Negotiating An Agreement Without Giving In*. United Kingdom: Penguin Group.

Fuente, Juanma de la, Julio Santiago, Antonio Román, Cristina Dumitrache, and Daniel Casasanto. 2014. "When You Think About It, Your Past Is in Front of You: How Culture Shapes Spatial Conceptions of Time." *Psychological Science* 25 (9): 1682–90. 10.1177/0956797614534695

Halbwachs, Maurice. 1992. *On Collective Memory*, edited by Lewis A. Coser. Chicago: University of Chicago Press.

Hall, Edward Twitchell. 1983. *The Dance of Life: The Other Dimension of Time*. New York: Anchor Books.

Hampden-Turner, Charles, and Fons Trompenaars. 2010. *Riding the Waves of Culture: Understanding Diversity in Global Business*. 3rd edition. New York: McGraw-Hill Education.

Hofstede, Geert, Gert Jan Hofstede, and Michael Minkov. 2010. *Cultures and Organizations: Software of the Mind*. New York: McGraw-Hill.

Hutton, Patrick H. 1993. *History as an Art of Memory*. New Hampshire: University Press of New England.

Ji, Li-Jun, Tieyuan Guo, Zhiyong Zhang, and Deanna Messervey. 2009. "Looking into the Past: Cultural Differences in Perception and Representation of Past Information." *Journal of Personality and Social Psychology* 96 (4): 761–9. 10.1037/a0014498

Kappmeier, Mariska, and Aurélie Mercy. 2019. "The Long Road from Cold War to Warm Peace: Building Shared Collective Memory through Trust." *Journal of Social and Political Psychology* 7 (1): 525–55. 10.5964/jspp.v7i1.328

Kelman, Herbert C. 2004. "Reconciliation as Identity Change: A Social-Psychological Perspective." In *From Conflict Resolution to Reconciliation*, edited by Yaacov Bar-Siman-Tov, 111–24. Oxford University Press. 10.1093/acprof:oso/9780195166439.003.0006

Lederach, John Paul. 1995. *Preparing for Peace: Conflict Transformation Across Cultures*. Syracuse, New York: Syracuse University Press.

Lederach, John Paul. 1997. *Building Peace: Sustainable Reconciliation in Divided Societies*. Washington, DC: United States Institute of Peace Press.

LeGoff, Jacques. 1992. *History and Memory*. New York: Columbia University Press.

Lewis, Richard. 2014. "How Different Cultures Understand Time." *Business Insider*, June 2, 2014. https://www.businessinsider.com/how-different-cultures-understand-time-2014-5

Li, Heng, and Yu Cao. 2018. "Karma or Immortality: Can Religion Influence Space-Time Mappings?" *Cognitive Science* 42 (3): 1041–56. 10.1111/cogs.12579

Maddux, William W., and Masaki Yuki. 2006. "The 'Ripple Effect': Cultural Differences in Perceptions of the Consequences of Events." *Personality and Social Psychology Bulletin* 32 (5): 669–83. 10.1177/0146167205283840

Mellor, David, Di Bretherton, and Lucy Firth. 2007. "Aboriginal and Non-Aboriginal Australia: The Dilemma of Apologies, Forgiveness, and Reconciliation." *Peace and Conflict: Journal of Peace Psychology* 13 (1): 11–36. 10.1037/h0094022

Meyer, Erin. 2014. *The Culture Map: Breaking Through the Invisible Boundaries of Global Business*. New York: Public Affairs.

Middleton, David, and Derek Edwards, eds. 1990. *Collective Remembering*. Thousand Oaks, CA: Sage.

Montville, Joseph. 2001. "Justice and the Burdens of History." In *Reconciliation, Justice, and Coexistence: Theory and Practice*, edited by Mohammed Abu-Nimer, 129–43. Lanham, MD: Lexington Books.

Nevins, Jennifer L., William O. Bearden, and Bruce Money. 2007. "Ethical Values and Long-Term Orientation." *Journal of Business Ethics* 71 (3): 261–74. 10.1007/s10551-006-9138-x

Nicholson, Cathy. 2016. "The Role of Historical Representations in Israeli-Palestinian Relations: Narratives from Abroad." *Peace and Conflict: Journal of Peace Psychology* 22 (1): 5–11. 10.1037/pac0000143

Nisbett, Richard E. 2004. *The Geography of Thought: How Asians and Westerners Think Differently … and Why*. New York: Free Press.

Nishishiba, Masami. 2017. *Culturally Mindful Communication: Essential Skills for Public and Nonprofit Professionals*. New York: Routledge. 10.4324/9781315277349

Noor, Masi, Nurit Shnabel, Samer Halabi, and Arie Nadler. 2012. "When Suffering Begets Suffering: The Psychology of Competitive Victimhood Between Adversarial Groups in Violent Conflicts." *Personality and Social Psychology Review* 16 (4): 351–74. 10.1177/1088868312440048

PBS. 2021. "Seven Generations—the Role of Chief." 2021. https://www.pbs.org/warrior/content/timeline/opendoor/roleOfChief.html

Peetz, Johanna, and Michael J. A. Wohl. 2019. "Perceiving Time through Group-based Glasses: Collective Temporal Orientation." *British Journal of Social Psychology* 58 (3): 609–29. 10.1111/bjso.12291

Pennebaker, James W., Darío Páez, and Bernard Rimé. 1997. *Collective Memory of Political Events*. Mahwah, NJ: Erlbaum.

Rafferty, Rachel. 2017. "Engaging with the Violent Past to Motivate and Direct Conflict Resolution Practice in Northern Ireland." *Conflict Resolution Quarterly* 35 (2): 197–221. 10.1002/crq.21204

Robinson, Michael D., Deirdre M. Cassidy, Ryan L. Boyd, and Adam K. Fetterman. 2015. "The Politics of Time: Conservatives Differentially Reference the Past and Liberals Differentially Reference the Future: Conservatives Differentially Reference the Past." *Journal of Applied Social Psychology* 45 (7): 391–99. 10.1111/jasp.12306

Samovar, Larry A., Richard E. Porter, Edwin R. McDaniel, and Carolyn Sexton Roy. 2016. *Communication Between Cultures*. Boston, Massachusetts: Cengage Learning.

Santayana, George. 1953. *The Life of Reason: The Phases of Human Progress*. Vol. 1. New York: Scribner.

Shi-xu. 2009. "Asian Discourse Studies: Foundations and Directions." *Asian Journal of Communication* 19 (4): 384–97. 10.1080/01292980903293262

Singer, Marshall R. 1987. *Intercultural Communication: A Perceptual Approach*. New Jersey: Prentice Hall.

Tint, Barbara. 2009. "Dialogue, Forgiveness, and Reconciliation." In *Forgiveness, Reconciliation, and the Pathways to Peace*, edited by Ani Kalayjian and Raymond F. Paloutzian, 269–85. New York: Springer.

Tint, Barbara. 2010a. "History, Memory, and Intractable Conflict." *Conflict Resolution Quarterly* 27 (3): 239–56. 10.1002/crq.258

Tint, Barbara. 2010b. "History, Memory, and Conflict Resolution: Research and Application." *Conflict Resolution Quarterly* 27 (4): 369–99. 10.1002/crq.20003

15
THE POLITICS OF INTERCULTURAL SPACE: INCLUSIVE, UNOBTRUSIVE, AND FAILED MEDIATION

Haynes Collins

Introduction: The agentive force of physical space

While there has been significant attention paid to the influence which virtual space now exerts upon society, the impact that embodied physical space has on social interaction often lies outside of most people's immediate awareness. This can be seen in Hall's (1966) labeling of the use of space or proxemics as "the hidden dimension." Patterns and regulation of movement such as which side of the road traffic should travel on or how pedestrians navigate through city centers, once learned, become second nature and usually no longer warrant much thought or attention. However, when encountering significantly different approaches to spatial use, the etiquette, understanding, and regulation of physical space can suddenly be revealed in the sense of what Agar (2006) terms a "rich point." For example, an uninformed escalator user in central London might be completely oblivious to the somewhat loose convention of standing on one side of the moving stairs during rush hour in order to let people who are in a hurry quickly overtake. A person who is unaware of this practice runs the risk of being publicly criticized by another who wants to go past. In this instance, suddenly the 'rule' (even though it may be both implicit and contested) becomes apparent in stark fashion to the person who is unfamiliar with it.

The COVID-19 pandemic, which in many respects has felt like one extended rich point, has served to draw attention to the increased regulation of movement through physical space. This has entailed increased control of the environment through an array of signage and rules governing activities ranging from how many customers are allowed in a business, which direction pedestrians are permitted to walk, and even whether people are allowed in public spaces at all. These new rules have served to illuminate the agentive force of physical space where it is no longer seen as neutral or disinterested, but as a 'historically configured phenomenon and as an actor' (Blommaert 2018, 62). The awareness that physical space is neither neutral nor disinterested is not only crucial for better architectural and planning approaches to civic design, but it is also important in highlighting the relationship between space, social interaction, and mediation.

Contested use of space and disputed claims of territorial ownership can provoke the need for mediation. This can occur at a macro level, as seen in international disputes over territory between nation-states, or in more micro everyday spaces that also have the potential for conflict. Yet, as a specific identity is attached to space thus rendering it as 'place,' it also holds the potential to draw

DOI: 10.4324/9781003227441-18

people together through a collective appreciation of its ethos and qualities. Moreover, inclusive public spaces can exert a positive influence on the relationship that humans have with each other and on the quality of social interaction. Klinenberg (2018) calls spaces which are accessible, shared and have few barriers to entry "social infrastructure" and he argues that social infrastructure is essential to community cohesion, health, and welfare. This resonates with Lofland's (1998) observation of how social spaces can contribute to everyday conviviality between strangers and with Staurides' (2019, 21) optimistic argument for shared space as a catalyst for social emancipation.

Building on these ideas and on previous research of mine, this chapter considers three examples of different spatial qualities and arrangements within publicly accessible swimming pools which demonstrate contrasting forms and degrees of mediation. The first case highlights how the use of collective memory of historic pool spaces can serve a mediating function through community building in areas which have seen a gradual decrease in public funding for local social infrastructure such as parks, libraries, and leisure facilities. This is followed by a second case that considers how spatial arrangement can serve as a form of 'pre-mediation' by increasing the potential for convivial social interaction and inclusivity. These examples are juxtaposed with a further case of ongoing contestation of pool space where differing approaches to swimwear expose the pool as a site of failed mediation. This chapter argues that space can be imbued with mediating properties if its organization and use is inclusive and informed by a close connection between users and regulators. These three examples are examined through McMurtrie's (2016) tripartite model for spatial analysis which was first applied to museum space but is equally applicable to swimming pools. This model considers space as having an agentive physical force made up of three diachronic texts (the 'architectonic text,' the 'curatorial text,' and the 'visitor text'), and, although each of these three texts are interconnected and interdependent, each will be discussed separately below in relation to the specific context that is being considered.

The context of publicly accessible pools is salient because these are everyday places where a diverse range of people converge to undertake a common activity and, in this sense, it can be viewed as an intercultural and diverse space. Here, interculturality and diversity are not used to signify the primacy of nationality as a membership category but stress the performative aspect of swimming which sees a wide range of people of different ages, sizes, abilities, and ethnicities approach it from different perspectives. In this sense, it is an interactive space where intersubjectivity must be considered given that swimmers rarely swim alone. This recognition acknowledges Dervin and Risager's (2014, 4) argument for the need to take intersubjectivity into account "in order to put into practice the essential idea that there is no self without an other and vice versa."

Collective memory in the architectonic text

The physical material structure of a building constitutes McMurtrie's (2016) notion of an architectonic text. While substantial variation exists in the choice of materials, architectural style, quality, and aesthetics, every building's architectonic text shares the common feature of having solid structures which, once built, are not easy to adapt. Thus, when a building's structure is not serving its users well, making changes to it is not an easy undertaking. The impact that the architectonic text can have on users of a space can be considerable and, put simply, buildings are much more than physical structures. A salient example can be found in the resurgent interest in historical baths and lidos within the United Kingdom (see, for example, Gordon and Inglis 2009; Pusill and Wilkinson 2019). One way in which these historic baths communicate a sense of community to pool users is by accentuating historical collective memories that offer a bridge to future possibilities for the pool. Tinkler (2013, xvii) provides an interpretation of collective memory, arguing:

Collective memory provides a cultural framework within which people articulate and interpret their personal memories. It is informed and shaped by the experiences and stories of people in communities and so, it is different from public history, which is imposed top down, usually by governments.

This emphasis on bottom-up community engagement emerged in Collins's (2021) ethnographic study of two historic baths in the United Kingdom (Bramley Baths and Moseley Road Baths) that have long and rich histories dating back to their respective openings in 1904 and 1907. The use of 'baths' in their name reflects their original purpose of serving as a public facility for washing at a time when few houses had piped running water. These baths are now indoor swimming pools and, despite constant cuts to public funding, have survived several threats of closure due to the work of the local community and many dedicated volunteers who now manage the pools as community-led charitable incorporated organizations. The history of the buildings has become an important part of each pool's identity and this history is accentuated and kept alive through marketing, the display of memorabilia and photographs in foyers, use of oral histories, and by retaining original features wherever possible (see Figure 15.1).

An example of the use of oral history is visible in past open-day events at Bramley Baths where visitors accessed recorded spoken memories through an old telephone handset which when lifted would play the voice of a pool user reflecting on the past and on the memories of the pool that have stayed with them over many years. Moseley Road Baths similarly collects and displays memories and in one example, a swimmer recounts her memory of attempting to swim in a knitted costume:

Figure 15.1 Bramley Baths 1903. Photo courtesy of Bramley Baths

> I came here around 1928/29 for swimming in the small bath. I brought my towel, my costume and wore a rubber swim cap. My mother knitted the costume and when I got in the bath it stretched and nearly came off.

These evocative memories combined with the historic ambiance of each building are important for shaping how current pool users experience the pools. The pools serve as a local connective tissue where users make an emotional commitment to the space and see it as a community asset which provides human connection. This is particularly salient in urban areas of low income which are prone to social exclusion and cuts in services and resources. These historic and community-led spaces exert a mediating effect in that the users enter the sites predisposed towards empathy and understanding and they are less likely to experience conflict due to their appreciation and relationship with the space. This emerges in how one Moseley Road Baths user ('Nuhra') explained her relationship to the pool in Collins' (2021) study:

> You know my husband sometimes says, 'You love those baths more than you love your house.' But it's my way of getting away from everything and I'm meeting people while I'm at it.

The commitment to providing affordable, accessible social space also stands in contrast to a consumerist and marketplace model. For example, in a transactional relationship with a private gym or swimming pool, broken facilities may produce a feeling of displeasure, of 'not getting one's money's worth' or even hostility that is manifested in a desire to complain or demand a refund. In a similar situation in a community-managed historic bath, swimmers might understandably be disappointed, but arguably are more likely to comprehend the challenges presented by very old facilities because they have a stake in the space and thus are even likely to contribute to the repair or know the person in charge of it. This sense of inclusivity is apparent in the data from another Moseley Road Bath user ('Sophie') from Collins' (2021) study who reflects on her relationship with the bath and the impact it has on her relationship with other users:

> [...] It is a community center, because these public spaces, these public buildings they are our common land, as it were. There is so much privatized space and having this as a public space, [...] it belongs to us and it's ours, and it's the one space where my daughter can come into the pool and she will be swimming with people and be conversing with people in the heart of the community, people we wouldn't necessarily meet in other aspects of our daily life, but they become your neighbors.

The historic baths have come to symbolize an alternative model to exclusive urban environments. Their power becomes even more tangible when contrasts are made through comparisons to what has been labeled 'hostile architecture' or 'defensive design' which includes features such as anti-homeless spikes; slanted, curved, or segmented benches and barred corners. These historic baths have made a commitment to inclusivity through principles that are founded on understanding the needs of the surrounding and changing urban locality. This begins with the buildings themselves as they provide a sense of continuity, stability and purpose allowing for a shared appreciation which, in turn, stimulates a sense of togetherness and the opportunity for human connections. This is the starting point for reducing the need for other forms of mediation as tensions are reduced through this shared commitment to historic places that belong to the community.

Meta-cognition and unobtrusive 'pre-mediation' in the curatorial text

Moving away from a building's solid physical structure, McMurtrie's (2016) curatorial text includes the arrangement of the building's more adaptable interior space, and it encompasses the choices involved in influencing how this interior is navigated and experienced by the users. While a curatorial text can be manipulated to meet the needs of different users, it also retains the potential to render the space as one which is heavily monitored for the purposes of control and surveillance. Awareness of the proxemics, or 'reading' the curatorial text, provides clues to the motivation of those who manage the space and their relationship to the users. This is particularly pertinent to publicly accessible swimming pools as they often attempt to cater for a range of swimmers with different abilities and approaches to swimming. Spatial organization in pools is frequently done by 'mapping' and partitioning the pool, and this is influenced by several factors starting with the available space provided by the architectonic text and the types of swimmers which the pool is catering for.

Although swimming pool taxonomy varies greatly across pools, loose distinctions can be made between 'leisure pools,' which are largely designed for play, and 'sport pools,' which are organized for lane swimming. Pools that cater for 'lane swimming' are generally arranged with physical barriers and restrictions such as lane ropes and signage that indicate where swimmers can swim depending on factors such as swimming ability. In addition to this physical layout, many pools also utilize a range of additional swim categories via a time table for special sessions which are open only or partially for those in that group (women only, family, general swimming etc.). In a well-functioning pool, the organization acts as a form of 'pre-mediation' allowing different swimmers of various ages and abilities to share the pool without conflict. Just as in the above section where pool users are predisposed towards empathetic social interaction based on their relationship with historic baths, well-planned pool space can similarly work to reduce the potential for conflict.

Clearly, the physical structure of the building and the layout of pool space are not the only determining factors contributing to how swimmers navigate this space. Scott (2010, 123) draws on negotiated order theory and Goffman's (1959) dramaturgical theory to argue that swimmers have three sets of tacit norms that they follow within pools: "respect for personal space," "respect for individuals' disciplinary regime," and "the desexualization of encounters." These norms are typically not explicitly stated in, for example, pool regulations and signage, but are learned over time. Thus, swimmers are influenced both by the organisation of the pool space as seen in the architectonic and curatorial texts, and by the intersubjective presence and movement of each other.

Collins and Pajak's (2019) ethnographic study focused on a publicly accessible pool on a university campus in the UK which attempted to attract a very wide range of pool users. To achieve this, the pool management dedicated substantial thought and energy to frequently adapting the curatorial text which included adding and taking away lanes regularly according to the time of day and number of users, changing signs stating the swimming direction (clockwise and anti-clockwise) and even raising and lowering the pool floor to accommodate children from local primary schools who were learning to swim. While these actions were not invisible to the swimmers, they were designed to be as inconspicuous as possible. This constant adjustment to the curatorial text is conducted with a view towards minimal intervention in the swimmers' routine and it signifies a form of unobtrusive mediation which, while not invisible, often goes unnoticed.

Despite implicit swim norms and the best intentions of pool management in organizing space, tension and even physical confrontations in swimming pools occur with some regularity and attract media attention (see, for example, BBC News 2017; Copland 2021; Wischgoll 2016; Paterson 2013; Rodger 2021). These disputes are frequently influenced by different approaches to pool use that can be amplified by gender, cultural, or racial issues. Collins and Pajak's (2019) study found that while there may appear to be a surface order to pool space, there can also be an underlying cognitive disorder and anxiety in the experience of pool users and swimmers manage this using different strategies. One such method is internal self-regulation through a meta-cognitive process as seen in data from one pool user, 'David,' in Collins and Pajak's (2019) study:

> I was saying about being an angry swimmer, but there is a definite reaction to people swimming in the wrong way and me thinking, they're not from round these parts [...]. I think there is something in, 'you're not obeying my rules.' Of course, what I do in my head is I say, they haven't got a clue what my rules are, how could they, and what's the problem of you, you nutcase [inner dialogue to self], but there is something in my reptilian brain, or whatever, that's just coming out fighting.

This user's data reveals an internal struggle to control his anger towards other swimmers which he self-manages through an inner dialogue. This anger results from his perception that the tacit rules and expectations within a pool are not consistently followed or universally understood. In addition to self-regulation, further data from this study reveals that David extends his coping strategy to dialogue with other swimmers:

> I can look at someone and hate them for the smallest reason and then you talk to them, and you think, ace, brilliant.

Although striking up a conversation in a 'sports' pool is neither straightforward nor always welcomed by other swimmers, David's attempt to humanize the environment through conversation works in defusing his own sense of annoyance and anxiety. Despite the carefully planned arrangement of pool space, the negotiated order, and the tactics that swimmers may use to manage their own anger or anxiety, conflict such as above can still manifest itself and, in these cases, the management is expected to intervene in the dispute. However, there are no assurances that this is always successful, and an element of risk remains where disputes can move beyond the specific pool through appeals to wider public opinion in an effort to exert a further governing effect on the pool space. This question of conflict in social relations is salient in considering the third text (the visitor text).

Failed mediation in the visitor text

Not only does pool taxonomy vary across neighborhoods, cities, regions, and countries, swimming regulations can differ considerably from pool to pool. Moreover, the ambiance of a pool often changes from quiet to busy over the course of the day and/or time of year. A swimmer may share the pool with friendly and considerate swimmers or may encounter an overly aggressive swimmer or one who is unaware of etiquette. These encounters exert an influence on the lived experience of the visitor, or in McMurtrie's (2016) term, the "visitor text."

This text takes account of how two swimmers can swim in the same pool at the same time but have two very different individual experiences particularly when pool rules are seen to be applied unevenly. The visitor text can be seen as the expression an individual's experience of the architectonic text, the curatorial text, and the encounter of others within the space. The above data from David represents his visitor text, and, in his case, he negotiates the space with other swimmers in a largely successful manner. However, visitor texts can also portray a much less positive experience. Wiltse's (2007) study of the social history of municipal pools in the United States revealed the discrimination, marginalization, and violence against African American swimmers throughout the twentieth century, resulting in very different experiences for black and white swimmers. Thus, the provision of social infrastructure on its own should not be seen as a panacea for resolving social tension particularly when, as Grodach (2010, 476) points out, "public space may serve to not only bring different groups together or bolster existing community relations, but also can function to reinforce existing social inequalities."

This tension can be seen in an impasse in Grenoble, France which has resulted in what is, at least interculturally, failed mediation of pool space. In 2019, five women in Grenoble were fined for wearing full-body swimming costumes in the Jean-Bron municipal swimming pool and banned from the facility for two months. Since this incident, the Citizen Alliance Association in Grenoble has held a series of protests outside two local swimming pools and, after raising 2,200 signatures, has engaged in a 'citizen initiative mediation' process that results when 50 citizens have signed and presented a petition to the municipal government. This mediation process allowed the petitioners three meetings with elected officials to find a resolution. However, on 19 January 2022, after meeting with representatives of the Citizen Alliance Association, the city of Grenoble officials decided not to take any action to change the regulations around swimwear for the pools nor to take steps towards compromise. This led to a high-profile resignation and determination from the Citizen Alliance Association to continue to protest what it sees as clear discrimination.

While it is not possible to detail the intricacies of French law or debate the rights and wrongs of this case in this chapter, it highlights what Leonard (2004, 942) calls "the multi-layered processes of inclusion and exclusion," which are to be found in the challenge of sharing space. This is clearly evident, as, after having set up a 'citizen initiative mediation' process, the local government was unable to reach any solution nor was it able to address the complaints raised by over 2,000 local citizens. This is tantamount to an admission that political calculations have rendered the municipal government unwilling or incapable of mediating this space. Moreover, this is now a space where preconceived ideas regarding nationality, religion, and culture have resulted in a form of 'othering' and a ban on swimmers who are seen to be outside of the rules and conventions of the pool.

Degrees of intervention in creating inclusive and intercultural social infrastructure

This chapter argues that physical space and its organization exerts an influence on social interaction and can provide beneficial effects under the right conditions. However, how this is realized in the lives of individuals can vary greatly. Just as there are examples of places which seem to be built for the specific purpose of exclusion, contrasting examples are evident of shared public spaces which encourage social interaction. The three different pool contexts each offer different points for consideration. The example of historic baths, through their community-led management, demonstrates the power and potential that spaces, if built inclusively from the bottom up, offer in combating social exclusion. Moreover, the use of collective memories which run through the fabric of these historic spaces are instrumental in encouraging users to develop a personal, tangible attachment to them. This connective bond can be further developed between users who have been aware of the historic value of the pool and new users visiting it for the first time.

However, creating and maintaining inclusive spaces takes effort, particularly in the face of economic challenges, and this is where the question of intervention is brought into sharp relief. It would be misguided to view pool space solely through a Foucault (1975, 1982) lens of biopower, which would render it as a highly regulated space with 'dividing practices' and lifeguards patrolling 'docile bodies.' Rather, this is a space, which, if attempting to attract a wide spectrum of swimmers, requires a degree of intervention. In a well-functioning and inclusive pool, this intervention is given with the consent of swimmers to serve their interests. Part of the pivotal work in managing pool space as seen in the second example is the constant need for decisions concerning the degree of intervention and mediation. The potential for disputes in public spaces is always present, but there are non-intrusive strategies for organizing space and humanizing cognitive steps that can be taken by the actors themselves that will contribute to conviviality.

Unfortunately, as the third example reveals, there are limits to inclusivity as 'othering' practices and discourses of culture, religion, and politics can enter a space, making it incapable of mediation. The protestors in Grenoble who were banned from pools are French citizens who want to take part in a communal activity and who believe that these spaces should be open to all. Their exclusion raises questions about the limits and balance of regulations and the difference between using regulations for the purpose of keeping people out or using regulations to encourage people in. The latter requires a bottom-up approach through dialogue and a close connection between the users of space and those in charge of regulating it. If this distance is too great or imbalanced, then the space becomes either exclusive or an overly regulated one, which only serves a limited segment of society.

References

Agar, Michael. 2006. "Culture: Can You Take It Anywhere?: Invited Lecture Presented at the Gevirtz Graduate School of Education, University of California at Santa Barbara." *International Journal of Qualitative Methods* 5 (2): 1–16. 10.1177/160940690600500201

BBC News 2017. "Equality complaint sinks women-only swimming class." *BBC News Online*, August 10. https://www.bbc.co.uk/news/uk-england-gloucestershire-40887393

Blommaert, Jan. 2018. *Dialogues with Ethnography: Notes on Classics, and How I Read Them.* Bristol; Blue Ridge Summit: Multilingual Matters. 10.21832/9781783099511

Collins, Haynes. 2021. "Mermaids, Knitted Costumes and Pink Carbolic Soap: Making Meaning and Translating Social Space in Community-Led Pools." *Language and Intercultural Communication* 21 (1): 6982. 10.1080/14708477.2020.1833899

Collins, Haynes, and Chris Pajak. 2019. "The Performance of Swimming: Disorder, Difference and Marginality within a Publicly-Accessible Pool." *Language and Intercultural Communication* 19 (1): 64–76. 10.1080/147084 77.2018.1545027

Copland, Jane. 2021. "As a Former International Swimmer, I've Been Abused by Men Countless Times for Swimming Fast." *The Independent Online*, 30 June. https://www.independent.co.uk/voices/swimming-abuse-women-catcalling-b1875324.html

Dervin, Fred, and Karen Risager, eds. 2014. *Researching Identity and Interculturality.* New York: Routledge. 10.4324/9781315816883

Foucault, Michel. 1975. *Discipline and Punish: The Birth of the Prison.* London: Allen Lane.

Foucault, Michel. 1982. "The Subject and Power." *Critical Inquiry* 8 (4): 777–95. 10.1086/448181

Goffman, Erving. 1959. *The Presentation of Self in Everyday Life.* Garden City, NY: Doubleday.

Gordon, Ian, and Simon Inglis. 2009. *Great Lengths: The Historic Indoor Swimming Pools of Britain. Played in Britain.* Swindon: English Heritage.

Grodach, C. 2010. "Art Spaces, Public Space, and the Link to Community Development." *Community Development Journal* 45 (4): 474–93. 10.1093/cdj/bsp018

Hall, Edward T. 1966. *The Hidden Dimension: Man's Use of Space in Public and Private.* New York: Anchor.

Klinenberg, Eric. 2018. *Palaces for the People: How to Build a More Equal and United Society.* London: The Bodley Head.

Leonard, Madeleine. 2004. "Bonding and Bridging Social Capital: Reflections from Belfast." *Sociology* 38 (5): 927–44. 10.1177/0038038504047176

Lofland, Lyn H. 1998. *The Public Realm: Exploring the City's Quintessential Social Territory.* New York: Routledge. 10.4324/9781315134352

McMurtrie, Robert James. 2016. *The Semiotics of Movement in Space.* New York: Routledge. 10.4324/9781315640273

Paterson, Tony. 2013. "Swiss Introduce Apartheid-like Restrictions: Local Authorities Ban Asylum Seekers from Public Places." *The Independent Online*, 7 August. https://www.independent.co.uk/news/world/europe/swiss-introduce-apartheidlike-restrictions-local-authorities-ban-asylum-seekers-from-public-places-8750765.html

Pusill, Emma, and Janet Wilkinson. 2019. *The Lido Guide.* London: Unbound.

Rodger, James. 2021. "Woman Held Underwater by Male Swimmer after Overtaking Him in Pool." *Birmingham Mail*, 5 July. https://www.birminghammail.co.uk/news/midlands-news/woman-held-underwater-male-swimmer-20974909

Scott, Susie. 2010. "How to Look Good (Nearly) Naked: The Performative Regulation of the Swimmer's Body." *Body & Society* 16 (2): 143–68. 10.1177/1357034X10364768

Staurides, Stauros. 2019. *Common Spaces of Urban Emancipation.* Manchester: Manchester University Press.

Tinkler, Penny. 2013. *Using Photographs in Social and Historical Research.* Los Angeles: Sage.

Wiltse, Jeff. 2007. *Contested Waters: A Social History of Swimming Pools in America.* Chapel Hill: University of North Carolina Press.

Wischgoll, Petra. 2016. "German Town Bars Asylum Seekers from Pool after Harassment Complaints." *Reuters Online*, January 15. https://www.reuters.com/article/us-europe-migrants-germany-pool-idUSKCN0UT1VL

PART III

De-centering Alternative Dispute Resolution (ADR)

16

IMAGINING A RACIALLY DIVERSE AND INCLUSIVE MEDIATION FIELD: UNCOVERING THE STRUCTURAL HURDLES

Maria R. Volpe and Marvin E. Johnson

Creating a racially diverse and inclusive mediation field has been largely acknowledged as essential by mediation organizations, programs, and practitioners in the United States. Despite the widespread consensus that race matters in the delivery of mediation related services, there is no consensus about how best to proceed. Historically, racially different groups in the United States have had remarkably and well documented different experiences. Central to this state of affairs has been the resulting ongoing racism that has prevailed, namely the marginalization of Black people through entrenched practices and structures which have been inextricably associated with cultural, economic, political, and social institutions existing since the first African slaves were brought to the United States. Changing this historic landscape has been daunting.

For the mediation field, its unique nature has multiplied the challenges of what it will take to diversify it. While virtually everyone finds it difficult to pursue mediation as a career, it is even more challenging for those from minority communities. In order to imagine a racially diverse and inclusive mediation field, not only do macro structures in American society need to change, but so do the challenges presented by the mediation field itself. This chapter will address the structural hurdles that continue to create explicit and implicit barriers for achieving a racially diverse and inclusive mediation field.

An overview: Racial diversity and inclusion matter

Given the resounding and recurrent interest in creating a diverse and inclusive mediation field, why is the field so challenged in achieving greater diversity? What are the barriers? What needs must be addressed? In the mediation field, like many other contexts, the oft-cited and now trite exhortation that there is a business case explanation for diversity gets widely repeated. It reminds everyone that it makes good business sense to have a diverse and inclusive field representative of the larger population.

In addition to all of the excellent reasons given for diversification and inclusion, for the mediation field, an important and compelling case can be made that the very nature of the field requires that special attention be paid to diversity since parties need to trust and feel comfortable with the interveners. In fact, the need for diversity is so strong that it is embedded in the Model Standards of Conduct for Mediators. Standard IX (2005), which focuses on the advancement of mediation

DOI: 10.4324/9781003227441-20

practice, states that mediators should engage in "Fostering diversity within the field of mediation." While enthusiasm and support for diversity among mediators is widespread and contagious, it is not sufficient to just hope that it will happen.

There are two main approaches to undertaking diversification for the mediation field. The first assumes that there is an established field awaiting the arrival of new practitioners. At informational events and conferences where sessions are held on how to become a mediator, presenters typically provide insights on how to become a mediator and their messages usually encourage the attendees to network, get to know mediators, find a mentor, shadow established practitioners, seek co-mediation opportunities, engage in public exposure of themselves by writing articles, presenting at events, creating a website, attending conferences, etc. In short, the message sent is that individuals who are interested in pursuing mediation work should be resourceful and creative in taking initiative to become a part of the field. This approach puts the burden on the interested party's shoulders. Regardless of who one is, the expectation is that if individuals are creative, persistent, and indefatigable in pursuing mediation, they will succeed.

A second approach assumes that what is needed is diversity awareness training for existing practitioners to create a welcoming environment for individuals from different backgrounds. The training could include bias awareness, racial awareness, microaggression awareness, micro inequities, etc. The thinking here is that after extensive training, everyone who is associated with the mediation field would know how to welcome practitioners from diverse backgrounds and everyone would feel comfortable and accepted. Related to this is the notion that if the field is known to be welcoming, people from all walks of life will pursue mediation and everyone will co-exist with ease.

In short, one could conclude that diversity and inclusion would be achieved if potential mediators took the initiative to build a practice or find employment opportunities in the mediation field or if those already in the field availed themselves of relevant awareness training programs. In fact, the aforementioned approaches do not address the deep-rooted structures, policies, practices, norms, and values that create unique challenges that transcend the stated approaches.

Pulling back the curtain on the mediation field

A close examination of the roots of any field provides invaluable understandings about what shapes its established ways of doing things. The explicit and implicit social structures, policies, practices, norms, and values become so internalized and normalized that they are taken for granted and are no longer visible to those who are impacted by them. This phenomenon of entrenched circumstances was vividly illustrated by Wallace (2005) who discussed the relationship of fish to water in the following parable:

> There are these two young fish swimming along and they happen to meet an older fish swimming the other way, who nods at them and says 'Morning, boys. How's the water?' And the two young fish swim on for a bit, and then eventually one of them looks over at the other and goes 'What the hell is water?'

Like the fish which are so surrounded by water that they are no longer aware of it, mediation embodies structural and philosophical features that are so embedded in its infrastructure and history that they are no longer noticed. They are recited as commonplace understandings of the field. As a result, despite the expressed commitments to diversification and all of the efforts launched over the years, the mediation context remains so unique that approaches that may work elsewhere are not as easily applied to the mediation field. Without addressing what creates mediation's current state of affairs, the field may continue to struggle with how to diversify long into the future.

Volunteerism

Contemporary mediation is rooted in volunteerism for the vast majority of entry-level mediators seeking entry level work. Volunteerism takes time and is uncompensated. How attractive or feasible is it for people interested in becoming a mediator to know that they will have opportunities to volunteer in order to gain experience or to do the work of a mediator, if such opportunities are even available? This approach is particularly challenging for those eager to enter the workforce as a mediator but are not in a position to do uncompensated work for a substantial period of time. Imagine being told that upon graduation from college, law school, or any other educational institution that what awaits you is the opportunity to do exciting work, but that you will not be compensated. Even worse, the potential job market awaiting once you have participated in a significant amount of volunteer work is very limited.

For those who are already employed elsewhere and interested in switching careers to become a mediator, they are cautioned to not leave their day job. This advice is part of the folklore of the mediation field. To pursue mediation as a new career, people are encouraged to do volunteer work, move slowly, and be prepared for a long, drawn-out preparation process with little or no compensation.

The roots of volunteerism in mediation are easy to find. A quick examination of how mediation has gotten to this point is explained by the prominent role that community mediation programs have played in recruiting and training citizens in local communities as mediators (Corbett and Corbett 2011). Once trained, community mediators helped their neighbors manage their conflicts at the local community mediation centers instead of resorting to the courts. Historically, the community mediation services have been provided by volunteers for free. The popularity of community-based mediation programs has grown since the late sixties with thousands of mediators being trained in the United States.

As the number of people interested in becoming mediators has grown, the opportunities to utilize them has not kept pace. First, the supply of mediators was always much greater than the number of individuals seeking services where one got to meet face to face with one's nemesis and work things out. Second, in addition to the community mediation programs, private trainers, and institutions of higher education, including law, business, and graduate schools, all began providing training programs. Finally, in response to the ongoing requests for trainings, the community mediation programs increased the number of training programs offered and started charging fees to create a new funding stream to sustain and expand their operations.

When community mediation programs provided opportunities for trained individuals to practice, the mediators typically conducted the mediation sessions for free. Many embraced the opportunity to utilize their newfound skills. As mediation gained popularity, many courts also began to offer mediation by volunteer mediators. While mediation was promoted as a better way to resolve court connected conflicts, it was operationalized as a less expensive way. Somehow, less expensive, more often than not, has gotten translated into pro bono services by providers. For aspiring mediators, the opportunity to mediate has always been attractive, even if uncompensated, since it provides an opportunity to gain experience.

Lack of career path and universal credentials

There is still no established or widely recognized path for those interested in becoming a mediator. Even when individuals figure out how to pursue entry, the pathway continues to be perplexing as they as attempt to gain experience and compensated work. Related to this is the lack of universal credentials. Many questions are raised, including: What should training to become a mediator consist of? How does one choose which education and/or training program one should pursue? Are there non-mediation credentials that are relevant? What about substantive background, does that matter?

Does one need specific experience, e.g., number of years in a specific industry? Does some experience work better than other types of experience, e.g., judicial, international relations, finance, real estate, etc.? Does lived experience matter, for example, life style, life circumstances, etc.? How much do personal qualities matter, for example: Emotional intelligence, resourcefulness, wisdom, persuasiveness, etc. What is the role of race, gender, sexual orientation, ethnicity, age, language skills, geographic origins, hobbies, etc. in becoming and serving as a mediator? For sure, some of the aforementioned criteria overlap and they matter differentially in different contexts.

The flexibility of credentials provides many opportunities, but it is confusing for those considering a mediation career. The challenge for not having a clearly defined path is that for those who are interested in pursuing mediation as a career, it can feel overwhelming. There is no identifiable academic home or identity to investigate. In addition to a vague entry into the field, there is no easy way to identify how one moves up in the field.

Given the current state of mediation, it is daunting to try to attract individuals from different backgrounds if they cannot identify what is needed to become a mediator. For young people considering careers, if credentials are not clear and compensated employment is scarce, they will find the pursuing the field unfeasible. Moreover, since older individuals who pursue mediation often come from every imaginable background, it would be near impossible to draw from their background information to promote mediation and recruit mediators as is done by other fields with clearly defined credentials and qualifications.

The high walls

Mediation sessions are typically held behind closed doors where parties are assured confidentiality. As a result, no one can see what is going on and people cannot observe firsthand what a mediator does. Mediators have to be careful about what they disclose about their cases. They are expected to be invisible. They help the parties but do not surface for accolades or explanations. TV shows typically do not showcase mediation. However, when they refer to it, the process may not be portrayed as mediators might describe it.

While the media are quick to highlight conflict, they rarely if ever report on mediated cases. Focusing on new stories that gain viewership or readership is what gets attention. Mediators take pride in discussing how they ensure privacy and confidentiality. Such walls work well for recruiting business from clients looking to keep their matter private. However, the same high walls that surround the process and are seen as beneficial, also create barriers in the recruitment of people to pursue a career as a mediator. Quite simply, the very practices that tout mediation's value also create a void in understanding what mediators do.

This raises a variety of questions, including: Who is the voice of the field? Who is the *go to* person(s) when expertise about conflicts is needed? Should mediators maintain a *low* profile? A low profile is fine, but out of sight here means out of mind. Neither potential users nor potential practitioners will hear about how mediation works. For those who might otherwise be interested in entering the mediation field, not hearing about the nature of the work, does not make it a sought-after destination.

Accessing the gatekeepers

Like many other fields, mediation has gatekeepers who make decisions about who might be selected for work opportunities. While networking is often referred to as vital in order to access those who make decisions about assigning, appointing, or referring mediators, in fact accessing, those who manage the upper reaches of the field can be out-of-reach. This is complicated by the fact that the mediation field relies not only on knowing individuals but trusting them on several levels, that the individuals will perform, and that the parties will respond favorably to them. When anyone like gatekeepers make a referral, it is like putting their seal of approval on who they suggest. The gatekeepers' own reputation may be at stake. It is not surprising that they stay within their own comfort zone of who is known to them.

As Johnson and Volpe (2017) have noted, implicit biases may play a role in who gets selected. Everyone has biases that impact how we think and see the world. Preferences or aversions toward others occur without conscious knowledge. While individuals may assert that they accept individuals from other groups, their actions may not even be aware that they are taking actions influenced by what is going on below the conscious level. While increasing attention is being paid to the importance of understanding how our actions are influenced by unintentional and uncontrollable biases, they are nonetheless detrimental to opening access in some contexts. Implicit biases create circumstances that reproduce what works well in one's comfort zone.

While uncompensated or nominally compensated opportunities may be available, the better compensated opportunities are not readily known to diverse segments of the field. According to Johnson and LaRue (2009), the practices of who chooses mediators can feel like one is confronted with a gated community. Only those who are members are let in.

Core values of mediation

Neutrality, impartiality, and self-determination are core values of mediation that are embedded in the Model Standards of Conduct for Mediators. By treating all parties fairly, not taking sides, and making space for parties to determine their own futures, mediators can ideally create a process where all participants feel welcome and perhaps even equal.

However, the mediation process does not lend itself well in resolving all kinds of matters, particularly where there is an expressed need or expectation that the intervener pay attention to injustices. For example, mediation's core values may be a deterrent for those embracing a social justice lens where a brave or more rights-based space is needed to address social inequities (Johnson and Volpe 2020). For mediators, remaining neutral means that the parties make decisions about their concerns. Clearly, this approach may not feel comfortable for those seeking a more assertive approach in achieving diversity and inclusion.

Limited data

Metrics for most aspects of the mediation field are buried or nonexistent (Volpe 2019). Basic information about the number of practicing mediators, the number of cases that are mediated, the demographics of who uses mediation services, and what the salary ranges for mediators remains virtually unknown. Some of this is a result of the limited or scattered recordkeeping since there is no entity that collects data about or mediators or their work. The American Bar Association (2018, 3) noted that "data on the diversity of neutrals within Dispute Resolution are scarce."

Without readily accessible data, information about how diverse the mediation field is remains unknown. Contributing to this vagueness is what is meant by the term 'diversity.' Who does it include? Depending on context, what it refers to can be very different. For example, with respect to race, when the broader concept *people of color* has been used, it has included many who self-define as POC who might not otherwise be included in a more specific classification of race.

Due to the complexity of the current state of the data for the mediation field and how diversity is defined, trying to establish a baseline or goals for diversifying the field can be daunting.

Domination of ADR field by legal profession

For a variety of reasons, there is an increasing association between mediation and the legal profession. Law schools are offering mediation courses. Bar associations have active ADR committees.

Law firms are adding ADR units. Courts are offering mediation as an option. As mediation increases its presence in the court systems, there is increasing reliance on attorneys. With this growth, in some contexts, the implications are that if one is not an attorney, one cannot pursue mediation. If the proliferation of attorneys continues for the mediation field and the pipeline to becoming a mediator includes a law degree, for diversification to occur, the legal field would have to undergo a diversity transformation in order for the mediation field to be diverse.

Additionally, as pressure arises for quality assurance, attention has been given to changing or raising the requirements for becoming a mediator. Since the mediation field has not established its own credentials, for some, a law degree has become a default credential. What this means then is if the legal field is has underrepresentation of racial groups, the pipeline to mediation will also have underrepresentation. Moreover, since the mediation field is less likely to have comparable compensated opportunities that are available for legal work, the potential pipeline of newcomers to mediation from the legal field can be even smaller than in the legal field itself.

Boundaries

Where does mediation work begin and end? Erickson and Johnson (2012) referred to the blurring of the boundaries of ADR processes as the larger dispute resolution field matures. The nuances between collaborative and competitive processes are difficult to distinguish. There are those who refer to mediators as decision makers, and others who refer to mediation and arbitration interchangeably. Such fuzziness contributes to the public's confusion about the distinction between ADR processes themselves.

Additionally, since so many professionals also respond to conflicts, the boundaries between mediation and other professions can be challenging. For some professions, boundaries are identified in the practice of the profession. For example, with respect to the legal field, boundaries are established about what constitutes acceptable professional behavior on the part of lawyers. For those who do not comply with the Rules of Professional Conduct established by the legal field, there are potential consequences. Violation could mean that complainants could file legal malpractice claims or report attorneys to the state's disciplinary board. The legal field has made attempts to keep the *good* practitioners in and the *violators* out. As a result, it safeguards itself from just anyone practicing law.

On the other hand, the boundaries for mediation are very amorphous and porous. Mediation work does not clearly identify its boundaries vis a vis many other fields such as social work, therapy, counseling, law, journalism, restorative justice, etc. Definitions like *mediators make talk work*, they help parties reach understandings, they are an extension of the negotiation process, help parties to reach understandings, etc. are what others do as well. Someone unfamiliar with the intricacies of the mediation field would not know that what they are doing is overreaching into the mediation field, particularly since there are no safeguards for being a mediator. And those who mediate poorly can give mediation a *bad* reputation without consequences.

In terms of diversifying the field, it is not easy for those who might be interested in becoming mediators to distinguish what mediators do from what others do in all of the other fields that attempt to help individuals who are experiencing conflict-related situations.

Impact of technology

While online dispute resolution has been growing steadily for over two decades, since the onset of COVID-19, interest and usage of online dispute resolution has grown exponentially. The restricted travel and social distancing policies all contributed to an almost overnight transformation of a field that had heretofore found in person presence the norm to one where virtual mediation now dominates how cases are processed.

Despite the growing enthusiastic use of online approaches, there is much to be learned about how the diversity of the field will be impacted by the new environment to which mediation is adapting. What role will it play in helping to make the mediation field more diverse and inclusive? Will it increase the diversity of practitioners and users, or will it serve as another structural barrier?

On the one hand, technology has increased access to the mediation field similar to what has occurred for many other fields. As a result, the potential to reach broader constituencies and users as well as the ability to make the process conveniently available to all from whereever they have increased. The use of technology can reduce the time and costs associated with learning about the process for those who are interested in becoming mediators as well as by disputants who could make use of it. On the other hand, the technology can also be limiting for those who are not tech savvy or do not have access to sufficient online resources, including computers, internet, software, etc. as well as necessary quiet space to be able to conduct a call virtually.

While it is relatively easy to assume that the online format can make mediation more accessible, how the diversity of the mediation field will be affected by this new environment remains unknown. The pandemic has provided every field with an opportunity to rethink how they package themselves, their products, and services. The use of technology has already dramatically changed the way mediators undertake their work. It will be important to stay abreast of research to understand how the other dynamics of in-person interactions, including those where implicit biases occur, play out online.

Rethinking: What can be done to diversify the mediation field?

In thinking about the diversification of the mediation field, it is crucial to keep in mind that its existing structures, policies, practices, and values are so embedded, internalized, and normalized that they are taken for granted and have become invisible. While mediators may release all of the appropriate sound bites about the necessity of diversity, the entrenched structures, policies, practices, and values are at the forefront of creating barriers to achieve a racially diverse and inclusive field.

A significant step for mediators is to think about how to increase compensated opportunities. Perhaps the most radical step would be for mediators to stop doing pro bono mediation. However, mediators are often so delighted to be included in some initiatives that they do not hesitate to offer their services for free. The recurrent question is, how can someone who cannot afford to do uncompensated work pursue mediation?

While the high walls that offer confidentiality are important for mediation work, it is imperative that mediators take leadership and responsibility to create and disseminate promotional pieces that describe what goes on behind the walls. They can vividly describe how mediation works in articles, talks, podcasts, blogs, and other social media without violating confidentiality. To attract individuals who have never heard about mediation and do not have mediation role models in their communities, there needs to be a way for them to fully understand how mediation works via readily available sources.

Diversity assumes that lived experience matters. However, diversity alone is not sufficient to become a good mediator. What else matters? What matters more? What criteria does the mediation field need to revisit: training standards, number of cases conducted, discipline of origin, past experiences, e.g., judicial, legal, counseling, etc.?

Uppermost, mediators need to brainstorm ways to address structures, policies, practices, norms, and values that contribute to stalling diversity efforts. Looking to how others external to the field address diversity is important. However, the infrastructure that the field has embraced is an internal matter that needs to be remedied by mediators themselves. The courts can make mediation available, but as long as the requests are for pro bono work, what would happen if all cases were settled within the allotted free time or if the parties chose to not continue their case if they had to pay? Is it conceivable that mediators could find themselves without any income after providing initial pro bono services?

Even if individuals networked, found mentors, shadowed experienced mediators, observed cases, and followed all of the suggested recommendations to become a mediator, the truth remains that it would still be challenging to diversify the mediation field without addressing the many structural barriers that are inherent in the very nature of the field itself. As Wallace (2005) noted, "The most obvious, important realities are often the ones that are hardest to see and talk about." For the mediation field, it will not be sufficient to replicate what many other fields have done to diversify. It will require tackling structures and practices that are deeply embedded in its history and have been passed down over the years.

References

American Arbitration Association, American Bar Association, Association for Conflict Resolution. 2005. *Model Standards of Conduct for Mediators*. https://www.americanbar.org/content/dam/aba/administrative/dispute_resolution/dispute_resolution/model_standards_conduct_april2007.pdf

American Bar Association. 2018. *Section of Dispute Resolution Report to the House of Delegates Resolution 105.* https://www.americanbar.org/content/dam/aba/images/abanews/2018-AM-Resolutions/105.pdf

Corbett, Justin, and Wendy Corbett. 2011. *The State of Community Mediation 2011*. Rochester, NY: Social Science Research Network. https://papers.ssrn.com/abstract=2030467

Erickson, Stephen K., and Marvin E. Johnson. (2012) "ADR Techniques and Procedures Flowing Through Porous Boundaries: Flooding the ADR Landscape and Confusing the Public." *Practical Dispute Resolution.* 5 (1): 1–15.

Johnson, Marvin E., and Homer C. LaRue. 2009. "The Gated Community: Risk Aversion, Race, and the Lack of Diversity in Mediation in the Top Ranks." *American Bar Association Dispute Resolution Magazine.* 15 (3): 17–20.

Johnson, Marvin E., and Maria R. Volpe. 2017. "The Color of Money: Compensation Opportunities and Barriers." *American Bar Association Dispute Resolution Magazine.* 23 (4): 14–8.

Johnson, Marvin E., and Maria R. Volpe. 2020. "Understanding the Deep-Rooted Complexity of Racism." *ACResolution.* November, 22–24. https://www.acresolution-digital.org/acresolutionmag/library/item/november_2020/3883762/

Volpe, Maria R. 2019. "Measuring Diversity in the ADR Field: Some Observations and Challenges Regarding Transparency, Metrics and Empirical Research." *Pepperdine Dispute Resolution Law Journal* 19 (2): 201–19.

Wallace, David Foster. May 21, 2005. *Transcription of the 2005 Kenyon Commencement Address.* https://web.ics.purdue.edu/~drkelly/DFWKenyonAddress2005.pdf

17

INTERCULTURAL MEDIATION FROM A EUROPEAN PERSPECTIVE

Agostino Portera

Introduction

The world in which we are living is undergoing dramatic changes. Today we are witnessing an increase in encounters, which often turn into clashes and conflicts, sometimes highly destructive. In all sectors of our lives there is a growing fluidity or liquidity. We are living in a time of "nowist culture" and "hurried culture" (Bertman 1998) with the lack of time and the (obsessive) seeking for something new and with the renegotiation of the meaning of our fundamental references. In the liquid-modern "society of consumers," Bauman (2016, 21) described the transition from linear to "pointillist time" [...] "broken up into a multitude of separate morsels, each morsel reduced to a point ever more closely approximating its geometrical idealization of non-dimensionality."

Migration and the advent of increasingly *multi-ethnic and multicultural societies* also contribute to several drastic changes (Bauman, Portera, and Mazzeo 2021). The emergence of a single market on a world scale, the concentration and internationalization of capital, and the persistent *economic wars* between nation States have caused an imbalance of wealth with consequences also of a political and social nature. Furthermore, the phenomenon of *neoliberalism*, has been considered as a shift towards dehumanizing ways of life. Schools and universities, traditionally spaces for education, culture, and democracy, are becoming more and more mere places of "performance and efficiency" (Giroux and Giroux 2006, 24) that promote excessive individualism (loss of the ability to perceive oneself as a part of social group with common humanity), indifference (toward needs and sufferings of plants, animals, and other human beings), competition (the detriment of cooperation), reductionism of complex phenomena and problems (experts in details, unable to grasp links), standardization (little or no consideration of individual and social differences and inequalities), and the promotion of a culture of *I don't care* (see also Portera 2016).

In the professional encounter, especially in educational and psychological fields, radical changes have also arisen. Teachers, mediators, counselors, and psychotherapists who are applying their own methods and practices (often unintentionally in ethnocentric ways) are facing new challenges. The encounter with people who hold different beliefs, values, behaviors, and *Weltanschauung*, complicate professional helping relationships. Language barriers, different communication styles, expectations, and understandings of problems become an obstacle, which leads to insecurities and new conflicts (Portera, Moodley, and Milani 2020). Here the central question refers to the forms of intervention in the field of mediation: How should traditional approaches be modified to deal with the new challenges?

DOI: 10.4324/9781003227441-21

Conflict and mediation

Conflict is inevitable in human life. The phylogenetic and ontogenetic development of the human being is inexorably linked with the presence of conflict. In order to live, we are *condemned* to destroy the lives of others. This is one of the deepest and ineluctable conflicts of human beings; "Am I indebted to being? Being, persisting in being, do I not kill? Being in the world, do I not take the place of someone else?" questioned Emmanuel Lévinas (1984, 148).

The concepts of *conflict* and *aggression* have been faced from the human sciences, especially sociology and psychology, as well as biology and ethology. Lately, they are also finding more and more attention in education. Historically, almost all disciplines have considered human aggression from a purely negative point of view, especially considering the tremendous damage it has caused. It was mainly thanks to psychology, in particular to the schools of psychotherapy, that the best conditions for the development of personality were understood in the ability to evaluate and positively address conflicts. For many years the educational visions have been predominantly conditioned by disruptive and often destructive forces associated with human aggression (Galtung 1996; Shultz 2007).

Etymologically, the word *aggression* refers to the Latin etymon *ad* and *gradi* (to go). In Latin, *ad* could also mean *against*: In this case it could actually refer to that negative aggressiveness (assault, destroy) of which Western literature is wedged. But *ad* may also indicate a positive attitude: *Towards*, which means growth, vitality, moving towards a goal in a secure way, attacking a problem (Fromm 1994). Therefore, in mediation it is necessary to start from the assumption that, despite some '*pacifistic utopias,*' basic aggressiveness is an ineliminable tendency of humans, which can neither be fully repressed nor allowed to be manifested in violent, uncontrolled, and destructive ways. Further, the term *conflict* comes from the Latin *conflictus*, from the verb *confligere*, which means *to bump, to bump against*. This is the common understanding of conflict as confrontation. The classical political thought of Plato and Aristotle was based on an idea of a society characterized by order and harmony where conflict was an imbalance of the natural condition: A pathological state of disharmony. A carefully study of its etymology reveals that *conflictus* can also take on the meaning of bringing together—aiming at an encounter. Machiavelli and Hobbes subvert the traditional conception of man and society, by developing an *anthropology of conflict*, where conflict is seen as the natural condition of the individual, which can only be regulated and managed through the exercise of reason, the only way of channeling man's passions and selfish spirit (Arielli and Scotto 1998, 5–9).

Today, globalization and the advent of pluralistic and multicultural societies imply not only an increase in conflict, but also add to it many novel aspects, especially on the level of communication. Therefore, especially in intercultural mediation, it is essential to reverse this trend and to begin considering conflict and aggression as unavoidable factors of human existence. The challenge consists in recognizing them in their specific entity (their disruptive and propulsive part) and learning to manage them in the most appropriate way both for the individual and for the community.

Among the positive aspects of the conflict, Johnson and Johnson (1995) indicate the intellectual stimulus (the capacity of reflection, reasoning, and *heterocentration*), as well as the promotion of a more intense and meaningful relationship with others. The scope of a positive mediation is to make conflicts explicit, by correctly identifying their nature, reasons, and background. At a closer look, conflicts can involve multiple levels, including some visible and others hidden, like positions, interests, personality problems, and significant past experiences (Besemer 1999). Conflicts also have several possible backgrounds, like the coexistence of different interests or needs, the involvement of hurt feelings, and the presence of disturbed relationships. Moreover, especially in multicultural settings, at the basis of a conflict there may be misunderstandings, communication problems, and a lack of information. In other cases, there might be structural conditions, environmental factors, economic injustice, or political oppression (see also Mitchell 1981). Nowadays, *mediation* is considered as a highly effective method of conflict management and is applied in many fields, from family mediation to school mediation, from law to economic, from health care to political international negotiations. In industrialized societies, especially in the West, discussion, argument, and negotiation are used as the main strategies of conflict resolution. Although *discussion* and *argumentation* have considerable advantages, they are based on thinking in terms of contrasts, which provokes the polarization of the conflict: Usually, one part wins, the other loses; the stronger point of view is imposed, not necessarily the better one. The risk of such a method is that the *fronts* become increasingly rigid; no new ideas are developed; time, energy, costs, and creativity are used only to weaken and overcome the ideas of others. Even the technique of *negotiation*, aimed at *compromise*, presents the risk of acting only within some limits, instead of seeking solutions in a creative way. If practitioners too overly focus on solving a given problem, they run the risk of seeing only a single and rather superficial cause, and thereby ignoring everything else; often because it is the easiest one to discover. Mediation instead wants to pass from fights to solutions. The method allows finding a solution, aims at promoting clients' communication and growth, so that they will be able to develop new solutions autonomously (De Bono 1989). In mediation, all interests are taken into account; people are acknowledged as distinctive from factual problems; it is possible to reflect about different possibilities of action before deciding what to do; all *truths* (all points of view) are considered; the union of means and purpose is practiced; only objectives valid for all parties are pursued; power is used not against others, but to achieve common goals (Folberg and Taylor 1984; Bercovitch, Anagnoson, and Wille 1991). At the root of mediation, in particular if intercultural, there is the awareness that: a) conflict is not negative in itself, only unresolved conflicts are dangerous; b) many conflicts arise from the difficulty of solving a problem, not from a lack of will to solve it; c) the best decisions about a conflict are those made by the parties involved; d) those who have reached an agreement are more respectful of the decisions if they themselves contributed to its achievement and if they accept the process that led to the agreement. Through successful mediation, conflicts can develop as opportunities for growth and enrichment. Rather than entrusting responsibility to specialists (such as lawyers or psychotherapists), even in the presence of an expert, the parties to the dispute maintain control of the problem. Instead of leaving room for the devastating forces of a destructive quarrel, participants can take responsibility and deal constructively with conflicts. Mediators, in their role as impartial third parties, can interrupt the process of escalation of conflicts and show participants the way to reach constructive solutions. Clients' attitudes towards a struggle to the bitter end, thinking in categories and defeating victory, can be transformed into mutual advantage towards creative solutions that take into account the interests of all the parties involved. By resolving conflicts without the use of power, force or violence, mediation can not only help to solve present difficulties, but can also prevent future problems, through promoting constructive solution-seeking, improving mutual relations, and developing lifelong conflict management skills (Mayer 2006).

In his research on the institutional barriers and critical factors that have hindered the quality of the relationship and the success in the management of conflicts in multicultural fields in Italy, Portera (2013) has identified difficulties between colleagues and among families with children of foreign origin because of a lack of time and/or reflectivity. In conflict situations, several teachers used communicative forms characterized by stigmatization, stereotypes, and prejudices. In the *health* sector (and similar in the business and law sectors), many conflicts arose for the lack of shared (or target) language (and use of relatives as translators) and the limited time available compared to the high number of tasks and roles required. Further barriers were the ethnocentric attitudes, stereotypes, and prejudices and also the poor (or absence) investment in intercultural training. With regard specifically to (intercultural) *mediation*, many practitioners found it difficult to identify tasks and boundaries of their work.

Intercultural mediation

Globalization, multicultural societies, and economic, political, and cultural interdependence are raising relevant questions for mediation. In countries with greater immigration, such as the United States,

Canada, and Australia, many new approaches and models have been developed (Moodley 1999). Portera (2020, 10–30) has summarized and analyzed the most relevant approaches to culture mentioned above. Four main directions have been recognized: Metacultural, transcultural, multicultural, and intercultural.

1   A first group of interventions could be described as *metacultural*. The term *meta-culture* refers to a *culture over the culture*, a *supra culture* (such as metaphysics in relation to physics or meta-communication in relation to communication). This group includes all forms of intervention aiming to work with clients, without taking into account the cultural differences, and without 'changing the culture' of people with an immigration background (Moodley 1999, 6). In my opinion, this assumption is faulty and misleading. No interpersonal encounter (above all mediation) can take place without changes in culturally related beliefs and behavior. Norms, values, and rules are involved in any interpersonal and professional encounter. Therefore, the metacultural model can be considered as inadequate and potentially dangerous, because it leads to assume that effective mediation can be conducted without a consideration of the clients' culture.

2   The second group of interventions could be associated with the term *transculture*. Generally, *cross-cultural* or transcultural strategies are based on universalism and are aimed at the development of universal and common characteristics, values (e.g., respect, honesty, autonomy), and concepts (e.g., peace, justice, environmental protection). In the psychiatric and psychological field, the transcultural approach was mostly applied by using ones' own method also for the treatment of people from foreign countries (an example is ethno-psychoanalysis by Devereux (1992) or Nathan (1993)). Although in mediation the transcultural approach brings many advantages, there are also several limitations: It could lead to a uniform view of the world while in reality it is very heterogenous. There is a risk of regarding one's own values, norms, and rules as universal, and to impose one's own values and *Weltanschauung*. Furthermore, this approach builds upon a static view of culture. So, its application could encourage an assimilationist orientation towards minorities. Instead, in the mediation field, all treatment methods should be considered as having deep cultural roots (having been developed and applied in a certain time and in a specific cultural background). They all contain their own rules, norms, and values, and reflect their own understandings of conflicts, disease, illness, and adequate treatment. Since as human beings we cannot be neutral, especially in the asymmetric professional settings. Mediators may thus run the risk of imposing (often unwittingly) their own thinking patterns on their clients.

3   A third group of interventions could be described as *multicultural*. These models are based on a philosophical orientation of cultural relativism, which emphasizes the uniqueness of every culture, and every culture's right to autonomy. Multiculturalism, aimed at a peaceful co-existence, in mediation shows many advantages. Strangeness is respected, and foreigners and immigrants are agreed the same rights as the locals. Moving through an ethnic awareness can lead to the strengthening of personal and cultural identity, with an overall positive development for the clients. Further, proper consideration of the physical and cultural differences and knowledge in relation to other cultures, languages or religions can help professionals to overcome many obstacles to understand culture-specific explanations of conflicts and attempts of solutions. In spite of the advantages of the multicultural perspective, mediators may risk adopting a homogeneous (nationalistic) view of cultures, which results in static and rigid thinking, with the danger of developing stereotypes and prejudices. The question remains open whether mediators should act as experts for their field across all cultures or if they shall only work with clients from their own country. In addition, by overly stressing cultural differences, many other important aspects of the clients' problems could be ignored (like vulnerability factors, marginalization, isolation, political and legal discrimination, poverty). And some deviant

behavior (such as hyperactivity or depression) could be misinterpreted as culture-specific behavior (spirited or shy).

4   A fourth group of interventions, in my opinion the most appropriate, is called *intercultural*. Although the term *intercultural* was previously used in the USA with a different meaning the intercultural approach was developed in Europe. The word *intercultural education* was first used in the USA in the early 1930. However, its strategies focused on assimilation and often ended in segregation and discrimination (McGee Banks 2011). The intercultural approach, in my opinion, represents a new 'Copernican' revolution (Portera 2010) because concepts like identity or culture are no longer considered as static but as dynamic. Further, emigration and life in a pluralistic and multicultural society are viewed not only as risk factors for disorders but also as opportunities for enrichment and personal and social development. Epistemologically, the intercultural approach includes all the positive aspects of universalism and relativism (by recognizing its limits) and adds something new. Beyond understanding and respecting differences (multicultural) and removing injustice by recognizing communal laws and roles (transcultural), it includes also the opportunity for genuine interaction, which means change through encounter, dialogue, confrontation, and conflict resolution. In the fields of mediation, the use of the intercultural approach involves overcoming the static and hierarchic conception of culture. The encounter with the foreigners is considered as an opportunity for dialogue, confrontation, and a positive change. Such positive development can best occur through the promotion of real communication, contact, encounters, and interaction. Clients with different cultural backgrounds are not (directly or indirectly) *forced* into singular elements of their cultural identities (which hides some dangers, especially for adolescents; Portera 1995). The professional encounter with the clients provides the possibility of open reflection and comparison of some culturally rooted concepts, ideas, and pre-judgments. Self-conceptualization can be reconsidered and (if wrong or maladaptive) changed through the assumption of a more dynamic and interactive way of thinking.

Intercultural mediation in Europe

In Europe, since the Treaty of Amsterdam (European Communities 1997), the inclusion of immigrants has been considered as the *first pillar*. The European Year of Intercultural Dialogue in 2008 (European Commission. Directorate-General for Education and Culture 2009) affirmed the "multicultural character of many countries" and the need for intercultural dialogue. Until today, intercultural mediation (IM) has been considered to be the most promising approach for inclusion and conflict management. IM is considered as an opportunity for individuals and cultural groups to cease living in isolation. Interpreting means that translators focus on what is said during interpersonal encounters and that they primarily focus on language structure but not on the inner meanings of a message. Intercultural mediation instead precisely emphasizes on cultural meanings and focuses on communication by combining elements from psychology, sociology, science of communication, and political science. It can be considered as a bridging of cultures and meanings (Wieviorka 2003).

After the most recent WHO report (Verrept 2019), intercultural mediators are highly effective in bridging linguistic and cultural barriers and are also indispensable to high-quality, comprehensive healthcare service for refugees and migrants. A comprehensive WHO literature review between August 2018 and January 2019 found that in healthcare systems, intercultural mediators are employed with the aim of reducing cultural and linguistic barriers and increasing the accessibility and quality of health care for refugees and migrants. Unfortunately, so far, no review of their roles or evaluation of their effectiveness have been published. In the 17 member states of the WHO European Region "intercultural mediation is a precarious, temporary occupation with an uncertain income" (Verrept 2019, VIII).

Another systematic literature review (Portera, Trevisan, and Milani 2020), focused on books and articles published in peer-reviewed journals, documents the high attractiveness that is ascribed do intercultural mediation in Europe. However, it remains unclear what intercultural mediation means and how it should be structured and supported as a profession. Across the 47 studies, different ideas about intercultural mediation were found. Many of these conceptual articles did not build on previous findings and definitions or even acknowledge previously published works. Nowadays, in Europe, most of the literature on IM refers to linguistic, translation, and interpreting (Dasli 2011; Liddicoat 2016). There are also notable works in the field of law and arbitration (Adeline and Hausmann 2009), economic relations (Broszkiewicz 2018), political conflicts, health care (Verrept 2019), family mediation (Nylund, Ervasti, and Adrian 2018), as well as school mediation (Catarci and Fiorucci 2020).

Considering the above results, in my opinion there is no particular method that is indicated for IM. Every approach shows positive aspects and limitations. Rather than identifying a particular approach as the most appropriate one, it is now more important to reflect on how traditional methods need to be improved by application in different cultural settings (Portera 2020). However, some elements must be considered necessary: First, an effective intervention in IM should necessarily recognize the *needs* of the clients. In previous research, I tried to identify the positive outcomes and opportunities, as well as the risks related with migration and living in a multicultural context (Portera 1995 and 1998). The method was a longitudinal, qualitative case study with 23 young people of Italian origin in Germany.

The study has identified several *main risk factors*, which are sudden, unprepared separation; frequent journeys between Germany and Italy; ambivalent behavior (especially that resulting from conflicting messages from school and family); social marginality and practical problems (debt, marginality, insufficient legal security); discrimination and stigmatization from peers or adults; isolation and loneliness; language problems; and strict upbringing (more than in the country of origin). It has additionally identified the following *protective factors*: Establishing a firm and secure relationship with a person of reference during childhood; parents' openness towards the German environment; parents' understanding and trust; readiness for separation; positive experience of acceptance and respect in the host country; understanding from teachers and educators; no pressure to assimilation; role of friends as a *bridge* between the cultures; external support also through counseling or therapy.

Furthermore, the study has also identified the most appropriate coping strategies. In many cases, the interviewed adolescents adopted coping strategies (e.g., passivity, submission) that were appropriate for solving conflicts in the country of origin or in the family, but not at school or in German society (Portera 1995, 211–2). On this basis, a theory of *fundamental needs of human development* has been developed, which takes into account the effects of globalization and life in the multicultural context. This theory is mainly based on the work of Maslow (1954), but also considering other psychological theories, mainly Rogers (1961) and Erikson (1968). The most important needs were: Physical well-being (metabolism, nutrition, sleep); social relations and sense of belonging (to feel part of a group, to feel similar to others and to interact with them); social bonds (to create a close relationship, with at least one main person of reference, possibly but not necessarily the mother); separation (to develop full autonomy); positive emotional regard (acknowledgment, respect, and acceptance), deep understanding (empathy), and congruence; trust (to oneself and to the external world); active participation (to live one's own life as a protagonist and not as a dominated); structure (clear, determined and reliable limits for orientation); continuity (internalize stable criteria for evaluating the external world; and not to be forced to remove or deny parts of one's own cultural standards, in order to be accepted). In a successive step, based on the research results, I also illustrated some correlations between fundamental needs, conflicts, and the development of psychic disturbances and disorders (Portera 1999) and also the implications for psychological support (Portera 2010). Next to considering risk, protective factors and fundamental needs, mediators need also to acquire intercultural competences (IC). Recently the *Centre for Intercultural Studies* in Verona carried out a study on intercultural competences needed in education, counseling, and mediation (Portera 2017). The results were used to develop a model of IC, which underlines its interactive aspects. This model places an *Area of the Self* in its center containing attitudes (like openness, sensitivity, decentralization, curiosity, humility, flexibility, respect, responsibility, critical thinking, acceptance, empathy, and congruence). In the model, this *Area of the Self* is surrounded by several different categories of *Knowledge* (awareness of the cultural self, knowledge of one's own culture and the culture of others), verbal-linguistic, nonverbal and paraverbal knowledge, disciplinary, multidisciplinary, and interdisciplinary knowledge) and *skills*, including linguistic and communicative skills, observation, analyzing and interpreting subjective reality, establishing positive relationships, building stable and trustful relationships, etc. Subsequently, Portera (2020) has validated the aforementioned model using the Delphi method. As a result, a new model of IC has been developed, which transcends the Eurocentric or North American conceptualization of IC and include competences rooted in Eastern traditions, mentioned in the philosophies of *Taoism* (like the importance of not rigidly dividing the world and persons) and *Chakra* (considering aspects like the divine or rooting in reality).

Final thoughts

Conflict is always a part of our lives. We will also need to discover its positive aspects:

> If you cannot remove conflict from life, why not adjust your thinking about it? If you can't beat it, join it. Why not try and see conflict as the salt of life, as a big energizer, the tickler, the tantalizer, rather than a bothersome nuisance, as a noise in a perfect channel, as disturbing ripples in otherwise quiet water! Why not treat conflict as a form of life? Particularly since we all know that it is precisely during the periods in our lives when we are exposed to a conflict that really challenges us. It is when we finally are able to master, that we feel most alive.
>
> *(Galtung 1975–80, Vol. 3: 501)*

Intercultural mediation, if properly intended as the facilitation of communication between persons with different linguistic and cultural backgrounds, may constitute a great help for adequately recognizing and for learning to manage conflicts in appropriate and constructive ways.

References

Adeline, Antoine, and Christian Hausmann. 2009. "Intercultural Mediation: Discussion and Reflection." *La Revue*, 25 November 2009. https://larevue.squirepattonboggs.com/Intercultural-mediation-discussion-and-reflections_a1755.html

Arielli, Emanuele, and Giovanni Scotto. 1998. *I conflitti: introduzione a una teoria generale*. Milano: Bruno Mondadori.

Bauman, Zygmunt. 2016. "Liquid Modern Challenges to Education". In *Neoliberalismo, educazione e competenze interculturali*, edited by Agostino Portera and Paola Dusi, 21–39. Milano: Franco Angeli.

Bauman, Zygmunt, Agostino Portera, and Riccardo Mazzeo. 2021. *Education and Intercultural Identity: A Dialogue between Zygmunt Bauman and Agostino Portera*, edited by Riccardo Mazzeo. London: Routledge. 10.4324/9781003123705

Bercovitch, Jacob, J. Theodore Anagnoson, and Donnette L. Wille. 1991. "Some Conceptual Issues and Empirical Trends in the Study of Successful Mediation in International Relations." *Journal of Peace Research* 28 (1): 7–17. 10.1177/0022343391028001003

Bertman, Stephen. 1998. *Hyperculture: The Human Cost of Speed*. Westport, CT: Praeger.

Besemer, Christoph. 1999. *Konflikte verstehen und lösen lernen: ein Erklärungs- und Handlungsmodell zur Entwurzelung von Gewalt nach Pat Patfoort*. Baden: Werkstatt für Gewaltfreie Aktion.

Broszkiewicz, Magdalena. 2018. "Mediation in International Economic Relations—Different Approaches and Cultural Background." *Ekonomia XXI Wieku* 3 (19): 98–109. 10.15611/e21.2018.3.07

Catarci, Massimo, and Massimiliano Fiorucci. 2020. "Interculturalism and Mediation in Education." In *Intercultural Mediation Counselling and Psychotherapy in Europe*, edited by Agostino Portera, Roy Moodley, and Marta Milani, 122–34. Newcastle: Cambridge Scholars.

Dasli, Maria. 2011. "Reviving the 'Moments': From Cultural Awareness and Cross-cultural Mediation to Critical Intercultural Language Pedagogy." *Pedagogy, Culture & Society* 19 (1): 21–39. 10.1080/14681366.2 011.527118

De Bono, Edward. 1989. *Konflikte: neue Lösungsmodelle und Strategien.* Düsseldorf: Econ.

Devereux, Georges. 1992. *Ethnopsychoanalyse complémentariste.* Paris: Flammarion.

Erikson, Erik H. 1968. *Identity, Youth and Crisis.* New York: Norton & Comp.

European Commission. Directorate-General for Education and Culture. 2009. *Highlights of the European Year of Intercultural Dialogue 2008.* LU: Publications Office. https://data.europa.eu/doi/10.2766/34067

European Communities. 1997. *Treaty of Amsterdam Amending the Treaty of European Union, the Treaties Establishing the European Communities and Certain Related Acts.* Luxembourg: Office for Official Publications of the European Communities. https://www.europarl.europa.eu/topics/treaty/pdf/amst-en.pdf

Folberg, Jay, and Alison Taylor. 1984. *Mediation: A Comprehensive Guide to Resolving Conflicts without Litigation.* San Francisco: Jossey-Bass.

Fromm, Erich. 1994. *On Being Human.* New York: Continuum.

Galtung, Johan. 1996. *Peace by Peaceful Means: Peace and Conflict, Development and Civilization.* Oslo: London; Thousand Oaks, CA: International Peace Research Institute; Sage.

Galtung, Johan. 1975–1980. *Essay in Peace Research.* 5 Vol. Copenhagen: Christian Ejlers.

Giroux, Henry A., and Susan Searls Giroux. 2006. "Challenging Neoliberalism's New World Order: The Promise of Critical Pedagogy." *Cultural Studies ↔ Critical Methodologies* 6 (1): 21–32. 10.1177/15327086052 82810

Johnson, David W., and Roger T. Johnson. 1995. *Teaching Student to be Peacemakers.* Edina: Interaction Book Company.

Lévinas, Emmanuel. 1984. *Etica e infinito.* Roma: Città Nuova.

Liddicoat, Anthony J. 2016. "Intercultural Mediation, Intercultural Communication and Translation." *Perspectives* 24 (3): 354–64. 10.1080/0907676X.2014.980279

Maslow, Abraham H. 1954. *Motivation and Personality.* New York, Evanston, London: Harper & Row.

Mayer, Claude-Hélène. 2006. *Trainingshandbuch interkulturelle Mediation und Konfliktlösung: didaktische Materialien zum Kompetenzerwerb.* Münster, New York: Waxmann.

McGee Banks, Cherry A. 2011. "Becoming American. Intercultural Education and European Immigrants." In *Intercultural and Multicultural Education: Enhancing Global Interconnectedness,* edited by Carl A. Grant and Agostino Portera, 124–37. New York: Routledge.

Mitchell, Christopher. R. 1981. *The Structure of International Conflict.* London: Palgrave Macmillan.

Moodley, Roy. 1999. "Psychotherapy with Ethnic Minorities: A Critical Review". *Changes. International Journal of Psychology and Psychotherapy* 17 (2): 109–25.

Nathan, Tobie. 1993. *Principle d'ethnopsychanalyse.* Paris: Éditions La Pensée Sauvage.

Nylund, Anna, Kaijus Ervasti, and Lin Adrian, eds. 2018. *Nordic Mediation Research.* Cham: Springer International Publishing. 10.1007/978-3-319-73019-6

Portera, Agostino. 1995. *Interkulturelle Identitäten. Faktoren der Identitätsbildung Jugendlicher italienischer Herkunft in Südbaden und Süditalien.* Köln, Weimar, Wien: Böhlau.

Portera, Agostino. 1998. "Multiculture, Identity, Educational Need and Possibilities of (Intercultural) Intervention." *European Journal of Intercultural Studies* 9 (2): 209–18. 10.1080/0952391980090211

Portera, Agostino. 1999. "Beitrag zur Ätiologie von psychischen Verhaltensauffälligkeiten und Störungen aus personenzentrierter Sicht". *Gesprächspsychotherapie und Personenzentrierte Beratung* 99 (1): 37–44.

Portera, Agostino. 2010. "Multicultural and Intercultural Education in Europe." In *Intercultural and Multicultural Education,* edited by Carl A Grant and Agostino Portera, 12–32. London: Routledge.

Portera, Agostino. 2013. "Competenze interculturali per la società complessa". In *Competenze interculturali,* edited by Agostino Portera, 140–52. Milano: Franco Angeli.

Portera, Agostino. 2016. "Educazione (interculturale) nel tempo del Neoliberalismo". In *Neoliberalismo, educazione e competenze interculturali,* edited by Agostino Portera and Paola Dusi, 40–7. Milano: Franco Angeli.

Portera, Agostino. 2017. "Intercultural Competences in Education." In *Intercultural Education and Competences: Challenges and Answers for the Global World,* edited by Agostino Portera and Carl A. Grant, 23–46. Newcastle upon Tyne: Cambridge Scholars Publishing.

Portera, Agostino. 2020. "Intercultural Competences in Mediation, Counselling and Psychotherapy." In *Intercultural Mediation Counselling and Psychotherapy in Europe,* edited by Agostino Portera, Roy Moodley, and Marta Milani, 10–30. Newcastle: Cambridge Scholars.

Portera, Agostino, Michael Trevisan, and Marta Milani. 2020. "A Status Report on School Intercultural Mediation in Europe." *Journal of Educational, Cultural and Psychological Studies,* no. 22 (December): 49–70. 10.7358/ecps-2020-022-port

A European perspective

Portera, Agostino, Roy Moodley, and Marta Milani. 2020. *Intercultural Mediation Counselling and Psychotherapy in Europe*. Newcastle: Cambridge Scholars.

Rogers, Carl R. 1961. *On Becoming a Person*. Houghton: Mifflin.

Shultz, Lynette. 2007. "Educating for Global Citizenship: Conflicting Agendas and Understandings". *The Alberta Journal of Educational Research* 53 (3): 248–58.

Verrept, Hans. 2019. *What Are the Roles of Intercultural Mediators in Health Care and What Is the Evidence on Their Contributions and Effectiveness in Improving Accessibility and Quality of Care for Refugees and Migrants in the WHO European Region?* Health Evidence Network Synthesis Report 44. Copenhagen: World Health Organization, Regional Office for Europe. https://apps.who.int/iris/bitstream/handle/10665/327321/9789289054355-eng.pdf

Wieviorka, Michel. 2003. *Mediation: A European Comparison*. Paris: Centre for Sociological Analysis and Intervention.

18

ISLAMIC FORMS OF INTERCULTURAL MEDIATION

Akram Abdul Cader

Introduction

As of 2015, roughly 1.8 billion people had reportedly identified as Muslims amounting to 24% of the world population (Lipka 2017). This number is expected to exponentially grow due to higher rates of conversion and growing birth rates in Muslim countries with some projections placing growth rates at 70% by 2060. The demographic indicators point to the significant influence Islam has on various societies (Lipka 2017). While Muslims only accounted for roughly 3% of the population in the Western world in 2010, this number is projected to double by 2030.

Islam refers to a complete submission to Allâh and the legislation that was revealed to His messenger, Muhammad (Ĝauhari 1987, 1952–1953). The religion of Islam is a comprehensive way of life for a Muslim that is based on the Shari'ah (legislation), which is derived from the Qur'an and the Prophetic tradition (Sunnah). The Qur'an is the final revelation of Allâh to the Prophet Muhammad, whose speech and actions constitute the Sunnah as a part of Islamic legislation. The theological influence of Islam is a significant moderator on the beliefs and behavior of Muslims (Abdul Cader 2017, 351–52). Cultural difference is the human condition (Quran, 11: 118–99). Therefore, conflict and dispute are an inevitable reality of this world and Islam provides Muslims with a guide to manage their lives.

Tawhid is the unification of God in all forms starting with the sincere belief and faith and actualized through behavior and legislated acts of worship. Behavioral guidance in Islam is tied to the foundational belief that Allâh created mankind for the purpose of worship (Qur'an, 51:56). This belief dictates all actions and decisions of a Muslim in every interaction across cultures (Abdul Cader 2017, 351–52). In order to understand the Islamic perspectives on mediation, it is imperative to understand the sources of Islamic legislation and what constitutes the correct interpretation of these texts. For the purpose of this chapter, the Islamic perspective is focused on the theological basis rather than a pseudo-cultural tradition that homogenizes Muslims into a singular tradition thereby allowing the discourse to include intercultural mediation between Muslims of different cultural tradition as well as between Muslims and non-Muslims regardless of culture. This is because Islam as a religion integrates throughout cultures given the Islamic principle that allows cultural tradition that does not contradict or oppose the tenants of Islam whereby Islamic belief takes precedence (al-Sa'di 2005, 116–20). With this understanding, interfaith mediation is a derivative of intercultural mediation in the Islamic perspective. This chapter lays a framework of intercultural mediation from an Islamic perspective based on Islamic sources.

172

DOI: 10.4324/9781003227441-22

Intercultural mediation

Researchers have studied the multi-faceted nature of intercultural mediation as a means to bridge the gap in the dynamic globalized multicultural world we inhabit. Continually expanding globalization has increased the number of multicultural societies in the span of decades. Saudi Arabia saw an increase in expatriate workers in the 1970s. While the native language is Arabic, Saudi Arabia started to integrate more southeast Asian, African, and English speakers leading to numerous linguistic barriers between locals and expatriates. Unfamiliarity between local and visiting cultures created numerous challenges to both parties. Regrettably, the transcultural nature of the modern world has also brought more reason for conflict thereby increasing the need for intercultural mediation (Mayer 2020, 249–50).

However, with the increasing interest in the field there has been few efforts to investigate principles of intercultural mediation from an Islamic perspective, despite the significant influence of Islamic legislation on nearly a quarter of the world's population. Many current studies continue to discuss the field through the lens of Western academia, thereby falling short of understanding how Islam guides Muslims in intercultural mediation. As Abdull Manaf, Shakri, and Mahyut (2018, 5171–3) argued, Islamic mediation provides both parties, regardless of religion or religiosity, with additional steps and principles that are not present in conventional models of mediation. Whether the gap is due to hesitancy of researching the Islamic approach through Islamic sources or due to linguistic and theological barriers, the result is that the Islamic mediation is a normative process among Muslims of various cultural backgrounds.

The goal of intercultural mediation is to bring both parties to mutual understanding via a third person intervening as a cultural broker (Katan 2013, 84–91). Interpreters often play this role as language is often one of the biggest barriers in addition to unfamiliarity with the other's culture (Liddicoat 2016, 354–8). Past studies have investigated this role through the lens of interpretation, dialogue, analytics, patient experience, and student integration among many other perspectives. However, there are barely a handful of studies that focus on Islamic mediation between cultures. Most studies on Islamic mediation have focused on peacebuilding and conflict resolution without a focus on culture (Abdul Cader 2017, 351–3). The majority of these studies blend Western concepts with some Islamic perspective to create a hybrid model of mediation. These models lack a robust Islamic foundation thereby leaning more on Western ideas of mediation without proper integration of Islamic principles. This is likely due to the reliance on English publications, which have significantly less contribution from Arabic speakers familiar with Islamic theology. It is necessary to establish prerequisite Islamic principles for any model of Islamic intercultural mediation. Applying the Islamic principles discussed in this chapter as a foundation allows for more salient integration of Western models of mediation with Islam and Muslims of various cultures. There are limitations to Islamic mediation, specifically when participants are not guided by Islamic beliefs, either as non-Muslims or through sectarian differences.

The sources of Islamic mediation

Muslims believe that the Qur'an is the ultimate guidance (Qur'an, 2:185). Muslims unanimously consider Prophet Muhammad as a guidance in Islam (Qur'an, 24:48). While the two fundamental references of Islamic mediation originate with the texts of Islamic legislation, other sources provide insight into its application and understanding. This chapter centers around traditional interpretation of Islam thereby limiting the focus to Sunni interpretations sourced from scholarly texts in creed, exegesis, jurisprudence, and Hadith. In addition to these areas of Islamic study, historical narratives are a significant contributor to understanding the Islamic perspective of mediation. Islamic scholars considered the attributes and behavior of the Prophet Muhammad as a defining factor in understanding the revelation. The wife of the Prophet, Aisha, was asked about his character wherein she responded that his character was an embodiment of the Qur'an (al-Qušairī 1955, 746). Therefore, the character of the Prophet informs the Islamic understanding of mediation. AbdulHak, Ahmed, and Oseni (2013, 15–22) noted that intercultural mediation in the Arabian Peninsula existed before the revelation of Islam, but was refined according to Islamic beliefs by the Prophet Muhammad.

For instance, prior to the first Qur'anic revelation to Muhammad, the different tribes of the Quraysh disputed over the placement of the black stone during the rebuilding of the Ka'bah. The four clans were prepared to go to war over this dispute. Al-Walid bin Al-Mughirah, one of the tribal leaders, announced that the first person to enter would decide who places the stone in its place. When Muhammad entered, the tribal leaders announced that they were pleased with him as he was truthful. His decision, based on shared benefit, was that everyone partook in the placement of the stone at the same time (Ibn Hishām 1978, 108–9). Researchers have used this narrative as an example for justice and truthfulness in Islamic mediation (Abdull Manaf et al. 2018, 5171–3; Pely 2016, 10–35). The character of Prophet Muhammad and of previous Prophets are integrated into Islamic theology, formulating Islamic understanding of mediation.

Mediation in the literature is often either translated as *Wisatah* (Manaf, Shakri, and Mahyut 2018, 5171–3; Hassan and Malik 2020, 47–54; Zaki et al. 2017, 219) or *Islāh* (Haeratun, Sulistiyono, and Isharyanto 2019, 115–8; Zartman 2020, 164–77). Wisatah is often used in the realm of governance and some researchers differentiate it from *Islāh*. The source of this understanding in current literature on Islamic mediation is based on Kitab al-Wuzara of the 9th-century 'Abbasid official and scholar, Al-Jahshiyārī who narrated an instance of mediation of Muhammad b. Muslim with property tax payers (Al-Jahshiyārī 1938, 142) and the dispute mediated by the Barmakids for Harun al-Rashid and a man from Bani Umayyah (Al-Jahshiyārī 1938, 187). The term '*Tawassut*' appears in the margins of the book as a subtext by the editors, but does not actually appear in the body of the work as seen in the manuscript housed in Österreichische Nationalbibliothek (Cod. Mixt. 916). However, the term was used interchangeably by the 10th-century Iraqi scholar, al-Māwardī (2006, 142–3). Zaki et al. (2017, 219–20) noted that *Sulh* is binding based on AbdulHak's research, which is based on the Ottoman code of law (*Majalla*). However, the Ottoman code, as cited by Bouheraoua (2008, 16–8), is a later legal code that does not factor the interchangeability of the terminologies used in early Arabic texts (al-Māwardī 2006, 142–3; al-Qurtubī 1964, 154–5). Islamic jurists have determined that mediation is when an impartial third person aids the disputants in removing differences with mutual agreement (al-Zahrānī 2010, 12–20). Mediation takes place only in the advent where a clear theological or juristic evidence is unavailable in resolving issues (Bouheraoua 2008, 16–8). Umar b. Al-Khattāb instructed Abu Musā Al-Ash'arī: "Mutual conciliation is permitted between disputing Muslims, except a *Sulh* that prohibits what is permissible (*halāl*) and permits what is forbidden (*Harām*)" (Anas 1994, 1037–50). Mediation appears as a mandate in the Qur'an where Allâh instructs the use of a mediator between disputing spouses (Qur'an, 4:35). The Qur'an also ordains reconciliation and mediation between two groups of Muslims engaged in conflict (Qur'an, 49:9).

Islam and culture

As the first mediator after the revelation of Islam, Prophet Muhammad stands as the best example for Muslims to model intercultural mediation. Islam is a way of life and a system of beliefs allows for adherents to practice and affiliate with their cultures on the condition that it does not contradict Islam. Islamic jurists have established a principle that Muslims can judge and govern in accordance to cultural norms. *Al-'Adah Muhakkammah*, is one of the goals, *Maqasid*, of the Islamic legislation. The reason is that Islamic legislation aims to create ease for people and incorporating culture that is in accordance with Islamic law makes it easy for followers to abide by the rules of Islam rather than create a purely Islamic 'culture.' Faruqi (1992, 482) argued that the application of local customs and cultures was a standard practice during the era of the rightly guided caliphates (*Khulafa al-Radhidun*).

The practice of integrating *'Urf* (customs) and *'Aadat* (cultural norms) in governance was later codified in Islamic jurisprudence by the *Fuqaha* (jurists) in all four major schools of thought (*madhahib*). In his *Al-Muwafaqat*, Al-Shatibi emphasizes the role of culture and customs in the *Shari'ah* (Shabana 2006, 87).

Salisu (2013, 133–48) described culture as ancillary rather than a source of legislation. Evolution of culture among local Muslims gave cultural authority more legitimacy as Islam began spreading around the world. As more people converted, local culture did not disappear, but was often implemented side by side. Islam had a strong influence on local culture and language without erasing it. Therefore, intercultural disputes between Muslims of different ethnic affiliations arose. A prime example is in the numerous disputes that arose between the Muslims in Arabia and in Persia that centered around culture and language. Another example is seen with the cultural grievances that occurred between the Turkish Ottomans and the Arabs during the Arab revolts of the 19th century. Mahmoud Fahmy Basha, a central figure in the Urabi revolt against the Ottoman viceroy in Egypt and the British governorate, describes numerous cultural conflicts with the Ottomans in his memoirs (Basha 2007, 221–30).

Recently, intercultural disputes and Islam often views Muslims as a homogenous culture in disputation with non-Muslims. For example, Sri Lankan Muslims are portrayed homogenous versus the Singhalese or Tamils while Muslims in Sri Lanka represent various cultural heritages of the Arab Moors, Malays, and Tamils. This perception is problematic as Islam itself is not a homogenous culture, but a religion encompassing numerous varying cultures. Therefore, it is imperative that a model of Islamic intercultural mediation is presented in a form that is applicable in every instance where there exists cultural variance.

Another recent example can be seen in the cultural clashes between Muslims in multicultural communities in America and Europe. Cultural differences between ethnic 'hyphenated' communities, such as the African-American Muslim community or the Pakistani-American Muslim community have witnessed disputes due to cultural differences pertaining to all matters of life from marriage to financial disputes (Kibria 2012, 227–40).

The traits of an intercultural mediator in Islam

The role of a mediator in Islam is better than charity (al-Kissī 1988, 275) and equivalent to enumerating prayer and charity (Anas 2006, 866). Abdull Manaf et al. (2018, 5171–3) suggested that the role of the mediator in the Islamic perspective usually requires them to be an Imam (leader) citing Al-Jahshiary's *Kitab al-Wuzaraa*. However, there is no source text from the Qur'an and Sunnah that places it as a condition. Rather, the Qur'an permits mediators, arbitrators, and conciliators to be regular Muslims as noted in the dispute between spouses (Qur'an, 4:35). Mediation in Islam is considered similar to an act of worship (al-Sijistānī, 2008) and thereby regulated by Islamic principles. Irani (1999) argued that this role is not only vital among Muslims, but it holds a reputable status that is promised a reward by Allâh. Therefore, along the lines of Abdull Manaf et al.'s (2018, 5171–3) proposition, not anyone can assume the role of an Islamic mediator. The indication in the Qur'an and Sunnah is that the mediator must have certain traits that quality them to mediate between disputants.

It is encouraged to use a Muslim in mediation between Muslim disputants. This is because Allâh describes mediation with Muslims as reconciliation between brothers. In the event a non-Muslim mediator is chosen, the condition is that the affair in dispute is not of a religious nature (Bouheraoua 2008, 16–8). Before mediation can occur, the potential candidate must meet the following attributes.

Sincerity

An Islamic mediator must be sincere in seeking reconciliation and mutual cooperation and understanding between disputants. Sincerity complements Tawhīd and Islam in moderating the role of an Islamic mediator. A major aspect of Islam, sincerity is the cornerstone of all actions (Qur'an, 4:35; 11:88; Bukharī 1966, 127). Researchers in Islamic mediation consider sincerity as the first binding trait of a mediator (Abdul Cader 2017, 354–356; Abdull Manaf et al. 2018, 5171–3; Bouheraoua 2008, 16–8; Sarif, Noordin, and Abdullah 2004, 107–22).

Knowledge

The Prophet Muhammad stated that knowledge precedes speech and action (Bukhārī 1996, 24). Acting upon ignorance is contrary to the role of a mediator. A mediator is tasked with verifying the facts of the disputes (Qur'an, 49:6). The mediator must have current understanding of Islamic law and the revelation (Abdul Cader 2017, 350–58). This is often why Islamic scholars were chosen as mediators (Köse and Beriker, 2012, 136–61). Abdull Manaf et al (2018, 5171–3) postulated that a mediator should specifically have knowledge of Islamic law and legal principles. Since Islam regulates all aspects of a Muslim's life, it is imperative that a mediator have working knowledge of Islamic laws and jurisprudence.

Trustworthiness

In the first noted incident of mediation between the tribal leaders, the Prophet Muhammad was viewed as a person that was trusted among disputants. Islamically, a Muslim cannot be deceptive in their dealings (Tirmidhī 1965, 626–30). A mediator accordingly must not be a person known for lying or cheating.

Justice

The mediator must have justice in their decisions, not favoring one over another (Qur'an, 5:8). This allows for a mediator to have affiliation to one party's culture provided they do not have any explicit or implicit biases that deter them from making a just decision. Justice in decision making is considered as piety and is a reflection of one's religiosity. This is why righteous people were called to mediate in Islamic history. The Qur'an cites behaving justly 23 times. Abdull Manaf et al. (2018, 5171–3) indicated that the emphasis in the Qur'an on justice and fairness is a requirement in mediation.

Reliability

A mediator should be one who is consistent in their behavior and their speech (Qur'an, 49:6) and scrutinizes information that they hear and transmit. An aspect of reliability is basing decisions on evidence and not speculation. Thereby, a key function of a mediator in Islam is *Tathabbut* (verification) of evidence (Abdul Cader 2017, 351–8). This does not make the mediator an investigator. The mediator's role is to verify the accuracy of the information between parties by asking clarifying questions to establish correct understanding.

Wisdom

Experience and wisdom are important elements of mediation that are sought after in the Qur'an. In Arabic, wisdom and judgement share the same linguistic root. References to wisdom appear 24 times throughout the Qur'an with the majority equating the revelation of the Sunnah as wisdom. What can be derived from the numerous verses on wisdom is that the mediator follows the example of the Sunnah. This behavior is exemplified by the disciples of the Prophet (Qur'an, 2:137; Bukhārī 1996, 349).

The Prophet Muhammad exemplified these traits in intercultural mediation such as in the case of the two men of different cultures in dispute over land ownership (al-Sijistānī 2009, 221). The

Prophet in this example applied justice and portrayed reliability when he acknowledged the lack of evidence in the case by hearing both sides and determining the validity of each evidence. Upon the lack of evidence, he used his wisdom to mediate by highlighting the warning of one who deceives in his oath.

The behavior of an intercultural mediator in Islam

Islamic theology describes the differences between cultures as a natural condition of creation with a purpose of mutual understanding (Qur'an: 49:13). The Qur'an notes that mutual understanding and cooperation is a mercy from Allâh as differing is innate in mankind (Qur'an, 11: 118–119). In addition to the aforementioned traits of an Islamic mediator, intercultural mediation has additional objectives and behaviors:

At-Ta'aruf

The Qur'an indicates that people were created and grouped into cultures and peoples in order for each one to know the other and not as a means of division between people. Therefore, Islam promotes multi-culturalism and intercultural understanding. This requires a mediator to learn about the cultures where the mediation is taking place so as to avoid judging upon ignorance. The moderator of this understanding one another is Islamic law. Therefore, a knowledgeable mediator would be able to decipher what aspects of each culture is not compatible with Islam and mediate accordingly. For example, in the mediation of Al-Fadl bin Rabi' and the people of Baghdad with the Caliph Al-Ma'mun in his decision to discontinue black as the color of the armies and police in place of green, which was the 'Alid colors promoted by the Persian factions; Al-Fadl bin Rabi' brought the viewpoints and cultural understanding of both parties during mediation. This approach defused a hostile situation that would have inevitably resulted in a civil war between the pro-'Abbasid Arabs and the pro-'Alid Persians that had building tension since Al-Ma'mun's rule (Anonymous 1971, 183–250). In the case of an intercultural dispute between a Muslim and a non-Muslim, the obligation of the mediator is to understand the perspective of both sides including the religious and cultural perspective of the non-Muslims so that the mediation is based on justice without partisanship.

At-Ta'akhi

The Qur'an orders Muslims of all cultures to behave in a brotherly manner towards one another (Qur'an, 49:10). As Muslims have been ordered to cooperate upon righteousness and piety (Qur'an, 5:2), the mediator must exert efforts to bring disputants together as brothers despite differences in their culture. The goal of this behavior is to spread mutual love between disputing parties. Brotherhood in Islam is a part of faith described as desiring the same outcomes for your brother as you want for yourself (Bukhārī 1996, 12–5). For instance, in the dispute between the 'Abbasid Caliph Harun Al-Rashid and the Ummayad from Damascus, the Persian minister, Yahya al-Barmaki mediated based on brotherhood despite their tribal differences (Al-Jahshiyārī 1938, 187–8).

An-Nasihah

The Prophet Muhammad stated that it is a part of the religion to give sincere advice (al-Qušairi 1955, 74). A mediator approaches disputants in the manner of giving sincere advice rather than instructions and orders. This method allows mediators to suggest compromise or cooperation. Specifically, the mediator advises disputants to align with Islamic principles and forgive one another and work together in resolution for the sake of Allâh. al-Zahrānī (2010, 21–35) noted that the mediator's role extends to advising an oppressed party to pardon the oppressor or to ease the re-tribution in cases of accidental death.

Ar-Rifq

Muslims have been ordered with gentleness in all issues related to their behavior and mannerisms (al-Qušairī 1955, 2593). This behavior was equated to good outcomes by the Prophet with a warning that the person who abstains from gentle behavior is not given positive outcomes (al-Sijistānī 2008, 254–55). When Prophet Moses and Aaron was instructed by Allâh to mediate between the Children of Israel and Pharoah, he was instructed to use gentle language and manners to soften the heart of Pharoah (Qur'an, 20:44). Hence, the mediator should present the best character and manners and not use harsh language.

At-Tasamuh and Al-'Afw

Among the behaviors of a mediator is to encourage disputants to forgive and pardon one another with sincerity (Qur'an, 2:182). Islam encourages disputants to forgive even when one has been wronged or oppressed (al-Zahrānī 2010, 23–30). The one who forgives and pardons when they have been wronged is promised a great reward by Allâh, and the mediator reminds and encourages participants to work towards resolution based on pleasing Allâh and achieving a greater reward (Tirmidhī 1965, 626–30).

Conclusion

An Islamic mediator holds a lofty status among Muslims when mediating between cultures. The importance of seeking a mediator that embodies the attributes discussed in this chapter and manifests the aforementioned behaviors cannot be understated as is seen throughout Islamic history. Regardless of what religious affiliation disputants hold, an Islamic mediator is expected to uphold justice through unbiased mediation. Islamic mediation is one of the most valued tools of inter-cultural dispute resolution. While many Muslim countries are experiencing increased globalization and multiculturalism through immigration and expatriate workforces, there is a growing need to understand how to Islamically mediate conflicts between cultures in all areas such as financial transactions, worker disputes, and marital discord. As many researchers, like AbdulHak, Ahmed, and Oseni (2013, 18–23) have noted, Muslims must embrace the use of Islamic mediation in dispute resolution and revive this tradition that has been taught and utilized throughout the ages in Muslim societies.

References

Abdul Cader, Akram. 2017. "Islamic Principles of Conflict Management: A Model for Human Resource Management." *International Journal of Cross Cultural Management* 17 (3): 345–63. 10.1177/1470595817740912
AbdulHak, Nora, Sa'odah Ahmed, and Omar A. Oseni. 2013. *Alternative Dispute Resolution (ADR) in Islam.* Malaysia: IIUM Press.
Al-Jahshiyārī, Muhammad b. 'Abdus. 1938. *Kitab Al-Wuzara Wa'l-Kuttab.* Cairo: Mustafa Al-Babi Al-Halabi.
al-Kissī, 'Abd Ibn-Ḥumaid, ed. 1988. *Al- muntaḥab Min Musnad'abd Ibn-Ḥumaid.* Beirut: 'Ālam al-Kutub.
al-Māwardi, 'Ali b. Muhammad. 2006. *Aḥkām Al-Sulṭāniyah.* Cairo: Dār Al-Hadith.
al-Quṣairī, Muslim Ibn-al-Ḥaǧǧāǧ. 1955. *Ṣaḥīḥ Muslim.* Cairo: Dār Iḥyā' al-Kutub al-'Arabiya.
al-Qurṭubī, Muhammad b. Ahmad. 1964. *Al-Jami' li-Aḥkām Al-Qur'an.* Cairo: Dār al-Kutub al-Masriyya, 154–70.
al-Sa'dī, 'Abd al-Raḥmān ibn Nāṣir. 2005. *Al-Qawā'id Al-Fiqhiyah.* Riyāḍ: King Fahad Library.
al-Sijistānī, Abū Dā'ūd Sulaymān ibn al-Ash'ath. 2008. *Sunan Abī Dawūd.* Beirut: Dar al-Kotob al-Ilmiyah.
al-Zahrānī, 'Ali b.'Bukhit. 2010. *Al-Minhāj fi Al- Islāḥ dhāt al-Bayn.* Makkah: Al-Lajnah Al- Islāḥ dhāt al-Bayn.

Anas, Mālik ibn. 1994. "Masalih Ba'd Al-Waritha 'An Mal Al-Mayyit." In *Al-Mudawwanah* 3: 379–80. Beirut: Dar al-Kotob al-Ilmiyah.

Anas, Mālik ibn. 2006. *Al-Muwaṭṭa'*. Beirut: Dār al- Kutub al-'Ilmīya.

Anonymous. 1971. *Akhbār Al-Dawlah Al-'abbāsīyah*. Beirut: Dār al-Ṭali'ah li-al-Ṭibā'ah wa-al-Nashr.

Basha, Mahmoud Fahmy. 2007. *Al-Bahr Al-Zakhir fi Tarikh Al-'Alam wal-Akhbar al-Awa'il wal Awakhir*. Cairo: Dār al-Kitāb.

Bouheraoua, Said. 2008. "Foundation of mediation in Islamic law and its contemporary application." In *4th Asia-Pacific Mediation Forum, International Islamic University Malaysia*. http://www.asiapacificmediationforum.org/resources/2008/11-_Said.pdf

Bukhārī, Muḥammad ibn Ismā'īl. 1966. *Sahih Bukhari*. Karachi: Karkhanah-i Tijarat-i Kutub.

Faruqi, Muhammad Y. 1992. "Consideration of 'Urf in the Judgments of the Khulafa' al Rashidun and the Early Fuqaha." *American Journal of Islam and Society* 9 (4): 482–98. 10.35632/ajis.v9i4.2536

Ğauhari, Ismā'īl Ibn-Ḥammād. 1987. *Ṣiḥāḥ tāğ Al-luğa Wa-ṣiḥāḥ Al-'arabīya*. Cairo: Dār al-Kitāb al- 'Arabī.

Haeratun, Adi Sulistiyono, and Isharyanto. 2019. "Mediation as an Alternative Institution of Disclaimer in Religion Court in Indonesia According to Justice Perspective." In *Proceedings of the 3rd International Conference on Globalization of Law and Local Wisdom (ICGLOW 2019)*. Surakarta, Indonesia: Atlantis Press. 10.2991/icglow-19.2019.29

Hassan, Abida, and Dil Mohammad Malik. 2020. "Alternative Dispute Resolution Processes in Islam." *The International Research Journal Department of Usooluddin* 4 (2): 47–54.

Ibn Hishām, 'Abd al-Malik. 1978. *Al-Sīrah Al-Nabawīyah Li-Ibn hishām*. Cairo: al-Maktabah al-Tawfīqīyah.

Irani, George E. 1999. "Islamic Mediation Techniques for Middle East Conflicts." *Middle East Review of International Affairs* 3 (2): 1–17. https://ciaotest.cc.columbia.edu/olj/meria/meria99_irg01.html

Katan, David. 2013. "Intercultural Mediation." In *Handbook of Translation Studies*, edited by Yves Gambier and Luc van Doorslaer, 4: 84–91. *Handbook of Translation Studies*. Amsterdam: John Benjamins. 10.1075/hts.4.int5

Kibria, Nazli. 2012. "Transnational Marriage and the Bangladeshi Muslim Diaspora in Britain and the United States." *Culture and Religion* 13 (2): 227–40. 10.1080/14755610.2012.674957

Köse, Talha, and Nimet Beriker. 2012. "Islamic Mediation in Turkey: The Role of Ulema: Islamic Mediation." *Negotiation and Conflict Management Research* 5 (2): 136–61. 10.1111/j.1750-4716.2012.00094.x

Liddicoat, Anthony J. 2016. "Intercultural Mediation, Intercultural Communication and Translation." *Perspectives* 24 (3): 354–64. 10.1080/0907676X.2014.980279

Lipka, Michael. 2017. "Muslims and Islam: Key Findings in the U.S. and around the World." *Pew Research Center*. https://www.pewresearch.org/fact-tank/2017/08/09/muslims-and-islam-key-findings-in-the-u-s-and-around-the-world/

Manaf, Azwina Wati Abdull, Asfarina Kartika binti Shakri, and Siti Marshita binti Mahyut. 2018. "Mediation in Islam." *Advanced Science Letters* 24 (7): 5171–3. 10.1166/asl.2018.11297

Mayer, Claude-Hélène. 2020. "Visions of Intercultural Mediation." In *Intercultural Mediation and Conflict Management Training*, edited by Claude-Hélène Mayer, 249–50. Cham: Springer. 10.1007/978-3-030-51765-6_24

Pely, Doron. 2016. *Muslim/Arab Mediation and Conflict Resolution*. London; New York: Routledge. 10.4324/9781315644554

Salisu, Taiwo Moshood. 2013. "'Urf/ 'Adah (Custom): An Ancillary Mechanism In Shari'ah." *Ilorin Journal of Religious Studies* 3 (2): 133–48.

Sarif, Suhaili, Kamaruzaman Noordin, and Ahmad Sufian Che Abdullah. 2004. "Managing Organizational Conflict from Islamic Perspective." *Jurnal Syariah* 12 (2): 107–22.

Shabana, Ayman. 2006. "'Urf and 'Adah within the Framework of Al-Shatibi's Legal Methodology." *UCLA Journal of Islamic and Near Eastern Law* 6: 87–100.

Tirmidhī, Muḥammad ibn 'Īsá. 1965. *Sunan Al-Tirmidhī*. Himṣ: Maktabat Dar al-Da'wah.

Zartman, Jonathan K. 2020. "Development and Peace Through Traditional, Cultural, Islamic Mediation." *Journal of Peacebuilding & Development* 15 (2): 164–77. 10.1177/1542316620905788

Zaki, Mohammad Hafiz Bin Mohd, Mazbah Termizi, Muhammad Ridhwan Saleh, Nina Syazmeen binti Mohd Din, and Siti Farhana binti Abu Hasan. 2017. "Mediation v. *Sulh*: A Comparative Study." In *International Conference on Dispute Resolution 2017. Modern Trends in Effective Dispute Resolution. 9–10 August 2017. Proceedings*, edited by Abdul Ghafur Hamid and Muhammad Laeba, 219–26. Kuala Lumpur, Malaysia: Ahmad Ibrahim Kulliyyah of Laws International Islamic University Malaysia.

19
TRANSFORMING CONFLICT CULTURES THROUGH MEDIATION

Kenneth Cloke

Introduction

José Ortega y Gasset (1961, 60) wrote, "The selection of a point of view is the initial action of culture." From the point of view of conflict resolution, we experience, engage in, resolve, transform, and transcend conflicts in three fundamental initial locations, arenas, or 'fields,' each with its own characteristics, rules, processes, algorithms, and dynamics:

1   *Internally* or personally, as sensory perceptions, neurophysiological responses, mental activities, emotional reactions, heartfelt desires, qualities of energy, and spiritual states that happen inside us;
2   *Relationally* or socially, as active and passive communications, responsive behaviors, relationships, and interactions with others that take place *between* us;
3   *Environmentally* or systemically, as cultures and contexts, rites and rituals, customs and practices, systems and structures that take place in couples and families, organizations and institutions, nations and societies; along with the backdrops and settings, histories and experiences, economic and political conditions, ethics and values, and countless other circumstances that occur *around* us.

Each of these interacts in complex, subtle, and intricate ways with the others. Each is a potential source of resistance and resolution, intractability and insight, revenge and reconciliation, instigation and prevention, retributive and restorative justice, stasis and transformation. None is conflict-neutral. Each contributes, often in veiled and unspoken, yet powerful ways to the nature, intensity, duration, impact, and meaning of our conflicts. Each *profoundly* impacts the quality of our lives, our personal capacity for joy and compassion, and our ability to collaborate in solving common problems.

Yet nearly all of our attention in mediation is directed at its social or relational aspects, with comparatively little to its internal emotional, spiritual, and heartfelt aspects, and nearly none to its cultural, environmental, and systemic aspects. Why is this, why is it important, and what can be done to improve our ability to transform and enhance our conflict cultures?

What is culture, and how does it generate conflict?

There are dozens of ways of defining culture, most of which focus on customs, norms, social behaviors, beliefs, arts, and learning. Broadly, culture is how we approach our environment, how we group and separate from one another, how food is produced and consumed, how gender is

180   DOI: 10.4324/9781003227441-23

perceived and displayed, how space and boundaries are established, how time is defined and used, how learning takes place, how people play and laugh, how goods are made, used, exchanged, and distributed.

Culture is how we perceive and process reality. It is shared beliefs, attitudes, behaviors, and customs. It is a way of life, a method for differentiating and integrating, a set of lessons on how to satisfy needs and navigate environments. It is an accumulation of successful adaptations, and agreed upon *meanings* of symbols, events, sensations, behaviors, and communications. It is what everyone knows and no one talks about.

Culture is shaped beneath the surface, at a level deeper than conscious attention, where we seek to avoid the uncertainty and chaos of conflict; to alleviate, resolve, and learn from the fear and pain they provoke; to encourage cohesion, collaboration, and community—all of which require *significant* conflict resolution skills.

Families, groups, organizations, communities, and nations create cultures that draw people together despite their diversity, yet also discriminate against them based on their differences, discouraging disobedience, and punishing dissent. Most cultures create stories or narratives that describe how people should and should not behave, how they get into conflicts, with whom, over what, how they get resolved, and what happens when they don't.

Most importantly for mediators, culture is a way of assigning *meaning*, and every conflict happens partly because people assign different meanings to what was said and done, or not said and done. It is therefore axiomatic that every conflict is, on some level, cross-cultural. As the meaning of our conflicts is most important to us; and as every unique meaning alters the *form* of our conflict, creating fresh meanings, openings, insights, and approaches, cultural methods in mediation can trigger transformation, transcendence, prevention, and restorative outcomes.

How cultures assign meaning

Cultural anthropologist Edward T. Hall outlined the most important elements of culture in his classic book, *The Silent Language* (1959), which he saw as creating rules for clarifying meaning—not only in interacting with the environment, but associating with others, assessing biases, competing and collaborating for sustenance, navigating space and time, learning and playing, using property and fighting over it.

According to Hall, culturally defined meanings are *evolutionary* tools for transmitting messages. Space, for example, is a consequence of an animal's instinctive defense of its lair, reflected in human society in office workers' defense of their cubicles, or fences around a home. Distinctions can be drawn between cultures in relation to their perceptions of space, for example, as closed vs. open, functional vs. aesthetic, separation vs. connection, empty vs. filled, thing vs. relationship, personal vs. social, face-to-face vs. side-by-side.

Similarly, contrasting meanings of time can give rise to conflicts, for example, as limited vs. unlimited, mono-chronic vs. poly-chronic, linear vs. circular, logical vs. emotional, being on time vs. being in time, time as money vs. time as sacred, controlled by schedule vs. flexible schedules, unitary vs. flowing. Conflicts commonly arise over other cultural issues, for example:

- precision vs. ambiguity in communication,
- open vs. closed in personal information,
- verbal vs. written as a basis for traditions,
- high vs. low context in establishing meaning,
- consensus vs. individualistic in decision making,
- formal vs. informal in processes,
- competitive vs. collaborative in relationships,

- direct vs. indirect in giving feedback,
- authoritarian vs. democratic in organization,
- deference vs. rebelliousness in relation to authority,
- exclusive vs. inclusive in relation to outsiders,
- linear vs. non-linear emphasis in thinking,
- Gestalt vs. detail in orientation,
- appropriateness vs. inappropriateness in humor and play,
- demonstrative vs. restrained in emotional expression,
- permissive vs. directive in child rearing,
- fixed vs. fluid attitudes toward rules,
- open vs. closed attitudes toward outsiders,
- individual vs. group orientation in norms and values,
- interests vs. power or rights orientation in dispute resolution.

Any of these can trigger conflicts that are mistaken, camouflaged, or superficially interpreted as 'personality differences,' yet can only be fully understood, resolved, and transformed by identifying their deeper cultural origins and collaboratively negotiating expectations for how they will be handled.

If we ask which of these conflicting cultural approaches is correct, it is clear that they are *all* correct, depending on context or circumstance. Therefore, collaborative, pluralistic *mediative* approaches to cultural diversity will predictably generate more complex, socially successful solutions to a wider range of problems than simpler, unitary ones.

We can also predict that conflict avoidant and highly competitive cultures will only be able to solve simple problems; and that collaborative cultures and advanced conflict resolution skills will increasingly be required as societies evolve and problems become more complex. This will happen because chronic cultural conflicts produce two fundamentally opposite outcomes:

1 exclusive, competitive, hierarchical, 'zero sum,' power- or rights-based, coercion-driven approaches in which one side wins and the other loses, and the dispute resolution process *itself* eliminates much of the complexity and collaboration needed to fully solve problems, causing them to turn chronic;
2 synergistic, collaborative, heterarchical, non-zero sum, interest-based, consensus-driven approaches in which diverse cultures communicate and engage in dialogue with each other in a search for collaborative, synergistic solutions that are *at least* as complex and diverse as the problems they need to solve.

Context, culture, and the attribution of meaning in conflict

In the everyday, unspoken give-and-take of diverse, conflicted human relationships, the 'silent language' of culture plays a critical role. Edward T. Hall analyzed the ways people 'talk' to one another without words, showing, for example, how the pecking order in a chicken yard is reflected in competition on a school playground or hierarchies at work.

One of the ways cultures assign meaning is through 'high and low context' communications (Hall 1976), in which meaning depends on the amount of context needed to accurately interpret what is said. If, for example, we regard law as a culture consisting of precise definitions, little or no context is required to elucidate their meaning.

Emotional, romantic, and sexual communications, on the other hand, are subtle, nuanced, imprecise, and highly dependent on context to accurately assess the meaning of any behavior or statement. Even the word 'hello' can be said in romantic, lewd, angry, curious, wistful, or happy ways. How, then, do we *know* what 'hello' means?

The answer depends on a set of cultural rules for turning context into meaning, *especially* the context of conflict, which requires enormous amounts of context to identify its meaning. This is why mediators need to be skilled in active listening, empathy, reframing, facilitated dialogue, nonviolent communication, appreciative inquiry, and similar methods; and able to elicit the parties' unique conflict cultures, including how each signals what things actually mean to them.

For these reasons, the resolution of any conflict is *necessarily* an act of culture. Indeed, if we look closely at the role played by culture in conflict, we can see that *every* conflict takes place in a rich cultural environment with myriad contextual elements that directly impact efforts to resolve it. Yet it is rare that mediators are trained in reading cultural contexts, or *'cultural intelligence,'* (Earley and Ang 2003) which consists partly of *interest-based* skills that aid us in:

1   recognizing, categorizing, surfacing, exploring, and deepening people's understanding of their 'conflict cultures,' and how they can obstruct or improve their capacity for empathy and collaboration, and make agreements more arduous or easy;
2   revealing and dismantling the sources of cultural bias, stereotyping, prejudice, and discrimination through facilitated dialogue, culturally informed conversations, and advanced bias awareness and prejudice reduction techniques;
3   assisting conflicted parties in clarifying the contexts that create meaning for them and collaboratively negotiating the cultural norms and expectations they want to live by in their relationship with each other;
4   identifying guidelines for *designing* cultural approaches to conflict resolution that are creative, collaborative, and grounded in otherwise unspoken interests and understandings;
5   encouraging and promoting transformation and transcendence in conflict cultures, by redefining approaches to conflict in ways that deepen understanding and restorative outcomes.

25 ideas on culture and mediation

In implementing these skills in mediation, it is important to understand the roles cultures play in creating and resolving conflicts. Based on this understanding, here is a summary of 25 generic ideas, lessons, and insights that have been useful to me in conducting cross-cultural mediations and dialogues in many countries and communities over several decades:

1   Everyone creates culture—every person, family, age group, and organization—partly through stories that re-imagine and re-interpret life experiences.
2   Culture is what people understand without having to define or specify. It is the subtle, often unspoken ways of understanding and living in the world.
3   Culture includes the ways people set expectations, how they meet needs, what they imagine, how they relate to one another, what they do and do not react to, and how they react when they differ.
4   Cultures are largely defined by their differences from other cultures—the greater the difference, the more defined the culture.
5   Culture pre-determines what and how we see, hear, think, and feel. Whatever conflicts with our cultural assumptions is less accurately received and understood.
6   Most cultures assume they are superior to other cultures, and their ways are 'right' or 'better.'
7   Conversely, opposing cultures are often seen as 'wrong,' or 'inferior,' and are judged, ridiculed, or insulted.
8   Most cultures value conformity, reward compliance, and punish dissent.
9   All cultures 'socialize' their members, teaching them the 'rules' and pressuring them to conform.

10   Among the teaching devices cultures use to socialize their members are myths about heroes and villains, parables about behaviors and consequences, metaphors for processing information, masks for defining the self, stereotypes, stories about conflict, narratives about people and groups, and 'scripts' for all occasions.

11   Tolerance and acceptance of diversity and dissent within a culture decrease as conflicts with other cultures increase, and increase as conflicts with others decrease.

12   No culture is innately 'better' or superior to any other. Each is capable of learning from others.

13   In *every* culture, people want to be accepted, listened to, acknowledged, and respected.

14   Cultural differences help define us, encourage positive values, and are reasons for celebration rather than fear.

15   All cultures have evolved methods for resolving conflicts and mediating differences, as well as sources of impasse and obstacles to resolution.

16   Cross-cultural conflicts arise even between members of the same culture, representing cracks in the culture, which are opportunities for adaptation, evolution, and improvement.

17   There are no absolute, universal 'correct' responses to conflict, only *relatively* 'right' or 'wrong' ones within a given culture.

18   Not every conflict between people who are different is based on cultural differences.

19   We can't know all things about all cultures.

20   There are no universal problem solving, mediation, or conflict resolution techniques, processes, or methodologies that are successful always, everywhere, in all cultures and conditions.

21   In every culture, people want to be understood, and respond favorably to curiosity and respectful communication.

22   We can increase the effectiveness of intercultural communication and problem solving by improving our communication and conflict resolution skills.

23   Cultural conflicts do not disappear when we ignore them.

24   There is ambiguity in diversity. Tolerance for diversity and keeping an open mind are therefore essential skills in mediating cross-cultural conflicts.

25   Cross-cultural collaboration improves through empathy and honesty, open dialogue, committed listening, integrity, and willingness to improve over time.

25 techniques for mediating cross-cultural conflicts

In mediating cross-cultural conflicts, it is helpful to adopt an attitude of curiosity, genuine caring, empathy, honesty, and commitment to respectful and transparent communications, processes, and relationships. As mediators, we want to ask questions that reveal the hidden contexts, silent languages, unspoken expectations, and implicit cultural assumptions beneath the veneer of contested issues. Instead of defining culture as something 'everyone knows and no one talks about,' we redefine it as something everyone talks about, to discover what each person means.

Here are 25 generic exercises, activities, questions, and techniques based on my experience conducting cross-cultural mediations, bias awareness and prejudice reduction workshops, public dialogues, and cross-cultural conversations:

1   Co-mediate in culturally diverse teams.

2   Ask people what they expect of the process, who they think you are, and what role they would like you to play.

3   Invite each party to suggest someone from their culture to act as a process observer, to offer feedback during and after the session.

Transforming conflict cultures

4   Establish common backgrounds, points of reference, and values for the process, for example, regarding the importance of cooperation, family, friendship, or education, then connect these to the issues.

5   Ask questions that elicit the role of culture in their conflict, for example:

- "What words do you use to describe the various kinds of conflict?" "What do people typically do in each case?"
- "What is the meaning in your culture, for example, of crime? Silence? Public criticism? Physical contact? Yelling? Confidentiality? Use of first names? Mediation?"
- "How are conflicts typically handled in your culture, for example, between insiders and outsiders? Younger and older? Women and men? Siblings? Employer and employee? Neighbors?"
- "How are conflicts typically handled in your culture, for example, between insiders and outsiders? Younger and older? Women and men? Siblings? Employer and employee? Neighbors?"
- "How are emotions expressed and communicated in your culture?" "Which are encouraged or discouraged?" "Why?"
- "How are mediations and negotiations typically conducted in your culture in relation to, for example, the role of the mediator? Aggressive or collaborative in style? Communication of emotions, 'bottom lines,' or hidden agendas? Role of outsiders? Compromise?"

6   Ask questions like: "What does that mean to you?" "What does the word '_____' mean in your culture?" Record agreed-upon meanings for later reference.

7   Periodically ask, especially when discussions get difficult, "What can I/we do to make this process work better for you?"

8   Elicit a hierarchy of conflicts by identifying which are most serious and which are least, compare similarities and differences, and do the same with conflict styles.

9   Ask parties to rank the options for resolution in their culture from war to surrender, elaborate those that lie in the middle, and explore reasons for choosing collaborative approaches.

10 Ask them to state, pantomime, role-play, draw, or script how conflicts are commonly handled in their cultures.

11 Ask them to list positive words that describe the other party's culture, and alongside, positive words that describe their own, then exchange lists and compare them, pointing out similarities and differences in perceptions.

12 Consider conducting the same exercise more dangerously by eliciting negative words and stereotypes regarding their own culture, then searching for neutral or positive words that reframe them, and discuss.

13 Surface, acknowledge, and model respect for cultural differences by asking people if they are proud of their culture. If so, why, and if not, why not.

14 Or, more dangerously, consider asking if there is anything they dislike about their culture, and why.

15 Ask them to describe a stereotype others have of their culture, say whether they think it applies, and why or why not.

16 Ask each person to describe the heroes, victims, villains, mediators, or others in their culture, then compare and contrast them.

17 Ask them to describe the most important lessons they learned from their culture, who taught them, why they were important, and how they might be used to resolve this dispute.

18 Ask them to bring photographs of their families, the homes they grew up in, or themselves as children, share these with each other, and describe three crucible events that made them who they are today.

19   Ask each party to write about the conflict as a story or fable, using neutral names and a third-person voice, perhaps starting with "Once upon a time …" and ending with "and they all lived happily ever after," then read them aloud to each other.
20   As the mediator, describe your own culture, the stereotypes others have of it, the stereotypes you were taught about your own or other cultures, and how you overcame them.
21   Create an appreciation of culture by asking what they would miss most if it disappeared.
22   Jointly design a consensus-based cross-cultural model for conflict prevention, resolution, transformation, and reconciliation.
23   Ask for honest feedback about how you did as mediator, and how you might do better next time.
24   Ask one thing each person learned, will do differently, or will take away from the mediation.
25   Ask each person to bring a song, dance, poem, ritual, work of art, food, etc. from their culture to the next mediation, break bread, and jointly celebrate your work together.

We can also ask people to meet in small groups and brainstorm elements of the 'old culture,' what elements they would like to include in the 'new culture,' and 3–5 ways of expressing them; or suggestions for how the mediators can encourage collaborative outcomes; or elements they would like to add to their culture to strengthen its mediative capacities.

In intractable and hostile disputes, we can target ways of assigning meaning by asking questions that elicit cultural filters and lenses. For example, in the midst of an argument, we can ask: "What do you think is the meaning of what she just said?" "Why do you think that is what she meant?" "Do you think she agrees with your understanding of what she meant?" "Would you like to find out?" "Why don't you ask her right now?" Or during a hostile exchange, we can ask, "Excuse me, is this conversation working?" "Why not?" "What is one thing the other person can do that would make it work better for you?" "Are you willing to do that, starting now?"

How to transform conflict cultures in mediation—two examples

Because cultures are partly *imagined*, they can be re-imagined. Because they are open, malleable, regenerative, and plastic, they can be reshaped in mediation. Here are two examples of deep, profound, simple, yet transformational changes that took place through culturally informed mediation processes.

1   Several years ago, I was asked to mediate nearly a dozen conflicts between doctors and nurses at a children's hospital. After conducting several interviews, it became clear that the hospital was a highly stressed, *chronically* conflicted cultural environment in which everyone was working long hours, children were dying and being saved, and there was no acknowledgment or support for a completely exhausted and massively burned-out staff.

Instead of mediating on a 'triaged,' case-by-case basis, I brought the staff together to report on what I found. I said we were not genies, but would like each person to offer one wish for how they might create a less stressful work environment. A nurse said he gave everything he had every week to the children who were his patients, and he wished that at the end of the week, someone would give him a flower, as a way of recognizing his efforts. This impressed me as a powerful suggestion, so I asked him, "Would you be willing to start, and give flowers to the people you work with?" He said he would, and I asked everyone else, "Raise your hand if you are willing to join him." Every hand went up. Within a week, every Friday, the hospital was *filled* with flowers.

The next person who spoke suggested creating a tone over the loudspeaker to mark every time a child died, so everyone could stop, just for a second, to say goodbye to that child; plus a different tone to mark every time a child's life was saved, so everyone could stop for a second to celebrate what they had achieved. In these small, seemingly insignificant ways, the *entire culture* of the hospital was transformed overnight, conflicts dramatically dropped in numbers and severity, morale improved significantly, stress declined, and people realized they could collaboratively re-imagine and transform their conflict culture.

2   In a different case, I was asked to help *prevent* conflicts that were about to emerge in a cardboard box factory that was located in a dilapidated, unpainted, concrete block building in a dirt lot that became muddy whenever it rained. The manager was an elderly Latino man who had been promoted from the ranks and was now retiring and being replaced by a younger Anglo woman being brought in from the outside. The workers were all middle-aged Latino men who the owners knew would resent and rebel against the new manager, creating costly, demoralizing conflicts.

I met with the new manager and we came up with a plan. On the weekend before her first day at work, she, her husband and two sons painted the factory inside and out, built a concrete walkway so no one had to walk through the dirt and mud, and planted flowers at the entrance. She put lace curtains on the windows, rugs on the floor, and paintings on the walls. She brought comfortable chairs for them to sit in, a coffee maker, small refrigerator and microwave, table and chairs to eat at, nice plates and cups for everyone, and a CD player to play their favorite music. When the workers arrived on Monday morning, she was there to greet them each by name, and they were utterly stunned by what she had done. They felt so deeply respected and acknowledged by her that for a long time there were *zero* conflicts.

By fundamentally transforming the culture of the factory, she made it harder for them to behave rudely, even in conflict, simply by putting lace curtains on the windows, rugs on the floors, paintings on the walls, soft chairs to sit in, coffee to drink, a table to sit and break bread at, and pleasant music to play.

In both examples, chronic conflicts were triggered less by high conflict personalities, disrespectful communications, and hostile behaviors than by stressful uncaring, disrespectful cultures, whose meanings could be negated by proactively identifying contrary meanings, then redesigning the environment and culture to express them.

Creating cultural maps in mediation

Culture is a kind of *map* that teaches people how to navigate their conflicts, and mediation can help them figure out what to do when they get lost or disoriented, or changes take place that alter the meaning of previously understood symbols and directions. We can get confused and move off course in any of the locations of conflict, especially when the map itself is changing. As philosopher William Irwin Thompson described it,

> A culture provides an individual with a mapping of time and space, but as the culture goes through a period of change and stressful transformation, this map becomes distorted. In periods of intense cultural distortion, the map becomes so changed as to be almost obliterated. For some this can be a moment of terror, for others, a time of release ... The old forms fall away, there comes a new receptivity, a new centering inward, and in an instant there flashes onto the screen of consciousness a new re-visioning of the map ... . [N]ew possibilities of time and space announce themselves, possibilities that lie beyond the descriptions of the old institutions of the old culture. This is the prophetic moment, the annunciation of a new myth, and the beginning of a new culture.
>
> *(Thompson 1978, 13)*

Mediation can assist people in becoming more aware of the ways their culture maps alternate paths through conflict and design new, *combined* maps that enable them to more successfully navigate their disputes, and to resolve, forgive, reconcile, and prevent them—not only internally and relationally, but culturally, systemically, and environmentally as well.

Cultural maps, unlike ancient atlases, are less depictions of what is known than cautionary tales, secret codes, cryptic guides, pious sentiments, moral rationalizations, and justifications for failure. To map conflicts in *transformational* ways, we need to 'cultivate' cultures that are less avoidant, accommodating, and adversarial, and more collaborative, consensus-based, and mediative; cultures that actively encourage diversity and dissent, dialogue and negotiation, mediation and restorative justice.

Margaret Mead perceptively suggested that,

> If we are to achieve a rich culture, rich in contrasting values, we must recognize the whole gamut of human potentialities, and so weave a less arbitrary social fabric, one in which each diverse human gift will find a fitting place.
>
> *(Mead 1935, 322)*

To do so, we need to strengthen the elements within our cultures that *discourage* bias and prejudice, conditioned passivity and reactiveness, hyper-competition and selfishness, cynicism and apathy, shaming and blaming, manipulation and demagoguery, stories of victimization and demonization, dependence on hierarchy and external authority, blind obedience and acceptance of covert behaviors, defenses against empathy and lack of ownership of 'someone else's problem.' And *all* of these are natural, transformational attributes of the culture of mediation.

Last, it is essential for mediators to appreciate that *culture* is intimately connected—not only to the *content* of conflict and meaning of the issues, but to its *processes* and *relationships*, as well. Indeed, every genuine transformation in mediation necessarily shifts all four aspects, strengthening them at their core, and generating a multidimensional map that allows us to transform and transcend conflicts in all these areas.

By doing so, we discover and design pioneering approaches that *invite* us to evolve to higher orders of conflict and resolution; to invent new maps, avert future conflicts, and restore justice and community to people who have been alienated from one another, which are the highest, most heartfelt, transformative, and *transcendent* purposes of every conflict culture.

References

Earley, P. Christopher, and Soon Ang. 2003. *Cultural Intelligence: Individual Interactions Across Cultures*. Stanford, CA: Stanford University Press.

Hall, Edward Twitchell. 1959. *The Silent Language*. Garden City, N.Y.: Doubleday.

Hall, Edward Twitchell. 1976. *Beyond Culture*. New York: Anchor Books; Random House.

Mead, Margaret. 1935. *Sex and Temperament in Three Primitive Societies*. New York: Morrow.

Ortega y Gasset, José. 1961. *The Modern Theme*. New York, Evanston, London: Harper & Row.

Thompson, William Irwin. 1978. *Darkness and Scattered Light: Four Talks on the Future*. Garden City N.Y.: Anchor Press.

20
INDIGENOUS CONFLICT MANAGEMENT STRATEGIES BEYOND THE ADR PARADIGM

Hamdesa Tuso

Introduction

The Alternative Dispute Resolution (ADR) emerged during the 1970s, mostly in North America. Its basic tenants proposed that conflict can be resolved more constructively outside of the legal process. Indeed, its very name suggests that mediation is an alternative to litigation. The rise of court cases relative to divorce and cost associated as well as the length of the time it took to ligate, the United States during the 1970s spurred some intellectuals and community leaders to seek an alternative mechanism to litigation (Scimecca 1991, 18–39). Also, the frequent occurrence of intergroup conflicts in Eastern Europe and the Global South during the end of the Cold War attracted the attention of peacemakers. As a result, the practice of ADR spread world-wide exponentially (Kriesberg 2007; Tuso 2012, 245–70). Original Dispute Resolution (ODR), on the other hand, has been practiced around the world for centuries. However, it has been ignored and undermined by the global state system dominated by the West for about five centuries. Also, it has been neglected by ADR (Tuso 2012). This chapter focuses on five major themes: (1) ADR and its discontent; (2) some critical issues, which explain the nature of ODR; (3) the basic elements pertaining to ODR; (4) the basic differences between ADR and ODR; and (5) a call for a paradigm shift.

ADR and its discontent

By early 1990s, some scholars began to observe that ADR, as conceptualized and practiced in North America, did not apply in non-Western cultures. Thus, they began focusing on the role of culture in the social construction of conflict. For example, John Paul Lederach (1995), in his widely read book *Preparing for Peace* (1995), posited that conflict is a socially constructed cultural phenomenon (9). Equally significant is the book by Kevin Avruch, Peter Black, and Joseph Scimecca (co-edited), published in 1991, entitled *Conflict Resolution: Cross-Cultural Perspectives*, where the authors presented case studies, explaining how peace-making is done in different cultures. Of a particular significance is the thesis by Avurch where he posited that negotiation theory as presented in the ADR negotiation theory is based in white middle class American culture (Avruch 1991, 4–5). He further asserted the same point in his later book, entitled *Culture and Conflict Resolution* (1998, 78). Also, David Augsburger (1992, 200–4) published *Conflict Mediation Across Cultures*. In this work, Augsburger wrote a detailed description comparing mediation in *modern* and *traditional* societies.

DOI: 10.4324/9781003227441-24

Some scholars began undertaking case studies regarding the system of conflict resolution, as practiced by the indigenous communities. One of the earliest inquiries on indigenous processes of peace-making is the study by anthropologist Cathie Witty (1980), who studied the *Sulaha* in Lebanon (Sulaha is the pre-Christianity and pre-Islam form of peacemaking in the Middle East). 16 years later, Mohammed Abu-Nimer (1996) wrote several articles on the Palestinian way of resolving conflict. He eventually wrote a book entitled *Nonviolence and Peacebuilding in Islam* (2003). Mark Davidheiser (2004) undertook a field work in the Gambia on how indigenous communities resolve conflicts. Also, several anthropologists began pursuing inquiry on this line of study. For example, Sponsel and Gregor (1994) wrote a book criticizing how anthropologists misunderstood, leading to some serious misrepresentation with respect to the nature of indigenous form of peacemaking. And finally, the work by Kemp and Fry which focused on peacemaking in peaceful cultures (cultures which avoid violence). As the time went on, some scholars began focusing in exploring the patterns of conflict resolution in the so-called traditional societies (continent wide). The book by William Zartman (2000) entitled *Traditional Medicine for Modern Conflict* (in Africa) fits this category of a newly evolving line of inquiry.

Some critical issues

Before proceeding further in this essay, some issues which are critical to the understanding the subject of under current study need to be clarified.

What do we mean by indigenous process of peacemaking? The term *indigenous* is complex and tends to generate some level of controversy. Generally, there are three categories of communities to whom the term *indigenous* applies. One category is those communities encapsulated in the modern state system; such groups reside in remote rural areas; they live separately from the dominant groups—they use their own languages and generally practice their cultures. The second category of communities to which the term *indigenous* applies is those segments of society who straddle between urban cultures and rural cultures. The third category to whom the term indigenous applies is the elite who have captured state power from the colonial masters; such groups straddle between Western cultures and their own cultures. For the purpose of the current work, the term *indigenous* is used in reference to the practices of peacemaking in non-Western cultures (Tuso and Flaherty 2016, 19).

Patterns of similarity within the different indigenous cultural communities

Indigenous communities live in a vastly different cultural and material ecology; the speak different languages and practice peace-making in their own cultural frames; is it therefore acceptable to use the reference *indigenous conflict resolution* to represent the patterns of activities in making peace in such communities? In some ways, these are the problems scholars who studied comparative religions encountered when attempting to categorize religious practices in non-industrialized societies. The general reference with respect to belief systems in such societies was framed as *religions in primitive societies*. One critical question was, is it indigenous religion or indigenous religions? After several scholars reported the existence of several patterns of unity within the diverse religious belief systems, a common understanding emerged among those who engage in comparative religions; thus, it was suggested that there were enough patterns of similarities, so that it is justifiable to use the reference *indigenous religion* (Cox 2017).

Collectivist vs individualist cultures: Scholars who have studied comparative cultures have observed that there are distinct differences with respect to the patterns of orientation in traditional societies and industrialized societies. The patterns of relationships in the traditional societies are identified as *collectivist* and those in industrialized societies are called *individualist*. According to this designation, collectivist culture focuses on the community interests as opposed individual interests.

Charlotte Nickerson (2021a; 2021b) provides the following summary, comparing and contrasting the main traits in individualist and collectivist cultures. The following is her summary relative to the main traits in individualist cultures: (1) individualist cultures emphasize the needs and desires over those of the group and relationships on individuals with respect to other individuals; (2) in individualist cultures, persons are expected to learn and discover what their values and interest are independent of the group's social structures. Such efforts focus on independence and self-sufficiency; and self-definition leads to social behavior motivated and driven by the desire of individuals; (3) individuals who are born in and grew up in individualist cultures tend to believe that independence, completion, and personal development are important goals in life; (4) the need of the individuals dictates social behaviors, rather than the needs of larger groups; and (5) fundamentally, individualism teaches a person that the individual goal is an end in itself. Therefore, such individuals cultivate their judgment, irrespective of the group's expectations.

In contrast, collective cultures focus in orienting the individual to frame and formulate their goals in life to accommodate and comply with the larger group.

The following is a summary by Nickerson (2021b) with respect to the traits in collectivist cultures: (1) Collectivism is a tendency on the individual and societal level, to view oneself as interdependent and a member of a group, rather than as an independent being; (2) in collectivist cultures, people feel as if they belong to a larger in-group or collectives which care for them in exchange of loyalty. As a result, collectivist cultures value collaboration, communalism, constructive interdependence, and conformity to roles and norms; (3) a collectivist culture is especially likely to emphasize the importance of social harmony, respectfulness, and group needs over individual needs.

Nickerson (2021b) further posits that there are four important cultural traits in collectivist communities: (1) The definition of the self as interdependent—in relation to other people rather than in the abstract traits of an individual; (2) secondly, an alignment of personal and communal goals—meaning that the individual makes decisions accounting for what the collective and what they are bringing or taking away from the group; (3) the greater consideration of social norms than the individual attitudes when making decisions; and (4) an emphasis on the relationships, even if disadvantageous for individuals (ibid.). The relevant point here is to suggest that the indigenous forms of peacemaking take place in the context of collectivist cultures.

Creating the Third Force: Indigenous conflict management strategy

The concept of *Creating the Third Force* was developed by William Ury. Although he was originally trained in the field of anthropology, as the new field of conflict resolution emerged during the 1970s, he embarked on doing research and practice in conflict resolution. As a result, he published several important works (e.g., *Getting Past No* (1993), *Conflict Resolution System Design* (1995)). Ury then returned to his original academic discipline of anthropology. Upon his field work in Southern Africa, he wrote an article entitled *Conflict Resolution Among the Bushmen: Lessons in Dispute Resolution Design* (1995). In his article he asserted that conflict resolution as imagined and practiced by the Bushmen community constituted "a complete and effective form of conflict resolution." In his study of the Bushmen community methods of conflict resolution, Ury made the following observations: (1) The Bushmen community viewed conflict as a disruptive force and invested considerable amounts of resources and energy in preventing conflict from occurring; (2) healing the wounds through dialogue facilitated by elders; (3) reconciling interests (sorting out claims) with the assistance of the elders; (4) balancing rights by providing council for the aggrieved and warning the aggressor that he would not violate the community norms; (5) testing relative power by discouraging its members not to use power when conflicts emerge within the community; (6) and containing violence from spreading in case of a conflict within the community (1995). In advancing his thesis relative to the concept of creating the *third force*, Ury authored a short book entitled *The*

Third Side: Why we fight and how we can stop it (2000), Ury further theorized that every social conflict involved three sides—(1) the aggressor party, (2) the aggrieved party, and (3) the outsiders. The outsiders include family members, friends, neutrals, outsiders, the onlookers, etc. According to Ury, if those members who are on the third side are mobilized in opposing to a conflict from spreading and escalating, the community can create the *third force.* Ury wrote the above cited book to inform/educate Western societies to reduce conflict escalation by learning from indigenous communities.

There are some other scholars who have studied the mechanism of dealing with conflicts in non-Western societies and who observed similar patterns of norms and practices. The work of three such scholars will be mentioned here. David Augsburger (1992), in his widely read book *Mediation across Cultures,* reported that the indigenous communities use 11 interrelated mechanisms in managing social conflicts, being: (1) family mediation, (2) clan resolution processes, (3) caste/panchayat adjudication, (4) third-party mediators, (5) community mediation, (6) tribal or village palaver, (7) political broker, (8) local or regional headmen, (9) religious leaders, (10) police law, and (11) court system. He further noted five key observations relative to the common features found in indigenous processes of peacemaking. (1) Peace-making is not left to the parties in conflict; the larger community becomes involved through facilitated procedures undertaken by trusted community leaders; (3) since face is a critical factor in such societies, the third-party mediators and other trusted individuals carry the messages between the conflicting parties—this mechanism avoids potential confrontations between the parties in conflict; (4) it is required and expected that the parties in conflict present their cases in the context of community concerns and interest of the larger community; and (5) peacemakers are members of the community.

Roger Mac Ginty (2008), in his extensive literature review in social anthropology relative to the subject of peacemaking in indigenous communities, made the following observations regarding the characteristics of peacemaking in traditional societies: (1) they hold a sophisticated view regarding peace; (2) the discussions regarding the peacemaking processes are transparent; (3) those who hold power in the community are accountable for their actions; (4) peacemaking involves elaborate ceremonies; (5) the peacemaking process focuses on the ongoing relationship rather than on change, which is common in modern commercial practices; (6) peacemakers use consensus processes in pursuing mediation; (7) the peacemakers focus on repairing damaged relationships; (8) some forms of compensation are made between the parties in conflict to ensure positive memory is created in the minds of the disputing parties. In a similar vein, Gloria Lee, who studied dispute resolution mechanism(s) among the indigenous community in Canada, reported the observation that the essential elements of peacemaking include the following: (1) elders take in the role of peacemaking; (2) disputes are handled by family members; (3) when this does not produce the desired results, it goes to the community forum; (4) when the community leadership takes over, they still involve the family in the peace process; (5) admission of wrongdoing by the offender party and his/her family is an essential element of peacemaking; (6) forgiving the offender by the party which had been wronged in the case is encouraged and expected; (7) rituals are performed to facilitate the process of healing, and (8) agreements at family and community levels are binding.

Kemp and Fry (2004), in their co-edited book entitled *Conflict Resolution in Peaceful Societies Around the World,* after reviewing nine cases of conflict resolution in peaceful societies around the world, found eight key patterns of non-violent conflict management approaches, as developed and practiced by those societies. Their findings about the traditions and practices of peace-making in such societies are summarized here: (1) societies who manifest a low level of aggression tended to have core values promoting non-violent behavior in the relationships; (2) the core leaderships in such societies emphasize avoidance, especially when confronted with incidents of violence; (3) in such societies self-restraint and self-control rather than pursuing or threatening the aggressive party is manifested; (4) the third-party peacemakers readily become involved in managing conflicts within the community; (5) in these societies decisions are made through consensus processes rather than imposed on the community members; through such processes hard feelings are minimized among community members; (6) in such societies the items such as drugs and alcohol, which can cause a person to be more aggressive, are discouraged, and shunned; (7) there are specific social norms that discourage aggression; and (8) in such societies children are socialized to respect the values of non-violence and peaceful co-existence.

The discussions in the foregoing sections are based on the scholarly works of researchers on the subject of the patterns of peacemaking in indigenous communities around the world. In the following section, the author of this chapter will present a summary of his research-based findings (and of his teaching a graduate course on the subject of indigenous processes of peacemaking over three decades). According to his findings, there are 12 common features in the indigenous processes of peacemaking: (1) Conflict resolution is mandatory; (2) the goal of conflict resolution is to establish the truth (the cause) and to bring about justice; (3) the individual, the family, and the community take over responsibility with respect to a conflict at hand; (4) elders are the key players in resolving a conflict at hand; (5) storytelling is used as a tool during the peacemaking process; (6) spirituality plays significant role in peacemaking; (7) in the discourse during peacemaking, connections are made between the individual, the community, nature, and the supernatural; (8) the process of peacemaking is used to maintain unity and tradition in the community; (9) justice is not based one's social status, wealth, and power in the social order where a given conflict occurs; (10) admissions of wrongdoing on the part of the offender and forgiving on the part of the aggrieved are essential parts of conflict resolution; (11) the main goal of dispute resolution is to repair damaged relationships—not to excert punishment; although restoration for the lost/damaged items are required; and (12) rituals play a significant role during the peacemaking process (Tuso 2016, 509–35).

The discussions in the foregoing sections suggest that there are common features which are present in the practices of peace-making by indigenous communities around the world. Based on this information we can conclude that the indigenous communities have strategies in managing conflict. Their strategies can be summarized as follows: (1) the indigenous communities work feverishly to prevent conflicts from occurring. Such efforts commence in the community by socializing children not to engage contentious behaviors; also, adults are encouraged to avoid conflicts; (2) once conflicts occur, peacemakers start mediation; (3) in the peacemaking efforts, the entire communities are mobilized (including families and friends) themselves to de-escalate the conflict (this is what William Ury calls *Creating the Third Force*); (4) once the disputes are ended, the elders lead the conflicting parties toward reconciliation.

ADR and ODR: The differences

Based on a literature review as presented in the previous sections as well as on the author's personal knowledge, basic features of the two models can be distinguished. As indicated in the introduction, ADR evolved in the 1970s primarily in North America, particularly in the United States, to deal with the rising cases of divorce and the resultant exorbitant legal costs. Also, as the Cold War ended, identity-based conflicts increased around the world; the West, as it had prominence in the world affairs, began sending out mediators to such hot spots. The key features of ADR include: (1) objectivity (rationalism); (2) professionalism (the mediator has to be a trained professional); (3) the satisfaction by the conflicting parties with the outcome of a given mediation. The classic model, which is based on Western values includes the following suggestions: (1) focus on interests instead of positions; (2) separate issues from people; (3) invent options for the parties so that there is a win–win situation; (4) insist on focusing on objective criteria (Augsburger 1992, 207). The mediator has to be from outside of circle of the group where the conflict occurs. Thus, ADR has an individualistic orientation. For example, participation in the mediation process is voluntary; the process of mediation ends when the conflicting parties agree on the recommendation by the mediator. There is no community involvement in the peace process. There is no ritual performed at the end of mediation. Spirituality has no place in ADR forms of mediation. ADR does not consider reconciliation as an essential part of peacemaking.

ODR, on the other hand, has a collectivist orientation in peacemaking. When conflict occurs, participation in mediation is mandatory. The mediator(s) are from within the community where a given conflict occurs, but they have to be trusted by both parties. In the worldview of the indigenous communities, a given conflict can cause harm to the cohesiveness of the community. Peacemaking involves the family members, friends and the larger community members. The peacemakers are elders who have been trained through long years of experience and they have earned their reputations as knowledgeable about the culture of the community and as competent in peacemaking. In such communities, peacemaking has a spiritual dimension. The main goal of peacemaking is to repair damaged relations—not to impose punishment for the sake of restitution, *per se*. Reconciliation is an essential part of the peace process.

A call for paradigm shift

As the journey of knowledge relative to indigenous processes of peacemaking progressed, the apparent deficiency in ADR in dealing with conflicts in cross-cultural situations became clearer. As a result, there have been some voices which have called for paradigm shift when approaching peacemaking in cross-cultural situations. Some of the voices emerged from scholars/practitioners from the West; they have developed a view that the Western-trained practitioners and their methods of mediation, which are based on their training from textbooks, should not come to the scene of conflict. John Paul Lederach (1995) who had been involved in making peace over 60 cases around the world, developed a concept of *elicitive mediation*. In his presentation on this subject, he distinguished the *elicitive* from the *prescriptive* model. According to Lederach, the *prescriptive* model implies that a trainer approaches the training events from a perspective of an expert who comes with well-planned models for confronting the situation at hand. However, the *elicitive model* proposes that trainers should solicit information from the audience. Lederach posits that the foundation of the elicitive model is culture in approaching peacemaking; thus, the trainer should look into the cultural norms and expectations of community members where a conflict occurs (Lederach 1995, 55–83).

Augsburger (1992) also suggested that traditional tradition is different from the mediation relative to *modern* cultures. In order to illustrate this point, he identified the following features: (1) mediation is a communal process with involvement of trusted leadership. The normal structures for data flow and dispute management are trusted. The pathways familiar to the participants, the time frames preferred, and the settings of familiar social interactions will be utilized; (2) Indirect, triangular, third-party processes of a go-between are more desirable to save face, reduce threat, balance power differentials, and equalize verbal or argumentative abilities. So, communication may be carried through others; demands may be carried by advocates, and agreements may be suggested by multiple participants. (3) Time is relational (multiple relationships and issues are interwoven; polychromic). Tasks and schedules are secondary to the relationships; so self-disclosure follows social rituals, personal agendas, and communal concerns; (4) Process is dynamic, rationally oriented and directed toward resolving tension in network and community. The responsibility of the disputants to their wider context and the reconciliation of injured parties are central; and (5) mediators are recognized community leaders or trusted go-betweens from the social context. They are personally embedded in the social networks and remain in relationship with the parties in dispute both during and after resolution (Lederach 1995, 204).

Polly Walker (2004), a scholar in indigenous studies (in the United States), in her bristling critique of ADR, has authored an article entitled 'Decolonizing of the Discipline of Conflict Resolution.' In her article, she argued that the new ADR, through its dominance, has made ODR invisible and thus undermined its historical role of peace-making in the indigenous communities. She further argued that ADR was formed and developed in the well-known colonial patterns treating indigenous cultures.

Debarati Sen, Ferdinand Kwaku Danso, and Natalia Menses, in their chapter on 'Culture and Conflict Management' included in the book *Indigenous Conflict Management Strategies*, edited by Adebayo, Benjamin, and Lundy (2014), have suggested that the concepts of culture and conflict management need a paradigm shift. The authors in pursuing the above indicated theme suggest that two issues have to be addressed: (1) there should be a paradigm shift in the way culture is understood and in the associated mechanisms of conflict resolution; (2) there should be radically different ways of valuing differences and new ways to think about social change where the Western epistemology is replaced with the epistemology based on indigenous cultures (Sen, Danso, and Meneses 2014, 257). According to this line of argument, such paradigm shifts will lead to (potentially) opening up a space in the world of ideas, which indigenous ways of thinking and managing conflicts can thrive for.

Schirch (2005), the author of *Ritual and Symbol in Peacebuilding*, strongly recommended that practitioners in ADR should integrate rituals in the process of mediation. In chapter 10 of her book, Schirch (2005, 161–75) provided some detailed approaches on how rituals can be incorporated in ADR mediations. Douglas Fry (2006) in his ambitious book entitled *The Human Potential for Peace* has argued passionately that the notion that human beings are naturally bent on aggression and violence is based on Western cultural assumptions. Based in his study, which examined the cultural orientation of some 80 indigenous societies around the world, he concluded that human societies are capable of creating cultural values that are able of avoiding aggression and curtailing violence. William Ury (2000) his book entitled *The Third Side: and How We Can Stop* has argued passionately that urbanized societies can learn from traditional societies on how to galvanize the third side (family members, friends, community members, etc.) and how to develop effective mechanisms of preventing conflict from escalating. Tuso and Flaherty (2016), in their co-edited book *Creating the Third Force*, have advanced a proposal that educators should include the subject of indigenous forms of peacemaking in the curriculum in all levels of academic structure; further, they have recommended that the countries in the Global South, where most of the indigenous communities reside, invest more resources in promoting substantive knowledge relative to indigenous worldviews and the peacemaking processes.

Conclusion

Indigenous processes of peacemaking are one of the oldest professions in human history. They survived against all odds. They survived colonialism and the accompanying racism and prejudice. They survived the negative stigma—being called rituals of the savages—by the proponents of the Semitic religions (Christianity and Islam), which penetrated the societies of the Global South over the last several centuries. They survived the state formation and the accompanying militarization, which has caused the marginalization of indigenous cultures. In the newly formed states, the legal system was promoted as an appropriate mechanism in dealing with conflict. Also, the new conflict resolution model (ADR) neglected indigenous processes of peacemaking. In one respect, the emergence of ADR was a welcomed development. For some five centuries, the orientation from the Global North has been dominated by intense competition and the desire to conquer, subjugate, and control.

Thus, the emergence of ADR spurred the indigenous communities to assert themselves in the world of ideas, claiming that their own model of peacemaking is the original form of peacemaking (Pinto 1998). Since the early 1990s, some scholars have recognized that ADR is not suitable for dealing with conflicts in the cultures of indigenous communities. Subsequently, several scholars commenced on exploring the nature of indigenous forms of peacemaking. As a result, we have learned more about indigenous processes of peacemaking. The indigenous processes of peacemaking still face some serious challenges. The state formation and control of population tend to cause manipulations, division, and violence. Migration of some groups from the indigenous communities to urban areas has caused such groups to form some kind of hybrid model of peacemaking. Some members from the indigenous community who acquire modern education tend to join the ruling class in the modern state system. There is a high rate of illiteracy in some of the indigenous communities, which poses some serious challenges. There is still more research needed to better understand the essence and the dynamics in indigenous processes of peacemaking.

References

Abu-Nimer, Mohammed. 1996. "Conflict Resolution Approaches: Western and Middle Eastern Lessons and Possibilities." *American Journal of Economics and Sociology* 55 (1): 35–52. 10.1111/j.1536-7150.1996.tb02706.x

Adebayo, A. G., Jesse J. Benjamin, and Brandon D. Lundy, eds. 2014. *Indigenous Conflict Management Strategies: Global Perspectives.* Lanham, Maryland: Lexington Books.

Augsburger, David W. 1992. *Conflict Mediation across Cultures. Pathways and Patterns.* Louisville, KY: Westminster/John Knox Pr.

Avruch, Kevin. 1991. "Introduction. Culture and Conflict Resolution." In *Conflict Resolution. Cross-Cultural Perspectives*, edited by Kevin Avruch, Peter W. Black, and Joseph A. Scimecca, 1–17. New York/Westport/London: Greenwood.

Avruch, Kevin. 1998. *Culture and Conflict Resolution.* Washington, DC: United States Institute of Peace Press.

Cox, James Leland. 2017. *From Primitive to Indigenous: The Academic Study of Indigenous Religions. Vitality of Indigenous Religions.* London, New York: Routledge.

Davidheiser, Mark. 2004. *The Role of Culture in Conflict Mediation: Toubabs and Gambians Cannot Be the Same.* Gainesville FL: Doctoral Dissertation, University of Florida. http://ufdc.ufl.edu/UFE0005520/00001

Fry, Douglas P. 2006. *The Human Potential for Peace: An Anthropological Challenge to Assumptions about War and Violence.* New York: Oxford University Press.

Kemp, Graham, and Douglas P. Fry, eds. 2004. *Keeping the Peace: Conflict Resolution and Peaceful Societies around the World.* New York: Routledge.

Kriesberg, Louis. 2007. "The Conflict Resolution Field. Origins, Growth, and Differentiation." In *Peacemaking in International Conflict: Methods & Techniques*, edited by I. William Zartman, Rev. ed, 25–60. Washington, D.C: United States Institute of Peace.

Lederach, John Paul. 1995. *Preparing for Peace. Conflict Transformation Across Cultures.* Syracuse, NY: Syracuse University Press.

Mac Ginty, Roger. 2008. "Indigenous Peace-Making Versus the Liberal Peace." *Cooperation and Conflict* 43 (2): 139–63. 10.1177/0010836708089080

Nickerson, Charlotte. 2021a. "Individualistic Cultures and Behavior." *Simply Psychology.* https://www.simplypsychology.org/what-are-individualistic-cultures.html

Nickerson, Charlotte. 2021b. "Understanding Collectivist Cultures." *Simply Psychology.* https://www.simplypsychology.org/what-are-collectivistic-cultures.html

Pinto, Jeane Marie. 1998. *The Original Dispute Resolution: An Analysis of the Peacemaker System of the Navajo Nation.* M. S. Nova Southeastern University.

Schirch, Lisa. 2005. *Ritual and Symbol in Peacebuilding.* Bloomfield, CT: Kumarian Press.

Scimecca, Joseph A. 1991. "Conflict Resolution in the United States: The Emergence of a Profession?" In *Conflict Resolution. Cross-Cultural Perspectives*, edited by Kevin Avruch, Peter W. Black, and Joseph A. Scimecca, 19–39. New York, Westport, London: Greenwood.

Sen, Debarati, Ferdinand Kwaku Danso, and Natalia Meneses. 2014. "Culture and Conflict Management: The Need for a Paradigm Shift." In *Indigenous Conflict Management Strategies: Global Perspectives*, edited by Akanmu G. Adebayo, Jesse J. Benjamin, and Brandon D. Lundy, 257–64. Lanham, Maryland: Lexington Books.

Sponsel, Leslie E., and Thomas Gregor, eds. 1994. *The Anthropology of Peace and Nonviolence.* Boulder: L. Rienner.

Tuso, Hamdesa. 2012. "Indigenous Processes of Peacemaking by the New Field of Conflict Resolution." In *Critical Issues in Peace and Conflict Studies. Theory, Practice, and Pedagogy*, edited by Thomas Matyók, Jessica Senehi, Sean Byrne, Ousmane Bakary Bâ, Thomas Boudreau, Jason J. Campbell, Paul Cormier, et al., 245–270. Lanham: Lexington Books.

Tuso, Hamdesa. 2016. "Creating the Third Force: Some Common Features in Indigenous Processes of Peacemaking, and Some Preliminary Observations." In *Creating the Third Force: Indigenous Processes of Peacemaking*, edited by Hamdesa Tuso and Maureen P. Flaherty, 509–35. Peace and Conflict Studies. Lanham: Lexington Books, an imprint of The Rowman & Littlefield Publishing Group, Inc.

Tuso, Hamdesa, and Maureen P. Flaherty, eds. 2016. *Creating the Third Force: Indigenous Processes of Peacemaking*. Lanham: Lexington Books.

Ury, William. 1993. *Getting Past No: Negotiating in Difficult Situations*. New York: Bantam Books.

Ury, William L. 1995. "Conflict Resolution among the Bushmen: Lessons in Dispute Systems Design." *Negotiation Journal* 11 (4): 379–89. 10.1111/j.1571-9979.1995.tb00753.x

Ury, William. 2000. *The Third Side: Why We Fight and How We Can Stop*. New York: Penguin Books.

Walker, Polly O. 2004. "Decolonizing Conflict Resolution: Addressing the Ontological Violence of Westernization." *American Indian Quarterly* 28 (3/4): 527–49.

Witty, Cathie J. 1980. *Mediation and Society: Conflict Management in Lebanon*. New York: Academic Press.

Zartman, I. William, ed. 2000. *Traditional Cures for Modern Conflicts: African Conflict "Medicine."* Boulder, CO: Lynne Rienner.

PART IV

De-essentializing culture in intercultural mediation

21
THE DISCOURSE OF THIRDNESS IN INTERCULTURAL MEDIATION

Malcolm N. MacDonald

Introduction

Intercultural mediation is conventionally characterized as a form of intercultural exchange whereby a third interlocutor arbitrates between two people with irreconcilable views. Within the field of intercultural communication this irreconcilability is often attributed to the interlocutors holding different attitudes, beliefs and values because they come from different 'cultures.' The classic understanding of intercultural mediation then attributes the cause of the irreconcilability of the two conflicting participants' viewpoints to a homology between the participants' 'culture' and their nation of origin. This classic conceptualization of intercultural mediation is co-terminous with the assumptions of a modernist paradigm. It is predicated on an objectivist ontology whereby the material and social worlds exist independently of the subject, and on a positivist epistemology whereby knowledge is verifiable through empirical observation and measurement. However, this understanding of intercultural mediation has been criticized as being static and over-reductive, not least through its essentializing of the two participants whose positions are in need of reconciliation (Busch 2016).

In this chapter I will set out a perspective on mediation from a more poststructuralist perspective, which emerges from a 'discourse of thirdness' in intercultural communication to consider its implications for our understanding of intercultural mediation. Arguably, intercultural mediation does not just take place through the intervention of a third actor in a dysfunctional exchange between two persons. Intercultural communication has also been conceived of through the positions different interlocutors occupy in an intercultural exchange being visualized through topographical metaphors. Specifically, the metaphors of 'Third Space'[1] and 'third place' have been adopted extensively in the field of intercultural communication to envisage the sets of new meanings which are generated through the syntheses or contradictions which arise out of the encounter between one set of meanings and another. More often than not, this way of envisaging intercultural communication arises not so much from the real-time conversations which take place between cultural actors, but rather from the engagement of a reader/listener/viewer from one 'culture' with a text which originates from another 'culture.' Here, a text is envisioned in its broadest sense as being any form of semiosis—a book, a webpage, a phone message, a film, or an artwork. This view therefore regards 'thirdness' as the symbolic space which opens up between any two sets of semiotic coding when they are 'decoded' differently by their receiver to the 'encoding' of their producer (after Hall 1973). By contrast with orthodox views of intercultural mediation, a topographical understanding of thirdness

DOI: 10.4324/9781003227441-26

is predicated on a constructionist ontology whereby the material and social worlds are inter-dependent with the person who is observing them, and a critical-interpretivist epistemology whereby meaning is socially constructed.

While the literature in intercultural communication commonly places the discourse of thirdness in the last decade of the 20th century, fewer scholars recognize that the idea of 'third culture' was first mentioned in the early 1960s the American social anthropologists John and Ruth Useem. Acknowledging that they were carrying out their fieldwork in the dying embers of the colonial system, the phrase 'third culture' was coined to theorize the experiences of expatriate Americans working in India and Vietnam, and those Indians and Vietnamese who worked within the orbit of the expatriate groups in the emerging post-colonial order (Useem 1963; Useem, Useem, and Donoghue 1963). The Useems' project was therefore set squarely within the emerging remit of cross-cultural studies as a "study of patterns generic to the intersections of societies." They define a third culture as: "… the behavioral patterns created, shared, and learned by men (*sic*) of different societies who are in the process of relating their societies, or sections thereof, to each other" (Useem, Useem, and Donoghue 1963, 169). In 1963, John Useem also wrote explicitly that a third culture performs "mediating functions" in as much as it incorporates aspects of the values, attitudes, and behaviors of both cultures on either side of the Useems' 'binational' equation.

> The third culture signifies the patterns generic to a community of men which spans two or more societies. It consists of more than the mere accommodation or fusion of two separate, juxtaposed cultures, for as groups of men belonging to different societies associate together and interact with each other, they incorporate into their common social life a mutually acknowledged set of shared expectations. A third culture cannot be understood fully without reference to its *mediating functions* between societies nor apart from the cultures of the several societies in which its participants learned how to behave as human beings. Nonetheless, each third culture generates a composite of values, role-related norms, and social structures which distinguish its patterns from any of the societies it spans.
>
> *(Useem 1963, 484, my emphasis)*

The Useems also anticipated the symbolic nature which would later come to characterize the mediational function of the 'third culture,' prophesying that "culture becomes more systematic and elaborated as it is stored in written word and recorded symbols …" (Useem, Useem, and Donoghue 1963 170).

Mediating third space

Two texts set out the seminal idea of 'Third Space': the essay *Commitment to Theory* (Bhabha 1994, 18–40, first published 1988); and an interview with the British cultural studies scholar, Jonathan Rutherford (Bhabha 1990). In the second half of *Commitment to Theory*, Homi Bhabha uses the notion of Third Space in order to problematize the role of critical theory within the postcolonial project (Bhabha 1994, 18–31). Bhabha proposes a "translation and transformation" of the role of critical theory within postcolonial critique in order for it to realize its full potential. To accomplish this, he distinguishes between "cultural diversity" and "difference." Cultural diversity is the re-lationship between cultures which is upheld by the liberal doctrine of multiculturalism, the prin-ciples of which not only inform the political relationship between various ethnic groups hypostatized within the state, but also the principle of communication that is promoted between members of different national cultures to whom discrete values, attitudes and beliefs are attributed in the strand of intercultural studies derived from social psychology. To achieve this variegation be-tween different cultural groups, the notion of 'cultural diversity' must assume a fixity in the meanings, values, and traditions of cultures. This static, totalizing conceptualization of 'culture'—similar to that predicated by the classic conceptualization of intercultural mediation—is one of the things which Bhabha challenges in this essay. By contrast, 'cultural difference' is proposed as the site where cultural meaning is constituted. For Bhabha, the moment of critical engagement takes place at the very moment in which difference is realized semiotically and transgressively interpreted: "... at the significatory boundaries of cultures, where meanings and values are (mis)read or signs are misappropriated" (ibid, 34). Later, Bhabha comments that while the articulation of policies of multiculturalism in liberal societies towards the end of the 20th century professed to promote "diversity," they in fact served not only to "contain" difference but also to actually 'encourage racism' through their implicit implementation of "ethnocentric norms, values and interests" (Bhabha 1990, 206). These 'significatory boundaries of cultures' bear a striking resemblance to—if not a direct homology with—the hermeneutic engagement which takes place between the two interlocutors in the process of intercultural mediation.

The 'Third Space' therefore arises from the ambivalence that resides in any cultural meaning which emerges from the nature of communication. Bhabha refers to the act of communication as a "moment of enunciation," and argues that there is always a "split" or a "disjuncture" between what he calls the "subject of a proposition" (*énoncé*) and the "subject of enunciation" (*enunciation*, Bhabha 1994, 36). This 'split' is based on the view that the *énoncé* ('statement' or 'proposition') is only the material realization of the performative act, not the totality of meaning itself. Meaning is only fully realized through its *enunciation*, glossed by Robert Young as the "what is said," or the "said" (2001, 401). In my view, it is here—within the 'moment of enunciation'—that the 'what is said' is subject to the cultural and historical conditions in which the statement or proposition is realized. The gap that opens up between the realization of a statement or proposition and its enunciation is where hegemonic understandings can be challenged by adopting alternative readings of authorized statements about culture.

> The pact of interpretation is never simply an act of communication between the I and the You designated in the statement. The production of meaning requires that these two places be mobilized in the passage through a Third Space, which represents both the general conditions of language and the specific implication of the utterance ....
>
> *(Bhabha 1994, 36)*

The 'ambivalence' within the 'pact of interpretation' arises from: on the one hand, it not being possible for a proposition to totally circumscribe the meaning which has been mobilized from the resources of language; and on the other, the conditions under which a proposition is transmitted not being solely determined by a proposition's meaning. Meaning is therefore a synthesis that is carried out by the reader of the interplay between the performative act (by the writer) and the conditions under which a text is transmitted. The Third Space is that moment of synthesis—or, if you like, 'mediation'—that takes place between the linguistic or semiotic articulation of a proposition and the realization of its cultural meaning; these are distinct and neither is reducible to the one or to the other. However, as we shall see (*pace* MacDonald 2019), the Third Space has more recently come to be regarded in intercultural studies as a form of hybridization of identity. This shift in meaning takes place despite Bhabha clarifying that the Third Space is

> not so much identity as identification: ... a process of identifying with and through another object, and another object, and an object of otherness, at which point the agency of identification—the subject—is itself always ambivalent, because of the intervention of that otherness.
>
> *(1990, 211)*

Now the force of this conceptualization of Third Space for postcolonial theory is that the very conditions of textuality render the potential for the reader to challenge, confront, and destabilize what at the time was being critiqued as the 'cultural authority' of the colonizing European nations. For Bhabha, the enactment of the Third Space opens up the possibility for the 'subaltern' to re-interpret, revise, and indeed appropriate, the cultural documents of the colonizer in order to de-stabilize the appearance of temporal stability in the traditional frameworks of hegemonic cultures:

> It is that Third Space, though unrepresentable in itself, which constitutes the discursive conditions of enunciation that ensure that the meaning and symbols of culture have no primordial unity or fixity; that even the same signs can be appropriated, translated, re-historicized and read anew.
>
> *(Bhabha 1994, 37)*

This is also where Third Space theory is germane to intercultural mediation. The problematic of intercultural communication is here articulated as being one of signification; and it is in the interstices that open up between the different semiotic realizations of 'culture' that meanings can be contested, and where misrepresentations, distortions and perversions can be challenged. However, we should understand that these encounters might be neither happy nor harmonious, but can often entail conflict and struggle, both with others and within ourselves. In this respect, Bhabha later emphasizes the "incommensurability" which can reside in the "difference between cultural practices, the difference in the construction of cultures within different groups" (1990, 209).

In his more recent exegesis which acknowledges the increasing flows of populations worldwide at the beginning of the 21st century, Bhabha (2011) develops the conceptualization of "third space" (*sic*) in relation to the 'recognition' of migrants by countries in the Global North. On this argument, recognition does not so much concern 'identity,' as the "*subject* of recognition." This subject "is the process by which 'agency' emerges through the mediating structures of alterity that constitute social representation" (10–1, my emphasis). Here, the third space is not confined to the ambivalence of textual interpretation but is extended to the nomadic forms of subjectivity which emerge *both* through the interplay between the *act of enunciation* whereby the speaker articulates her experience through language, and the *site of enunciation* in which the subject is positioned through the ideological and institutional discourses of the nation state. The conceptualization of the third space is therefore reconstituted for the 21st century as the liminal location of migrancy that arises out of the interstices between discourse and language. It is informed by an ethic of 'hospitality' (after Levinas 1999; Derrida 2000) which is at once 'conditional' (by way of the statist discourses of social services, medicine and the law) and 'unconditional' (by way of the 'universal' right to dignity and equality).

From third place to symbolic competence

Just as the concept of 'Third Space' was becoming common parlance within postcolonial theory and cultural studies, the other most prominent topographical image of the discourse of thirdness, "third place," was coined by Claire Kramsch as a more specific metaphor for the development of 'interculturality' on the part of language learners (1993, 206). As with postcolonial theory, the third place was predicated on the socially constructed nature of language and culture, where 'culture' and 'self' were conceived not so much as non-negotiable *a prioris*, but rather as sets of meanings which are produced, transmitted and reproduced by social agents through language and discourse. At a time when *Landeskunde*, or the transmission of facts and knowledge about 'other cultures,' still prevailed in the teaching of modern and foreign languages, Kramsch proposed the 'third place' as a virtual location in which learners could realize difference, "not only between self and others but between one's personal and one's social self" (1993, 234). On this argument, language learning is seen as a point of engagement between, first, two imagined but bounded cultures 'C1' and 'C2'; and then between learners' subjective perceptions of the 'C1' and the 'C2' and the 'real,' externalized 'C1' and 'C2.' Here, 'culture' is not confined to the boundaries of the nation state, but also can also include clusters of meanings centered on a person's "age, gender, regional origin, ethnic background, and social class" (Kramsch 1993, 216).

There are three characteristics of this 'third culture.' First, engagement with it as a 'popular culture' presents language learners with the potential for setting their own stamp on "the dialectic of meaning production" (1993, 239), which arises from the tension between the role of the educational institution to transmit knowledge and skills, and the capacity of learners to make these their own by bringing to the classroom their personal—and sometimes "oppositional" (Kramsch 2009, 238)—appropriation of popular texts and cultural practices. Secondly, the third place does not just involve learners in unreflectingly mimicking the different 'discourse worlds' of the target language, and subsuming themselves to the norms of the 'native speaker.' Rather, the third place demands a 'critical' pedagogy that involves an engaged, questioning approach towards not only the immediate situational context of the classroom, but also the wider global context in which meanings constituted in the multiple languages of the pedagogic context circulate. Finally, the third place is also an 'ecological culture' that engages with the politics of teaching and learning a foreign language. In this, it is conceived as a pedagogical space which resists dominant constructions of educational policy and practice (1993, 247).

However, in a paper delivered in 2010, Kramsch challenges her own notion of third place and explicitly introduces the idea of mediation into the discourse of thirdness: "How can one mediate, that is, interpret one's own and the other's culture each in terms of the other, if at the same time one's interpretation is culturally determined?" (Kramsch 2011, 355). On this argument, while the third place did good service for the more dichotomous times of the late 20th century, it no longer appears adequate to capture the plethora of modalities and meanings which confront literate language users—both young and old—at the beginning of the 21st. First, the solid notions of 'NS' and 'NNS,' 'C1' and 'C2' which are mediated through the third place, cannot capture the experience of the 'decentered' postmodern subject who is required to produce and decode meanings across several different symbol systems: quite possibly shifting across different registers of multiple languages, and combining different modalities of semiosis daily through electronic media (Kramsch 2009/2013). Second, like Bhabha, Kramsch concedes that the concept of a hybrid third place has too readily been appropriated by the political 'ideology of cultural diversity' generated by nations comprising a number of ethnic minority populations. And finally, neither the term 'third place' or 'third culture' acknowledges the agency of the multilingual subject in changing "social reality through the use of multiple symbolic systems" (2009/2013). Thus, Kramsch proposes superseding the more bounded concepts of 'third place' and 'third culture' with the more fluid idea of 'symbolic competence': "… the notion of third culture must be seen less as a PLACE than as a symbolic PROCESS of meaning-making that sees beyond the dualities of national languages (L1–L2) and national cultures (C1-C2)" (2011, 255).

Recontextualization and reinterpretation

It is therefore possible to discern the historical trajectory of the discourse of thirdness through the second half of the 20th century. *Third culture* emerges in the prototypical discourse of cross-cultural studies which appeared in the early 1960s; then *Third Space* is coined in the late 1980s in the neighboring field of postcolonial studies; in the early 1990s the concept of *third culture* is reprised in applied linguistics and augmented by the enduring figure of the *third place*; finally, in the early 21st century, it is proposed that these metaphors of spatialization are superseded entirely by the less spatially fettered concept of *symbolic competence*.

However, while both Bhabha and Kramsch both position themselves *contra* the appropriation of the discourse of thirdness by the national ideologies of interculturalism which prevailed in the late 20th century, we can discern that these images still proved amendable to appropriation by the dominant ideology of multiculturalism which was circulating during this period in European and Anglophone societies. All three metaphors of thirdness hypostatized an imagined site of mediation between one symbolic system of meanings and an alternative symbolic set, and thus served essentially as metaphors for the interpretation of meaning which any social agent who dwells in the interstices between two semiotic systems undertakes as part of their ongoing, day-to-day, activity. Nevertheless, the principal distinction between them resides in the directionality of the flow of power between the two sets of meanings which are mediated. While 'third culture' was originally coined to signify a mental and social state intermediate between a residual, indigenous past and a colonized, globalized future, the 'Third Space' signified the appropriation, recontextualization, and repurposing of the meanings of the colonizer by the subaltern. By contrast, the 'third place' was conceived more specifically as a pedagogical site, which posited an agentive language learner empowered by heuristic activities to selectively mobilize and recontextualize sets of meanings from both 'their own' and 'the other' languages and cultures for their own ends.

As the figures of the 'third culture,' 'Third Space,' and 'third place' were delocated from their original discourses and relocated in the emergent discourse of intercultural studies, the original discourse of thirdness has been subjected to reinterpretation by language teachers and applied linguistics scholars. MacDonald (2019) carried out a corpus analysis of 220 articles written between 1977 and 2017 in the 12 leading intercultural communication journals to analyze the ways in which the phrases 'third culture,' 'Third Space,' and 'third place' have become recontextualized within the field. The analysis of the different linguistic contexts within which the meanings of these three metaphors have been reconfigured revealed some 'discontinuities' and 'ruptures' (after Foucault 1972) with the meanings set out in the autochthonous literature in which the terms were originally located. This relates in particular to the extent to which the figures of 'Third Space' and 'third place' are conceived as bounded spatial metaphors, which has been their main axis of criticism in the intervening years (Crawshaw, Callen, and Tusting 2001).

A discernible transformation has taken place in the meaning of the term 'Third Space' in the process of its recontextualization into the discourse of intercultural studies. First of all, key lexis used in the discourse of intercultural studies appears to have actually *consolidated* the aspect of spatialization, which I would argue was only implicit in Bhabha's original conceptualization (MacDonald 2019, 99–101). But more importantly, 'Third Space' appears to have lost its specific association with textual interpretation for which it was originally conceived. Despite Bhabha's caveats, the idea of 'Third Space' has instead been reconfigured to signify a zone which encompasses the complex identities of subjects who inhabit more than one 'culture,' or traverse multiple 'cultures.' And the appropriation of this term within intercultural studies has, crucially, led to the evacuation of the transgressive and potentially transformational nature of Bhabha's conceptualization of Third Space in favor of a more harmonious, and arguably liberal, constitution of 'identity.' In this, identity has become conceived as a form of a relatively frictionless form of 'hybridity,' substantially evacuated of a sense of power relations. In this context, 'Third Space' has shifted from its emergence within the philosophy of a potentially revolutionary postcolonial moment to its appropriation by an ideology of liberal multiculturalism, very much in accord with the state policies of late 20th-century Europe and North America.

By contrast with 'Third Space,' 'third culture' emerged as the least spatialized term within MacDonald's corpus (2019, 13–4). In its original conceptualization (Useem 1963; Useem et al. 1963), the term 'third culture' appears to have been suggestive of a state of 'inbetweenness' which was strangely prescient of the forms of 'hybrid identity' that have become so popular nowadays. However, over the years the term appears to have been appropriated into a rather 'harder' formation within the literature which developed out of the Useems' original work. Particularly within the cognitivist paradigm of intercultural studies, 'third culture' appears to become constituted as some form of 'model' which is 'built,' exhibiting the characteristics of 'solidity,' 'rigidity,' and 'scientificity' (in the style of Geertz 1983). 'Third culture' is also constituted as an attribute which is ascribed to intercultural subjects, such as 'third culture individuals' or 'third culture kids' with sometimes pathological overtones (Pollock and Van Reken 1999). From this it appears that the term 'third culture' has become recontextualized within the social psychological paradigm of intercultural studies to signify some form of cognitive process. Here, the well-worn cognitivist metaphors of 'model' and 'building' associated with 'third culture' contrast with the properties of 'flexibility' and 'fluidity' that are associated with the poststructuralist conditions of subjectification connotated by 'Third Space.'

However, Kramsch takes up the term 'third culture' rather differently, using it more or less synonymously with 'third place' (Kramsch 1993; Kramsch 2009). Not least, in its original iteration, 'third culture' appears to transfer to an intercultural pedagogy some of the attributes of criticality which have become disassociated with the recontextualized notion of the 'Third Space.' In her later work, Kramsch (2009) expands the more narrowly pedagogic focus of 'third culture,' to suggest that it can be used more broadly as a "metaphor for eschewing other dualities on which language education is based" (238). In this, Kramsch begins to envisage 'third culture' as a position where speakers can draw in the multiplicitous discursive resources of different symbol systems in order to use them purposively for the creation and re-creation of their selves. In contrast to 'Third Space,' 'third place' exhibited fewer indications of operating as a spatial metaphor within the discourse of intercultural studies, than as the signifier of an *actual* or virtual space in which intercultural pedagogy takes place. Thus, the 'third place' is reproduced in the discourse of intercultural studies not so much as metaphor for a state of hybrid identity, but rather as a pedagogic site—both as a material 'place' (such as a university, school, or classroom) or as a virtual 'place' (such as an internet chat room or a virtual learning environment)—in which a relationship between language learning and interculturality can be developed. The learning which takes places in these pedagogic sites also becomes associated with a constellation of civic values which we recognize from other constructions of 'intercultural competence' within our field such as democracy, citizenship, and critical thinking (c.f. Byram 2008). In the discourse of intercultural studies, therefore, 'third place' emerges as a term with similar values to 'Third Space,' but also distinct: as a pedagogic site where the 'hybrid' identity of the language learner qua intercultural subject can be worked out.

Symbolic mediation

This chapter concludes by emphasizing the role of 'symbolic mediation' as another alternative to the terminology of thirdness as we move into the third decade of the 21st century (c.f. Kramsch, 2009/2013, 74). Now, young people in particular are engaging with ever more complex multicultural and multimodal symbol systems in which communication is carried out in increasingly hybrid forms. From the rallying of popular protests and uprisings through the distribution of evocative imagery posted on the smartphones of sympathizers, to the sexually indeterminate videos posted by internet influencers on TikTok, evocative or ironic meanings are mediated through symbol systems circulated from the producer to the end-user through words (written and spoken), music and images without any intercultural intermediary. Through the dispersion of electronic media, it is now possible (although by no means presumed) that control of the cultural imaginary resides in the hands of individual producers and end-users, often independent of any of the prevailing institutional or pedagogical order.

While each decade has had its own nuanced constructions of 'thirdness,' there are three functions which the discursive construction of thirdness through the metaphors of 'space' and 'place' have performed in intercultural communication. First, the autochthonous descriptions of thirdness mostly entail the subjects' engagement in a symbolic relation rather than real-time conversational interaction. Second, these symbolic resources serve to actualize a form of mediation which takes place between two intercultural actors, without requiring the intervention of a third 'mediating' actor (c.f. Busch 2016). Third, the production of a novel synthesis of meaning by way of this process of symbolic mediation leads to a transformation in the subject's consciousness: at its most liberal changing both the promise and the practice of symbolic resources (Kramsch 1993); at its most radical, leading to a shift in the power relations between subordinate and hegemonic cultures (Bhabha 1994).

However, we have also seen in this chapter, that in recent times the idea of intercultural mediation has become appropriated by political regimes of various hues to 'make everything all right' between different peoples, whether in pursuit of ostensibly harmonious multicultural societies or the resolution of conflicts, both local and international. If symbolic mediation is to retain something of Bhabha's original conceptualization of Third Space, it will make us always question in whose interests intercultural mediation ultimately lies; and in conditions where asymmetrical distribution of resources maintain (not least with regard to the recent uneven availability of coronavirus vaccines worldwide), it remains difficult to dispute that 'difference' does not still maintain, despite the continued prevalence of shallow policies of 'diversity.'

Acknowledgment

Some of the material in this chapter has previously been published as: Malcolm N. MacDonald. 2019. 'The discourse of "thirdness" in intercultural studies.' *Language and Intercultural Communication*, 19 (1), 93–109. https://doi.org/10.1080/14708477.2019.1544788.

Note

1 Homi Bhabha (1994) capitalizes the phrase 'Third Space.' Elsewhere 'third place' and 'third culture' are written in small case (Kramsch 1993).

References

Bhabha, Homi K. 1988. "The Commitment to Theory." *New Formations* 5: 1–23.
Bhabha, Homi. K. 1990. "The Third Space". In *Identity: Community, Culture, Difference*, edited by Jonathan Rutherford, 207–21. London: Lawrence and Wishart.
Bhabha, Homi K. 1994. "The Commitment to Theory". In *The Location of Culture*, edited by Homi K. Bhabha, 8–40. New York: Routledge.
Bhabha, Homi K. 2011. *Our Neighbours, Ourselves: Contemporary Reflections on Survival*. Hegel Lectures Series: Berlin, New York: De Gruyter, 10.1515/9783110262445
Busch, Dominic. 2016. "Does Conflict Mediation Research Keep Track with Cultural Theory?" *European Journal of Applied Linguistics* 4 (2): 181–206. 10.1515/eujal-2015-0037
Byram, Michael. S. 2008. *From Foreign Language Education to Education for Intercultural Citizenship*. Clevedon: Multilingual Matters.
Crawshaw, Robert, Beth Callen, and Karin Tusting. 2001. "Attesting the Self: Narration and Identity Change During Periods of Residence Abroad." *Language and Intercultural Communication* 1 (2): 101–19. 10.1080/14 708470108668067
Derrida, Jacques. 2000. *Of Hospitality*, translated by Rachel Bowlby. Stanford: Stanford University Press.
Foucault, Michel. 1972. *The Archaeology of Knowledge*. London: Tavistock.
Geertz, Clifford. 1983. *Local Knowledge*. New York: Basic Books.
Hall, Stuart. 1973. "Encoding and Decoding in the Television Discourse." *University of Birmingham. Paper for the Council of Europe Colloque on Training in the Critical Reading of Television Language*. University of Leicester, September.

The discourse of thirdness

Kramsch, Claire J. 1993. *Context and Culture in Language Teaching*. Oxford: Oxford University Press.

Kramsch, Claire. J. 2009. "Third culture and language education." In *Contemporary Applied Linguistics, Vol. 1, Language Teaching and Learning*, edited by Vivian Cook an Li Wei, 233–54. London: Continuum.

Kramsch, Claire. 2009/2013. "The Multilingual Subject." *International Journal of Applied Linguistics* 16 (1): 97–110. 10.1111/j.1473-4192.2006.00109.x

Kramsch, Claire. 2011. "The Symbolic Dimensions of the Intercultural." *Language Teaching* 44 (3): 354–67. 10.1017/s0261444810000431

Levinas, Emmanuel, 1999. "Peace and Proximity." In *Alterity and Transcendence*, translated by Michael B. Smith, 133–44. New York: Columbia University Press.

MacDonald, Malcolm N. 2019. "The Discourse of 'Thirdness' in Intercultural Studies." *Language and Intercultural Communication* 19 (1): 93–109. 10.1080/14708477.2019.1544788

Pollock, David, and Ruth Van Reken. 1999. *Third Culture Kids: The Experience of Growing Up Among Worlds*. Yarmouth: Intercultural Press.

Useem, John. 1963. "The Community of Man: A Study in the Third Culture." *The Centennial Review* 7 (4): 481–98.

Useem, John, Ruth Useem, and John Donoghue. 1963. "Men in the Middle of the Third Culture: The Roles of American and Non-Western People in Cross-Cultural Administration." *Human Organization* 22 (3): 169–79. 10.17730/humo.22.3.5470n44338kk6733

22

THE TRIADIC CHARACTER OF INTERCULTURAL LEARNING: INSIGHTS FROM EDUSEMIOTICS

Juming Shen and Ying Zhou

Intercultural learning, widely seen as an approach to developing intercultural communication competence (Messner and Schäfer 2012), has been explored both in research and practice (UNESCO 2007). The majority of existing studies have focused on the outcomes of learning, such as the development of individuals' awareness of cultural differences and skills for interacting in different cultural contexts, while insufficient attention has been paid to the process of learning and the rationales underpinning the learning practices. A primary reason may be that intercultural learning has been largely taken as a type of educational practice, and thus inevitably affected by the Cartesian Dualism that has dominated the education sector in English-speaking countries (Semetsky 2014). In line with the 'body-mind' dualism featured by analytical philosophy and ignorance of the 'middle' within between (Semetsky 2014), 'outcome' has been made naturally an orientation for explorations of intercultural learning. A typical example of such outcome-oriented perspective may be the tools and models developed for evaluating individuals' intercultural competence (Byram 1997; Chen 2018; Deardorff 2006; Shen and Gao 2015), which have developed the general dichotomy of competence/performance into more specific perspectives like knowledge/cultural norms or traditions, awareness/cultural differences, skills/verbal or nonverbal behaviors, and attitudes/evaluations (Shen, Sheng, and Zhou 2020).

Although we cannot deny that the perspectives derived from Cartesian Dualism have contributed to the cognition and analysis of the outcomes of intercultural learning, they provide very limited investigation into the 'middle' of the dichotomy, or the process of how the outcomes are achieved through practices of learning. Such ignorance is problematic because excluding the investigation into the process may lead to inadequate understandings or perceptions of learning as an integrated and dynamic activity. A typical example of such problematization may be the reflection of Benjamin Bloom on the educational taxonomy raised by himself. Bloom's Taxonomy, which is still prevalent in the educational sector today, renders the concept of 'competence' to be measurable, and hence the development of the competence, or learning, possible to be planned or guided via instruments based on cognitive, affective, or conative studies. Nevertheless, Bloom also admitted that the achievements of learning into categories of cognition, affection, and physics/kinesthetics "might lead to a fragmentation and atomization of education purposes such that the parts and pieces finally placed into the classification might be different from the more complete objective with which one started" (Bloom 1994, 3).

Different from Descartes's dualistic philosophy, semiotics, especially the semiotic framework established by Charles Sanders Peirce, advocates that human activity such as communication and

210

DOI: 10.4324/9781003227441-27

learning, which involves creation, production, or exchange of meaning, are realized through the action of signs—a dynamic process embedded in triadic relations. For Peirce, meaning is produced in the interpretation process of signs, or semiosis, which consists of the interaction between the objects (knowledge or understanding), the representamen (observable signs of language, behavior, etc.), and interpretant (interpretation between objects and representamen) (Peirce 1978a, 484). Peirce defined such interaction as follows:

> A sign ... is something which stands to somebody for something in some respect or capacity. It addresses somebody, that is, creates in the mind of that person an equivalent sign, or perhaps a more developed sign. That sign which it creates I call the interpretant of the first sign. The sign stands for something, its object. It stands for that object, not in all respects, but in reference to a sort of idea, which I have sometimes called 'the ground of the representamen.'
>
> *(Peirce 1932, 228)*

The trichotomy proposed by Peirce is often presented by a triangular model as in Figure 22.1.

This triadic viewpoint renders it possible to explore the 'middle' ignored in the theories derived from Cartesian dualism and the triadic framework has been applied in various studies ranging from culture and literature to communication and even artificial intelligence (Raza, Bakhshi, and Koshul 2019). In the past two decades, the framework has been increasingly influential in educational studies with edusemiotics developing rapidly. Edusemiotics composes a range of semiotic perspectives with a focus on the process of learning, or the 'middle' between the dichotomy of performance/competence so as to problematize the dualistic educational theories and practices (Kull 2018; Olteanu 2014; Semetsky 2010; Semetsky and Stables 2014; Stables et al. 2018). For edusemioticians, learning is a process of signification that mediates between learner and environment. Such a viewpoint also echoes with the perspective of intercultural mediation which was first defined as resolutions to problems upon its creation and has been increasingly associated with the process for participants in intercultural contexts to develop interpretation of cultural diversities as well as shared understanding between each other (Meyer 1991; Liddicoat and Scarino 2013; Liddicoat 2016).

Based on the Peircean semiotic framework, this chapter will elicit the triadic character of intercultural learning with a focus on the dynamicity it involves. First, the triadicity underpinning the process of intercultural communication will be presented. We will elaborate the process that a message transmits between participants through semiosis, which is embedded in the interpretation of the participants involved in the communication process. This will shed light on how the participants' intercultural competence may affect their performance in intercultural communication via the process of semiosis. By highlighting the dynamicity of the triadic relations of semiosis, we will unveil the ways in which intercultural learning may contribute to development of intercultural communication competence.

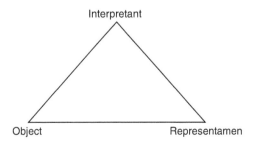

Figure 22.1 Model of Peirce's trichotomy

The triadic character of intercultural communication

In studies of intercultural communication, analyzing the impact of participants' cultural background and the process of communication has been a major theme as both would impact the effectiveness of the communication (Samovar et al. 2017; Shen 2010). From the perspective of semiotics, culture is semiotic in that culture phenomenon embeds a dichotomy of two aspects: The concrete materialistic denotation as the signifier/representamen, and the abstract ideological connotation as the signified/object. For individuals, culture is manifested in one's thoughts and behaviors such as the perceptions of norms, ways of reaction, etc. and it is also largely a result of the operation of signs, i.e., the semiosis process (Shen 2010). The semiotic feature of communication has also been acknowledged by researchers of intercultural communication:

> [...] humans are symbol-making creatures [...] we are able to generate, receive, store, and manipulate symbols. This sophisticated system allows us to use a symbol—be it a sound, a mark on paper, a statue, Braille, a movement, or a painting,—to represent something else [...].
>
> *(Samovar et al. 2017, 26)*

In other words, information can only be carried by the material mediums and communication cannot be conducted unless the signs can be interpreted by the interpreters (Shen 2010).

In intercultural contexts, the process of communication consists of two different types of semiosis. The semiosis for the message sender is an encoding process which starts from an object and ends with a representamen, while that for message receiver is a decoding process that starts from the representamen and ends with an object. The representamen, taking the form such as verbal or nonverbal language, serves the medium between the message sender and receiver. Moreover, semiosis takes place in *semiosphere*, a term raised by Lotman's (1990) to conceptualize the semiotic form of cultures such as conventions, rules, and norms. The whole process of intercultural communication is illustrated in a model as in Figure 22.2 (Shen 2010, 135).

The model above aligns with the widely accepted viewpoint that culture and communication are both ever-changing; they can be transformed, shaped, transmitted (Samovar et al. 2017). Such

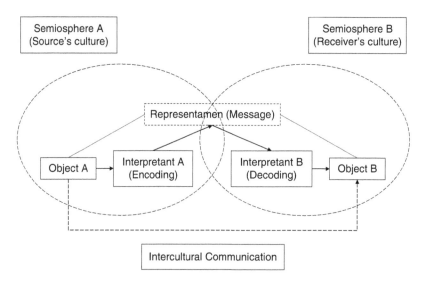

Figure 22.2 Semiotic model of an intercultural communication process

Insights from edusemiotics

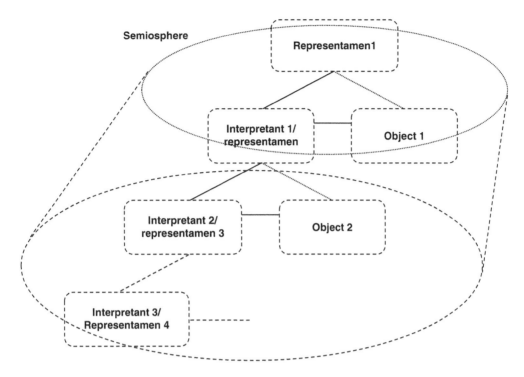

Figure 22.3 Semiosis and the expansion of the semiosphere

dynamicity lies in the infinity of semiosis, of which representamen is infinite of further interpretant both proceed and precede from any given representamen and this process would produce new objects as well (Merrell 2001). That is, the interpretation of the signs can be within the existing knowledge scope (semiosphere), as well as bring up new understandings, i.e., new interpretant and object, so as to contribute to the development of knowledge, i.e., the expansion of semiosphere. In other words, the dynamic interpretation of semiosis may contribute to the development of participants' semiosphere constituted by the knowledge scope of cultural norms, conventions, rules, etc. We have established a model to illustrate such process as in Figure 22.3 (Shen and Su 2015, 147).

Although the dynamicity of intercultural communication can be affected in multiple ways, such as the different type of signs as we have explored in another study (Shen and Su 2015), the models above highlight two aspects that can contribute to the exploration of role of learning in intercultural contexts. First, interpretant plays a crucial role in intercultural communication as the whole process is affected by the collaboration between all the elements involved in semiosis, among which interpretation can be the most important. This is because interpretant is "not an interpreter but rather the sense made of the sign" (Peirce 1932, 303). That is, how a sign/representamen can be interpreted from or into an object is flexible and up to the individual, though it is far from an arbitrary action as we will discuss in the next section. Second, the models also indicate that communicators' cultural background, or semiosphere, can be developed constantly because it is a result of semiosis. Communicators are able to keep learning and expand their knowledge scope through the semiosis in the communication process.

Eliciting such dynamicity is meaningful because it allows us to foresee the possibility of improving one's intercultural communication competence, which falls in line with the research and practice of intercultural learning. To explore how intercultural learning can bring about such positive impact, we will introduce the detailed perspectives from edusemiotics in the next section to illustrate learning as a semiosis process itself. Afterwards, we will discuss in detail regarding how intercultural learning may contribute to the development of individuals' intercultural communication competence following the edusemiotic perspectives.

Edusemiotics and the semiotic framework of learning

Since its inauguration in the Foreword by Marcel Danesi in *Semiotics Education Experience* authored by Semetsky (2010), edusemiotics has been developing rapidly in both theoretical and practical explorations (Semetsky 2015, 2014; Deely and Semetsky 2017). One of the most influential perspectives raised in edusemiotics is the conceptualization of learning as semiosis that involves choice-making, which can be referred to as *abduction* and can be habituated, and sheds much light on understanding the role of intercultural learning.

As we have discussed, dynamicity is a key feature of semiosis and the source of the dynamicity is the individuals' choice involved in interpretation (Eco 2018). Kull explained such semiosis-as-choice in detail to further illustrate Peirce's triadic model (Kull 2018, 455):

> The aspects in the choice process that correspond to the three relata can be described as follows. *Representamen* by itself is ambiguous, as it is possible to interpret it in various ways. This means that representamen may refer to different objects. In semiosis, a choice is made between these possibilities, which appear as options, and representamen becomes related to a particular object. This relation is a decision, which is the same as *interpretant*. Representamen, object and interpretant emerge together at the event of choice-making […] semiosis supposes a choice between options.

Yet from the perspective of Peircean semiotics, the choice-making embedded in interpretation or semiosis is not an arbitrary act. For Peirce, such choice or arbitrariness is explainable by means of *abduction*, which is conceptualized as an insightful and intuitive mode of reference (Semetsky 2015). As Peirce stated,

> Abduction, in the sense I give the word, is any reasoning of a large class of which the provisional adoption of an explanatory hypothesis is the type. But it includes processes of thought which lead only to the suggestion of questions to be considered, and includes much besides.
> *(Peirce 1932, 544)*

In other words, abduction is a form of reasoning; it is irreducible and indispensable but different from *deduction* and *induction* (Psillos 2011). For Peirce, abduction is a type of reasoning that introduces new ideas:

> abduction is the process of forming explanatory hypotheses. It is the only logical operation which introduces any new idea. […] All the ideas of science come to it by the way of Abduction. […] Abduction consists in studying facts and devising a theory to explain them. Its only justification is that if we are ever to understand things at all, it must be in that way.
> *(Peirce 1978a, 145 & 171)*

Therefore, from Peirce's perspective, abduction is a process for a sign or a sign-relation to develop from unconsciousness into consciousness; such process takes an integrated form which is peculiar, indistinguishable, and not verbally articulated (Shen, Sheng, and Zhou 2020). For Peirce, abduction is essential to the growth of intelligibility, or *learning* or *becoming* in educational contexts. As Peirce states,

It is the only logical operation which introduces any new idea; for induction does nothing but determine a value, and deduction merely evolves the necessary consequences of a pure hypothesis. Deduction proves that something must be; Induction shows that something actually is operative; Abduction merely suggests that something may be.

(Peirce 1978a, 172)

To be specific, abduction brings what is now unconscious into conscious in the future; the unconscious realm as a deep psychological ground now determines the acts and behaviors in the future (Peirce 1978b, 156). That is, processes like learning or changing which generate meaning take place via semiosis which is based on on choice-making. Meanwhile, such choice-making is not a simple action of choosing from options; instead, it involves bringing what was unconscious in the past into conscious and projecting what is unconscious now into conscious in the future (Shen, Sheng, and Shen 2020; Shen, Sheng, and Zhou 2020).

Furthermore, such learning, or abduction, or the choice-making that brings unconscious into conscious is not arbitrary or uncontrollable either, but rather can be shaped via *habituation*. Peirce developed the conceptualization of *habit* with a much broader sense,

in which it denotes such a specialization, original or acquired, of the nature of a man, or an animal, or a vine, or a crystallizable chemical substance, or anything else, that he or it will behave, or always tend to behave, in a way describable in general terms upon every occasion that may present itself of a generally describable character.

(Peirce 1978a, 538)

This viewpoint was further elaborated by Kull (2018) so as to explain how habituation is correlated with choice-making, and thus learning:

Habituation is generally a fine-tuning of the connection made by learning. This occurs in repeated use of the same, or nearly the same, sign or choice-making. It means that when choosing, the same connection is found as in some earlier choices, thus the choice does not make a new connection, but it repeats already existing ones, still possibly deepening traces or slightly shifting constraints. Repeated decision usually strengthens the connection and causes further choices in an analogical situation to be more automatic. However, on certain occasions, if the difference is greater, a habit may reverse, and sensitization takes place.

(Kull 2018, 459)

To sum up, from the perspective of edusemiotics, learning is based on semiosis/interpretation which involves choice-making, and such choice-making can be habituated. This is because choice-making is realized through abduction, an action of tracing back to the past experience and predicting the future possibilities. When the abduction is habituated, learning can be realized and achieved (Shen, Sheng, and Zhou 2020). Such conceptualization of learning from the edusemiotic perspective is of significant value to intercultural learning as it highlights the role of personal choice in the development of intercultural communication competence.

An edusemiotic perspective on intercultural learning

Since the concept of intercultural communication competence (ICC) was initiated by Hymes (1972) and expanded by Canale and Swain (1980) from the linguistic perspective, the research into the conceptualization of ICC has attracted scholars from various disciplines (Shen and Gao 2015; Gao 2014; Byram 1997; Spitzberg and Changnon 2009; Deardorff 2006; Chen 2010). The explorations have reached consensus on some key conceptualizations of ICC, among which the most important is the acknowledgement that it is through individual's own effort of changing or *adaptation* that ICC can be developed. For example, Kim (1991) defined intercultural adaptability as the core of intercultural communication competence; through adaptation, individuals are able to change the existing personal and environmental status to fulfill requirements or meet expectations.

However, it seems these theoretical approaches have stopped furthering their investigation into what *adaptation* is. Discussion is limited regarding how adaptation may take place through the interaction between different aspects of ICC or that between the internal aspects and external contexts (Shen, Sheng, and Zhou 2020). For example, Byram did not give much explanation on how the entwining in his model actually takes place (1997) while for Guo-ming Chen, more investigation is needed for his ICC model to elicit the relationship, interaction, or integration between the different aspects of intercultural communication competence:

> […] it is important to go one step further to examine the relationships between or among dimensions or components in the compositional model so that the hierarchical or determinative order of the dimensions or components toward intercultural communication competence can be specified.
>
> *(Chen 2014, 11)*

Following the semiotic framework, the process of adaptation and the role of learning in the development of intercultural communication competence can be illustrated. According to the perspectives of edusemiotics discussed in the previous section, though individuals have the freedom of interpretation and making choices, it is through abduction—tracing back to the past experience and predicting to the future—that the choices could be made. For individuals, learning takes place when abduction is being habituated in accordance with the cultural norms. Therefore, for individuals from different cultures, the habituation of abduction they have experienced would be different so that the abduction they are used to in intracultural contexts may no longer be appropriate in intercultural contexts (Shen, Sheng, and Zhou 2020). Thus, to ensure the effectiveness of communication, individuals may have to adopt a different approach to abduction, which can be essential to adaption and thus the development of intercultural communication competence.

More importantly, the process of adapting the abduction is actually realized through abduction as well and thus can habituated too, which echoes with studies on the development of intercultural communication competence. For example, in Byram's view (1997), the savoir of knowledge, be it about the self, others, or society, and the skills, be them of interpreting, relating, discovering, or interacting, as well as the 'cultural awareness' referring to what an individual has acquired, are the past traces. Yet the tracing of these past traces could be affected by the savior être, meaning (various) attitudes, (possible) relativization, valuing/devaluing others. Scholars have also proposed directions of such habituation, such as the attitudes of 'respect,' 'openness,' and 'curiosity and discovery' (Deardorff 2006). Hence, in other words, if individuals can be habituated to be more inclusive, tolerant, willing to learn about or accept new or different opinions, and to abide with principles such as cultural relativism when tracing their past experience and predicting the future, the choices they make when interpreting the messages in intercultural contexts could be more inclusive and situations such as misunderstandings and conflicts may be better avoided.

In a word, adaptation is a core part in intercultural learning which aims at developing individual's intercultural communication competence. Following the semiotic framework of learning-as-semiosis-as-abduction, adaptation is realized through changing the abduction as actions that have been habituated in intracultural contexts to actions that cater to intercultural contexts. Moreover, the action of changing the abduction can be habituated as well since it is realized through abduction, too. By means of intercultural learning, individuals can be habituated to conduct interpretation in intercultural

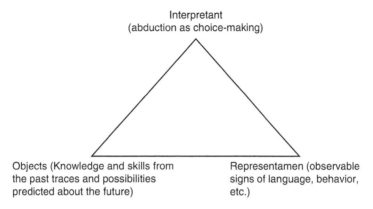

Figure 22.4 Intercultural learning: Modification of Peirce's trichotomy

contexts in manners that contribute to successful communication, though the definition of success may vary in different scenarios. We have illustrated the triadic relation incorporated in intercultural learning by means of a modified triangular mode of Peirce's dichotomy (Shen, Sheng, and Zhou 2020, 621). Figure 22.4

Conclusion

In conclusion, the essence of intercultural learning lies in what Semetsky has termed for the core part of edusemitoics: "a series of interpretants that leads to new meanings arising as the outcomes of learning from lived experience and elicits the transformation of habits due to revaluation of this experience" (Semetsky 2014, 495). A possible and perhaps essential means that intercultural learning may promote the development of individuals' intercultural communication competence lies in habituating individuals to be more adaptative. A further inquiry would be how the habituation could be realized through learning. For us, the answer would still be centered on abduction, i.e., tracing the past experience and predicting the future. This also aligns with the educational philosophy of John Dewey (1916/1924) who asserted that "to learn from experience is to make a backward and forward connection [that] […] becomes instruction—discovery of the connection of things" (164).

References

Bloom, Benjamin S. 1994. "Reflections on the Development and Use of the Taxonomy." In *Bloom's Taxonomy. A Forty-Year Retrospective*, edited by Lorin W. Anderson and Lauren A. Sosniak, 1–8. Chicago, IL: University of Chicago Press.
Byram, Michael. 1997. *Teaching and Assessing Intercultural Communicative Competence*. Clevedon, Philadelphia: Multilingual Matters.
Canale, Michael, and Merrill Swain. 1980. "Theoretical Bases of Communicative Approaches to Second Language Teaching and Testing." *Applied Linguistics* 1 (1): 1–47. 10.1093/applin/I.1.1
Chen, Guo-Ming. 2010. *Foundations of Intercultural Communication Competence*. Hong Kong: China Review Academic Publishers.
Chen, Guo-Ming. 2014. "Intercultural Communication Competence: Summary of 30-Year Research and Directions for Future Study." In *Intercultural Communication Competence*, edited by Xiaodong Dai and Guo-Ming Chen, 14–40. Newcastle upon Tyne, UK: Cambridge Scholars Publishing.
Chen, Guo-Ming. 2018. "A Yin-Yang Theory of Human Communication." *China Media Research* 14 (4): 1–15.

Deardorff, Darla K. 2006. "Identification and Assessment of Intercultural Competence as a Student Outcome of Internationalization." *Journal of Studies in International Education* 10 (3): 241–66. 10.1177/1028315306287002

Deely, John, and Inna Semetsky. 2017. "Semiotics, Edusemiotics and the Culture of Education." *Educational Philosophy and Theory* 49 (3): 207–19. 10.1080/00131857.2016.1190265

Dewey, John. 1916/1924. *Democracy and Education: An Introduction to the Philosophy of Education.* New York: Macmillan Company.

Eco, Umberto. 2018. "Giorgio Prodi and the Lower Threshold of Semiotics." *Sign Systems Studies* 46 (2–3): 343–51. 10.12697/SSS.2018.46.2-3.07

Gao, Yongchen. 2014. "Developing a Conceptual Framework for Assessing Chinese College Students' Intercultural Communication Competence." *Foreign Language World* 4: 80–8.

Hymes, Dell H. 1972. "On Communicative Competence." In *Sociolinguistics. Selected Readings*, edited by John B. Pride and Janet Holmes, 269–93. Harmondsworth: Penguin.

Kim, Young Yun. 1991. "Intercultural Communication Competence: A Systems Theoretic View." In *Cross-Cultural Interpersonal Communication*, edited by Stella Sage and Felipe Korzenny, 259–75. Newbury Park, CA: Sage.

Kull, Kalevi. 2018. "Choosing and Learning: Semiosis Means Choice." *Sign Systems Studies* 46 (4): 452–66. 10.12697/SSS.2018.46.4.03

Liddicoat, Anthony, and Angela Scarino. 2013. *Intercultural Language Teaching and Learning.* Hoboken, N.J: Wiley-Blackwell.

Liddicoat, Anthony J. 2016. "Intercultural Mediation, Intercultural Communication and Translation." *Perspectives* 24 (3): 354–64. 10.1080/0907676X.2014.980279

Lotman, Iurii Mikhailovich. 1990. *Universe of the Mind: A Semiotic Theory of Culture.* Bloomington: Indiana University Press.

Merrell, Floyd. 2001. "Charles Sanders Peirce's Concept of the Sign." In *The Routledge Companion to Semiotics and Linguistics*, edited by Paul Cobley, 28–39. London, New York: Routledge.

Messner, Wolfgang, and Norbert Schäfer. 2012. *The ICCA™ Facilitator's Manual: Intercultural Communication and Collaboration Appraisal (ICCA™).* Createspace.

Meyer, Meinert. 1991. "Developing Transcultural Competence: Case Studies in Advanced Language Learners." In *Mediating Languages and Cultures: Towards an Intercultural Theory of Foreign Language Education*, edited by Dieter Buttjes and Michael Byram, 136–58. Clevedon, Philadelphia: Multilingual Matters.

Olteanu, Alin. 2014. "The Semiosic Evolution of Education: The Semiosic Evolution of Education." *Journal of Philosophy of Education* 48 (3): 457–73. 10.1111/1467-9752.12077

Peirce, Charles S. 1932. *Collected Papers of Charles S. Peirce (Volume II): Principles of Philosophy and Elements of Logic*, edited by C. Hartshorne and P. Weiss. Cambridge: Harvard University Press.

Peirce, Charles S. 1978a. *Collected Papers of Charles S. Peirce (Volume V): Pragmatism and Pragmaticism*, edited by C. Hartshorne and P. Weiss. Cambridge: Harvard University Press.

Peirce, Charles S. 1978b. *Collected Papers of Charles S. Peirce (Volume VI): Scientific Metaphysics*, edited by C. Hartshorne and P. Weiss. Cambridge: Harvard University Press.

Psillos, Stathis. 2011. "An Explorer upon Untrodden Ground." In *Handbook of the History of Logic*, 10: 117–51. Elsevier. 10.1016/B978-0-444-52936-7.50004-5

Raza, Asim, Asim D. Bakhshi, and Basit Koshul. 2019. "An Application of Peircean Triadic Logic: Modelling Vagueness." *Journal of Logic, Language and Information* 28 (3): 389–426. 10.1007/s10849-019-09287-2

Samovar, Larry A., Richard E. Porter, Edwin R. McDaniel, and Carolyn S. Roy. 2017. *Communication between Cultures.* Ninth edition. Boston, Massachusetts: Cengage Learning.

Semetsky, Inna. 2010. *Semiotics Education Experience.* Boston: Brill.

Semetsky, Inna. 2014. "Taking the Edusemiotic Turn: A Body~mind Approach to Education: Taking the Edusemiotic Turn." *Journal of Philosophy of Education* 48 (3): 490–506. 10.1111/1467-9752.12082

Semetsky, Inna. 2015. "Edusemiotics: The Tao of Education." *Language and Semiotic Studies* 1 (1): 130–43.

Semetsky, Inna, and Andrew Stables. 2014. *Pedagogy and Edusemiotics: Theoretical Challenges/Practical Opportunities.* Rotterdam, Boston, Taipei: Sense Publishers.

Shen, Juming. 2010. "The Process of Intercultural Communication: A Semiotic Perspective." *Chinese Semiotic Studies* 3 (1): 75–133. 10.1515/css-2010-0109

Shen, Juming, and Xiaojun Su. 2015. "Photographic Illustrations in Chinese College English Textbooks: A Semiotic Analysis." *Language and Semiotic Studies* 1 (1): 144–60.

Shen, Juming, and Yongchen Gao. 2015. "Construction of Intercultural Communication Competence Inventory for Chinese College Students Based on Knowing-and-Doing Model." *Foreign Languages in China* 2015 (3): 14–21.

Shen, Juming, Yu Sheng, and Xingchen Shen. 2020. "Umwelt-Semiosis: A Semiotic Perspective on the Dynamicity of Intercultural Communication Process." *Language and Semiotic Studies* 6 (2): 1–22.

Shen, Juming, Yu Sheng, and Ying Zhou. 2020. "Learning for Adaptation: An Edusemiotic Perspective on Intercultural Communication Competence." *Chinese Semiotic Studies* 16 (4): 603–25. 10.1515/css-2020-0032

Spitzberg, Brian H., and Gabrielle Changnon. 2009. "Conceptualizing Intercultural Competence." In *The Sage Handbook of Intercultural Competence*, edited by Darla K. Deardorff, 2–52. Thousand Oaks, London, New Delhi, Singapore: Sage.

Stables, Andrew, Winfried Nöth, Alin Olteanu, Sébastien Pesce, and Eetu Pikkarainen. 2018. *Semiotic Theory of Learning: New Perspectives in the Philosophy of Education*. New York, London: Routledge. 10.4324/97813151 82438

UNESCO. 2007. "UNESCO Guidelines on Intercultural Education." In *Education for Peace and Human Rights, Division for the Promotion of Quality Education*. Paris: UNESCO.

23
THE BRIDGE METAPHOR IN INTERCULTURAL MEDIATION

John Corbett

Introduction

The act of mediation is central to intercultural communication. That act is often conceptualized as building bridges. This chapter reflects critically on the 'bridge metaphor' in intercultural mediation and its consequences for the conceptualization and practice of mediation.

Metaphor is often deployed to conceptualize mediation since the act of mediation is abstract, complex, and polysemous. Corbett (2021) discusses some of the different possible meanings of 'mediation' in intercultural communication and language education. 'Mediation' in intercultural communication draws on the use of the term in translation studies to refer to the transfer of common concepts across languages; on its use in Vygotskyan psycholinguistics to refer to the transformation of thought into language; and on its use in conflict resolution to refer to the search for common ground in order to achieve, for example, reconciliation among parties in dispute. All three senses can be found in the updated *Common European Framework of Reference* document (North, Goodier, and Piccardo 2018). While the process of mediation in all three senses can be conceptualized as building bridges, here we will focus on intercultural mediation as the search for common ground between parties from different cultural backgrounds, who find themselves in dispute or conflict, or simply in need of services such as health care. The differences in their cultural backgrounds might be based on race, ethnicity, nationality, class, gender, age, and so on. That is, the different parties will have been socialized into a different set of assumptions, attitudes, beliefs and worldviews, in accordance with their membership of a given social category. When these divergent worldviews result in irreconcilable demands, disputes or conflict, bridges might need to be built between the different parties.

Metaphors and frames

Jones and Hughes (2003) suggest that relatively recent ways of thinking about human cognition and rationality have precipitated an intellectual revolution that rivals those of the Renaissance and Enlightenment. The innovations in thinking derive largely from work in cognitive linguistics and neuroscience, and they include the insights that humans are emotional beings who are capable of reason, rather than rational beings who are capable of feeling, and that much of our thinking is metaphorical in nature. The latter insight derives, of course, from the influential work by Lakoff and Johnson (1980) in which metaphor was presented primarily as a cognitive rather than a purely linguistic phenomenon. Their argument was that much of our understanding of concepts,

220

DOI: 10.4324/9781003227441-28

particularly abstract concepts in a complex world, is founded on metaphorical extensions of our embodied experiences. Thus, to take one of the more obvious examples that is pertinent to our later discussion, the complex and abstract notion of an individual's 'life' can be understood with reference to the less complex and concrete notion of a 'journey,' resulting in the common conceptual metaphor, LIFE IS A JOURNEY. In Lakoff and Johnson's terms, a concept is mapped from one cognitive domain onto another; in more traditional linguistic terms, the Tenor or Topic ('life') is understood with reference to a Vehicle ('journey'). The incidents in an individual's life as they progress temporally from birth to death can be seen as spatial points in the course of a journey. The basic conceptual metaphor thus generates others that are thematically related and coherent with it: choices are conceptualized as crossroads, challenges as obstacles or barriers, life goals as destinations, and so on.

The metaphorical conceptualization of complex and abstract concepts allows for the possibility of framing and reframing. A commonly quoted example is Lakoff and Johnson's ARGUMENT IS WAR, which is evidenced by utterances such as 'she attacked my point of view', or 'I defended my proposition' and so on. A verbal debate is commonly framed in terms of armed conflict; however, other framings are possible. An alternative framing would be ARGUMENT IS A DANCE, which might generate a different form of behavior. Lakoff and Johnson (1980: 5) speculate that such a framing would result in a culture in which

> the participants are seen as performers, and the goal is to perform in a balanced and aesthetically pleasing way. In such a culture, people would view arguments differently, experience them differently, carry them out differently, and talk about them differently.

While Lakoff and Johnson do not draw on evidence of any culture that does frame argument in this fashion, their speculation clearly inspired Harriet Lerner to write *The Dance of Anger* (1985), a popular self-help book for women who wish to change aspects of their relationships with their male partners.

The key point, then, is that much of our thinking about concepts such as mediation is unconsciously metaphorical, and the nature of the metaphor may frame our understanding in such a way that it prompts certain types of behavior. Different cultural frames are associated with different metaphors, which in turn trigger different conceptualizations of the mediation process, and so, by reframing them, we might change our understanding and our behavior.

The *bridge* metaphor

A bridge may seem to be a useful and obvious vehicle for a metaphorical conceptualization of mediation. Its utility is evident in the characterization of the frame that the embodied experience of a bridge offers to the understanding. This characterization is coded, for example, in the Berkeley *FrameNet* project which positions *bridge* within the conceptual domain of *roadways* and defines it as "a structure carrying a road, path, or railway across a river, road, etc." The verbs associated with *bridge* are largely physical actions: "build, construct, continue, cross, lower, pass, rebuild, use, walk" (International Computer Science Institute, University of Berkeley, 1997). The FrameNet project gives a brief summary of the literal sense of the noun, for use in semantic role labeling. It is this literal sense that is available to be mapped onto other conceptual domains.

Metaphorical extensions of this core meaning can be traced through the *Historical Thesaurus of English* (Kay, Roberts, Samuels and Wotherspoon, 2009). This lexicographical project has coded all the senses of every word in the history of English; the different codes for each lexical item indicate the metaphorical shifts in the meanings of words in English over time (Anderson, et al. 2016). *The Historical Thesaurus of English* confirms that the literal sense of *bridge* extends from the Old English period: The noun is *brycg* and associated verbs are *oferbrycgian* and *gebrycgian to span with a bridge*. Over time, these senses radiated to other semantic domains. The lexicographic record, for example shows the following shifts to the domain of physical alignment, which again extend further into personal relationships:

•	That which connects/bond	a1225 + 1742-
•	Relate/connect one thing to another	1853-
•	Connect to give continuity (*bridge a gap*)	1879-

There are other senses of *bridge*, from the bridge of one's nose to the upper structure of a ship, but the metaphorical meanings that express physical and personal relationships are those most relevant to mediation.

Mediation in the sense that it is used here is also, of course, metaphorical in nature. The earliest records of the use of the word in English, from the 15th century onwards, indicate a set of sometimes contradictory physical senses (*divide in two, be usable in more than one position, connect*) and metaphorical extensions that map onto the domain of personal and professional relationships (*intercede, be advantageous to, bring peace to people in discord/strife*, and so on). The mutual core senses relating to positionality that link *bridge* and *mediation*' are available for framing the process of intercultural mediation in a particular way: Two cultural positions are separated, and an intervention is required to *bridge the gap*. The cultural basis of the *gap* might be religion, race, ethnicity, social class, gender, age or another social variable; however, the assumption is that bridging that gap is both necessary and possible. The bridge metaphor is congruent with other metaphors mentioned above. If LIFE IS A JOURNEY, then the cultural gap is an obstacle to progress that needs to be bridged. If ARGUMENT IS WAR, then the two opposing parties are positioned in an aggressive or hostile stance over the cultural gap; a bridge will connect the two and facilitate constructive communication, and other mutually beneficial exchanges and collaborations, such as trade.

The bridge metaphor in action

There is in the research literature on conflict and mediation abundant evidence that the bridge metaphor is used in the discourse of conflict resolution and reconciliation. Cameron (2007) shows that bridging is one of the key metaphors used in a series of conversations between Jo Berry, whose father was killed in Brighton by a bomb, and Pat Magee, a member of the Irish Republican Army responsible for planting the bomb. Cameron is interested in the metaphors used by both parties in their mutual and voluntary attempt to achieve a measure of reconciliation after the bombing. The main metaphors Cameron identifies are

- RECONCLIATION IS A JOURNEY
- RECONCILIATION IS CONNECTION
- RECONCILIATION IS CORRECTING A DISTORTED IMAGE
- RECONCILIATION IS LISTENING TO THE OTHER'S STORY

The bridge metaphor is pertinent to the first two conceptual domains: A bridge allows a stopped journey to continue, and it connects parties separated by an ideological divide and/or a history of violence. It arises overtly in the discourse of both parties in the reconciliation talk: Jo Berry actually presents Pat Magee with a poem on the need to build bridges which becomes a topic in one of their conversational exchanges (Cameron 2007: 213, presentation slightly adapted...):

PAT ... (3.0) that's a very beautiful poem.
and er –

The bridge metaphor

... (1.0) in the er −
the journey,
... (1.0) coming ... to a bridge,
... you [know].
JO [hmh]
PAT ... with two ends,
... (1.0) er −
... (2.0) that's −
... that's why this is so important.

The except suggests that Pat Magee is negotiating the meaning of the bridge metaphor; as Cameron observes, Magee's insistence on the importance of the "two ends" is "a move that enables Pat to distance himself slightly from Jo while at the same time maintaining alignment through repeating her *bridge* metaphor" (Cameron 2007: 213).

The spatial properties of separation, distance, alignment, connection, and proximity are an important resource in conceptualizing the relationship of self to other in this reconciliation scenario. The bridge metaphor is not the only way of organizing these spatial qualities: The participants in the reconciliation also draw upon images of barriers and obstacles to be broken down and they talk about *opening up* to the perspective of the other. As noted above, the reconciliation discourse also moves beyond spatial metaphors to metaphors of seeing without distortion (that is, precise and empathic understanding), a faculty enabled by listening to a story (mutual sharing of experiences).

The mediation in this case study was prompted by one of the key players, Jo Berry, because she wanted to understand the reasons behind the murder of her father in a politically motivated act of violence. The cultural divide between them can be construed in terms of religion, nationality, and ideology. It is Berry who takes the initiative in prompting the attempt to find connection and achieving whatever resolution is possible; other mediators are largely confined to setting up the meetings, and recording and analyzing them. It is Berry and Magee who are building their metaphorical bridge towards a deeper understanding of and empathy for the other.

In different situations, however, the mediator is a third party who takes on a more central role and it is the mediator who can be conceptualized as the bridge between the parties in conflict. One such situation is bilingual medical health interpreting, in which interpreters might be construed as, or construe themselves as, bridges (Hsieh 2009). In Hsieh's interviews with medical interpreters, the bridge metaphor is again invoked explicitly:

[The goal of medical interpreting is] to help other people to bridge the gap, that's pretty much the theme of all the [training] classes. To help other people from our own country who do not speak English, who don't know the system and who don't know the culture, just to help them, guide them along, and help them as much as you can, to get through it.
(Hsieh 2009: 140)

Hsieh contrasts the bridge metaphor with what she calls the *conduit* metaphor; she argues that one way in which third-party mediators understand themselves is as neutral facilitators of cross-cultural communication, that is, as neutral conduits through which messages pass backwards and forwards. The core sense of positionality and alignment of the bridge metaphor expands this self-conceptualization: It is the mediating interpreter's role not just to act as a channel of communication but to guide the patient through the system (to *cross the gap*), and to align one set of cultural assumptions with another. The bridge metaphor allows the conceptualization of greater agency for the mediator than the conduit metaphor. Hsieh notes, however, that there are limits to the extent to which interpreters are willing to *build bridges*. She illustrates these limits by quoting the words of one interpreter, *Colin* (Hsieh 2009: 141):

Colin talked about how interpreters are bridges between two languages, providing cultural frameworks to other conversational partners; however, when one of his patients was asked to leave the clinic because of the lack of funds, Colin decided to not get involved because 'It's not my battle. Being an interpreter, that's not our battle.' In other words, although interpreters were aware of their functions in bridging the gaps between the provider and the patient in various aspects (e.g., linguistic, cultural, educational, and socioeconomic aspects), they still strived to be and saw themselves as conduits. Nevertheless, the interpreters' use of the bridge metaphor highlighted the fact that their understanding of the 'conduit' role has extended beyond the conduit model envisioned in their training programs and the ideology of translation and interpretation.

There are a number of salient issues arising from Hsieh's observations. The metaphor of the bridge allows for the conceptualization of the mediator as seeking potential mutual alignment (linguistic, cultural, educational, and sociolinguistic) between different parties, but, as Colin's example shows, the mediator might withdraw from 'the battle' if the parties in conflict are not willing to adjust to each other's demands and expectations. Hsieh also raises the issue of training: Metaphors of conduits and bridges are resources used in the training of interpreters, so that individuals involved in mediation have a graspable sense of their function, their potential, and the limits to their responsibilities. The mediator's ability to be a bridge or bridge-builder, then, can be seen as part of his or her intercultural communicative competence.

Bridge building: Developing intercultural communicative competence

Despite a proliferation of models of intercultural communicative competence over the past two decades (Deardorff 2009), the most extensive and widely used set of guidelines for language educators is the *Common European Framework of Reference (CEFR)*, and its updated Companion (Council of Europe 2001; North, Goodier, and Piccardo 2018). The latter volume, with revised and updated descriptors of many aspects of intercultural communicative competence, gives a much more central role than its predecessor did to the concept of intercultural mediation, an activity introduced but underdeveloped in the 2001 framework (North, Goodier, and Piccardo 2018: 22):

> However, for mediation, an important concept introduced in the CEFR which has assumed even greater importance with the increasing linguistic and cultural diversity of our societies, no validated and calibrated descriptors existed. The development of descriptors for mediation was, therefore, the longest and most complex part of the project that led to the production of this CEFR Companion Volume. Descriptor scales are provided for mediating a text, for mediating concepts, for mediating communication, as well as for the related mediation strategies and plurilingual/pluricultural competences.

Not surprisingly, the authors of the revised framework invoke the bridge metaphor in relation to the various forms of mediation being discussed (North, Goodier, and Piccardo 2018: 103):

> In mediation, the user/learner acts as a social agent who creates bridges and helps to construct or convey meaning, sometimes within the same language, sometimes from one language to another (cross-linguistic mediation). The focus is on the role of language in processes like creating the space and conditions for communicating and/or learning, collaborating to construct new meaning, encouraging others to construct or understand new meaning, and passing on new information in an appropriate form. The context can be social, pedagogic, cultural, linguistic or professional.

Table 23.1 CEFR achievement scales for 'overall mediation' (North, Goodier, and Piccardo 2018: 105)

Overall mediation
C2 Can mediate effectively and naturally, taking on different roles according to the needs of the people and situation involved, identifying nuances and undercurrents and guiding a sensitive or delicate discussion. Can explain in clear, fluent, well-structured language the way facts and arguments are presented, conveying evaluative aspects and most nuances precisely, and pointing out sociocultural implications (e.g., use of register, understatement, irony, and sarcasm).
C1 Can act effectively as a mediator, helping to maintain positive interaction by interpreting different perspectives, managing ambiguity, anticipating misunderstandings and intervening diplomatically in order to redirect talk. Can build on different contributions to a discussion, stimulating reasoning with a series of questions. Can convey clearly and fluently in well-structured language the significant ideas in long, complex texts, whether or not they relate to his/her own fields of interest, including evaluative aspects and most nuances.

The intercultural language learner, as mediator, is here presented in a fashion that echoes to some extent the self-conceptualization of the health interpreters mentioned above: The intercultural language learners may not themselves be bridges, but they create bridges. This creation involves the construction of meaning (*building metaphor*), the transfer/passing on of information (*conduit metaphor*) and the creation of metaphorical *space* for collaborative meaning-making. The description of C1 and C2 levels of mediation (Table 23.1) indicates the authors' concept of how an intercultural mediator should be able to behave:

While the bridge metaphor is not explicitly evoked here, the underlying metaphorical structures are congruent with it: The mediator is in a position to observe different *undercurrents*, guiding conversational partners, possibly redirecting them, in such a way as to proceed on their journey.

The affordances and limitations of the bridge metaphor

So far, the use of the bridge metaphor in intercultural mediation might seem natural and un-controversial. The metaphor is grounded on a spatial relationship that seems easily to map onto intercultural relations: There are two distinct and different points, separated by a gulf or an obstacle, that must be bridged so that travel is possible between those points. This physical scenario easily maps onto a metaphorical scenario in which the different points are people from different cultural backgrounds whose divergent beliefs or assumptions, and possibly hostility to each other, become a gulf or obstacle that must be bridged. The mediator takes the role of that bridge or takes the role of creating that bridge. In doing so, the mediator must take up a position between the two distinct parties and align them so that constructive communication is possible. Insofar as a bridge is an inanimate conduit, the mediator is also a neutral broker; however, the role of the bridging mediator extends beyond that of a conduit, to embrace guidance and, in cases of hostility, diversion.

It is clear that there are affordances in framing intercultural mediation as the process of con-structing bridges. Parties such as Jo Berry and Pat Magee can conceive of themselves as separated by ideology, nationality and moral framework, and attempt to align themselves in such a way as to make constructive communication and a degree of empathy possible. A healthcare interpreter can also imagine his or her role as bringing patients and the healthcare system into some kind of connection and constructive alignment. An intercultural language learner can conceive of mediation as enabling connection, too, by attending to undercurrents, and co-constructing meaning with conversational participants, resolving ambiguity and directing discussion away from sensitive areas that might cause conflict. However, even in the examples that we have seen, there are tensions that suggest that the bridge metaphor might be at least limited in its application, and, at worst, inappropriate in certain situations.

The bridge metaphor depends on the presence of three participants: Two opposing parties and an interceding mediator. There also has to be a gap or obstacle between the opposing parties and the mediator needs to have the possibility of bridging it. One immediate problem with this metaphor lies in the conceptualization of the mediator as being or constructing a bridge between the opposing parties. Cohen (2001) argues that the concept of a mediator varies substantially in Arabic, Hebrew and Anglo-American languages and cultures, a fact that has added to the difficulty of *bridge building* by American mediators in the Israel-Arab conflict. In Anglo-American culture, a mediator tends to be visualized as a neutral, honest broker between opposing parties. In Arabic culture the translation of *mediator* is *wasit*, someone of accepted moral authority and wealth, who might use his own financial capital as a sweetener to persuade opposing sides to lay aside their differences. In the Hebrew language, according to Cohen, the translation of *mediator*, *metavich*, tends to evoke a professional, like a lawyer, hired to bring opposing parties together. The mediator is expected to benefit from any agreement reached. Given these different and largely conceptions of a mediator and his or her role, the process of bridge-building will be a considerably different proposition for each of the parties involved in the mediation. In short, their assumptions about each other's *positionality* in the dispute would diverge. In fact, as Cohen (2001: 50) argues, the initial departure for the mediation process would be for all the parties involved to agree on what mediation involves. The metaphor for building a bridge would only function with initial reflection by all parties leading to some kind of consensus about the responsibilities and expectations of those at each end, and those interceding.

The other elemental constituent of the bridge metaphor is the obstacle or the gulf to be bridged. There is an assumption that this obstacle or gap is blocking progress on life's journey for all parties. However, it may be that those parties involved in conflict rely on the perceived gap or obstacle to constitute and sustain their community identity. Brigg (2003) presents examples of largely non-western cultures who do not consider their engagement in violent conflict as requiring mediation; rather, conflict with the out-group helps to sustain internal social cohesion amongst the warring parties. There is possibly an echo of this attitude in Pat Magee's response to Jo Berry in the dialogue quoted earlier: When she recited her poem on building bridges, he responded to it positively, but commented that the salient fact was that there must be two ends to the bridge. Without the gulf between them, the validity and cohesion of the opposing communities will be compromised, and their distinctive identity might not be maintained. A mediator who succeeds in *bridging* a gap necessarily also changes the identity of the opposing parties. Building a bridge does not, then, necessarily connect—it also threatens. This factor, and the anxieties it provokes, also needs to be addressed in intercultural mediation.

Alternatives to the bridge metaphor

Perhaps the most fundamental constituent of the bridge metaphor is that there must be a spatial configuration of two distinct points separated by a gulf or obstacle. The bridge metaphor assumes that the two opposing parties are indeed different. The illustrations we have drawn upon in this chapter seem to give ample evidence that they are. Jo Berry and Pat Magee are separated by their adherence to different national mythologies, their divergent political ideology, and a moral perspective that either disavows or legitimates the use of violence for political ends. They are also separated by the fact that Magee was directly responsible for the violent death of Berry's father. The healthcare scenario is also predicated on patients whose language, expectations, and healthcare beliefs separate them from providers in a foreign healthcare system. Intercultural language learners interact with a myriad of people with different assumptions about how discourse and the world operate; they may find, for example, that *mediator* can be translated in many different ways and that the roles and expectations of mediators vary across different communities. Gulfs to be bridged do seem to exist.

However, as we have already seen, alternatives to the bridge metaphor are evident in the range of metaphors that Berry and Magee draw upon to try to make sense of their developing relationship (Cameron 2007). Alternative conceptualizations do not necessarily rely on metaphorical separation or bringing divergent beliefs into alignment. The two main ones that Cameron identifies are:

- RECONCILIATION IS CORRECTING A DISTORTED IMAGE
- RECONCILIATION IS LISTENING TO THE OTHER'S STORY

The metaphors are related: By attending to the experiences and grievances of the other, ideally the self comes to a more accurate, less stereotypical, more empathic understanding of his or her position. The other is not necessarily seen as separate or even very different from the self. The parties need to accept that their understanding of the other's position is partial and perhaps inaccurate, and that attending to the other's experience will redress that inaccuracy to some extent. The process of mediation is perhaps less goal-directed, more reflexive than building a bridge. But by reframing the process of mediation as *seeing with greater clarity* or *listening attentively to a story* the mediator, at least, is alerted to the fact that there might be different ways to reach consensus or reconciliation.

Conclusion

Cognitive linguists claim that our thinking and behavior is at least to some extent conditioned by perspectives on the world that are structured metaphorically. Embodied experiences are mapped onto more abstract concepts in order for us to make sense of a broad range of intangible phenomena. Thus, spatial distance is a means of understanding interpersonal relationships. There are, however, different ways of extending experience into the realm of metaphor, and so concepts can be framed in different ways according to how we structure them metaphorically. A powerful metaphor for intercultural mediation is, as we have seen, bridge building. But, like other metaphors, it has its limitations, and alternative metaphors are available for the mediator to deploy.

References

Anderson, Wendy, Ellen Bramwell, and Carole Hough, eds. 2016. *Mapping English Metaphor through Time.* Oxford: Oxford University Press.

Brigg, Morgan. 2003. "Mediation, Power, and Cultural Difference." *Conflict Resolution Quarterly* 20 (3): 287–306. 10.1002/crq.26

Cameron, Lynne J. 2007. "Patterns of Metaphor Use in Reconciliation Talk." *Discourse & Society* 18 (2): 197–222. 10.1177/0957926507073376

Cohen, Raymond. 2001. "Language and Conflict Resolution: The Limits of English." *International Studies Review* 3 (1): 25–51. 10.1111/1521-9488.00224

Corbett, John. 2021. "Revisiting Mediation: Implications for Intercultural Language Education." *Language and Intercultural Communication* 21 (1): 8–23. 10.1080/14708477.2020.1833897

Council of Europe. 2001. *Common European Framework of Reference for Languages: Learning, Teaching, Assessment.* Strasbourg: Council of Europe; Cambridge University Press. https://www.coe.int/en/web/common-european-framework-reference-languages

Deardorff, Darla K., ed. 2009. *The Sage Handbook of Intercultural Competence.* Thousand Oaks, CA: Sage.

Hsieh, Elaine. 2009. "Bilingual Health Communication. Medical Interpreters' Construction of Mediator Role." In *Communicating to Manage Health and Illness*, edited by Dale E. Brashers and Daena J. Goldsmith, 135–60. New York: Routledge.

International Computer Science Institute, University of Berkeley. (1997-). *FrameNet*. https://framenet.icsi. berkeley.edu/fndrupal/

Jones, Wendell, and Scott H. Hughes. 2003. "Complexity, Conflict Resolution, and How the Mind Works." *Conflict Resolution Quarterly* 20 (4): 485–94. 10.1002/crq.42

Kay, Christian, and Christian Kay, eds. 2009. *Historical Thesaurus of the Oxford English Dictionary: With Additional Material from "A Thesaurus of Old English."* Oxford; New York: Oxford University Press.

Lakoff, George, and Mark Johnson. 1980. *Metaphors We Live By*. Chicago: University of Chicago Press.

Lerner, Harriet Goldhor. 1985. *The Dance of Anger: A Guide to Changing the Pattern of Intimate Relationships*. New York: Harper and Row.

North, Brian, Tim Goodier, and Enrica Piccardo. 2018. *Common European Framework of Reference for Languages: Learning, Teaching, Assessment: Companion Volume with New Descriptors*. Strasbourg: Council of Europe. https://www.coe.int/en/web/common-european-framework-reference-languages/home

24

USING CREATIVE NON-FICTION TO PINPOINT MOMENTS OF DECENTERING IN INTERCULTURAL MEDIATION

Adrian Holliday

To connect the three elements in the title, I will first explain the principle of deCentering and its cruciality for intercultural mediation, and then how creative non-fiction is a useful methodology for this purpose. I will then demonstrate how this works with an example of a previously published creative non-fiction account and conclude with what can be learned from this.

DeCentering and starting from the small

DeCentering is necessary to contest a false, dominant, Center perception of culture as suggested by a number of postcolonial and critical cosmopolitan writers (Bhabha 1994, 56; Baumann 1996; Stuart Hall 1996, 619; Beck and Sznaider 2006; Kumaravadivelu 2007; Quijano 2007; Delanty, Jones, and Wodak 2011; Canagarajah 2011). In summary:

- *The Center perception* is that cultures exist as separate homogeneous collectivities that exclusively associate language, culture, nation and civilization that define and confine who we are, and that hybridity is the product of blurring globalization.
- *The deCentered perception* is of a natural hybridity of multiple shifting and porous cultural realities that have always lived creatively alongside each other, and that:
- *The Center reality* has been constructed by Western colonial and nation-state organizing and reification of culture. This encourages 'us'-'them' essentialism and racism that hides and does not recognize the deCentered reality and its contribution.

The Center perception is seductively powerful in academic and popular narratives because of the apparent science of methodological nationalism, apparent opportunities that it offers the colonized, and grand narratives of nation. Therefore, particular and focused efforts need to be made to see the natural hybridity that exists all around us. This require entering into a difficult third space (Soja 1996; Holliday forthcoming).

DeCentering therefore requires beginning not with presuppositions about cultural differences and in-compatibilities, but, instead, starting with direct observation of the normal hybridity of cultural life from the small, or the 'bottom-up' (Stuart Hall 1991, 35). It is this direct observation of 'small culture formation on the go' (Holliday 2019) that is served, not only, but very usefully, by creative non-fiction.

DOI: 10.4324/9781003227441-29

The relevance of creative non-fiction

Creative non-fiction is an ethnographic method that collects together the researcher's experience of social events that cannot easily be captured through more established modes of data collection and analysis. Agar (1990) explains that more 'formal' data, such as interview transcripts, can only ever be a partial representation of the multiplicity of probable ethnographic interpretations. Creative non-fiction represents this multiplicity through a series of characters with different and sometimes conflicting positions. Rather than focusing on the Center perception of conflict between reified cultures, this enables a focus on conflicting Center and deCentered discourses *about* culture with which we often express our positioning and social alignments—reifying culture while at the same time 'making' it as a hybrid flow (Baumann 1996, 31).

This deCentered creative non-fiction thus acknowledges the intersubjectivity recognized by post-modern, constructivist ethnography (Clifford and Marcus 1986), and also required in the decoloniality project (Quijano 2007, 172). It therefore employs the ethnographic disciplines of making the familiar strange and thick description. Because the researcher is also implicated through their own intersubjective positioning, the discipline of allowing meanings to emerge also ensures that the creative non-fiction takes on its own life beyond their initial preoccupations.

Creative non-fiction is therefore employed as text to educate readers in the nature of intercultural conflict and how it may be addressed (Holliday 2019), as well as data in empirical research texts (Holliday and Amadasi 2020).

Demonstrating how it works

The example of creative non-fiction in this chapter concerns four characters, Stefan, Alicia, Roxana, and Jane, in a workplace setting, taken verbatim from Holliday (2019, 101–2), where an earlier analysis can be found. It describes an instance of conflict in which a dominant group marginalizes newcomers. While much of my creative non-fiction is based on particular interview and observation data, this one is based on what I commonly see and hear happening around me. The characters are therefore composites of a wide range of people. I have chosen this example because of its particular focus on how the actions and positions taken by the characters represent personal scripts derived from the splintered normalization of Center and deCentered positions (see Lyotard 1979, 22; Goodson 2006; Wodak 2021, 105–6). It also demonstrates how apparently innocent cultural stereotyping leads to 'unwitting' racism, as described by the Macpherson report (1999, 6.4, 6.17) following the murder of black teenager Stephen Lawrence, and how Bourdieu's concept of symbolic violence leads to between-the-lines micro-aggression by the ostensibly well-wishing West against migrants (Flam and Beauzamy 2011).

Following is the full text with numbered paragraphs for ease of reference:

It's what you wear

1   When Stefan first met his new colleague, Roxana, he was so pleased to see someone different around the place. She was also personable and friendly and clearly knew her job very well. He knew he had to be careful though and that he mustn't just jump to conclusions that she was foreign. He had been through the company's online diversity training course and knew all about that. He had found the course a bit of a chore and had been quite cynical about it, but on meeting Roxana he began to see its relevance.

2   Roxana did announce that she was born and brought up in Ex, but that she had been living here since her late teens when her parents came to this country. He imagined

Using creative non-fiction

that, therefore, he could refer to her as 'foreign.' Indeed, once they got to know each other better, he found her very easy to talk to and her 'foreignness' became one of the topics of their banter.

3   Anyway, it was so clear to him that Roxana was different. Stefan couldn't work out exactly what it was until one of the other women in the office said that Roxana was 'flashy,' 'extravagant,' 'materialistic,' and 'a bit of a show-off.' Roxana certainly did come over as being quite exotic. Somebody said that she dressed as though she was going to a cocktail party rather than the office. Stefan thought it odd that they should say this when he considered the expensive power dressing of some of his more senior women colleagues. But then he heard Roxana talking about how she missed the servants they had in Ex and how it was so good when she and her family visited their friends who had a villa in the South of France and were able to retain some of their 'old lifestyle.' Roxana actually had quite a lot to say and didn't seem to notice the stony silence that these comments were met with. She certainly wasn't the submissive image that everyone imagined of women from Ex.

4   On further reflection, Stefan wondered if Roxana's growing unpopularity had anything to do with her being foreign. Everyone knew someone who was annoying because they talked things up instead of the general preference here to talk things down. With Roxana, it was something more.

5   He got an answer when he met with his friend, Alicia. When he told her about Roxana, Alicia said that it wasn't just a matter of Roxana's personality and that there was an important factor connected with her being foreign and even coming from a particular part of the world. Alicia said that she herself was from a part of the world which meant that she also had experienced at least part of what Roxana must be going through and that when she started reading about post-colonial politics as part of her university course, she could see how a lot of things began to connect.

6   Alicia explained that there were deep national grand narratives that traced themselves right back to things like the war between the Greeks and Persians in the fifth century BC, and even the story of David and Goliath, which represented the small person defeating the powerful giant. Alicia said that the idea of the clever, agile, self-directed, free-thinking small nation defeating the huge, corrupt, wealthy, and depraved empire underpinned much of how people here pictured the rest of the world. She said that these narratives were all around them, whether it was endless references to defeating the 'Evil Empire' in games and movies, or government rhetoric about spreading 'democracy' across the world when what they are really interested in is oil money. Stefan said he understood all of this but couldn't see what it had to do with Roxana. He knew that Alicia was going to go on and on about this, but he did want to get to the bottom of it.

7   Alicia said that it was all also connected with a Protestant religious thing which disapproved of anything materially wasteful or inefficient. Stefan said that this was surely something in the past because there was so much wastefulness and inefficiency. Alicia replied that this wasn't the point. It is what's in people's minds that's important. A conviction of functional superiority can exist quite well alongside waste and inefficiency. She said that this is probably why people get so angry when they see blatant and open showiness in people like Roxana, when they themselves are so mixed up about it. They associate Roxana's whole demeanor—her dress and open expression of luxury—with the extravagant corruption of the Evil Empire.

8   Stefan thought about the issue of functional superiority. He remembered that even though Roxana was very good at her job, people kept praising her as though it was

unexpected, as though she had learned it from them. Then Alicia began to go on about how she felt so intimidated by people here. She said they repeatedly talked down at her, refused to take her behavior seriously, calling it 'theatrical.' She said that women seemed afraid of her stealing their men, as though she was some sort of siren. She said this was evident in the way these women shot possessive looks at their husbands if the latter got into any sort of conversation with her during social occasions. Then, the husbands themselves seemed extremely cautious and uncomfortable about saying anything to her at all when their wives were not present. Alicia said she hated how these so-called 'feminist' women referred to her as being nothing more than 'glamorous' and 'decorative.' She said that where she comes from women are far more adult, trusting, and less possessive of how men and women behave with each other.

9 At this point Stefan had had enough and told Alicia that, as much as he liked her, she needed to stop taking all this too seriously. He really was surprised that someone with such a strong personality could feel so intimidated.

10 Later on, back in the office, Stefan's colleague, Jane, was talking about Roxana. She said that Roxana's behavior could be explained in terms of her culture—that Roxana didn't realize, even after 'being here so long,' that in the culture of the country she was living in people were critical of women being submissive regarding material gender roles. Stefan immediately remembered what Alicia said about feminism and felt even more confused.

Countries of origin?

As a general rule I do not reveal the characters' countries of origin because this would invoke in the reader national or civilizational culture stereotypes. Even if known to be false, they would get in the way of analysis (Baumann 1996, 1–2). They are voiced or implied only by the characters to indicate that they are their constructions.

I do however employ 'Ex' (also in Holliday and Amadasi 2020) as Roxana's fictitious heritage, to represent the tacit construction of the so-imagined 'exotic' that seems recognized by all the characters. Alicia's announcement that she comes from the same part of the world as Roxana (par. 5) also allows the implication that Stefan and his colleagues are, by contrast, Western, and that her resistance is against the 'viscerally felt' power of the West (see Jabri 2013, 11, 5).

Leaving of statements of origin to the characters also recognizes how the imposition of where one 'comes from' can itself be a form of micro-aggression when implying a lack of right to 'be here.' It therefore heeds Quijano's assertion that decoloniality recognizes 'a freedom to choose between various cultural orientations' (2007, 178) in resistance against colonialism and nation-states organizing people into separate 'geocultural identities' (171). That this labeling may indeed change dependent on who is speaking to whom is well-reported in Baumann's (1996) ethnography of a multicultural London suburb. That Alicia says that she is 'from a part of the world' that enables her to understand what is going on with Roxana therefore implies not a Center-defining 'nation' or 'culture' but a geopolitical area that has, in her terms, particular power relations with the West.

Stefan and searching disbelief

I pursue what I think is a common disbelief in micro-aggression by presenting Stefan as ambivalent about what he sees going on with Roxana. I present him as a partially non-committed onlooker (par. 3) to better show his perception of the different 'sides' to what is going on and how he forms his views. Although his initial observation of how Roxana is treated (par. 1) makes him appreciate the required diversity training, he is still unsure that aggression is actually taking place (par. 6, 8, 9). He gets bored with Alicia 'going on' about it (par. 8). The possible, in his terms, innocence of Roxana's treatment is also implicit in my choice of title, 'It's what you wear'—as though 'it is not us who are marginalizing *you* until *you* break the rules that *we* have established for ourselves.' He does nevertheless seem to appreciate what a cruelly excluding topic 'what you wear' can also be. Situating the aggression amongst women colleagues, while corresponding with what people upon whom I have based the characters of Roxana and Alicia have told me, also enables Stefan to distance himself from it as somehow 'their affair' rather than his. While the micro-aggression is explained to him by Alicia (par. 5–8), it is not explicitly stated to him until the final paragraph, when, despite thinking more about the connections she has presented to him, it is still not certain what he concludes.

Even if Stefan disapproves of Roxana's treatment, I show him recognizing the narrative of the 'wasteful and extravagant' Other as a fact with which he possibly colludes. Therefore, even when Roxana breaks the stereotype of the 'passive non-West' by being talkative, she still falls into the corrupt extravagance narrative by 'talking things up' (par. 4), especially when referring to 'the South of France' (par. 3) as the beginning of the 'extravagant' South and East—all of which fit the grand narrative proposed by Alicia (par. 7). However, again, while Stefan recognizes the grand narrative, he still might not think it is Othering or indeed racist. This therefore hints at how we are all, to use Fairclough's (1995, 36) phrase, 'standardly unaware' of the racist nature of narratives which we employ.

This depiction of disbelief is based on my personal insider knowledge of Stefan's implied 'whiteness,' and its denial of its Other-defining, Center, colonizing racism on account of its claimed 'well-wishing' Western gaze (Delanty, Jones, and Wodak 2011) which I refer to elsewhere as the West as steward dis¬course (Holliday 2019, 79–80).

Alicia and the Orientalist grand narrative

I also keep Roxana's perception of how she is treated unclear throughout the account. I voice this instead through Alicia (par. 5–8), based on her own felt injustice at being thought of as having brought nothing of value from her background. This is partly to indicate that it can take others to rationalize the nature of such aggression. I place what is in effect the Orientalist grand narrative (Edward Said 1978), which I believe to be a major source of intercultural prejudice (Holliday 2011, 71–4; 2022), into her words to indicate a personal sense-making of the theory, as it is meaningful to her, with whatever accuracies and inaccuracies that might involve. This also reflects how I, like Stefan, first heard about Orientalism as recounted by a friend who is one of the inspirations for Alicia, and was set upon a personal learning trajectory to find ways to deCenter. I aim to show that the authenticity of these theories therefore depends on how they resonate with our lives and how we speak into them.

Alicia's critique of 'so-called "feminist" women' (par. 8) has some basis in critiques of 'Western feminism' not appreciating Eastern women's long-standing fight against patriarchy (Afshar 2007; Rostami-Povey 2007, 113, 119). It is, again, her relating her own life experience of this that makes it important—to recount her personal anger at having her personal feminism and gender-related social skills doubted because of 'where she comes from.' It is also important to note that Alicia herself essentializes the presumably 'Western' women who attack her as lacking 'adult' attitudes to gender relations because of where *they* 'come from.' Again, I leave it to readers to surmise whether she believes this also racist stereotyping, or whether this is 'strategic essentialism' (Danius and Jonsson 1993, interviewing Spivak)—what she needs to do in her struggle to claim Center ground for herself, in her own terms (see Stuart Hall 1991, 35).

Roxana's silence

By keeping Roxana only spoken about by others, I wish to imply how aggression can go on relentlessly without being mentioned by many of its victims. I have heard numerous successful professional people, who have lived 'here' for many decades, tell me that they have learnt silently to 'put up' with racist aggression. This perhaps unexpected phenomenon is well reported by Kebabi's (forthcoming) study of high-status employees in British universities, including of 'nearby' Southern European origin. As with Alicia and Roxana, the hesitancy with which I name their 'origin' represents the ambivalence of Kebabi's respondents regarding the common labels imposed upon them.

I do though present Roxana as being vocal in ways that annoy her colleagues (par. 2–3). We do not however know what is behind her statements and whether or not they are her own attempt at strategic essentialism—feeding back the stereotype that is expected of her to gain personal space, or as her way of opposing, by exaggerating 'extravagance,' the dominant Western imagery that Alicia complains about.

Jane, the punchline, and food for discussion

In the very final paragraph of the account, I introduce Jane, one of the colleagues that Stefan has heard talking about Roxana. This is the first time that I allow an explicit voicing of the essentialist narrative that Alicia has described. Hardly any of the detail that Alicia has recounted is there though. Readers, like Stefan, are therefore left wondering about the extent that what she says amounts to Orientalist racist Othering. The key 'evidence' is in Jane saying what Roxana should have learned after 'being here so long,' thus denying that she has brought anything of value to the 'culture' in which she now lives—implying that she is a foreigner from an incompatible 'other culture.'

Leaving much in the creative non-fiction open to interpretation and discussion is one of the aims in engaging readers in a discussion about what is going on. It is hoped that the characters are sufficiently recognizable and unfinished to allow readers to find multiple resonances that lead them also to question themselves.

The nature of intercultural mediation

The picture of intercultural mediation supported by this use of creative non-fiction is not one of people from distinct cultures, large or small, learning how to understand each other and find resolution. It is not a vignette of 'intercultural contact' or 'intercultural dialogue,' as in, e.g., Kramsch and Uryu (2020) and Deardorff (2020), respectively. Creative non-fiction is instead a device that helps to explore and make sense of the *blocks* that substantiate intercultural prejudices and the deCentring *threads* that dissolve them (Amadasi and Holliday 2018). Intercultural here is not between cultures but refers to how we position and reposition in the everyday experience of hybrid cultural diversity.

A map of this process is my grammar of culture (Holliday 2011, 131; 2019; 2022, 20) in Figure 24.1, following C Wright Mills' (1959/1970, 234–5) "grammar of the socio¬logical imagination." It indicates the potential for threads and the sources of blocks (in italics) that come to play in the everyday practice of small culture formation on the go (center right).

Regarding the creative non-fiction example in this chapter, also discussed in Holliday (2019, 103–4), the grammar helps us to understand that:

- Alicia brings the *cultural resources* (left of the figure) of knowledge of postcolonial theory and gender agency from her background and *personal cultural trajectory* (right center) which she also associates with Roxana. She claims this as a deCentered *thread* that she carries to the West.
- Jane makes the *essentialist statements about 'culture'* (right of figure) that 'we are critical of women being submissive regarding material gender roles.' This is a Center block that excludes Roxana and represents the *'us'-'them' grand narrative* (bottom left) referred to by Alicia.

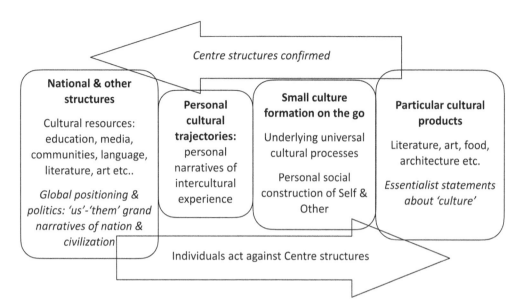

Figure 24.1 Grammar of culture

- Stefan refers to the *cultural product* (right of the figure) of power dressing as an attempted thread with Roxana.
- Regarding the arrows (top and bottom), depressingly, despite Alicia's attempted *action against Center structures*, the major *block* is that the *Center structures are confirmed*.

This list is by no means exhaustive and does not claim to be a definitive interpretation. The grammar invites readers to continue to explore what is going on in the creative non-fiction.

The outcome in this particular case may indeed seem depressing in that there is no resolution for Roxana; and Alicia does not allude to success in being recognized for who she is at a personal level. However, the story in this creative non-fiction is by no means finished. Readers have witnessed and may identity with Alicia's analysis and Stefan's ambivalence in at least remembering what she has told him when he hears Jane's statement. They have been exposed to a deCentered narrative. It is not in the necessary nature of creative non-fiction that things are not resolved within the storyline. However, even in cases where characters do show evidence of successful mediation, these are only small steps in an ongoing story of intercultural conflict and prejudice that is created by the continuing 'us'-'them' politics of the world we live in.

At the same time, the particular example in this chapter demonstrates the deeply difficult nature of the decoloniality project—in finding deCentered threads to connect with such as Roxana's ostensibly 'well-wishing' colleagues and overturning the West as steward discourse.

References

Afshar, Haleh. 2007. "Muslim Women and Feminisms: Illustrations from the Iranian Experience." *Social Compass* 54 (3): 419–34. 10.1177/0037768607080838

Agar, Michael. 1990. "Text and Fieldwork: Exploring the Excluded Middle." *Journal of Contemporary Ethnography* 19 (1): 73–88. 10.1177/089124190019001004

Amadasi, Sara, and Adrian Holliday. 2018. "'I Already Have a Culture.' Negotiating Competing Grand and Personal Narratives in Interview Conversations with New Study Abroad Arrivals." *Language and Intercultural Communication* 18 (2): 241–56. 10.1080/14708477.2017.1357727

Baumann, Gerd. 1996. *Contesting Culture: Discourses of Identity in Multi-Ethnic London*. Cambridge, New York: Cambridge University Press.

Beck, Ulrich, and Natan Sznaider. 2006. "Unpacking Cosmopolitanism for the Social Sciences: A Research Agenda." *The British Journal of Sociology* 57 (1): 1–23. 10.1111/j.1468-4446.2006.00091.x

Bhabha, Homi K. 1994. *The Location of Culture*. London, New York: Routledge.

Canagarajah, Suresh. 2011. "Translanguaging in the Classroom: Emerging Issues for Research and Pedagogy." *Applied Linguistics Review* 2 (2011): 1–28. 10.1515/9783110239331.1

Clifford, James, and George E. Marcus, eds. 1986. *Writing Culture. The Poetics and Politics of Ethnography*. Berkeley, Los Angeles, London: University of California Press.

Danius, Sara, and Stefan Jonsson. 1993. "An Interview with Gayatri Chakravorty Spivak." *Boundary 2* 20 (2): 24. 10.2307/303357

Deardorff, Darla K. 2020. *Manual for Developing Intercultural Competencies: Story Circles*. New York: Routledge. 10.4324/9780429244612

Delanty, Gerard, Paul Jones, and Ruth Wodak. 2011. "Introduction: Migration, Discrimination and Belonging in Europe." In *Identity, Belonging and Migration*, edited by Gerard Delanty, Ruth Wodak, and Paul Jones, 1–18. Liverpool: Liverpool University Press. 10.5949/UPO9781846314537.001

Fairclough, Norman. 1995. *Critical Discourse Analysis. The Critical Study of Language*. London: Longman.

Flam, Helena, and Brigitte Beauzamy. 2011. "Symbolic Violence." In *Identity, Belonging and Migration*, edited by Gerard Delanty, Ruth Wodak, and Paul Jones, 221–40. Liverpool: Liverpool University Press. 10.5949/UPO9781846314537.012

Goodson, Ivor. 2006. "The Rise of the Life Narrative." *Teacher Education Quarterly* 33 (4): 7–21.

Hall, Stuart. 1991. "The Local and the Global: Globalization and Ethnicity." In *Culture, Globalization and the World System: Contemporary Conditions for the Representation of Identity*, edited by Anthony D. King, 19–40. New York: Palgrave.

Hall, Stuart. 1996. "The Question of Cultural Identity." In *Modernity: An Introduction to Modern Societies*, edited by Stuart Hall, David Held, Don Hubert and Kenneth Thompson, 595–634. Oxford: Blackwell.

Holliday, Adrian. 2011. *Intercultural Communication and Ideology*. Los Angeles, London, New Delhi, Singapore, Washington DC: Sage. 10.4135/9781446269107

Holliday, Adrian. 2019. *Understanding Intercultural Communication: Negotiating a Grammar of Culture*. 2nd edition. Milton Park, Abingdon, Oxon; New York, NY: Routledge: Routledge. 10.4324/9781351139526

Holliday, Adrian. 2022. *Contesting Grand Narratives of the Intercultural*. London: Routledge. 10.4324/9781003039174

Holliday, Adrian, and Sara Amadasi. 2020. *Making Sense of the Intercultural. Finding DeCentered Threads*. London, New York: Routledge. 10.4324/9781351059190

Jabri, Vivienne. 2013. *The Postcolonial Subject. Claiming Politics/Governing Others in Late Modernity*. London: Routledge. 10.4324/9780203112250

Kebabi, Amina. forthcoming. 'Identity' and 'Belonging' in the Personal Lives of High-Status Professionals Living in the UK: Racism, and Freedom in Material and Non-Material 'Culture'. Unpublished PhD project in preparation. Faculty of Arts Humanities & Education, Canterbury Christ Church University.

Kramsch, Claire, and Michiko Uryu. 2020. "A Global Agenda for Ethical Language and Intercultural Communication Research and Practice." In *The Routledge Handbook of Language and Intercultural Communication*, edited by Jane Jackson, 204–18. London: Routledge.

Kumaravadivelu, Balasubramanian. 2007. *Cultural Globalization and Language Education*. New Haven, CT: Yale University Press.

Lyotard, Jean-François. 1979. *The Postmodern Condition. A Report on Knowledge*. Manchester, U.K.: Manchester University Press.

MacPherson, William. 1999. *The Stephen Lawrence Inquiry: Report of an Inquiry*. Command Papers 4262–1. London: The Stationery Office.

Mills, Charles Wright. 1959/1970. *The Sociological Imagination*. Reprint. A Pelican Book. Harmondsworth: Penguin Books.

Quijano, Aníbal. 2007. "Coloniality and Modernity/Rationality." *Cultural Studies* 21 (2–3): 168–78. 10.1080/09502380601164353

Rostami-Povey, Elaheh. 2007. *Afghan Women: Identity and Invasion*. New York: Zed Books.

Said, Edward W. 1978. *Orientalism*. London: Routledge & Kegan Paul.

Soja, Edward W. 1996. *Thirdspace: Journeys to Los Angeles and Other Real-and-Imagined Places*. Cambridge, MA: Blackwell.

Wodak, Ruth. 2021. "Re/Nationalising EU-Rope: National Identities, Right-Wing Populism, and Border- and Body-Politics." In *National Stereotyping, Identity Politics, European Crises*, edited by Jürgen Barkhoff and Joep Leerssen, 95–121. Amsterdam: Brill. 10.1163/9789004436107_007

25
EMIC AND ETIC PERSPECTIVES ON CULTURE IN MEDIATION

Alena L. Vasilyeva

Introduction

Mediation is a form of dispute resolution that gives disputants an opportunity to manage their conflict with the help of a third party, that is, a mediator. The institution of mediation is a cultural feature, as it does not exist in all cultures (Vasilyeva 2017). Besides, in the course of mediation, a local view of communication is realized through interaction, thus giving an idea what is valued and appropriate and what is not valued and inappropriate in terms of communication practices in a particular culture (Vasilyeva 2017). Understanding peculiarities of a culture and its complexities is especially salient for intercultural mediators. Mediation is considered to be intercultural when at least one of the participants (a mediator or a disputant) assumes that participants "have different cultural backgrounds or that the conflict itself may result from cultural differences" (Busch 2016, 183). Intercultural mediation focuses on the exploration of culturally specific worldviews to manage conflict and thus requires from a mediator to have intercultural competence, understanding, awareness, and an ability to apply appropriate techniques depending on the situation (Mayer 2018). In the following sections, I will discuss emic and etic approaches to culture and how these perspectives are used in mediation.

Emic and etic approaches to culture

The terms 'etic' and 'emic' were coined by Kenneth Pike (1967) in regards to two perspectives on culture, namely, outsiders' vs. insiders' views of a culture. According to Pike (1990), an emic unit is any item, mental or physical, that is "treated by insiders as relevant to their system of behavior" (28), whereas etics denotes an approach, in which an outsider interprets an inside system using their emics. Marvin Harris (1990), who also contributed to the development of these concepts, disagrees with Pike's treatment of etic analysis as a starting point for discovering an emic system and argues that etic analysis has a value on its own. Lett (1990) synthesizes Pike's and Harris's views and offers their definition of these concepts. In their view, emic constructs are those that are in accord with the conceptual system of an insider's culture. Etic constructs are those that are considered meaningful and appropriate by the community of scientific observers. According to Lett, any etic construct should "be applicable cross-culturally" (131).

While etic and emic approaches emphasize the importance of taking culture into consideration, they differ in their focus and methods of study. Pike underlines creation vs. discovery in regard to the differences of these perspectives, stating, "The etic organization of a world-wide cross-cultural scheme

DOI: 10.4324/9781003227441-30

may be created by the analyst. The emic structure of a particular system must ... be discovered" (38). The etic approach is considered to be culture-general, as it privileges universal concepts (e.g., the cultural dimension of individualism-collectivism) and is based on the outsider's accounts of culture (Zhu and Bargiela-Chiappini 2013). The research in this tradition focuses on external, measurable features (e.g., measuring perceptions of justice and variables associated with it). Researchers usually use surveys and brief observations of multiple settings and cultural groups to conduct their studies (Morris et al. 1999). The emic approach focuses on cultural-sensitive dimensions and gives prominence to insiders' perspectives on culture (Zhu and Bargiela-Chiappini 2013). Researchers use ethnographic methods (e.g., long-term observations and interviews) to explore the complexities of some culture from the viewpoint of members of that culture. Research in this tradition is driven by the following question: How do local people understand their cultural processes and practices? Instead of imposing existing categories derived from a researcher's culture or the ones that exist in the discipline to understand some phenomenon, researchers are interested in what is meaningful for insiders, what concepts and constructs they use, and how they perceive the world.

Comparing the assumptions and the goals of these two perspectives, Morris et al. (1999) note that these perspectives differ in their views on culture itself. Researchers taking the emic perspective "describe the cultural system as a working whole," while the etic perspective focuses on describing "the ways in which cultural variables fit into general causal models of a particular behavior" (783). Emic researchers see a culture as the interconnection of all components. In contrast, etic researchers tend to study isolated components.

Morris et al. (1999) point out that adherents of emic or etic perspectives often diminish the significance of the other tradition. For example, etic researchers are critiqued for being distant from respondents and, thus, are likely to miss the nuances of a studied culture and to be insensitive to how their questions affect respondents. The emic approach, in its turn, is discounted on the basis of potentially incorporating the misconceptions of insiders about their own culture and relying on the researchers' interpretations (Morris et al. 1999; Zhu and Bargiela-Chiappini 2013).

Both approaches, however, are valid and necessary for cross-cultural research (Gudykunst 2003). What approach is appropriate to take depends on research questions a study aims to answer (Gudykunst 2003). According to Pike (1967), emic and etic standpoints should not be seen as a dichotomy but as different viewpoints on the same event. Similarly, Lett (1990) suggests viewing emic and etic as epistemological constructs that have nothing to do with the ontological status of a phenomenon. In their opinion, the understanding of a phenomenon can be etic or emic, while the phenomenon itself stays unchanged. Lett argues that it is necessary to obtain both emic and etic knowledge in order "to fully understand the relationship between the particular and the general" (133).

Berry (1990) introduces the following sequence to illustrate how emic and etic approaches interplay. A researcher starts with the emic approach to understand their own culture. Using this knowledge to study a phenomenon in another culture means taking the etic approach. The next step is to learn about the phenomenon of interest from natives' viewpoints, putting aside one's own cultural baggage. Finally, the two conceptual systems (i.e., an emic understanding from one's own culture and an emic understanding from the studied culture) are compared. If there are shared features, an etic understanding is achieved that can be used for comparing the phenomenon in both cultures. In this respect, Berry introduces the concepts *imposed etic* and *derived etic*. *Imposed etic* refers to the situation when a researcher uses concepts or instruments from their own culture to study another one, while *derived etic* refers to the common aspects emerged as a result of doing emic research in two cultures. Furthermore, Berry distinguishes between the notions of *derived etic* and *universal*. A *derived etic* is limited to a set of cultures under study. For a *universal* to be established, a *derived etic* should be attained from all the cultures.

Similarly, Morris et al. (1999) and Zhu and Bargiela-Chiappini (2013) argue that emic and etic approaches should not be seen as oppositions but as a continuum, as they can be used at different stages of research and enrich one another. The emic approach is best suited for exploratory research, and the etic approach is useful for testing hypotheses (Morris et al. 1999). Also, the accounts of culture obtained in the course of the former can serve as grounds for formulating transcultural dimensions and constructing generalizations that can be used to compare cultures (Zhu and Bargiela-Chiappini 2013).

At the same time, researchers emphasize that the etic approach is legitimate, only if equivalence (e.g., functional, conceptual, metric, linguistic, and sample equivalence) of phenomena in the cultures under study is established (Berry 1990; Gudykunst 2003). For example, conceptual equivalence presupposes that concepts have the same meaning for the compared cultures (Berry 1990). After emic aspects of studied concepts are generated in each culture, culture-specific and culture-general aspects should be integrated in one instrument, translated and tested in each culture. The final instrument will incorporate only items that are appropriate in all the studied cultures (Gudykunst 2003).

Emic and etic approaches to culture in mediation

Exploring how cultural influences on mediation practices are reflected in research on conflict management, Busch (2016) conducted a content analysis of a representative sample of articles published in the journal *Conflict Resolution Quarterly* that focus on the interplay of culture and mediation. One of the dimensions that this project investigated is the category of emic vs. etic perspectives. The research shows that most articles on mediation (44 out of 72) used the etic approach. Busch identifies the following features of etic studies: 1) declaring the focus of their research as non-Western; 2) comparing non-Western practices to corresponding Western ones; and 3) entertaining the idea of transferring conflict management techniques employed in one culture or context to another one. Khachaturova and Poimanova's (2015) study can serve as an example of this approach. Their quantitative research examines the effectiveness of mediators' strategies in solving interpersonal conflict between teenagers in high schools in Russia. The study is based on mediation strategies taken from Wall and Chan-Serafin (2014) and Kressel (2007), which illustrates the third aspect of the etic perspective on culture in mediation at two levels: 1) using Western conflict management techniques in a non-Western culture, and 2) applying them in the context of interaction between teenagers.

The application of this approach, however, can be problematic. One of the issues with bringing Western mediation practices into non-Western cultures is the lack of awareness about differences in understanding of what conflict is and what role it plays in the respective society (see e.g., Brigg 2003). In Western cultures, conflict is usually seen as destructive and unproductive. Even when conflict is seen as constructive, it is still treated as an obstacle to overcome. Hence, the goal of mediation is conflict resolution, and the value is placed on reaching some agreement at the end of the session. As Brigg (2003) states, "while mediation values engagement with conflict, this is so in order to achieve peace; conflict is thus subordinated to peace" (289). For some non-Western cultures, however, conflict can have constitutive and beneficial roles. It can serve as a means of forming groups and maintaining them (Brigg 2003). Also, in cultures where the self does not exist outside of interpersonal ties, conflict does not function as a threat to social bonds but, on the contrary, as a reaffirmation of them, as Macdonald (1990), for example, illustrates for the Wiradjuri.

Depending on culture and interpersonal situation, mediation is not necessarily an appropriate way of dealing with conflict, and mediators have to be familiar with the culture and the context of the conflict to know whether that conflict requires mediation (Polley 1988). Moreover, enforcing formal mediation in cultures that have their own traditions of conflict resolution can meet resistance from members of that culture. For example, introducing community mediation programs in Israel intensified conflicts between residents and authorities instead of resolving them (Li-On 2009).

Besides, cultures differ in their argumentation styles and their views on the role of emotions and rationality in argumentation. In Western cultures, it is expected that disputes will be managed in a rational way, and dealing with them in an emotional way is considered inappropriate and ineffective (Kochman 1981). Thus, emotions are usually discouraged in mediation sessions. It does not mean that feelings are totally ignored in dispute mediation. For example, Jacobs and Aakhus (2003) identify a therapeutic model of mediation, a characteristic of which is probing for disputants' feelings and attitudes to help them understand each other's point of view. Nevertheless, this model is not used frequently, and feelings and attitudes are explored only because they are seen as obstacles to conflict resolution. There are, however, cultures where emotions are not separate from cognition. Thus, if mediators promote a rational way of dealing with disagreement in non-Western cultures (e.g., Aboriginal Australian), they enforce a culturally specific technique that would be inappropriate in this setting (Brigg 2003).

Research on mediation from emic perspective focuses on understanding conflict within a particular context. Among the characteristics of this type of scholarship, Busch (2016) highlights the following ones: 1) the focus on some cultural setting of conflict management without relating to others; 2) the use of terminology shared by the members of the studied social or cultural group; and 3) warning against comparing non-Western practices and Western forms of mediation, as it would not allow for an appropriate understanding of the practices under study. Brigg (2003) calls for an ethical approach to cultural differences and argues that not doing this "reinforces Western values as universal, therefore disavowing and disrespecting other worldviews and lifeways" (298). Brigg emphasizes the importance for mediation practitioners to become aware of their cultural assumptions, including understanding their own culture, orientation to conflict, and the mode of selfhood.

Brigg (2003) encourages mediators to be ready to embrace the unknown that may arise during mediation and to diverge from the predominant Western standards of facilitative mediation. For example, neutrality, which is often emphasized in Western mediation, is considered to be unattainable and undesirable in the mediation model of the Navaho nation (Pinto 2000). Mediation also varies in forms depending on a culture. For example, a type of dispute mediation utilized in the Philippines is a three-person panel, in which mediators are chosen by the disputants from volunteers in the barangay (i.e., a village in rural communities or the smallest political unit in a big city) (Tabucanon, Wall, and Yan 2008). The proceeding of dispute resolution there is public and informal.

Another cultural peculiarity is the establishment of who is right or wrong (e.g., in the Philippines (Tabucanon et al. 2008)), which is not a characteristic of mediation in Western cultures. In the Philippines, it is important to determine right and wrong parties, as the person who is right is pressured to modify their claim and to forgive the opponent, while the one who is wrong would apologize and have their obligation reduced.

Some practices that Brigg (2003) suggests for improving intercultural mediation include accepting non-neutrality of mediation and de-professionalizing (e.g., allowing themselves to be affected by emotions), experimenting with the structure of mediation sessions (e.g., to eliminate agendas and to employ stories), integrating spiritual and emotional spheres into the process, and allowing political and social contexts to be part of the interaction. For example, Li-On (2009) argues that in multicultural settings (specifically, in Israel), mediation is linked to political and social issues and the sources of power and counterpower. Minority groups there see the roots of conflicts in social and cultural oppression rather than as a consequence of cultural characteristics. While dominant groups view the establishment of formal mediation primarily as a method for dealing with cultural heterogeneity and pushing cultural groups to unity and coexistence, minorities associate the use of mediation with social and political circumstances. In this respect, Li-On recommends using context-related mediation practices that take into account power dynamics as well as the political situation of the society in general. Similarly, Mayer (2018) emphasizes the importance of using local practices in mediation to increase a chance of conflict

Emic and etic perspectives on culture

resolution such as physical techniques (e.g., breathing exercises), faith-related rituals (e.g., reference to a higher power), and nonverbal techniques (e.g., sculpture work).

At the same time, some studies do not fall neatly into emic or etic categories, as they have features of both approaches. One example is Polley's (1988) work on mediation in the United States and Norway. Polley developed a model of group dynamics and used it to compare polarization patterns in the U.S. and Norwegian organizational context. They collected their data using a questionnaire administered to U.S. American and Norwegian groups from a variety of settings. The Norwegian subjects received a translated version of the questionnaire. These aspects of research (i.e., using surveys as a method and the translation of the original instrument instead of employing concepts from the local culture, and making a cross-cultural comparison) are of the etic nature. However, in contrast to etic research on mediation that advocates the transfer of mediation techniques from one culture to another, Polley argues against the validity of this position and questions the assumptions that mediation techniques successfully used in the United States will work in another culture. They emphasize the necessity of a culturally sensitive approach to mediation and suggest seeing mediation not as a set of behaviors but as a relationship which needs to be taken into account to figure out appropriate behaviors for conflict management.

While it is important for mediators to be culturally sensitive, it is not easy to apply that in practice. Researchers draw attention to the complexity of culture (Davidheiser 2007; Mayer 2018) that creates a challenge for mediators. First of all, culture can be defined in different ways. Some scholars see it in terms of ethnic and national groups, whereas others understand culture in a broader way, for example, including religious, professional, and gender dimensions that influence individuals. Thus, individuals share multiple cultures, and even within the same culture there are variations (Avruch 2003). Quek Anderson and Knight (2017) note, "Mediators thus face very complex individuals who may not necessarily manifest the characteristics that are traditionally attributed to their group" (2). For example, the traditional model of North American mediation with its focus on problem-solving and such features as a turn-taking system that excludes interruptions, the prevention of direct exchanges between disputants, and mediator neutrality, does not work in mediation that involves Black Americans, as in their style of communication turn-taking is driven by the exchange of ideas arising during the discussion and the participants' passion, and not by outside authority (Davidheiser 2007). Also, according to Davidheiser, a factor that can contribute to intragroup variation is class belonging. Mediators' techniques of probing questions to collect information is not efficient in interaction with poor Black American disputants, as direct queries are usually avoided, especially in communicating with a person associated with power (e.g., a mediator), due to their experiences of structural violence.

Moreover, according to the constructivist view of culture (Avruch 2003), culture is dynamic, and what cultural identity becomes relevant at a given moment depends on the context of interaction. This is connected to another challenge that culturally sensitive mediation programs face, namely, matching a mediator with disputants in terms of cultural backgrounds. These programs often carry out a matching based on ethnonational similarities (Davidheiser 2007) and leave out other salient identities. Davidheiser raises a question about the validity of matching practices, even in those cases, when other variables such as religious and sexual orientation are taken into account. One of the problems Davidheiser indicates is the issue of social justice and power, as the matched mediator may be perceived as acting on behalf of that disputant, which may undermine the fairness of mediation. Moreover, the mediator who is matched with a disputant based on some stereotypical identity category may differ from the disputant in their worldviews, which may disadvantage that individual (Davidheiser 2007).

In this respect, some researchers (Davidheiser 2007; Goldberg 2009) suggest incorporating the notion of worldviews rather than culture. Worldviews are defined as "particular modes of perception and interpretation that ... shape action" (Davidheiser 2007, 61). Worldviews are affected by a variety of factors that are not necessarily related to cultural aspects. The social marginalization of Blacks may be a better explanation of their avoidance of direct questioning than ethnic or racial identities. Also, while mediators may attribute interracial or interethnic conflicts to cultural differences, they can be in fact rooted in societal issues (e.g., structural violence). According to Davidheiser, the term 'worldviews' is preferable to culture as it is "less suggestive of a single homogenous cognitive-interpretive mazeway shared among all the members of a given group" (67). Worldviews are dynamic and multidimensional; they embrace shared norms and behavioral patterns, as well as individual experiences across and within groups.

Taking an emic-constructivist approach, Quek Anderson and Knight (2017) emphasize the importance of understanding individuals' cultural preferences and study how these individuals act in a specific dispute with a specific person. They encourage mediators to abandon their own assumptions about what cultures are relevant in the given situation and to embrace the disputants' cultural complexity. They note that quite often mediators start interaction based on misinformed generalizations, and when they get a better idea about the parties' characteristics, it can be too late to adjust the mediation process. Quek Anderson and Knight suggest incorporating pre-mediation intake interviews as a way of figuring out the disputants' cultural dimensions related to the given situation, which will help mediators to design an appropriate mediation process. The instrument that the researchers developed include questions that are based on general dimensions of culture (e.g., power distance). In contrast to etic research that uses these constructs to create generalizations about some culture, the researchers incorporate these dimensions to examine each individual's preferences in connection to the context of a particular conflict situation. For example, the proposed interview questions related to the dimension 'preference for indirect versus direct communication' ask about the ways the disputant communicated their concerns to the other party involved in conflict. Based on the received information, the mediator is expected to adjust their strategies to avoid clashes with the disputant's preferred way of communication. When the disputants differ in their styles, the mediator has to manage interaction (e.g., to use reframing) to facilitate understanding between the parties. Quek Anderson and Knight argue that getting a nuanced insight into the parties' preferences will help mediators to become more culturally responsive and to create an effective mediation process.

Goldberg (2009), in their turn, emphasizes the importance for mediators, especially those who are involved in intercultural mediation, to self-reflect and know their own worldviews. Moreover, expanding one's worldview and encompassing new ones is an asset for mediators, as they can "move back and forth along continuums and access more profiles" (428). Goldberg argues that if mediators share their worldviews with their clients, it will be beneficial for the disputants, as mediators will be able to explain better to them why they are the best match to deal with their case.

Conclusion

Mediators use various interactional resources, including culture, to craft mediation activity, which requires from mediators to be culturally sensitive, especially in intercultural mediation settings. Beyond cognitive skills, mediators need to have emotional competence and an understanding of the complexity of cultural processes to conduct successful mediation sessions. This entails not just having the knowledge of a particular culture, but being able to work with intersectionalities in mediation such as "the intersection of age, gender, cultural group, nationality, (dis)-ability and mother tongue" (Mayer 2018, 2) among others. Besides, it is important for mediators to be aware of their own cultural assumptions and identities.

While both approaches to culture, etic and emic, have their own values and challenges, the latter provides a greater opportunity for getting a more nuanced insight into cultures, which will enable intercultural mediation practitioners to design an appropriate and effective mediation activity. Nevertheless, understanding mediation practices requires culture-specific and culture-general information. Findings from these two perspectives can challenge, stimulate, and complement each other to create richer accounts of culture (Morris et al. 1999).

References

Avruch, Kevin. 2003. "Type I and Type II Errors in Culturally Sensitive Conflict Resolution Practice." *Conflict Resolution Quarterly* 20 (3): 351–71. 10.1002/crq.29

Berry, John W. 1990. "Imposed Etics, Emics, and Derived Etics: Their Conceptual and Operational Status in Cross-Cultural Psychology." In *Emics and Etics: The Insider/Outsider Debate*, edited by Thomas N. Headland, Kenneth L. Pike, and Marvin Harris, 84–99. Newbury Park, CA: Sage.

Brigg, Morgan. 2003. "Mediation, Power, and Cultural Difference." *Conflict Resolution Quarterly* 20 (3): 287–306. 10.1002/crq.26

Busch, Dominic. 2016. "Does Conflict Mediation Research Keep Track with Cultural Theory?: A Theory-Based Qualitative Content Analysis on Concepts of Culture in Conflict Management Research." *European Journal of Applied Linguistics* 4 (2): 181–206. 10.1515/eujal-2015-0037

Davidheiser, Mark. 2007. "Race, Worldviews, and Conflict Mediation: Black and White Styles of Conflict Revisited: Race, Worldviews, and Conflict Mediation." *Peace & Change* 33 (1): 60–89. 10.1111/j.1468-0130. 2007.00476.x

Goldberg, Rachel M. 2009. "How Our Worldviews Shape Our Practice." *Conflict Resolution Quarterly* 26 (4): 405–31. 10.1002/crq.241

Gudykunst, William B. 2003. "Issues in Cross-Cultural Communication Research." In *Cross-Cultural and Intercultural Communication*, edited by William B. Gudykunst, 149–61. Thousand Oaks, CA: Sage.

Harris, Marvin, 1990. "Emics and Etics Revisited". In *Emics and Etics: The Insider/Outsider Debate*, edited by Thomas N. Headland, Kenneth L. Pike, and Marvin Harris, 48–61. Newbury Park, CA: Sage.

Jacobs, Scott, and Mark Aakhus. 2003. "What Mediators Do with Words: Implementing Three Models of Rational Discussion in Dispute Mediation." *Conflict Resolution Quarterly* 20 (2): 177–203. 10.1002/crq.19

Khachaturova, Milana R., and Daria M. Poimanova. 2015. "The Role of Mediation Strategies in Solving Interpersonal Conflicts." *Conflict Resolution Quarterly* 33 (1): 35–55. 10.1002/crq.21131

Kochman, Thomas. 1981. *Black and White Styles in Conflict*. Chicago: Univ. of Chicago Press.

Kressel, Kenneth. 2007. "The Strategic Style in Mediation." *Conflict Resolution Quarterly* 24 (3): 251–83. 10. 1002/crq.174

Lett, James. 1990. "Emics and Etics: Notes on Epistemology of Anthropology." In *Emics and Etics: The Insider/Outsider Debate*, edited by Thomas N. Headland, Kenneth L. Pike, and Marvin Harris, 127–42. Newbury Park, CA: Sage.

Li-On, Lee. 2009. "The Politics of Community Mediation: A Study of Community Mediation in Israel." *Conflict Resolution Quarterly* 26 (4): 453–79. 10.1002/crq.243

Macdonald, Gaynor. 1990. "Where Words Harm and Blows Heal." *Australian Dispute Resolution Journal* 1: 125–32.

Mayer, Claude-Hélène. 2018. "Methodological Challenges in Intercultural Communication." *Newsletter of the European Forum for Restorative* Justice 19: 7–9.

Morris, Michael W., Kwok Leung, Daniel Ames, and Brian Lickel. 1999. "Views from Inside and Outside: Integrating Emic and Etic Insights about Culture and Justice Judgment." *Academy of Management Review* 24 (4): 781–96. 10.5465/amr.1999.2553253

Pike, Kenneth. 1967. *Language in Relation to a Unifies Theory of the Structure of Human Behavior*. The Hague, the Netherlands: Mouton.

Pike, Kenneth L. 1990. "On the Emics and Etics of Pike and Harris." In *Emics and Etics: The Insider/Outsider Debate*, edited by Thomas N. Headland, Kenneth L. Pike, and Marvin Harris, 28–47. Newbury Park, CA: Sage.

Pinto, Jeanmarie. 2000. "Peacemaking as Ceremony: The Mediation Model of the Navajo Nation." *The International Journal of Conflict Management* 11 (3): 267–86.

Polley, Richard Brian. 1988. "Intervention and Cultural Context: Mediation in the US and Norway." *Journal of Management* 14 (4): 617–29. 10.1177/014920638801400411

Quek Anderson, Dorcas, and Diana Knight. 2017. "Managing the Inter-Cultural Dimensions of a Mediation Effectively—A Proposed Pre-Mediation Intake Instrument." *Australasian Dispute Resolution Journal* 28 (2): 89–97.

Tabucanon, Gill Marvel P., James A. Jr Wall, and Wan Yan. 2008. "Philippine Community Mediation, Katarungang Pambarangay." *Journal of Dispute Resolution* 2: 501–13.

Vasilyeva, Alena L. 2017. "Mediation Discourse in the United States and Belarus: Culturally Shaped Interactions." In *The Handbook of Communication in Cross-Cultural Perspective*, edited by Donal A. Carbaugh, 273–84. New York: Routledge.

Wall, James A., and Suzanne Chan-Serafin. 2014. "Friendly Persuasion in Civil Case Mediations: Friendly Persuasion in Civil Case Mediations." *Conflict Resolution Quarterly* 31 (3): 285–303. 10.1002/crq.21092

Zhu, Yunxia, and Francesca Bargiela-Chiappini. 2013. "Balancing Emic and Etic: Situated Learning and Ethnography of Communication in Cross-Cultural Management Education." *Academy of Management Learning & Education* 12 (3): 380–95. 10.5465/amle.2012.0221

26

PROFESSIONAL DISPUTE MEDIATORS' NOTIONS OF CULTURE

Dominic Busch, Emilian Franco, and Andrea Hartmann-Piraudeau

Introduction

Intercultural mediation is a very open term that allows for various interpretations. In research and practice, this openness leads to theoretical and practical concepts for different fields of application that hardly seem to have anything in common anymore. Mediation and intercultural mediation have been described primarily from a researchers' point of view, trying in principle to take some form of external perspective on mediation. It is entirely plausible that the actors' assessments of their situations most significantly determine how they manage these situations, including their assessment of the role of culture. Still, this actor's perceptions of the explicit role of culture—not only in mediation—are hardly explored yet.

This chapter examines notions of culture and interculturality among professional conflict mediators in Europe from family mediation, business mediation, and community mediation. These mediators follow mediation techniques taught in Western and North American mediation training programs, standardized by professional mediators' associations in Europe, and recently framed by European and national legislation. In sum, the mediators in the study work in very different fields and contexts. On the other hand, they all share cultural and structural backgrounds.

Translation research critically reflects the ambitious idea of a neutral interpreter, and its chances have been questioned from very early on (cf. Santamaría Ciordia in this volume). In contrast, mediation research has strongly preferred an etic perspective describing mediators' work by naming and identifying different mediator styles and techniques (for a recent overview, cf. Cominelli and Lucchiari 2017, 226–29). Instead of departing from mediation practice, mediation research relies on prescriptive mediation strategies. Mediators' actual practices instead were seen from a critical perspective as deviating from the norm—and thus to be rejected. Deviations from the prescriptive norm were usually interpreted as a deception or manipulation in that mediators were doing something other than what they claimed to be doing according to the principles of mediation (cf. Greatbatch and Dingwall 1999; Jacobs 2002). Bush and Folger (1994) go even further and see the most significant dilemmas as inherent in the process itself so that mediators would be powerless in any case. Alternatively, Folger and Bush focus more on the mediation process to change it accordingly.

Pignault, Meyers, and Houssemand (2017, 1589) challenge this external view on mediation because these categorizations can hardly be put in relation to the concrete results of mediation talks. Cheevers (2020) points out that mediators and their clients often understand entirely different things about central principles of mediation, such as neutrality. The mediators themselves, these authors argue, might be able to provide much more accurate assessments, for example, of the factors for success in mediation.

DOI: 10.4324/9781003227441-31

Ethnographic approaches to analyzing mediation

Suppose mediators' real conceptions and perceptions towards culture and interculturality are to be elicited. This will require an empirical approach that avoids any predetermined reference to these terms if possible. Ethnographic approaches seem particularly suitable for this purpose, as they allow for in-depth observation and reflect the role of the researcher. Problem-centered expert interviews aim to preserve these epistemological gains while even more boiling the empirical data down to relevant information for the question under research (Döringer 2021).

Indeed, also contexts of mediation have already been studied in this way. Raines Pokhrel and Poitras (2013) interviewed experienced mediators worldwide about what they see as the biggest challenges in mediation. The authors put their results into the following categories: "getting and keeping clients, getting parties to the table, educating the parties and the public about mediation, professional development, and work-life issues" (Raines, Pokhrel, and Poitras 2013, 85). In a similar vein, Pignault, Meyers, and Houssemand (2017) conducted semi-structured interviews with mediators from different fields of work in the French-speaking regions of Europe. The authors conclude that mediators' attitudes align with the prescriptive mediational principles, so they are not entirely detached from them. Nevertheless, there are variabilities. Listening and letting parties talk it out are seen by many mediators as their core competencies that lead to success. Mediators tend to see these competencies less as part of mediation training but rather as something mediators will need to learn by experience (Pignault, Meyers, and Houssemand 2017, 1601).

In addition, mediators consider mutual support within the profession to be essential. This need is repeatedly addressed by storytelling projects in which mediators report on their work. Accordingly, these projects do not always have a primarily scientific agenda. However, they are well suited to providing insights into mediators' perspectives, and they do indeed lend the mediators a voice. Galton and Love (2012) have published many such reports from mediators primarily based in the United States under the title *Stories Mediators Tell*. Love and Parker (2017b) continue this series of narrations with their *Stories Mediators Tell—World Edition* inviting more international and global authorship, and thus, also a wider variety and a higher diversity of mediation contexts. Here, the section headings organizing the contributions may indicate how the editors see mediation internationally and prefer to envision mediation in intercultural contexts. Thus, the editors assume that there may be cultural differences, but mediation can deal with them in flexible, productive, and creative ways. The editors also present mediation as a culture-universal tool, and they explore how mediators can work best without prior knowledge of their field under mediation. Finally, the editors see mediation as a vehicle for improving the world. Mediation here is conceived as a "worldwide movement" (Love and Parker 2017a, xi) that creates unity (among the adherents to mediation) worldwide.

Raines (2018) supposes that mediators feel this great need to tell their stories because they are seeking advice and feedback from their colleagues and because mediation work can significantly change mediators' whole lives in the medium term. Accordingly, mediators see the key challenge as maintaining their equilibrium in a context that tends never to resolve or improve. They will always be approached with new conflicts and problems. While Raines still anticipates fundamental success for mediators, Harmon-Darrow and Xu (2018) turn the spotlight on volunteer community mediators in the United States, most of whom quit after four years. Harmon-Darrow and Xu's quantitative survey shows that the quality and existence of social relationships of the mediators (with each other as well as with the umbrella organization, as well as in their private lives) was the strongest predictor of whether they would develop burnout symptoms and/or stop working as a mediator.

Culture's relevance for action: Subjective notions of culture

Analyzing the influence of culture on mediators' actions will require a research framework with notions of culture that ensure that what they capture will indeed be relevant for action (as stated for the whole field of research on intercultural communication: Busch 2012, 18). In recent decades, research on intercultural communication has shifted from a preference for essentialist to constructivist understandings of culture. Therefore, this also entails a preference for notions of concepts based on people's perceptions and actions. We can now pursue this tendency to derive concepts of culture even a bit further on. In their everyday lives and discourse, people do not only construct ways of handling culture but also understandings of culture itself.

While it has always been challenging to agree on an adequate notion of culture, one thing should be sufficiently clear: People talk about culture in academia and their everyday lives. People participate in discourses about culture. They perceive, help create, and adopt them in their contexts. Therefore, it can be assumed that every person has a subjective understanding of culture. This understanding includes what culture is, how it affects one's own and others' actions, and how best to deal with it oneself. Gender studies is a discipline that has realized this construction of its object of research much earlier and more decisively than research on intercultural communication (Butler 1993, 4). Mae (2007, 41–4) has made a case for applying these findings from gender studies to intercultural research. These discourses about culture will always have a normative orientation, and power imbalances also mark them. This is the case not only in academic discourse (Busch 2021) but also in everyday discourses about culture, whereby these fields are linked together.

For an empirical inquiry into these subjective notions of culture, methods are suitable that can capture how subjects make unsolicited and explicit references to culture (Busch 2010). For this, inquiry techniques should be used that are open and record the subjects' utterances in the spoken word. Busch (2010) demonstrated this with a conversation analytic study of sales conversations. As a part of ethnomethodological conversation analysis, membership categorization analysis (Sacks 1974; Moerman 1988) may capture people's explicit understandings of culture and their associations with culture, and how to cope with it. Conversely, this paradigm holds that if subjects do not express things independently, they are not relevant to them.

Research design

As part of the project *In-Medias* funded by the European exchange program Erasmus+ in the years 2020 to 2023, the authors conducted a total of 21 guided interviews with mediators from the countries of Austria, Bulgaria, Cyprus, Georgia, Germany, Hungary, Ireland, Lithuania, the Netherlands, Poland, Portugal, Spain, and Turkey in the winter of 2019/2020.[1] The interviews were conducted via videocalls (Archibald et al. 2019), partly in German and English. The interviews were conducted partly by the authors themselves and partly by mediators whom the authors had already interviewed. Mediators were asked about their professional backgrounds, the structural situation of mediation in their countries, and their perceived major challenges and opportunities of mediation. Finally, an open-ended question was also asked about their assessment of and experience with intercultural mediation without defining the latter more precisely. However, the following analysis does not only draw from this last question. Instead, cultural and culturalizing references can be found in numerous other interview passages. From this, subjective constructions of culture in mediation from the perspective of mediators can be drawn.

Results

In this study, these uses of culture could be identified and merged into the following categories:

* mediation as a culture,
* mediation culture in contrast to national culture,
* national cultures as discursive constructions,

culture requires specific mediation strategies,
rejecting the idea of culture as a cause of conflict.

The following examples illustrate these categories.

Mediation as a culture

Mediators fairly often describe mediation itself as a culture. Mediators perceive their field of work as different and distinct from the rest of society. Mediators share a specific and exclusive range of professional knowledge that they master and also favor. Beyond the mediators' circle, this knowledge is not applied and simply does not exist. In this way, mediators create their distinct world around them. At the same time, this distinctiveness is the central pillar for the preservation of this mediatory culture. Mediation is perceived as the better concept for society, but unfortunately, it does not establish itself. Mediators are familiar with this concept and are committed to it. They want to help the rest of the world and provide access to this tool. Therefore, mediation is the better culture in the end. The following interview passage illustrates this view:

> [...] mediation is the new Esperanto. It's a new language in a very individualized, victimized society of individuals who are only concerned about their rights and not about their duties. And so it's a new language in society where there's a huge polarization where people do not talk with each other or to each other and do not listen and where the whole atmosphere has become very positional. We see that in in U.S. we see it in Europe you see it with the woke and the political correctness. Everyone is right and you are wrong and that's the discussion. So we are far away from a dialogue and I think that mediation is a tool. A Language so to say that you could learn to speak. And mediators are the facilitators who can teach you that language and can help you speak that language in in order to get into more constructive and more empathic but also assertive discussion dialogues.

Mediation thereby eradicates the injustices of the ordinary world. Our everyday world is full of power imbalances. Mediation instead pursues a social justice project and invites and includes everyone:

> The opportunity to change in an inclusive way. That's what it means to me. If I if I go back to my childhood and follow the trail through the ones saying that I feel disrupts my spirit. Most is being exclusive. Being broken, the thing that really the core of mediation is that inclusive problem solving. It offers that the creative inclusivity if you want so that to me is the heart of it. You don't lose anybody.

Mediation culture in contrast to national cultures

In this perception, the country's national culture in which the respective mediators work often constitutes the counterpart to which mediation culture is set apart. Not least because mediation is still an exclusive knowledge, it almost necessarily goes without saying that people from this respective national culture do not know mediation properly. Moreover, from a mediation point of view, these people are not competent in arguing properly and well.

> And so they're going to do an entire mediation, use assumptions as certainties and so asking questions as if this were an acknowledged fact. It's very easy. [...] which is why. It ends up

being much more of a of a positional mediation. At the end of the day. Because it's, you say, you you say versus you say. And they don't question as much what each party says, yeah, but if you stay in the positions he will never come to an agreement with you. I don't know that that's my assumption that they do because it ends up being a concession. It said concession based on location.

In another example, a mediator complains that the parties tend not to accept the mediator:

Regarding with the challenges, um, there is an issue in both countries, um, to accept the mediator. So you know to agree to to the to the mediator itself. You know it's not easy because you have to educate them that. The mediator is not to judge. The mediator isn't an arbitrator, so you don't lose anything if you give your consent to a certain person to be the mediator, because it's not the mediator of part A in the mediators party is going to be. It's going to be the mediator for both of you, so this is something that it's not, think about it, it's not easy. You know it's basic, but it's not easy. And to accomplish in every case.

This view of culture also incorporates academic knowledge from intercultural communication. Hofstede's cultural dimensions have been adopted into many people's everyday knowledge and cement their concept of culture. For example, mediators draw on Hofstede's dimensions, among others, to try to explain why people from a given national culture are so alienated from mediation. This mediator justifies this sense of strangeness with the dimension of power distance:

And so, in terms of mediation, acceptance, or the acceptance of having a third party, that's never an issue in […], because in […] you really look to with authority and you respect the authority of those who have authority. So when, when you take the Hofstede dimension of power distance, that is extremely high in […]. So somebody was hired from the outside because they have expertise and skill, and both parties recognize that in that person, whatever that person says is going to be. And it would be like the ultimate truth right? And So what ends up happening is a lot of frustration sometimes from the parties when they realize that that person is not there to decide or is not there to to help or recommend or or give their opinion.

Culture requires specific mediation strategies

When culture is brought up in the interview, mediators usually reject culture-specific mediation methods. Instead, they propagate universal strategies, as this mediator puts it:

My rule number one that I tried to share with my students and it's something that's very hard for them, is never assume anything.

Another mediator does acknowledge the need to be considerate of different worldviews and ways of communicating. However, on the other hand, at the same time, they warn against giving culture too much weight and tend to leave the actual influence of culture unclear:

Yeah, but these are all very different conflicts, so let me let me say linking it to culture. It's over estimated an under estimated. Okay culture is overestimated in the sense that people think. Oh, I'm now negotiating or mediating with the Chinese. Now I need to be very careful with culture and do lots of studies. Um, that's overestimated. Obviously when I have cases with China, I have a Chinese in my team. I wanna make sure that that I can understand the clues and that I can in my strategy obviously connect with them in the right way. But it's overestimated in the sense that these Chinese there are also people, and they may have different clues, but on the human level. It's all the same thing, and so you need to be able to read the clues and and the signs and not to misinterpret them, and that that is why culture obviously has a relevance, but it's overestimated in the sense that all of a sudden people think. Now it's a completely different ball game because we are dealing with the Chinese. That's not the case. [...] and so that's why my advice is always. I look at every human being an in mediation of presentation every party as a unique person.

The mediator rejects culturalizations, and at the same time, this has the effect of preserving mediation as a universal tool. This underscores the already existing central competence of the mediator, that is, being able to be sensitive to people.

Rejecting the idea of culture as a cause of conflict

Mediators also tend to reject the idea that culture or cultural differences could be a cause of conflict.

I'm actually doing it right now. Can't see I can't see that's very intercultural. [...] So just like international let's. Uh huh. Put it that way. But I think that when it when it comes to Europe, it's not that different, but you can still can still see some differences of how, especially when there are children involved, like how they see how their child has to be has to be raised. And of course legal systems are different and support system is different. So I think these are these kind of the main aspects, but I wouldn't call that. You know that really intercultural, different religions. Different completely different backgrounds. I haven't had that example, but I would be very interested to have.

Again, the mediator gives examples that could potentially be understood as cultural but de facto considers them to be non-cultural. In the research literature on intercultural mediation, Busch (2016) distinguished six different notions of intercultural mediation. The insights above may signal that one of these categories, i.e., '"Intercultural mediation" deals with conflicts arising from cultural differences' (Busch 2016, 187), may have existed in the literature but is hardly advocated in mediation practice at the time of the study.

Discussion

The mediators' views of culture found in this study confirm the assumptions of some previous studies. Thus, it can be confirmed that the practitioners' views do not strikingly diverge from the literature. However, ruptures and contradictions prove that this particular knowledge in mediatory practice is the product of mediators participating in discourses on culture and interculturality. For example, on the one hand, mediators complain about how much local cultures' conflict management preferences oppose mediation or are unwilling to embrace it. In this context, mediators then refer to national-cultural characteristics of conflict management. On the other hand, they strongly reject the relevance of culture to mediation elsewhere. Mediation is portrayed as a tool that addresses the individual and can be applied in any culture. As early as 2003, Avruch argued that mediators had to be prepared to deal with actual cultural differences as well as pretended, constructed claims of difference. What Avruch still presented as a both/and, in mediation discourse emerges as an either/or. Also, Love and Parker's (2017b) *World Edition* of *Stories Mediators Tell*, on the one side, in its concept and title, assumes international diversity. On the other side, and at the same time, puts some efforts into maintaining mediation as a culture-universal tool that does not need to stop at presumed cultural boundaries.

This observation also corresponds with Busch (2016, 203), who showed that mediation as a tool had been confronted with an increasingly complex variety of challenges, especially in the intercultural context. Paradoxically, however, this insight never leads to conclusions about the potential limitations of mediation. Instead, the most that happens is that new tools and perspectives are established, through which mediation remains ever more universally viable. Given this primacy of perpetual viability, it cannot be denied from a perspective of dispositive theory (Busch 2021) that what is implicitly at stake here is to maintain the tool of mediation as viable in a world that is becoming increasingly complex.

Conclusion

What role culture plays in mediation is also significantly influenced by what mediators themselves think about culture in mediation. Mediators, like all people, participate in discourses from which they draw their worldview. These discourses incorporate ideologies, and powerful hegemonies structure them. As the data from the study presented show, mediators often feel that they belong to a culture of mediation that unites them and delineates mediation to the outside world. In this way, a mediatorial culture is created with internal discourses that ensure immunity and permanent preservation of this culture. For mediators, the outside world vis-à-vis mediation is characterized on the one hand by national cultures with culture-specific characteristics of disputing. On the other hand, mediators often participate in discourses in which it is vital to avoid culturalizations and essentializations. For the preservation of the culture of mediation, this has the positive effect of preserving mediation as a culturally universal tool and legitimizing its global applicability. This insight, in turn, confirms Busch's (2016, 198) finding that authors in mediation literature tend to choose one definition of culture for their study that best covers and cements their previous assumptions. The idea of intercultural mediation is thus a component of mediation practice discourses that helps to consolidate and sustain mediation itself in an increasingly complex world.

Note

1 No financial funding has been spent for this part of the project.

References

Archibald, Mandy M., Rachel C. Ambagtsheer, Mavourneen G. Casey, and Michael Lawless. 2019. "Using Zoom Videoconferencing for Qualitative Data Collection: Perceptions and Experiences of Researchers and Participants." *International Journal of Qualitative Methods* 18 (January): 160940691987459. 10.1177/16094 06919874596

Avruch, Kevin. 2003. "Type I and Type II Errors in Culturally Sensitive Conflict Resolution Practice." *Conflict Resolution Quarterly* 20 (3): 351–71. 10.1002/crq.29

Busch, Dominic. 2010. "Shopping in Hospitality: Situational Constructions of Customer–Vendor Relationships among Shopping Tourists at a Bazaar on the German–Polish Border." *Language and Intercultural Communication* 10 (1): 72–89. 10.1080/14708470903452614

Busch, Dominic. 2012. "Cultural Theory and Conflict Management in Organizations: How Does Theory Shape Our Understanding of Culture in Practice?" *International Journal of Cross Cultural Management* 12 (1): 9–24. 10.1177/1470595811413106

Busch, Dominic. 2016. "Does Conflict Mediation Research Keep Track with Cultural Theory?" *European Journal of Applied Linguistics* 4 (2): 181–206. 10.1515/eujal-2015-0037

Busch, Dominic. 2021. "The Dispositive of Intercultural Communication." *International Journal of Bias, Identity and Diversities in Education* 6 (1): 1–16. 10.4018/IJBIDE.2021010101

Bush, Robert A. Baruch, and Joseph P. Folger. 1994. *The Promise of Mediation: Responding to Conflict through Empowerment and Recognition.* 1st edition. The Jossey-Bass Conflict Resolution Series. San Francisco, CA: Jossey-Bass.

Butler, Judith. 1993. *Bodies That Matter: On the Discursive Limits of "Sex."* New York: Routledge.

Cheevers, Aonghus. 2020. "Neutrality in Irish Mediation, One Concept, Different Meanings." *Conflict Resolution Quarterly* 37 (3): 253–72. 10.1002/crq.21273

Cominelli, Luigi, and Claudio Lucchiari. 2017. "Italian Mediators in Action: The Impact of Style and Attitude: Italian Mediators." *Conflict Resolution Quarterly* 35 (2): 223–42. 10.1002/crq.21206

Döringer, Stefanie. 2021. "'The Problem-Centred Expert Interview'. Combining Qualitative Interviewing Approaches for Investigating Implicit Expert Knowledge." *International Journal of Social Research Methodology* 24 (3): 265–78. 10.1080/13645579.2020.1766777

Galton, Eric, and Lela P. Love, eds. 2012. *Stories Mediators Tell.* Chicago: American Bar Association, Section of Dispute Resolution.

Greatbatch, David, and Robert Dingwall. 1999. "Professional Neutralism in Family Mediation." In *Talk, Work and Institutional Order*, edited by Srikant Sarangi and Celia Roberts, 1999th edition, 1: 271–92. Language, Power and Social Process. Berlin, New York: Mouton de Gruyter. 10.1515/9783110208375.3.271

Harmon-Darrow, Caroline, and Yanfeng Xu. 2018. "Retaining Volunteer Mediators: Comparing Predictors of Burnout." *Conflict Resolution Quarterly* 35 (4): 367–81. 10.1002/crq.21216

Jacobs, Scott. 2002. "Maintaining Neutrality in Dispute Mediation: Managing Disagreement While Managing Not to Disagree." *Journal of Pragmatics* 34 (10–11): 1403–26. 10.1016/S0378-2166(02)00071-1

Love, Lela P., and Glen Parker. 2017a. "Introduction." In *Stories Mediators Tell. World Edition*, edited by Lela P. Love and Glen Parker, xi–xvi. Chicago, Illinois: ABA, Section of Dispute Resolution.

Love, Lela P., and Glen Parker, eds. 2017b. *Stories Mediators Tell. World Edition.* Chicago, Illinois: ABA, Section of Dispute Resolution.

Mae, Michiko. 2007. "Auf dem Weg zu einer transkulturellen Genderforschung." In *Transkulturelle Genderforschung*, edited by Michiko Mae and Britta Saal, 37–51. Wiesbaden: VS Verlag für Sozialwissenschaften. 10.1007/978-3-531-90625-6_3

Moerman, Michael. 1988. *Talking Culture: Ethnography and Conversation Analysis.* University of Pennsylvania Publications in Conduct and Communication. Philadelphia: University of Pennsylvania Press.

Pignault, Anne, Raymond Meyers, and Claude Houssemand. 2017. "Mediators' Self-Perception of Their Work and Practice: Content and Lexical Analysis." *The Qualitative Report* 22 (6): 1589–1606. 10.46743/2160-3715/2017.2676

Raines, Susan S. 2018. "Becoming the Change We Wish to See: The Unexpected Benefits of Conflict Resolution Work." *Conflict Resolution Quarterly* 35 (3): 319–27. 10.1002/crq.21213

Raines, Susan S., Sunil Kumar Pokhrel, and Jean Poitras. 2013. "Mediation as a Profession: Challenges That Professional Mediators Face: Mediation as a Profession." *Conflict Resolution Quarterly* 31 (1): 79–97. 10.1002/crq.21080

Sacks, Harvey. 1974. "On the Analysability of Stories by Children." In *Ethnomethodology. Selected Readings*, edited by Roy Turner, 216–323. Harmondsworth: Penguin.

27
DESIGN THINKING AND DESIGN COMMUNICATION FOR INTERCULTURAL CONFLICT MANAGEMENT

Patrice M. Buzzanell, Sean Eddington, Evgeniya Pyatovskaya, and Aliah Mestrovich Seay

Introduction

Design is utilized in every subject area, often as a method for approaching and evaluating information and pragmatic applications in particular contexts, including intercultural mediation. At its heart, design is a problem-solving system: problem identification, idea generation and selection according to project specifications, and prototyping and testing for sustainable solutions. Design has many forms, including Design Thinking (DT), Human-Centered Design (HCD), Communication as Design (CAD), Empathic Design, and Intercultural Design. Each variation emphasizes different aspects of design processes and outcomes. These range from innovative project generation (DT, IDEO n.d.) and co-design with users (HCD, Zoltowski et al. 2012), to interactivity to shape communication possibilities (CAD, Aakhus 2007, 112), feelings about the design (empathic), and incorporation of complex cultural understandings (intercultural).

However, all variations and foci are essential to good design. Good or effective design typically includes such criteria as feasibility, viability, and sustainability. In intercultural mediation, good or effective design incorporates qualities such as relational development, reflexivity, recognition that all design decisions are ethical choices, valuing different cultural ways of constructing knowledge and being in the world. Shifting from one to others of these emphases throughout projects can enhance the quality of design. The shifting enables new aspects to come to light, thus producing robust products, needed or desirable services, and/or effective cultural interactions. For instance, Buzzanell (2014) describes how a global engineering team tasked with work toward integrated water-energy-sanitation-education and women's empowerment systems in rural Ghanaian villages evolved through intercultural mediation of diverse parties' views and goals.

Intercultural mediators engage in activities that fit design processes although they may not label them as such (Baraldi 2018; Farini 2013). These mediators explain problems, provide context for language translations, intercede between institutions and group members, and socially construct situations advantageously for different parties. Prototypes and negotiated solutions result from co-ordinated interactions and outcomes of the designs. As Mayer (2020) notes, a key to any type of mediation is to "reconcile the superficially different interests of the conflict parties at a deeper level to search for a common denominator and thus expand the room for manoeuvring and discussion"

DOI: 10.4324/9781003227441-32

(57). This maneuvering is creative and disciplined; it often takes place under time constraints with incomplete data and limited resources (Radcliffe and Fosmire 2014). Constraints and opportunities mean that co-designers and stakeholders ideally allow themselves to be steeped in historical-cultural understandings. They also are vulnerable to mistakes and constant learning, and cognizant that design outcomes often fit users' interests only temporarily (Buzzanell 2017, 2014, 2020).

Often these mistakes and missed opportunities result from a lack of understanding of those people for whom design is intended and who are more-or-less involved in design processes. For example, intercultural mediation during refugee resettlement programs typically focuses on the refugees. However, not attending to "how the volunteers position themselves within their [unfolding] narratives of interactions with and about the refugees" can limit possibilities for effective processes and outcomes (McAllum 2020, 58). In this positioning, volunteers attend to their own cultural frameworks and reflect upon who is authoring and has decision authority in particular circumstances. This movement among and within micro-meso-macro contexts, and between reflection and confrontation, in uncertain situations is a hallmark of current scholarship on intercultural ethics (Busch 2021). This movement and ethical orientation fit the tensional and negotiation processes within design and intercultural mediation.

Design and intercultural mediation decision authority or expertise negotiations at every phase are constituted via interconnections of human and material agencies. Material agents or artifacts—visual process depictions, 3D models, video, simulations and models of complex systems, sketches, virtual reality spaces, and others—assist intercultural mediation. These material agents have varied aims. They can explain or strategically construct ambiguities, persuade and dissuade, create boundaries, legitimize stakeholder concerns, trigger conversation, and imagine new realities (Buzzanell and Zoltowski, forthcoming). Broadly, written texts and human actors can constitute conjunctive vectors, centering on compatibilities, and disjunctive vectors, maintaining distance and disagreement within relational webs and emerging results (Brummans, Higham, and Cooren 2022). On micro-levels, design team members break, make, and personalize sensemaking to implement design work (Austin et al. 2020) that can affect outcomes of intercultural mediation and other design goals.

With this overview in mind, we next discuss (1) intercultural mediation approaches. We progress in complexity from one perspective to the next, building on key understandings and needed communication expertise. We conclude by recommending (2) justice-oriented design communication for intercultural mediation.

Intercultural mediation approaches

In this section, we describe (a) intercultural conflict management and developmental challenges so that we can then contrast this perspective with that of (b) intercultural mediation design. Our third approach goes a step further by centering (c) empathy in intercultural mediation design.

Intercultural conflict management and developmental challenges

Local societies are impacted by global economic and social changes such that people negotiate cultural differences daily in work and interpersonal relationships (Ting-Toomey 2010). To do so, they learn how to navigate intercultural conflict through intercultural competence development on relational through societal and global levels. Ting-Toomey (2010) encourages competence development "to manage emotional frustrations and interaction struggles mindfully due primarily to cultural group membership differences" (21). She notes that a key indicator of cultural conflict is cultural distance.

Although conflict is a normal process in unfolding relationships, the larger the cultural distance between the parties, the greater the likelihood that meaning-making and conflict negotiating can be hampered by intercultural differences. These conflicts are even more likely when people come from ethnocentric mindsets in which they do not realize or attend to cultural differences (Bennett 2018). This inattention can increase miscommunication through polarization and disengagement (Canary, Lakey, and Sillars 2006). In these cases, the interacting conflict parties are at odds with each other because of differences in worldviews as well as in socio-political, cultural, and historical backgrounds. Parties' diverse expectations can produce dysfunctional results and/or can become openings for intercultural engagement.

An example of needed intercultural competence development and conflict management is diversity, equity, and inclusion (DEI) efforts in the United States and around the globe. There are many reasons why DEI is essential. These range from recruitment and retention of talent to innovation, growth, and social justice (Buzzanell 2020). While such efforts often combine business, economic, and moral reasons, they typically do not challenge majority members' worldviews (Carrillo Arciniega 2021) meaning that intercultural conflicts persist and opportunities to create inclusive cultures are missed. Based on Bennett's (2018) Developmental Model of Intercultural Sensitivity, the Intercultural Development Inventory (IDI) offers a psychometric tool that measures people's abilities to shift their behaviors and adapt to cultural commonalities and differences (Hammer 2011). The IDI helps explain how individuals and organizations navigate cross-cultural experiences using an ethnocentric-transitional-ethnorelative continuum.

Ethnocentrism means that individuals and organizational systems operate from mindsets of denial or polarization with no real interest in understanding cultural differences. Ethnocentrism avoids systemic issues and conversations about diversity. When difference is discussed, exchanges can resemble polarizing, 'us-vs-them' encounters. Underlying such discussions are feelings of superiority regarding dominant cultural values and beliefs with only non-threatening cultural differences, such as food or dress, being acknowledged. Individuals from non-dominant backgrounds may not feel valued, seen, or heard.

In the *transitional organizational mindset of minimization*, equality and equity are conflated and used interchangeably (Pearce, Wald, and Ballakrishnen 2015). Most people would say they are unbiased and point out overt acts of discrimination never considering they could be part of the DEI problem. Minimization provides a space where difficult DEI issues are overlooked. Although there are understandings that difference exists, people focus on cultural similarities as sources of comfort and resist systemic change. Individuals and organizations with this mindset overestimate intercultural competence, minimize cultural conflict, and support 'color-blind' policies. Moreover, microaggressions or daily (linguistic and interactional) microinvalidations and microinsults (Sue et al. 2019), are tolerated and invisible to dominant cultural groups which can lead to non-dominant individuals' disengagement and organizational exit.

Finally, in *ethnorelativism*, acceptance and adaptation are intercultural mindsets that exemplify appreciation of cultural differences and intentional efforts dedicated to equity and inclusionary practices. In the early stages of acceptance, there may be struggles to incorporate effective systems. When these struggles incorporate intercultural humility, competence, and conflict management as part of the organizational mission and identity, then there are possibilities for sustainable DEI designs for transformative systemic change (Buzzanell 2017; 2020).

Thus, intercultural conflict management offers diagnostic skills and developmental approaches to mindsets and behaviors that can enable parties to engage productively in intercultural mediation. These kinds of communication skills and awareness are necessary but not sufficient for effective and sustainable intercultural mediation. The reason that they are insufficient is that DEI is a wicked problem (Buzzanell 2017; Eddington et al., 2020). Wicked problems are seemingly intractable concerns so deeply embedded in contexts that efforts to address one part often reveal and create other problems, thus exacerbating problems. Such is the case with DEI where disparities in health, education, water, food, mentoring, and other resources thwart attempts to achieve intercultural mediation resolutions and harmony. To work with these intractable conflicts and discursive-material issues, what is needed is design.

Intercultural mediation design

When harmony is thrown out of balance by misunderstandings based on cultural differences or inequitable resources, intercultural conflicts may emerge. Engaging in intercultural mediation requires the skills and mindsets already mentioned. Intercultural mediation operationalized through design thinking is one possible response to entangled cultural concerns and material considerations.

Intercultural mediation, or "the act of establishing social links between people from different cultures" (Adeline 2009), involves complex processes incorporating knowledge generated from communication studies, linguistics, management, psychology, and culture. In considering how mediation may be done, design thinking's problem-solving position, strategy, and method offer different points of entry from cognitive approaches (Kimbell 2011) to interactive frameworks that can promote dialogue across differences (Eddington et al. 2020). Design is inherently suitable to solve complex problems, such as intercultural conflicts, that are rooted in human behavior and directly connected to the growing speed of development, diversity, and change (Kummetz Brunetto 2018). In a world that is increasingly dynamic and multifaceted and where cultures meet, mingle, and clash, questions like 'How can we successfully navigate conflict in the world increasingly interconnected?' or 'How do we support different cultural mindsets and expression?' can stimulate design thinking sessions that use 'what if' approaches (Kimbell 2011).

Design, especially DT and HCD, iteratively seeks to understand the 'user' (Stevens 2021) in varied contexts in which intercultural conflicts and desires for change occur (Kimbell, 2011; Pande and Bharathi 2020). Design thinking provides tools to challenge assumptions and problems from new perspectives that are co-constructed by all participants (Eddington et al. 2020). A new level of understanding is shaped through identifying alternative strategies to those previously and unsuccessfully used. Participants are encouraged to question their initial frames of reference against the desired states they are collectively constructing and envisioning. DT can transform intercultural mediation, not only by developing solutions that are "desirable, viable, and feasible" (Brown, n.d.) but also by assuming that wicked problems such as DEI are never fully resolved. DT does not necessarily produce answers or solve a conflict, but rather "converts problems into opportunities" (Kimbell 2011, 294) with HCD reminding intercultural mediators that these opportunities are user-specific, co-designed, and context-bound.

For instance, Eddington et al. (2020) describe design processes incorporating DT and HCD. They utilized surveys about engineering identities and identifications; individuals' journey maps in their disciplinary majors and careers; interviews and design session discussions for deep understandings and checkpoints with co-designers; and other methods to engage members of two different engineering schools in designing new insights and possible interventions to promote DEI. Since DT is both communal and creative, it can facilitate and enable increasingly humane transformation in situations of intercultural conflict and mediation. Its ability to create opportunities to share perspectives (empathize), openly negotiate the best acceptable solution (prototype), and encourage individual self-reflection, perspective-taking, and joint sense-making (ideate) is highly efficient in precarious conflicts that stem from cultural differences. Empathy acts as a core moral orientation for those involved in the design process. Understanding what another sees as meaningful can be productive of new levels of understanding among participants and creating "solutions that meet both expressed and unexpressed needs" (Glen et al. 2015, 657). By encouraging people to "remain open and curious, to assume nothing, and to see ambiguity as an opportunity" (IDEO, n.d.), design becomes a framework that creates space for reconciliation between culturally (in) sensitive, (mono/multi)lingual, (open/closed)-minded participants to engage in meaningful communication about topics of importance to everyone involved.

At the same time, design is neither unproblematic in its application to intercultural mediation, nor the only one. One potential pitfall is the unreflexive generalization of DT-related practices that can ignore the ways DT is implemented in very concrete situations. Because design and culture are intertwined (Fallan and Lees-Maffei 2016), DT is informed by the culture in which it is practiced while it simultaneously aims to transcend boundaries to facilitate intercultural dialogue in which alternative cultures are created (Casmir 1993). For instance, Eddington et al. (2020) found that Schools of Electrical and Computer Engineering and Biomedical Engineering had very different views about DEI and design, meaning that prototypes were developed for these particular schools with hopes for some transferability in the future. Another problematic area is how the DT process can privilege the designer. In intercultural mediation, it is especially important that neither processes nor cultural differences be centered on designers at the expense of individuals engaging in design thinking. Situated and embodied experiences guide design procedures but HCR can provide the means of achieving co-design (Zoltowski, Oakes, and Cardella 2012). 'Caring design,' a concept that couples care ethics, with its emphasis on attention, empathetic response, and relationships with DT, can be effective in addressing the issues mentioned (Hamington 2019).

Empathy in intercultural mediation design

As mentioned throughout our chapter, design is used in varied contexts including workplaces, teams, and societies (Brown 2008). Tools can be leveraged to solve and address business problems (Elsbach and Stigliani 2018), and to diagnose and identify issues existing within organizational cultures (Eddington et al. 2020). Moreover, the cultivation of 'designerly ways of thinking' can help address complex problems (Donaldson and Smith 2017). Yet, our chapter notes that a central requirement is the cultivation of empathy (Dell'Era et al. 2020; Devecchi and Guerrini 2017; Jamal, Kircher, and Donaldson 2021; Kolko 2014), or the ability to 'feel what it's like to be another person' (Kolko 2014, 75). More specifically, empathy is constituted via cognitive, affective, and conative processes—the former being the ability to engage in perspective-taking, the second resulting in acknowledgment and responsiveness to individuals with appropriate emotions, and the latter being practice- and action-orientations (Brown 2008; Jamal, Kircher, and Donaldson 2021).

Design communication privileges cognitive empathy as if the designer's interpretation of perspective-taking is the key to understanding another. Much of the design literature discusses the importance of perspective-taking vis-à-vis design tools (e.g., customer journey maps, empathy mapping, and affinity diagramming) that can be adopted to promote empathic thinking, or the cultivation of "the various perspectives of real and imaginary individuals for whom the problem is tangible and solutions would be beneficial" (Donaldson and Smith 2017, 5). Elsbach and Stigliani (2018) argue that "given the empathetic engagement with other people that design thinking tools promote, these tools may lead to an increased level of empathy in the organizational members who use them" (2301); however, as stated above, these tools often privilege designers as all-knowing about another's lived experience (Ray Murray et al. 2021). Critics of this form of DT argue that, despite its claims for innovation and transformation, the process is inherently problematic and colonizing (i.e., reproducing many of the same problems and issues that occurred before the design process) and can be considered "a mechanism for the reproduction of whiteness" (Constanza-Chock 2020, 16). In intercultural mediation processes, cognitive empathy may be contra-productive in fostering constructive interactions among individuals.

However, when considering the prevalence of wicked problems and intractable conflicts that design processes are adept at addressing (Brown 2008), some argue for reframing DT toward justice-oriented design approaches (e.g., Costanza-Chock 2020). Thus, the promotion of affective and conative empathy may be central to addressing justice-oriented processes (Afroogh et al. 2021) through the "infrastructuring for community care" (Ray Murray et al. 2021, 5). This type of infrastructure is similar to how Jamal and colleagues (2021) describe affective and conative empathy as necessary components of cultivating praxis and care ethics for vulnerable communities, as well as helping to center "diverse ways of knowing' that 'embrace pluralistic worldviews and values" that seek to decolonize and democratize design processes for and with diverse communities (17). A justice-oriented design approach takes HCD a step further for DEI by foregrounding and prioritizing all peoples as central to making change within society and affirms "the dignity of human beings as they act out their lives in varied social, economic, political, and cultural circumstances" (Buchanan 2001, 37). Justice-oriented design processes are constituted through democratic empowerment that acknowledges individuals' right to be part of design processes (Walton 2016); however, the affective and conative approaches to empathy are critical since they help inform how individuals approach social justice issues from a design perspective. That is, the affective and conative forms of empathy serve as an essential aspect of relationship-building. Affective and conative states of empathy can only go so far (and, at times, can minimize or erase minoritized individuals' contributions in design processes).

What is needed in design processes to enact social justice is critical empathy. Drawing from Remke (2006), critical empathy "is a testament to the realization that one can never really truly and deeply understand the lived experience of another person, especially when that person identifies as coming from another cultural background" (Mestrovich Seay et al. forthcoming). Thus, in considering the myriad ways that social justice issues are complex, entangled, and configured in society, critical empathy is key to understanding and communicating across differences and power. That is, critical empathy acknowledges how power and empathy are entangled. In "identifying with a morally specific variety of suffering that arises from social pathology and injustice," critical empathy catalyzes transformation (Lobb 2017, 597).

To illustrate the potential of critical empathy, Bennett and Rosner (2019) critiqued two design examples aimed at addressing disability experiences. These examples are an accessible voting booth and a prototype empathy activity that helped designers cultivate an understanding of disabled experiences. In their critique, they argued that the empathic aims of the design cases focused on 'being like' someone over 'being with' someone. In 'being like' someone, cognitive empathy and perspective-taking are central to design processes. In the case of the voting booth, designers incorporated the perspectives of disabled people but did not acknowledge their contributions to the design process—in essence erasing the experiences of key designers. In the empathy activity, designers used cards to help understand disabled experiences, but through the lens of the designer (not the one with the lived experience). To "be with" someone "involves learning to be affected and attending to difference without reifying that difference once again." In so doing, designers make room for "affective partnerships" that help them "destabilize and reimagine imposed boundaries" (Bennett and Rosner 2019, 10). In considering how design communication strategies can engage social justice and intercultural communication, a critical empathic stance is a necessary aspect of how intercultural mediation vis-à-vis design may be made possible.

Conclusion: Design communication for intercultural mediation

Throughout our chapter, we have suggested possibilities for engaging in intercultural mediation from design theories, applications, and methodologies. We encourage the use of multiple design approaches so that the different needs, interests, material circumstances, human and non-human agents, and cultural differences can be examined from different lenses. For instance, intercultural conflict management can equip parties and organizations with skills and mindsets that better enable them to embrace difference and create inclusionary cultures. Intercultural mediation through design engages productively with wicked problems underlying grand challenges such as DEI but may be problematic in particular circumstances. Toward productive and transformational intercultural

Design thinking and design communication

mediation, we encourage justice-oriented design grounded in critical empathy and aspirational longings for inclusion and co-design among all parties.

References

Aakhus, Mark. 2007. "Communication as Design." *Communication Monographs* 74 (1): 112–7. 10.1080/0363775 0701196383

Adeline, Antoine. 2009. "Intercultural Mediation: Discussion and Reflection." *La Revue* (25 November 2009). https://larevue.squirepattonboggs.com/Intercultural-mediation-discussion-and-reflections_a1755.html

Afroogh, Saleh, Amir Esmalian, Jonan Donaldson, and Ali Mostafavi. 2021. "Empathic Design in Engineering Education and Practice: An Approach for Achieving Inclusive and Effective Community Resilience." *Sustainability* 13 (7): 4060. 10.3390/su13074060

Austin, Jasmine T., Brittney S. Wallace, Britney N. Gilmore, and Ryan S. Bisel. 2020. "The Micro-Skills of Collective Communication Design Work: An Academic Team's Development of Sensebreaking Messages." *Communication Studies* 71 (2): 295–314. 10.1080/10510974.2020.1722720

Baraldi, Claudio. 2018. "Interpreting as Mediation of Migrants' Agency and Institutional Support. A Case Analysis." *Journal of Pragmatics* 125: 13–27. 10.1016/j.pragma.2017.11.012

Bennett, Cynthia L., and Daniela K. Rosner. 2019. "The Promise of Empathy." In *Proceedings of the 2019 CHI Conference on Human Factors in Computing Systems*, edited by Stephen Brewster, Geraldine Fitzpatrick, Anna Cox, and Vassilis Kostakos, 1–13. New York: ACM. 10.1145/3290605.3300528

Bennett, Milton J. 2018. "Developmental Model of Intercultural Sensitivity." In *The International Encyclopedia of Intercultural Communication*, edited by Young Y. Kim, 1–10. Hoboken: Wiley-Blackwell. 10.1002/978111 8783665.ieicc0182

Brown, Tim. 2008. "Design Thinking." *Harvard Business Review* June 2008: 1–9.

Brown, Tim. n.d. *Design Thinking Defined*. Palo Alto, CA: IDEO Design Thinking. https://designthinking.ideo.com

Brummans, Boris HJM, Lise Higham, and François Cooren. 2022. "The Work of Conflict Mediation: Actors, Vectors, and Communicative Relationality." *Human Relations* 75 (4): 764–91. 10.1177/0018726721994180

Buchanan, Richard. 2001. "Human Dignity and Human Rights: Thoughts on the Principles of Human-Centered Design." *Design Issues* 17 (3): 35–9. 10.1162/074793601750357178

Busch, Dominic. 2021. "The Changing Discourse of Intercultural Ethics: A Diachronic Meta-Analysis." *Journal of Multicultural Discourses* 16 (3): 189–202. 10.1080/17447143.2020.1803887

Buzzanell, Patrice M. 2014. "Reflections on Global Engineering Design and Intercultural Competence: The Case of Ghana." In *Intercultural Communication Competence: Conceptualization and Its Development in Cultural Contexts and Interactions*, edited by Xiaodong Dai and Guo-Ming Chen, 315–34. Newcastle upon Tyne, UK: Cambridge Scholars Publishing.

Buzzanell, Patrice M. 2017. "Constituting Intercultural Harmony by Design Thinking: Conflict Management In, For, and About Diversity and Inclusion Work." In *Conflict Management and Intercultural Communication. The Art of Intercultural Harmony*, edited by Xiaodong Dai and Guo-Ming Chen, 66–84. London, New York: Routledge.

Buzzanell, Patrice M. 2020. "Design of Meaningful Work in Diversity and Inclusion: Enactment of Inclusionary Engineering Design and Partnerships in Rural Ghana." In *Organizing Inclusion: Moving Diversity from Demographics to Communication Processes*, edited by Marya L. Doerfel and Jennifer L. Gibbs, 215–34. New York, NY: Routledge. 10.1093/acprof:oso/9780198739227.003.0009

Buzzanell, Patrice M., and Carla B. Zoltowski. forthcoming. "Communication and Media/technology Affordances in the Ways We Teach and Communicate Across Boundaries." In *Teaching Communication Across Disciplines*, edited by J. Burchfield and April A. Kedrowicz. Lexington.

Canary, Daniel J., Sandra G. Lakey, and Alan L. Sillars. 2006. "Managing Conflict in a Competent Manner: A Mindful Look at Events That Matter." In *The SAGE Handbook of Conflict Communication: Integrating Theory, Research, and Practice*, edited by John G. Oetzel and Stella Ting-Toomey, 185–210. Los Angeles: Sage.

Carrillo Arciniega, Luzilda. 2021. "Selling Diversity to White Men: How Disentangling Economics from Morality Is a Racial and Gendered Performance." *Organization* 28 (2): 228–46. 10.1177/1350508420930341

Casmir, Fred L. 1993. "Third-Culture Building: A Paradigm Shift for International and Intercultural Communication." *Annals of the International Communication Association* 16 (1): 407–28. 10.1080/23808985.1993.11678861

Costanza-Chock, Sasha. 2020. *Design Justice: Community-Led Practices to Build the Worlds We Need*. Cambridge, Massachusetts, London, England: The MIT Press.

Dell'Era, Claudio, Stefano Magistretti, Cabirio Cautela, Roberto Verganti, and Francesco Zurlo. 2020. "Four Kinds of Design Thinking: From Ideating to Making, Engaging, and Criticizing." *Creativity and Innovation Management* 29 (2): 324–44. 10.1111/caim.12353

Devecchi, Alice, and Luca Guerrini. 2017. "Empathy and Design. A New Perspective." *Design Journal* 20 (sup1): S4357–64. 10.1080/14606925.2017.1352932

Donaldson, Jonan Phillip, and Brian K. Smith. 2017. "Design Thinking, Designerly Ways of Knowing, and Engaged Learning." In *Learning, Design, and Technology*, edited by Michael J. Spector, Barbara B. Lockee, and Marcus D. Childress, 1–24. Cham: Springer. 10.1007/978-3-319-17727-4_73-1

Eddington, Sean, Danielle Corple, Patrice M. Buzzanell, Carla B. Zoltowski, and Andrew Brightman. 2020. "Addressing Organizational Cultural Conflicts in Engineering with Design Thinking." *Negotiation and Conflict Management Research* 13 (3): 263–84. 10.1111/ncmr.12191

Elsbach, Kimberly D., and Ileana Stigliani. 2018. "Design Thinking and Organizational Culture: A Review and Framework for Future Research." *Journal of Management* 44 (6): 2274–306. 10.1177/0149206317744252

Fallan, Kjetil, and Grace Lees-Maffei. 2016. "Real Imagined Communities: National Narratives and the Globalization of Design History." *Design Issues* 32 (1): 5–18. 10.1162/desi_a_00360

Farini, Federico 2013. "Interpreting and Intercultural Mediation in Italian Healthcare Settings." *Journal of Intercultural Communication* 33: 1–19. https://immi.se/intercultural/nr33/farini.html

Glen, Roy, Christy Suciu, C. Christopher Baughn, and Robert Anson. 2015. "Teaching Design Thinking in Business Schools." *The International Journal of Management Education* 13 (2): 182–92. 10.1016/j.ijme.2015.05.001

Hamington, Maurice. 2019. "Integrating Care Ethics and Design Thinking." *Journal of Business Ethics* 155 (1): 91–103. 10.1007/s10551-017-3522-6

Hammer, Mitchell R. 2011. "Additional Cross-Cultural Validity Testing of the Intercultural Development Inventory." *International Journal of Intercultural Relations (IJIR)* 35 (4): 474–87. 10.1016/j.ijintrel.2011.02.014

International Development Enterprise Organization. n. d. *HCD Human-Centered Design: Toolkit.* 2nd edition. www.hcdconnect.org/toolkit/en

Jamal, Tazim, Julie Kircher, and Jonan Phillip Donaldson. 2021. "Re-Visiting Design Thinking for Learning and Practice: Critical Pedagogy, Conative Empathy." *Sustainability* 13 (2): 964. 10.3390/su13020964

Kimbell, Lucy. 2011. "Rethinking Design Thinking: Part I." *Design and Culture* 3 (3): 285–306. 10.2752/1754 70811x13071166525216

Kolko, Jon. 2014. *Well-Designed: How to Use Empathy to Create Products People Love.* Boston, Mass: Harvard Business Review Press.

Kummetz Brunetto, Sebastian. 2018. *When to Use Design Thinking and When NOT to?*LinkedIn. https://www.linkedin.com/pulse/glimpse-design-thinking-when-use-sebastian-kummetz-brunetto-1

Lobb, Andrea. 2017. "Critical Empathy." *Constellations* 24 (4): 594–607. 10.1111/1467-8675.12292

Mayer, Claude-Hélène. 2020. *Intercultural Mediation and Conflict Management Training.* Cham: Springer. 10.1007/978-3-030-51765-6

McAllum, Kirstie. 2020. "Refugee Resettlement Volunteers as (Inter)Cultural Mediators?" *Journal of International and Intercultural Communication* 13 (4): 366–83. 10.1080/17513057.2019.1653953

Pande, Mandaar, and S. Vijayakumar Bharathi. 2020. "Theoretical Foundations of Design Thinking – A Constructivism Learning Approach to Design Thinking." *Thinking Skills and Creativity* 36: 100637. 10.1016/j.tsc.2020.100637

Pearce, Russell G., Eli Wald, and Swethaa S. Ballakrishnen. 2015. "Difference Blindness Vs. Bias Awareness: Why Law Firms with the Best of Intentions Have Failed to Create Diverse Partnerships." *Fordham Law Review* 83 (5): 2407–55.

Radcliffe, David F., and Michael Fosmire, eds. 2014. *Integrating Information into the Engineering Design Process.* West Lafayette, IN: Purdue University Press.

Ray Murray, Padmini, Naveen L. Bagalkot, Shreyas Srivatsa, and Paul Anthony. 2021. "Design Beku: Toward Decolonizing Design and Technology Through Collaborative and Situated Care-in-Practices." *Global Perspectives* 2 (1). 10.1525/gp.2021.26132

Remke, Robyn Virginia. 2006. *(Ir)Rationalities at Work: The Logics, Heart, and Soul of Head Start.* Unpublished diss., Purdue University, West Lafayette, IN.

Seay, Aliah K. Mestrovich, Mac T. Benavides, Sean M. Eddington, and Jurdene A. Coleman. 2022. "Beyond Perspective Taking: Fostering Equity Through Critical Empathy and Intercultural Listening." In *Achieving Equity in Higher Education Using Empathy as a Guiding Principle*, edited by Catherine Ward, 141–71. Hershey, PA: IGI Global. 10.4018/978-1-7998-9746-0.ch007

Stevens, Emily. 2021. "What Is Design Thinking? A Comprehensive Beginner's Guide." *CareerFoundry Blog.* https://careerfoundry.com/en/blog/ux-design/what-is-design-thinking-everything-you-need-to-know-to-get-started/

Sue, Derald Wing, Sarah Alsaidi, Michael N. Awad, Elizabeth Glaeser, Cassandra Z. Calle, and Narolyn Mendez. 2019. "Disarming Racial Microaggressions: Microintervention Strategies for Targets, White Allies, and Bystanders." *The American Psychologist* 74 (1): 128–42. 10.1037/amp0000296

Ting-Toomey, Stella. 2010. "Intercultural Conflict Interaction Competence: From Theory to Practice." In *The Intercultural Dynamics of Multicultural Working*, edited by Maria Manuela Guilherme, Evelyne Glaser, and María C. Del Méndez-García, 21–40. Multilingual Matters. 10.21832/9781847692870-005

Walton, Rebecca. 2016. "Supporting Human Dignity and Human Rights." *Journal of Technical Writing and Communication* 46 (4): 402–26. 10.1177/0047281616653496

Zoltowski, Carla B., William C. Oakes, and Monica E. Cardella. 2012. "Students' Ways of Experiencing Human-Centered Design." *Journal of Engineering Education* 101 (1): 28–59. 10.1002/j.2168-9830.2012.tb00040.x

PART V

Theorizing intercultural mediation

28
THEORIZING MEDIATION FROM THE PERSPECTIVE OF LEGAL ANTHROPOLOGY

Marc Simon Thomas

Introduction

This chapter argues that the legal anthropology literature on disputes and dispute settlement offers useful insights for understanding mediation from a 'legal research' point of view. This is because a lot of current common knowledge on mediation has its roots in a legal anthropological understanding. The argument that is set forth in this chapter is that the most important lesson that can be learned is that mediation should not be seen in isolation, but as part of a social process. This chapter is a shortened and slightly revised version of Simon Thomas (2016).

Mediation involves a wide range of practices and practitioners, and the use of various strategies to resolve disputes. Mediation is based on the premise that disputes often concern more than a strictly legal conflict. In this regard, mediation can be distinguished from a formal court procedure. Consequently, mediation is seen as a form of 'alternative dispute resolution,' which in practical terms means an alternative to litigation in formal courts of law. Most of mediation's considered benefits are pragmatic in nature, holding that solutions reached via mediation are more effective (e.g., in terms of costs, duration, anticipated outcome, etc.), and offer a more sustainable solution for the parties involved, than a court decision. Settling disputes in courts provides a win-lose decision, while mediation leads to a win–win settlement. Since most disputes touch on more than just a strict legal conflict (e.g., in terms of the 'history' of the conflict, parties and stakeholders involved, and the possible impact of the settlement in the future) this first explanation contends that, in most cases, both parties are better off when they settle the case themselves via dialogue mediated by a professional who stands between them (i.e., win–win), instead of a judge who stands above them and who rules in favor of just one of the parties (i.e., win-lose). The bulk of the literature on mediation underscores these arguments, although there has also been some cogent criticism regarding mediation that cannot easily be dismissed. Perhaps the most incisive of these criticisms is the argument that not everybody is equally well equipped in terms of power, education, etc., to stand up for one's interests; Laura Nader (2002), for example, can be seen as one of the earliest and most formative criticasters of the emergence of ADR in the United States. As we shall see, legal anthropological literature is the basis of this as well as other critical views of mediation.

This chapter argues that insights drawn from legal anthropology literature on disputes and dispute settlement can be fruitfully applied to mediation. Many contemporary, generally known insights regarding mediation can actually be traced back to earlier legal anthropological research. Knowledge derived from legal anthropological literature does not only explain why mediation proves to be an effective and

DOI: 10.4324/9781003227441-34

265

sustainable solution in so many cases. It can also be used to draw conclusions as to what will happen when the legal playing field with regard to mediation changes. The most important lesson here is that mediation should not be seen as an activity that occurs outside of particular social contexts (Merry 1987, 2063).

This chapter starts with an overview of legal anthropological literature. Since the 1940s, much of the focus of legal anthropological research has been on studying disputes, with researchers consistently stating the view that state law is just one of the alternatives to settle disputes. The next section is on understanding disputes, and here it is emphasized that disputing is a dynamic process that comprises distinct phases and permutations. In the subsequent paragraph, knowledge derived from legal anthropological research on disputes and the disputing process is applied to mediation activities. The main argument in that section is that the practice of mediation could benefit from applying the insights offered by legal anthropology.

Legal anthropology and dispute settlement

An overview of legal anthropology

Legal anthropology (also called anthropology of law) initially was regarded as a sub-discipline of cultural anthropology (Donovan 2007; Pirie 2013), but eventually developed into an independent discipline, offering its own theories of dispute settlement. Legal anthropology specifically focuses on rules and processes within a specific social, legal, economic, political, and cultural context (Comaroff and Roberts 1981; Nader and Todd 1978). Legal anthropological research is holistic in nature in that it appreciates and addresses the multiplicity of legal systems and dispute resolution mechanisms that exist in any society. The approach of legal anthropology is actor-centered, examining the ways individuals control and are controlled by the institutions and persons that govern them. 'The law in action,' from a legal anthropological perspective, refers to a study and interpretation of the way in which people think and make use of law in their daily reality. Legal anthropology's main activity is field-based ethnography, and its methodology involves participant observation, interviews, and occasionally archival research (Starr and Goodale 2002). Studying and analyzing the daily practice of law in a particular local setting (e.g., what happens in a court, an organization, a specific cultural setting, or during a mediation process) provides a framework for deriving tentative general hypotheses as to why these things happen.

In legal anthropology, while 'socio-legal' aspects include formal juridical institutions and their social surroundings, they also encompass other activities related to the law, as well as processes of disputing and dispute settlement in other social domains, whether officially or unofficially. Legal anthropologists do not ask themselves what disputes are in terms of law, or how the latter should be enforced. Instead, they address the fundamentally different question of how the law works in practice. A legal anthropological approach thus looks at who makes the rules, how these rules are normalized and enforced, and the way in which these rules are morally justified. Yet another typical line of inquiry within legal anthropology is the important question of what lies outside of the norm-governed domain and is thus open to individual or group interpretation. Finally, legal anthropologists not only ask questions about how people deal with the law, but also about how they avoid doing so (Donovan 2007; Just et al. 1992; Moore 1978; Sack and Aleck 1992). In short, from a legal anthropological point of view, law provides a point of entry into broad questions about regular and irregular, and official and unofficial social arrangements concerning disputes and dispute settlement.

Originally, legal anthropology concerned the study of small-scale, traditional or 'unknown' societies and how they dealt with crime, conflicts, and sanctions. The foundation for legal anthropology's development was laid by—among others—the jurist and historian Henry Maine and the sociologist Emile Durkheim. Bronislaw Malinowski ([1926] 1985), one of the most prominent early legal ethnographers (Moore 2005), emphasized themes such as reciprocity, social pressure, and tradition. According to Malinowski, all societies have some kind of law, although he introduced a division of norms with and

The perspective of legal anthropology

without a formal authority that served as their guarantors. Later, Alfred Reginald Radcliffe-Brown (1952), one of the founding fathers of structural functionalism, took as his point of departure the notion that solidarity and norms together defined equilibrium in society. He held that norms were guaranteed by the use of coercive force, applied by a tribunal or specialized body, and that the aim of sanctions was to restore balance. In the work of both men, the focus had shifted from larger questions of change and historical development (i.e., the work of Maine and Durkheim) towards a focus on very detailed studies of individual societies, even single communities. In contrast to Malinowski, Radcliffe-Brown concluded that some 'simpler' societies had no law (Nader 2002, 85). It was, however, Malinowski's view that every society could be said to have some sort of law, and this became the predominant assumption for future generations of researchers studying law in primitive societies (Nader 2002, 86).

Viewed in retrospect, Malinowski and Radcliffe-Brown were mainly concerned with whether traditional societies could be considered to have laws. Among their followers, a new debate arose around the question of how to study law. The first theoretical conceptualization in this regard posited the existence of general rules which applied to everyone, and which aimed at the maintenance of order within a society. Their research concentrated more on authorities and institutions and less on social processes. Conflicts were considered deviant behavior, and—according to this view—one could infer the underlying rule through analyzing the decisions of authorities and institutions in combination with the power they exercise. This line of thought regarding customary law, which prevailed during the first half of the last century, is called the normative paradigm (Sierra and Chenaut 2002) or rule-centered paradigm (Comaroff and Roberts 1981). Beginning in the 1940s, this view was criticized on the ground that it appeared to overestimate the importance of authorities and institutions. Such an overemphasis led the anthropologist Evans-Pritchard, for example, to declare that the Nuer of the Southern Sudan did not have laws (Comaroff and Roberts 1981, 9). Dissatisfaction with the characterization of such societies as 'lawless' prompted later scholars to shift their focus to the study of disputes (Griffiths 2002, 292).

Thereafter, a second paradigm, which arose in the 1940s and fell out of favor in the 1960s, considered disputes to constitute normal rather than exceptional social behavior. This view held that, when analyzing norms and conflicts, one should also pay attention to the arguments, negotiations and compromises of the concerned parties, instead of focusing solely on authorities or institutions. The earlier interest in rules and practices was thus replaced by the assumption that order could only be understood as the product of the actions and strategies of living men and women. Consequently, conflicts and their resolution became the focus of legal anthropology. The joint work of the jurist Llewellyn and the anthropologist Hoebel on 'trouble cases' and Cheyenne law can be regarded as one of the first studies conducted according to this second paradigm (Llewellyn and Hoebel 1987; see also Gulliver 1968 and Turner 1957). Their work was followed by several major studies (Bohannan 1957; Pospisil 1958). Pospisil (1958, 255) studying the Kapauku in New Guinea, stated that it was not "the abstract rule that affects the Kapauku people, but the actual decision of the headman," thus emphasizing the importance of the process, rather than rules.

Eventually, this second, process-oriented paradigm (Comaroff and Roberts 1981) for the study of disputes came under attack. Specifically, critics held that studying the settlement of disputes alone was too limited. Among other things, this meant that if one studied problem cases, one also had to study 'non-problematic' cases in order to get a complete picture of everyday life. As Holleman (1973, 599) stated:

> In the study of substantive law and its practice, and in a field of law in which litigation is rare, a fieldworker relying mainly on a case method focused upon actual [problematic] cases may get a skewed idea of the accepted principles and regularities in this particular field (...). The [non-problematic] case then becomes a necessary check on the [problematic] case, rather than the other way around.

More importantly, in the 1970s, legal anthropologists began to advocate a shift in research focus "to the description and analysis of behavior connected with disputing" (Just et al. 1992, 374). An integration of the two paradigms was sought, one in which the broader context would also be taken into account (i.e., a shift from rules or processes, via rules and processes, to rules and processes within their social, cultural, and political context) (Nader and Todd 1978).

As noted previously, during the early years legal anthropology mainly concerned the study of law in 'traditional' societies; cutting their units of research off from their surroundings, and treating customary law independently form state law. The paradigm had shifted from rule-centered to process-oriented. Starting in the 1970s, a third, more pluralistic paradigm was embraced, meaning that the customary law of the societies under research could not be studied without paying attention to colonialism and post-colonial dynamics and holding that it should be studied in relation to state law. The interrelationships among small-scale, 'simple' societies, the state, and the greater, outside world began to attract the interest of legal anthropological researchers in the late 1970s (Fitzpatrick 1980; Benda-Beckmann 1979). At that time, the study of legal pluralism became one of the main focuses of legal anthropology (Benda-Beckmann 2002; Griffiths 1986; Merry 1988). The idea that state law is not the only source of organized social order also paved the way to an analysis of law in the context of history and power relations (Starr and Collier 1989). The main focus of research in legal anthropology thus shifted to the interaction between customary law and state law, or more precisely to "the dialectic, mutually constitutive relationship between state law and other normative orders" (Merry 1988, 880), while this legal pluralism "is [best] understood as a relation of dominance and resistance" (Sieder 1997, 10). Or, in more general terms, legal anthropological research in mostly non-Western societies has taught us that people can have more normative orders to refer to than only state law, and that the significance of disparities in power should not be underestimated.

But perhaps most important of all, nowadays legal anthropological research is not only reserved for post-colonial, non-Western research settings (Hertzfeld 1992), and is conducted in all kinds of settings around the world. Current research takes into account not only normative rules, but also political events, economic realities and social inequalities. And it does this while studying legal practices in daily life in both non-Western and Western countries. Themes that are of interest for legal anthropologists include struggles over property, human rights, multiculturalism and collective rights, and law and religion. Disputes and dispute resolution remained on the research agenda of legal anthropology as well, while some overlap with socio-legal studies cannot be denied (see the next section). Current legal anthropological research is not only concerned with the experiences of indigenous people. It is emphatically concerned with ordinary Western people's experience and use of state law and courts, while the focus in such research has often been on litigants' interests and strategies (Moore 2005). In sum, legal anthropological research takes a different perspective on law. Instead of looking at the different ways that law handles conflicts, legal anthropologists examine the various ways conflicts are resolved, with law presenting only one possible approach (Merry 1987, 2060). This insight can be easily applied to the study of mediation; as a matter of fact, to a certain extent, this has been happening in the United States (Avruch and Black 1996; Greenhouse 1985; Merry 1987), where academics who went to Africa in the 1960s and 1970s to teach law in universities there became interested in how people settled disputes without courts, and their observations and analyses had an effect on the teaching and adaption of ADR (Abel 1982; Gibbs 1963; Greenhouse 1985; Krishnan 2012).

Understanding disputes

But before this chapter turns to the significance of legal anthropological research for the field of mediation, a basic understanding of disputes and disputing processes is essential. Basically, a dispute is a dynamic process comprising distinct phases, in which parties' standpoints and interests seem to

The perspective of legal anthropology

grow less flexible as the process evolves. The legal anthropologist Snyder, for example, recognizes the pre-conflict or grievance stage, the conflict stage, and the dispute stage, as three phases of the dispute process (Snyder 1981). Broadly speaking, two kinds of disputes can be distinguished: Those concerning material resources and power, and those of a social-emotional nature, which involve matters of perception and belief (Avruch 1998). In a way, the two negotiation models in mediation derived from social psychology (i.e., the so-called Harvard rational choice model and the trans-formative model, emphasizing empowerment of the disputing parties) respectively mirror these two classes of disputes, although there is by no means a strict one-to-one correspondence between material disputes and the rational-choice model, on the one hand, and social-emotional disputes and the transformative model, on the other. It is generally understood that the events and circumstances that occur during one phase influence happenings during the next phase.

A classic scholarly model for studying the process of disputing is the "naming, blaming, claiming ..." framework, developed by socio-legal scholars William Felstiner, Richard Abel and Austin Sarat (1980), in which they argue that disputes follow different phases. They show that during the 'claiming' phase, it is that an initial grievance becomes transformed into a dyadic disagreement. As soon as the parties are not able to solve the problem themselves and decide to turn to a third party to help them settle their conflict, a dyadic disagreement turns into a triadic disagreement. Following Felstiner et al., others also emphasize that the process of disputes contains different phases. Friedrich Glasl, for example, has developed a nine-stage model of conflict escalation (Glasl 2000). His nine stages can be grouped in three main phases: In the first phase, conflict is considered a 'problem' that can still be resolved jointly; the parties are on speaking terms and a win–win solution is still within reach. In the second phase, conflict is considered to be a battle that needs to be won (win-lose), while during the third phase each party basically tries to harm the other as much as possible, even at its own expense (lose-lose). Glasl also implies that a dispute moves from one stage to another as a result of certain events or changing circumstances. Given the fact that not every phase or stage needs to occur in every case, the models by Felstiner et al. and Glasl constitute so-called pyramid models (Miller and Sarat 1980). At the bottom of the pyramid, any kind of problem can be found, while at the top only really seriously escalated disputes can be detected. Depending on the degree of escalation, mediation is considered to provide a workable solution, and what a mediator then basically does is to help parties to walk down the pyramid of escalation in order to reach the phase in which they can settle their dispute themselves via dialogue.

While the above-mentioned authors emphasize the different phases preceding the settlement of a dispute, Keebet von Benda-Beckmann (2003) argues that the dispute process should not be considered after the final ruling has been issued. She in fact takes up a point previously made by Felstiner et al. (1980, 639), namely that "there is always a residuum of attitudes, learned techniques, and sensitivities that will, consciously or unconsciously, color later conflict." Felstiner et al. also argue that any given dispute might continue even after a settlement, or that the end of one dispute might lead in turn to a new grievance. Von Benda-Beckmann consequently argues that the transformation process enters a new phase when a dispute is settled by mediation, a court, or another authority and (together with the parties involved) returns to the social environment from which it originated. It is in this old (or more often: changed) social setting where the real outcome of the settlement is negotiated. Thus, it is possible to not only distinguish a pre-trial and a trial phase in the disputing process, but also a post-trial phase. And it is in this post-trial phase that disputes can continue in new forms or with new definitions over prolonged periods, with the trial simply being a point at which the dispute enters a new phase or becomes transformed in some way. It is because of this that social science research on disputing sometimes talks about dispute processing rather than dispute resolution (Merry 1987, 2065).

However, more important than subdividing disputes into phases or stages is the emphasis of Felstiner et al. on the transitions between the various phases. Such transitions (Mather and Yngvesson 1980) are caused by, and have consequences for, the parties involved, the scope of the conflict, and the entities adjudicating disputes. Furthermore, these transitions lead to a further development, in which the dyadic disagreement eventually evolves into a triadic process. According to Felstiner et al. (1980), such transformations are subjective, unstable, reactive, complicated, and incomplete. However, they need to be taken into account because they provide insight into parties' individual perceptions, behavior, and decision making; or in broader terms, into the why and how of the dispute process. For example, when a dispute is likely to be brought to court (a dispute institution), or when a lawyer becomes involved (a representative added), this will likely narrow the conflict down to a strictly legal case (i.e., the scope of the conflict changes). This change in scope in turn influences the potential tactics used and the relative probabilities of particular outcomes. Felstiner et al. emphasize that it is not possible to present subjects (i.e., what is being transformed) and agents (i.e., those who do the transformation) by means of a simple matrix, since every factor can be construed as both. In other words, during transformations the parties involved, the scope of the conflict, and the entities adjudicating disputes, among other factors, appear to be interactive.

In sum, disputes provide information about more than just law. Studying disputes is not only about trials. It is about disputing processes—including the pre-trial and the post-trial phase, in which the law plays a role. In other words, in contemporary legal anthropology research, disputes do not primarily serve as a means to understand law, but rather provide an insight into dispute processes, the behavior of human beings involved in the dispute, and the role of law in its resolution.

Lessons to be learned

A lot of knowledge in the field of mediation can be traced back to earlier legal anthropological research that aimed at describing and analyzing disputes and dispute settlement. As Simon Roberts has written, in most societies, even early nomadic hunters, 'meeting and talking' has been used to resolve disputes (Roberts 1979). Accordingly, legal anthropology has analyzed a wealth of information regarding alternative dispute resolution. In a way, legal anthropologists challenge traditional understandings of the centrality of adjudication to the maintenance of social order in modern society, and so does mediation. Mediation expresses a certain 'anti-law ideology' by claiming that non-adversarial ways of resolving conflict can create more sustainable solutions (Merry 1987, 2058).

Perhaps the most important lesson that can be learned from legal anthropology is that a dispute is a social construct. In other words, it is a process which takes place within a wider social context. As Merry argues, the definition of a dispute shifts with the audience to which it is presented, and each audience may actually redefine it, expressing the interactive relationship between mediation and its context (Merry 1987, 2061). Disputes and dispute settlement have been at the core of legal anthropological research since the 1940s. With the integration of the above-mentioned rule-centered paradigm and the process-oriented paradigm, scholars came to acknowledge that rules are applied and processes occur within a social, cultural and political context. Disputing, from the perspective of legal anthropology, is social behavior. It is informed by the parties' moral views about how to disagree, the meaning parties attach to consulting a mediator or going to court, social practices that indicate when and how to escalate disputes from a dyadic disagreement to a triadic one, and parties' notions of rights and entitlement. Therefore, legal anthropological research lies at the basis of the major premise that disputes often concern more than just a strict legal conflict (e.g., in terms of the background of the conflict, the parties, stakeholders and institutions involved, and the possible impact of the resolution in the future). Anthropology of law provides us with the tools for a holistic view on disputes and, as such, underscores the benefits that are often attributed to mediation.

Legal anthropological research, in combination with socio-legal research, has also taught us that disputing is a dynamic process and that disputes develop in stages or phases. Snyder, Felstiner et al., Glasl, and von Benda-Beckmann, respectively, identified pre-conflict, conflict, and dispute stages; naming, blaming, and claiming; problem, conflict, and 'war'; and the pre-trial, trial, and post-trial phases. In line with what Kritzer (2011) views as the 'naming-blaming-claiming' schema as an abstraction of a more complex reality, it is fair to argue that this counts for the other models as well. Different phases overlap, and parties and institutions easily switch between being an object or a subject during the whole process. But still, these models prove to be very helpful in analyzing disputes in a scholarly way, as well as for mediators in a more practical way. It is the transitions among these phases that deserve special attention, in theory as well as in practice. This is very relevant for mediators de-escalating a dispute in order to reach the phase in which disputing parties can settle their dispute themselves via dialogue.

In addition to these broad lessons that it has to offer, legal anthropology has had an impact on mediation in a couple of more specific ways as well. First, the well-known assumption that mediation leads to win-win settlements, while court decisions provide win-lose solutions, has its origin in legal anthropological research. The distinction between court decisions and mediated settlements in terms of outcome and processes was first introduced by Philip Gulliver (1979) more than 30 years ago. He has become famous for his positing a sharp dichotomy between negotiations (i.e., joint-decision making) and adjudication (i.e., decision making by a third party). It is this sharp distinction that paved the way for acknowledging the differences in the outcome of these two alternatives. In general, anthropological studies indicate that when disputants are bound by multi-stranded social relationships, they will seek to compromise their differences (win-win), but when they have only single-stranded social ties, they will seek victory in adversarial contests (win-lose) rather than attempt to reach compromise (Merry 1987, 2061), and this is reflected in the way they choose institutions.

Second, the principle of voluntariness in a mediation process supposes a parties' free choice for an alternative institution. And this idea of parties choosing among different institutions in order to select the one they feel best serves their own interests obviously stems from the pluralistic paradigm in legal anthropology. The phenomenon of selecting parties is described in the literature as 'forum shopping,' and this concept was introduced into legal anthropology by Keebet von Benda-Beckmann (1981). Legal anthropological research, however, proves that forum shopping does not involve a strictly rational choice that takes place within a context of different legal forums operating on the same level playing field. The decision-making process is often far more complex than just "a simple outcome of a rational deliberation of pros and cons" (Shahar 2013). Legal anthropological research shows that forum shopping practices are embedded in social, cultural, and political contexts that render legal scholars' voluntary rational choice assumptions invalid (Shahar 2013). As a matter of fact, it was Keebet von Benda-Beckmann herself who, more than 30 years ago, suggested that "social control at the village level" influenced people's choice-making behavior (Benda-Beckmann 1981, 143). And, as demonstrated by legal anthropology's pluralistic approach, there is no reason to suggest that such social control does not play a role in contemporary Western contexts as well. Therefore, we need to acknowledge that forum shopping (or in the context of this chapter: Selecting mediation rather than resorting to courts of law) might not be possible under all circumstances. Differences in power, education, social class, and culture, in relation to 'access to mediation' (or in general: Access to justice), might very well influence parties' ability to choose (Simon Thomas 2015).

The significance of disparities in power is another thing we have learned from legal anthropological research. The argument that the preconditions for access to mediation are not equally distributed constitutes one of the most cogent criticisms of mediation. Similarly, wide disparities in individuals' ability to stand up for their own interests would certainly seem a valid argument against mandatory mediation. In a negotiated process such as mediation, the danger of the negative influence of power imbalances on the final outcome cannot be understated, according to certain critics. Accordingly, these critics hold that people should not be pushed into an alternative in which they have to rely so heavily on their own skills. There are still other reasons for withholding an endorsement of mandatory mediation (which is expected to soon be proposed in the Netherlands). For example, based on what we know about the different stages and phases of a conflict, and the consequences of transformations, the whole idea of a mandatory institution introduces an a priori transformation of the dispute. Additionally, parties' awareness that, if mediation fails, a court procedure will follow (and this is another part of the proposed Dutch rules) is a factor which is certain to affect the course of any given mediation process. The dynamics of the mediation in such a case will differ sharply from 'pure mediation,' because the expectation of an imposed settlement will inevitably alter the meaning of the event for all actors (Merry 1978, 2066). In general, as courts or legislators move to make alternatives mandatory, the ability to choose forums is being transferred from individual disputants to the institutions that assign cases to particular forums, and this very process transforms the scope of the conflict.

Conclusion

This chapter has shown that there is a comprehensive legal anthropological literature on disputes and disputing processes that can be usefully applied to mediation. First, legal anthropology teaches us to turn the legal paradigm upside down. Thus, instead of looking at different ways that laws can be applied to conflicts, legal anthropologists examine the ways conflicts are resolved, with law representing only one possible approach. This paves the way for a scholarly perspective of mediation, as part of a set of alternative dispute resolutions, on the part of an established legal discipline. Second, legal anthropological studies on disputing afford the important insight that there is a dynamic interaction between dispute resolution and social practice. Legal anthropology thus shows that dispute settlement is a dynamic process, embedded within a structure of social relationships, practices of handling conflict, and normative principles, within which positions become transformed in the course of that process. Consequently, mediation should not be seen as an isolated process, disconnected from the outer world, and instead it should be studied in relation to the social reality in which it takes place. Legal anthropology can therefore be viewed as providing a clarifying prism that allows scholars who study mediation to draw empirically and theoretically grounded conclusions as to what it really means for people, why it sometimes provides effective and sustainable solutions, and in which cases its results prove unsatisfactory.

References

Abel, Richard L., ed. 1982. *The Politics of Informal Justice. Volume1. The American Experience.* New York: Academic Press.

Avruch, Kevin. 1998. *Culture & Conflict Resolution.* Washington, D.C: United States Institue of Peace Press.

Avruch, Kevin, and Peter W. Black. 1996. "ADR, Palau, and the Contribution of Anthropology." In *Anthropological Contributions to Conflict Resolution*, edited by Alvin W. Wolfe, Honggang Yang, and Michael V. Angrosino, 29: 47–63. Athens, GA; London: The University of Georgia Press.

Benda-Beckmann, Franz von. 1979. *Property in Social Continuity: Continuity and Change in the Maintenance of Property Relationships Through Time in Minangkabau, West Sumatra.* The Hague: Martinus Nijhoff.

Benda-Beckmann, Franz von. 2002. "Who's Afraid of Legal Pluralism?" *The Journal of Legal Pluralism and Unofficial Law* 34 (47): 37–82. 10.1080/07329113.2002.10756563

Benda-Beckmann, Keebet von. 1981. "Forum Shopping and Shopping Forums: Dispute Processing in a Minangkabau Village in West Sumatra." *The Journal of Legal Pluralism and Unofficial Law* 13 (19): 117–59. 10.1080/07329113.1981.10756260

Benda-Beckmann, Keebet von. 2003. "The Environment of Disputes." In *The Dynamics of Power and the Rule of Law: Essays on Africa and Beyond*, edited by Wim van Binsbergen, 235–45, Leiden: African Studies Centre.

Bohannan, Paul. 1957. *Justice and Judgment Among the Tiv.* London: Routledge. 10.4324/9781351037303

Comaroff, John L., and Simon Roberts. 1981. *Rules and Processes: The Cultural Logic of Dispute in an African Context.* Chicago: University of Chicago Press.

Donovan, James M. 2007. *Legal Anthropology: An Introduction.* Lanham, MD: Altamira Press.

Felstiner, William L.F., Richard L. Abel, and Austin Sarat. 1980. "The Emergence and Transformation of Disputes: Naming, Blaming, Claiming … ." *Law & Society Review* 15 (3–4): 631–54. 10.2307/3053505

The perspective of legal anthropology

Fitzpatrick, Peter. 1980. *Law and State in Papua New Guinea*. London: Academic Press.

Gibbs, James L. 1963. "The Kpelle Moot: A Therapeutic Model for the Informal Settlement of Disputes." *Africa* 33 (1): 1–11. 10.2307/1157793

Glasl, Friedrich. 2000. *Help! Conflicten*. Zeist: Christofoor Uitgeverij.

Greenhouse, Carol J. 1985. "Mediation: A Comparative Approach." *Man. New Series* 20 (1): 90–114.

Griffiths, Anne. 2002. "Legal pluralism." In *An Introduction to Law and Social Theory*, edited by Reza Banakar and Max Travers, 289–310. Oxford: Hart Publishing.

Griffiths, John. 1986. "What Is Legal Pluralism?" *The Journal of Legal Pluralism and Unofficial Law* 18 (24): 1–55. 10.1080/07329113.1986.10756387

Gulliver, Philip. 1968. *Social Control in African Society: A Study of the Arusha: Agricultural Masai of Northern Tanganyika*. London: Routledge and Kegan Paul.

Gulliver, Philip Hugh. 1979. *Disputes and Negotiations: A Cross-Cultural Perspective. Studies on Law and Social Control*. New York: Academic Press.

Hertzfeld, Michael. 1992. *The Social Production of Indifference: Exploring the Symbolic Roots of Western Bureaucracy*. Chicago: University of Chicago Press.

Holleman, J.F. 1973. "Trouble-Cases and Trouble-Less Cases in the Study of Customary Law and Legal Reform." *Law & Society Review* 7 (4): 585–610. 10.2307/3052962

Just, Peter, June Starr, Jane F. Collier, Laura Nader, and Lawrence Rosen. 1992. "History, Power, Ideology, and Culture: Current Directions in the Anthropology of Law." *Law & Society Review* 26 (2): 373. 10.2307/3 053902

Krishnan, Jayanth K. 2012. "Academic SAILERS: The Ford Foundation and the Efforts to Shape Legal Education in Africa, 1957–1977." *American Journal of Legal History* 52 (3): 261–324. 10.1093/ajlh/52.3.261

Kritzer, Herbert M. 2011. "The Antecedents of Disputes: Complaining and Claiming." *Oñati Socio-Legal Series* 1 (6): 1–31. 10.2139/ssrn.1631796

Llewellyn, Karl and Edward Hoebel. 1987. *The Cheyenne Way: Conflict and Case Law in Primitive Jurisprudence*. Norman, OK: University of Oklahoma Press.

Malinowski, Bronislaw. [1926] 1985. *Crime and Custom in Savage Society*. Totowa: Rowman & Allanheld Publishers.

Mather, Lynn, and Barbara Yngvesson. 1980. "Language, Audience, and the Transformation of Disputes." *Law & Society Review* 15 (3–4): 775–821. 10.2307/3053512

Merry, Sally Engle. 1987. 'Disputing without culture." *Harvard Law Review* 100 (8): 2057–73.

Merry, Sally Engle. 1988. "Legal Pluralism." *Law & Society Review* 22 (5): 869–96. 10.2307/3053638

Miller, Richard E., and Austin Sarat. 1980. "Grievances, Claims, and Disputes: Assessing the Adversary Culture." *Law & Society Review* 15 (3–4): 525. 10.2307/3053502

Moore, Sally Falk. 1978. *Law as Process: An Anthropological Approach*. London: Routledge and Kegan Paul.

Moore, Sally Falk, eds. 2005. *Law and Anthropology: A Reader*. Malden, Oxford, Carlton: Blackwell.

Nader, Laura. 2002. *The Life of the Law: Anthropological Projects*. Berkeley, Los Angeles, London: University of California Press.

Nader, Laura, and Harry Todd Jr., eds. 1978. *The Disputing Process: Law in Ten Societies*. New York: Colombia University Press.

Pirie, Fernanda. 2013. *The Anthropology of Law*. Oxford: Oxford University Press. 10.1093/acprof:oso/97801 99696840.001.0001

Pospisil, Leopold. 1958. *Kapauku Papuans and Their Law*. New Haven: Department of Anthropology, Yale University.

Radcliffe-Brown, Alfred. 1952. *Structure and Function in Primitive Society: Essays and Addresses*. London: Cohen and West.

Roberts, Simon. 1979. *Order and Dispute: An Introduction to Legal Anthropology*. Harmondsworth: Penguin.

Sack, Peter and Jonathan Aleck, eds. 1992. *Law and Anthropology*. Aldershot: Dartmouth Publishing.

Shahar, Ido. 2013. "Forum Shopping Between Civil and Shari'a Courts: Maintenance Suits in Contemporary Jerusalem." In *Religion in Disputes: Pervasiveness of Religious Normativity in Disputing Processes*, edited by Franz von Benda-Beckmann, 147–64, New York: Palgrave.

Sieder, Rachel. 1997. *Customary Law and Democratic Transition in Guatemala*. London: Institute of Latin America Studies.

Sierra, María Teresa and Victoria Chenaut. 2002. "Los debates recientes y actuales en la antropología jurídica. Las corrientes anglosajonas." In *Antropología jurídica. Perspectivas socioculturales en el estudio del derecho*, edited by E. Krotz, 116–23. Rubí: Anthropos.

Simon Thomas, Marc. 2015. "Access to Mediation." http://blog.montaignecentre.com/index.php/en/

Simon Thomas, Marc. 2016. "Theorizing Mediation: Lessons Learned from Legal Anthropology", *Utrecht Law Review* 12 (1): 50–60. 10.18352/ulr.325

Snyder, Francis G. 1981. "Anthropology, Dispute Processes and Law: A Critical Introduction." *British Journal of Law and Society* 8 (2): 141–80. 10.2307/1409719

Starr, June and Jane Collier (eds.). 1989. *History and Power in the Study of Law: New Directions in Legal Anthropology*. Ithaca, NY: Cornell University Press.

Starr, June and Mark Goodale. 2002. *Practicing Ethnography in Law: New Dialogues, Enduring Methods*. New York: Palgrave Macmillan.

Turner, Victor. 1957. *Schism and Continuity in an African Society: A Study of Ndembu Village Life*. Manchester: Manchester University Press.

29
ANTHROPOLOGICAL APPROACHES TO CULTURE IN CONFLICT MEDIATION

Rebecca Golbert

Introduction

I loved my first mediation class. I loved learning about the form and the process of mediation and putting it into practice in simulated sessions. However, as an anthropologist, I was struck by the lack of consideration of who the parties might be, what cultural values, behaviors, and expectations they might bring to the table, and more broadly, whether mediation might take different forms in different social and cultural contexts. This was a universal model of mediation and of mediator, subsuming all parties within the rightness of its flow and the purpose of its form. As a student of mediation, I loved the simplicity of this model; as an anthropologist, I knew it did not reflect the more complicated social and cultural reality of our world. This duality resulted in my first paper on the topic, 'An Anthropologist's Approach to Mediation' (Golbert 2008), attempting to problematize the North American model of mediation I was learning in the classroom in the context of a broader comparative and cross-cultural literature on mediation and conflict resolution.

Anthropologists have in fact been studying dispute processes within and across cultures for a very long time. They rely on and contribute to a rich body of ethnographic literature to examine case studies of conflict and wide-ranging modes of conflict resolution in the field (see Merry 1984; Greenhouse 1985; Nader 1972; Wehr and Lederach 1991; Avruch 1998; Augsburger 1992; Fry 2000). These scholars approach the fields of law and dispute resolution with a distinctly anthropological lens, often building on one another's scholarship. Sally Engle Merry, Laura Nader, and Carol Greenhouse have shaped the current field of legal anthropology; Jean Paul Lederach and Kevin Avruch have lent their dual expertise in anthropology and mediation to the field of international peacebuilding. Writing from the field of international relations, Jacob Bercovitch nonetheless approaches international mediation with the subjectivity of an anthropologist (1991; Golbert 2008, 94–5). Marc Simon Thomas writes, "There is quite an extensive and excellent legal anthropology literature on disputes and dispute settlement and this article argues that insights drawn from these writings can be fruitfully applied to mediation" (Simon Thomas 2016, 52). Sally Engle Merry describes the underlying concerns of anthropologists in the following way:

> Anthropologists are interested in the mechanisms that exist for the maintenance of order in a society. They seek to determine the range of processes which produce order and induce individuals to confirm to social rules. The courts are only one such process. Many small-scale societies lack state organization and any formal legal apparatus, yet maintain order

DOI: 10.4324/9781003227441-35

through a wide range of informal mechanisms such as gossip, fear of ostracism, dependence on others for economic assistance and political support, and mediation by village elders. These informal systems are pervasive and far older than the earliest states. They persist even within contemporary state societies. Consequently, the legal system itself should rightly be viewed as an alternative, rather than the other way around.

(Merry 1984, 277)

Merry draws a connection between "modes of dispute resolution and social structure," suggesting that informal social pressures work best in small-scale societies and highly interdependent social communities (Merry 1984, 280). In a similar vein, Carol Greenhouse notes that the framework and style of mediation may be shaped by access (or lack thereof) to wider sources of authority and legitimacy (Greenhouse 1985, 97–8). At the same time, Merry suggests that "[d]ispute-resolution systems are additive," and in complex societies, informal and formal systems of dispute resolution may be layered one upon another (Merry 1984, 280).

Despite the long history of anthropology studying dispute processes, anthropological perspectives are often absent from the discourse and practice of conflict mediation (Magistro 1997, 9). In the international realm, John Magistro suggests that conflict mediation is dominated by political science and international studies frameworks, which lack the "field-based, microanalytical understanding of intra- and inter-community relations deriving from an anthropological perspective" (1997, 9). The alternative dispute resolution (ADR) framework of my mediation handbook (Kovach 2004[1994]) and curriculum, while a comprehensive overview of theory and practice, also omitted anthropological perspectives on mediation and dispute resolution, from decades of ethnographic case studies in the field, triggering my initial attempt to rectify this omission (Golbert 2008). Simon Thomas describes the literature on mediation as a largely descriptive and applied field, addressed to practicing mediators and aimed at putting mediation into practice (2016, 50, 52). Even in this more applied context, Magistro asserts the importance of including an anthropological perspective in understanding and practicing mediation:

Anthropologists are trained holistically to understand a broad range of social, economic, political, and environmental processes that shape ethnic and cultural identities. Interestingly, our anthropological knowledge and preoccupation with core concepts like culture, ethnicity, conflict, and indigenous knowledge and practices have not been widely translated into the institutional practice of peace building or conflict mediation. We need only to look within our own communities to see that the economic, political, and social (read ethnic) tensions are rapidly rising here at home. This begs the fundamental question of our role as educators in mitigating conflict both domestically and abroad.

(Magistro 1997, 9)

So, what does anthropology have to offer the current field of conflict mediation? What does it mean to take an anthropological approach to the field?

Culture, conflict, and mediation

In exploring the relevance of anthropology to mediation, it is important first to examine the interconnections among anthropology, culture, conflict, and mediation and to define these concepts more thoroughly. Although the practice of mediation exists across cultures, the North American model of mediation is not universally applied. Cultural variation shapes the modes of conflict resolution from one culture to the next, including whether an intervention takes the form of mediation or another form of conflict management, prevention, or de-escalation, and whether and in

Anthropological approaches to culture

what capacity a third party becomes involved. Douglas Fry describes the careful balance between universalism and particularism in dispute resolution in this way:

> On the one hand, conflict management mechanisms can be viewed as highly specific to the particular cultural system within which they operate (Avruch 1991). On the other hand, cross-cultural comparisons reveal general mechanisms of conflict management. For example, a comparative perspective shows that mediation (i.e., third-party assisted negotiations of a settlement) occurs in many cultures, whereas at a more specific level, the subtleties of mediation processes vary with the plethora of cultural values, beliefs, institutions, social roles, and so on found in different societies.
>
> *(Fry 2000, 334)*

So how do scholars understand culture and its role? It is helpful to start by defining what it is not. On one recent morning, I received a blog post in my inbox, entitled "How to Overcome Cultural Barriers in Negotiation" (PON staff Dec. 16, 2021). The title jarred me. Farther down the page, after scanning some descriptions of what to expect in negotiating with Germans, or Chinese, or Mexicans, I read that the blog had been adapted from another article, 'Coping with Culture at the Bargaining Table.' Both framings approach culture as an obstacle, a hurdle, or a problem, that requires 'coping' strategies to 'overcome.' Let's examine more holistic ways of understanding culture and its role in human interactions, conflict, and conflict mediation. In his seminal book, *The Interpretation of Cultures*, Clifford Geertz defines culture as value-laden and meaning-centered, a fundamental quality of human existence and experience:

> Believing, with Max Weber, that man is an animal suspended in webs of significance he himself as spun, I take culture to be those webs, and the analysis of it to be therefore not an experimental science in search of law but an interpretive one in search of meaning.
>
> *(Geertz 1973, 5)*

Kevin Avruch approaches the concept of culture through the lens of the individual rather than the group, noting the role that individuals play in creating, bearing, and transmitting culture within a group or across generations: "This reorientation supports the idea that individuals reflect or embody multiple cultures and that 'culture' is always psychologically and socially distributed in a group" (1998, 5). Avruch strives for a destabilizing definition of culture, one that is flexible and complicated, a social quality of individuals and groups, and at the same time, can be reflected through multiple, diverse cultural encounters on the part of individuals. In my article, 'An Anthropologist's Approach to Mediation' (Golbert 2008), I propose a definition that builds on Geertz and Avruch:

> Culture may be defined as a set of values, beliefs, symbols, and traditions, socially transmitted within a group and across generations, constituting the framework through which individuals in that group interpret and give meaning to their own and others' experiences.
>
> *(2008, 85)*

In refashioning this definition today, I would, like Avruch, take greater store in the multiplicity of cultures that individuals embody, and through which they interpret and give meaning to their experiences and encounters. If we approach culture as an anthropologist, we grasp a more dynamic, multifaceted notion of culture, one that is constantly in flux; this notion of culture-in-motion is no less true when we explore the relationship between culture and conflict. In this framing, culture is not something that can be mastered, or overcome, or reduced to a simplistic cultural understanding of social reality. So too, we cannot assume any single approach to conflict and conflict resolution based on an individual's social and cultural affiliations (Golbert 2008, 85).

Before turning to conflict mediation, it is worth defining what meanings and values scholars ascribe to the terms conflict or dispute. A conflict might arise from diverging worldviews, or from the perception of irreconcilable differences over an issue, value, or belief. Conflict may also escalate over land, power, or resources (Simon Thomas 2016, 56). Is conflict inherently bad or good? Is it destructive or constructive? Is conflict always something to be resolved? The conflict diagram (or Mode instrument), a significant teaching tool for ADR, displays the range of individual approaches to conflict, suggesting that individuals operate on a scale from assertiveness to cooperativeness, alternatively competing, avoiding, accommodating, compromising, or collaborating (Kilmann and Thomas 1977). Cultural approaches to conflict take a broader view and suggest that such individual responses are also culturally informed. For example, Douglas Fry writes, "In some societies, avoidance is the culturally favored way of dealing with conflict" (2000, 335). Drawing from legal anthropology, Marc Simon Thomas describes a dispute as a "social construct" and disputing as "social behaviour." Moreover, he places disputes and disputing within the larger social, cultural, and political contexts in which they occur. So too, Simon Thomas suggests that disputes often develop in stages—such as "naming-blaming-claiming" (2016, 58–9). One can imagine that the stages experienced by parties to a conflict may also vary according to social practice. David Augsburger further complexifies these definitions when he writes, "Conflicts are universally similar, culturally distinct, and individually unique" (1992, 17). Like individuals who embody multiple cultures, conflicts are complex, reside across cultures, and yet, are both culturally specific and individuated. Drawing from John Paul Lederach, Augsburger suggests that conflicts emerge from a clash of social realities, when the single reality we assumed to exist is shattered to reveal multiple realities (1992, 17).

Conflict resolution, then, is the renewed search for a common meaning, the renegotiation of a shared reality, after the rupture and recognition of multiple realities and frames of reference (Augsburger 1992, 17). Individually, socially, culturally, and cross-culturally, this negotiation of a new consensus may take different forms. Scholars point out a range of conflict management tools for addressing conflict in different societies: "Across cultural settings, persons engage in avoidance and toleration, attempt negotiations, exercise aggressive self-help, and rely on the assistance of various kinds of third-party settlement agents to resolve conflicts. Particular cultures use some procedures more than others" (Fry 2000, 347). Scholars also emphasize the prevalence of mediation across cultures. Augsburger asserts "[t]hroughout virtually all traditional societies, mediation of conflicts by trusted persons or groups is the most frequently used process of dispute settlement" (1992, 191–2). Avruch writes, that "in small-scale societies, [...] mediation has much to recommend it. This is because mediation aims to preserve and restore social relationships by leaving the parties in charge of their own negotiation and its outcome" (1998, 82). This emphasis on preserving and restoring relationships suggests the importance of mediation in close-knit communities and societies, where familial, social, cultural, and economic networks and structures overlap (Avruch 1998, 82; Golbert 2008, 87). However, what constitutes mediation—as form, process, third-party intervention, and goals and outcomes—may be shaped by distinctive cultural contexts as well as the relationship of mediation to sources of authority and the state (Fry 2000, 336; Greenhouse 1985, 97–8).

Here anthropologists contrast other cultural models of mediation to the North American model of mediation. In a recent volume entitled *On Mediation*, the authors offer the following definition:

> Mediation is commonly defined as a non-violent, cost-saving mode of negotiating, regulating, or settling conflicts and disputes between two or more actors using the help of a third party as mediator who, in contrast to an adjudicator, has no authority to pass final judgement.
> *(Härter, Hillemanns, and Schlee 2020, 1)*

Anthropological approaches to culture

Despite this seemingly neutral and broad definition of mediation, the model of mediation taught and applied in the United States and exported abroad includes distinct assumptions about the practice of mediation and the role of mediators. In my earlier article, I suggest:

> The approach to mediation that has developed in North America has distinctive ideas about the structure and process of mediation, the qualifications and role of the mediator, the relationship of the mediator to the parties, and the relationship between the parties. Debates about many of these issues abound within the field of North American mediation, raising ethical issues about the practice of mediation and professional issues about the boundaries of mediation as a field. [...] An examination of mediation as it is perceived and practiced in other national and cultural settings, and in cross-cultural and international settings, may place these and other issues within a broader comparative framework and allow us to rethink some of our assumptions about what makes mediation work in differing cultural contexts.
>
> *(Golbert 2008, 83)*

The North American model, applied by mediators and taught in mediation seminars and trainings, frames mediation as a discrete process, with a beginning, middle, and end. Identifying ground rules, delivering opening statements, identifying the problem, brainstorming and problem-solving solutions, looking for common ground or zones of agreement, seeking consensus for a mediated agreement—these structural elements form stages in the process toward a mediated settlement. The third-party mediator facilitates the transition between the stages and coaxes the parties toward consensus (Kovach 2004[1994], 34–8). Ethical considerations emerge concerning the selection of the mediator, the relationship of the mediator to the parties, and the relationship between the parties, impacting whether the parties meet face to face, or express their concerns, interests, and needs to one another only through caucusing with the mediator, who shuttles between the parties to reach a resolution. In this framework, the mediator is generally expected to be neutral, impartial, and without conflict of interest or prior relationship to the parties (Davidheiser 2008, 61–2; Simon Thomas 2016, 50; Kovach 2004[1994], 44–7, 211–4).

The qualifications and role of the mediator, in particular, speak to cultural distinctions within the practice of mediation. As Avruch asserts, the notion that the ideal mediator should be neutral, impartial, and without prior relationship to the parties is unsupported by the ethnographic record (1998, 84). Avruch writes, for example, 'that "mediator" is a complex term that covers many different sorts of third-party roles, so that potential variations on the theme (including cultural ones) are to be expected' (1998, 83). The mediation literature sometimes distinguishes between mediator styles—more facilitative or more directive—in guiding the parties toward settlement. However, Augsburger proposes a continuum of mediator roles—observer, chairperson, enunciator, prompter, leader, arbiter—and suggests that a mediator may shift from facilitative to evaluative along with the stages of mediation (1992, 194). Both scholars build on the framework of third-party involvement developed by Paul Wehr and John Paul Lederach for Central American disputes, particularly the concept of the "insider-partial" (Wehr and Lederach 1991; Golbert 2008, 88). This concept captures the importance of a mediator's trust and connectedness in many mediation contexts: "The insider-partial is the 'mediator from within the conflict,' whose acceptability to the conflictants is rooted not in distance from the conflict or objectivity regarding the issues, but rather in connectedness and trusted relationships with the conflict parties" (Wehr and Lederach 1991, 87). Pointing to the prevalence of outsider mediators in international peacemaking processes, Kristina Roepstorff and Anna Bernhard emphasize the importance of including insider mediators, who have the "advantage of an in-depth knowledge of the conflict context, its dynamics, as well as the involved parties and their interests" (2013, 164). Noting that insider and outsider are "relative terms" and "fluid categories," they nonetheless define insiders as "actors who are directly affected by and have a stake in the conflict and the impact of the conflict resolution initiatives" (2013, 164–5). Insider-partials are invested in the resolution of the conflict and will remain to implement the terms of the agreement in the aftermath of the mediation. Unlike the outsider mediator, they cannot leave the conflict context to go home (Roepstorff and Bernhard 2013, 168).

The importance of a trustworthy relationship between the mediator and the parties relates to cultural variations in other aspects of mediation, including its level of formality, the presence or absence of additional stakeholders to the conflict, the goals of the mediation, and the place of mediation within the broader system of dispute resolution of the society, the state, or the international community. Some examples from ethnographic and empirical studies reveal both the prevalence of mediation and its cross-cultural variation.

Case studies of mediation across cultures

Douglas Fry draws on cases studies from the ethnographic literature to examine conflict management in cross-cultural perspective. His examples reflect the fluidity of boundaries between different modes of dispute resolution as well as the unique cultural contexts in which these practices emerge (2000, 341–5). In one distinctive example, Fry describes the becharaa', a mediation process among the Semai of Malaysia. According to Fry, the Semai uphold strong cultural values of nonviolence; however, when a dispute cannot be averted, the headman of the Semai band convenes a *becharaa'* assembly that includes the disputants, their relatives, and other members of the community. This group mediation process emphasizes the cohesiveness and interdependency of the band community. The disputants thus address their grievances to the whole group, rather than to one another. The headman, whose role as third-party mediator mirrors the insider-partial closely connected to the parties and the dispute, plays an active and directive role in guiding the *becharaa'* process, examining the dispute from all angles and evaluating the disputants' behaviors, with the goals of diffusing the emotions of the conflict, addressing the substantive issues, and promoting reconciliation. The focus remains on relationship preservation and social harmony. In his closing statement, the headman shifts toward the role of arbitrator, voicing the consensus of the community on how the dispute should be resolved and applying social pressure on the disputants to accept the proposed resolution. As Fry notes, "the *becharaa'* has elements of both mediation and arbitration," and the process is defined strongly by the social and cultural values and practices of the group (2000, 341–3).

In their empirical study, Jacob Bercovitch and Ole Elgström explore culture in international mediation, seeking to understand its impact on the management and resolution of international conflict (2001). They write against a long history in international relations of emphasizing national interests, power, and diplomacy and minimalizing both the relevance of culture and its interconnectedness with these phenomena (2001, 9–10). Although Bercovitch and Elgström begin with a complex, dynamic, and multifaceted definition of culture in social life, the authors in fact seek to operationalize culture to measure its effect on mediation outcomes (2001, 5–6, 11–2). They acknowledge that cultural differences weave throughout the international mediation process, affecting the parties, the mediator, the context, and the process of mediation. They thus hypothesize the following: "Cultural differences exert a significant impact on mediation outcomes, so that the greater the differences the less likelihood of a successful outcome" (2001, 14). In their research design, the authors review empirical data on international conflicts and international mediation (in the period of 1945–1995), and they apply a somewhat cruder measurement of culture, including geographical proximity, type of political system, level of political rights, level of civil liberties, and religion. Although international conflicts tend to occur within the same region, the states in conflict often have significant political, social, cultural, and religious differences (2001, 15–6). The authors' analysis of the data set suggests a strong correlation between culture and mediation outcomes:

Anthropological approaches to culture

> Cultural differences present some of the most formidable challenges to mediators. [...] [W]hen conflicts take place within the same geographical region, and thus presumably between states with some convergent perceptions, hopes and fears, the success rate for mediation is 40%. When countries belong to different geographical regions, mediation's success rate is only 24%. Mediation is also much more likely to be successful when the countries in conflict share the same level of political rights, civil liberties and religion.
>
> *(Elgström and Bercovitch 2001, 17)*

The authors acknowledge the risks of reducing the complexity and dynamism of culture to more crude, measurable elements (2001, 15). I would add to this critique, that focusing primarily on elements of national culture—religion, geography, political system, social and political rights—obscures the diversity of identities and cultures, both of individuals and social groups, from within the state, that can also impact outcomes of cross-cultural and international mediation processes. Bercovitch and Elgström's empirical study would best be accompanied by in-depth ethnographic case studies of international conflicts and mediations. Nonetheless, the authors successfully demonstrate that culture and context matter a great deal in international mediation, shaping the behaviors and experiences of the parties and the mediator and impacting significantly the mediation process; culture and context, thus, should not be overlooked.

Mark Davidheiser searches for a methodology of intercultural mediation that will be responsive to the complexity and diversity of culture and worldviews by drawing on his own experience as a mediator in the United States and his field research on third-party peacemaking in West Africa (2008). At the macro level, Davidheiser contrasts the Gambian model of mediation to his experience with American mediation, noting that the Gambian mediators he encountered were more connected to the parties and the conflict and more directive in their style—reflective of the insider-partial profile defined by Lederach and others. So too, Gambian mediators focused more on reconciliation than on issues and interests. At the same time, at the meso level, Davidheiser finds significant variation in mediation behavior among and within Gambian social groups. He writes, for example, that "even members of the same ethnic, gender, religious, and age group exhibited marked divergences in worldview and mediation styles" (2008, 70–1). This finding of sociocultural diversity within the Gambian case study of conflict mediation has implications for American mediation. Davidheiser evaluates existing methods for making intercultural mediation more culturally sensitive—such as awareness of differing communication styles, ethnic matching of mediators and participants, or cultural competency—and finds them crude and simplistic. He describes a particularly salient example of the deficiencies of matching, cited in a Canadian study by Viswanthan and Ptak, in which the interplay of gender and ethnicity reveals the complexity of identity. A Chinese woman in a divorce mediation requests not to be matched with a Chinese mediator for fear that patriarchal attitudes about women and divorce within Chinese culture will impinge upon her ability to make claims on her former spouse (2008, 71–4). Davidheiser concludes:

> In summation, matching, like most intercultural methodologies, generally cannot be said to do justice to worldviews. Whether due to practical limitations or otherwise, matching reduces culture to stereotypical identity categories that may not correspond with disputants' worldviews.
>
> *(Davidheiser 2008, 74)*

Conclusions

Davidheiser's research on intergroup and intragroup variation within Gambian mediation informs his approach to intercultural mediation in the U.S. domestic context, and particularly his call for mediation methodologies to address the complex, multifaceted cultural frameworks within which individuals and groups interpret and give meaning to social practices and experiences. Conflict and conflict resolution are part and parcel of social practice. Davidheiser worries about the ability of current mediation models and methodologies to be flexible and adaptive to cultural diversity, and he suggests the "need for an open and integrative approach, underlying the value of process flexibility" (2008, 77).

Culture and context matter. Davidheiser's call to complexify our model of intercultural mediation is similar to my conclusions in *An Anthropologist's Approach to Mediation*: "An approach to cross-cultural and international mediation that is truly responsive to context and culture must do more than explain and translate important cultural differences; it must attempt to incorporate dimensions of cultural difference into the mediation model" (Golbert 2008, 97). Today, I might go a step further and argue for the need to train mediators to hold an anthropological approach to mediation that takes culture and worldview seriously and understands them not as superficial and secondary concerns but as fundamental to the ways in which the parties give meaning to all aspects of the mediation process—the dispute itself, the role of the mediator, the relationship of the parties, the goals and outcomes of mediation, and the parties' own behaviors, needs, and responses throughout the difference phases of dispute resolution.

So too, an anthropological approach to culture in conflict mediation should take "an open and integrative approach" that includes multiple dimensions of identity and belonging, such as gender, sexuality, socioeconomic status, geography, language, and religion, as part of a broad and complicated understanding of culture, context, and worldview and the multifaceted ways they may shape the mediation process, the parties, the mediator, and their interactions. Scholars such as Laura Nader have expressed concerns about equity and the imbalance of power in mediation, whether tied to race, class, or education level. Not all parties may be equipped to represent themselves or stand up for their interests in mediation. Some scholars have further argued that an emphasis on culture risks obfuscating other types of power differences and inequalities (Nader 2002; Simon Thomas 2016, 52, 60; Davidheiser 2008, 64, 66). However, as Avruch clarifies, a definition of culture that considers and incorporates the multiple realities of individuals and groups should encompass questions and concerns about equity and power as well. As Avruch writes,

> [B]y linking culture to individuals and emphasizing the number and diversity of social and experiential settings that individuals encounter, we expand the scope of reference of culture to encompass not just quasi- or pseudo-kinship groupings (tribe, ethnic group, and nation are the usual ones) but groupings that derive from profession, occupation, class, religion, or region.
>
> *(Avruch 1998, 5)*

An anthropological approach to mediation, then, must also address "[d]ifferences in power, education, social class and culture, in relation to 'access to mediation' (or in general: access to justice)" (Simon Thomas 2016, 60). Anthropologists and mediators must nimbly resolve these questions and incorporate them into the mediation model, while also considering the relationship of mediation to other modes of dispute resolution, including the courts and the broader social and legal system, in the given society, state, or international community. In the contexts of pluralistic legal and social institutions, parties should continue to have a choice about whether to resolve their conflicts through mediation, based on the flexibility and resiliency of mediation and of mediators to be responsive to their needs, values, and worldviews. Anthropological approaches to culture in mediation matter. We ignore them at our own peril.

References

Augsburger, David W. 1992. *Conflict Mediation across Cultures. Pathways and Patterns.* Louisville, KY.: Westminster/John Knox Pr.

Avruch, Kevin. 1991. "Introduction. Culture and Conflict Resolution." In *Conflict Resolution. Cross-Cultural Perspectives*, edited by Kevin Avruch, Peter W. Black, and Joseph A. Scimecca, 1–17. New York; Westport; London: Greenwood.

Avruch, Kevin. 1998. *Culture and Conflict Resolution.* Washington, DC: United States Institute of Peace Press.

Bercovitch, Jacob. 1991. "International Mediation." *Journal of Peace Research* 28 (1): 3–6. 10.1177/0022343391 028001002

Davidheiser, Mark. 2008. "Race, Worldviews, and Conflict Mediation: Black and White Styles of Conflict Revisited: Race, Worldviews, and Conflict Mediation." *Peace & Change* 33 (1): 60–89. 10.1111/j.1468-013 0.2007.00476.x

Elgström and Bercovitch. 2001. "Culture and International Mediation: Exploring Theoretical and Empirical Linkages." *International Negotiation* 6 (1): 3–23. 10.1163/15718060120848937

Fry, Douglas P. 2000. "Conflict Management in Cross-Cultural Perspective." In *Natural Conflict Resolution*, edited by Filippo Aureli and Frans B. M. de Waal, 334–51. Berkeley: University of California Press.

Geertz, Clifford J. 1973. "Thick Description: Toward an Interpretive Theory of Culture." In *The Interpretation of Cultures*, edited by Clifford J. Geertz, 3–30. New York: Basic Books.

Golbert, Rebecca. 2008. "An Anthropologist's Approach to Mediation." *Cadorzo Journal of Conflict Resolution* 11 (1): 81–97.

Greenhouse, Carol J. 1985. "Mediation: A Comparative Approach." *Man* 20 (1): 90–114. 10.2307/2802223

Härter, Karl, Carolin Hillemanns, and Günther Schlee, eds. 2020. *On Mediation: Historical, Legal, Anthropological, and International Perspectives.* New York, Oxford: Berghahn Books.

Kilmann, Ralph H., and Kenneth W. Thomas. 1977. "Developing a Forced-Choice Measure of Conflict-Handling Behavior: The 'Mode' Instrument." *Educational and Psychological Measurement* 37 (2): 309–25. 10.1177/001316447703700204

Kovach, Kimberlee K. 2004 [1994]. *Mediation: Principles and Practice.* St. Paul, MN: Thomson/West.

Magistro, John. 1997. "An Emerging Role for Applied Anthropology: Conflict Management and Dispute Resolution." *Practicing Anthropology* 19 (1): 5–9. 10.17730/praa.19.1.a566422474m82421

Merry, Sally Engle. 1984. "Anthropology and the Study of Alternative Dispute Resolution." *Journal of Legal Education* 34 (2): 277–83.

Nader, Laura. 1972. "Some Notes on John Burton's Papers on 'Resolution of Conflict.'" *International Studies Quarterly* 16 (1): 53–8. 10.2307/3013472

Nader, Laura. 2002. *The Life of the Law: Anthropological Projects.* Berkeley: University of California Press.

PON Staff. Dec. 16, 2021. "How to Overcome Cultural Barriers in Negotiation." International Negotiation Daily. https://www.pon.harvard.edu/daily/international-negotiation-daily/coping-with-culture-at-the-bargaining-table/

Roepstorff, Kristina, and Anna Bernhard. 2013. "Insider Mediation in Peace Processes: An Untapped Resource?" *Sicherheit & Frieden* 31 (3): 163–9. 10.5771/0175-274x-2013-3-163

Simon Thomas, Marc. 2016. "Theorizing Mediation: Lessons Learned from Legal Anthropology." *Utrecht Law Review* 12 (1): 50–60. 10.18352/ulr.325

Wehr, Paul, and John Paul Lederach. 1991. "Mediating Conflict in Central America." *Journal of Peace Research* 28 (1): 85–98. 10.1177/0022343391028001009

30

ANTHROPOLOGY AND MEDIATION IN AN ENVIRONMENTAL CONFLICT: WORLDVIEW TRANSLATION AS SYNTHESIS

Brenda J. Fitzpatrick

Introduction[1]

Every so often, a scholar calls for greater integration between the potentially synergistic fields of anthropology and conflict and peace studies (for example, Brown 2013; Denskus and Kosmatopoulos 2015; Sponsel 1994; Wolfe and Yang 1996). Indeed, anthropology and peace and conflict research and practice have much to offer each other. These fields share not only an interest in conflict but an emphasis on understanding without judging (through empathetic listening in conflict resolution and cultural relativism in anthropology) and intermediary roles involving the translation of perspectives, whether between conflicting parties or between ethnographic protagonists and audience. They also have complementary strengths. Anthropology's participant observation and elicitive ethnographic methods are well adapted for drawing out nuanced accounts of the cultural aspects of conflict. In contrast, conflict studies supplies knowledge of conflict dynamics and an applied orientation which anthropological studies of conflict have generally lacked. Yet these calls for integration have so far fallen flat. Scholars of conflict have rarely drawn on anthropology's profound explorations of how people belonging to various identity groups relate to the world, while anthropologists have rarely directed their knowledge to the practical resolution of conflicts.

For the controversy over the 'Site C Clean Energy Project,' however, a combined anthropological and conflict-informed research strategy seemed particularly applicable. The multi-billion-dollar hydro-electric dam project on the Peace River in northeastern British Columbia, Canada, which was at the proposal stage during my research, has been hotly disputed since its inception, and, though now under construction, remains subject to a court challenge. BC Hydro (the provincial power utility) championed the project, and many locals supported it because of the 1100 megawatts of renewable power it would generate, but First Nations, farmers, ranchers, and other local residents resisted the threatened inundation of 5500 ha of wilderness, prime farmland, and Indigenous traditional territory under treaty.

Given the ethnic, occupational, urban/rural, political, and other intersecting cultures presumably bound up in the dispute, in-depth, holistic ethnographic methods seemed ideally suited to unearthing the values and assumptions, the understandings of the proper relationships among humans, and between humans and the non-human world, that underlay the conflict. At the same time,

284

DOI: 10.4324/9781003227441-36

Worldview translation as synthesis

intercultural communication theory suggested the significance of differing communication styles in conflict. Finally, both anthropological and conflict transformation (Lederach 2003) lenses highlighted the need to consider the systemic context in which the conflict played out. I hoped that a hybrid approach, incorporating all these elements and considering both sides of the conflict equally, would enhance understanding of the conflict and even produce openings for some form of intercultural mediation.

The research results both upheld the value of anthropology and conflict studies integration in environmental conflicts and pointed to the obstacles to such integration. Ethnographic research techniques and cultural relativism produced rich new insights about the substantive, relational, systemic, and cultural issues in the Site C conflict. At the same time, the hybrid research strategy not only revealed methodological and ethical challenges with using anthropological research to address conflict, but by revealing the structural and cultural violence embedded in both the dam project itself and in the official environmental consultation and decision-making process that authorized it, it underlined the limitations of facilitative conflict resolution.

Anthropology and conflict

Despite overlapping interests and approaches, the realms of anthropology and conflict have remained largely separate. Overall, conflict and peace studies fields have hesitated to focus on anthropology's central concept—culture—as a factor in conflict. Reflecting the dominance of political science and social psychology in the origins of the field, some authors and practitioners have outright denied its importance in conflict resolution (Avruch 2007; see Burton and Sandole 1987; Zartman 1993). Nevertheless, Lederach struck a chord with his (1995) call for elicitive conflict resolution training models that drew on participants' knowledge and experience of conflict, rather than the culture-blind, prescriptive transfer of mostly North American mediation and training models to diverse contexts, which had been the norm.

D'Estrée and Parsons describe a "wave" of research concerning the "psychosocial dimensions" affecting conflict perceptions and practice in the late 1990s and into the 2000s (d'Estrée and Parsons 2018, 11). Although authors often warned that these dimensions existed along spectra, rather than as dichotomies, the temptation to attach them to national groups in a "shorthand, essentialist way," (d'Estrée and Parsons 2018, 11) led to work on national negotiating styles (such as Cohen 1997). Counteracting "concerns about cultural oversimplification," a "myriad of case studies" then began to document "indigenous and traditional perceptions of conflict and conflict resolution" around the world (see d'Estrée and Parsons 2018) with greater ethnographic richness (Avruch 2018, 392).

Some scholars of conflict and peace, however, continue to see 'culture' as "a vague, political, and notoriously difficult term," (Brigg 2010, 329). Furthermore, despite the potential benefits of ethnography as a research method in complex conflicts, anthropology's purported "obsession with details," the long timelines and expense of extended fieldwork, and lack of communication across disciplines and between practitioners and academics, along with language barriers and security issues in conflict-affected areas (Bräuchler 2018, 34), as well as the perceived lack of transferability of ethnographic insights from one conflict context to another, have also hampered the take-up of genuine ethnography in peace research.

Anthropology, for its part, has always enjoyed the study of conflict in its various forms (from disputes to oppression) (Davidheiser and Treitler 2007, 12), with the sub-field of legal anthropology focusing explicitly on conflict and its resolution in socio-cultural context. Early classics in legal anthropology (Nader and Todd 1978; Gulliver 1979; Gibbs 1963) produced a body of knowledge on conflict resolution across cultures, particularly in small-scale societies without formal legal systems. Advocates of Alternative Dispute Resolution (ADR) in the United States in the 1970s drew on such ethnographic research concerning 'tribal' conflict settlement mechanisms as examples of "more humane, organic, therapeutic, non-adversarial" judicial processes (Avruch 2007, 13). In turn, a few legal anthropologists turned a critical lens on ADR (Conley and O'Barr 2019; Merry 1990) with Nader (1998), for example, protesting the imposition of a "harmony ideology" that "subverts access to justice" (in Avruch 1998). Legal anthropology then became "mostly marginal" to early conflict resolution (Avruch 2007), and, as of 2007, the average conflict resolution practitioner would "be unable to identify any anthropological contribution" to the field beyond the sense that "culture is important" (Davidheiser and Treitler 2007, 12).

Meanwhile, anthropologists rarely ventured into applied conflict work. Not only might efforts to intervene in conflict run counter to a neo-Marxian view of the social benefits of conflict, but applied anthropology in general has a mixed history, lacking prestige at best (Davidheiser and Treitler 2007). At worst, it is associated with colonialist collaborations and, more recently, co-optation into the war on terror (Bräuchler 2018). Neither do anthropological nuance and jargon necessarily translate well into mainstream or practice-oriented literature. Yet anthropology, with its strengths in participative, richly qualitative, and interpretative research, and focus on layers of meaning within social context, is ideal for the elicitation of perspectives and motivations in complex conflicts. Millar argues that ethnographic approaches offer many potential benefits to peace [and conflict] research; these include thick description, the ability to explain the 'why' and 'how' of social processes (rather than simply the 'what'), reflexivity, the potential for "collaborative and emancipatory" methodologies, and diverse and flexible methods. At the same time, anthropologists have much to learn from peace scholarship regarding the dynamics of conflict, violence, and peace (2018, 6–10).

Although culture "is always the lens through which the causes of conflict are refracted" (Avruch 1998, 30), the need for a holistic, multi-layered research strategy with attention to cultural factors seems particularly acute in environmental conflicts, in which "economic, social, legal, political, and ecological issues" are entangled with "deeply held values that lie at the core of many individual and group identities" (Blechman et al. 2000, 5). With the exception of some work on process and "framing" (for example, Lewicki, Gray, and Elliott 2003) and sometimes values (Schmidtz 2000), conflict and peace studies have primarily considered the environment in terms of material resources, and as a variable in the outbreak or duration of armed hostilities. Environmental conflicts, however, often constitute examples of "worldview conflicts," in which "the parties appear [...] to be speaking different languages and occupying different realities" (Docherty 2001, 28). Such worldview conflicts result from "a clash" of symbolic, but "very real" "inner worlds" incorporating ontological, epistemological, and ethical elements. Although much conflict resolution writing assumes that participants in conflict resolution processes partake of a single shared reality, in many cases reality itself must be "negotiated" before concrete issues can be dealt with since, worldviews cannot be simply altered or bargained over. Nevertheless, few theoretical or practical models exist for working with worldviews. Docherty, however, suggests observing language and actions of people in conflict, and exploring "stories [...], metaphors [...], institutionalized practices, [and other] carriers of [...] worldmaking," to arrive at a tentative and imperfect worldview analysis (Docherty 2001, 72). She further suggests making use, in conflict resolution processes, of "worldview translators" who understand or partake of conflicting worldviews and can not only "mediate between [...] ways of seeing and enacting the world," but "demonstrate the interaction" between them (Docherty 2001, 298–9, original emphasis)—a role that nicely combines the functions of both anthropologists and mediators.

Anthropology, then, dovetails with the notion of worldview analysis and translation. Not only does the discipline espouse a nuanced, fluid, multi-dimensional view of conflict that is "variable both across and within groups" (Davidheiser 2008, 67) that is underdeveloped in mainstream conflict studies, but it offers elicitive ethnographic research techniques for bringing to light unquestioned, unarticulated perceptions and worldviews, complementing conflict resolution's understanding of conflict patterns and practical strategies for reaching agreement. A research approach that drew on both fields thus appeared promising in the conflict over Site C. Although worldview

Worldview translation as synthesis

conflict was manifest among the parties to the conflict—Indigenous communities who have made their home on the land for millennia and more recent arrivals with a strong sense of home connected to their Peace River valley farms, on one side, and BC Hydro, the provincial government, and residents interested in increased non-combustion energy generation and economic growth on the other—the official Consultation and Environmental Assessment (EA) process did not recognize worldview differences, much less offer opportunities to negotiate reality. Though I had no official role in the Site C conflict, I hoped conceptual and research resources from anthropology would yield insights that would suggest pathways for informal mediatory activities that would increase mutual understanding and, in turn, contribute in some small way to a just resolution.

Research challenges

My research consisted of a year of participant observation in the Peace River Valley, as well as semi-structured interviews with 18 opponents and 14 supporters of the dam, and attendance at approximately half of the 28 days of public hearings held as part of the EA. I read all the public hearing transcripts and analyzed a selection, supplemented with other documents from the EA process.

The research involved methodological and ethical complications. Most significantly, although I planned to give equal ethnographic attention to both pro- and anti-dam perspectives, due to conflict circumstances and my own demographics and personality, my research access to pro- and anti-Site C groups and individuals was not symmetrical, as I have described elsewhere (Fitzpatrick 2020). At the same time, although my goal was to understand competing perspectives on Site C, not to evaluate the project itself, the more I learned, the more I became convinced that the negative impacts—on the environment, agriculture, and First Nations rights and culture—outweighed the potential benefits of the dam. Moreover, like many opponents of Site C, I became angry and frustrated with the inequities of the EA process.

This reaction left me wondering how to position myself and manage my obligations to research participants on both sides of the conflict (Fitzpatrick 2020). Although anthropology is increasingly comfortable with "engagement" (Low and Merry 2010), anthropologists' first responsibility is to the people they study, which poses a dilemma when those people are in active, explicit conflict with each other. Furthermore, neutrality expectations for intervenors in conflict are more stringent: "an elementary principle of conflict resolution practice" demands that facilitators be nonpartisan (Rubenstein 2017, 137). Thus, the ethnography of conflict approach generated new insights into the "content" of the conflict and the divergent views of the human place within the natural environment that underpinned it, but it also revealed the violence inherent in the project and the EA process. Far from pointing to avenues for mediation, it left me wondering how to apply, or even write about, my findings, wavering between the commitment to honor competing perspectives and the responsibility to call out injustice.

Findings

Competing visions for the future and views of the human place within the natural environment were pivotal to the Site C conflict. While both supporters and opponents of Site C who resided in the valley had some relationship to the land, supporters were willing to accept the impacts of the proposed dam in exchange for the opportunity, as they saw it, to use resources for the greater good, to fuel "progress" cost-effectively and without worsening climate change. They saw the impacts of the project, if properly managed, as compatible with their enjoyment of an outdoor lifestyle, in line with continuous processes of environmental transformation, and even as possible improvements. Site C opponents, on the other hand, often had deeper roots in the area and expressed a stronger attachment to place. Their environmental ethic mandated, not maximizing resource development, but preserving viable and productive ecosystems for humans and other organisms. They regarded anthropogenic changes to cherished and "irreplaceable" landscapes inevitably as degradation; Site C for them represented destruction, waste, and loss.

Site C opponents' language, their imagery of battle and violation, however, pointed to something beyond competing worldviews—the violence inherent in both the project and the consultation process. Opponents believed that Site C would cause avoidable physical and psychological harm to them as affected First Nations and valley residents, while its purported benefits would primarily land elsewhere. By flooding heritage sites, sacred places, ancestral graves, multi-generational family farms, and traditional territory ostensibly protected by a treaty, the dam threatened their rights, their history, their future livelihoods, and their cultural existence. These harms would be especially acute because of Site C opponents' worldviews and relationships to place—the dam would rupture their bond with personally and culturally beloved places and offend their senses of right environmental relations.

Their worldviews, however, did not meet the pro-development worldview(s) on an equal footing. In addition to the financial and political advantages BC Hydro enjoyed, the techno-rational orientation of the EA process obscured proponents' biases, while highlighting those of opponents. Overall, the consultation and EA process suggested that the project would, indeed, be carried out "properly," though many questions remained unresolved, particularly questions of environmental justice. The case for Site C as a project in the public interest resonated with a dominant worldview that valued progress and economic growth, while looking to technology to contain environmental impacts. Because the consultation process did not recognize this perspective as a worldview, in competition with other worldviews, however, Site C opponents fought a losing battle in challenging it.

Being consulted demanded much from Site C opponents in terms of financial and personal resources. The process was not equitable, they could not engage on their own terms, and they had good reason to expect that it would ultimately legitimize a foregone conclusion to proceed with a project that would greatly harm their lives and communities; thus, it was disempowering and psychologically distressing. Again, their embattled language testified to the latent violence, in this case of the consultation process.

Furthermore, ethnographic attention to the relational "context" and social "structure" as well as the worldview clash or conflict "content" (Lederach 2003, 12) revealed that the conditions of encounter were not just. The Site C conflict revealed the importance of incorporating attention to socio-cultural context and power dynamics when undertaking worldview analysis, and particularly, of identifying "structural violence"—violence consisting not of an individual action, but which is "built into the [social] structure and shows up as unequal power and consequently as unequal life chances," sometimes causing as much harm as "direct" or "personal" violence (Galtung 1969, 171). The Site C project, which prioritized economic growth and energy generation at the expense of First Nations' and other Peace Valley residents' physical, social, and cultural well-being, was a clear case of structural violence. In addition, an uneven distribution of "the power to decide over the distribution" of resources, as was exhibited in the Site C EA process, is also a form of structural violence (Galtung 1969, 171).

Moreover, when violence is "inherent in particular social, economic, and political formations," it is often normalized or "misrecognized"—not perceived as violence (Scheper-Hughes and Bourgois 2004, 21). Domination may operate invisibly "through discursive practices, narratives, worldviews, knowledge, behaviors and thoughts that are assimilated by society as true without public questioning" (Rodríguez and Inturias, 2018, 95). Such "aspects of culture, the symbolic sphere of our existence ... [that] justify or legitimize" social injustice are what Galtung calls "cultural violence" (1990, 291). Worldview analysis, attuned not only to discourses, narratives, and institutional arrangements, but to their implicit power, revealed the importance of cultural violence in legitimating Site C: appearing to consult affected people, presenting Site C as the conclusion of an impersonal, unbiased analysis, and treating the interests and values of First Nations (and other Site C opponents) as minority concerns, worth sacrificing for the "common good" of "economical" and "clean" power, camouflaged the decision to discount consequences for marginalized people.

Discussion

Thus, although the research improved my understanding of the worldviews underlying the conflict, it also pointed away from mediation as a possible solution, without suggesting a clear alternative use for the findings. I continue to believe that *where conflicting parties are relatively equal in power*, ethnographers have much to contribute to nuanced intercultural mediation. The messiness of worldviews, and their tendency to spill over identity boundaries (Blechman et al. 2000, 28), may daunt many conflict practitioners and put them off worldview analysis and translation. Anthropology, however, provides conceptual tools to cope with the "dynamic and diffuse nature of worldviews," and its emic, elicitive, ethnographic approach is well suited to the "replicable yet adaptive [conflict transformation] practice modality" that Davidheiser suggests is the most "promising" (2008, 79).

In the Site C conflict, however, there was no obvious institutional framework or source of funding for such mediation. With the provincial government, BC Hydro, and the pro-Site C public content with the status quo, and Site C critics deeply cynical on the issue, a facilitated process held little appeal for anyone. More significantly, though, in structural conflicts, where unequal power results in injustice, facilitation may not be appropriate. According to Curle, mediation will not succeed in conflicts where power is highly unbalanced, because the stronger party has no incentive to compromise (Curle 1986 in Avruch 2013).

If not facilitation, however, then what? Power is a "root problem" in conflict resolution, given the prevalence of power asymmetry in conflict (Avruch 2013, 143), and one for which the field has yet to develop—perhaps cannot develop—any really satisfactory solutions. Authors and practitioners do, though, often suggest "empowerment" of the weaker party, inside and outside the resolution process (Avruch 2013), with implications for the role of conflict specialists. Although the "strong bias of the profession [remains] toward facilitation" rather than advocacy, Rubenstein (2017, 145), suggests that the aim of systemic transformation requires greater political awareness and action on the part of conflict practitioners and even that in the presence of a "violence-generating system," the practitioner is "obliged to recognize" its existence and to "practice her trade in a way that reflects this recognition" through participation in various forms of political advocacy (Rubenstein 2017, 137).

This call to advocacy creates a quandary for an ethnographer of conflict, in trying to draw on anthropology's strengths both to mitigate conflict and uphold justice, while respecting their (the researcher's) obligations to all participants (Fitzpatrick 2020). Inspired by the notion of worldview translation, my original intention was to produce an even-handed ethnography that would promote understanding, not evaluate or blame. But recognition of the violence inherent in the Site C project raised difficult questions: whether to concentrate on understanding "the situation as a human reality," or on changing it to address injustice (Riesman, in Scheper-Hughes 1995, 416)? How to listen non-judgmentally, without neglecting political economy? And how to acknowledge the limitations of individual agency in structural violence, while calling institutions to account?

Worldview analysis and translation are one way to walk that fine line—working to understand challenging perspectives, precisely in order to reduce power abuses and violence. They offer an approach somewhere between facilitation and advocacy. By revealing competing worldviews as worldviews, on an equal footing, by illuminating "particular ways of knowing the world," and the modes by which they are imposed "at the expense of oppressing others" (Rodríguez and Inturias 2018, 92), worldview analysis undermines the hegemony of dominant assumptions and their potential for cultural violence. In so doing it can interrupt the cycle whereby cultural violence legitimizes structural violence, and structural violence reinforces the culture. At the same time, worldview translation, pointing out not only the harms that structures such as EAs may cause, but why they make sense to some people and why they are invested in them, while treating their representatives with respect and ethnographic empathy, may be more effective in promoting reform than simply denouncing them would be.

Conclusion

A combined anthropological and conflict research lens on the conflict over Site C demonstrated that anthropology, with its strengths in cultural analysis, along with participant observation, discourse analysis, and other holistic, elicitive ethnographic research methods, can provide perspectives on conflict and tools for articulating worldviews that may enrich intercultural mediation efforts. Anthropology's theoretical resources for the analysis of subtle forms of power and violence can also, however, help to identify situations when injustice makes mediation inappropriate. Although anthropologically informed conflict analysis cannot solve the problem of power asymmetry, it offers one way to empower the subordinate party—by undermining the cultural violence that sustains structural violence.

Note

1 Portions of this chapter previously appeared in Fitzpatrick, Brenda J. 2021. "Studying Across: Anthropology, Conflict Transformation and Cultural Violence in Environmental Conflict." *Vibrant: Virtual Brazilian Anthropology* 18: e18701 and Fitzpatrick, Brenda J. 2021. "Power Relations: Environment, Emotion, and Violence in the Site C Dam Approval Process (T)." University of British Columbia. http://hdl.handle.net/2429/78068.

References

Avruch, Kevin. 1998. *Culture & Conflict Resolution*. Washington, D.C: United States Institute of Peace Press.
Avruch, Kevin. 2007. "A Historical Overview of Anthropology and Conflict Resolution." *Anthropology News* 48 (6): 13–4. 10.1525/an.2007.48.6.13
Avruch, Kevin. 2013. *Context and Pretext in Conflict Resolution: Culture, Identity, Power, and Practice*. New York: Routledge. 10.4324/9781315635446
Avruch, Kevin. 2018. "Towards the Fourth Wave of Conflict Resolution Practice." In *Cultural Encounters and Emergent Practices in Conflict Resolution Capacity-Building*, edited by Tamra Pearson d'Estrée and Ruth J. Parsons, 387–401. London, England: Palgrave Macmillan. 10.1007/978-3-319-71102-7_13
Blechman, Frank, Jarle Crocker, Jayne Seminare Docherty, and Steve Garon. 2000. "Finding Meaning in a Complex Environmental Policy Dialogue: Research into Worldviews in the Northern Forest Lands Council Dialogue, 1990–1994." 14. ICAR Working Paper, Fairfax, VA.
Bräuchler, Birgit. 2018. "The Cultural Turn in Peace Research: Prospects and Challenges." *Peacebuilding* 6 (1): 17–33. 10.1080/21647259.2017.1368158
Brigg, Morgan. 2010. "Culture: Challenges and Possibilities." In *Palgrave Advances in Peacebuilding*, edited by Oliver P. Richmond, 329–46. London: Palgrave Macmillan UK. 10.1057/9780230282681_18
Brown, Anne M. 2013. "Anthropology and Peacebuilding." In *Routledge Handbook of Peacebuilding*, edited by Roger Mac Ginty, 132–46. London: Routledge.
Burton, John W., and Dennis J.D. Sandole. 1987. "Expanding the Debate on Generic Theory of Conflict Resolution: A Response to a Critique." *Negotiation Journal* 3 (1): 97–100. 10.1111/j.1571-9979.1987.tb00396.x
Cohen, Raymond. 1997. *Negotiating across Cultures: International Communication in an Interdependent World*. Rev. edition. Washington, D.C: United States Institute of Peace Press.
Conley, John M., and William O'Barr. 2019. *Just Words: Law, Language and Power*. 3rd edition. Chicago: University of Chicago Press.
Curle, Adam. 1986. *In the Middle: Non-Official Mediation in Violent Situations*. Oxford: Berg.
Davidheiser, Mark. 2008. "Race, Worldviews, and Conflict Mediation: Black and White Styles of Conflict Revisited." *Peace & Change* 33 (1): 60–89. 10.1111/j.1468-0130.2007.00476.x
Davidheiser, Mark, and Inga E. Treitler. 2007. "An Analytic Introduction and a Call for Interdisciplinary Engagement." *Anthropology News* 48 (6): 12–3. 10.1525/an.2007.48.6.12

Denskus, Tobias, and Nikolas Kosmatopoulos. 2015. "Anthropology & Peacebuilding: An Introduction." *Peacebuilding* 3 (3): 219–23. 10.1080/21647259.2015.1081124

Docherty, Jayne Seminare. 2001. *Learning Lessons from Waco: When the Parties Bring Their Gods to the Negotiation Table.* Syracuse, N.Y: Syracuse University Press.

d'Estrée, Tamra Pearson, and Ruth J. Parsons. 2018. "The State of the Art and the Need for Context-Grounded Practice in Conflict Resolution." In *Cultural Encounters and Emergent Practices in Conflict Resolution Capacity-Building*, edited by Tamra Pearson d'Estrée and Ruth J. Parsons, 1–29. Cham: Springer International Publishing. 10.1007/978-3-319-71102-7_1

Fitzpatrick, Brenda J. 2020. "Anthropology and Conflict Transformation. Promises and Dilemmas of Worldview Translation." In *Anthropology and Activism*, edited by Anna J. Willow and Kelly A. Yotebieng, 160–74. New York: Routledge.

Galtung, Johan. 1969. "Violence, Peace, and Peace Research." *Journal of Peace Research* 6 (3): 167–91. 10.1177/0022343369006003001

Galtung, Johan. 1990. "Cultural Violence." *Journal of Peace Research* 27 (3): 291–305. 10.1177/0022343390027003005

Gibbs, James L. 1963. "The Kpelle Moot: A Therapeutic Model for the Informal Settlement of Disputes." *Africa* 33 (1): 1–11. 10.2307/1157793

Gulliver, Philip H. 1979. *Disputes and Negotiations: A Cross-Cultural Perspective.* New York: Academic Press.

Lederach, John Paul. 1995. *Preparing for Peace: Conflict Transformation Across Cultures.* Syracuse: Syracuse University Press.

Lederach, John Paul. 2003. *The Little Book of Conflict Transformation.* Intercourse, PA: Good Books.

Lewicki, Roy, Barbara Gray, and Michael Elliott, eds. 2003. *Making Sense of Intractable Environmental Conflicts: Frames and Cases.* Washington, D.C.: Island Press.

Low, Setha M., and Sally Engle Merry. 2010. "Engaged Anthropology: Diversity and Dilemmas—An Introduction to Supplement 2." *Current Anthropology* 51 (S2): S203–26.

Merry, Sally Engle. 1990. *Getting Justice and Getting Even: Legal Consciousness among Working-Class Americans.* Chicago: University of Chicago Press.

Millar, Gearoid. 2018. "Introduction: The Key Strengths of Ethnographic Peace Research." In Ethnographic Peace Research. Rethinking Peace and Conflict Studies, edited by Gearoid Millar, 1–19. Palgrave Macmillan, Cham. 10.1007/978-3-319-65563-5_1.

Nader, Laura. 1998. "Harmony Models and the Construction of Law." In *Conflict Resolution: Cross-Cultural Perspectives*, edited by Kevin Avruch, Peter W. Black, and Joseph A. Scimecca. Westport, CT: Praeger.

Nader, Laura, and Harry F. Todd. 1978. *The Disputing Process—Law in Ten Societies.* New York: Columbia University Press.

Rodríguez, Iokiñe, and Mirna Liz Inturias. 2018. "Conflict Transformation in Indigenous Peoples' Territories: Doing Environmental Justice with a 'Decolonial Turn.'" *Development Studies Research* 5 (1): 90–105. 10.1080/21665095.2018.1486220

Rubenstein, Richard E. 2017. *Resolving Structural Conflicts.* London: Routledge. 10.4324/9781315665764

Scheper-Hughes, Nancy. 1995. "The Primacy of the Ethical: Propositions for a Militant Anthropology." *Current Anthropology* 36 (3): 409–40. 10.1086/204378

Scheper-Hughes, Nancy, and Philippe Bourgois. 2004. "Introduction: Making Sense of Violence." In *Violence in War and Peace: An Anthology*, edited by Nancy Scheper-Hughes and Philippe Bourgois, 1–27. Malden, MA: Blackwell.

Schmidtz, David. 2000. "Natural Enemies: An Anatomy of Environmental Conflict." *Environmental Ethics* 22 (4): 397–408.

Sponsel, Leslie E. 1994. "The Mutual Relevance of Anthropology and Peace Studies." In *The Anthropology of Peace and Nonviolence*, edited by Leslie E. Sponsel and Thomas Gregor, 1–36. Boulder: Lynne Rienner.

Wolfe, Alvin, and Honggang Yang, eds. 1996. *Anthropological Contributions to Conflict Resolution.* Athens: University of Georgia Press.

Zartman, William I. 1993. "A Skeptic's View." In *Culture and Negotiation: The Resolution of Water Disputes*, edited by Guy Olivier Faure and Jeffrey Z. Rubin, 17–21. Newbury Park, CA: Sage.

31

WEAVING TOGETHER THREE STRANDS OF RESEARCH: CULTURE, COMMUNICATION, AND CONFLICT

Deborah A. Cai and Edward L. Fink

"Strife is the father of all things."
Heraclitus, ca. 500 B.C.E. (as quoted in Collins, 1994, 47).

This chapter uses a metaphor from the book of Ecclesiastes (4:12, CSB), which says a cord of three strands is not easily broken. Although Solomon (the assumed author) was referring to the protection that three people have over two if they are overpowered by another person, the metaphor is used here to represent the inseparability—the tying together—of culture, communication, and conflict. Our goal is to demonstrate how, over the 20th century, researchers already integrated the study of culture, communication, and conflict, treating these areas as inseparable. We begin by first looking at the origins typically cited for these three areas. We then examine some important works outside the canon of the culture, communication, and conflict literature, but that, nonetheless, contribute important insights into how we understand their interdependence.

Communication

Jefferson Pooley and David Park (2012) have provided an insightful look at the histories that have been written about communication as a field. These authors considered the areas of study under the communication umbrella, including journalism, rhetoric, and media and they reviewed the scholars who are reported to be the founding disciplinary parents. They noted that the field's history is largely presented from a Western, especially a North American and European, perspective, with little focus on the international scholarship that has shaped the discipline.

Jesse Delia (1987) traced the social science roots of communication as a discipline to the early 20th century. Communication research began with sociologists, psychologists, political scientists, and literary scholars. At the same time, in response to changes in the United States toward mass production and consumption, businesses were changing, and there was a greater need for people—especially men—to sell products. It was within this context that Dale Carnegie wrote the book *How to Win Friends and Influence People* (1936), which focused on public communication and social interaction and remains one of America's best-selling books.

When researchers identified common interests in communication, those interests began coming together. Wilbur Schramm is often considered the first professor of communication

292

DOI: 10.4324/9781003227441-37

(1947), and Michigan State University had the first college of communication (1958). A turning point of the field was the information flow model, in Claude Shannon and Warren Weaver's 1949 book, *The Mathematical Theory of Communication*, which was the first book that focused on the communication process. Academic departments began to include speech communication, or simply *communication*, in their names. This shift mid-20th century led to the creation of the discipline of communication, with its own journals, theories, departments, and academic associations.

Intercultural communication

Textbooks of intercultural communication typically point to Edward T. Hall's work as the start of this scholarly field. Hall worked for the U.S. State Department, teaching intercultural communication to foreign service officers to prepare them for overseas assignments. He developed new concepts to explain cross-cultural differences in communication. His first book, *The Silent Language* (1959), laid out aspects of nonverbal behavior that varied across cultures and across contexts within those cultures and that create complications in communication.

Hall's books set the stage for the growing attention to what it means to communicate with people from different cultures and to identify what differences affect communication. Throughout the 20th century, anthropology and psychology contributed significantly to the study of intercultural communication with typologies such as value orientations theory by Florence Kluckhohn and Fred Strodtbeck's (1961) in their book *Variations in Value Orientations*. This work was followed by Milton Rokeach's (1979) study of individual and societal values, Geert Hofstede's (1980, 2001) comparison of cultural values among IBM employees around the world, Shalom Schwartz's (1992) examination of universal values, and Harry Triandis's (1995) investigation of individualism and collectivism.

The shift in the study of culture and communication over the 20th century reflects the shift in Western societies from a societal to an individual focus. Early conceptualizations of culture were influenced by sociologists such as Ferdinand Tönnies (German; citation 1887), David Émile Durkheim (French; citation 1893/1933), and Max Weber (German; citation 1922); they considered how societies moved from communal and organic structures, such as farms and villages, to created larger structures, such as businesses and organizations developed by individuals. Over the 20th century, however, conceptualizations shifted to focusing less on societies and more on the individuals who were influenced by the society in which they were enculturated.

Conflict

The study of interpersonal conflict also takes off during the middle of the 20th century. Morton Deutsch defined conflict as occurring whenever one person's action is "incompatible with another action" so that it "prevents, obstructs, interferes with, injures, or in some way makes the latter [action] less likely or less effective" (1973, p. 10).

Interpersonal conflict is pervasive in history, literature, and scholarship. Early Biblical conceptualizations of interpersonal conflict provide directives such as *an eye for an eye* as well as the New Testament's Golden Rule: Whatever you want others to do for you, do also the same for them (Matt. 7:12, CSB). Confucian teaching provides a slightly different version: Do not treat others in ways that you would not like to be treated. In contrast, Sigmund Freud (1922) addressed the aggressive drives within people that affect interpersonal relationships.

One of the earliest 20th-century considerations of social conflict was written by Georg Simmel (1904), who wrote that conflict is inevitable and important to societal development, noting that complete unity in relationships and society is neither realistic nor desirable. Later research by Lewis Coser (1956) argued that social conflicts serve several relational functions such as binding groups together as they seek to manage differences with out-groups. Coser laid the groundwork for later efforts by scholars in psychology and communication to understand how conflict affects many different types of relationships (William Donohue and Deborah Cai, 2022).

By the mid-20th century, the study of culture, communication, and conflict each developed into separate fields of study. Yet earlier in the century, these three areas were already being investigated as inseparable threads for understanding people's attitudes and behaviors toward others.

Attitudes and actions

In 1924, Emory Bogardus, a sociologist, developed one of the earliest measures of attitudes, the Bogardus Social Distance Scale (Bogardus 1924). The scale measured the prejudice of one group (A) toward another group (B) by asking a series of questions, such as would a person be willing to marry a member of another group, such as an immigrant from a particular country, and would a person be willing to have a person from that other group as a close friend or neighbor or colleague. The values reported by participants represented the social distance between the groups. Bogardus wanted to understand the racial and ethnic prejudice held by Americans toward immigrant groups during a time of rising racist immigration restrictions.

One of the restrictive immigration laws passed that would have concerned Bogardus was the U.S. Immigration Act of 1924. In addition to the Chinese Exclusion Act of 1882, these immigration policies barred or restricted many non-Northern European immigrants from entering the United States and prevented most Asian immigrants already in the United States from becoming citizens or owning land. It was during this time that Richard T. LaPiere (1899–1986), a sociologist, set out to better understand the relationship between people's attitudes and their actions regarding racial and ethnic relations.

Beginning in 1930, LaPiere took a Chinese couple on a road trip across the United States. They visited 67 hotels, auto camps, and tourist homes, and 184 restaurants and cafes. On this trip, LaPiere asked the proprietors if they (LaPiere plus the couple) would be allowed to visit as hotel or restaurant guests; only one place out of the 251 they visited refused to do so. Six months later, LaPiere issued a questionnaire to these same establishments, along with others, asking "Will you accept members of the Chinese race as guests in your establishment?" (LaPiere, 1934, p. 233). Of the 128 places that they had previously visited, all but one said 'no,' meaning that they would not serve Chinese people in their establishment.

When LaPiere and his fellow travelers communicated initially with the establishments, it was face-to-face, and he and his Chinese companions were welcomed in all but one place. But when asked, via a questionnaire six months later, if they would be welcome, they were refused. The mode of communication changed the results: As LaPiere stated, "those establishments who had provided for our needs so graciously were, some months later, verbally antagonistic towards hypothetical Chinese" (p. 234). Gordon W. Allport (1979, p. 390) summarized this finding this way:

The 'verbal' situation aroused more hostility than the actual situation.

LaPiere's work (1934) followed a few years after the development of the Bogardus Social Distance Scale. This scale confirmed that the attitudes assessed represented prejudice, but the attitudes were not consistent with how the Chinese couple was initially treated face to face. That said, when LaPiere sought to examine the question of attitudes versus actions, he understood rejecting a Chinese couple was consistent with the then-existing American cultural bias.

Cultural experience and expression of pain

In 1952, Mark Zborowski (1908–1990), an anthropologist, examined different responses to pain exhibited by American men from different cultural backgrounds (i.e., Italian, Irish, Jewish, and what he termed *Old American*, meaning "White, native-born individuals, usually Protestant, whose grandparents, at least, were born in the United States and who do not identify themselves with any foreign group. [...]" (Zborowski 1952, 19). The study focused on patients at a veterans' hospital in the Bronx. Findings were based on the observations and interviews with the hospital's medical staff and long interviews with the patients and their family members.

Differentiating cultural responses to pain provides several insights for understanding the inseparability of the study of culture, communication, and conflict. First, the doctors' and nurses' observations provided a glimpse of the assumptions that the medical staff made about these different culture groups based on differences in communication. For example, the medical staff described Italians and Jews as having very emotional and exaggerated responses, and they concluded that these responses reflect high sensitivity and a low threshold for pain. In comparison, people from Nordic groups were described as having a higher threshold for pain because they were less expressive. In other words, the expression of pain was assumed (falsely it turns out) to reflect the physical state of pain.

Similarly, when people from different cultures use verbal or nonverbal expressions that may be perceived as communicating frustration, such loud voices, they may be perceived as complaining, rude, or annoying by people who do not expect this type of communication. Zborowski differentiated a culture's experience of pain into *pain expectancy* and *pain acceptance*. For example, labor pain may be *expected* across cultures, but in Poland, for example, labor pain (at that time) was also *accepted*, so little was done to alleviate it. In contrast, in the United States, labor pain was *expected* but not *accepted* because interventions were employed to alleviate the pain as much as possible. Similarly, in cultures that accept war as an inevitable part of national life, battle wounds tend to be viewed as both expected and accepted. But in pacifistic cultures, battle wounds may be expected but they are not accepted, which affects how others respond to those who suffer from such wounds.

Zborowski identified how people from different backgrounds respond to pain given their expectations and acceptance of pain, how pain is treated, and how the pain may be treated in the future. He described Italians as present-oriented toward pain and pain relief: They were concerned with the immediate pain sensation and expressed their discomfort, but once they were no longer suffering, they would no longer express concerns. In contrast, he described the Jewish response to pain as future-oriented pessimism, because Jews were more likely to be concerned with the symptomatic meaning of the pain and the potential meaning of the pain for the long-term welfare of the patient and the patient's family. Jewish patients expressed greater concern about drugs that could alleviate their present suffering because of the risks of long-term addiction. They were also more likely to remain concerned even once the pain was alleviated because of the possibility that the pain might return.

The medical staff described 'exaggerated and over-emotional' responses to pain as sowing seeds of mistrust with both Italian and Jewish patients (Zborowski 1952, 23). Yet the responses were rooted in different concerns and goals: For Italians, pain was expressed to seek the immediate alleviation of the pain, and for Jews, it was to seek to understand the causes of the pain and to prevent it in the future.

In contrast, 'Old American' patients were characterized as approaching pain with a future-oriented optimism. These patients were described as detached and unemotional observers, less likely to complain because "it won't do any good" (25), more likely to "avoid being a 'nuisance'" (25), and more concerned with seeking approval. Not only did Old Americans view emotional expression as a hindrance to healing; the medical staff was also expected to approach pain and its treatment with this type of detached response.

Several lessons can be drawn from Zborowski's description and explanation of how people from different cultural backgrounds respond to pain. First, Zborowski's framework can be used to consider how cultures differ in their expectation and acceptance of conflict and argument. The way people express themselves about issues is interpreted by others based on their own culture's acceptance and expectation of that type of expression. If vocal expression of conflict, including argument, is expected and accepted, then communication styles that are direct, less mitigated, and argumentative are not likely to be perceived as aggressive or offensive. However, if conflict behaviors are neither expected nor accepted, direct styles of communication may be perceived as rude and off-putting, because behaviors that convey being nice and that avoid the appearance of conflict may be generally preferred. But these are external perceptions of other people's behaviors, not what the people themselves believe they convey.

Second, Zborowski differentiated cultures by their level of pain apprehension and pain anxiety. Pain apprehension results in people avoiding pain as much as they can. Pain anxiety is the response people have to the experience of pain, which is based on their understanding of the meaning of pain and its significance for the welfare of the person and the person's family. Pain anxiety is affected by the intensity, quality, and duration of the pain that is experienced.

These differences can be used to understand cultural approaches to conflict. Conflict apprehension can result in avoidance of conflict at all costs, whereas conflict anxiety is how members of this culture differ in their experience of conflict and its potential outcomes for personal and group relationships.

A third observation is the vast difference between the perceptions of the medical staff based on the patients' expression of pain and the meaning those expressions have for the patients themselves. The expression of pain was assumed by the medical staff to reflect the reality of the physical state. But that was not the case: Similar expressions across culture groups did not reflect similar attitudes about the pain that was experienced. Instead, similar reactions served very different functions and purposes for people from different cultural backgrounds.

This observation is important for understanding how people may make mistakes about what they perceive others are expressing. Applying Zborowski's differentiation between present, future-pessimistic, and future-optimistic orientations to conflict, the vehemence of an idea for people using a present orientation may be perceived as complaining and trying to get one's own way; however, people from a future-pessimistic orientation may need to understand an issue, challenging the ideas until they are understood, and arguing from multiple points of view. From a future-optimistic orientation, vehemence may be avoided generally because it is not conducive to good relationships and is therefore perceived as not constructive to conversation.

Understanding how people from different cultures express themselves and how these differences can be misinterpreted affect the role of argument across cultures: How argument is used, what it expresses, and how it can lead to misinterpretation.

Argument as conversation or conflict

The documentary film, *Arguing the World* (Joseph Dorman 1997, and the book by the same name, Joseph Dorman 2000), looks at the role that argument played, during the mid to late 20th century, in shaping the abilities of four New York intellectuals to critique and criticize the ideas of others. Daniel Bell (1919–2011), Nathan Glazer (1923–2019), Irving Howe (1920–1993), and Irving Kristol (1920–2009) each grew up in a borough of New York City; all four were sons of working-class Jewish immigrants from Russia or Eastern Europe. They each attended City College of New York, where they argued about Trotsky and Stalin; socialism, fascism, and liberalism; literature and history; and much more. Each of them became an elite scholar in top American universities.

Significant to their development as scholars is the role of argument in the ethnic culture in which they were raised. As sons of Jewish immigrants, they learned argument as part of everyday life. As Irving Howe explained, "The immigrant Jews brought with them memories of the old country, legends and stories of things that had happened there. So you absorbed this kind of historical consciousness at the kitchen table, literally at the kitchen table" (Dorman 1997). Schiffrin (1984) described *Jewish argument* as follows:

> In sociable argument, speakers repeatedly disagree, remain nonaligned with each other, and compete for interactional goods. Yet they do so in a nonserious way [...]. The analysis [in Schiffrin's article] also demonstrates the cultural relativity of norms of evaluation about dispute.
>
> *(Schiffrin 1984, 311)*

These four scholars were eventually responsible for a remarkable amount of communication, as lecturers and through the written word. Their cultural inheritance as Jews greatly influenced both their historical and religious knowledge and provided a foundation for arguing, frequently, vehemently, and discerningly. Like Zborowski's depiction of future-oriented pessimism, argument for this group of first-generation New York Jews was used to do *intellectual battle*: "They had thought that argument would help to confirm the correct path toward political salvation [...]." (Dorman 2000, 3).

Contrast this style of conversation with that of the *Minnesota nice* stereotype, which expects people to behave with politeness, friendship, courtesy, and restraint. One of the peers of the New York intellectuals contrasted Southern conversation with the communication within their group: "They're always praising one another and we're always attacking each other" (Dorman 2000, 7).

When conflict becomes aggression, and aggression becomes violence

The implications of this contrast can be found in Richard Nisbett and Dov Cohen's book, *Culture of Honor* (1996), which describes how cultural norms *require* Southern White men to insist on being seen as strong and tough. Nisbett and Cohen argued that this does not apply to all White men or to all Southerners; instead, these norms are associated with a culture that was historically tied to the life of being a herdsman. The herding culture created expectations to protect one's land and family and evolved into an unwillingness for men to tolerate insult, so insult came to require retaliation and revenge.

Nisbett and Cohen provide a remarkable amount of evidence to support their thesis about the culture of honor, comparing people from different regions on homicide rates, attitudes toward violence, responses to insults, physiological ties to aggression, social policies, support for war, behaviors such as spanking children, and so on. They examined the strong impact of culture and communication on conflict, and this example is the most impactful of the examples that we have discussed: Conflict was not merely displayed with rudeness; it often meant torture or death. We can use the NAACP's (2022) discussion of lynching to provide a powerful example:

> Many victims of lynching were murdered without being accused of any crime. They were killed for violating social customs or racial expectations, such as speaking to white people with less respect than what white people believed they were owed.
>
> *(NAACP, 2022)*

In the Netherlands, Fieke Harinck and colleagues (2013) compared Dutch people with Turkish immigrants, who also came from an honor culture. They found that the culture of honor also yielded more constructive responses—not just aggressive or violent ones—to conflict, as long as the people involved were not insulted by the other side, because their communication norms were shaped by an effort to avoid offending others. Contrast this view with that of argument in *Arguing the World*:

City College alumnus Philip Selznick recalled, 'in those days having a discussion meant arguing about something and doing it at the top of your lungs!'

(Dorman 2000, 2)

In one context, argument yielded engagement, new ways of thinking about age-old problems, and relational connection. In the other context, it could be perceived as threatening and offensive, and it could result in violence.

Conclusions

The *Oxford English Dictionary* dates the use of the term *communication* to 1382, of culture, to 1450, and of *conflict*, to 1440. This chapter has considered ways these terms emerged in research over the 20th century. This research can be summarized in the following propositions:

1   What people do, and what they say they will do, are not the same.
2   How people express themselves, and what they mean through their expression, can be misinterpreted by others.
3   How people express disagreement is rooted in their ethnic or cultural values.
4   How people communicate can have serious consequences.

In conclusion, if people who serve as a formal or informal mediator do not understand these complexities of communication and culture, they may exacerbate the conflict between the mediated parties.

In LaPiere's study, the conflict was between him and the proprietors; he was a surrogate for the Chinese couple. When asked via a questionnaire about the possibility of serving the Chinese couple, the proprietors responded with "verbally antagonistic [responses]." The response was clearly conflictual. Zborowski reported conflict regarding some patients not accepting medical treatment and the associated pain that they suffered, the possibility of responses from family members who were not supportive, and the perceived standoffishness of the medical staff who could look down upon their patients.

In these two studies, communication was influenced by the cultural differences and conflict was a product of the intertwining of communication and culture. The resulting conflict ranged from the communication being clear, loud, and aggressive with the medical staff, sometimes speaking in *sotto voce* to each other, while uncomfortable or embarrassed with each other.

In the culture of honor, the antagonism impelled by the culture of the adversaries can range from verbal attacks to serious physical attacks. The culture is at the foreground of the behavior, and that culture + communication can easily make 'conflict' an understatement.

In *Arguing the World*, we see conflict as schizophrenic, revealing unity and enmity, and it also may reveal authority and humility. Here conflict can be more like a formal tournament than a rout. In our example, the culture here is Jewish culture, with a background of centuries of *pilpul* (Hebrew: פלפול, loosely meaning 'sharp analysis').

Georg Simmel (1904) argued that society cannot have complete harmony and that conflict serves to strengthen societies. Yet when cultural differences affect communication, the conflict that ensues can be more disruptive than unifying because of misunderstandings about how people from other cultures communicate. The studies we have examined show that there are differences in how people from different cultural backgrounds express themselves, different reasons for the way they express themselves, and different perceptions by others about what the expression means. Further, our review has shown that what people experience and what they say they experience, as well as what they do and what they say they will do, can differ quite significantly. Therefore, conflict that arises from these types of misunderstandings about the perceived meaning of communication may be more disruptive than unifying, unless we seek to find ways to appreciate, rather than disparage, such different forms of communication.

We have shown different forms of communication, different styles of culture, and different decibel levels of conflict. Of course, there are more, but our goal is for the reader to (a) appreciate these differences; (b) employ this knowledge for interpersonal, intergroup, and international understanding and application; and (c) understand how communication and culture can become catalysts for conflict.

References

Allport, Gordon W. 1979. *The Nature of Prejudice*. Unabridged, 25th anniversary ed. Reading, MA: Addison-Wesley.

Bogardus, Emory S., ed. 1924. *Fundamentals of Social Psychology*. New York, London: D. Appleton-Century.

Carnegie, Dale. 1936. *How to Win Friends and Influence People*. New York: Pocket Books.

Collins, Randall, ed. 1994. *Four Sociological Traditions: Selected Readings*. New York: Oxford University Press.

Coser, Lewis A. 1956. *The Functions of Social Conflict*. New York: Free Press.

Delia, Jesse. 1987. "Communication Research: A History." In *Handbook of Communication Science*, edited by Charles R. Berger and Steven H. Chaffee, 20–98. Beverly Hills: Sage Publications.

Deutsch, Morton. 1973. *The Resolution of Conflict: Constructive and Destructive Processes*. New Haven: Yale Univ. Press.

Donohue, William A., and Deborah A. Cai. 2022. "Interpersonal Conflict, History Of." In *Encyclopedia of Violence, Peace, & Conflict*, 616–25. Elsevier. 10.1016/B978-0-12-820195-4.00124-2

Dorman, Joseph. 2000. *Arguing the World: The New York Intellectuals in Their Own Words*. New York: Free Press.

Dorman, Joseph, dir. 2005 1997. *Arguing the World*. DVD. New York: Riverside Productions.

Durkheim, Émile. 1933. *The Division of Labor in Society*. New York: Macmillan.

Freud, Sigmund. 1922. *Beyond the Pleasure Principle*. London; Translated by C.J.M. Hubback. Vienna: The International Psycho-analytical Press.

Hall, Edward Twitchell. 1959. *The Silent Language*. Garden City, N.Y.: Doubleday.

Harinck, Fieke, Saïd Shafa, Naomi Ellemers, and Bianca Beersma. 2013. "The Good News about Honor Culture: The Preference for Cooperative Conflict Management in the Absence of Insults." *Negotiation and Conflict Management Research* 6 (2): 67–78. 10.1111/ncmr.12007

Hartwig, Daniel. 2010. *Guide to the Richard T. LaPiere Papers*. Stanford: Stanford University. Libraries. Department of Special Collections and University Archives. https://oac.cdlib.org/findaid/ark:/13030/kt1199r6zd/

Hofstede, Geert. 1980. *Culture's Consequences: International Differences in Work-Related Values*. Beverly Hills, CA: Sage.

Hofstede, Geert. 2001. *Culture's Consequences: Comparing Values, Behaviors, Institutions, and Organizations Across Nations*. Thousand Oaks: Sage.

Kluckhohn, Florence Rockwood, and Fred L. Strodtbeck. 1961. *Variations in Value Orientations*. Evanston, IL: Row, Peterson and Company.

LaPiere, Richard T. 1934. "Attitudes vs. Actions." *Social Forces* 13 (2): 230–7. 10.2307/2570339

NAACP. 2022. *History of Lynching in America*. https://naacp.org/find-resources/history-explained/history-lynching-america

Nisbett, Richard E., and Dov Cohen. 1996. *Culture of Honor: The Psychology of Violence in the South*. Boulder, CO: Westview Press. 10.4324/9780429501142

Pooley, Jefferson D., and David W. Park. 2012. "Communication Research." In *The Handbook of Communication History*, 76–90. New York: Routledge. 10.4324/9780203149119.ch3

Rokeach, Milton, ed. 1979. *Understanding Human Values: Individual and Societal*. New York: Free Press.

Schiffrin, Deborah. 1984. "Jewish Argument as Sociability." *Language in Society* 13 (3): 311–35. 10.1017/S0047404500010526

Schwartz, Shalom H. 1992. "Universals in the Content and Structure of Values: Theoretical Advances and Empirical Tests in 20 Countries." In *Advances in Experimental Social Psychology*, 25: 1–65. Elsevier. 10.1016/S0065-2601(08)60281-6

Shannon, Claude Elwood, and Warren Weaver. 1949. *The Mathematical Theory of Communication*. Urbana, IL: The University of Illinois Press.

Simmel, Georg. 1904. "The Sociology of Conflict. I." *American Journal of Sociology* 9 (4): 490–525. 10.1086/211234

Tönnies, Ferdinand. 1887. *Gemeinschaft und Gesellschaft*. Leipzig: Fues's Verlag.

Triandis, Harry C. 1995. *Individualism and Collectivism*. New York: Routledge. 10.4324/9780429499845

Weber, Maximilian Carl Emil (1922). *Wirtschaft und Gesellschaft*. Tübingen: Mohr.

Zborowski, Mark. 1952. "Cultural Components in Responses to Pain." *Journal of Social Issues* 8 (4): 16–30. 10.1111/j.1540-4560.1952.tb01860.x

32

INTERCULTURAL MEDIATION AS INTERCULTURAL COMPETENCE[1]

Jan D. ten Thije

Introduction

The title of this chapter reads: *Intercultural mediation as intercultural competence*. Mediation has several meanings (see other chapters in this handbook). The most commonplace meaning is that of mediating in conflicts, which can prevent the pressing of legal charges (Busch and Schröder 2005). Another meaning of mediation is *bridging*. This meaning is filled in in a more abstract way within the social sciences and humanities. One refers to a medium that makes communication and image formation possible (Baraldi 2017). It concerns the medium by which and through which communication takes place, for communication is of course more than sending messages back and forth. The way in which a communicative medium is or must be used determines the communicative result in a conversation, newspaper, film, blog, website, or catalogue (Gautheron-Boutchatsky et al. 2004, Agha 2011). Using the concepts of *mediating and bridging*, I would like to explain how researchers from different disciplines work together to shape the interdisciplinary field of intercultural communication, especially in relation to intercultural competence. To this end, I am going to discuss five scientific approaches.

We will see that in the past 30 years there have been shifts in the definition of intercultural communication. Initially, researchers assumed that *every* communication between people from *different* linguistic and cultural backgrounds concerns intercultural communication (Samovar and Porter 1991). Nowadays, we use a more limited definition: Intercultural communication only occurs when people *change* their attitude, knowledge, and skills of languages and cultures through *reflection* on their own language and culture (Rehbein 2006, Jackson II 2014, Zhu 2018). In this context, one speaks of a move from an *essentialist* conception of intercultural communication towards a *non-essentialist* conception (Dervin and Gross 2016). I will get back to that at the end of this chapter.

First acquaintance with five approaches

I am going to introduce the five approaches to intercultural communication. Therefore, I have put these five approaches in a diagram (see Figure 32.1), which also shows the special position of intercultural mediation.

The first approach is called the *contrastive approach*. This is about comparing languages and cultures: What are differences and what are similarities? This comparison is on the one hand about finding universal principles in languages (Lado 1957), and on the other hand about the characteristics that are important for learning a foreign language (Fisiak 1984).

DOI: 10.4324/9781003227441-38

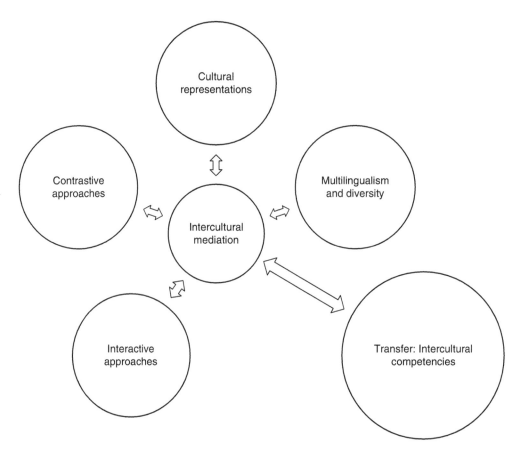

Figure 32.1 Interrelations of five approaches to intercultural communications (ten Thije 2020a, 7)

When researching cultural differences, you can also think of the work of organizational psychologist Hofstede, who developed universal dimensions with which cultures can be compared to one another (Hofstede 1980), for instance collectivist vs. individualistic cultures. His work is well known, but also controversial, because it is considered essentialist. In his model, a culture is equated with a country. Nowadays this is considered too simple (Dervin and Gross 2016).

The second approach focuses on research into *cultural representation and imaging*: How does one see oneself, the other, and vice versa. How does cultural identity come about (S. Hall 2001, Leerssen 2007)? Research into discrimination and racism also fits within this approach (Reisigl and Wodak 2005). Here, a fruitful exchange has been established between research into intercultural communication and literature studies, media and gender studies and research into post-colonialism (Leurs 2019).

The third approach is about the *interaction* itself: How does face-to-face interaction between people in multilingual and multicultural situations take place? This is the domain of interaction researchers and ethnographers (Gumperz 1982). In America, linguistic anthropology is an established discipline. It is of great importance to research Intercultural Communication. Other important contributions are Agar's work (Agar 1994) with his Rich Points and European interaction-research such as functional pragmatics (Koole and ten Thije 1994).

The fourth approach focuses on research into *linguistic diversity and multilingualism*: How do organizations deal with multilingual situations and how do you describe, for instance, the development of children who learn several languages side by side at home? What is the influence of language

Mediation as intercultural competence

policies at school and at home (Jessner-Schmid and Kramsch 2015)? This approach is in the domain of sociolinguists and language psychologists (Le Pichon-Vorstman and Baauw 2019).

Finally, the fifth approach is called the *transfer approach*. This approach is about how intercultural knowledge and skills are transferred (Deardorff 2004). This starts with the crucial question of what is meant by intercultural competences. This approach includes, on the one hand, research into language learning and the training of competences (Ahmed, Al-kadi, and Hagar 2020). On the other hand, it involves research into transfer in the form of advice, counselling, and training (Byram 1997; Beerkens et al. 2020).

To summarize: The contrastive approach is about the comparison of languages and cultures, the representation approach is about the representation between cultures. The interaction approach answers the question: What do people do when they communicate face to face in multilingual situations? The multilingualism approach is about how diversity is dealt with in practice and in policy. Finally, transfer is about the transfer of knowledge and experience in the form of education, training, or advice.

All these approaches provide building blocks for scientific research into intercultural communication. By focusing on mediation, we get a specific view on the contributions from the different approaches that are important for mediation and bridging in intercultural communication (Busch 2016). This chapter concentrates on the key aspects and gives some examples of the interactive approach, the multilingual approach, and the transfer approach, since these approaches contribute the most to the concept of intercultural competence.

Interactive approach

The interactive approach of intercultural communication has its origins in sociolinguistic and discourse-analytical studies of language contact and focuses on face-to-face interaction (Gumperz 1982; Koole and ten Thije 1994).

Therefore, I would like to refer to my research in Volgograd (ten Thije 2014). The example shows how the interpreter acts as an intercultural mediator between languages and cultures. In this example, the Dutch colleague announces that he would like to make a second toast. In the transcript in Table 32.1, on the left you can see what the Dutch coordinator says. On the right, you can see how the interpreter translated his words into Russian. For this presentation, I have translated his words into English, but he speaks Russian.

The Dutchman says "*Alec, may I make another toast. In Holland I'm not used to making so many toasts.*" In the translation of the interpreter, I have reconstructed three steps so that the importance of this second toast for the Russian host is made clear. I have called these steps *generalizing*, *perspectivising*, and *contrasting* (ten Thije 2006).

Table 32.1 Transcript of mediation by a non-professional interpreter (ten Thije 2020a, 19)

Interpreter as intercultural mediator *Speaker in English*	*Interpreter in Russian*
1. Alec	1. —
2. May I bring another toast	2. —
3. In Holland I am not used to bring so many toasts.	3. In Holland it is not customary to bring so many toasts,
	4. but
	5. here in Russia
	6. he would like to say one more

In step 1—generalizing—the sentence "*In the Netherlands I am not used to making so many toasts*" is translated as "*In the Netherlands it is not customary to make so many toasts.*" The words of the speaker are generalized so that they express a cultural standard in the Netherlands. Step 2 connects directly to this: "*here in Russia.*" The request of the Dutchman is explicitly placed in the current communicative situation in Russia. In step 3, the two cultural standards in the Netherlands and Russia are juxtaposed and connected with the conjunction "*but*": "*In the Netherlands it is not common to make many toasts, but here in Russia he would like to make another one.*" The interpreter makes his own position clear by changing "*me*" into "*him.*" For Russians it is very common for people to make several toasts during dinner. Because of this contrast, the interpreter makes it clear to the Russian host that the fact that the Dutchman makes a second toast should be regarded as a special form of courtesy. If the interpreter had translated literally, this form of intercultural politeness would have been lost.

In actual fact, a speaker can also present his own actions as an expression of a cultural norm and then compare this norm with the cultural norm of the other. In this way, the other person comes to a better understanding. This intercultural strategy of perspectivizing is a good example of intercultural mediation, where the speaker meditates his own goals.

Multilingualism approach

Multilingualism refers to two types of multilingualism: Additive and inclusive multilingualism (Rindler-Schjerve and Vetter 2012). Additive multilingualism is about different languages working side by side. When the European Community was founded, all national languages were considered equal. Since then, additive multilingualism in Europe has been referred to in Brussels as the equivalence of national languages. This view stems from the emergence of European nation states in the 17th and 18th centuries. Each state chose one language. There was an ideology of *one nation state, one culture,* and *one language.* Switzerland, Belgium, and Luxembourg are the exceptions. With European unification and increased migration and mobility, another form of multilingualism has become increasingly important. Citizens are increasingly confronted with situations in which several languages are used at the same time. Backus et al. (2013) have called this form inclusive multilingualism. In this case, it is about using multiple languages at the same time.

As an elaboration on inclusive multilingualism, I would like to discuss *Luistertaal* or *Lingua Receptiva* (ten Thije 2018). I am going to discuss an example from the research of Roos Beerkens (2010). She did ethnographic research in the border region between the Netherlands and Germany. One of the cases was the Dutch-German spatial planning team that met twice a year to discuss cross-border projects. In these teams, civil servants from the German *Bezirksregierungen* (district governments), from the Dutch provinces, from the Euroregion, and sometimes from ministries worked together. These officials consciously decided that both sides would speak their own language. Dutch people would speak Dutch and German people would speak German. Their receptive knowledge of the other's language was sufficient to understand each other.

Luistertaal, which is also known internationally as lingua receptiva, turns out to be an optimal form of intercultural communication (Rehbein, ten Thije, and Verschik 2012). After all, it shows great respect for the other person that he or she is given the opportunity to use the language that he or she controls best in the given situation. In this way, the fear of making mistakes is also removed from people who would otherwise have to use a foreign language.

Beerkens' research (Beerkens 2010, 193–96) contains a good example of an intercultural discussion. It is about the train connection between Rotterdam and Oberhausen. The Dutch know this as the *Betuwelijn.* In the Netherlands, the connection to the border has been ready for a long time, but in Germany it is not progressing. A German newcomer to the discussion did not understand why the connection is called the *Betuwelijn* and why his German colleagues also referred to the connection between Arnhem and Oberhausen that way. It was explained to him that in the

Netherlands, the train runs through a region called the *Betuwe*. It finally made sense and the colleague understood the name and that his German colleague also referred to it that way, because the train was already running in the Netherlands and not in Germany. For the sake of clarity, this communication was conducted entirely in Dutch-German lingua receptiva.

The intercultural reflection of the German colleague shows how intercultural mediation works in Lingua Receptiva. Language differences in a multilingual situation are bridged so that intercultural understanding arises. The *Betuwelijn* in Germany is still not ready, much to the annoyance of the Netherlands. A German website states that this connection will be extended to Genoa. From the point of view of intercultural mediation, one could advise Dutch policymakers to have another good thought about the name *Betuwelijn*. Wouldn't a name like *Trans Europa Express One* be more likely to prompt Germans, Swiss and Italians to invest billions?

Transfer approach: Intercultural competences

The transfer approach summarizes the results of the other approaches and focuses on the formulation of intercultural competences. Intercultural mediation plays a central role in this.

Intercultural competence is described by Deardorff (2004, 194) as: "the ability to communicate effectively and appropriately in intercultural situations based on one's intercultural knowledge, skills and attitudes." The fundamental issue common to all transfer studies is how self-reflection can be taught and integrated in intercultural education. Self-reflection, or reflective learning, is the key to teaching and learning intercultural competences (Alred and Byram 2002, McConachy and Liddicoat 2016).

The last example in this chapter shows a nice summary of the argument on intercultural mediation in practice. It concerns an Education Innovation Project at Utrecht University: Intercultural Competences for Utrecht University: ICUU. In that context, a training course was developed for staff members of the university. These are colleagues who work at the international office, at HR, or as a study advisor. These are people who have to deal with internationalization on a daily basis in their work and who want to increase their competencies. The training is based on the wonder of the *Rich Point* (Agar 1994). The training illustrates the critical reflection brought forward by the non-essentialist approach of intercultural communication.

Severs, Schoutsen, and Thije (2022) describe how this approach is incorporated into a type of text that the older readers will remember. It is a large notepad that used to be on everyone's desk with all the months of the year following. You could take small notes on it, and it was called a desk pad. (In Dutch: *Bureau Onderlegger Blok* is abbreviated to *BOB*). On this modern desk pad, employees can write their observations about intercultural communication on a daily basis, so that they can discuss them in their team meetings or in their conversations with managers (Severs, Schoutsen, and Thije 2022).

I will briefly explain this structure. At the top you write a *Rich Point*. Then, there are three columns. The left column represents the institutional perspective. What are organizational conditions for communication? This prevents something from being seen as intercultural too quickly, when actually the cause lies in the formal or informal organization of the university. The second column questions all sorts of aspects of interculturality and the third column focuses on the reflection process itself. Reflection is a cyclical process of observing, naming, trying out, and experiencing again (Kolb 1984).

Intercultural communication: From essentialism to non-essentialism

We have come to the end of this chapter and a summary of the results: What insights do the interfaces between the five approaches provide? What do we understand by intercultural communication, and what is the meaning of mediation in relation to intercultural competence?

Since the concept of intercultural communication was first used in 1959, there has been a shift in the interpretation of this concept (E. T. Hall 1959). One speaks of a development from an essentialist to a non-essentialist conception of the field. I can summarize this development here based on three definitions.

The oldest and still best-known definition states that intercultural communication is understood as *all* communication between people from different linguistic and cultural backgrounds. From this definition, the focus is on the explanation of misunderstandings. Hofstede's (1980) research into universal cultural dimensions can serve as an example here. In his model, culture is equated with country. Smaller cultural units within countries, such as regions, cities, or neighborhoods, are ignored (Krase and Uherek 2017). Cultural identity is seen as static and unchanging. In the analysis and comparison of different languages, the native speaker is the norm. Intercultural training focuses on learning *do's and don'ts* with the motivation that more knowledge about other languages and cultures prevents misunderstandings (Müller-Jacquier and ten Thije 2000).

Influenced by research within all approaches, the field has developed in a more non-essentialist direction. This is expressed in the second definition: Intercultural Communication *only* exists when linguistic and cultural differences become *relevant* for the course and outcome of multilingual or multicultural communication (Spencer-Oatey and Franklin 2009).

Of course, national cultures remain important, but researchers have become more aware of the fact that identity is a construction shaped and reformed by new and old media all over the world (Ponzanesi 2016). Think in this context of globalization, localization, and glocalization. Cultural identities are seen as more hybrid and plural. Attention is paid to racism, discrimination, and post-colonialism as forms of intercultural communication. Besides the attention for these forms of oppression, there is also attention for how to play creatively with the concepts of race, ethnicity, gender, and social position (ten Thije 2020b).

The interaction approach has played a major role in this development by showing how you can deduct from the reaction of the other if and how you understand each other (Di Luzio, Günthner, and Orletti 2001). Think of the interpreter in Volgograd. In this way, you can show that successful intercultural communication exists and that it differs from monolingual communication, as we have seen in lingua receptiva (Rehbein, ten Thije, and Verschik 2012). In research into multilingualism, attention has shifted from the native speaker to efficient communication (Backus et al. 2013). Education and training are no longer just about learning about other languages and cultures, but also about which strategies you can use to promote intercultural understanding.

The third definition is the most narrowed down. It states: Intercultural communication only occurs when people *change* their attitudes, knowledge or skills of languages and cultures through reflection on their own language use and culture in multilingual and multicultural situations (Rehbein 2006). Interestingly, this definition presupposes a combination of the essentialist and non-essentialist approaches (Siapera 2010). You can reflect better on your own behavior if you have knowledge of how others view your language and culture. In other words: How can you avoid the essentialist trap in intercultural education (Cole and Meadows 2013)? For efficient multilingual communication you do not always need to use the native or national cultural standard, but it is necessary to know when this standard is absolutely necessary and therefore you need to seek help to meet it (Sweeney and Zhu 2010). The key to this approach is that learning is cyclical, and that people understand how different factors affect communicative success at the same time (Deardorff 2004, McConachy and Liddicoat 2016).

As I have shown, scientific research into intercultural communication is a product of many, very diverse theories. With the help of intercultural mediation, I have shown how different approaches can be linked in a meaningful way.

Note

1 This chapter is a shortened version of the inaugural lecture 'Intercultural Communication as mediation,' spoken at the assumption of the chair of Intercultural Communication at Utrecht University on Friday 31 January 2020.

References

Agar, Michael. 1994. *Language Shock: Understanding the Culture of Conversation*. 1st edition. New York: Morrow.

Agha, Asif. 2011. "Meet Mediatization." *Language & Communication* 31 (3): 163–70. 10.1016/j.langcom.2011.03.006

Ahmed, Rashad, Abdu Al-kadi, and Trenton Hagar, eds. 2020. *Enhancements and Limitations to ICT-Based Informal Language Learning: Emerging Research and Opportunities*. Hershey, PA: IGI Global. 10.4018/978-1-7998-2116-8

Alred, Geof, and Mike Byram. 2002. "Becoming an Intercultural Mediator: A Longitudinal Study of Residence Abroad." *Journal of Multilingual and Multicultural Development* 23 (5): 339–52. 10.1080/01434630208666473

Backus, Ad, Durk Gorter, Karlfried Knapp, Rosita Schjerve-Rindler, Jos Swanenberg, Jan D. ten Thije, and Eva Vetter. 2013. "Inclusive Multilingualism: Concept, Modes and Implications." *European Journal of Applied Linguistics* 1 (2). 10.1515/eujal-2013-0010

Baraldi, Claudio. 2017. "Language Mediation as Communication System." *Communication Theory* 27 (4): 367–87. 10.1111/comt.12118

Beerkens, Roos. 2010. "Receptive Multilingualism as a Language Mode in the Dutch-German Border Area." Dissertation.

Beerkens, Roos, Emmanuelle Le Pichon- Vorstman, Roselinde Supheert, and Jan D. ten Thije, eds. 2020. *Enhancing Intercultural Communication in Organizations: Insights from Project Advisers*. Routledge Focus on Communication Studies. New York, London: Routledge.

Busch, Dominic. 2016. "Does Conflict Mediation Research Keep Track with Cultural Theory?" *European Journal of Applied Linguistics* 4 (2): 181–206. 10.1515/eujal-2015-0037

Busch, Dominic, and Hartmut Schröder. 2005. *Perspektiven interkultureller Mediation: Grundlagentexte zur kommunikationswissenschaftlichen Analyse triadischer Verständigung*, edited by Dominic Busch and Hartmut Schröder. Frankfurt am Main: Lang.

Byram, Michael. 1997. *Teaching and Assessing Intercultural Communicative Competence*. Clevedon: Multilingual Matters.

Cole, Debbie, and Bryan Meadows. 2013. "Avoiding the Essentialist Trap in Intercultural Education." In *Linguistics for Intercultural Education*, edited by Fred Dervin and Anthony J. Liddicoat, 29–47. Amsterdam: John Benjamins. 10.1075/lllt.33.03col

Deardorff, Darla K. 2004. *The Identification and Assessment of Intercultural Competence as Student Outcome of Internationalization*. Raleigh, NC: North Carolina State University Press.

Dervin, Fred, and Zehavit Gross, eds. 2016. *Intercultural Competence in Education*. London: Palgrave Macmillan. 10.1057/978-1-137-58733-6

Di Luzio, Aldo, Susanne Günthner, and Franca Orletti. 2001. *Culture in Communication. Analyses of Intercultural Situations*. Amsterdam: John Benjamins. 10.1075/pbns.81

Fisiak, Jacek, ed. 1984. *Contrastive Linguistics. Prospects and Problems*. De Gruyter Mouton.

Gautheron-Boutchatsky, Christina, Marie-Christine Kok Escalle, Georges Androulakis, and Karl Rieder. 2004. "Representations of the Concept of Otherness in Advertising and Cultural Mediation." In *Cultural Meditation in Language Learning and Teaching: Research Project*, edited by Geneviève Zarate, 155–79. Strasbourg.

Gumperz, John J. 1982. *Discourse Strategies*. Cambridge: Cambridge University Press.

Hall, Edward Twitchell. 1959. *The Silent Language*. Garden City, NY: Doubleday.

Hall, Stuart. 2001. *Representation. Cultural Representation and Signifying Practices*. London/ Thousand Oaks/ New Delhi: Sage.

Hofstede, Geert. 1980. *Culture's Consequences: International Differences in Work-Related Values*. Beverly Hills, London: Sage.

Jackson II, Ronald L. 2014. "Mapping Cultural Communication Research. 1960s to the Present." In *The Global Intercultural Communication Reader. Second Edition*, edited by Molefi K. Asante, Yoshitaka Miike, and Jing Yin, 76–91. New York, London: Routledge.

Jessner-Schmid, Ulrike, and Claire J. Kramsch, eds. 2015. *The Multilingual Challenge: Cross-Disciplinary Perspectives*. De Gruyter. 10.1515/9781614512165

Kolb, David Allen. 1984. *Experiential Learning: Experience as the Source of Learning and Development.* Englewood Cliffs, N.J.: Prentice-Hall.

Koole, Tom, and Jan D. ten Thije. 1994. *The Construction of Intercultural Discourse: Team Discussions of Educational Advisers.* Amsterdam: Rodopi.

Krase, Jerome, and Zdeněk Uherek, eds. 2017. *Diversity and Local Contexts.* Cham: Springer. 10.1007/978-3-319-53952-2

Lado, Robert. 1957. *Linguistics Across Cultures: Applied Linguistics for Language Teachers.* Ann Arbor, MI: University of Michigan Press.

Leerssen, Joep. 2007. "Imagology: History and Methods." In *Imagology: The Cultural Construction and Literary Representation of National Characters. A Critical Survey*, edited by Manfred Beller and Joep Leerssen, 17–32. Amsterdam: Rodopi.

Le Pichon-Vorstman, Emmanuelle, and Sergio Baauw. 2019. "EDINA, Education of International Newly Arrived Migrant Pupils." *European Journal of Applied Linguistics* 7 (1): 145–56. 10.1515/eujal-2018-0021

Leurs, Koen H.A. 2019. "Community Media Makers and the Mediation of Difference—Claiming Citizenship and Belongingness." In *Cultures, Citizenship and Human Rights*, edited by Rosemarie Buikema, Antoine C. Buyse, and Antonius C.G.M. Robben. 1st edition, 31–48. New York: Routledge.

McConachy, Troy, and Anthony J. Liddicoat. 2016. "Meta-Pragmatic Awareness and Intercultural Competence: The Role of Reflection and Interpretation in Intercultural Mediation." In *Intercultural Competence in Education*, edited by Fred Dervin and Zehavit Gross, 13–30. London: Palgrave Macmillan UK. 10.1057/978-1-137-5 8733-6_2

Müller-Jacquier, Bernd, and Jan D. ten Thije. 2000. "Interkulturelle Kommunikation: interkulturelles Training und Mediation." In *Linguistische Berufe: Ein Ratgeber zu aktuellen linguistischen Berufsfeldern*, edited by Michael Becker-Motzek, Gisela Brünner, Hermann Cölfen, and Annette Lepschy, 39–56. Forum angewandte Linguistik 37. Frankfurt am Main: Lang.

Ponzanesi, Sandra. 2016. *Connecting Europe: Postcolonial Mediations.* Utrecht: Utrecht University.

Rehbein, Jochen. 2006. "The Cultural Apparatus: Thoughts on the Relationship between Language, Culture, and Society." In *Beyond Misunderstanding. Linguistic Analyses of Intercultural Communication*, edited by Kristin Bührig and Jan D. ten Thije, 144: 43–96. Amsterdam: John Benjamins. 10.1075/pbns.144.04reh

Rehbein, Jochen, Jan D. ten Thije, and Anna Verschik. 2012. "Lingua Receptiva (LaRa)—Remarks on the Quintessence of Receptive Multilingualism." *International Journal of Bilingualism* 16 (3): 248–64. 10.1177/13 67006911426466

Reisigl, Martin, and Ruth Wodak. 2005. *Discourse and Discrimination. Rhetorics of Racism and Antisemitism.* London: Routledge. 10.4324/9780203993712

Rindler-Schjerve, Rosita, and Eva Vetter. 2012. *European Multilingualism: Current Perspectives and Challenges.* Bristol; Buffalo: Multilingual Matters.

Samovar, Larry A., and Richard E. Porter, eds. 1991. *Intercultural Communication: A Reader.* 6th edition. Belmont, CA: Wadsworth.

Severs, Rosanne, Karen Schoutsen, and Jan D. ten Thije. (2022, to appear). Becoming Interculturally Competently Aware: The Usage of a Reflection Tool to Enhance Intercultural Competences, a Case Study at Utrecht University. In: *The Riches of Intercultural Communication (Vol. 2) Multilingual and Intercultural Competences Approaches*, edited by Roselinde Supheert, Gandolfo Cascio, and Jan D. ten Thije. 2022b, to appear, Leiden: Brill.

Siapera, Eugenia. 2010. *Cultural Diversity and Global Media: The Mediation of Difference.* Chichester, UK: Wiley. 10.1002/9781444319132

Spencer-Oatey, Helen, and Peter Franklin. 2009. *Intercultural Interaction: A Multidisciplinary Approach to Intercultural Communication.* London: Palgrave Macmillan UK. 10.1057/9780230244511

Sweeney, Emma, and Hua Zhu. 2010. "Accommodating Toward Your Audience: Do Native Speakers of English Know How to Accommodate Their Communication Strategies Toward Nonnative Speakers of English?" *Journal of Business Communication* 47 (4): 477–504. 10.1177/0021943610377308

ten Thije, Jan D. 2006. "The Notions of *Perspective* and *Perspectivising* in Intercultural Communication Research." In *Beyond Misunderstanding. Linguistic Analyses of Intercultural Communication*, edited by Kristin Bührig and Jan D. ten Thije, 144: 97–151. Amsterdam: John Benjamins. 10.1075/pbns.144.05thi

ten Thije, Jan D. 2014. "The Self-Retreat of the Interpreter. An Analysis of Teasing and Toasting in Intercultural Discourse." In *Translational Action and Intercultural Communication*, edited by Kristin Bührig, Juliane House, and Jan D. ten Thije, 114–51. London, New York: Routledge.

ten Thije, Jan D. 2018. "Receptive Multilingualism." In *Twelve Lectures on Multilingualism*, edited by David M. Singleton and Larissa Aronin, 327–63. Bristol, Blue Ridge Summit: Multilingual Matters.

ten Thije, Jan D. 2020a. Intercultural Communication as Mediation. Inaugural lecture, 31 January 2020, Utrecht University (Dutch and English), last visited 6 January 2022: https://issuu.com/humanitiesuu/docs/oratie-jan-ten-thije_2020_en_totaal

ten Thije, Jan D. 2020b. "What Is Intercultural Communication?" In *The Cambridge Handbook of Intercultural Communication*, edited by Guido Rings and Sebastian Rasinger, 1st edition, 35–55. Cambridge University Press. 10.1017/9781108555067.004

Zhu, Hua. 2018. *Exploring Intercultural Communication: Language in Action*. 2nd edition. London: Routledge. 10.4324/9781315159010

33
IT TAKES THREE TO TANGO. A SOCIOLOGICAL TRIADOLOGY

Ulrich Bröckling

Postmodernity's enthusiasm for triads as a symptom of crisis

Preoccupation with 'the third' can produce paranoia. Wherever one looks, third parties look back; triadic, ternary, triangular or even trinitarian constellations lurk everywhere. There is no alter ego relationship in which a *tertius* or a *tertia* is not present, no duality in which a *tertium* is not embedded, no social structure, no matter how complex, that cannot be broken down into elementary triangular elements. Charles S. Peirce gave name to the disease from which he himself was said to suffer: "triadomania" (Spinks 2012).

Of course, susceptibility to this 'haunting' depends on the perspective of the observer and thus itself on the influential manifestation of the third. One sees what one expects to see, and those who look for third parties will find them everywhere. So far, so trivial. In terms of the sociology of knowledge, of greater interest is the question of what it is that leads the observer's gaze precisely in this direction. What causes numerous contemporary social and cultural theories to distrust binary schemes of order and turn instead to figurations of the third? What are the questions to which thinking responds with the transition from two-valued to three-valued models?

This is the first theme examined here. It places this shift in terms of contemporary diagnosis and interprets it as a symptom of a crisis in both the epistemic and the political order. The second part of this chapter, based on Georg Simmel's remarks on the "quantitative conditioning of the group," examines exemplary sociological contributions that elaborate the constitutively triadic structure of socialization and the diversity of triadic constellations. Finally, I present a triadic social experiment, which provides a playful utopian counter-draft to the asymmetries of triangular relationships.

The conclusions of present analyses regarding the third party seem unambiguous: A multitude of mediator, transgressor and hybrid figures, of included and excluded thirds populates contemporary theoretical landscapes. For example, René Girard's *scapegoat*, which was the founding figure of his social anthropology of violence (Girard 1977, 1986). Michel Serres called into play the figures of the parasite (Serres 1982a) and Hermes (Serres 1982b), the messenger of the gods and the god of merchants and thieves. Giorgio Agamben described *Homo sacer* as leading an ostracized threshold existence, reduced to his "naked life" (Agamben 1998). For cultural anthropology, the shape-shifting trickster is relevant, whilst postcolonial studies examine the creolised inhabitants of "third spaces" (Bhabha 1994). As already referred to, the observer occupies a key position in Niklas Luhmann's systems theory. Concepts of difference or rather *différance*, of impurity and ambiguity

310

DOI: 10.4324/9781003227441-39

have superseded those of identity and contradiction. More than the two sides of the respective distinction, the process of distinguishing itself becomes the problem.

This shift in focus is part of the catchy meta-narrative of a transition from modernity to postmodernity, as prominently formulated by Zygmunt Bauman on the part of sociologists. According to this narrative, modernity, by which Bauman, like postmodernity, does not mean a clearly defined epoch, but a specific "state of mind" (Bauman 1992, vii), a way of being-in-the-world and shaping the world, is characterized by a frenzy of putting things in order. This is supposed to banish the horrors of contingency. Since the order of the world is no longer given unquestioningly, it must be created through human effort, and it can only be created as a continuous struggle between disorder and chaos. For Bauman, the general model of the creation of order is the naming/classifying function of language, which operates via binary oppositions:

> Each act of naming splits the world into two: entities that answer to the name; all the rest that do not. Certain entities may be included into a class—made a class—only in as far as other entities are excluded, left outside. Invariably, such operation of inclusion/exclusion is an act of violence perpetrated upon the world, and requires the support of a certain amount of coercion. [...] Ambivalence is a side-product of the labour of classification; and it calls for yet more classifying effort. Though born of the naming/classifying urge, ambivalence may be fought only with a naming that is yet more exact, and classes that are yet more precisely defined: that is, with such operations as will set still tougher (counter-factual) demands on the discreteness and transparency of the world and thus give yet more occasion for ambiguity.
>
> *(Bauman 1991, 2 f.)*

The violence inherent in the dream of the Great Order and the war against ambivalence is multiplied, Bauman continues, because the modern world and its inhabitants are not only linguistically classed, but also practically segregated and condemned. The nation state in particular radicalizes the logic of inclusion and exclusion and translates the principle of *Tertium non datur* into a socio-technological program with possibly murderous consequences: Those who do not fit into the binary schemes are forced to fit and assimilate, or they are disenfranchised, exiled; in extreme cases persecuted and killed. To the same extent that the sovereign power either absorbs or expels everything foreign and different, it establishes itself as lawgiver, judge, and monopolist of violence and thus as the only legitimate instance of the third. Wherever two citizens or groups of citizens enter into contracts or disputes, the agencies of state law and the state apparatus of coercion are present behind the scenes as rule-setting and sanctioning *third-party enforcers*, even if they do not actively intervene.

Bauman emphasizes the "horticultural" ambitions of the modern nation-state. In order to create a system committed to the phantasm of purity and homogeneity, it not only meliorates the usable human material, but above all removes those elements "that neither fit the visualized perfect reality, nor can be changed so that they do" (Bauman 1989, 65). Racism and anti-Semitism are therefore constitutively inscribed in it. In this perspective, the National Socialist murder of the Jews does not prove to be a breach of civilization, but rather its most consistent realization, "as a rare, yet significant and reliable, test of the hidden possibilities of modern society" (Bauman 1989, 12). The Jews were exterminated as ostracized third parties. For the anti-Semites, Jews embodied the hated principle of universal mediation—money—which functions as a *Tertium comparationis* in every act of purchase, whilst also conversely the no less perhorrescent scandal of a "non-national nation" (Bauman 1989, 52). The anti-Semites did not see Jews as an enemy nation, but—far worse—as the enemies of the *völkisch* principle. 'The Jews' were the included, excluded third party and thus the personified negation of the nation form, writes Klaus Holz in a critical continuation of Bauman's reflections:

> The national anti-Semitic image of the Jews is paradoxical insofar as it constructs the 'Jews' as the tertium non datur of this distinction [of one's own and another nation, UB]. According to this distinction, they do not exist as a third party, but the third party only exists according to this distinction. They personify an ambivalent or non-identical identity.
>
> *(Holz 2000, 281)*

In the projections of a Jewish world conspiracy, the hatred of a supposedly cosmopolitan mode of existence that eluded the division of the world by nation manifested itself. The danger that was to emanate from the Jews was not that they were different, but that they were neither different nor the same.

Postmodernism does not mark the end or the absolute 'other' of modernity, but is its reflexive variant that has become a problem in itself. It is characterized above all by the fact that it liquefies fixed demarcations and privatizes the management of ambivalences. As a singular order no longer seems attainable and/or desirable, heterogeneous concepts of order, each of limited scope and duration, compete. Phenomena of the alien, the ambiguous, the hybrid, which the modern cleansing rage had fought against equally and throughout this struggle had always created itself anew, are now readily welcomed or at least taken into account as unchallengeable. The ambivalent third party mutates from troublemaker to not infrequently emphatically charged guarantor of a diversity that is aesthetically consumed, or which forms the starting point of particular identity politics, which are then in turn thwarted by identity-critical strategies of disambiguation. Nomads, queers, tricksters, cyborgs, and other boundary crossers who subvert the pressure of homogenization with a conundrum of blurred or shifting positionings have become leading figures of theoretical reflection as well as of a political practice critical of domination.

The privatization of ambivalence management in no way breaks with the logic of exclusion and inclusion, but merely multiplies the instances and sorting rules. The violence of 'whoever is not for us is against us' diffuses into neo-tribalisms, which define themselves through religious confessions, ethnic ascriptions of the self, and other and/or clientelistic allegiances. It has long been apparent that postmodernism also produces its ostracized third parties: the 'superfluous,' who fall out of the social functional systems as irrelevant and are not even suitable as objects of exploitation and social oppression. Likewise, the migrants, against whose stream the rich states seal themselves off and who, if they have nevertheless overcome the border fortifications, are pushed into the illegalized existence of *sans-papiers*.

The position of the third is occupied by disparate entities in both modernity and postmodernity, as the contemporary diagnostic outline has shown: There are guardians of order as well as disruptors of order, border guards and border violators, stabilizing as well as dynamizing forces, figures of sovereignty who apply and enforce the law, but also outlawed people who are denied the status of legal subjects. Regardless of whether the various figurations of the third are idealized, demonized, or observed from a neutral position, regardless of whether their irritating or instituent potential is in the foreground or the background, in each case they embody the problematic side of social order—its fragility and contingency, its conflictuality, and its indelible propensity for violence.

Georg Simmel: Triads are the foundations of sociation

The fact that social order is not self-evident and is therefore highly problematic is also the starting point of Georg Simmel's reflections on the third party. "How is Society Possible?" he asks in an excursus at the beginning of his *Sociology* (Simmel 1908/2009, 40), the subtitle of which is perhaps the most postmodern of the founding writings of this profoundly modern discipline in its anti-systematic structure—"Investigations into the Construction of Social Forms." Simmel conceives of society neither as an ontological fact nor as a subjectless construct, but as a process continually actualizing itself by the interactions of its members, precisely as sociation (Bedorf 2003, 107). "Sociation continuously emerges and ceases and emerges again. Even where its eternal flux and pulsation are not sufficiently strong to form organizations proper, they link individuals together" (Simmel 1917/1950, 9-10). It is sociologically relevant, because going beyond the merely psychological, such interactions are those that gain a contour independent of the persons involved in the individual case, i.e., that occur with a certain regularity and which solidify into institutions.

Simmel describes sociation as an interdependent process between individuals, therefore he attaches particular importance to the number of participants and dedicates a separate chapter to 'The Quantitative Conditioning of the Group,' which to a certain extent forms the original text of sociological preoccupation with the third party. The transition from the dyad to the triad marks the decisive threshold for Simmel. For him, the third is "a sociological archetype" (Freund 1971, 91). Although the isolated individual remains socialized insofar as society is present in his solitude, "be it as echoes of past or anticipation of future relations, be it as yearning or as voluntary seclusion" (Simmel 1908/2009, 79), it is presented exclusively in a negative way. Conversely, the dyad, whether it is an intimate or friendly connection, the conflict between two parties, a cooperative or an exchange relationship, embodies interaction in its purest, most elementary form. However, its existence depends directly on the presence of its two members: "The departure of either individual would destroy the whole, so it does not attain the same supra-personal life that one feels as independent of oneself" (Simmel 1908/2009, 83). Dyadically conceived theories of intersubjectivity are therefore as incapable of establishing sociality as anthropological Robinsonades. Only with a third party do interactions acquire the historicity and objectivity that are indispensable for the emergence of social institutions, but also their disintegration and transformation (Berger and Luckmann 1991, 76). Two parties in a relationship can love each other and quarrel, they can cooperate, give each other gifts, exchange goods, but without a third party there would be neither family nor market nor law nor other forms of sociation (Fischer 2000: 130). The third party is also paradigmatic for Simmel insofar as he is convinced that "the further expansion to four or more in no way modifies the essence of the grouping correspondingly more" (Simmel 1908/2009, 95). His thesis suggesting that the triad already contains *in nuce* the entire complexity of social relations does, of course, ignore the particularities of larger associations. For example, the dynamics of mass actions, or the institutions that, like the social insurance system, operate on the basis of statistically normal distributions and therefore require large numbers to be taken into account. As plausibly as Simmel elaborates the emergent function of the third party in relation to the dyad, his attempt to cancel out the multiplicity of modes of sociation within it is unconvincing.

Personal third parties or institutions as supra-personal third parties are neither temporally nor logically added to the interaction between two. Triadic constellations are rather structurally anterior to dyadic ones because interpersonal relationships and, even more so, their institution are always socially pre-structured: Every human being is part of a family triangle from birth (or, in the consciousness of his parents, long before his birth), however this may be structured. Further, *ego* and *other* can only understand themselves as *ego* and *other* because their relationship is distinct from other relationships. Dyad and triad must therefore be thought of in a kind of time loop: The seemingly elementary is already endowed by the complexity to which it evolves.

In Simmel's social grammar the third party appears as either an element of divisiveness or as one of unification. It either destabilizes an existing dyad to its own or another's advantage, profiting from the courting of two opponents for his favor, or mediates or settles an antagonism between two parties (Bedorf 2003, 118). In the basic figures of the third party that Simmel derives from this—firstly, impartial and mediator, secondly, *tertius gaudens*, thirdly, the one who acts according to the maxim *divide et impera*—elementary social institutions can easily be identified. The figures of the arbitrator and mediator embody the nucleus of law, the customer as a smiling third-party competitor is at the center of all market activity, and the principle of 'divide and conquer' provides a key to understanding political rule (Fischer 2000).

The social grammar is, admittedly, not yet exhausted by this typology; Simmel's triadic figure theory needs supplementation. It recognizes sovereign but not ostracized third parties, the *tertius gaudens* but not the complementary figure of the *tertius miserabilis*, as manifested in the figures of the "servant of two masters," the bone of contention, the whipping boy and the neglected or rejected "weeping third party" (Scharmann 1959). Simmel himself thematizes one figure of the hybrid third in the famous "Excursus on the Stranger." Like Bauman, he takes the Jewish diaspora experience as his starting point and like Bauman, he emphasizes the precarious position of the stranger "as one who comes today and stays tomorrow" (Simmel 1908/2009, 601). Contrary to Bauman's victim of the modern terror of order and writing before the macro-crimes of the 20th century, however, Simmel's stranger is allowed to stay as "an organically unrelated add-on" but "still an organic member of the group whose unified life includes the particular conditions of this element" (Simmel 1908/2009, 605). Simmel's third may be antagonized, the first and the second may conspire against him, they may exploit or oppress him, but he does not fall out of the world of social interactions. The radically excluded, ostracized third, threatened with annihilation, marks an empty space in his theory.

Triadological insights are challenging game theory

Simmel's triadology was embraced in the 1950s and 1960s by a number of U.S. social scientists who combined his thoughts on coalition formation in triadic constellations with the mathematical game theory of John von Neumann and Oskar Morgenstern and translated them into an empirical research program. Theodore Caplow (1956, 1959, 1968) is particularly worthy of mention, while important contributions were also made by Theodore M. Mills (1953, 1954, 1956) and William A. Gamson (1961).

Von Neumann and Morgenstern theorized that every social interaction can be modelled as a strategic game in which the players seek to minimize their costs and maximize their gains. While in two-person games the main problem for each player is to find the optimal strategy, i.e., the general principles for choosing moves, under given rules, success in three- and multi-person games depends mainly on the choice of coalition partners.

> In a zero-sum three-person game a particular move of a player—which, for the sake of simplicity, we assume to be clearly advantageous to him—may be disadvantageous to both other players, but it may also be advantageous to one and (a fortiori) disadvantageous to the other opponent. Thus some players may occasionally experience a parallelism of interests [...]. It may happen, in particular, that a player has a choice among various policies: That he can adjust his conduct so as to get into parallelism of interest with another player, or the opposite; that he can choose with which of the other two players he wishes to establish such a parallelism, and (possibly) to what extent.
>
> *(Neumann and Morgenstern 1944/1953, 220)*

Neumann and Morgenstern illustrated this with a simple game. Each player, unaware of the choices of his two fellow players, chooses one of them as his partner. Thus, in each game there is either a pair or no pair. If two players have chosen each other, each of them receives half a unit as a reward, while the third player loses a unit. If there is no pair, no one receives any winnings. Of particular sociological relevance is that Neumann and Morgenstern must introduce an external influence. The coalitions necessary in the context of a theory of rational choice actions can only be the results of social negotiation processes. In order to act rationally, the players must reach agreements outside the game itself. Communication with its double or triple contingency, with its vagueness, idiosyncrasies, and cultural biases contaminates the strictly mathematical theory of decision making.

This social dimension of coalition formation, which cannot be mathematized, is the starting point for sociological coalition theory, which formalizes the possible alliances in a triad on the basis of the distribution of power between its members. In doing so, like Simmel, its assumption is that the mechanisms of coalition formation change with the number of actors in the system but are largely independent of whether the actors are children in the playground, political parties in the formation of government or competing nation states. If one quantifies the relative initial strength, eight possible types of triads emerge, each of which makes certain coalitions seem rational (Caplow 1968, 6). Figure 33.1 illustrates six of them:

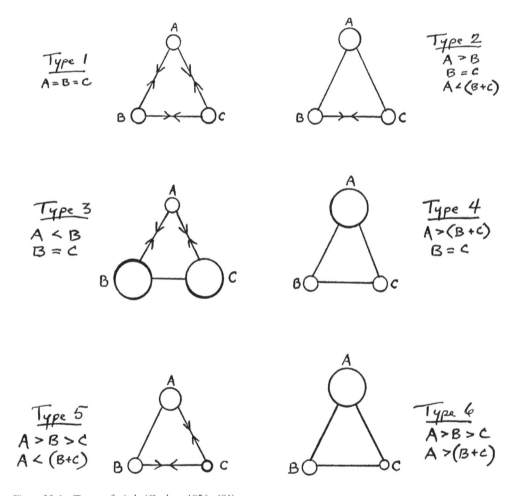

Figure 33.1 Types of triads (Caplow 1956, 491)

Caplow introduces further differentiation distinguishing between different types of games. *Continuous* three-person games are those in which the participants are in permanent relationships with each other and the reliability of reciprocal behavioral expectations plays an important role. *Episodic* games are those where relative power is only fixed for one game, e.g., one election period, where the game partners try to obtain the largest possible share of gains in this game. Finally, *terminal* games include those in which the triad dissolves after the conclusion of a game because all participants pursue the goal of eliminating their fellow players and only enter into alliances if they can thereby protect themselves against their own elimination. With the terminal game scenario, Caplow models a lethal confrontation of two against one and thus, unlike Simmel, includes the possibility of the annihilation of the third party in his considerations.

According to Caplow's hypothesis, depending on the nature of the game, different coalitions will arise with the same initial strength. Thus, in the case of the theoretically particularly productive triad of type 5, in which $A > B > C$ and at the same time $A < (B + C)$, the coalitions AB and AC are equally probable in the case of a continuous game: C needs a partner in either case in order not to be dominated. B would remain inferior in a coalition with A and is therefore interested in forming a coalition with the weaker C in order to be able to dominate A. To prevent this coalition, A is also interested in joining forces with C, so that C has the choice of which of the two to ally with. In an episodic game, each player seeks the most favorable position with regard to the distribution of winnings in the respective game. In the case that the prize is divided equally between the coalition partners, the same result is to be expected as in continuous play. If, on the other hand, the winnings are distributed asymmetrically according to the initial strength, coalition BC becomes more likely, since C will prefer it in order to increase his share of the gains. Under the conditions of a terminal game, no alliance of two is likely to come about at all, as in any possible coalition the weaker link would be helplessly at the mercy of the stronger one, after they had previously jointly eliminated the third. Caplow sees an example of this constellation in the fragile balance of power between the nuclear powers USA, Soviet Union, and China during the Cold War (Caplow 1968, 5ff.).

The observation that in coalitions of two against one, where original strength often turns into weakness and weakness into strength is perhaps the most important insight of a game-theoretically informed sociology of the third. It once again confirms Simmel's fundamental finding that in triadic relationships the construction of order and its destabilization are indissolubly intertwined. Caplow, however, not only elaborates on Simmel's reflections on three-way constellations, he also narrows them down. By focusing exclusively on the problem of coalition formation, he overlooks the mediator and arbitrator function of the third party; by constructing only *win-lose* games and consequently analyzing only two-against-one coalitions, he remains blind to the variant of a grand coalition that includes A, B, and C. In terms of outcome, Caplow's third parties merely function as catalysts of dyadic cooperation. They are necessary for two to find each other, but superfluous once they have found each other. Because Caplow sets out from pre-existing triadic constellations, he is not interested in the processes of the constitution of a triad or its elements, such as the social dynamics triggered by the addition of a rival or the birth of a child in a love relationship or the appearance of a competing supplier in an existing buyer-seller interaction. In other words, he examines the relationship starting from the positions, not the position starting from the relationships. In comparison to Simmel, his understanding of power is also one-dimensional. By generally conceiving of power relations in purely quantitative terms and also assuming that all participants know their own strength as well as the strength of the others, he is able to adequately describe coalitions that fulfil these conditions, such as the formation of a government after a parliamentary election, but not confrontation or cooperation games, in which power is only realized *in actu* and the rules of the game are not necessarily fixed in advance (Bedorf 2003, 141 ff.). Finally, he concludes by stating that one dominates over two or two over one, but does not ask in what way power is exercised.

According to their status, Caplow's coalition predictions, even if he introduces them as the only rational strategies of the actors involved in the sense of maximizing utility, are no more than probabilistic hypotheses that can guide empirical research. His typology has found resonance in above all social psychology, where it has been tested, modified, and supplemented in numerous small group experiments with regard to age, gender, and other influencing factors (cf. Vinacke and Arkoff 1957, Vinacke 1959, Stryker and Psathas 1960, Borgatta 1961, Borgatta and Borgatta 1962, Uesugi and Vinacke 1963, Chertkoff 1967). Von Neumann and Morgenstern had to introduce the search, comparison, and negotiation processes that precede coalition formation as a contaminating moment, without being able or willing to describe them more precisely. Caplow and the small-group researchers who succeeded him, however, try to clarify these communicative impurities by either converting them into quantifiable relations of forces or transferring them into replicable experimental arrangements.

Triads prove to be a particularly suitable unit of analysis for this purpose because they are complex enough to model social relationships beyond the first-person age binary, but they are simple enough to still be able to represent them mathematically and/or to reproduce them experimentally in the social psychology laboratory. "Larger subgraphs than triads are not usually investigated," says a textbook on social network analysis:

> This is partly due to the large number of possible subgraphs with more than three nodes. If there were 22 = 4 possible states of a dyad, there would already be 26 = 64 possible states of a triad: for each of the six ordered pairs of three nodes, the border can exist or not. For tetrads (subgraphs of four nodes and all edges between them) there are already 12 ordered pairs and thus 212 = 4096 different possible states.
>
> *(Trappmann, Hummell, and Sodeur 2005, 184)*

This is decidedly too much even for computer-based modeling. Social network analysts therefore resort to the so-called triad census. This involves examining the relationships in larger social associations by analytically disaggregating the overall group into triad units, classifying the mutual, unilateral, or non-relationships in these triads using graph notation, and then calculating the frequency distributions for the different types of triads. The procedure is based on methodological reductionism: first, a social structure, e.g., a clique or school class, is broken down to the smallest possible actor constellations, to triads, and these in turn function as a combination of two-way relationships. These units are then mathematically formalized and statistically aggregated in order to finally derive probability statements about the structure to be analyzed, i.e., to predict its future development from the existing friendships in the clique or school class. In short, in order to be able to make mathematically exact statements, even if it is only in the sense of probability calculations, one cuts the phenomenon to be investigated until one can model it, and then describes exclusively those sides of the phenomenon that correspond to the selected cut. What cannot be modelled is left out—not only the nation state, but also social science evidently harbors horticultural ambitions.

Three-sided football: A postmodern triadic social experiment

If one takes up Zygmunt Bauman's distinction between modernity and postmodernity, then the game and network theoretical approaches, in contrast to Simmel's dazzling essayistics, undoubtedly fall under the epistemic order of modernity. They assume, at least in the sense of a plausible as-if assumption for forecasts, that people act rationally on the basis of their preferences and the information available to them, i.e., that they always decide in favor of the alternative from which they expect to derive the greatest possible benefit. Human behavior appears as a continuous series of choices that excludes ambivalence because either a subjectively better and a worse alternative exists, or a pure decision is either inevitable, as sufficient information is lacking, or risk-free, since costs and benefits are identically distributed on both sides. This includes aporetic decision-making situations, in which orientation towards individual utility maximization leads to worse results than cooperative strategies, which, in turn however, have to fall back on a precarious resource, because it cannot be generated exclusively by rational choice actions: That of trust. The best-known example is the prisoner's dilemma with its radically asymmetrical three-way constellation between both delinquents and the prosecutor. What is clear in any case though, is that a decision must be made. The freedom

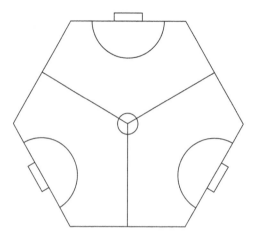

Figure 33.2 Playing field three-sided football[1]

to choose is coincidently the compulsion to have to choose. Thus, although Caplow's social geometry describes power relations in which no coalition is formed or in which several options seem equally plausible, it does not consider the possibility of non-decision. It is the excluded third of rational choice theory. Bartleby's "I would prefer not to" is beyond the horizon of thought (Figure 33.2).

The triadic social experiment of the three-sided football pitch attempts to playfully undermine precisely this compulsion for unambiguity in social interactions (cf. Bedorf 2003). The Danish artist and political activist Asger Jorn, co-founder of the avant-garde movement CoBrA and at times a member of the Situationist International, invented it to illustrate his concept of "triolectics" crossing dialectical dualisms. In three-sided football, three teams of seven players each compete on a hexagonal pitch with three goals. A referee is superfluous or rejected because there is to be no sovereign authority above the parties. The game already has a third party. It happens that some players of one team cooperate simultaneously with one opponent, the others with the second. The unavoidable confusion and the constant change of coalitions are deliberate, for they always lead to new constellations of alliances and oppositions, which do not solidify into a permanent hierarchy and/or opposition, but also do not dissolve into a harmonious game without losers.

National teams, cups, and leagues, etc. do not exist in three-sided football. Although there are references circulating on the internet to a Three-sided Football League with members in Great Britain, Italy, Serbia, Austria, and Australia, it cannot be ruled out that this is the hoax of a communications guerrilla. In any case, the first tournament is said to have taken place in Glasgow in 1993 as part of an anarchist summer school; in 2014, Jorn's birthplace, Silkeborg, hosted the first World Cup, and in 2017, Kassel in Germany hosted the second.

One would like to recommend the three-sided football game as an antidote to all kinds of bread-and-circus spectacles and the idiocy of national self-enthusiasm, but this social experiment is like anarchism in general: *it would be a good idea*. More important than devising sociological triadologies, therefore, would be to critically apply interest in the third and examine why the equally stupid and fatal binary of the 'us' and the 'them' still has such a power of fascination—and not only in football.

Note

1 Ed g2s (https://commons.wikimedia.org/wiki/File:Three sided football pitch.svg), "Three sided football pitch," colors modified by Dominic Busch, https://creativecommons.org/licenses/by-sa/3.0/legalcode.

It takes three to tango

References

Agamben, Giorgio. 1998. *Homo Sacer: Sovereign Power and Bare Life.* Stanford: Stanford University Press.

Bauman, Zygmunt. 1989. *Modernity and Holocaust.* Cambridge: Polity Press.

Bauman, Zygmunt. 1991. *Modernity and Ambivalence.* Ithaca, N.Y.: Cornell University Press.

Bauman, Zygmunt. 1992. *Intimations of Postmodernity.* London and New York: Routledge.

Bedorf, Thomas. 2003. *Dimensionen des Dritten. Sozialphilosophische Modelle zwischen Ethischem und Politischem.* München: Fink.

Berger, Peter L., and Thomas Luckmann. 1991. *The Social Construction of Reality: A Treatise in the Sociology of Knowledge.* London: Penguin Books.

Bhabha, Homi. 1994. *The Location of Culture.* London and New York: Routledge.

Borgatta, Edgar F., and Marie L. Borgatta. 1962. "Coalitions and Interaction Concepts of Support in Three-Person Groups." *Social Forces* 41 (1): 68–75. 10.2307/2572922

Borgatta, Marie L. 1961. "Power Structure and Coalitions in Three-Person Groups." *Journal of Social Psychology* 55 (2): 287–300. 10.1080/00224545.1961.9922184

Caplow, Theodore. 1956. "A Theory of Coalitions in the Triad." *American Sociological Review* 21 (4): 489–93. 10.2307/2088718

Caplow, Theodore. 1959. "Further Development of a Theory of Coalitions in the Triad." *American Journal of Sociology* 64 (5): 488–93.

Caplow, Theodore. 1968. *Two against One. Coalitions in Triads.* Englewood Cliffs and New Jersey: Prentice-Hall.

Chertkoff, Jerome M. 1967. "A Revision of Caplow's Coalition Theory." *Journal of Experimental Social Psychology* 3 (2): 172–77. 10.1016/0022-1031(67)90020-0

Fischer, Joachim. 2000. "Der Dritte. Zur Anthropologie der Intersubjektivität." In *wir/ihr/sie. Identität und Alterität in Theorie und Methode*, edited by Wolfgang Eßbach, 103–36. Würzburg: Ergon.

Freund, Julien. 1971. "Der Dritte in Simmels Soziologie." In *Ästhetik und Soziologie um die Jahrhundertwende: Georg Simmel*, edited by Hannes Böhringer and Karlfried Gründer, 90–104. Frankfurt am Main: Klostermann.

Gamson, William A. 1961. "A Theory of Coalition Formation." *American Sociological Review* 26 (3): 373–82.

Girard, René. 1977. *Violence and the Sacred.* Baltimore and London: The Johns Hopkins University Press.

Girard, René. 1986. *The Scapegoat.* Baltimore: The Johns Hopkins University Press.

Holz, Klaus. 2000. "Die Figur des Dritten in der nationalen Ordnung der Welt." *Soziale Systeme* 6: 269–90.

Mills, Theodore M. 1953. "Power Relations in Three-Person Groups." *American Sociological Review* 18: 351–57. 10.2307/2087546

Mills, Theodore M. 1954. "The Coalition Pattern in Three-Person Groups." *American Sociological Review* 19 (6): 657–67. 10.2307/2087912

Mills, Theodore M. 1956. "Developmental Processes in Three-Person Groups." *Human Relations* 9: 343–55. 10.1177/001872675600900305

Neumann, John von, and Oskar Morgenstern. 1944/1953. *Theory of Games and Economic Behavior.* Princeton: Princeton University Press.

Scharmann, Theodor. 1959. *Tertius miserabilis.* Berlin: Duncker & Humblot.

Serres, Michel. 1982a. *The Parasite.* Baltimore and London: Johns Hopkins Univ. Press.

Serres, Michel. 1982b. *Hermes: Literature, Science, Philosophy.* Baltimore and London: The Johns Hopkins University Press.

Simmel, Georg. 1908/2009. *Sociology: Inquiries into the Construction of Social Forms.* Leiden and Boston: Brill.

Simmel, Georg. 1950. *The Sociology of Georg Simmel*, edited by Kurt H. Wolf. New York: The Free Press.

Spinks, Cary W. 2012. *Peirce and Triadomania. A Walk in the Semiotic Wilderness.* The Hague: De Gruyter Mouton.

Stryker, Sheldon, and George Psathas. 1960. "Research on Coalitions in the Triad: Findings, Problems and Strategy." *Sociometry* 23 (3): 217–30. 10.2307/2785887

Trappmann, Mark, Hans J. Hummell, and Wolfgang Sodeur. 2005. *Strukturanalyse sozialer Netzwerke. Konzepte, Modelle, Methoden.* Wiesbaden: Springer VS.

Uesugi, Thomas K., and W. Edgar Vinacke. 1963. "Strategy in a Feminine Game." *Sociometry* 26 (1): 75–88. 10.2307/2785726

Vinacke, Edgar W. 1959. "Sex roles in a Three Person Game." *Sociometry*, 22 (4): 343–60. 10.2307/2786051

Vinacke, Edgar W., and Abe Arkoff. 1957. "An Experimental Study of Coalitions in the Triad." *American Sociological Review* 22 (4), 406–14.

34

A FRAMEWORK FOR UNDERSTANDING INTERCULTURAL MEDIATION FROM THE STANDPOINT OF A SYSTEMIC THEORY OF COMMUNICATION

Claudio Baraldi

Introduction

This chapter is based on the assumption that the analysis of intercultural mediation requires an investigation into its theoretical and methodological presuppositions. Theory explains *what* intercultural mediation is, while methodology explains the *way* in which intercultural mediation is achieved. From a theoretical point of view, the concept of 'intercultural mediation' may be split in two parts, i.e., the substantive 'mediation' and the adjective 'intercultural': the point of departure is the substantive, but the adjective is important to understand a specification—and a limitation—of the general concept of mediation. From a methodological point of view, the analysis concerns the possible ways of achieving mediation in general and the possibility to apply them to intercultural mediation.

This chapter suggests a specific theoretical and methodological framework which explains mediation as achieved through communication. Mediation is conceived as a communication system realized through interactions. Against this background, this chapter deals with two problems: (1) the conditions of intercultural mediation, i.e., mediation as an intercultural communication system; (2) the methodological problem of identifying the specificity of intercultural mediation.

The organization of the chapter is thus based on the distinction between (1) the general concept of mediation and the concept of intercultural mediation, and on the distinction between (2) theory and methodology. The first section presents the concept of mediation, the second section the concept of intercultural mediation, and the third section the methodological presuppositions of mediation as a general concept and intercultural mediation. The concluding section discusses the most important consequences of the use of the concept of intercultural mediation from a theoretical and methodological point of view.

Mediation

Mediation is defined here as a communication system, in which the role of one participant (the mediator) consists in dealing with problems of communication involving the other participants.

Understanding intercultural mediation

Dealing with these problems means enhancing reflexivity in the mediation system. Reflexivity (Luhmann 1995) means that one communicative event refers to the communication process, focusing on the way in which this process is produced. In particular, the communicative event can highlight the possible alternatives in producing further communication. In the case of mediation, reflexivity is achieved through the mediator's *reflexive coordination* of the communication process of mediation. The mediator's utterances focus on communication in whatever way it manifests itself.

The function of reflexive coordination is (1) to clarify opportunities of communication and/or (2) to stress problems or doubts about the production of communication. By focusing on the conditions of the communication process, the mediator's utterances pave the way to alternative ways of producing communication, i.e., resolving problems and taking opportunities. Reflexive coordination is important when participants' utterances need further investigation, because they include relevant information or intentions, because they are complex or unclear, or because they deal with delicate issues Reflexive coordination gives priority to the participants' ways of clarifying their points of view, experiences, and/or emotions. Thus, reflexive coordination enhances *transformative relaying* (Heritage and Clayman 2010, 209) in communication, which means that the mediator's utterances modify the position of one participant to invite response from the other participant.

Mediation is the production of reflexivity in problematic conditions, in particular when problems of understanding or acceptance of communication arise; these problems originate two specific forms of mediation, i.e., language mediation and conflict mediation, which include similarities and differences (Baraldi 2017). Language mediation deals with problems of mutual understanding whereas conflict mediation deals with lack of acceptance. The common function of these two forms of mediation is repairing problems (of either understanding or acceptance) emerging in other communication systems, such as problems in involving children in schools or patients in healthcare services, or in reaching agreements in international politics.

The accomplishment of mediation requires agency on the part of the mediator, who chooses "a set of positions and not others" (Winslade and Monk 2008, 113). The concept of agency highlights the importance of choices: agency is shown by *intelligible* choices of actions (Van Langenhove and Harré 1999), that is actions which clearly show the mediator's autonomous selection among a range of options. Mediators are active distributors of opportunities to talk, they induce parties to introduce and deal with particular issues, reinforce certain positions, make some outcomes more likely than others. In other words, mediators are agents because they *produce* knowledge in communication, making this production intelligible through their actions. Thus, mediators' skills "are less about unique personal qualities than the qualities of being a unique person" (Cloke 2003, 52). Mediators' actions are expressions of agency when they lead to social change, since they introduce unpredictability in the communication system, changing the conditions of either conflict (conflict mediation) or understanding (language mediation).

The mediator's agency alone, however, is not sufficient to achieve reflexive coordination and social change. Mediators' agency both enhances and is enhanced by the agency of the other participants, all of whom contribute to reflexive coordination and change. Agency is a communicative construction, rather than an individual achievement, and reflexive coordination is a way of diffusing agency among the participants. Thus, mediation may be seen as a communication system based on all participants' contributions, i.e., as a mediation system. The mediators' actions can trigger changes in the mediation system since change is the result of a structure of communication.

The mediation system is based on a specific structure which orients mediated communication to (1) a basic distinction between positive equality and negative inequality of participation, (2) the positioning of empowering (the mediator) and empowered participants, and (3) sensitivity for personal expressions. This means that the mediation system is based on dialogue. According to Wierzbicka, in dialogue participants make efforts to understand each other and make themselves understood, dialogue

321

implying "that each party makes a step in the direction of the other" (2006, 692). In short, dialogic mediation is based on the structure enhancing equity, empowerment, and sensitivity.

Mediation is realized through interactions, which do not necessarily imply participants' physical presence, although this is a frequent condition. In a broader view, interactions are based on reciprocal (reflexive) perception, whereby each participant perceives that s/he is perceived by the other participants (Luhmann 1995), which may be also achieved remotely. In the mediation system, reflexive perception is necessary since it allows participants to take action and respond to each other immediately, thus enabling participants to exercise their agency. In the mediation system, reflexivity extends from perception to coordination and to diffusion of agency among participants. Mediation, however, is not limited to specific interactions; rather, it is observed as a generalized mediation system based on a generalized structure of dialogue. The mediation system is reproduced through several specific interactions, while its function and structure are not limited to any specific interaction. Interactions are specific realizations of a general mediation system.

Intercultural mediation

Intercultural mediation means that the mediation system is a system of intercultural communication. For a long time, intercultural communication has been conceived as based on cultural difference, i.e., on the difference of cultural membership, and thus cultural identity of participants in communication (Spencer-Oatey and Franklin 2009; Ting-Toomey 1999). This conception has been applied to intercultural conflict resolution and mediation (Avruch and Black 1991, 1993; LeBaron 2003a; Rubenfeld and Clément 2012; Fritz 2014). In this view, which criticizes the misleading universalism of mediation, mediation is intercultural because participants are influenced by their own cultures, which make their identities 'cultural.' If participants' cultural identities are different, communication becomes intercultural. This approach can also be found in several specialized sites and in training about intercultural mediation.

The concept of intercultural communication is based on an essentialist epistemology, in that it presents "people's individual behavior as entirely defined and constrained by the cultures in which they live so that the stereotype becomes the essence of who they are" (Holliday 2011, 4). A non-essentialist view of intercultural communication stresses the prefix inter and warns against insisting on a predefined cultural identity (Byrd Clark and Dervin 2014). Such a view focuses on the construction of *narratives* of cultural identity in communication processes (Baraldi 2015; Holliday and Amadasi 2020). Since the meaning of 'cultural' identity is constructed in communication processes, it is contingent, fluid, and malleable (Dervin and Liddicoat 2013). Holliday (2011) defines the construction of narratives of cultural identities as *small cultures*, i.e., negotiated constructions in specific social groups or social activities. The interactional formation of small cultures is based on narratives of participants' personal cultural trajectories, which lead to constructing the meaning of diversity and identity (Holliday and Amadasi 2020). The production of small cultures, based on narratives of personal cultural trajectories, is a hybrid construction of identity (Holliday and Amadasi 2020; Kramsch and Uryu 2012). Here, the concept of 'hybrid' refers to the *way of constructing* narratives in situated communication processes: hybrid refers to the communicative construction of a variety of narratives related to personal experiences.

In this view, 'intercultural' mediation is based on the communicative construction of personal narratives concerning cultural meanings, rather than on the participation of individuals with different cultural identities. Mixed views of mediation, drawing on essentialism and constructivism, may be observed in an analysis of mediated conversations which presupposes a culturally predefined context (Garcia 2013), and in an analysis of mediation as 'third culture,' which focuses on ways of mediating based on presupposed cultural differences (Salamandra 2002). A more radical non-essentialist view explains mediation of intercultural conditions as the production of small cultures and a fluid identity (Brownlie 2017, 2018).

Intercultural mediation is a system of intercultural communication based on reflexive co-ordination and enhanced by the mediator's agency. In this sense, intercultural mediation is a specific form of mediation, which depends on the type of problem dealt with, i.e., either a problem of understanding or acceptance of narratives of personal cultural trajectories. The production of an intercultural mediation system depends on the way in which this type of problems becomes relevant, i.e., *structural coupling*.

The mediation system fulfils the function of 'repairing' communication problems in another system, for instance medical communication in which doctors and patients do not speak the same language or engage in conflicts. Thus, mediation is provided in a given communication system (e.g., the healthcare system) when the reproduction of communication in this system is difficult due to problems of mutual understanding or acceptance. This implies a coupling between the structure of the mediation system and the structure of the system in which mediation is provided. Structural coupling means that the different structures of different systems influence each other, but without determining each other. In particular, coupling between the structures of different communication systems is achieved in a specific communication process (Luhmann 2013): communication is simultaneously achieved in both systems (mediation and, e.g., the healthcare system) and structural coupling maintains the autonomy of both systems, since the same communication has different meanings in the two systems (for instance, communication is both mediated and medical). Each structure influences the communication process; thus, the mediation system needs to take into account the structure it is coupled with (e.g., taking care of illness), and the other system needs to take into account the structure of the mediation system (equity). This implies that the mediation system can trigger new conditions of equity in the other communication system, while restoring its structure; for example, the way illness is taken care of becomes more equally participated through the empowerment of participants. The mediation system cannot empower one participant's agency (e.g., patient's agency) without empowering the other participant's agency (e.g., doctor's agency). Mediation is dialogic since it implies the positive acknowledgement of different perspectives: each participant is led to observe and consider the others' competent and legitimate perspectives. Thus, dialogic mediation provides transformation in other communication systems: it produces change of the structuration of specific interactions (e.g., doctor-patient interactions) and, when applied extensively, it has an impact on the structure of the larger communication system (e.g., the healthcare system).

Structural coupling determines the conditions of intercultural mediation. Social structures are also cultural presuppositions (Gumperz 1992; Gumperz and Cook-Gumperz 2009) of communication systems, i.e., the semantics which guides communication (Luhmann 2013). Thus, structuring a communication system also means establishing a cultural orientation for communication processes. For instance, in the healthcare system, the semantics of taking care of illness and of providers and patients' roles guides medical communication. This semantics may become problematic when users (e.g., migrants) who get access to the communication system do not share the symbols of cultural presuppositions (e.g., care of illness and/or relevant roles). In this case, negotiation of different cultural meanings—a small culture—is needed, and intercultural mediation becomes relevant. On the one hand, mediators are asked to help internal roles (e.g., doctors) to explore problems of understanding or acceptance expressed by users (e.g., patients), negotiating relevant cultural meanings with them. On the other hand, mediators are asked to give users the opportunity to explain their understanding and/ or their views on the cultural presuppositions of communication (e.g., care of illness). This mediation is intercultural since it clarifies the semantics of cultural presuppositions which is not understood or accepted by all participants. Intercultural mediation produces re-interpretations of these cultural presuppositions through mediated communication, which re-interpret—and change—them within the local interactional context. Thus, intercultural mediation can promote a structural change in another communication system. Its function is enhancing positive intercultural communication, i.e., avoiding or transforming essentialist positions, making the contingent production of small cultures evident and enhancing the positive meaning of hybridity.

The intercultural meaning of mediation does not depend on participation of individuals of different nationalities, migrant individuals, members of minorities, nor on lack of mutual language understanding. Mediation can create the conditions for the empowerment of participants' agency, for instance migrants' agency (Baraldi and Gavioli 2017; Inghilleri 2005) and the promotion of equal relationships, but without highlighting or treating cultural meanings and identities when participants do not express any cue of cultural diversity in communication. In all cases, the cultural work of mediators consists in narrowing the gap between different opportunities of exercising agency, including participants' perspectives, indicating that diverse positions are taken into account, avoiding stereotypes and forms of dominant behaviors or actions ignoring other participants; however, mediation can only be defined as intercultural when communication explicitly shows cues of cultural diversity.

The relevance of intercultural mediation in the mediation system is a matter of empirical investigation. Mediation is properly intercultural when it deals with explicit and evident cultural problems or concerns. Intercultural mediation proper means intercultural adaptation (Baraldi 2017; Baraldi and Gavioli 2017), i.e., the communicative negotiation of cultural values and behaviors, which shows the way in which cultural presuppositions are adapted to specific conditions of communication, and interlaced personal cultural trajectories are produced as small cultures. In this sense, the specific function of intercultural mediation is to enhance empowerment and recognition of cultural diversity, abolish or at least reduce ethnocentric communication (us-them distinctions), promote change of the dominating cultural presuppositions within a communication system, and treat cultural diversity as a plurality of options. This means both enhancing all participants' agency in expressing these options and opening up spaces to negotiate these options. Intercultural mediation may transform cultural diversity from a communication block based on an essentialist view of cultural belonging into a thread for hybrid communication processes based on negotiated constructions of personal cultural trajectories.

Methodological presuppositions of (intercultural) mediation

Methodology sets out the ways in which mediation is achieved. The analysis of methodology requires empirical observations, i.e., either external observations provided by researchers or self-observations provided by mediators themselves. Research and literature reveal different ways of achieving mediation; however, some general reflections are possible.

Methodology concerns the mediator's actions which can implement the mediation system. These actions are observable only in the interaction, in particular through the effects on other participants' actions. While the features of mediation actions have been very frequently described in the literature (Benjamin 2003; Brownlie 2018; Garcia 2013; Picard and Melchin 2007), theories of *transformative mediation* (Bush and Folger 1994) and *narrative mediation* (Winslade and Monk 2008) are particularly important for this description. On the one hand, the action of mediation is identified as able to transform the relationship between the participants through the promotion of their mutual recognition and empowerment. On the other hand, the action of mediation is identified as the construction of alternative narratives, with respect to existing ones in which one party is subjugated to or marginalized by the other. Alternative narratives encourage the participants to consider new ways of dealing with different and conflicting or not understandable perspectives. Mediation can create opportunities for the participants to introduce their own stories and for recovering their unstoried experiences, dealing with the participants as the producers and editors of their own stories.

To sum up, dialogic mediation implies that mediators actively intervene as distributors of opportunities to communicate, inviting the parties to introduce and deal with particular issues and giving voice to their stories. Re-authoring stories requires the recognition and empowerment of the participants' agency. Empowerment and re-authoring define mediation as creation of space for different voices which do not hinder each other. Reflexive coordination can sustain both re-cognition and empowerment, and the enhancement of alternative narratives, building on stories of cooperation. Mediation is based on systematic intuition and ethics of deception (Benjamin 2003). The mediator is a 'trickster,' a boundary crosser, a shape-shifter, a creative disrupter, and a storyteller (LeBaron 2003b).

Mediators' dialogic actions are made evident in communication systems, in particular in in-teractions. These actions may be identified through research based on audio- or video-recorded mediated encounters and include summarizing, de-escalating emotion, reframing, providing in-sightful comments, and non-prescriptive suggestions, asking circular questions (Brownlie 2018; Garcia 2012). They also include active listening, through both verbal (e.g. acknowledgment tokens, continuers, repetitions) and nonverbal (glances, smiles, gestures, posture) signals; ques-tions (including circular questions) allowing participants' expansions and clarifications; formula-tions of the meanings of previous content uttered by the participants in such a way as to summarize, explicate, or develop its gist; and positive connotation and appreciation of different positions (Baraldi 2010, 2019, 2021; Baraldi and Iervese 2010). All these actions show sensitivity to both explicit stories and opportunities for opening alternative stories, i.e., double listening (Winslade and Monk 2008).

Mediators' dialogic actions invite to reflect on different communicative constructions of pro-blems, avoiding judgments, proposing a deconstruction of negative identities, and activating pro-posals of alternative narratives. Formulations are particularly important, since they provide definitional reframing (Mayer 2000) and transformative relaying (Heritage and Clayman 2010) of participants' positions, opening stories of cooperation. Formulations provide reframing since they support "the process of changing the way a thought is presented so that it maintains its fundamental meaning but is more likely to support resolution efforts" (Mayer 2000, 132). Circular questioning is important since it allows the co-construction of more complex narratives, avoiding isolation of participants and the corresponding construction of their negative identities.

Despite preoccupation for the inadequate universalism of mediation, these methodological suggestions seem to apply to intercultural mediation. The reason for this is that, from a metho-dological point of view, mediation focuses on communication processes through reflexive co-ordination. The ways of focusing on communication and providing reflexive coordination do not change culturally since they are basic principles of enhancing communication. Rather, commu-nication and reflexive coordination can highlight and explore possible cultural identities and di-versity expressed as small cultures in the mediation system.

Mediation can be defined as intercultural when dialogic actions signal, explore, and mediate the linguistic cues of different cultural presuppositions (Gumperz 1992); in this respect, dialogic actions are cues for sensitivity to, recognition, and empowerment of diverse cultural presuppositions, and thus produce different cultural narratives of identity as small cultures showing different personal cultural trajectories. Intercultural mediation means enhancing and mediating personal knowledge of cultural meanings of places, people, and identities, i.e., enhancing participants' agency in telling stories about themselves and their experiences.

Intercultural mediation invites participants to assess what they know about themselves, rather than what they know (or think they know) about other people. Thus, it discourages the con-struction of ethnocentrism. Participants can certainly express, but also ignore, underscore, or reject narratives of their own cultural diversity. They can reject their categorization as members of cultural groups as well as the narrative of their cultural identity. The mediator's agency in reframing (for-mulating) cultural diversity can be taken by the participants as a proposal on which they have the last say. Ultimately, dialogic intercultural mediation is a hybrid process that can lead to either con-struction or deconstruction of narratives of cultural identity.

Conclusions

In this chapter, I have highlighted some theoretical and methodological presuppositions to understand, describe and explain mediation as a dialogic mediation system. I have shown that mediation is an intercultural communication system when it deals with problems of understanding or acceptance of cultural presuppositions of the communication systems in which it is applied. In these cases, intercultural mediation means promoting adaptation of cultural presuppositions (intercultural adaptation) by constructing hybrid communication processes as negotiated small cultures in which personal cultural trajectories become relevant and are mediated. Thus, intercultural mediation gives the participants the opportunity to express their personal cultural trajectories and therefore their cultural identities, if they wish to do so.

Despite the preoccupation for an abstract universalism of mediation, the methodological presuppositions of the dialogic mediation system seem to apply to intercultural mediation as well. This methodology of (intercultural) mediation can be tested in the interactions in which it is performed. The analysis of interactions is important in order to understand the dialogic actions which can effectively implement (intercultural) mediation. This type of analysis shows the dialogic actions that can create the conditions for participants' empowerment and construction of new and alternative narratives. In this chapter, however, it was not possible to discuss empirical examples of mediated interactions for reasons of space.

In the dialogic mediation system, the process of enhancing the participants' exercise of agency, through the mediator's reflexive coordination, is more important than the type of narratives produced, which are always unpredictable. The methodological presuppositions, and the focus of the analysis, concern the *process* rather than the contents or results of mediation. Mediators can develop 'cultural awareness' (LeBaron 2003a) by adopting a methodologically guided way of enhancing reflexive coordination and double listening in communication.

However, limitations of intercultural mediation should not be underestimated. First, in some contexts power differences and/or radical disagreements may prevent any intercultural form of dialogue (Phipps 2014; Ramsbotham 2010), and thus mediation can fail. Second, mediation can fail in providing equity and empowerment of participants' agency, enhancing instead ethnocentric communication, when mediators replace the other participants, downgrading their agency (Baraldi 2017; Baraldi and Gavioli 2017). These critical aspects should warn against an unconditioned appreciation of intercultural mediation and invite to analyze local, authentic, mediated communication processes to understand its form and effectiveness.

References

Avruch, Kevin, and Peter W. Black. 1991. "The Culture Question and Conflict Resolution." *Peace and Change* 16 (1): 22–45. 10.1111/j.1468-0130.1991.tb00563.x

Avruch, Kevin, and Peter W. Black. 1993. "Conflict Resolution in Intercultural Settings: Problems and Prospects." In *Conflict Resolution Theory and Practice. Integration and Application*, edited by Dennis J.D. Sandole and Hugo van der Merke, 131–45. Manchester: Manchester University Press.

Baraldi, Claudio. 2010. "Is Cross-cultural Mediation a Technique? Theoretical/Methodological Frameworks and Empirical Evidence from Interaction." In *International and Regional Perspectives in Intercultural Mediation*, edited by Dominic Busch, Claude-Hélène Mayer and Christian Martin Boness, 99–126. Frankfurt am Main: Peter Lang.

Baraldi, Claudio. 2015. "Intercultural Communication Systems and Discourses of Cultural Identity." *Applied Linguistics Review* 6 (1): 49–71. 10.1515/applirev-2015-0003

Baraldi, Claudio. 2017. "Language Mediation as Communication System." *Communication Theory* 27 (4): 367–87. 10.1111/comt.12118

Baraldi, Claudio. 2019. "Using Formulations to Manage Conflicts in Classroom Interactions." *Language and Dialogue* 9 (2): 193–216. 10.1075/ld.00038.bar

Baraldi, Claudio. 2021. "Conflicts in the Classroom." In *Promoting Children's Rights in European Schools. Intercultural Dialogue and Facilitative Pedagogy*, edited by Claudio Baraldi, Erica Joslyn and Federico Farini, 133–51. London: Bloomsbury.

Baraldi, Claudio, and Laura Gavioli. 2017. "Intercultural Mediation and '(non)professional' Interpreting in Italian Healthcare Institutions." In *Non-professional Interpreting and Translation*, edited by Rachele Antonini, Letizia Cirillo, Linda Rossato, and Ira Torresi, 83–106. Amsterdam: John Benjamins. 10.1075/btl.129.05bar

Baraldi, Claudio, and Vittorio Iervese. 2010. "Dialogic Mediation in Conflict Resolution Education." *Conflict Resolution Quarterly* 27 (4): 423–45. 10.1002/crq.20005

Benjamin, Robert D. 2003. "Managing the Natural Energy of the Conflict: Mediators, Tricksters and the Constructive Uses of Deception." In *Bringing Peace into the Room. How the Personal Qualities of the Mediator Impact the Process of Conflict Resolution*, edited by Daniel Bowling and David Hoffman, 79–134. San Francisco: Jossey-Bass Publishers.

Brownlie, Siobhan. 2017. "Mediation through an Intercultural Communication Lens." *Mediation Theory and Practice* 2 (1): 34–53. 10.1558/mtp.32579

Brownlie, Siobhan. 2018. "Using Cultural Categories for Opposition and Brokering in Cultural Mediation." *Language and Intercultural Communication* 18 (1): 90–106. 10.1080/14708477.2017.1400506

Bush, Baruch Robert A., and Joseph P. Folger. 1994. *The Promise of Mediation: Responding to Conflict through Empowerment and Recognition*. San Francisco: Jossey-Bass.

Byrd Clark, Julye S., and Fred Dervin. 2014. *Reflexivity in Language and Intercultural Education*. London: Routledge. 10.4324/9781315879604

Cloke, Kenneth. 2003. "What Are the Personal Qualities of the Mediator?" In *Bringing Peace into the Room. How the Personal Qualities of the Mediator Impact the Process of Conflict Resolution*, edited by Daniel Bowling and David Hoffman, 49–56. San Francisco: Jossey-Bass.

Dervin, Fred, and Anthony J. Liddicoat, eds. 2013. *Linguistics for Intercultural Education*. Amsterdam: John Benjamins. 10.1075/lllt.33

Fritz, Jean Marie. 2014. "Cultural Considerations." In *Moving Toward a Just Peace. The Mediation Continuum*, edited by Jean Marie Fritz, 17–34. Dordrecht: Springer. 10.1007/978-94-007-2885-1_2

Garcia, Angela Cora. 2012. "Advice-Giving and Disputant Empowerment in Divorce Mediation Sessions." *Language and Dialogue* 2 (3): 398–426. 10.1075/ld.2.3.05gar

Garcia, Angela Cora. 2013. "Mediation Talk in Cross-Cultural Perspective: The Contribution of Conversation Analysis." *China Media Research* 9 (4): 85–101.

Gumperz, John. 1992. "Contextualization and Understanding." In *Rethinking Context: Language as an Interactive Phenomenon*, edited by Alessandro Duranti and Charles Goodwin, 229–53. Cambridge: Cambridge University Press.

Gumperz, John, and Jenny Cook-Gumperz. 2009. "Discourse, Cultural Diversity and Communication: A Linguistic Anthropological Perspective." In *Handbook of Intercultural Communication*, edited by Helga Kotthoff and Helen Spencer-Oatey, 13–29. Berlin: Mouton de Gruyter. 10.1515/9783110198584.1.13

Heritage, John, and Steven Clayman. 2010. *Talk in Action. Interactions, Identities, and Institutions*. Chichester: Wiley-Blackwell.

Holliday, Adrian. 2011. *Intercultural Communication and Ideology*. London: Sage. 10.4135/9781446269107

Holliday, Adrian, and Sara Amadasi. 2020. *Making Sense of the Intercultural. Finding DeCentred Threads*. London: Routledge. 10.4324/9781351059190

Inghilleri, Moira. 2005. "Mediating Zones of Uncertainty. Interpreter Agency, the Interpreting Habitus and Political Asylums Adjudication." *The Translator* 11 (1): 69–85. 10.1080/13556509.2005.10799190

Kramsch, Claire, and Michiko Uryu. 2012. "Intercultural Contact, Hybridity, and Third Space." In *The Routledge Handbook of Language and Intercultural Communication*, edited by Jane Jackson, 211–25. London: Routledge.

LeBaron, Michelle. 2003a. *Bridging Cultural Conflicts. A New Approach for a Changing World*. San Francisco: Jossey-Bass.

LeBaron, Michelle. 2003b. "Trickster, Mediator's Friend." In *Bringing Peace into the Room. How the Personal Qualities of the Mediator Impact the Process of Conflict Resolution*, edited by Daniel Bowling and David Hoffman, 135–50. San Francisco: Jossey-Bass.

Luhmann, Niklas. 1995. *Social Systems*. Stanford: Stanford University Press.

Luhmann, Niklas. 2013. *Theory of Society*, vol. 2. Stanford: Stanford University Press.

Mayer, Bernard. 2000. *The Dynamics of Conflict Resolution*. San Francisco: Jossey-Bass.

Phipps, Allison. 2014. "'They are bombing now'. 'Intercultural Dialogue' in Times of Conflict." *Language and Intercultural Communication* 14 (1): 108–24. 10.1080/14708477.2013.866127

Picard, Cheryl A., and Kenneth R. Melchin. 2007. Insight Mediation: A Learning-Centered Mediation Model. *Negotiation Journal* 23 (1): 35–53. 10.1111/j.1571-9979.2007.00126.x

Ramsbotham, Oliver. 2010. *Transforming Violent Conflict. Radical Disagreement, Dialogue and Survival*. London: Routledge. 10.4324/9780203859674

Rubenfeld, Sara, and Richard Clément. 2012. "Intercultural Conflict and Mediation: An Intergroup Perspective." *Language Learning* 62 (4): 1205–30. 10.1111/1467-9922.2012.00723.x

Salamandra, Christa. 2002. "Globalization and Cultural Mediation: The Construction of Arabia in London." *Global Networks* 2 (4): 285–99. 10.1111/1471-0374.00042

Spencer-Oatey, Helen and Peter Franklin. 2009. *Intercultural Interaction. A Multidisciplinary Approach to Intercultural Communication*. Basingstoke: Palgrave. 10.1057/9780230244511

Ting-Toomey, Stella. 1999. *Communication across Cultures*. New York: The Guilford Press.

Van Langenhove, Luk, and Rom Harré. 1999. "Introducing Positioning Theory." In *Positioning Theory*, edited by Rom Harré and Luk van Langenhove, 14–31. Oxford: Blackwell.

Wierzbicka, Anna. 2006. The Concept of 'Dialogue' in Cross-Linguistic and Cross-Cultural Perspective. *Discourse Studies* 8 (5): 675–703. 10.1177/1461445606067334

Winslade, John, and Gerard Monk. 2008. *Practicing Narrative Mediation: Loosening the Grip of Conflict*. San Francisco: Jossey-Bass.

PART VI

Linguistic explorations of intercultural mediation

35

RESEARCH FROM CONVERSATION ANALYSIS ON INTERCULTURAL MEDIATION

Angela Cora Garcia

Introduction

This chapter addresses how cultural differences can impact the interactional process in mediation sessions.[1] Because it provides for the direct observation of human action and the analysis of the techniques and procedures participants use to engage in and coordinate their interactions with others, conversation analysis has much to offer those seeking a deeper understanding of the role of culture in mediation. Conversation analysis is an approach to analyzing naturally occurring interaction in its sequential context (e.g., Garcia 2013a; Heritage and Clayman 2010; Schegloff 2007a). It grew out of the ethnomethodological perspective (Garfinkel 1967) as a way to investigate human action and how social organization and social order are created through action, including talk (Sacks 1992). Conversation analysis lets us analyze participants' actions in context and to explore the techniques and procedures they use to act and respond to the actions of others.

A significant body of previous conversation analytic research on mediation has been done, most of which focuses on facilitative mediation sessions conducted in a variety of contexts (such as small claims, consumer, neighborhood, family, and divorce, etc.). This research explores the interactional organization of mediation and how neutrality is accomplished in mediation (e.g., Garcia 2019; Greatbatch and Dingwall 1997; Heisterkamp 2006; Jacobs 2002). While intercultural mediation has not yet been sufficiently studied with conversation analysis, conversation analytic studies of other contexts and settings can be used enhance our understanding of the process of mediation and how it can best be designed and executed for intercultural mediation.

This chapter explores how conversation analytic research can illuminate aspects of intercultural communication in mediation, including issues of language difference; cultural group membership and identity; cultural differences in values, religion, or attitudes; and the pragmatics of communication. Issues related to access to mediation, including the choice to participate in mediation, the intake process, and the interaction within mediation will also be addressed. Finally, I provide a conversation analytic perspective on what is 'intercultural' mediation, and discuss examples from mediation sessions in which religion and race/ethnicity illustrate this perspective.

---

[1] The data excerpts cited in this chapter were collected by the author with grant SBR-9411224 from the "Law and Social Sciences" program of the National Sciences Foundation.

DOI: 10.4324/9781003227441-42

Language difference and the accomplishment of turn taking

Mediators facilitating sessions between native and non-native speakers may experience language-related challenges in the coordination of turn exchange. Interactants attend to a current speaker's utterance in order to project its possible completion, when a unit of talk (e.g., a word, phrase, or sentence) is analyzably complete in the interactional context in which it occurs (Sacks, Schegloff, and Jefferson 1974). However, the grammatical structures of languages differ, and may have implications for turn taking.

For example, Korean speakers may typically place the verb at the end of their turn, or delete it entirely, while English speakers typically use the subject, verb, object order (Park 2016). Korean speakers may use intonation to signal that they have reached a transition relevance place, even if the final verb has not been produced (Park 2016). In addition, Park found that word order is much more flexible in Korean than in English; this also complicates the projection of possible turn completion points.

In an intercultural mediation session, mediators would do well to pay attention to how non-native speakers signal they are done with a turn to avoid either cutting a speaker off before they have completed their turn or waiting for an explicit turn completion that may not appear.

Language difference and access to mediation

Language differences between participants in mediation could discourage potential clients from seeking out mediation or otherwise present barriers to their participation. Several conversation analytic studies in emergency phone calls illustrate how language difference can impact access to services.

Raymond (2014) found that non-native speakers of English who called emergency services often requested translation services. While most of these requests were handled unproblematically, some call taker responses were less accommodating even when the caller displayed through their talk that they had limited or no ability to speak English. Mediation programs should consider the need for translation and interpreter services to assist both during the intake process and the mediation session itself.

In addition to language differences, political differences, economic inequality, inter-group conflict, and/or racism or discrimination may impact accessibility of services. For example, in a study of emergency telephone calls in South Africa there were not only a variety of languages spoken, there were also ethnic group and political tensions (Penn, Watermeyer, and Nattress 2017). Translators were at times provided for speakers of majority and minority group's languages, but the minority group's language preferences were not as readily accommodated (Penn, et al. 2017). Similarly, Svennevig (2012) analyzed an emergency service call between a Turkish caller and a Swedish call taker during a time in which the political climate in Sweden involved some tension between the two groups. The call taker's failure to successfully manage the emergency service call from the non-native speaker led to a tragic delay in service.

If a non-native speaker agrees to participate in mediation, effective techniques to avoid or repair misunderstandings during the session can be used. Osvaldsson et al. (2013) showed how a native Swedish-speaking emergency services call taker successfully managed a call from a non-native speaker by using confirmation checks, reformulations, and repair techniques to avoid or repair any misunderstandings that emerged.

Mediators and mediation programs serving communities with multiple languages, nationalities or ethnic groups should be aware not only of the barriers to access to mediation that can be caused by language difference, but also that political, cultural, and historical inequalities or conflicts may also affect an individual's access to mediation.

Institutional procedures as barriers to access to mediation

Participants in intercultural mediation sessions may have different levels of knowledge of the institutional or organizational procedures of the mediation program, the role of the mediator, and the process of mediation itself which may create barriers to receiving services. For example, in some cultural contexts, location-giving may be done by describing landmarks and routes rather than by giving precise addresses, while an emergency services call taker may be working under different institutional requirements (Nattrass, et al. 2017; Paoletti 2012). These types of cultural differences in institutional procedures or conventions may provide challenges in mediation if the mediator does not share the cultural context of one or more of the disputants, regardless of the level of language competence of the participants.

In addition to expectations about institutional procedures and knowledge, there may be cultural differences in expectations for social roles. Conversation analytic studies reveal cultural differences in patient deferral to the authority of doctors and in doctor's acknowledgment of patient's rights to make their own decisions. A study of Nigerian doctor/patient interactions showed that while patients at times resist doctors' authority, the doctors may be very directive and assertive in their instructions to patients (Boluwaduro 2021). While mediation may typically be treated as a relatively informal context, in some cultures the mediator may be perceived as having more (or less) authority and power than they actually have. The mediator should be aware of cultural differences in these types of expectations and work to defuse them if they seem apparent.

Creating, confirming, or correcting comprehension

In intercultural interactions, especially those including non-native speakers, not only may misunderstandings occur more frequently due to differences in language, vocabulary, accent, or cultural expectations, participants may not share conventions for repairing misunderstandings (Garcia 2013b). If conventions for repair are not shared, participants can make accommodations and adjustments if they are aware of these differences.

The repair of troubles in talk or misunderstandings in interaction depend on the ability to produce a repair move soon after the problematic utterance has been produced (Jefferson 1974; Schegloff, Jefferson, and Sacks 1977). The interactional organization of facilitative mediation involves a turn taking system in which disputants typically address their remarks to the mediators and wait until selected to speak to respond to the opposing disputant's accusations or complaints (Garcia 2019). This turn-taking system can be functional for the mediation process by minimizing arguing, but may also inadvertently compromise the repair of misunderstandings (Garcia 2013b). In mediation sessions, delay of the opportunity to initiate other-repair can extend the duration of the misunderstanding because of the inability of an opposing disputant to self-select to produce an other-initiation of repair at the appropriate juncture (Garcia 2019).

Svennevig et al. (2019) studied a simulated interaction with a native speaker giving first aid instructions to a non-native speaker. They found that the native speakers used four main strategies for accommodating the non-native speaker's level of language proficiency to avoid misunderstandings or mistakes: Lexical substitutions, reformulations, left-dislocation (prefacing an explanation with a key word from the explanation, and then using that word in context), and decompositions (breaking the full instruction into increments). The success of each of these techniques depends on their placement and timing relative to the responses of the native speaker. Each of the techniques identified by Svennevig et al. (2019) could be useful for mediators in the context of conducting a mediation session with one or more non-native speakers.

Cultural differences in how active listenership is displayed can lead to misunderstandings or to perceptions that the speaker is not being supported. Landmark et al. (2017) found cultural differences affecting intersubjective understanding in doctor-patient interactions. Patients who were non-native speakers of Norwegian failed to produce verbal listener responses in consultations with Norwegian-speaking doctors, leaving the doctors unsure if they had been understood. This type of cultural difference in listener responses could also cause problems in the context of mediation.

Embodied interactions can be an additional source of problems in intercultural mediation, if there are not shared understandings of what gestures mean or which gestures are appropriate in given contexts. Birlik and Kaur (2020) studied a German firm with employees who spoke a variety of native languages, in which English was the shared language for meetings. They found cultural differences in the meaning of different methods of pointing and therefore varied the gesture used depending on the culture of the person they were addressing.

A conversation analytic perspective on intercultural mediation

In order to attribute aspects of an interaction to membership categories such as race/ethnicity, gender/s, or nationality, participants must in some way act to display the relevance of these categories to the talk (Schegloff 1992). This may be done through how persons are referred to or how membership categories and the actions/characteristics connected to them are conveyed; the category must have procedural consequentiality for the talk (Sacks 1992; Schegloff 2007b).

Cultural differences between mediation participants or membership categories such as religion, nationality, race/ethnicity, etc. may or may not be known to the mediators or other participants; the line between *intra-* or *inter-*cultural mediation therefore may not be apparent. If cultural differences are made relevant in the interaction, mediators must have the skills and resources necessary to manage them. The next section of this chapter first reviews some ways in which religion can be either intra or intercultural, and second how race/ethnicity may be made relevant in mediation.

Religion and intra/intercultural mediation

Whether mediation clients share the same religion or not does not necessarily make their membership in a *religion* category relevant for the mediation, and does not automatically make the interaction 'intercultural mediation.' For example, in a family mediation session (see Garcia (2019) for a description of the data set) Bob and Kate are in disagreement about an issue which they frame in terms of their religious beliefs. They state they have the same religion and share beliefs against living together without being married; they are nevertheless in conflict over this issue. As the discussion gets argumentative, Excerpt 1 shows Mediator A intervening by trying to bridge their expressed positions (lines 1–3, 7). Kate responds by challenging Bob's religious values (line 9). Bob then rebuts her challenge in line 12; claiming to share the same religious values. Mediator A interrupts the incipient argument to make another attempt at bridging their perspectives (starting in line 13).

Excerpt 1:   Bob & Kate Mediation, Session 2

1	MA:	[WE:LL? I=THINK=I'VE I HEARDJU] <u>BOTH</u> say your=the reasons. (0.8) .h
2		Bob >Bob is the< reason beCAUSE >he's not ready to-< (0.4) to (0.5) <u>ACT</u>ually
3		take the marriage <u>VOWS</u>!
4		(0.4)
5	Kate:	Right.
6		(0.9)
7	MA:	On <u>your</u> part? (0.9) You're unwilling to live in his <u>HOUSE</u> for religious reasons
8		[so]
9	Kate:	[°Right.°] Which are supposed to be his same religious values too.
10		(0.4)
11	MA:	Yeah. [but BY- (thing-)]
12	Bob:	[Well they <u>are</u>! I] understand it. I'm not [( ).]
13	MA:	[I=THINK=IT'S] CLEARLY
14		<u>BOTH</u> OF=YOU! who=are saying? (0.7) that (1.1) that >that=this=is <u>HAP</u>pening
15		because=of–< (0.3) reasons on both sides.

Studying talk in intercultural mediation

16		(0.7)
17	B:	°Mm hm.°
18		(2.6)
19	MA:	Bob >would be HAPPY t'have you <u>stay</u> there? i[f the religious is]sue

While their shared religion is clearly an issue for the couple, it seems to be treated by the participants more as an 'intercultural' than an 'intracultural' issue. The mediator's interventions also reference the issue of religion; she works to help both partners feel supported in their religious beliefs while helping them each understand the other's position. In contrast, a divorcing couple in another mediation session presents themselves as 'intercultural' with regard to religion, stating that they have different religions (Jon is Catholic and Liz belongs to a different denomination of Christianity). The religious difference is not introduced until their second mediation session, in the context of a discussion of how they will share decisions about their daughter once the divorce is final. Liz is concerned that Jon will have their daughter baptized, which would be against her religion's rule that only adults be baptized. This religious difference is not only a cultural difference between the spouses, it is made relevant by the participants for their discussion of the issues under dispute in the mediation session. Once the spouses agree not to baptize their daughter, the mediator intervenes (Excerpt 2):

Excerpt 2: Jon & Liz Mediation, Session 2 (Garcia 2021 ©2020 Wiley Periodicals LLC)

1	MA:	Well, [THIS IS A, THIS IS SOME]THING THAT
2	MA:	OFTEN GETS REAL HARD for people, um, YOUR
3		ATTITUDES toward religion, <u>change</u> as you get older. So, this
4		MIGHT be a discussion that you'll need to bring UP, in a few
5		<u>years</u>, when she gets into school for instance. Um, you MIGHT
6		decide Jon that you <u>WANTED</u> her to attend religious education,
7		but she <u>couldn't</u> receive the sacraments without <u>baptism</u>.
8	Jon:	Right.
9	MA:	So, you MIGHT if, you MIGHT, if you FELT <u>differently</u>
10		enough about it then, you'd have to engage Liz in, in a discussion,
11		and see what you could work out.
12	Jon:	Okay.

Analogous to Whitehead's (2020) analysis of how race can be implicitly identified in interactions, Mediator A may be implicitly identifying herself as Catholic by displaying knowledge about why not baptizing their daughter is problematic from the point of view of the Catholic religion (line 7). This implicit self-identification risks a lack of neutrality in her response to the spouses. While the mediator is using the same techniques and interventions they might use in an 'intracultural' mediation, they may need to examine their own cultural position (in this case regarding religion) to make sure their group membership does not lead to cultural bias in their interventions during the session. The intercultural aspects of this mediation session are not visible or available to any participants until the spouses bring up the issue in the context of the session, and the possibility that the mediator may also be part of the intercultural dynamic with regard to religion is also not visible until this part of the interaction occurs.

Angela Cora Garcia

Race and intra/intercultural mediation

As with religion, racial/ethnic difference may be made relevant during the interaction in a mediation session. Conversation analytic research has discovered a range of ways of representing or referring to membership in a racial/ethnic category. Race may be treated as a default category (Whitehead and Lerner 2009), may be explicitly referred to or made a topic of discussion (West and Fenstermaker 2002; Whitehead 2015), or may be implicitly referred to (Whitehead 2020).

Whitehead's (2015) study of radio call in shows in South Africa shows how racial categories or identities can be claimed explicitly or implicitly, and stereotypes tied to these categories can be challenged or let stand. Racial identities can be inferred from accents, region, occupation, or expressed positions, and the use of pronouns (such as the collective 'we') can be used to express default membership in a racial/ethnic group by creating an alignment between the speaker and the host (Whitehead 2020). Stokoe (2015) showed that some callers to a mediation program's intake service use explicit racial/ethnic categories and tie them to negative stereotypes. While some call takers responded ambiguously toward the negative stereotypes, others explicitly disaffiliated with the caller's expressed positions.

Mediators who are trained to recognize uses of racial/ethnic categories, particularly when linked to negative stereotypes or racial prejudice, would be better able to intervene if necessary. However, the techniques a mediator uses to handle these types of challenges may be the same techniques they would use to handle any problem the clients are experiencing. For example, in the family mediation between Bob and Kate discussed below, the first mention of race (explicitly or implicitly) occurs more than halfway through their third mediation session. The issue is how the racial prejudice Bob's parents have against Kate is connected to their disagreement over when to get married. When they start talking about Bob's parents, Bob admits that his parent's attitudes have been a concern, but believes they will accept Kate in the end. Kate is upset because he has not yet informed his parents of their intended marriage. When Kate reveals that she wants to be present when Bob talks to them, Mediator A intervenes and argues that it would be better if Bob talked to his parents alone first (lines 1, 4–9):

Excerpt 3:   Bob & Kate Mediation, Session 3

1	MA:	[AND THEY DE]SERVE A <u>CHANCE</u>, (0.2) to <u>wrestle</u> with this. because
2		(0.2)
3	Bob:	Yeah! I think [so!]
4	MA:	[even]=though prejudic:e (0.4) is a terrible thing, (1.3) there's no
5		doubt that (0.4) our culture (0.7) has a lot of adjustments to make. and a lot of
6		progress to make in this area. and (0.5) this can be an oc<u>ca</u>sion for (1.0) <u>building</u>
7		some of those bridges. (3.5) I guess I'd have to say Kate that I su<u>pport</u> Bo:b, (0.4)
8		in wanting a chance to TALK to his parents, and then <u>asking</u> them? (1.5) <u>would</u>
9		you come over for dinner!

In terms of how mediators handle intercultural issues in mediation, the mediator's response in Excerpt 3 is potentially problematic. Mediators risk a failure of neutrality if they express affiliation with the perspective of one disputant against the other (Garcia 2019). Shortly after this exchange, the disagreement between Bob and Kate on this issue becomes more pronounced. When Bob appears to defend his parents by arguing that they are not racist, Kate sarcastically invokes negative racial stereotypes to convey how she feels unsupported by Bob (Excerpt 4):

Studying talk in intercultural mediation

Excerpt 4:   Bob & Kate Mediation, Session 3

1	Bob:	It doesn't mean they don't like black people. They've had (0.4).h we went to
2		<u>church</u> with black [people.] they [had, y'know-]
3	Kate:	[I know,] [>One of his< be]st friends was black, the old=
4	Bob:	=>shoot yeah the [old–<]
5	Kate:	[(the old)] pa[t on]='uh h[ead?]
6	Bob:	[exactly.] [SO] so they [weren't-]
7	Kate:	[I like] darkies,
8		you know? mammie, [we] eat pumpkin [pie, ( )]
9	MA:	[tch] [But HEAR WHAT 'E'S SAY]ING
10		NOW.
11		(0.3)
12	MA:	hear [what='e's] saying now, Kate. (0.7) he's TRYING not to defend his
13	Bob:	[o<u>ka:</u>y?]
14	Kate:	[( )]
15	MA:	parents but they've got a <u>lo:ng</u> history (0.9) that (0.5) <u>doe:s</u> explain somewhat-
16		why they are where they are today.

Notice that the mediator is essentially performing a topic shift with her intervention starting in line 9. She does not explicitly address the racial stereotypes Kate has sarcastically introduced in response to Bob's defense of his parent's racism. Instead, she resumes her previous efforts to encourage Kate to move to agreement. She works to help Kate to hear Bob's perspective rather than responding to Kate's perspective on the racial discrimination she has experienced. This could be considered ignoring or sidelining the issue of racism in their family and how it affects their relationship.

In short, racial/ethnic difference and racial prejudice are topics of discussion in this mediation and points of conflict between the partners, both in terms of their interaction in the session and in terms of the conflicts they are in mediation to resolve. The mediator works hard to mediate between the two to make sure that Kate hears and understands Bob's underlying message. However, it could be argued that the mediator's response relegates Kate's concerns about racism in Bob's family to the sidelines, while foregrounding the mediation work of facilitating agreement. Mediators in intercultural mediations would do well to consider whether issues of cultural, racial/ethnic differences, or conflict are being ignored or made into a side issue by the mediator's intervention.

Conclusion

This chapter has reviewed a number of conversation analytic studies and considered how their findings about interaction in situations involving language and/or cultural difference can affect the interaction in ways that may be consequential for mediation.

Differences in language and/or cultural conventions can affect turn transition, impede inter-subjective understanding, and impact the effectiveness of repair mechanisms and other interactional procedures designed to avoid misunderstanding and check comprehension; any of these types of challenges may become a barrier to accessing mediation or participating in it effectively. In addition, political or economic inequality, intergroup conflict, or tensions may impact not just the need for mediation but also how members of different groups communicate about their concerns. Cultural differences in or knowledge about institutional or organizational procedures or social roles may lead to a misfit in approaches that may cause problems in interaction.

Further research on intercultural mediation should address the extent to which mediation can be designed to make it culturally compatible to both sides in a dispute. In other words, it is not just different ways of communicating or different cultural values that may make intercultural mediation more challenging, it is the process of mediation itself and how fundamentally compatible that process is for the individuals participating. A conversation analytic investigation of how the interaction in various types of mediation works can provide the detailed understanding of the nature of the interaction required to decide what approach to mediation should be used for a given set of disputants.

References

Birlik, Seval, and Jagdish Kaur. 2020. "BELF Expert Users: Making Understanding Visible in Internal BELF Meetings through the Use of Nonverbal Communication Strategies." *English for Specific Purposes* 58 (April): 1–14. 10.1016/j.esp.2019.10.002

Boluwaduro, Eniola. 2021. "Patients' Compliance and Resistance to Medical Authority in Nigerian Clinical Encounters." *Journal of Pragmatics* 171 (January): 8–19. 10.1016/j.pragma.2020.09.033

Garcia, Angela Cora. 2013a. *An Introduction to Interaction: Understanding Talk in Formal and Informal Settings.* London; New York: Bloomsbury.

Garcia, Angela Cora. 2013b. "Mediation Talk in Cross Cultural Perspective: The Contribution of Conversation Analysis." *China Media Research* 9 (4): 85–101.

Garcia, Angela Cora. 2019. *How Mediation Works: Resolving Conflict Through Talk.* London: Cambridge University Press. 10.1017/9781139162548

Garcia, Angela Cora. 2021. "Locations for Advice-Giving and the Production of Neutrality in Divorce Mediation Sessions." *Conflict Resolution Quarterly* 38 (3): 189–208. 10.1002/crq.21292

Garfinkel, Harold. 1967. *Studies in Ethnomethodology.* Englewood Cliffs, NJ: Prentice-Hall.

Greatbatch, David, and Robert Dingwall. 1997. "Argumentative Talk in Divorce Mediation Sessions." *American Sociological Review* 62 (1): 151–170.

Heisterkamp, Brian L. 2006. "Taking the Footing of a Neutral Mediator." *Conflict Resolution Quarterly* 23 (3): 301–315. 10.1002/crq.139

Heritage, John, and Steven Clayman. 2010. *Talk in Action: Interactions, Identities, and Institutions.* Chichester: Wiley-Blackwell.

Jacobs, Scott. 2002. "Maintaining Neutrality in Dispute Mediation: Managing Disagreement While Managing Not to Disagree." *Journal of Pragmatics* 34 (10–11): 1403–1426. 10.1016/S0378-2166(02)00071-1

Jefferson, Gail. 1974. "Error Correction as an Interactional Resource." *Language in Society* 3 (2): 181–199. 10.1017/S0047404500004334

Landmark, Anne Marie Dalby, Jan Svennevig, Jennifer Gerwing, and Pål Gulbrandsen. 2017. "Patient Involvement and Language Barriers: Problems of Agreement or Understanding?" *Patient Education and Counseling* 100 (6): 1092–1102. 10.1016/j.pec.2016.12.006

Nattrass, Rhona, Jennifer Watermeyer, Catherine Robson, and Claire Penn. 2017. "Local Expertise and Landmarks in Place Reformulations during Emergency Medical Calls." *Journal of Pragmatics* 120 (October): 73–87. 10.1016/j.pragma.2017.09.001

Osvaldsson, Karin, Daniel Persson-Thunqvist, and Jakob Cromdal. 2013. "Comprehension Checks, Clarifications, and Corrections in an Emergency Call with a Nonnative Speaker of Swedish." *International Journal of Bilingualism* 17 (2): 205–220. 10.1177/1367006912441420

Paoletti, Isabella. 2012. "The Issue of Conversationally Constituted Context and Localization Problems in Emergency Calls." *Text & Talk* 32 (2). 10.1515/text-2012-0010

Park, Jae-Eun. 2016. "Turn-Taking in Korean Conversation." *Journal of Pragmatics* 99 (July): 62–77. 10.1016/j.pragma.2016.04.011

Penn, Claire, Jennifer Watermeyer, and Rhona Nattrass. 2017. "Managing Language Mismatches in Emergency Calls." *Journal of Health Psychology* 22 (14): 1769–1779. 10.1177/1359105316636497

Raymond, Chase Wesley. 2014. "Negotiating Entitlement to Language: Calling 911 without English." *Language in Society* 43 (1): 33–59. 10.1017/S0047404513000869

Sacks, Harvey. 1992. *Lectures on Conversation.* Oxford, UK and Cambridge, USA: Blackwell.

Sacks, Harvey, Emanuel A. Schegloff, and Gail Jefferson. 1974. "A Simplest Systematics for the Organization of Turn-Taking for Conversation." *Language* 50 (4): 696–735.

Studying talk in intercultural mediation

Schegloff, Emanuel A. 1992. "On Talk and its Institutional Occasions." In *Talk at Work: Social Interaction in Institutional Settings*, edited by Paul Drew and John Heritage, 101–134. Cambridge: Cambridge University Press.

Schegloff, Emanuel A. 2007a. *Sequence Organization in Interaction: A Primer in Conversation Analysis*, Volume 1, Cambridge, UK: Cambridge University Press.

Schegloff, Emanuel A. 2007b. "Categories in Action: Person-Reference and Membership Categorization." *Discourse Studies* 9 (4): 433–461. 10.1177/1461445607079162

Schegloff, Emanuel A., Gail Jefferson, and Harvey Sacks. 1977. "The Preference for Self-Correction in the Organization of Repair in Conversation." *Language* 53 (2): 361–382.

Stokoe, Elizabeth. 2015. "Identifying and Responding to Possible -Isms in Institutional Encounters: Alignment, Impartiality, and the Implications for Communication Training." *Journal of Language and Social Psychology* 34 (4): 427–445. 10.1177/0261927X15586572

Svennevig, Jan. 2012. "On Being Heard in Emergency Calls. The Development of Hostility in a Fatal Emergency Call." *Journal of Pragmatics* 44 (11): 1393–1412. 10.1016/j.pragma.2012.06.001

Svennevig, Jan, Jennifer Gerwing, Bård Uri Jensen, and Meredith Allison. 2019. "Pre-Empting Understanding Problems in L1/L2 Conversations: Evidence of Effectiveness from Simulated Emergency Calls." *Applied Linguistics* 40 (2): 205–227. 10.1093/applin/amx021

West, Candace, and Sarah Fenstermaker. 2002. "Accountability in Action: The Accomplishment of Gender, Race and Class in a Meeting of the University of California Board of Regents." *Discourse & Society* 13 (4): 537–563. 10.1177/0957926502013004455

Whitehead, Kevin A. 2015. "Everyday Antiracism in Action: Preference Organization in Responses to Racism." *Journal of Language and Social Psychology* 34 (4): 374–389. 10.1177/0261927X15586433

Whitehead, Kevin A. 2020. "The Problem of Context in the Analysis of Social Action: The Case of Implicit Whiteness in Post-Apartheid South Africa." *Social Psychology Quarterly* 83 (3): 294–313. 10.1177/0190272519897595

Whitehead, Kevin A., and Gene H. Lerner. 2009. "When Are Persons 'White'?: On Some Practical Asymmetries of Racial Reference in Talk-in-Interaction." *Discourse & Society* 20 (5): 613–641. 10.1177/0957926509106413

36

MANAGING CULTURALITY IN MEDIATION SESSIONS: INSIGHTS FROM MEMBERSHIP CATEGORIZATION ANALYSIS AND DISCURSIVE PSYCHOLOGY

Siobhan Brownlie

Introduction

Membership categorization analysis and discursive psychology can be used in the study of many types of discourse but have more typically been applied to spoken exchanges. In this chapter, we will discuss the application of membership categorization analysis and discursive psychology to the analysis of the form of alternative dispute resolution known as mediation where a third party, the mediator, facilitates a discussion and agreement between two parties in conflict (Herrman 2006). Data is discussed that consists of recordings of meetings from a particular context of mediation, a family mediation service, where the clients are couples who have decided to separate and divorce. With regard to the term *intercultural mediation*, what is meant here is instances of conflict mediation during which cultural differences and sometimes similarities between the parties are made relevant; they play a part in a party's narrative and in the other party's and mediator's responses. Such cultural matters relate to identity categories. Although ethnicity/nationality/national language may be perceived as key factors of cultural identity, there are other important aspects too that concern notably gender, sub-national region, socio-economic class, educational level, profession, age, (dis) ability, faith, and sexual orientation (Zhu 2013, 204). These categories are no less culturally shaped than ethnicity. Zhu (2013, 209) has used the term *interculturality* to describe the interactional practice of self- and other-ascription of identity categories as well as the analytical paradigm whereby rather than seeing cultural memberships in identity groups as uniquely given and static, they are viewed as emergent and discursive. In the context of mediation, identity categories may be used by a party to set up an oppositional narrative, and conversely can also be worked with by the mediator to further bridging between the parties. The aim of this chapter is to illustrate how the sociological/linguistic and discursive approaches of Membership Categorization Analysis and Discursive Psychology can be applied in analyzing mediation sessions with regard to interculturality and its implications. Combining these two approaches offers a method for revealing how culture is present in mediation sessions and for tracing how cultural categories are used and managed by interactants in the course of exchanges.

340

DOI: 10.4324/9781003227441-43

Managing culturality in mediation sessions

Membership categorization analysis

The interculturality paradigm described by Zhu (2013) is largely inspired by Membership Categorization Analysis (MCA). This is a method for analyzing interactional and textual practices that along with Conversation Analysis (CA) stems from Harvey Sacks' (1979) ground-breaking *Lectures on Conversation*. The focus of conversation analysis has been on revealing patterns in everyday communication in terms of sequencing of utterances in short or long sequences of talk (Schegloff 2007), whereas membership categorization analysis examines categories that people orient to during conversation as well as features attributed to those categories (Stokoe 2012). In an ongoing dynamic process of construction, as well as relating to cultural identity, these categories may be *turn-formed*, e.g., questionnaire and answerer, and some are *omnirelevant*, that is, relevant throughout an exchange, such as mediator and party in a mediation session (Fitzgerald and Housley 2015). Both fields, MCA and CA, espouse an ethnomethodological approach that eschews a priori theorization and analytical imposition by the researcher, and rather seeks to explore the interactants' point of view. Analysis must be warranted by the interactants' discourse. One may wonder, though, how this approach can fully apply to the use of language which is naturally inference-rich, and therefore meanings are often not made linguistically explicit. Rather than inferences being stated as the analyst's suppositions, MCA shows how participants in an interaction orient endogenously to inferences by various means. A participant may repair, that is, modify what he/she previously said, showing an awareness of inferences of particular terms, and interactions call on a *common knowledge component* such that the use of categories between participants without repair works on the basis that knowledge and unspecified inferences are shared (Stokoe 2012, 290–1).

In her call for a more systematic approach to membership categorization analysis, Stokoe (2012) argues that the concerns of conversation analysis and membership categorization analysis overlap in that sequential matters can be attended to in the study of categorial issues. Stokoe (2012, 280) outlines five steps for the undertaking of MCA: 1) Collect data. 2) Build a collection of explicit categories, e.g., *man*, *membership categorization devices* (superordinate frameworks), e.g., gender, and category-resonant descriptions, e.g., "don't be so testosterony." The latter may be descriptions of category-bound activities or category-tied predicates (characteristics). Standardized relational pairs, e.g., parent-child are also to be noted. 3) Locate the sequential position of each categorial instance. 4) Analyze the design and action orientation of the turn/text in which the category or resonant description appears. 5) Look for evidence of how participants orient to the category, device, or description; look for sequential features related to categorial formulations; and study interactional consequences of a category's use, and how speakers within and between turns build and resist categorizations. In her study of a data set where the membership categorization device of gender is made relevant, Stokoe (2012) indeed finds evidence of sequential and interactional patterns. For example, in police interviews the suspect gives a type-conforming response (yes, no) to a question, followed by an account in which the suspect supplies a category-based denial, e.g., "I've never hit a woman in my life." A *woman* is a general category, and the statement also implies a certain type of man. As seen from this example, categorial formulations draw legitimacy through operating as idiomatic summarizing devices that are difficult to test empirically. Of potential use in studying the intricate communication that occurs in mediation sessions is a refinement of the relationship between category features (activities, characteristics) and categories, such as that proposed by Reynolds and Fitzgerald (2015). Firstly, the link between category and category feature may be treated by participants as not taken for granted and needing to be made explicit. Secondly, features are treated as naturally related to a category in a taken-for-granted but nevertheless explicit way. Thirdly, a category feature is directly implied by the operation of a membership device or category (Reynolds and Fitzgerald 2015).

With regard to MCA studies of the category of ethnicity/nationality, a major point of interest has been how such cultural memberships are brought about across an interaction. Studies have shown that through discourse, participants can make their cultural membership (e.g., as a Chinese person) relevant or irrelevant in the particular context; can ascribe membership to others; can claim membership to groups that they don't normally belong to; and can resist membership ascribed by others (Zhu 2013, 211). Nishizaka (1995) uses data from a radio talk show featuring a Japanese host and a Sri Lankan student. He shows how the categories *Japanese* and *foreigner* were made relevant and sometimes irrelevant through topics of talk. An example of the latter case occurred when the host suggested that learning and speaking Japanese would be difficult for the student as a foreigner, and the student replied that he had mastered Japanese technical terms for his work, thus making the *Japanese/foreigner* relational pair irrelevant, and the categories *specialist/layperson* relevant at this point. Resistance to proffered category-bound activities and predicates is significant because it potentially plays a role in the change of social attitudes. The *specialist/layperson* categories in Nishizaka's (1995) study indicate an opening up beyond the issue of ethnicity to embrace a wider sense of the (inter)cultural described above. Thus, 'interculturality' (Zhu 2013) becomes the complex and shifting play of various cultural categories and their associated features and activities that are used and refuted in the course of a stretch of interaction.

Discursive psychology

Sharing the ethnomethodological approach and emphasis on the close study of discursive interaction to justify analytic findings, the field of discursive psychology (as developed by Edwards and Potter 1992) is linked to conversation analysis. What distinguishes it is the aim to study how psychological concepts such as memory, attitudes, identity, emotions, and causal attribution are worked up, managed, and have consequences in discourse, including discursive interactions. Discursive psychology is quite revolutionary with regard to mainstream cognitive psychology, since it makes no claims about thought as an internal object, and in fact asserts that there is no way of getting behind discourse. Discursive psychology does not deny that cognition exists, but talk is seen as a part of social practices, rather than being a direct reflection of inner cognitive processes (Wiggins 2017, 4). Of course, such a radical departure from cognitive psychology is not without its detractors. With regard to memory, Brown and Reavey (2015, 7) argue that to treat remembering purely in terms of interactional formulations is to miss an aspect of memory that is crucial for all of us, the felt connection between what we are doing now and our personal or collective histories that we draw on in making sense of a given interaction.

Several strands of discursive psychology have been delineated in terms of focus of study. A first strand is re-specification. Psychological concepts are re-specified since they are theorized and studied as discursive practices rather than cognitive states. For example, *scripting* (evoking normative procedures) may be studied as a means to manage responsibility for one's actions, rather than being interpreted as evidence of a particular cognitive schema. The second strand is the *psychological thesaurus*: Psychological terminology and categories are examined for the interactional business they perform. Thirdly, managing psychological business refers to examining psychological themes (e.g., prejudice, emotional investment, etc.) for how they are managed in interaction, and finally the discursive psychology of institutions focuses on how psychological concepts perform institutional business (Wiggins 2017, 198).

Core principles of discursive psychology are the following: Discourse constructs different versions of the world, bringing particular accounts of reality into being; discourse is situated in a specific context of interaction, rhetoric, and turn-taking; and discourse acts on and in the context in different ways (Wiggins 2017, 9). A wide variety of discursive devices, means for completing actions through discourse, have been distinguished; the interaction or text shows evidence of these devices regardless of whether they may be consciously or unconsciously employed by the speaker. In what follows, discursive devices will be discussed that relate to discursive remembering, causal attribution, and factuality. Remembering in interaction is a matter of producing a particular version of past events.

The version makes available inferences that act to attribute causes, responsibility, and complicity. Causes may be portrayed as being internal to a person (for example, personality) or external (elements of the situation). A link between membership categorization analysis and the focus on causal attribution in discursive psychology is that categories and category-tied predicates (characteristics) can support causal inferences. The choice of category has implications, for example *white men, black sisters,* and *only human* perform indirect attributional, motivational, or mitigating work. Importantly, in the production of a version of events there is a dilemma in that the speaker is making specific inferences available, but at the same time does not want to appear to be biased. Therefore, he/she resorts to certain discursive devices for making the version appear descriptive and factual in order to offset suspicion of interest or stake, and the production of a counter-version by the other party. This process is termed *stake inoculation.* Factuality is constructed through various means: An impersonal data-oriented discourse style, precise details, and graphic descriptions, *voicing* whereby what other people said during the event reported on is quoted, and corroboration from independent sources, in particular those who have expert knowledge of the situation or matter at hand (their *category entitlement*). There are also other devices of stake inoculation. The speaker may change *footing,* typically attributing opinions to others and acting as a mouthpiece without responsibility for the point of view expressed, or he/she may present a counter-interest, for example an assessment of a negative trait in a person is countered by the assertion of being a close friend. Speakers are thus concerned not only with accountability of the actors within the version of events, but also with their own accountability for the version. Certain devices reinforce a version making it more difficult to rebut, such as the use of a coherent narrative structure, a logical argument, three-part lists which project a sense of completion, idiomatic expressions and vagueness (both of which are difficult to challenge), *extreme case formulations* (e.g., all, very, the most), *ontological gerrymandering* (the formulation of one realm of entities to the exclusion of another), the appeal to common knowledge, and script formulations that assert normality and normativity (Edwards and Potter 1992; Potter 1996; Wiggins 2017).

Discursive psychology is highly relevant to the study of mediation, since each party in a mediation presents an account, a version, of past events that while asserting itself as factual actually supports their own position and typically lays responsibility for problems on the other party. The following analysis will bring together MCA and discursive psychology in a practical application to show how the ongoing production of cultural categorizations during interaction links to inferred responsibility.

Data analysis

The data studied consists of three transcribed recordings of meetings of 30 to 50 minutes' duration between a client and a mediator at a National Family Mediation affiliated service in the South of England.[1] Couples who have decided to separate and divorce come to mediation as an alternative to solicitor negotiation or litigation in order to agree on arrangements with respect to the division of assets and matters of custody and access to the couple's children. The recordings comprise the initial meeting between the mediator and one party. At an initial meeting in this family mediation service, the mediator asks the party to tell their story, the role of mediation is discussed, and the party is asked about their wishes for a future agreement with the other party (Morris 2015). It is important to note that at an initial meeting we are presented with one spouse's perspective and version of events. Following Stokoe (2012), the aim of the analysis is to look for patterns across the three meetings that concern the cultural category-based narratives of the parties produced during the interaction between party and mediator.

The main pattern of note across the three mediation sessions is that the party in the session ascribes contrasting cultural categories to the other party, the spouse, and to him/herself. In the first session to be studied, Terence[2] has an autistic son, Andreas, from a previous marriage. He explains that the problems in his current marriage stem from how his wife, Esmeralda, relates to the boy. At the very start of his narrative, he states:

T: My wife is from Brazil
M: Yes
T: So she came here (.) when we were married really
M: Right

Terence provides a category-resonant description which ascribes to his wife the category of *person from Brazil* or *foreigner* from his perspective. The initial positioning in the narrative gives importance to this ascribed cultural category. In the following extract, "she doesn't speak English very well" is descriptive of the category *limited proficiency speaker of English*. Furthermore, Terence describes Esmeralda as having a particular communication style which upsets his son:

T: The problem with Esmeralda is that she doesn't speak English very well
M: Right
T: And when she does speak to Andreas she speaks <u>extreme</u>ly fast and extremely loud
M: [Yes
T: [which is not good for him
M: Yes
T: heh with the things he's got
M: Yes
T: He just doesn't understand what she's saying
M: Right
T: and the high pitch
M: Yes
T: It's very difficult for him

Terence also recounts that Esmeralda is demanding on the boy, which makes him angry, and he has become violent. Esmeralda is thus depicted implicitly as *a person with an inappropriate communication style*. In contrast, Terence performs and paints himself as a *well-educated proficient communicator*, and in the following passage points out that he is a *successful parent* in managing Andreas:

T: What I've found is that when Esmeralda's been away
M: hm
T: for a month in Brazil
M: Right
T: So it was supposed to be three weeks but it got extended because of the problems at the airport.
M: Yes
T: He's a lot calmer (.) when I deal with Andreas (one on one)
M: Yes

At a later stage in the mediation session, Terence mentions that social services are involved with Andreas. When probed by the mediator about this, he says that Andreas has been excluded from two schools due to his physical violence in damaging property. It is established that the boy is violent outside the house independently of the wife. It thus becomes obvious that another narrative version would be possible starting with the history of the boy's behavioral issues as an *autistic child* rather than starting with the wife's foreignness and deficient communication. The particular version told by Terence seems to be a factual description, but it in fact performs causal attributions that can be understood by the hearer (Potter 1996; Edwards and Potter 1992): Blame is placed on the wife both for the boy's behavior, and for the couple's separation.

In the second mediation session under study, Anne-Marie explains that the major reason why her marriage with husband Roger is not viable is that Roger is *a person who is non-communicative and non-emotional*, whereas she, in contrast, is an *emotional, tactile, and communicative person*. This is resonant of the gender stereotype whereby women are more communicative and emotionally expressive than men, and according to Anne-Marie, Roger is an extreme case. In the following passage, Anne-Marie supports her opinion through voicing the alleged views of a counsellor:

A: And the counsellor ↑only met him I think ↑once by himself and then this might have been our first session together and it was like a lightbulb going on. And he said he looked at me and he said "Most people in their lives follow two tracks (.) the practical track" there was a word for it but I can't remember what it was ( ) and ( ) "and the emotional track."
M: mm
A: And he said to me "you Anne-Marie work on parallel tracks."
M: mm
A: And he said to Roger "you don't have that emotional track."
M: mm
A: And I thought that's why I find it so difficult to talk to him about how I feel

Anne-Marie's intonational emphasis on *only* and *once* seems to indicate that her husband's character is so obvious that it took only a small amount of contact with him for the counsellor to be able to make his diagnosis. The inference in Anne-Marie's voicing of the counsellor's words is that Roger is lacking a normal human capacity, as he is not like *most people*. Voicing tends to support factuality of a report, and voicing a specialist lends credibility to the ideas by virtue of his *category entitlement* (people in particular categories are expected to know certain things) (Edwards and Potter 1992).

So far, the membership categorization devices (Stokoe 2012) of nationality/language and gender have been drawn on. In the third case of mediation, the relevant membership categorization device is social class. The following descriptions of Gordon's wife, Sally, when he first met her are resonant of the category *person of a low socio-economic class*:

G: When I met my wife (2) you know (.) she she was living on an Estate. She had a two bedroom flat (.) no food in the cupboard (.) you know (.) no central heating you know. And you know my mum (.) obviously families take sides ( ) my mum said ah she'll have to go back to eating beans on toast

There is a lot of hesitancy and repetition of "you know" in Gordon's speech which indicate some difficulty in articulation. Gordon categorizes himself as a *family man* who has worked hard, "bringing the bacon home":

G: ( ) You know I really am a family man.
M: Yes
G: I don't drink (.) I don't gamble. (4) All I've ever done is work really.

In Gordon's account his hard work as a *family man*, highlighted by emphatic sentence stress in the above quote, has allowed his wife to lead a "charmed life" of improved socio-economic status as a *lady of relative leisure*, indulging in her passion for horses:

G: she said 'Well I've worked. I've brought the kids up'. I said 'Well yeah no I'm not disputing that (.) you know (.) but I've paid the bills and put the food on the table and paid for all your holidays and diamonds and paid for your horses and your cars and you know
M: mm

This category-based portrayal implicitly supports the notion that it is unfair that Sally should demand the majority of equity in the marital house, an issue of disagreement which has brought mediation to a stand-still.

In all three mediation cases, contrasting cultural categories are ascribed in the manner of Zhu's (2013) *interculturality* in order to attribute the cause of the problems in the marital relationship or problems in the divorce negotiations to the other party, and to portray the party speaking in a positive light. However, the clear-cut nature of this pattern of blame is tempered.

The last quote above from Gordon displays another pattern, *stake inoculation* (Potter 1996). In order to provide the inference that the category-based version of affairs is not biased and thus to support the factuality of the account, the absent spouse is not painted in an entirely negative light. Thus, in the previous quote Gordon affirms that Sally has worked in that she has brought up the children of the marriage. Elsewhere, he says that she has "been a good mum" and has cooked and cared for the home. The same pattern occurs in the other mediation sessions under study. Despite the difficult relationship between Terence's wife, Esmeralda, and his son, Terence admits that this stepmother has provided "some amount of bonding" and "continuity." He also suggests that her communication style comes across as demanding, but "she may not mean it quite this way." For her part, Anne-Marie says that her husband is "a really good man, he's a fantastic father." These positively connoted descriptions that relate in all three cases to the membership categorization device of *parent* are juxtaposed with more qualified evaluations; the quote from Anne-Marie, for example, is followed by the clause "but we're just so different."

Stake inoculation regarding the potential bias of the proffered categories and category-resonant descriptions is undertaken in two other ways: The party describes his/her own drawbacks, and the party reports the contrasting point of view of their spouse that is also in the form of a category. Following on from the earlier quote when speaking of his ability as a parent to manage his autistic son, Terence indicates his potential imperfection as a parent:

T: He's a lot calmer when I deal with Andreas (one on one)
M: Yes
T: It may not be perfect how I deal with him but I <u>can</u> manage him
M: Yes
T: on my own (.) in my view anyway

Despite the self-deprecation, Terence stresses his capacity orally, "<u>can.</u>" For his part, Gordon reports a classification that his wife has made of him. This provides the inference that his account is not one-sided since he gives the other party's point of view.

G: Ah. My wife says I'm a manic depressive. Ah
M: (4) Do you think you're a manic depressive?
G: Well (.) I don't really know what a manic depressive is. I mean I get fed up with being taken for a ride.

Gordon appears to rebut the category provided by his wife, but later on he admits that he has been depressed, not only because of the marital situation of "thirty years gone down the drain," but also because he has been unemployed.

Other category-based patterns across these three mediation sessions can be observed, but it is hoped that the above analysis, although limited, has provided insight into how membership categorization analysis and discursive psychology can be applied.

Conclusion

Membership categorization analysis allows the exploration of interculturality (Zhu 2013), the dynamic use of cultural categories by participants across a stretch of interaction. Discursive psychology contributes further to the analysis of the use of cultural categories through its focus on causal inference and the construction of factuality which are important issues when an interactant is presenting a particular version of the past, as in mediation sessions. The close analysis of discourse in the MCA/DP approach shows how people manage cultural categories, category-resonant descriptions, and their causal inferences in sometimes explicit and sometimes subtle ways. The aim of the approach is to reveal patterns in the use of language in interaction. In the analysis of some family mediation data above, shared patterns of discursive structure were found across three mediation cases. It was shown that a party in mediation ascribes categories (with category-resonant descriptions) to him/herself and to the other party in order to attribute responsibility for problems to the other party. In order that the party's account should not be perceived as biased, stake inoculation with regard to the attribution of categories is undertaken in various ways, for example the other party is not painted entirely negatively. In the data studied here, the mediator did not challenge the party's account because this would not be appropriate in the context of family mediation (Morris 2015). However, in other types of conflict mediation where the aim is to improve the relationship between the parties, the mediator may take a more active role with regard to the party's construction of cultural categories that disculpate and attribute blame. Despite its limited scope, the analysis provided an illustration of how membership categorization analysis and discursive psychology can provide useful approaches for the purpose of analyzing and better understanding mediation, and more specifically intercultural mediation through tracing interactants' management of cultural categories.

Transcription conventions

(.)	small pause
(3.6)	pause to tenth of a second
( )	inaudible/incomprehensible speech
(yes)	transcriber not entirely sure of the words
[	overlapping speech
heh	laughter particle
<u>can</u>	strong stress
↑	noticeable rising intonation

Notes

1 The family mediation recordings were initially gathered by Paulette Morris for her PhD project in 2010. I thank Paulette warmly for entering into a data sharing agreement with me.
2 All names are pseudonyms.

References

Brown, Steven D., and Paula Reavey. 2015. "Dilemmas of Memory: The Mind is not a Tape Recorder." In *Discursive Psychology: Classic and Contemporary Issues*, edited by Christian Tileagă and Elizabeth Stokoe, 210–223. London: Routledge.

Edwards, Derek, and Jonathan Potter. 1992. *Discursive Psychology*. London: Sage. 10.1002/casp.2450050106

Fitzgerald, Richard, and William Housley. 2015. "Introduction." In *Advances in Membership Categorization Analysis*, edited by Richard Fitzgerald and William Housley. 1–22. London: Sage. 10.1002/9781118611463.wbielsi018

Herrman, Margaret, ed. 2006. *The Blackwell Handbook of Mediation: Bridging Theory, Research and Practice.* Malden, MA: Blackwell. 10.1111/j.1744-1617.2007.00134.x

Morris, Paulette. 2015. *Screening for Domestic Violence in Family Mediation: An Investigation into How Mediators Manage Disclosures of Domestic Abuse and Associated Emotions.* PhD thesis. London: Brunel University.

Nishizaka, Aug. 1995. "The Interactive Constitution of Interculturality: How to Be a Japanese with Words." *Human Studies* 18: 301–326. 10.1007/BF01323214

Potter, Jonathan. 1996. *Representing Reality: Discourse, Rhetoric and Social Construction.* London: Sage.

Reynolds, Edward, and Richard Fitzgerald. 2015. "Challenging Normativity: Re-appraising Category Bound, Tied and Predicated Features." In *Advances in Membership Categorization Analysis*, edited by Richard Fitzgerald and William Housley. 99–122. London: Sage. 10.4135/9781473917873.n5

Sacks, Harvey. 1979. *Lectures on Conversation.* Vols I and II. Edited by Gail Jefferson. Oxford: Blackwell.

Schegloff, Emanuel. 2007. *Sequence Organization in Interaction: A Primer in Conversation Analysis.* Cambridge: Cambridge University Press. 10.1017/CBO9780511791208

Stokoe, Elizabeth. 2012. "Moving Forward with Membership Categorization Analysis: Methods for Systematic Analysis." *Discourse Studies* 14 (3): 277–303. 10.1177/1461445612441534

Wiggins, Sally. 2017. *Discursive Psychology: Theory, Method and Applications.* London: Sage. 10.4135/9781473983335

Zhu, Hua. 2013. "Language, Identity and Interculturality: A Paradigm-shifting Question." In *Exploring Intercultural Communication: Language in Action*, 201–220. London and New York: Routledge.

37

INTERCULTURAL MEDIATION FROM THE PERSPECTIVE OF LINGUISTIC PRAGMATICS

Anthony J. Liddicoat

Introduction

In linguistics, pragmatics refers to the ways that language is used in context to communicate and interpret meaning. Pragmatics recognizes that communication is not simply achieved through syntactic and lexical means, but that context, both linguistic and non-linguistic, is a central part of what and how human beings communicate. Meanings are always constructed, communicated, and interpreted within a context and context shapes both what is said or written and what is understood. Context is thus a central element of meaning-making practices (Verschueren 2008). In any language, there are multiple ways of expressing similar meanings and such alternatives are not simply synonymous ways of expressing the idea but represent contextually adapted ways of speaking that interact with context to produce elements of meaning beyond the strictly linguistic.

Most work in pragmatics has tended to focus on the ways in which linguistic forms are used to realize actions (e.g., requests, compliments, promises, etc.) and how these realizations differ in terms of their social functions (e.g., politeness/impoliteness) (Mey 1993). There has, however, been a significant comparative perspective in pragmatics that has compared and contrasted the ways that different languages use linguistic resources to create similar actions (Verschueren 2016). However, this perspective has ended to adopt a with-in language approach to analysis in which the language use of (monolingual) native speakers of different languages is compared. More recently, there been a developing interest in intercultural pragmatics, which studies how language is used in social encounters between speakers who have different first languages and is interested in understanding how meanings are made and interpreted by participants in such interactions (Kecskes 2013, 2016). It is within the context of intercultural pragmatics that thinking has begun to emerge about how differences in meaning-making and interpretation are mediated in intercultural communication. This chapter will explore how meaning-making and interpretation are understood in intercultural pragmatics and then discuss how mediation has come to be understood as a form of action within the field. It will then consider the place that meta-pragmatic awareness has in understanding the mediational processes involved.

Intercultural pragmatics

The focus on meanings as contextualized has increasingly led to consideration of the ways in which cultures constitute a part of this context, and of the ways that cultures are a constituent part of

DOI: 10.4324/9781003227441-44

linguistic meaning-making and interpretation rather than being simply the backdrop against which communication occurs (Liddicoat 2009). Pragmatics has thus come to be understood as

> a form of culturally embedded practice within which patterns of language use represent pathways for meaning established by and for cultural groups at different scales of social organization, from small cultural groups such as families and local clubs to larger scale groups such as national and transnational communities of practice.
>
> *(McConachy and Liddicoat 2021, 4–5)*

Pragmatics provides communicators with sets of norms that they draw on to construct and interpret meanings.

Pragmatic norms do not simply involve normative rules for the construction and interpretation of utterances but also provide resources for presenting and interpreting identities and self-concepts in interaction. They are thus closely connected to assumptions, whether explicit or implicit, about social roles and relationships, and to the constitution of normal ways of being and doing in the social world. The field of intercultural pragmatics research has increasingly come to show that ways of speaking are not simply judged in terms of the appropriateness of linguistic choices to the linguistic and extra-linguistic contexts in which they are produced and understood but they also involve moral judgments about the nature of social conduct and of the people who perform it (Spencer-Oatey and Xing 2019). Pragmatic norms constitute not only descriptive norms—what is likely to be said and how in a particular context—but also injunctive norms—what ought to be said and how (Cialdini 2012). Pragmatics, as a fusion of language and culture in making and interpretating meanings, is thus a confrontation between language forms and the moral order of value judgments of speakers based in the wider universe of cultural values and ideologies (Blitvich and Kádár 2021). This moral order can be understood as the constellation of normative assumptions and principles that members of a cultural group use to construct their perceptions of how things should be and to make evaluative judgments of the comportment of others, and of those comporting themselves on such ways (Spencer-Oatey and Kádár 2020). Different ways of constructing utterances, that is differences in descriptive norms, therefore may be associated with different moral judgments about the person using a particular way of speaking. In intercultural contexts, therefore, differences in pragmatic norms are not simply differences in the ways that utterances are constructed and interpreted but may also represent differences in moral judgments about self and other (McConachy 2019).

Recognizing that pragmatic norms are not simply neutral constructs for organizing linguistic behavior has significant consequences for how we understand the place of language in intercultural communication. Language is not a neutral vehicle through which communication occurs but a morally laden set of practices that draw social relationships and power relations into processes of interpretation in ways that make possible moral stereotyping of speakers, entire language communities, nations, or even supranational groupings (e.g., East-West, Europe-Asia, etc.) (Pizziconi 2021).

In intercultural interactions, although one language may be used to carry out the communication, it is not the case that only one set of pragmatic norms will be in action as pragmatic norms themselves are not closely bound with language forms. Those communicating in intercultural contexts may thus draw on the same linguistic resources to construct their communication but may draw on multiple sets of pragmatics norms to construct and interpret the meanings being communicated (Kecskes 2013). In such contexts, there has been a tradition of privileging one set of norms, those of native speakers, as 'correct,' over those of non-native speakers and of discounting their interpretations as deviant (Kecskes 2019; McConachy and Liddicoat 2021). However, this view grossly oversimplifies the internal variability within pragmatic norms, the contingency of their application in any context, and cognitive, emotional, and political realities involved in communicating across languages and cultures. Given these complexities, intercultural communication requires mediation of the norms that are at play and understanding how those norms contribute both to how something is communicated and to how it is interpreted.

The understanding of mediation in intercultural pragmatics

In the field of intercultural pragmatics, mediation is understood in a range of different but inter-related ways (Liddicoat in press) and the term has been critiqued for its unacknowledged polysemy (Piccardo 2012; Tapia 2011) that includes three main dimensions of meaning: 1) resolving conflicts or problems, 2) acting as an intermediary, and 3) learning through practices of interpretation. In many discussions of mediation some or all of these may be present and influence how mediational work is understood. The idea of mediation as a process of problem solving is probably the most common understanding of mediation outside the field. This view of mediation represents cultural contact as being largely shaped by problems of miscommunication that result from cultural differences. This view of the relationship between languages, cultures, and communication has, however, been widely criticized within the linguistics literature (for example, see Piller 2011; Sarangi 1994). Where culture is viewed as the source of miscommunication, intercultural mediation is seen as needed to restore communication and re-establish understanding between participants (Gohard-Radenkovic et al. 2004).

In many fields, mediation is understood as a specialist capability that is drawn on in the context of solving problems that the participants in the communication cannot resolve for themselves (Rubenfeld and Clément 2012). Mediators are thus understood as intermediaries external to the communication itself, who can intervene to restore problems in communication that have led to communication breakdown. When mediation is applied to language, such mediators may commonly be seen as interpreters or translators who enable meanings created in one language to be communicated to recipients who do not speak that language (Katan 2002, 2004; Pöchhacker 2008). Mediation is therefore conceptualized as a communicative act in which the mediator is a third party who negotiates meaning between participants as an intermediary and who re-expresses or re-languages the meanings of others. This view of the mediator as always outside the main communication is problematic in the field of intercultural pragmatics as problem solving is not usually understood as a macro-level communicative problem but rather as a micro-level phenomenon that occurs moment by moment in communication and needs to be resolved locally by the participants themselves inside the communication.

Within intercultural pragmatics, while the external mediator remains one possibility within the system of mediation, other possibilities are also brought into the scope of mediational work. Liddicoat (2014; 2017; in press) has argued that to understand intercultural mediation in relation to pragmatics, it is important to consider both external and internal mediational processes because mediation can be for the self as well as the other. Mediation for others involves operating on meanings that are present in the interaction, but which cause difficulties for comprehension by others. This mediation is enacted by someone who understands the meanings that are involved in the interaction, who may be, and usually is, a participant within the interaction itself. This form of mediational work for others can be seen in Extract 1, where Ana, who is a Chilean exchange student, takes on a mediating role in an interaction with two Australian interlocutors in order to help them come to understand Ana's own personal meanings.

Extract 1   (source Liddicoat 2014, 271–2):

1.	Cara:	So I don't get why- why she is- why she got upset you know. Her son was just being nice.
2.	Ana:	Where I come from, I don't say 'thank you' if my mother cooked dinner for us. It would not sound good to her. It's like she does something unusual. My mother always cooks dinner. If I say thank you, she might be sad.

3.	Beth:	You mean she- if you said thank you she wouldn't like it.
4.	Ana:	Yeah. She think I was saying she was bad mother.
5.	Cara:	But you're just being nice.
6.	Ana:	It's nice here. I think you thank people for more things. You tell people you like what they do. You thank for everything not just special things.
7.	Cara:	Like saying thanks to the bus driver.
8.	Ana:	We don't do that. They just drive a bus. They're supposed to do that. It's not they're doing you favour.
9.	Beth:	It's their job.
10.	Ana:	Yeah. We don't thank for doing job. That's not special. If they just do what they're supposed to.
11.	Beth:	What if they're especially nice.
12.	Ana:	If they do something good. Something not usual. You would say thank you. Not just for the driving. For something else.
13.	Beth:	So if I thank my mother when she cooks dinner that is like I say she did something unusual.
14.	Cara:	Like she doesn't cook for you. She did it specially this time.
15.	Ana:	Or I am guest not part of family. She does it special because I am guest. She's not my mother.
16.	Beth:	So what do I do? Do I say I like what she cooked?
17.	Ana:	I think if I say 'dinner is nice' she says 'isn't it always?'. We say is nice, when is special, when is different. If she make my favorite, I say that.

This interaction takes place in a classroom in which students have been discussing a transcription of an interaction between a mother and a son in which the son has thanked his mother for helping him and the mother has reacted negatively to the thanking (see Liddicoat 2009 for a fuller discussion). While her interlocutors have difficulties comprehending the mother's reaction, Ana recognizes the ways that the thanking has been meaningful for both sets of participants and associates the mother's meanings with her own expectations about linguistic conduct. As she interacts, she provides interpretations of the meanings at play both from the perspective of her interlocutors and from her own (and the mother's) perspectives. In her mediational work, Ana makes evident the multiple interpretative possibilities for understanding the talk and brings these into relation.

An example of mediation for self can be seen in Extract 2, which James reports on his experience as a learner of Japanese experiencing an interpretive dissonance that he needed to resolve for himself. While he was outside the interaction in which the communicative issue occurred, it is his own interpretations of the situation and their dissonance with the meaning-making he has witnessed that he must resolve, and he reports on how he worked through these problems in meaning-making.

Extract 2 (source, Liddicoat and McConachy 2019, 14–15):

1. James: On one of my visits to Japan, I was in a restaurant at Tokyo station and there was this uh older guy at one of the tables an' he really shocked me.

2. Researcher: What did he do?

3. James: Well um it was a restaurant, right? And he was at a table and they were eating and he just turns around and calls out to the waitress '*nama:::*' ((draught beer)), just like that. And I was just like shocked. He didn't even look at her, just called out.

4. Researcher: hmm.

The perspective of linguistic pragmatics

5.	James:	And I like thought that's so rude. Um, I mean, you always think of Japanese people as super polite. But he just said '*nama::::*' and he got his beer. And like you know I didn't think they would do that.
6.	Researcher:	So why did you think it was rude?
7.	James:	Well um you know, it's not the way we would do it here. You can't just say that. You have to ask and say please and stuff. So, it wasn't my way. But it wasn't like what we learn in class either. It's always 'oh you've got to be so polite' and 'Japanese people are all polite' and stuff. And we spend so much time learning polite stuff.
8.	Researcher:	mhm
9.	James:	It was um sorta like the first time I'd seen it. But you know after a while, you seen it happen and you think they're not all like what we learn in class. There's other stuff, like a whole range of things people do.
10.	Researcher:	So how do you understand what he did?
11.	James:	Well uh it's like it all depends who's there. I guess, um like it's because he's a man and old and that and she was just a young girl. So I thought it was a bit sexist, you know, when it happened. And that's something you get in Japan.
12.	Researcher:	mhm.
13.	James:	And I've seen other times, that people sometimes are polite to waiters and people in shops. They just say what they want or point or something and that's all. And the waiters and shop people are all like so super polite. Um, it's like in Japanese they say something like *kyaku-sama, kami-sama* ((the customer [is a] god)). You know, the customer is like a god. So if you're a god, I guess you don't have to be polite. But for me it's a bit shocking, you know.
14.	Researcher:	mm. So how do you sort this out for yourself?
15.	James:	Well in the restaurant I started saying like '*onegaishimasu*' for everything. Cos I hadn't ordered yet. Like I was trying to show I wasn't like that guy. So not '*nama*'. I don't want people to think I speak like that to them. '*nama onegaishimasu*'. Heh, heh I used to just say '*kudasai*' cos in class they said it was the word for please. But I wanted to be um politer than that to sorta show, I'm not like that. Now it's '*onegaishimasu*', just cos of that guy who said '*nama*' and not you know wanting to be that person.

In this extract, James is discussing a communicative event in which his own injunctive norms were in conflict with both his understanding of Japanese pragmatics norms and his own norms for inter-action in this context. Here James is dealing with the injunctive norms that he understood to be in operation in service encounters in restaurants and relates the judgments he made about the language use he observed and about the speaker. He discusses how he came to understand the injunctive norms here in new ways as he began to understand better the associations between ways of speaking and the expectations and values at play in this particular context. In discussing this event he draws out the ways that he approached the problem of interpreting language in context and how he resolved it, both for understanding the specific event and also for developing a set of pragmatic norms that allowed him to resolve the communicative problem his new understanding brought into being.

Mediation and metapragmatic awareness

The approach to mediation discussed here ultimately depends on the mediator's metapragmatic awareness, a concept first proposed by Verscheuren (2000); it involves language in use itself becoming the object of thinking and articulation (McConachy 2013; McConachy and Liddicoat 2016, 2021). However, in intercultural contexts, metapragmatic awareness needs to be conceptualized more broadly than has often been in the case when the concept has been applied to communication in a single language. In such cases, metapragmatic awareness has often been limited to the linguistic aspects of language in use that allow for the recognition of the linguistic action being performed by particular utterances in context (Verschueren 2000; Mey 1993). In some work, metapragmatic awareness has also applied to awareness of the mapping linguistic forms onto context and of the contextual constraints on linguistic resources for achieving particular pragmatic acts and in making judgments of pragmatic appropriateness (Safont Jordá 2003; Alcón Soler and Safont Jordà 2008; Kinginger and Farrell 2004). In intercultural contexts, metapragmatic awareness also involves a recognition of the multiplicity of meanings potentially present in interaction, how such meanings come to be present at any moment in communication and how such meanings constitute valid ways of understanding communication. Metapragmatic awareness is not therefore simply an act of identifying speakers' meanings but rather of interpreting the multiple meanings present for interlocutors (Liddicoat and Scarino 2013; Liddicoat 2021).

In intercultural communication, interpretation is complex as there may be multiple interpretations present for participants that result from different potential understandings and interpretative possibilities that exist in the use of each language available to the participants and their culturally based assumptions about language use. Mediation in this context is not simply finding the interpretation that is the 'correct' representation of a speakers' meaning of the language used in the context (c.f. Schleiermacher 1977). Such an understanding would imply the validating on one potential understanding of the mapping of language and context over others and assume that the intended speaker meaning was unitary and/or unambiguous at the moment of its production. In any use of language for communication, and particularly in intercultural communication, multiple meanings are potentially present and potentially valid (see Gadamer 2011; Ricoeur 1965). Gadamer argues that reaching a shared interpretation involves a fusion of horizons—that of the maker of meaning and that of its interpreter—through dialogue between different interpretations. For Ricoeur, similarly, the focus of interpretation needs to be placed on exposing multiple possible meanings to highlight the motivations behind and the implications of each. This dialogue of interpretations is thus a central element of the mediational process, and such dialogues can be seen in Extracts 1 and 2 above in which the participants acknowledge and interrelate the various potential meanings they have discovered. Such mediational work involves using metapragmatic awareness as a hermeneutic resource for coming to know the ways that meaning is being made and interpreted. This process of dialogic negotiation of meaning is fundamentally a linguistic act in which the languages(s) of the participants provide a resource though which meanings can be articulated and shared.

However, mediation is not simply an interpretative process that seeks to identify multiple possible meanings but also requires the mediator to work to bring diverse interpretations into relationship. This is a reflective process in which mediators construct the meaningfulness and consequentiality of talk for themselves and/or for others (McConachy and Liddicoat 2016). Thus, the process of mediating requires an understanding and awareness of, and a reflection on, the process of meaning-making itself (see Kramsch 2006; 2011 on symbolic competence). Mediation involves an intervention into the processes of meaning-making and interpretation in which the multiplicity of meanings identified serves to progress communication by giving insight into how linguistic features and context interact to create meanings. Metapragmatic awareness is thus a reflexive form of understanding that involves deeper awareness of how language functions in the creation of interpersonal meaning within and across languages and cultures (McConachy 2018).

Concluding remarks

Intercultural mediation in pragmatics has developed a particular take on mediation that reflects the needs of interlocutors to manage problems in meaning-making and interpretation locally as they occur in communication. Current work in the field has shown that when participants need to make sense of different potential meanings of language in context, they draw on a range of reflective and interpretative resources, most especially metapragmatic awareness, to identify and interrelate different potential meanings. It has also shown that quite similar processes are used by participants in communication to resolve problems of meaning whether they are co-present with their interlocutors, as in the case of face-to-face interactions, or distanced from them, as in the case of problems of meaning arise in written or media communication. Nonetheless, research on intercultural mediation in the field of pragmatics is new and remains underdeveloped and there is much work to do to understand exactly what linguistic, conceptual and hermeneutic resources mediators draw on to develop their interpretations, how they manage the diversity of interpretations that results, and how they enact mediational roles.

References

Alcón Soler, Eva, and Maria Pilar Safont Jordà. 2008. "Pragmatic Awareness in Second Language Acquisition." In *Encyclopedia of Language and Education*. Vol. 6, edited by Jasone Cenoz and Nancy H. Hornberger, 193–204. New York: Springer. 10.1007/978-0-387-30424-3_149

Blitvich, Pilar Garcés-Conejos, and Dániel Z. Kádár. 2021. "Morality in Sociopragmatics." In *The Cambridge Handbook of Sociopragmatics*, edited by Michael Haugh, Dániel Z. Kádár, and Marina Terkourafi, 385–407. Cambridge, UK: Cambridge University Press. 10.1017/9781108954105.021

Cialdini, Robert B. 2012. "The Focus Theory of Normative Conduct." In *Handbook of Theories of Social Psychology*. Vol. 2, edited by Paul A.M. van Lange, Arie W. Kruglanski, and E.T. Higgins. 2 vols, 295–312. London: Sage. 10.4135/9781446249222.n41

Gadamer, Hans-Georg. 2011. *Wahrheit und Methode. Grundzüge einer philosophischen Hermeneutik* [Truth and method. Fundamentals of a philosophical hermeneutics]. Berlin: Akademie Verlag.

Gohard-Radenkovic, Aline, Denise Lussier, Hermine Penz, and Geneviève Zarate. 2004. "La Médiation Culturelle en Didactique des Langues Comme Processus." [Cultural mediation in language learning and teaching as a process]. In *La Médiation Culturelle et Didactique des Langues*, edited by Geneviève Zarate, Aline Gohard-Radenkovic, Denise Lussier, and Hermine Penz, 225–238. Strasbourg: Council of Europe Publishing.

Katan, David. 2002. "Mediating the Point of Refraction and Playing with Perlocutionary Effects: A Translator's Choice?" In *Critical Studies: Interdiciplinarity and Translation*, edited by Stefan Herbrechter, 177–195. Amsterdam & New York: Rodolphi.

Katan, David. 2004. *Translating Cultures: An Introduction for Translators, Interpreters and Mediators*. Manchester, UK: St Jerome.

Kecskes, Istvan. 2013. *Intercultural Pragmatics*. Oxford: Oxford University Press.

Kecskes, Istvan. 2016. "Can Intercultural Pragmatics Bring Some New Insight into Pragmatic Theories?" In *Interdisciplinary Studies in Pragmatics, Culture and Society*, edited by Alessandro Capone and Jacob L. Mey, 43–69. Cham: Springer. 10.1007/978-3-319-12616-6_3

Kecskes, Istvan. 2019. "Impoverished Pragmatics? The Semantics-Pragmatics Interface from an Intercultural Perspective." *Intercultural Pragmatics* 16 (5): 7–31. 10.1515/ip-2019-0026

Kinginger, Celeste, and Kathleen Farrell. 2004. "Assessing Development of Meta-Pragmatic Awareness in Study Abroad." *Frontiers: The Interdisciplinary Journal of Study Abroad* 10 (1): 19–42. 10.36366/frontiers.v10i1.131

Kramsch, Claire. 2006. "From Communicative Competence to Symbolic Competence." *The Modern Language Journal* 90(2): 249–52. 10.1111/j.1540-4781.2006.00395_3.x.

Kramsch, Claire. 2011. "The Symbolic Dimensions of the Intercultural." *Language Teaching* 44(3): 354–67. 10.1017/S0261444810000431.

Liddicoat, Anthony J. in press. "Intercultural Mediation and Intercultural Pragmatics." In *Cambridge Handbook of Intercultural Pragmatics*, edited by Istvan Kecskes. Cambridge: Cambridge University Press.

Liddicoat, Anthony J. 2009. "Communication as Culturally Contexted Practice: A View from Intercultural Communication." *Australian Journal of Linguistics* 29 (1): 115–133. 10.1080/07268600802516400

Liddicoat, Anthony J. 2014. "Pragmatics and Intercultural Mediation in Intercultural Language Learning." *Intercultural Pragmatics* 11 (2): 259–277. 10.1515/ip-2014-0011

Liddicoat, Anthony J. 2017. "Interpretation and Critical Reflection in Intercultural Language Learning: Consequences of a Critical Perspective for the Teaching and Learning of Pragmatics." In *The Critical Turn in Language and Intercultural Communication Pedagogy: Theory, Research and Practice*, edited by Maria Dasli and Adriana Díaz, 22–39. London, New York: Routledge.

Liddicoat, Anthony J. 2021. "Interprétation/Interpreting." In *La Médiation Interculturelle en Didactique des Langues et des Cultures/Intercultural Mediation in Teaching and Learning Languages and Cultures*, edited by Anthony J. Liddicoat, Martine Derivry-Plard, George Alao, Jacqueline Breugnot, Daniel Kwang Guan Chan, Wai M. Chan, Seo W. Chi et al. Paris: Editions des archives contemporains.

Liddicoat, Anthony J., and Angela Scarino. 2013. *Intercultural Language Teaching and Learning*. Chichester: Wiley-Blackwell.

Liddicoat, Anthony, and Troy McConachy. 2019. "Meta-Pragmatic Awareness and Agency in Language Learners' Constructions of Politeness." In *Pragmatic and Cross-Cultural Competences. Focus on Politeness*, edited by Thomas Szende and George Alao, 22–25. Bruxelles: Peter Lang.

McConachy, Troy. 2013. "A Place for Pragmatics in Intercultural Teaching and Learning." In *Linguistics for Intercultural Education*, edited by Fred Dervin and Anthony J. Liddicoat, 71–86. Amsterdam: John Benjamins.

McConachy, Troy. 2018. *Developing Intercultural Perspectives on Language Use in Foreign Language Learning*. Bristol: Multilingual Matters.

McConachy, Troy. 2019. "L2 Pragmatics as 'Intercultural Pragmatics': Probing Sociopragmatic Aspects of Pragmatic Awareness." *Journal of Pragmatics* 151:167–176. 10.1016/j.pragma.2019.02.014

McConachy, Troy, and Anthony J. Liddicoat. 2016. "Metapragmatic Awareness and Intercultural Competence: The Role of Reflection and Interpretation in Developing Intercultural Understanding." In *Intercultural Competence: Alternative Approaches for Different Times*, edited by Fred Dervin and Zehavit Gross, 3–30. New York: Routledge.

McConachy, Troy, and Anthony J. Liddicoat. 2021. "Introduction: Second Language Pragmatics for Intercultural Understanding." In *Teaching and Learning Second Language Pragmatics for Intercultural Understanding*, edited by Troy McConachy and Anthony J. Liddicoat, 1–18. New York: Routledge, Abingdon.

Mey, Jacob. 1993. *Pragmatics: An Introduction*. Oxford, Cambridge, MA: Blackwell.

Piccardo, Enrica. 2012. "Médiation et Apprentissage des Langues: Pourquoi est-il Temps de Réfléchir à cette Notion." [Mediation and language learning: Why is it time to reflect on this notion]. *Ela. Études de linguistique appliquée* 167: 285–297.

Piller, Ingrid. 2011. *Intercultural Communication: A Critical Introduction*. Edinburg: Edinburgh University Press.

Pizziconi, Barbara. 2021. "Exploring Framing Categories in Language Learners' Intercultural Positioning: "Asia" and "The West"." In *Teaching and Learning Second Language Pragmatics for Intercultural Understanding*, edited by Troy McConachy and Anthony J. Liddicoat, 60–82. New York: Routledge, Abingdon.

Pöchhacker, Franz. 2008. "Interpreting as Mediation." In *Crossing Borders in Community Interpreting: Definitions and Dilemmas*, edited by Carmen V. Garcés and Anne Martin, 9–26. Amsterdam: John Benjamins. 10.1075/btl.76.02poc

Ricoeur, Paul. 1965. *De L'Interprétation: Essai Sur Freud* [On interpretation: Essay on Freud]. Paris: Seuil.

Rubenfeld, Sara, and Richard Clément. 2012. "Intercultural Conflict and Mediation: An Intergroup Perspective." *Language Learning* 62 (4): 1205–1230. 10.1111/j.1467-9922.2012.00723.x

Safont Jordá, Maria Pilar. 2003. "Metapragmatic Awareness and Pragmatic Production of Their Language Learners of English: A Focus on Request Acts Realizations." *International Journal of Bilingualism* 7: 43–69.

Sarangi, Srikant. 1994. "Critical Perspectives on Intercultural Communication." Pragmatics. Quarterly Publication of the International Pragmatics Association (IPrA) 4 (3): 409–427. 10.1075/prag.4.3.05sar

Schleiermacher, Friedrich. 1977. *Hermeneutik und Kritik: Mit einem Anhang sprachphilosophischer Texte Schleiermachers* [Hermeneutics and criticism: With an appendix of Schleiermacher's philosophical texts]. Frankfurt am Main: Suhrkamp.

Spencer-Oatey, Helen, and Dániel Kádár. 2020. *Intercultural Politeness*. Cambridge: Cambridge University Press. 10.1017/9781316810071

Spencer-Oatey, Helen, and Jianyu Xing. 2019. "Interdisciplinary Perspectives on Interpersonal Relations and the Evaluation Process: Culture, Norms, and the Moral Order." *Journal of Pragmatics* 151:141–154. 10.1016/j.pragma.2019.02.015

Tapia, Claude. 2011. "Médiation: Définition et Problématique." [Mediation: Definition and problematic]. *Le Journal des psychologues* 288 (5): 16. 10.3917/jdp.288.0016

Verscheuren, Jef. 2000. "Notes on the Role of Metapragmatic Awareness in Language Use." *Pragmatics. Quarterly Publication of the International Pragmatics Association (IPrA)* 10 (4): 439–456. 10.1075/prag.10.4.02ver

Verschueren, Jef. 2008. "Context and Structure in a Theory of Pragmatics." *Studies in Pragmatics* 10 (1983): 14–24.

Verschueren, Jef. 2016. "Contrastive Pragmatics." In *Handbook of Pragmatics*, edited by Jan-Ola Östman and Jef Verschueren, 1–34. Amsterdam: John Benjamins. 10.1075/hop.20.con18

38
STORYTELLING, CULTURE, AND IDENTITY IN MEDIATION

Brian L. Heisterkamp

Storytelling in mediation

Fundamentally, mediation is a process of storytelling. Court-based mediation programs provide scholars with a view of the interplay between storytelling, culture, and identity. Mediators typically open the hearing, explain the mediation process, introduce the parties, and then invite each disputant to tell their story (Garcia 2000). Many mediators are trained to ask disputants to "tell their stories" (Docherty 2004), which solidifies the place of storytelling in mediation. The story-as-told can be viewed as the structure of a party's accounting of the dispute with the mediator serving as the manager of the storytelling process (Rifkin, Millen, and Cobb 1991). The disputants' stories convey their values and conflict-related behavior while potentially bringing facts into clearer focus when conveyed through narrative (Duryea and Potts 1993). The goal is that through the telling of the story, disputants are able to move from story to settlement (Stewart and Maxwell 2010).

Stories in mediation should not be considered monolithic entities that are self-contained and uninfluenced by emerging factors. Parties tell separate stories that may contain side stories, deviate based on another party's story, and emerge based on mediator questioning. Mediators may assist less powerful disputants in developing co-created stories about identity, validation, and respect (Stewart 2008). And mediators solicit second or third stories from disputants (Garcia 2000) with the aim of seeking clarification, balancing disparities between the parties, and moving the dispute to settlement.

Distinctions can be made between different types of stories that surface during mediation sessions. Many mediation scholars have examined the canonical narrative with a distinct beginning and ending and a description of events outlined in mostly chronological order (Stewart and Maxwell 2010; Jones 1988). Conversation analysis scholars have made contributions to understanding the sequential organization of stories, particularly how stories enter and exit routine conversation (Mandelbaum 2012). Within the context of mediation and peacebuilding, stories may be characterized as constructive or destructive where constructive stories inspire and promote settlement and destructive stories convey negative values and encourage conflict (Coburn 2011). More recently, Georgakopoulou (2015) articulated how "small stories", that do not fit into canonical narrative analysis, foster understanding of how this form of storytelling unfolds through co-construction between teller and audience in non-linear, non-chronological ways. These different story types offer unique analytic lenses through which scholars can better understand various aspects of the mediation process.

358

DOI: 10.4324/9781003227441-45

These different story types serve valuable functions important to conflict management and mediation. Stories frame the conflict for both the mediator and the disputing parties. Given that a conflict exists between the parties, the telling of these different frames enables both the parties and the mediator to identify possible routes to settlement. The stories convey the perspectives of the disputants and offer the opportunity for the mediator to find areas of congruence that may lead to rapprochement. The stories convey values held by the disputants in ways that may be better understood because of the familiarity of the narrative form. And stories hold the potential to unlock commonalities related to cultural identity.

Because stories hold the ability to make cultural connections, they are useful in developing, understanding, and finding common purpose (Aidman and Long 2017). Cultural exchange occurs through narrative and stories may move the parties toward settlement through the information generated during the storytelling engrained in the mediation process (Duryea and Potts 1993). The stories function as frames of orientation through which disputing parties can recognize aspects of another's cultural values with which they can identify.

Intercultural approach to storytelling during mediation

Intercultural mediation occurs when "either the researcher or at least one of the participants to a mediation assume that the participants have different cultural backgrounds or that the conflict itself may result from cultural differences" (Busch 2016, 3). Culture can be defined as the "sum total of a society's signifying practices" (Rings and Rasinger 2020, 61) or "the composite of cohesive behavior within any social grouping" (Holliday 1999, 247). Analysis of storytelling enables researchers to describe culturally relevant behaviors and since the knowledge transmitted through stories has the potential to be "reinterpreted, reframed, and resisted by individual tellers" stories have been used for many analytic purposes, including examining mediation (Senehi 2009, 211). When mediators ask the parties 'what is this conflict about,' disputants often provide a broad frame of their view of the conflict in the form of the story (Docherty 2004).

More specifically, stories are a means of forming cultural identity, creating membership boundaries, and constructing the self (Nasrollahi Shahri 2019). Cultural identity construction within stories (Ta and Filipi 2020) has often been examined from an essentialist perspective where aspects of an individual's identity, particularly related to nationality and ethnicity, are characterized as fixed, leading to the view that one's cultural identity causes certain behaviors (Brownlie 2017). An alternative, small cultures, viewpoint is proffered by Holliday (1999) in which a group's cohesive behavior is not essentialized and groups are not viewed as subordinate to other groups. Mediation is a process of small culture creation through the shared understandings the parties form (Brownlie 2017). The idea of *small* represents an alternative paradigm for examining cohesive social groupings (Holliday 1999). One such social grouping mediation parties employ is the identification of cultural categories in an ongoing, dynamic process based on community knowledge (Brownlie 2017).

Traversing from storytelling to the construction of cultural identities in those narratives leads to the relevance of interculturality as a means of understanding how those identities are formed during narrative production. From an intercultural pragmatics stance, interculturality is a "situationally emergent and co-constructed phenomenon that relies both on relatively definable cultural norms and models as well as situationally evolving features" (Kecskes 2013, 98). Constructing culturally relevant identity categories becomes one resource participants employ when building narratives that ascribe identity categories on themselves or others (Zhu 2018; Brownlie 2018). Because participants belong to multiple cultural categories, they likely make specific categories—for themselves or another—relevant during the social interaction in ways that appear beneficial to the mediation outcome they may favor (Zhu 2018; Brownlie 2018).

Constructing cultural identities

The data discussed here were collected as part of a broader study of conflict resolution in contexts including high schools, community outreach centers, and court-based mediation programs. The mediation sessions examined here were obtained from a court-based mediation program located in the southwestern United States that required all small claims disputes to be referred to mediation. Cases involved landlord-tenant disputes, consumer complaints, automobile accident disputes, and disagreements between neighbors. Fifty different sessions with 41 mediators were video recorded. The volunteer mediators received approximately 40 hours of training. Disputes not resolved during mediation were referred to the judge. For this analysis, mediation sessions and data extracts were selected that showed self or other ascriptions of cultural categories. The court-based mediation session data include stories where cultural categories based on gender, educational roles, age, and sport team roles emerge.

Because identity is a multifaceted construct, mediators and disputing parties benefit from being cognizant of the identity framework being conveyed by others. The following extract is from a mediation session involving a rental dispute in which the landlord is seeking to recover a lost rental incentive from the tenant and his father, who co-signed the lease agreement. As discussed below, another portion of this dispute was previously litigated before the judge.

Extract 1: Mediation 20. Participants: M: Mediator; A: Arturo (father/defendant); E: Ernie (son/defendant)

(1)	A:	See, my understanding was when he came to court, that the judge even told the
(2)		lady to put him in another apartment, okay, but the lady says, no, I want him
(3)		out. That is when he had the move out.
(4)	M:	Okay.
(5)	A:	See he didn't want to move out at all, period.
(6)	M:	Are you a student?
(7)	E:	Pardon?
(8)	M:	Are you a student?
(9)	E:	No.
(10)	M:	Oh, okay.
(11)	A:	And finally, my wife tells him you better move because they're not going to let
(12)		you in peace. Because they're going to be nagging and nagging at you for every
(13)		little thing that goes on there. They're going to blame you.

Through the mechanism of interculturality, the mediator attempts to ascribe the category *student* to the participant Ernie (lines 6 and 8). After seeking clarification (line 7), Ernie rejects being placed into the category of *student* (line 9). Earlier in the mediation—for reasons that were not stated—the landlords clarified that Ernie was evicted for noncompliance with the lease agreement. The mediator attempts to ascribe the category *student* onto Ernie and link that category to one who would be evicted from an apartment. This would not be an uncommon occurrence at this court-connected mediation program that is in the jurisdiction of a large university where cultural stereotypes of students being evicted from apartments resonate with community members. Nonetheless, the category is rejected by Ernie. But his father, Arturo, still indicates that Ernie is someone who would be nagged (line 12) and blamed for wrongdoing (line 13).

Later in the same mediation session, the landlord describes Ernie and provides some explanation for the eviction.

Storytelling in mediation

Extract 2: Mediation 20. Participants: M: Mediator; A: Arturo (father/defendant); J: Jan (landlord/plaintiff)

(1)	A:	He was willing to stay there as long as he wanted.
(2)	J:	But if I may?
(3)	M:	Sure.
(4)	J:	But unfortunately, the residents in that particular building that he was in did not
(5)		want him there, and we didn't want to take the chance of him moving to another
(6)		part of the complex and causing the same type of disturbances. That's just not
(7)		something we don't want to do. We had people saying that they were going to
(8)		move if he didn't.
(9)	M:	Okay. So —
(10)	J:	And we're not going to hold somebody — a good resident that, you know, we're
(11)		not going to make them move, after being there, because of somebody that's
(12)		there that's causing a disturbance.
(13)	M:	So
(14)	J:	So moving him to another part of the building was not an alternative.

The categorical description of Ernie develops and contrasting identities emerge. Jan describes Ernie as someone who causes *disturbances* (lines 6 and 12). That is contrasted with Arturo's description of his son as someone willing to stay (line 1). From an interculturality view, there are dual attempts by the mediator and the plaintiff Jan to create a negative identity for the defendant Ernie. The mediator attempts to ascribe the category *student* onto Ernie and the plaintiff Jan links him to an individual who causes *disturbances*. Divergent categorical descriptions of Ernie emerge with his father's describing him as not wanting to move out (Extract 1, line 5) and *willing to stay* (Extract 2, line 1) and the mediator attempting to ascribe the category of *student* onto him (Extract 1, lines 6 and 8) and the plaintiff describing him as *causing a disturbance* (Extract 2, line 12). These oppositional constructions emphasize cultural differences rather than similarities (Brownlie 2018) and may limit the ability of disputants to find common ground.

The mediation in the following extract concerned an automobile-bicycle accident. The bicycle and the automobile collided and responsibility for the accident and resulting damage to both the automobile and the bicycle is being disputed. The bicyclist was a minor who could not be absent from school so is represented by his father, Mr. Hillstrom. This extract occurs after a caucus and Mr. Hall, the automobile driver, is explaining why he waited 3–4 months after the accident to file the claim (Extract 3).

Extract 3: Mediation 14. Participants: M: Mediator; HA: Mr. Hall; HI: Mr. Hillstrom

590	HA	And finally, I mean, my friends were talking to me, and like I was just saying, I felt
591		bad, and they were saying just sue him for the damages. So I decided to go and
592		get an estimate on it and find out.
593	M	That's about as honest as you can make it.
594	HI:	Uh huh
595	M	Very refreshing to hear that because that's exactly how it happened and that's
596		exactly why mediation works.
597	HI	How old are you?
598	HA	Uh: Twenty-five.
599	HI	Yeah well Uhm I'd like to give you a little profile on the kid uh that you had the

---

361

600	accident with. He's an outstanding student and athlete. He uhm He's not that
601	kind of person — he's the kind of person you could trust to take care of your
602	house while you are on vacation.
603	He's he's honest.
604	He'll be paying for that accident through his insurance for the next — til he's
605	twenty five years old because of the ticket that he got, whether it's resolved and
606	probably will be at at court because it's going to be on his record regardless of
607	what happens here. Plus the loss of the bike, plus uh — this isn't one of those kids
608	that uh is going up intentionally wreckin other people's stuff. He isn't the kind of
609	kid that you're going to find out has taken your lawn mower or something over
610	the weekend. He's a very good, honest kid.

Interestingly, following Mr. Hall's explanation about the delay in filing the claim, the mediator lends credibility to the account by indicating that it is an *honest* (line 593) and *refreshing* (line 595) account that lends to the effectiveness of mediation. Through the operation of interculturality, Mr. Hillstrom then ascribes the cultural categories of *student* and *athlete* onto his son (line 600). He provides descriptions of those categories: *person you could trust* (line 601), *honest* (line 603), and *very good* (line 610). The ascription of these cultural categories onto his son may be in response to the mediator pronouncing the honesty of Mr. Hall, thus developing competing constructions of the *honest* individuals involved in the accident.

The following mediation also involves a rental dispute. In this case, the plaintiff is seeking to recoup the cost of damages he claims were caused by the defendant. This extract occurs during a caucus between the mediator and the plaintiff, Vince. Rosalind, the on-site property manager, is also present but remains silent during this period (Extract 4).

Extract 4: Mediation 1a. Participants: M: Mediator; V: Vince (plaintiff)

869:	M:	Okay (2.0) And are you seeing that Uh with what you can present the judge you
870		would probably just say yeah, let's give Vince the max?
871	V:	Well, yeah, I think so. I think my costs are are pretty clear.
572	M:	Uh hum
573	V:	I wasn't there. I've had Rosalind uh for years uh taking care of the property for
574		me. She's been very good, very helpful. She's a very credible (1.0) witness.
575	M:	Uh huh
576	V:	I think that she comes across as a believable person. She's honest. Uhh And you
577		don't find many people out there that do this type of work that are. And that's
578		why I've had her for many years. She sold me the property back in eighty three.
579		So uhh And I've had experience with other property managers and other
580		properties and all that, and none come (1.0) close to what Rosalind.
581	M:	It must be nice to have a good relationship.
582	V:	That's right.
583	M:	A business relationship
584	V:	So, you know, when she tells me something's wrong, I believe it. And I think a
585		judge would believe it. uhh I think he'll come across as being a young, uh uh uh
586		uh cocky (1.) guy, party, rugby player, had large parties there. Trashed the
587		apartment. Didn't give a damn. uh Supposedly takes care of his mother's real
588		estate uh I don't know if that's true. But.

Victor creates oppositional constructions of his property manager Rosalind and the former tenant Mark, who is not present during this caucus. Rosalind is described as *very credible* (line 574), *a believable person* (line 576), and *honest* (line 576). Adversely, the former tenant Mark is described as *young* (line 585) and *a cocky guy* (line 586). He questions the former tenant's veracity indicating that he "supposedly takes care of his mother's real estate" (lines 587–588). Vince creates a picture he believes the judge will see when comparing the type of witness Rosalind would be versus the former tenant Mark. These contrasting characterizations emerged when the mediator asks Vince to speculate about his prospects in court should the case not be resolved during this mediation session (lines 869–870).

Vince also ascribed the categorical description *rugby player* onto the former tenant, Mark (line 586), in the manner of Zhu's interculturality (2019). Earlier in the mediation session, Mark indicated that he "plays on the ruby team" for the nearby university. Vince is reconfirming that categorical descriptor but linking that category to the negative attributes of being *cocky* and having *large parties*. Rather than ascribe positive characteristics of athletes who play team sports, Vince elects to ascribe negative characteristics that affirm his supposition that Mark would not be viewed as a credible witness. Interestingly, the mediator does not challenge or probe the identity ascriptions Vince imposes on Rosalind or Mark. In fact, the mediator compliments the positive *business relationship* Vince has with Rosalind (lines 581 and 583).

This next mediation session involves a disputed real estate transaction. The plaintiff is seeking to recover costs associated with that matter from the brokerage firm that oversaw the real estate deal (Extract 5).

Extract 5: Mediation 35. Participants: M: Mediator: T: Tim (plaintiff)

552	M:	Okay. Okay. Uhm. Well, I'm interested at this point to talk to you what you think
553		your options are in this case on on both sides. How do you see (.) how do you
554		see your options?
555	T:	Well
556	M:	You can
557	T:	From the beginning I said hey, you know you didn't do your job right. Why don't
558		you just you know come forward like a man and say hey, you know something,
559		anybody's neck's got a little bit too much or whatever — and there would have
560		been no ethics thing. I would have hey, you know something, this guy is a
561		stand-up guy, you know. I got hurt a little bit because I had to sit there with the
562		million dollars not doing anything for a month, but no problem. I'll just get on
563		with my life, and that's it. But no, he has got to stand there and says, I didn't do
564		anything wrong, and now he's got ethics problems. And if he keeps it up, we'll
565		go to court and even get to pay, too, and uh or the broker. I don't know who's
566		ultimately responsible, but I renamed him personally from under his broker.
567	M:	Okay.

During this portion of the narrative, Tim ascribes *man* (lines 558) and *stand-up guy* (line 561) onto Jim, the defendant. Tim indicates that a *man* or a *stand-up guy* would admit wrongdoing, do his job right, and avoid ethics problems, which are categorical descriptions that resonate with cultural stereotypes of cisgender males. But, according to Tim's ascription, Jim implicitly does not have those cultural characteristics of a man and is thus liable for the damages he incurred because of this real estate transaction. With these categorical ascriptions, mediators and disputants may be able ask more sophisticated question because of the cultural information being conveyed through the stories (Duryea and Potts 1993). Taking an interculturality studies stance, these stories could function to negotiate membership in a group but the mediators in these instances did not question the boundaries of categorical ascription being applied to disputants.

Concluding remarks

This chapter explored the interconnectedness of storytelling, identity, and culture in a court-based mediation setting. Cultural categories and their associated identities were embedded within the stories disputants told to state their positions in the dispute. The process of interculturality was evidenced through the self and other ascription of cultural categories. Generally, disputing parties ascribed favorable categories onto themselves and unfavorable categories onto the opposing parties. These oppositional constructions often invoked cultural stereotypes based on gender, educational roles, and age. In most cases, mediators did not refute, contradict, or challenge the categorical ascriptions participants ascribed.

The communication in these mediation sessions is the site of cultural negotiation in which disputants use these categories as an interactional resource to construct their respective positions. As interactional resources, these cultural categories enable participants to build their own narratives and to blame the other party in some way and to stress differences over commonalities to achieve an advantage. Interculturality plays a role in conflict mediation to the extent that it enables researchers to examine how cultural categories create convergence or divergence between the parties. If, for example, both parties are portrayed as honest and ethical, a pathway to settlement may be likely. Alternatively, if parties portray each other in contradictory ways, settlement may be more elusive.

Individuals are complex with multiple identities that are made relevant at different interactional moments. This small culture approach accounts for the existence of "tentative, contradictory, diverse identities that emerge in certain context as selves-in-the-making, rather than as settled and reflected-upon projects" (Georgakopoulou 2015). This fluidity provides mediators the opportunity to probe or challenge the negative cultural categories ascribed to opposing parties. This could involve emphasizing the positive attributes of cultural categories rather than negative qualities. For instance, more emphasis could be placed on students and athletes as hard working and dedicated.

Successful mediation involves the creation of a microculture that develops through commonalities in meaning and behavior between the parties (Brownlie 2018). Certainly, there are a number of factors that contribute to settlement in court-based mediation including mediator tactics (Salmon et al. 2013), the source of the dispute (Galin 2014), and mediator rapport with the parties (Georgakopoulos 2017), to name a few. Perhaps mediators and parties who can recognize shared rather than dissimilar cultural categories and their inherent values and interests may be equipped to identify pathways to settlement.

References

Aidman, Barry, and Tanya A. Long. 2017. "Leadership and Storytelling: Promoting a Culture of Learning, Positive Change, and Community." *Leadership and Research in Education* 4 (1): 106–126. https://files.eric.ed. gov/fulltext/EJ1160822.pdf

Brownlie, Siobhan. 2017. "Mediation through an Intercultural Communication Lens." *Mediation Theory and Practice* 2 (1): 34–53. 10.1558/mtp.32579

Brownlie, Siobhan. 2018. "Using Cultural Categories for Opposition and Brokering in Conflict Mediation." *Language and Intercultural Communication* 18 (1): 90–106. 10.1080/14708477.2017.1400506

Busch, Dominic. 2016. "Does Conflict Mediation Research Keep Track with Cultural Theory?: A Theory-Based Qualitative Content Analysis on Concepts of Culture in Conflict Management Research." *European Journal of Applied Linguistics* 4 (2): 181–206. 10.1515/eujal-2015-0037

Storytelling in mediation

Coburn, Clare. 2011. "Storytelling as a Peacebuilding Method." In *The Encyclopedia of Peace Psychology*, edited by Daniel J. Christie, 1072–1076. Oxford, UK: Blackwell. 10.1002/9780470672532.wbepp268

Docherty, Jayne Seminare. 2004. "Narratives, Metaphors, and Negotiation." *Marquette Law Review* 87 (4): 847–851.

Duryea, Michelle LeBaron, and Jim Potts. 1993. "Story and Legend: Powerful Tools for Conflict Resolution." *Mediation Quarterly* 10 (4): 387–395. 10.1002/crq.3900100407

Galin, Amira. 2014. "What Makes Court-Referred Mediation Effective?" *International Journal of Conflict Management* 25 (1): 21–37. 10.1108/IJCMA-09-2012-0071

Garcia, Angela Cora. 2000. "Negotiating Negotiation: The Collaborative Production of Resolution in Small Claims Mediation Hearings." *Discourse & Society* 11 (3): 315–343. 10.1177/0957926500011003003

Georgakopoulos, Alexia, ed. 2017. *The Mediation Handbook: Research, Theory, and Practice.* 1st ed. Routledge. 10.4324/9781315648330

Georgakopoulou, Alexandra. 2015. "Small Stories Research: Methods - Analysis - Outreach." In *The Handbook of Narrative Analysis*, edited by Anna De Fina and Alexandra Georgakopoulou, 255–271. Hoboken, NJ: John Wiley & Sons, Inc. 10.1002/9781118458204.ch13

Holliday, A. 1999. "Small Cultures." *Applied Linguistics* 20 (2): 237–264. 10.1093/applin/20.2.237

Jones, Tricia S. 1988. "Phase Structures in Agreement and No-Agreement Mediation." *Communication Research* 15 (4): 470–495. 10.1177/009365088015004007

Kecskes, Istvan. 2013. *Intercultural Pragmatics.* Oxford University Press. 10.1093/acprof:oso/9780199892655.001.0001

Mandelbaum, Jenny. 2012. "Storytelling in Conversation." In *The Handbook of Conversation Analysis*, edited by Jack Sidnell and Tanya Stivers, 492–507. Chichester, UK: Wiley. 10.1002/9781118325001.ch24

Nasrollahi Shahri, Mohammad Naseh. 2019. "Second Language User Identities in Stories of Intercultural Communication: A Case Study." *Language and Intercultural Communication* 19 (4): 342–356. 10.1080/14708477.2018.1544253

Rifkin, Janet, Jonathan Millen, and Sara Cobb. 1991. "Toward a New Discourse for Mediation: A Critique of Neutrality." *Mediation Quarterly* 9 (2): 151–164. 10.1002/crq.3900090206

Rings, Guido, and Sebastian Rasinger, eds. 2020. *The Cambridge Handbook of Intercultural Communication.* 1st ed. Cambridge University Press. 10.1017/9781108555067

Salmon, Elizabeth D., Michele J. Gelfand, Ayşe Betül Çelik, Sarit Kraus, Jonathan Wilkenfeld, and Molly Inman. 2013. "Cultural Contingencies of Mediation: Effectiveness of Mediator Styles in Intercultural Disputes." *Journal of Organizational Behavior* 34 (6): 887–909. 10.1002/job.1870

Senehi, Jessica. 2009. "Building Peace: Storytelling to Transform Conflict Constructively." In *Handbook of Conflict Analysis and Resolution* edited by Dennis J. Sandole, Sean Byrne, Ingrid Sandole-Staroste, and Jessica Senehi, 201–214. London: Routledge. 10.4324/9780203893166.ch12

Stewart, Katherine A. 2008. *"Interactive Construction of Dispute Narratives in Mediated Conflict Talk."* PhD diss. University of Texas, Austin.

Stewart, Katherine A., and Madeline M. Maxwell. 2010. *Storied Conflict Talk: Narrative Construction in Mediation.* Amsterdam: John Benjamins. 10.1075/sin.12

Ta, Binh Thanh, and Anna Filipi. 2020. "Storytelling as a Resource for Pursuing Understanding and Agreement in Doctoral Research Supervision Meetings." *Journal of Pragmatics* 165 (August): 4–17. 10.1016/j.pragma.2020.03.008

Zhu, Hua. 2018. *Exploring Intercultural Communication: Language in Action.* 2nd ed. Routledge. 10.4324/9781315159010

PART VII

Psychological tools for analyzing intercultural mediation

39
CULTURAL INTELLIGENCE IN INTERCULTURAL MEDIATION

Gabriela Gonçalves and Cátia Sousa

Introduction

Globalization has increased contact between individuals from diverse cultural backgrounds with positive effects on intergroup relations and group performance in educational, social, and organizational contexts, such as innovation, communication, learning processes, etc. (e.g., Boone et al. 2019; Luo et al. 2021; Verkuyten and Yogeeswaran 2020). Despite the positive effects, cultural diversity results in a greater likelihood of intercultural conflicts and disputes (Salmon et al. 2013). These disputes entail additional difficulties arising from differences in language and communication norms (e.g., Hall 1976), values, cultural distance (Hofstede 1980), threat to identity, stereotypes, discrimination, and prejudices (e.g., Allport 1954). To Caputo et al. (2019), cultural intelligence can mitigate such difficulties, especially when values and beliefs differ, as individuals with high levels of cultural intelligence more easily grasp cultural differences and, as such, are able to adopt their behavior to different values, norms, and beliefs. Cultural intelligence (CQ) is a competence that has more than 20 years of research, hundreds of studies in several countries (Rockstuhl and Van Dyne 2018), and refers to the ability of individuals to relate and work effectively in complex and culturally diverse situations (Livermore, Van Dyne, and Ang 2021). Investigations within the scope of CQ have shown that individuals with higher levels of this competence are more likely to adapt to situations characterized by cultural diversity (Livermore 2014), as they are able to capture signals from the environment to understand cultural particularities, identifying what is or is not culturally acceptable (Rego and Cunha 2009). Whereas the psychological approach demonstrates a concern to describe potential parallels between cultural particularities (e.g., norms, preferences, different styles of conflict resolution) (Busch 2019), Gonçalves et al. (2016) suggest the CQ as a possible solution, since, according to Livermore, Van Dyne, and Ang (2021), this allows you to develop explicit processes to analyze a situation and generate possible solutions. Thus, it is expected that CQ presents itself as an effective competence in intercultural mediation processes. Intercultural mediation can be understood as an intervention by third parties, in and on situations of significant multiculturalism, oriented towards the recognition of the Other and the approximation between the parties (Giménez 2010). It is, therefore, a process that implies mutual communication and understanding, learning and the development of coexistence, as well as the regulation of conflicts between actors from different cultural contexts (Giménez 2010). By involving the mediation of knowledge and information between members of different cultures, with different styles and ways of life, mutual understanding across linguistic and cultural obstacles is of central importance in intercultural mediation. Thus, CQ may help individuals identify the best conflict resolution strategies

DOI: 10.4324/9781003227441-47

369

for a given situation, especially because it encompasses four dimensions (metacognitive, cognitive, behavioral and motivational) that allow individuals to be more efficient in decision-making in intercultural situations and are more likely to adapt to situations characterized by cultural diversity (e.g., Van Dyne, Ang, and Nielsen 2007). Although studies on cultural intelligence have been growing in the last two decades, there are still few that deepen their relationship with intercultural mediation. This chapter seeks to briefly reflect on the role and influence of cultural intelligence in mediation processes, since, from our point of view, culturally intelligent individuals can better understand the dynamics of cultural differences, thus presenting better results in an intercultural mediation process.

Cultural intelligence

In a world where crossing borders has become routine, cultural intelligence becomes a vital skill and competence.

(Earley and Mosakowski 2004, 139)

In recent years, various types of intelligence have emerged (e.g., Gardner 1993) that enhance the ability to adapt to others, such as emotional intelligence (e.g., Goleman 1996), social intelligence (Cantor and Kihlstrom 1985; Goleman 2006), or interpersonal intelligence (e.g., Gardner 1993). Cultural intelligence (CQ), being compatible with the conceptualizations of intelligence, adaptability, and adjustment to the environment (Gardner 1993; Sternberg 2000), differs from other types of intelligence because it specifically focuses on interactions characterized by cultural diversity (Van Dyne, Ang, and Koh 2008). Despite being strongly linked to emotional intelligence, CQ gains ground where emotional intelligence loses (Earley and Mosakowski 2004). An individual with a high emotional intelligence embraces what makes us human and simultaneously different from each other. In turn, an individual with high CQ is able to capture from human behavior certain distinctive characteristics that are specific to this person or that group, as well as those characteristics that are neither universal nor idiosyncratic. The vast territory that lies between these two poles is culture (Earley and Mosakowski, 2004). Earley and Ang (2003), to explain why some individuals perform more effectively than others in multicultural situations, took the multidimensional perspective of intelligence of Sternberg and Detterman (1986) to develop a conceptual model of CQ. CQ can then be defined as a set of abilities and skills that facilitate adaptation to different cultural situations and allow the interpretation of unfamiliar behaviors and situations (Van Dyne et al. 2012).

Dimensions of CQ

Earley and Ang (2003) consider CQ as a multidimensional construct comprising four dimensions: metacognition, cognition, motivation, and behavior. Since initial research on this new construct was typically focused on more global conceptualizations, more specific sub-dimensions have recently been constructed that allow for better theorizing and testing (Van Dyne et al. 2012). Thus, and through a literature review, the authors added 11 sub-dimensions to the initial 4 dimensions.

a. Metacognition—corresponds to cultural awareness and awareness during interaction with different cultures, being a crucial component as it promotes active thinking about people and situations in an unfamiliar environment. On the other hand, it triggers critical thinking about habits and beliefs, as well as allowing an assessment and revision of mental maps, thus increasing the capacity for understanding (Van Dyne, Ang, and Koh 2008), i.e., those who are a little 'uprooted' from their own culture, they can more easily adopt the habits and customs, and even the body language, of an unknown culture (Earley and Mosakowski 2004). This dimension can be divided into three sub-dimensions:

Cultural intelligence

- Plan: corresponds to a strategy prior to the cultural encounter. It includes careful preparation of goals, in-depth thinking about the culture, and anticipating needs. It can be related to the individual (self), to others, or to the resulting interdependence (Van Dyne et al. 2012).
- Awareness: while planning relates to preparation, this sub-dimension describes the degree to which the individual has real-time awareness of how culture influences behavior, mental process (yours and others), and the intercultural situation (Van Dyne et al. 2012).
- Verification: is defined as a process of reviewing hypotheses and adjusting mind maps when actual experiences differ from expectations. This component of metacognitive CQ involves questioning and reflecting on deep-rooted hypotheses and adapting mental models based on new data (Van Dyne et al. 2012).

In short, planning must take place before the interaction, awareness (or being aware of) must always be present, and verification must take place during and after interactions.

b. Cognition—refers to cultural knowledge of norms, behaviors, practices, and conventions in different cultures, gained through experience and education, and encompasses knowledge of the economic, social, and legal system of different cultures and subcultures as well as knowledge of cultural values (Che Rose et al. 2010). This dimension is composed of two sub-dimensions:

- General knowledge: corresponds to the knowledge of the general elements that constitute the cultural environment, which allows individuals to identify the similarities and differences of cultures (Van Dyne et al. 2012).
- Specific knowledge: is related to theoretical knowledge about cultural manifestations in a specific context and a practical knowledge of how to be effective in that context.

Individuals with high levels of cognitive CQ must possess a general knowledge of culture to understand the vast diversity of cultures and must possess specific knowledge to function efficiently and effectively in a specific culture (Van Dyne et al. 2012).

c. Motivation—conceptualizes the ability to direct attention and energy in relation to cultural differences, that is, it is a form of self-efficacy and intrinsic motivation in intercultural situations (Van Dyne, Ang, and Koh 2008). For example, CQ can facilitate the management of stress caused by multicultural contexts at work, in the social space, in mediation situations, etc. This ability gives individuals the confidence to overcome the obstacles that characterize these situations. The motivational dimension comprises three sub-dimensions:

- Intrinsic interests: correspond to an appreciation of culturally diverse experiences, which include an intrinsic satisfaction gained through intercultural relationships and a pleasure in working with people from other cultures (Van Dyne et al. 2012).
- Extrinsic interests: are defined as an appreciation of the tangible and personal benefits that can be derived from the intercultural experience (Ryan and Deci 2000).
- Self-efficacy to adjust: is related to the ability to deal with the stress of adjustment to new cultures, which implies having the confidence to interact with places of other cultures and the confidence to work with groups and in situations characterized by cultural diversity (Van Dyne et al. 2012).

When these sub-dimensions are activated, people with a high motivational CQ are attracted to intercultural situations because they value the benefits they derive from them and are confident that they can deal with the challenges inherent to cultural differences.

d.   Behavior—is one of the most visible dimensions of social interaction, and refers to the ability to express, verbally and non-verbally, appropriate behaviors when interacting with people from different cultures (Van Dyne, Ang, and Koh 2008). In other words, you will not be able to convince the foreign hosts only by showing that you understand their culture, it is necessary to prove, through attitudes, that you are effectively integrated in their world (Earley and Mosakowski 2004). This dimension is composed of three sub-dimensions:

- Verbal behavior: corresponds to flexibility in vocalization (e.g., accent, tone), including behaviors such as speaking faster or slower, louder or quieter, warm demonstrations, enthusiastic, formal, use of pause and silence (Varner and Beamer 2011; Van Dyne et al. 2012).
- Non-verbal behavior: corresponds to the communicational flexibility transmitted through gestures, facial expressions, and body language. The ability to be flexible in non-verbal behavior includes changing facial expression and gestures depending on whether you are facing a more neutral and formal culture, or a more expressive culture; it also includes behaviors such as sitting closer to or further away from another person, paying attention to the amount and nature of physical and visual contact with others (e.g., the manner of greeting varies from culture to culture), as well as clothing and use (formal or informal) and body language (Van Dyne et al. 2012).
- Act of speaking: is defined as the flexibility in how to communicate certain specific types of messages, such as requests, invitations, apology, gratitude, disagreement, and saying 'no,' which must be properly expressed in accordance with the norms of the culture (Bowe, Martin, and Manns 2014). The act of speaking is important because cultures have different conceptualizations of the appropriate behavior style to convey this type of messages, such as the words used or the degree of frankness (Van Dyne et al. 2012).

Those with a high level of behavioral CQ can overcome the natural human tendency to trust habits, demonstrating behavioral flexibility in cross-cultural situations, which includes a change of code and an adjustment to the cultural context (Molinsky 2007).

Individuals with a high level of CQ have a repertoire of strategies and behaviors to guide them when faced with unfamiliar perspectives and behaviors. So, when something bizarre or random happens, they have a mindset to discern what is cultural and what is particular to a person or organization (Livermore 2011).

Investigations within the scope of CQ

Studies carried out in the context of CQ showed that individuals who have a higher CQ are more efficient in decision-making in intercultural situations and are more likely to adapt to situations characterized by cultural diversity (Van Dyne, Ang, and Nielsen 2007). The higher the metacognitive dimension of CQ, the higher the performance capacity, and the higher the behavioral dimension, the better the performance in cultural diversity scenarios (Van Dyn, Ang, and Nielsen 2007). The motivational dimension showed positive results in the way individuals manage their life and work in a new culture (Templer, Tay, and Chandrasekar 2006). Both the behavioral dimension and the motivational dimension are significantly related to cultural adjustment.

Investigations carried out have shown the importance of CQ for the expatriates' adjustment (Stoermer, Davies, and Froese 2021), for the socialization of immigrants to the host country (Malik, Cooper-Thomas, and Zikic 2014), the relationship between CQ and personality (Sousa et al. 2019) and with the style of conflict management (Gonçalves et al. 2016), among others.

The results of these investigations show that CQ is an important attribute for any individual, regardless of being in an unknown culture. Individuals with CQ are more flexible, more open to change and the unknown, communicate more easily, and are more confident. Thus, it is expected that this competence is a positive predictor of other behaviors, namely in the context of intercultural mediation, allowing a more effective interaction of the parties involved in mediation processes.

Intercultural mediation and CQ

Mediation can be defined as

> a process of conflict management where disputants seek the assistance of, or accept an offer of help from, an individual, group, state, or organization to settle their conflict or resolve their differences without resorting to physical force or invoking the authority of the law. (Bercovitch, Anagnoson, and Wille 1991, 8)

In other words, mediation is a process that involves a third person, guided by principles of non-intervention or minimal intervention, which places the decision-making power on those involved in the process, creating communication opportunities with a view to building workable and re-sponsible commitments (ACM 2016, 12).

While all conflicts present their challenges, disputes between parties from different cultures are more likely to raise difficulties that can impact the mediation process (Adair et al. 2004; Salmon et al. 2013). These difficulties stem mostly from cultural differences between the parties, namely different expectations, norms, habits, style of conflict management (Gonçalves et al. 2016), personality and above all different communication styles that guide the behavior adopted in conflicting situations (e.g., Hall 1976; Salmon et al. 2013). In this context, intercultural mediation is extremely important, constituting a modality of intervention by third parties, in and on social situations of significant multiculturality, with particular attention to the other, its revaluation and recognition in this dif-ference (ACM 2016). That is, intercultural mediation does not only contemplate the resolution of communication problems, but also the development of shared understandings among commu-nication participants. Thus, mediation has as its main objectives the approximation of the parties, communication and mutual understanding and the learning, and development of peaceful coex-istence (ACM 2016). The intercultural mediator is responsible for analyzing the meanings con-structed by both parties, within different cultural frameworks, and providing the means for both parties to understand each other. In other words, mediators are involved in a complex process of understanding, explaining, commenting, interpreting, and negotiating phenomena (Liddicoat 2016). The results of mediation go beyond the objective itself. That is, opponents can obtain the desired results, but the process can have affective and relational costs that affect the relationship between individuals and the post-agreement motivation to adhere to the application of decisions or for future mediations (e.g., Hart and Schweitzer 2020).

Given the complexity associated with intercultural mediation, it is expected that certain intercultural competences will facilitate the resolution of intercultural disputes. Among the various intercultural competences (e.g., intercultural communication, multicultural personality, intercultural competence) CQ has emerged as a construct that focuses specifically on interactions characterized by cultural di-versity (Van Dyne, Ang, and Koh 2008), so individuals with high levels of CQ adopt strategies and behaviors that guide them in situations that are unfamiliar to them. For example, when the sub-dimensions of metacognitive CQ are activated, individuals with a higher level of metacognitive in-telligence consciously question their own cultural norms and the assumptions they have about other cultures. Individuals plan, reflect on what is happening (or is not) during cultural interactions and adjust their mental model based on these interactions (e.g., an intercultural mediator with high metacognitive CQ easily identifies cultural characteristics, so he/she may be able to anticipate what parties from different cultures (e.g., individualistic and collectivist cultures) value, conducting a negotiation more effectively. Together, the metacognitive sub-dimensions emphasize the dynamic nature of CQ, representing a critical component of CQ, as they represent proactive thinking about people and situations in culturally diverse environments (Van Dyne et al. 2012), which is fundamental for intercultural mediation processes. Also, the sub-dimensions of cognitive CQ are important and complementary. Having a broader knowledge of the objective and subjective elements of culture facilitates a deeper understanding of how people in a specific cultural context are shaped/influenced by the cultural environment in the way they think and act (Van Dyne et al. 2012). Thus, an intercultural mediator who has these skills will be better able to identify and understand the behavior of the parties involved in the mediation process, acting more effectively in the mediation process. It is also important that an intercultural mediator has a high level of motivational QC, as it activates and supports the energy directed to an efficient functioning in intercultural situations even when the situations are more complex, unexpected, or difficult (Van Dyne et al. 2012).

Another extremely relevant aspect in intercultural mediation is the ability to understand and communicate, so the behavioral dimension is assumed to be crucial in intercultural mediation. On the one hand, because the verbal flexibility increases the effectiveness of communication and non-verbal flexibility allows you to demonstrate respect for cultural norms, and is especially critical as it functions as a *silent language* and allows you to interpret slight indicators of sincerity, honesty, competence, etc. (Hall 1959). On the other hand, the flexibility in the act of speaking allows for a demonstration that communicational norms are understood, putting others at ease. Since behavior is what is most visible and accessible to others, these three sub-dimensions are the most critical of CQ.

Although studies on CQ have proliferated in the last decade, there are still few that reflect its influence on intercultural mediation. We can highlight some studies on the impact of this competence in business and conflict management contexts. For example, Imai and Gelfand (2010) sought to observe the effect of CQ on the effectiveness of intercultural negotiation. In their study, they concluded that CQ provides individuals with advantageous psychological characteristics for intercultural negotiation, and that those with higher CQ levels tend to have greater cooperative motives and epistemic motivation than individuals with lower CQ. They further observed that such psychological characteristics allow negotiators with higher CQ to overcome obstacles endemic to intercultural negotiation contexts, adopting more integrative negotiation strategies and investing more cognitive effort to grasp their culturally unknown counterparts more accurately (Imai and Gelfand 2010). In the same line of thought, Liu and Liu (2006) consider that a negotiator with a high CQ has a deeper knowledge of the counterpart's culture, thus being able to anticipate and adapt verbal and non-verbal cues sent by others, which also allows him/her to reduce the probability to suffer culture shock. These authors also consider that negotiators with higher levels of CQ are more confident in cross-cultural negotiations and more optimistic, as they can consciously adapt their behavior to the negotiation partner, facilitating interaction (Earley 2002) to achieve joint gains and individual gains, promoting the possibility of future collaboration (Liu and Liu 2006). Also noteworthy is the perspective of Salmon et al. (2013) who consider that the motivational dimension of CQ can play a crucial role in facilitating the resolution of intercultural disputes, as this dimension refers to an individual's ability to learn and act in situations with culturally diverse people. Also, Groves, Feyerherm, and Gu (2015) showed that CQ predicted negotiation performance and, in particular, that high levels of CQ were positively related to cooperative bargaining styles. Gonçalves et al. (2016) observed that in terms of dispositional measures used to predict conflict management styles, CQ presents itself as a reasonable predictor of conflict management styles, highlighting the metacognitive dimension as a predictor of problem-solving style. The authors thus showed that if individuals are more aware of each other's individual differences during social interactions and behave in ways that emphasize their connection with others, then, in a conflict situation, they choose strategies that benefit not only themselves as the other and, more importantly perhaps, strengthening and maintaining their relationship with that individual at the same time (Gonçalves et al. 2016). A more recent study by Caputo et al. (2019) showed that cultural values have a direct influence on negotiating styles, as well as an indirect effect, which is mediated by CQ, thus highlighting the importance of cultural values and CQ in the styles of negotiation.

In short, in cross-cultural settings, negotiators must be able to recognize cultural differences and adapt their negotiating style to the cultural contingencies necessary to succeed (Caputo et al. 2019). A culturally intelligent mediator can more easily adapt to local customs and better understand the dynamics of a foreign culture, feeling more confident and managing emotions better in a process of intercultural mediation.

Final considerations

Studies on CQ in intercultural mediation are still scarce, at least to our knowledge. Research in the scope of intercultural negotiation and conflict management style has a greater prominence in the literature of the area. But the results evidenced by the studies reinforce that CQ plays an extremely important role in intercultural contexts and can ease the difficulties of intercultural disputes. CQ is thus an asset in all areas of life, so it is important to reinforce the importance of developing this competence in managers, diplomats, teachers, expatriates, among others, as it will allow greater effectiveness in negotiation and intercultural mediation. In a world where there are growing opportunities for cooperation as well as threats of conflict at the global level, CQ is a key competence for managing global interdependence (Imai and Gelfand 2010).

References

ACM. 2016. *Entre Iguais e Diferentes: A Mediação Intercultural*. Lisboa: Alto Comissariado para as Migrações.

Adair, Wendi, Jeanne Brett, Alain Lempereur, Tetsushi Okumura, Peter Shikhirev, Catherine Tinsley, and Anne Lytle. 2004. "Culture and Negotiation Strategy." *Negotiation Journal* 20 (1): 87–111. 10.1111/j.1571-9979.2004.00008.x

Allport, Gordon. 1954. *The Nature of Prejudice*. Cambridge: Perseus Books.

Bercovitch, Jacob, J. Theodore Anagnoson, and Donnette L. Wille. 1991. "Some Conceptual Issues and Empirical Trends in the Study of Successful Mediation in International Relations." *Journal of Peace Research* 28 (1): 7–17. 10.1177/0022343391028001003

Boone, Christophe, Boris Lokshin, Hannes Guenter, and René Belderbos. 2019. "Top Management Team Nationality Diversity, Corporate Entrepreneurship, and Innovation in Multinational Firms." *Strategic Management Journal* 40 (2): 277–302. 10.1002/smj.2976

Bowe, Heather, Kylie Martin, and Howard Manns. 2014. *Communication across Cultures: Mutual Understanding in a Global World*. 2nd ed. Cambridge: Cambridge University Press. 10.1017/CBO9781107445680

Busch, Dominic. 2019. "Intercultural Conflict Mediation." In *Oxford Bibliographies in Communication*, edited by Patricia Moy. New York: Oxford University Press. 10.1093/obo/9780199756841-0229

Cantor, Nancy, and John Kihlstrom. 1985. "Social Intelligence: The cognitive basis of personality". *Review of Personality and Social Psychology* 6: 15–33.

Caputo, Andrea, Oluremi B. Ayoko, Nii Amoo, and Charlott Menke. 2019. "The Relationship between Cultural Values, Cultural Intelligence and Negotiation Styles." *Journal of Business Research* 99 (June): 23–36. 10.1016/j.jbusres.2019.02.011

Che Rose, Raduan, Subramaniam Sri Ramalu, Jegak Uli, and Naresh Kumar. 2010. "Expatriate Performance in International Assignments: The Role of Cultural Intelligence as Dynamic Intercultural Competency." *International Journal of Business and Management* 5 (8): 76–85. 10.5539/ijbm.v5n8p76

Earley, P. Christopher. 2002. "Redefining Interactions across Cultures and Organizations: Moving Forward with Cultural Intelligence." *Research in Organizational Behavior* 24 (January): 271–299. 10.1016/S0191-3085(02)24008-3

Earley, P. Christopher, and Soon Ang. 2003. *Cultural Intelligence: Individual Interactions across Cultures*. Stanford, CA: Stanford University Press.

Earley, P. Christopher, and Elaine Mosakowski. 2004. "Cultural intelligence." *Harvard Business Review*, October: 139–153. http://hbr.org/2004/10/cultural-intelligence/ar/1

Gardner, Howard. 1993. *Frames of Mind: The Theory of Multiple Intelligences*. New York: Basic Books.

Giménez, Soriano. 2010. "El perfil professional de un mediador intercultural." *Llegó Para Quedarse* (blog). October 19, 2010. https://mediadoresinterculturales.blogspot.com

Goleman, Daniel. 1996. *Inteligência Emocional.* Lisboa: Círculo de Leitores.

Goleman, Daniel. 2006. *Inteligência Social. A nova ciência das relações humanas.* Barcelos: Círculo de Leitores.

Gonçalves, Gabriela, Marta Reis, Cátia Sousa, Joana Santos, Alejandro Orgambídez-Ramos, and Peter Scott. 2016. "Cultural Intelligence and Conflict Management Styles." *International Journal of Organizational Analysis* 24 (4): 725–742. 10.1108/IJOA-10-2015-0923

Groves, Kevin S., Ann Feyerherm, and Minhua Gu. 2015. "Examining Cultural Intelligence and Cross-Cultural Negotiation Effectiveness." *Journal of Management Education* 39 (2): 209–243. 10.1177/1052562 914543273

Hall, Edward T. 1959. *The Silent Language.* New York: Anchor Books.

Hall, Edward. T. 1976. *Beyond Culture.* New York: Doubleday.

Hart, Einav, and Maurice E. Schweitzer. 2020. "Getting to Less: When Negotiating Harms Post-Agreement Performance." *Organizational Behavior and Human Decision Processes* 156 (January): 155–175. 10.1016/j.obhdp.2019.09.005

Hofstede, Geert. 1980. *Culture's Consequences: International Differences in Work-Related Values.* Beverly Hills, CA: Sage Publications.

Imai, Lynn, and Michele J. Gelfand. 2010. "The Culturally Intelligent Negotiator: The Impact of Cultural Intelligence (CQ) on Negotiation Sequences and Outcomes." *Organizational Behavior and Human Decision Processes* 112 (2): 83–98. 10.1016/j.obhdp.2010.02.001

Liddicoat, Anthony J. 2016. "Intercultural Mediation, Intercultural Communication and Translation." *Perspectives* 24 (3): 354–364. 10.1080/0907676X.2014.980279

Liu, Wu, and Leigh Anne Liu. 2006. *Cultural Intelligence in International Business Negotiation.* Montreal: IACM 2006 Meetings Paper. 10.2139/ssrn.905460.

Livermore, David A. 2011. *The Cultural Intelligence Difference: Master the One Skill You Can't Do without in Today's Global Economy.* New York: AMACOM, American Management Association.

Livermore, David A. 2014. *Leading with Cultural Intelligence: The Real Secret to Success.* New York: American Management Association.

Livermore, David, Linn Van Dyne, and Soon Ang. 2021. "Organizational CQ: Cultural Intelligence (CQ) for 21st Century Organizations." *Business Horizons,* November 6, 2021, 10.1016/j.bushor.2021.11.001

Luo, Kun, Edwin KiaYang Lim, Wen Qu, and Xuan Zhang. 2021. "Board Cultural Diversity, Government Intervention and Corporate Innovation Effectiveness: Evidence from China." *Journal of Contemporary Accounting & Economics* 17 (2): 100256. 10.1016/j.jcae.2021.100256

Malik, Amina R, Helena D. Cooper-Thomas, and Jelena Zikic. 2014. "The Neglected Role of Cultural Intelligence in Recent Immigrant Newcomers' Socialization." *International Journal of Cross Cultural Management* 14 (2): 195–213. 10.1177/1470595813507245

Molinsky, Andrew. 2007. "Cross-Cultural Code-Switching: The Psychological Challenges of Adapting Behavior in Foreign Cultural Interactions." *Academy of Management Review* 32 (2): 622–640. 10.5465/amr.2007.24351878

Rego, Arménio, and Miguel Pina e Cunha. 2009. *Manual de Gestão Transcultural de Recursos Humanos.* Lisboa: RH Editora.

Rockstuhl, Thomas, and Linn Van Dyne. 2018. "A Bi-Factor Theory of the Four-Factor Model of Cultural Intelligence: Meta-Analysis and Theoretical Extensions." *Organizational Behavior and Human Decision Processes* 148 (September): 124–144. 10.1016/j.obhdp.2018.07.005

Ryan, Richard M., and Edward L. Deci. 2000. "Intrinsic and Extrinsic Motivations: Classic Definitions and New Directions." *Contemporary Educational Psychology* 25 (1): 54–67. 10.1006/ceps.1999.1020

Salmon, Elizabeth D., Michele J. Gelfand, Ayşe Betül Çelik, Sarit Kraus, Jonathan Wilkenfeld, and Molly Inman. 2013. "Cultural Contingencies of Mediation: Effectiveness of Mediator Styles in Intercultural Disputes: Cultural Contingencies of Mediation." *Journal of Organizational Behavior* 34 (6): 887–909. 10.1002/job.1870

Sousa, Cátia, Gabriela Gonçalves, Joana Santos, and Alejandro Orgambídez-Ramos. 2019. "The Relationship between Multicultural Competencies and Intercultural Contact: Multicultural Personality and Cultural Intelligence." *Psicologia & Sociedade* 31: 1–17. 10.1590/1807-0310/2019v31166867

Sternberg, Robert. 2000. *Handbook of Intelligence.* New York: Cambridge University Press.

Sternberg, Robert, and Douglas Detterman. 1986. *What is Intelligence? Contemporary Viewpoints on its Nature and Definition.* Norwood, NJ: Ablex.

Stoermer, Sebastian, Samuel Davies, and Fabian Jintae Froese. 2021. "The Influence of Expatriate Cultural Intelligence on Organizational Embeddedness and Knowledge Sharing: The Moderating Effects of Host Country Context." *Journal of International Business Studies* 52 (3): 432–453. 10.1057/s41267-020-00349-3

Templer, Klaus J., Cheryl Tay, and N. Anand Chandrasekar. 2006. "Motivational Cultural Intelligence, Realistic Job Preview, Realistic Living Conditions Preview, and Cross-Cultural Adjustment." *Group & Organization Management* 31 (1): 154–173. 10.1177/1059601105275293

Van Dyne, Linn, Soon Ang, and Christine Koh. 2008. "Development and validation of the CQS". In *Handbook of Cultural Intelligence. Theory, Measurement and Applications*, edited by Soon Ang and Linn Van Dyne, 16–38. New York: Sharpe.

Van Dyne, Linn, Soon Ang, and Tjai Nielsen. 2007. "Cultural intelligence." In *International Encyclopedia of Organization Studies* edited by Stewart Clegg and James Bailey, 345–350. Thousand Oaks, CA: Sage.

Van Dyne, Linn, Soon Ang, Kok Yee Ng, Thomas Rockstuhl, Mei Ling Tan, and Christine Koh. 2012. "Sub-Dimensions of the Four Factor Model of Cultural Intelligence: Expanding the Conceptualization and Measurement of Cultural Intelligence: CQ: Sub-Dimensions Of Cultural Intelligence." *Social and Personality Psychology Compass* 6 (4): 295–313. 10.1111/j.1751-9004.2012.00429.x

Varner, Iris I., and Linda Beamer. 2011. *Intercultural Communication in the Global Workplace*. 5th ed. New York: McGraw-Hill/Irwin.

Verkuyten, Maykel, and Kumar Yogeeswaran. 2020. "Cultural Diversity and Its Implications for Intergroup Relations." *Current Opinion in Psychology* 32 (April): 1–5. 10.1016/j.copsyc.2019.06.010

40
RESEARCH FROM PSYCHOLOGY ON INTERCULTURAL MEDIATION: CULTURAL VALUES AND EMOTIONAL INTELLIGENCE

Marjaana Gunkel, Christopher Schlägel, and Vas Taras

Introduction

Intercultural mediation is a broad term that has been used in various research fields (e.g., intercultural communication, conflict resolution, translation, international politics). At the heart of the concept is interculturality, i.e., individuals from different cultural backgrounds interact with each other, which may result in misunderstandings, conflicts, or situations where additional clarifications and actions are needed to enable cooperation. In some cases, the intercultural differences may lead to conflicts, though they often result from minor miscommunications (Ting-Toomey and Oetzel 2001). However, intercultural conflicts may largely influence the dynamics at work. Conflicts are emotional events and may threaten the self-worth of individuals, thereby influencing processes and relationships at work (Brett 2018). Thus, meditating such conflicts becomes an important issue for the management of organizations.

Given the emotionality of conflict, the psychological approaches to research on conflict mediation have become a growing field of research in the last decades. In this area, studies have examined psychological concepts in connection to conflict in intercultural settings (e.g., Caputo, Ayoko, and Amoo 2018; Gunkel, Schlaegel, and Taras 2016), showing that psychological concepts, such as cultural intelligence (CQ) or emotional intelligence (EQ) can aid conflict resolution in an intercultural setting.

Some concepts, such as CQ, are explicitly related to understanding and reacting to cultural differences. Other psychological concepts have been assumed to be universal. The examination of these *universal* concepts in an intercultural setting is an important research field contributing to the better understanding of these concepts in an intercultural context. Thus, this chapter will focus on the concepts of conflict and EQ related to intercultural cooperation.

Gunkel, Schlaegel, and Taras (2016) combined the so far rather independent research streams of cultural value orientations and EQ as antecedents of conflict handing styles, thereby providing a comprehensive picture of how cultural dimensions affect the conflict handlings style preferences through EQ. Holt and DeVore (2005) meta-analytically integrated earlier research on conflict handling styles and examined the role of selected cultural value orientations. This chapter follows the same lines of argumentation; however, it extends these studies by performing a meta-analytic synthesis, which integrates the existing empirical evidence.

DOI: 10.4324/9781003227441-48

Conflict handling styles and intercultural mediation

Conflict handling style, the way how people prefer to behave in conflict situations, is a widely researched topic. This chapter focuses of examining how the different conflict-handling styles and the preference for the styles may be influenced by national culture. For defining and measuring national culture, the five dimensions of Hofstede (2001) will be utilized. In a further step, the relation between EQ and the conflict-handling styles is examined.

Conflict handling styles

When people work together, conflicts occur. Unsolved conflicts may have a negative impact on the interactions between the individuals (Thomas 1992), leading to negative emotions (Wall and Callister 1995) that may result in reduced job satisfaction (Derr 1977) and lower motivation and performance (Bergmann and Volkema 1989). Given the importance of conflict on the outcomes of human interactions, there has been a large interest in studying various conflict-handling styles resulting in a vast number of studies. Conflict handling styles, namely the ways how individuals prefer to behave in a conflict situation, are often not planned strategies, but rather predetermined by different factors (Gunkel, Schlaegel, and Taras 2016).

Already the early literature on conflict handling (Blake and Mouton 1964; Rahim 1983) suggested two dimensions of handling interpersonal conflict, namely "concern for self" and "concern for others." Different combinations of these two dimensions result in five conflict-handling styles: Integrating, avoiding, dominating, obliging, and compromising. The obliging style focuses on finding the commonalities between the parties and reducing possible differences. The integrating style of conflict handling requires problems-solving and is related to exchanging information and examining differences to find a solution. These two styles are often referred to as the positive-sum of win-win styles. On the other hand, dominating and avoiding styles are referred to as zero-sum (win-lose or lose-lose) styles. The dominating style is associated with forcing behavior to obtain one's position. That often leads to ignoring the other party's needs and expectations. The avoiding style of conflict handling results in not satisfying the concern of none of the parties and is, thus, related to withdrawal. The last style, compromising, is a mixed style of conflict handling (no-win/no-lose) that results from the parties giving up something to reach an acceptable solution for all parties.

Societal culture and the preference for conflict handling styles

Though the conflict-handling styles are often selected based on the specific conflict situation (e.g., Rahim 1983), the preferences for certain conflict-handling styles are relatively stable and influenced by demographic (Gbadamosi, Baghestaj, and Al-Mabrou 2014) as well as individual characteristics (e.g., Antonioni, 1998; Park and Antonioni 2007). Previous studies (e.g., Ting-Toomey et al. 1991) have shown that national culture may influence the conflict handling style preferences of individuals. In intercultural interactions, individuals often do not adapt the communications and interaction style of the other party, but rather stick to their own culturally dominant behaviors, displaying behaviors consistent with their own culture (Laurent 1983). Hofstede (2001), in his large international study examining national cultures, defined five cultural value dimensions, namely, individualism/collectivism, masculinity/femininity, power distance, uncertainty avoidance, and long-term/short-term orientation. Given the culturally dominant behaviors in intercultural interaction, these cultural dimensions most likely influence the conflict handling style preferences of individuals.

According to Hofstede (2001), collectivism is related to the responsibility to a collective or a group that one belongs to. Thus, collectivistic societies view the well-being of the group to be more important than individual achievements. Thus, individuals from collectivistic cultures prefer conflict handlings styles increasing the outcome of all related parties (Gunkel, Schlaegel, and Taras 2016). That is also shown by previous studies, in which collectivism has been related to the conflict-handling styles of compromising, avoiding, and integrating, whereas the dominating style has been related to individualism (Holt and DeVore 2005). *Thus, we propose that collectivism is related to the integrating, avoiding, obliging, and comprising the styles of conflict handling.*

As societies with high uncertainty avoidance prefer structured, regulated, and organized situations (Hofstede 2001), individuals from such societies most likely seek conflict-handling styles that reduce (or at least do not increase) uncertainty. Thus, the integrating or compromising styles of conflict handling, seeking for a win-win solution, may be preferred. On the other hand, avoiding and obliging styles of conflict handing may be preferred in societies with high uncertainty avoidance as these cultures may be interested in avoiding conflict in general, and thus, prefer to accept the demands and positions of the other party to avoid conflict in general (Gunkel, Schlaegel, and Taras 2016; Purohit and Simmers 2006). *Therefore, we propose that uncertainty avoidance is related to the conflict-handling styles of integrating, avoiding, obliging, and compromising.*

In long-term oriented societies, today's hard work is expected to result in future rewards (Hofstede 2001). Thus, individuals from long-term oriented societies are expected to focus on conflict handling styles likely to provide positive outcomes to the involved parties as such styles may result in long-term relations between the parties (Gunkel, Schlaegel, and Taras 2016; Xie et al. 1998). *Thus, we propose that long-term orientation is related to conflict handling styles of integrating, obliging, and compromising.*

The cultural dimension of power distance is related to accepting inequalities of power and the distribution of wealth within societies (Hofstede 2001). Thus, conflict-handling styles that allow a party to maintain power may be preferred in such societies. As the avoiding and dominating conflict-handling styles are not related to collaborative behaviors, individuals from high power distance societies may feel more comfortable with these styles as avoiding may restore or even increase the inequality between the parties (Gunkel, Schlaegel, and Taras 2016, Purohit and Simmers 2006). *Therefore, we propose that power distance is related to the conflict-handling styles of dominating and avoiding.*

Masculinity is related to achievement, control, and power (Hofstede 2001). Thus, more assertive as well as non-cooperative styles of conflict handling styles may be preferred in masculine societies (Gunkel, Schlaegel, and Taras 2016; He et al. 2002). Thus, the styles of integrating, avoiding, obliging, and avoiding might not be the preferred styles for individuals from masculine societies. A dominating style, which is related to accomplishing own wishes and fulfilling the party's needs, may be more preferred in other societies than the other styles of conflict handling (Oudenhoven et al. 1998). *Thus, we propose that masculinity is related to the conflict-handling style of dominating.*

Emotional intelligence and the preference for conflict handling styles

Emotional intelligence—"the ability to monitor one's own and others' feelings and emotions, to discriminate among them and to use this information to guide one's thinking and actions" (Salovey and Mayer 1990, 189)—may be considered as an individual characteristic influencing the conflict handling style, as conflicts are often rather emotional events (Jordan and Troth 2004). Previous research has suggested that EQ plays an essential role in solving and mediating conflict as the ability to recognize and regulate emotions may be necessary in finding an acceptable solution (Schlaerth et al. 2013). Thus, EQ may enable more productive conflict solving (Jordan and Troth 2004) as well as more constructive management of conflict (Schlaerth et al. 2013).

Gunkel, Schlaegel, and Engle (2014) show that EQ is determined by national culture. Especially the dimensions of collectivism, uncertainty avoidance, and long-term orientation seem to be positively related to EQ. Individualistic cultures tend to display emotions more than collectivistic ones (Matsumoto, Yoo, and Nagawa 2008), and open communication about emotions is considered rather normal (Matsumoto 1989). Recognizing the emotions is rather associated with collectivistic cultures, and thus, EQ is rather related to collectivism (Gunkel, Schlaegel, and Engle 2014). Uncertainty avoidance is associated with emotional expression. Studies (e.g., Palmer, Gignac, Ekermans, and Stough 2008) show that high uncertainty avoidance is related to emotional expression. Observing emotions may be seen as a way to reduce uncertainty. That is why uncertainty avoidance is related to EQ (Gunkel et al. 2014). Individuals from long-term oriented countries are interested in building long-term relationships (Hofstede 2001) Thus, individuals are willing to suppress, but also observe the emotions of others to create better long-term relationships (Gunkel, Schaegel, and Taras 2016). Therefore, long-term orientation is related to higher EQ.

As these three cultural dimensions are also related to conflict-handling styles (as discussed above), we propose that EQ *mediates the positive relationship between the cultural dimensions of collectivism, uncertainty avoidance, and long-term orientation and the conflict-handling styles of integrating, obliging, and compromising.* We also suggest that EQ *mediates the negative relation between the cultural dimensions of collectivism, uncertainty avoidance, and long-term orientation and the conflict-handling styles of avoiding and dominating.*

Methodology

Literature search and selection criteria

We test the hypotheses based on meta-analytic procedures. We searched the literature in four steps to identify empirical studies that have examined the association between cultural value orientations, EQ, and the various conflict handling styles. First, we searched previous qualitative reviews (e.g., Gunkel, Schlaegel, and Taras 2016) and related meta-analyses (Holt and DeVore 2005; Tehrani and Yamini 2020). Second, we searched electronic databases using various keywords. Third, we conducted an issue-by-issue search and examined in-press articles in relevant journals. Finally, we performed a forward and backward search.

Inclusion criteria, coding, and meta-analytic procedures

We used five inclusion criteria. First, we focus on quantitative empirical findings of articles that reported effect sizes and sample sizes. Second, we used heuristics to identify articles that are based on the same data to ensure the independence of samples. If several articles used the same data set, we only included the article that reported the most information. If a study was based on more than one sample (e.g., different countries), we used the respective correlation coefficients as if coming from separate studies. Finally, this meta-analysis focuses on associations at the individual level of analysis and, thus, we excluded studies at the team and the organizational level. An overview of all studies included in our meta-analysis is available from the authors. We coded the articles based on a structured and standardized coding scheme (Lipsey and Wilson 2001). Two of the authors independently coded all articles for sample size, effect sizes, reliability, study country, and year of data collection. The intercoder reliability (Cohen's kappa: 0.81) across the coding categories was excellent. Any discrepancies in the coding were resolved through discussion among the author team. We used Hunter and Schmidt's (2004) approach for the bivariate meta-analysis. We adjusted the mean meta-analytic correlation coefficient for measurement error (i.e., Cronbach's alpha) in the independent and dependent variables. To test the hypotheses, we used meta-analytic structural equation modeling (MASEM) and the harmonic mean of the meta-analytic correlation matrix.

Results

Table 40.1 presents the meta-analytic correlation matrix, which summarizes the results of the bivariate meta-analyses. We used this correlation matrix as the basis for the MASEM. Figure 40.1

Table 40.1 Meta-analytic correlation matrix

Variable	1	2	3	4	5	6	7	8	9	10	11
1. Power distance		36,354	36,354	36,354	36,354	23,594	7,614,483	6,713,210	7,914,792	7,914,792	5,510,807
2. Collectivism	0.06		36,354	36,354	36,354	23,594	156,043	156,043	156,043	156,043	156,043
3. Masculinity	0.46	0.11		36,354	36,354	23,594	7,614,483	6,713,210	7,914,792	7,914,792	5,510,807
4. Uncertainty avoidance	-0.16	0.35	-0.03		36,354	23,594	7,614,483	6,713,210	7,914,792	7,914,792	5,510,807
5. Long-term orientation	-0.13	0.20	-0.06	0.38		23,594	7,614,483	6,713,210	7,914,792	7,914,792	5,510,807
6. Emotional intelligence	-0.26	0.13	-0.09	0.25	0.22		174,384	123,238	163,922	164,106	143,579
7. Integrating	-0.08	0.21	-0.10	0.33	0.38	0.40		218,128	259,832	259,832	207,849
8. Obliging	0.16	0.19	-0.08	0.06	0.19	0.17	0.36		218,128	218,128	197,621
9. Dominating	0.22	-0.12	0.18	0.10	0.14	0.15	0.19	-0.17		259,832	197,621
10. Avoiding	0.24	0.17	0.25	0.10	0.11	-0.08	-0.11	0.47	0.00		197,730
11. Compromising	-0.07	0.12	-0.13	-0.14	-0.22	0.23	0.46	0.48	0.02	0.11	

Note: Meta-analytic correlations are presented below the diagonal. The number of effect sizes and the total number of study participants for each association are presented above the diagonal.

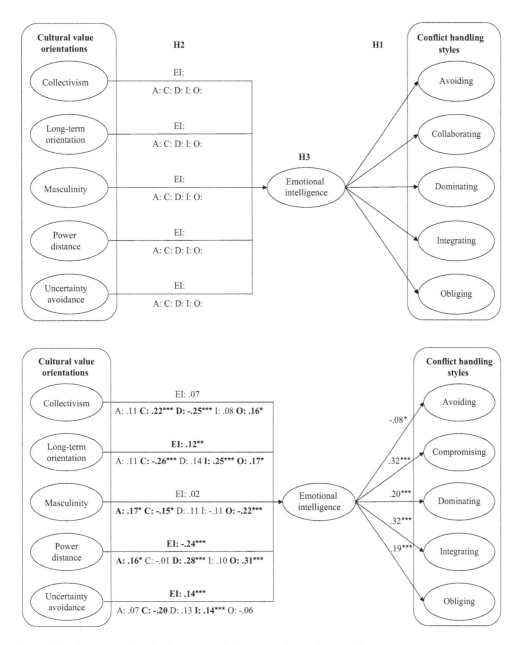

Figure 40.1 Summary of results for meta-analytic structural equation modeling.

presents the conceptual model and the MASEM results. The results show that EQ has a significant positive effect on collaborating (0.32), dominating (0.20), integrating (0.32), and obliging (0.19) conflict-handling style and a significant negative effect on the avoiding (−0.08) conflict-handling style. Furthermore, the results show that long-term orientation (0.12) and uncertainty avoidance (0.14) are positively and that power distance (−0.24) is negatively associated with EQ.

Based on theory and previous empirical findings, we proposed in our conceptual model that EQ partially mediates the relationship between cultural value orientations and conflict handling styles. Our results support this model as the partial mediation model fitted the data significantly better than the full mediation model. Our results show that various cultural value orientations are significantly associated with different conflict-handling styles. Masculinity (0.17) and power distance (0.16) are positively associated with an avoiding conflict-handling style. Collectivism is positively (0.22), and long-term orientation (−0.26), masculinity (−0.15), and uncertainty avoidance (−0.20) are negatively associated with a compromising conflict-handling style. Collectivism (−0.25) is negatively, and power distance is positively, related to a dominating conflict-handling style. Long-term orientation and uncertainty avoidance are positively associated with an integrating conflict-handling style. Collectivism (0.16), long-term orientation (0.17), and power distance (0.31) are positively, and masculinity (-0.22) is negatively associated with an obliging conflict-handling style. Additional analyses of the indirect effects of the cultural value orientations on the different conflict-handling styles through EQ supported the partial mediation.

Discussion

In summary, the results of the bivariate meta-analysis and the MASEM show that EQ is substantially related to four of the five conflict-handling styles, specifically to the compromising and integrating styles, indicating that the ability to understand own and others' emotions, as well as the ability to regulate and use emotions, is of particular relevance in developing a preference for a moderate to deep concern for self and the other party involved in the conflict. Our results further show that EQ is determined by cultural value orientations, specifically power distance has a negative relationship with EQ, indicating that individuals that to a higher degree accept inequality in social relationships possess lower EQ and, in turn, a lower preference for a compromising and integrating conflict-handling style. Our results also reveal that EQ partially mediates the influence of individual cultural value orientations on conflict handling styles, indicating that only specific cultural value orientations function through EQ in their association with specific conflict-handling styles and that cultural value orientation are also directly related to the preference of specific conflict handling styles. More specifically, our results show that an individual's preference for a compromising style is specifically related to collectivism, long-term orientation, and uncertainty avoidance. The preference for a dominating style is specifically associated with collectivism and power distance. An integrating style is specifically related to long-term orientation. An obliging style is in particular associated with masculinity and power distance.

Practical implications

From a practical point of view, the results of this study have far-reaching implications for managers and workgroup members. Conflict is common in any group, particularly in workgroups that work on demanding projects with high stakes and uncertainty, and disagreements often arise among the group members. A wrong approach to handling the conflict can amplify the conflict and hurt team dynamics and performance. In contrast, wise management of emotions and a constructive conflict-handling approach could not only lower the tension in the group but turn a disagreement and constructive argument that aids team productivity and problem-solving.

The present study showed a link between cultural values and EQ, which in turn relates to conflict-handling styles, and the findings have implications for recruitment and selection, as well for personnel training and development. Compromising and integrating are perhaps the most often preferred conflict resolution styles. However, under certain circumstances, such as when the work is routine and must be completed quickly without wasting time on discussions and deliberations (e.g., law enforcement or emergency room situations) might be preferred, particularly if the group leader leans towards a dominating conflict resolution style, while the subordinates tend towards obliging or avoiding. All of these are significantly predicted by EQ, which, in turn, is associated with certain sets of cultural values. Accordingly, selecting personnel with the values associated with higher EQ would likely result in a greater probability of effective conflict resolution in the workplace. Testing for cultural values and EQ could be incorporated in the selection procedures, or the recruitment could be focused on the groups that tend to display cultural values associated with high EQ and the preferred conflict-handling styles.

Perhaps even more importantly, the results of the present study have implications for personnel training and development. EQ is a trainable trait—and, thus, investing in training programs that develop EQ would result in numerous benefits, particularly more effective conflict handling in the workplace. According to the results of our study, such training would particularly be useful for employees to display high power distance orientation tendencies, and they tend to score low on EQ.

References

Antonioni, David. 1998. "Relationship between the Big Five Personality Factors and Conflict Management Styles." *International Journal of Conflict Management* 9 (4): 336–355. 10.1108/eb022814

Bergmann, Thomas J., and Roger J. Volkema. 1989. "Understanding and Managing Interpersonal Conflict at Work: Its Issues, Interactive Processes and Consequences." In *Managing Conflict: An Interdisciplinary Approach*, edited by M. Afzalur Rahim, 7–19. New York: Praeger.

Blake, Robert Rogers, and Jane Srygley Mouton. 1964. *The Managerial Grid: The Key to Leadership and Excellence*. Houston, TX: Gulf Publishing.

Brett, Jeanne. 2018. "Intercultural Challenges in Managing Workplace Conflict—A Call for Research." *Cross Cultural & Strategic Management* 25 (1): 32–52. 10.1108/CCSM-11-2016-0190

Caputo, Andrea, Oluremi B. Ayoko, and Nii Amoo. 2018. "The Moderating Role of Cultural Intelligence in the Relationship between Cultural Orientations and Conflict Management Styles." *Journal of Business Research* 89 (August): 10–20. 10.1016/j.jbusres.2018.03.042

Derr, C. Brooklyn. 1977. *Career Switching and Organizational Politics among Naval Officers*. Monterey, CA: Naval Postgraduate School.

Gbadamosi, Oluwakemi, Abbas Ghanbari Baghestan, and Khalil Al-Mabrouk. 2014. "Gender, Age and Nationality: Assessing Their Impact on Conflict Resolution Styles." *Journal of Management Development* 33 (3): 245–257. 10.1108/JMD-02-2011-0024

Gunkel, Marjaana, Christopher Schlaegel, and Vas Taras. 2016. "Cultural Values, Emotional Intelligence, and Conflict Handling Styles: A Global Study." *Journal of World Business* 51 (4): 568–585. 10.1016/j.jwb.2016. 02.001

Gunkel, Marjaana, Christopher Schlägel, and Robert L. Engle. 2014. "Culture's Influence on Emotional Intelligence: An Empirical Study of Nine Countries." *Journal of International Management* 20 (2): 256–274. 10.1016/j.intman.2013.10.002

He, Zhou, J. H. Zhu, and Shiyong Peng. 2002. "Cultural Values and Conflict Resolution in Enterprises in Diverse Cultural Settings in China." In *Chinese Conflict Management and Resolution*, edited by Guo-Ming Chen and Ringo Ma, 129–147. Westport, CT: Ablex.

Hofstede, Geert H. 2001. *Culture's Consequences: Comparing Values, Behaviors, Institutions, and Organizations across Nations*. 2nd ed. Thousand Oaks, CA: Sage Publications.

Holt, Jennifer L., and Cynthia James DeVore. 2005. "Culture, Gender, Organizational Role, and Styles of Conflict Resolution: A Meta-Analysis." *International Journal of Intercultural Relations* 29 (2): 165–196. 10.1016/j.ijintrel.2005.06.002

Hunter, John E., and Frank L. Schmidt. 2004. *Methods of Meta-Analysis: Correcting Error and Bias in Research Findings*. 2nd ed. Thousand Oaks, Calif: Sage.

Jordan, Peter J., and Ashlea C. Troth. 2004. "Managing Emotions During Team Problem Solving: Emotional Intelligence and Conflict Resolution." *Human Performance* 17 (2): 195–218. 10.1207/s15327043hup1702_4

Laurent, André. 1983. "The Cultural Diversity of Western Conceptions of Management." *International Studies of Management & Organization* 13 (1–2): 75–96. 10.1080/00208825.1983.11656359

Lipsey, Mark W., and David B. Wilson. 2001. *Practical Meta-Analysis*. Thousand Oaks, CA: Sage.

Matsumoto, David. 1989. "Cultural Influences on the Perception of Emotion." *Journal of Cross-Cultural Psychology* 20 (1): 92–105. 10.1177/0022022189201006

Matsumoto, David, Seung Hee Yoo, Sanae Nakagawa, and Multinational Study of Cultural Display Rules. 2008. "Culture, Emotion Regulation, and Adjustment." *Journal of Personality and Social Psychology* 94 (6): 925–937. 10.1037/0022-3514.94.6.925

Oudenhoven, Jan Pieter, Lonneke Mechelse, and Carsten K. W. Dreu. 1998. "Managerial Conflict Management in Five European Countries: The Importance of Power Distance, Uncertainty Avoidance, and Masculinity." *Applied Psychology* 47 (3): 439–455. 10.1111/j.1464-0597.1998.tb00037.x

Palmer, Benjamin R., Gilles Gignac, Gina Ekermans, and Con Stough. 2008. "A Comprehensive Framework for Emotional Intelligence." In *Emotional Intelligence: Theoretical and Cultural Perspectives*, edited by Robert J. Emmerling, Vinod K. Shanwal, and Manas K. Mandal, 17–38. New York: Nova Science Publishers.

Park, Heejoon, and David Antonioni. 2007. "Personality, Reciprocity, and Strength of Conflict Resolution Strategy." *Journal of Research in Personality* 41 (1): 110–125. 10.1016/j.jrp.2006.03.003

Purohit, Yasmin S., and Claire A. Simmers. 2006. "Power distance and uncertainty avoidance: a cross-national examination of their impact on conflict management modes." *Journal of International Business Research* 5 (1): 1–19.

Rahim, M. Afzalur. 1983. "A Measure of Styles of Handling Interpersonal Conflict." *Academy of Management Journal* 26 (2): 368–376. 10.5465/255985

Salovey, Peter, and John D. Mayer. 1990. "Emotional Intelligence." *Imagination, Cognition and Personality* 9 (3): 185–211. 10.2190/DUGG-P24E-52WK-6CDG

Schlaerth, Andrea, Nurcan Ensari, and Julie Christian. 2013. "A Meta-Analytical Review of the Relationship between Emotional Intelligence and Leaders' Constructive Conflict Management." *Group Processes & Intergroup Relations* 16 (1): 126–136. 10.1177/1368430212439907

Tehrani, Hossein Dabiriyan, and Sara Yamini. 2020. "Personality Traits and Conflict Resolution Styles: A Meta-Analysis." *Personality and Individual Differences* 157 (April): 109794. 10.1016/j.paid.2019.109794

Thomas, Kenneth W. 1992. "Conflict and Conflict Management: Reflections and Update." *Journal of Organizational Behavior* 13 (3): 265–274. 10.1002/job.4030130307

Ting-Toomey, Stella, Ge Gao, Paula Trubisky, Zhizhong Yang, Hak Soo Kim, Sung-Ling Lin, and Tsukasa Nishida. 1991. "Culture, Face Maintenance, and Styles of Handling Interpersonal Conflict: A Study in Five Cultures." *International Journal of Conflict Management* 2 (4): 275–296. 10.1108/eb022702

Ting-Toomey, Stella, and John G. Oetzel. 2001. *Managing Intercultural Conflict Effectively*. Vol. 5. Thousand Oaks, CA: Sage. 10.4135/9781452229485

Wall, James A., and Ronda Roberts Callister. 1995. "Conflict and Its Management." *Journal of Management* 21 (3): 515–558. https://doi.org/10.1177/014920639502100306

Xie, Jinhong, X. Michael Song, and Anne Stringfellow. 1998. "Interfunctional Conflict, Conflict Resolution Styles, and New Product Success: A Four-Culture Comparison." *Management Science* 44 (12-part-2): S192–S206. 10.1287/mnsc.44.12.S192

41

MEASURING INTERCULTURAL MEDIATION IN THE CONTEXT OF INTERGROUP CONFLICT: CLASSICAL AND MODERN TEST THEORY APPROACHES TO SCALE ASSESSMENT

Sara Rubenfeld and Richard Clément

In the sphere of language education, having the competence and willingness to act as a cultural mediator is considered a goal of second/foreign language learning (Wilkinson 2020). The Common European Framework of Reference for Languages (Council of Europe 2001, 2018) was proposed as a consensual perspective in which to view second-language education as a vector of social and intercultural harmony. It specifically held the ability to establish a positive collaborative environment as a goal of second-language learning (Byram and Golubeva 2020). Until recently, it has not been possible to empirically examine the conjectures presented above. To address aspects of this gap, the goal of this chapter is to describe the construction and assessment of a tool designed to measure willingness to mediate as a third party in the context of intergroup conflict.[1]

Intercultural competence

The ability and inclination to mediate between cultures arises from being an *intercultural speaker*. Intercultural speakers are said to be able to navigate between cultures and be at ease negotiating interactions between languages (Kramsch 1998), with knowledge of the languages involved being a key factor in defining the ability to act as a mediator (Byram 2012; Fantini 2012). The related concept of intercultural competence was defined by Byram as "the ability to establish a community of meanings across cultural boundaries" (1989, 5). By virtue of their ability to understand, interpret, and identify with individuals from distinct cultural backgrounds, bi- or multi-lingual individuals would have the competence and impetus to act as linguistic and cultural brokers, facilitating intercultural contact (Gohard-Radenkovic et al. 2004; Irishkanova, Röcklinsberg, Ozolina, and Zaharia 2004). If second/foreign language learning imparts an understanding of cultural differences and an ability to bridge intercultural communication, this would suggest that interculturally competent individuals may be good candidates to mediate in situations of intercultural conflict.

DOI: 10.4324/9781003227441-49

Measurement

Scales exist to evaluate individual approaches to intercultural conflict resolution (e.g., Hammer 2005), or intercultural communicative competence (e.g., Fantini 2019). However, none of these addresses the tendency to intervene in an intercultural conflict as a third party. To fill this gap, Lussier, Auger, Urbanicová, et al. (2004) and Lussier, Auger, Lebrun, and Clément (2004) developed a measure of intercultural mediation, which uses a scenario-based approach to determine participants' likelihood of acting as an intercultural mediator. Specifically, bilingual participants are asked to read about a conflict between individuals from differing linguistic groups and are then asked to indicate their likelihood of using specific mediational behaviors to respond to the conflict. Employing this measure, Rubenfeld et al. (2007) found that among Francophone respondents, mediation behaviors can be separated into two dimensions: Direct (e.g., I would mediate to reduce the tension) and avoidant (e.g., I would avoid the situation) mediational strategies. However, anomalous results prompted further psychometric testing of the measure (Rubenfeld and Clément 2007). This testing indicated that further revision to the measure is necessary, particularly with respect to the clarity of the scenarios and the items mapping onto avoidant mediation strategies.

The intercultural mediation scale

To address the aforementioned concerns, the Intercultural Mediation Scale (IMS) includes modified scenarios and items. In particular, more elaborate details of the context and individuals involved in the conflict are provided and tailored to the participant groups (i.e., Anglophones and Francophones) being examined. Further, new items have been developed to improve upon earlier shortcomings with the items tapping into avoidant mediation strategies. As well, given results (Rubenfeld and Clément 2007) demonstrating variability in minority (Francophone) and majority (Anglophone) group members' response to in-group perpetration of conflict, scenarios have been created to reflect perpetrator and victim scenarios (i.e., members of the linguistic group to which the participants belong perpetrating and being victimized by discrimination, respectively). The current goal is to assess the psychometric properties of the IMS.

Method

Participants

Anglophone and Francophone participants were invited to complete this study on the condition that their mother tongues were English and French, respectively. These two linguistic groups are official languages in Canada and frequently come in contact (in some regions of the country). Their history of contact is such that the scenarios described would be relatable or plausible for participants. The pool of participants included introductory psychology students from the University of Ottawa, a bilingual institution in Canada's national capital which provides instruction in both official languages.

Participants indicating that their country of origin was not Canada or that their mother tongue differed from the language of the questionnaire they completed were eliminated from further analyses. Following this, a total of 580 Anglophones and 310 Francophones remained. Of this total, 290 Anglophones (228 female, 61 male, and 1 transgender) and 200 Francophones (154 female and 46 male) were randomly selected for inclusion in the current study.

Measures

Intercultural mediation scale (see Annex for English version). This scale measures the extent to which participants endorse a range of responses during intercultural conflict scenarios. The scale consists of different cultural mediation scenarios that describe situations where those involved in the scenarios (Francophones or Anglophones) are either the perpetrator or the target of an intercultural conflict. Participants responded to a total of four scenarios, two scenarios where members of their linguistic group are perpetrators of a conflict and two scenarios where they are targets. After reading each scenario, participants were asked to respond to eight items on a 5-point Likert scale, ranging from 1 (Not at all probable) to 5 (Extremely likely).

Procedure

Participants were selected from undergraduate psychology classes participating in the University of Ottawa's Integrated Subject Research Pool (ISRP) who indicated that their mother tongues were English and French in a pre-test given to all ISRP participants. Students choosing to participate in the English or French studies completed the study online.

Results

As a preliminary step, the mean of like items (e.g., item one in both perpetrator scenarios) from the two perpetrator and two victim scenarios were computed, minimizing the number of scale assessments to one perpetrator composite score and one victim composite score for Francophones and Anglophones, each. This was done to simplify the analysis and was supported by moderately high correlations among like English perpetrator (range = 0.49–0.68) and victim (range = 0.34–0.50) items and French perpetrator (range = 0.55–0.67) and victim (range = 0.29–0.50) items. This suggests a common response pattern despite scenario differences.

The examination of the psychometric properties of the IMS's items was conducted using a combined Classical Test Theory (CTT) and Modern Test Theory (MTT) approach. The incorporation of both approaches provides the opportunity to exploit the advantages of each approach when determining whether the measure offers an accurate assessment of individuals' willingness to act as a mediator when witnessing intercultural conflicts.

CTT: Dimensionality

As a CTT approach, Confirmatory Factor Analysis (CFA) allows for a test of the dimensionality of a construct through an a priori specification of a pattern between observed and unobserved variables (Byrne 2006). The *a priori* specification of a model is particularly useful in this case because past evaluations of an earlier version of this measure have yielded by both one and two factor models (Rubenfeld and Clément 2007; Rubenfeld et al. 2007). A series of CFAs were conducted using AMOS 16.0 (Arbuckle 2007). Given that scenarios differ according to both language (English and French) and role of the in-group (perpetrator and victim), four separate sets of analyses were used for each eight composite cultural mediation items (see Tables 41.1 and 41.2 for correlation matrices for Francophone and Anglophone groups, respectively).

Fit indices, produced by Maximum Likelihood estimation, were compared to determine whether a one- or two-dimensional model best described the data. As represented in Table 41.3, in all cases the bidimensional models demonstrated a better fit than the uni-dimensional models.

In all cases, the CFI values indicated very good fit, 0.95 and above (Hu & Bentler 1999), for the bidimensional models, but were unacceptably low for the uni-dimensional models. The RMSEA values are not indicative of a well-fitting model, particularly the values for the perpetrator scenarios. Although substantively justifiable post hoc modifications reduce the value of the RMSEA, these modifications are not consistent across languages and scenarios. Given our desire to determine a consistent model for mediational behaviors, a somewhat less than ideal fit was sacrificed for the sake

Sara Rubenfeld and Richard Clément

Table 41.1 Intercorrelations among cultural mediation items for the Francophone group, including perpetrator (above diagonal) and victim (below diagonal) scenarios

	1	2	3	4	5	6	7	8
Item 1		0.74**	0.57**	0.56**	−0.32**	−0.36**	−0.33**	−0.13
Item 2	0.76**		0.63**	0.69**	−0.41**	−0.41**	−0.47**	−0.22*
Item 3	0.60**	0.79**		0.61**	−0.24**	−0.16*	−0.17*	−0.06
Item 4	0.60**	0.79**	0.74**		−0.22*	−0.20*	−0.20*	−0.04
Item 5	−0.25**	−0.29**	−0.16*	−0.21*		0.70**	0.69**	0.45**
Item 6	−0.27**	−0.28**	−0.17*	−0.17*	0.63**		0.64**	0.47**
Item 7	−0.20*	−0.25**	−0.16*	−0.12	0.66**	0.66**		0.58**
Item 8	0.03	−0.02	0.05	0.11	0.30**	0.41**	0.40**	

Notes
* $p < 0.05$
** $p < 0.001$

Table 41.2 Intercorrelations among cultural mediation items for the Anglophone group, including perpetrator (above diagonal) and victim (below diagonal) scenarios

	1	2	3	4	5	6	7	8
Item 1		0.89**	0.52**	0.71**	−0.31**	−0.42**	−0.32**	−0.17*
Item 2	0.87**		0.54**	0.78**	−0.31**	−0.39**	−0.34**	−0.13*
Item 3	0.76**	0.82**		0.58**	−0.22**	−0.23**	−0.16*	−0.05
Item 4	0.77**	0.87**	0.79**		−0.27**	−0.31**	−0.27**	−0.19*
Item 5	−0.33**	−0.36**	−0.34**	−0.35**		0.66**	0.62**	0.38**
Item 6	−0.28**	−0.30**	−0.25**	−0.25**	0.60**		0.58**	0.51**
Item 7	−0.19**	−0.22**	−0.21**	−0.24**	0.67**	0.51**		0.44**
Item 8	0.01	0.00	0.01	0.02	0.16*	0.33**	0.21**	

Notes
* $p < 0.05$
** $p < 0.001$

Table 41.3 Fit indices of one and two factor models

Model	X2	df	CFI	RMSEA	(lower)	(upper)	SRMR	AIC
Anglophone Perpetrator								
1 Factor	403.93**	20	0.71	0.26	0.24	0.28	0.17	435.93
2 Factor	71.54**	19	0.96	0.10	0.07	0.12	0.04	105.54
Anglophone Victim								
1 Factor	323.83**	20	0.80	0.23	0.21	0.25	0.16	335.83
2 Factor	47.98**	19	0.98	0.07	0.05	0.10	0.05	81.98
Francophone Perpetrator								
1 Factor	322.74**	20	0.63	0.28	0.25	0.30	0.18	354.74
2 Factor	57.75**	19	0.95	0.10	0.07	0.13	0.065	91.76
Francophone Victim								
1 Factor	310.22**	20	0.67	0.27	0.24	0.30	0.20	342.22
2 Factor	45.92**	20	0.97	0.08	0.05	0.12	0.07	79.92

Notes
** $p < 0.001$
χ2 chi-square; df—degrees of freedom; CFI—Comparative Fit Index; RMSEA—Root Mean Square Error of Approximation; RMSEA CI—Confidence Intervals based on RMSEA; SRMR—Standardized Root Mean Square Residual; AIC—Akaike Information Criterion.

of consistency. As well, in addition to the CFI values being very good, the SRMR values for the bidimensional model are all quite good (less than 0.08; Hu & Bentler 1999).

MTT: *Item Response Theory*

Using Item Response Theory (IRT), an MTT approach, over a CTT approach has some advantages when it comes to assessing the quality of questions being asked following each scenario. In particular, IRT models have the capacity to measure both person characteristics and item properties, which allows for a distinction between scores based on trait levels (e.g., a person's inclination to intervene directly) and item difficulty (e.g., a question that is only likely to be endorsed by those who are highly willing to intervene; Embretson and Reise 2000; Hambleton, Swaminathan, and Rogers 1991; Reise and Henson 2003). When it comes to analyzing polytomous data (e.g., Likert-type items), the Graded Response Model (Samejima 1969, 1972, 1996) allows for an estimation of both participants' trait levels (Θ) and item properties, difficulty (β), and discrimination (α). IRT analyses were conducted using Multilog 7.03 (Thissen, Chen, and Bock 2003).

Item difficulty. Item difficulty indicates the degree to which individuals must possess the latent trait in order to receive a particular item score. In Likert-type measurements, k-1 (k = number of response choices) difficulty values are produced per item where each value represents the level of trait a participant must have to endorse the response choice 50% of the time (Hays, Morales, and Reise 2000). Therefore, items with higher β values would require more of the cultural mediation trait (i.e., a greater willingness to act as a cultural mediator) in order to be endorsed.

Item discrimination. Item discrimination, represented by a slope value (α), delineates how well an item differentiates participants with varying levels of the trait. The higher the value of the slope, the more response options differentiate among trait levels. For example, a high discrimination value would suggest that the item is highly related to the cultural mediation trait and would, therefore, be sensitive to individual variations in trait levels.

Discrimination and difficulty values for the perpetrator and victim scenarios are produced for involved and avoidant factors for both Francophones (Table 41.4) and Anglophones (Table 41.5). With the exception of the slope for the first involved item in the victim scenario, which was quite low for the Anglophone group, all remaining discrimination values were acceptable.

Together, the β and α values form the Test Information Curve. This (solid line) curve represents the amount of information the test is able to provide at varying levels of theta (i.e., willingness to mediate during intercultural conflicts; see Figures 41.1 and 41.2). Balancing out the information provided, the measurement error (dotted line) represents variation in the responses that cannot be attributed to theta. High levels of error at lower portions of the abscissa indicate a limited ability to measure mediational responses among participants in the specified range of the outcome of interest, involved or avoidant mediation behaviors.

In some scenarios, it would be preferable to have more information as trait values vary from the mean. For example, the curves representing avoidant-Anglophone-perpetrator, involved-Anglophone-victim, and avoidant-Francophone-perpetrator indicate that the measure has a limited capacity to represent participants whose trait levels fall further than one standard deviation below the mean. Although this is not a critical problem, it does speak to some limitations in the IMS's ability to represent participants at all levels of the mediation trait.

Discussion

The assessment of the IMS represents a further step in the examination of non-discriminatory behavior. By systematically evaluating the dimensionality of the measure as well as the quality of the items, the results of the current study contribute to ascertaining the validity of the constructs being measured.

Sara Rubenfeld and Richard Clément

Table 41.4 IRT results of discrimination (α) and difficulty (β) for involved and avoidant factors for Francophone group.

Factor	Scenario	Item	α	$\beta1$	$\beta2$	$\beta3$	$\beta4$
Involved	Perpetrator	1	2.96	−2.02	−1.22	−0.35	0.66
		2	5.31	−1.96	−1.35	−0.48	0.49
		3	2.05	−1.95	−1.11	0.06	1.27
		4	2.46	−1.80	−1.10	−0.27	0.95
	Victim	1	2.60	−1.19	−0.08	0.86	1.76
		2	6.82	−1.30	−0.38	0.56	1.31
		3	3.59	−1.13	−0.20	0.66	1.45
		4	3.40	−1.19	−0.29	0.60	1.55
Avoidant	Perpetrator	5	3.56	−0.49	0.54	1.33	2.27
		6	3.23	−0.83	0.44	1.24	2.45
		7	3.93	−0.07	0.88	1.65	2.10
		8	1.74	−0.40	0.99	1.89	2.66
	Victim	5	2.74	−0.93	0.07	1.07	2.14
		6	2.73	−1.42	−0.14	0.72	1.70
		7	3.60	−0.57	0.39	1.15	2.17
		8	1.12	−0.58	0.71	2.15	3.92

Table 41.5 IRT results of discrimination (α) and difficulty (β) for involved and avoidant factors for Anglophone group.

Factor	Scenario	Item	α	$\beta1$	$\beta2$	$\beta3$	$\beta4$
Involved	Perpetrator	1	1.99	−3.18	−1.83	−0.42	0.93
		2	2.13	−3.37	−1.86	−0.54	0.98
		3	1.20	−2.38	−0.79	0.70	2.23
		4	1.88	−3.13	−1.70	−0.24	1.19
	Victim	1	0.23	−6.06	−2.05	1.41	5.60
		2	5.13	−0.64	0.29	1.09	1.69
		3	6.81	−0.86	−0.01	0.90	1.69
		4	3.67	−0.79	0.02	1.17	1.91
Avoidant	Perpetrator	5	2.75	−0.24	1.16	2.12	2.97
		6	3.51	−0.32	1.07	2.06	2.72
		7	2.47	0.47	1.66	2.66	3.41
		8	1.43	−0.09	1.44	2.88	4.63
	Victim	5	2.82	−1.34	0.04	1.15	1.91
		6	2.06	−1.63	−0.08	1.18	2.40
		7	2.61	−0.71	0.62	1.67	2.37
		8	0.72	−0.69	1.71	3.92	8.13

Upon contrasting a one- and two-factor model, it became clear that a bidimensional model would best describe the data. Although the involved and avoidant dimensions are related, the results of the dimensionality analyses suggest that individuals may simultaneously endorse both involved and avoidant mediation tactics when faced with situations of intercultural conflicts. By the same token, bidimensionality of the constructs suggests that individuals could endorse neither form of response.

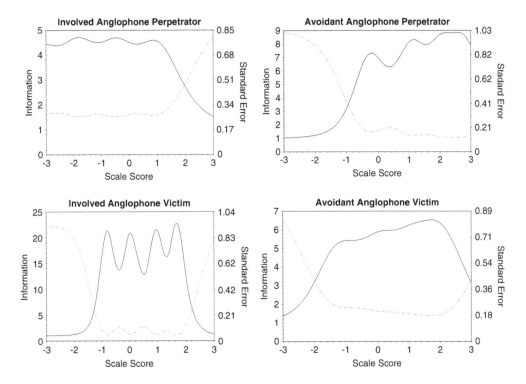

Figure 41.1 Test information curve—Anglophone

Note: Information and standard error axes vary between visuals.

When it comes to the assessment of items, the IRT analyses demonstrated that, for the most part, the newly developed and revised items are informative about the underlying constructs they represent. The slope of one item in a victim scenario was unacceptably low and should, therefore, be eliminated or re-examined in future uses of this scale.

Future research

The next step in better understanding cultural mediation behaviors is to establish what factors predict such mediational responses. Will intercultural competence, as Alred and Byram (2002) suggest, lead to an increased willingness to take social action and act in non-discriminatory ways? Does second-language competence and confidence influence intervention behavior? In addition to these substantive questions, the use of scenarios that vary the role of the in-group (perpetrator or victim) and is administered to groups in contact with different status (e.g., majority/minority) allows for an examination of how contextual factors influence mediational strategies.

Limitations

As with many self-report questionnaires, consideration must be given to a potential divergence between the participants' reported responses and their actual behaviors. In the case of mediation behaviors, this divergence might be particularly likely given the conflictual nature of scenarios being described. However, short of exposing participants to fabricated real-time conflicts, any method of capturing participants' responses to a conflict would be susceptible to questions regarding its ecological validity.

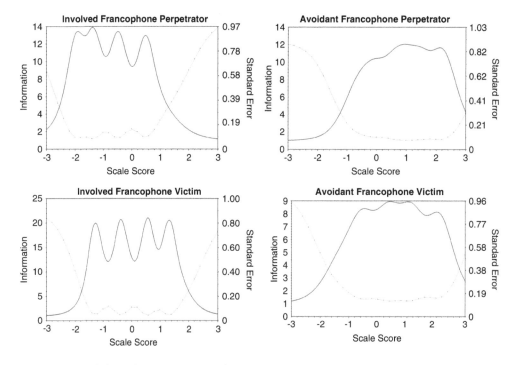

Figure 41.2 Test information curve—Francophone

Note: Information and standard error axes vary between visuals.

Conclusion

Through the development of the IMS, it becomes possible for researchers to investigate non-discriminatory behaviors. In addition to being an improvement of the initial measure, this measure allows for both the evaluation and future juxtaposition of responses to scenarios where the in-group perpetrates or is victimized by discrimination. As such, this work lays the groundwork for future substantive studies of non-discriminatory behaviors and its nomological network.

Note

1 © Her Majesty the Queen in right of Canada as represented by the Minister of National Defence (2023).

References

Alred, Geof, and Mike Byram. 2002. "Becoming an Intercultural Mediator: A Longitudinal Study of Residence Abroad." *Journal of Multilingual and Multicultural Development* 23 (5): 339–352. 10.1080/01434630208666473.
Arbuckle, James L. 2007. *Amos 16.0 User's Guide* [Computer software]. Chicago, IL: AMOS Development Corporation.
Byrne, Barbara M. 2006. *Structural Equation Modeling with EQS: Basic Concepts, Applications, and Programming* (2nd ed.). Mahwah, NJ: Lawrence Erlbaum. 10.4324/9780203726532
Byram, Michael. 1989. *Cultural Studies in Foreign Language Education.* Cleveland, UK: Multilingual Matters.
Byram, Michael. 2012. "Language Awareness and (Critical) Cultural Awareness—Relationships, Comparisons and Contrasts." *Language Awareness* 21 (1–2): 5–13. 10.1080/09658416.2011.639887
Byram, Michael, and Irina Golubeva. 2020. "Conceptualising Intercultural (Communicative) Competence and Intercultural Citizenship." In *The Routledge Handbook of Language and Intercultural Communication*, edited by Jane Jackson, 2nd ed., 70–85. London, New York: Routledge. 10.4324/9781003036210-6

Council of Europe. 2018. *Common European Framework of Reference for Languages: Learning, Teaching, Assessment: Companion Volume with New Descriptors.* Strasbourg: Council of Europe Publishing.

Council of Europe. 2001. *Common European Framework of Reference for Languages: Learning, Teaching, Assessment (CEFR).* Strasbourg: Council of Europe Publishing.

Embretson, Susan E., and Steven P. Reise. 2000. *Item Response Theory for Psychology.* London: Lawrence Erlbaum.

Fantini, Alvino E. 2012. "Language: An Essential Component of Intercultural Communicative Competence." In *The Routledge Handbook of Language and Intercultural Communication,* edited by Jane Jackson, 263–278. London: Routledge.

Fantini, Alvino E. 2019. *Intercultural Communicative Competence in Educational Exchange: A Multinational Perspective.* New York: Routledge. 10.4324/9781351251747

Gohard-Radenkovic, Aline, Denise Lussier, Hermine Penz, and Geneviève Zarate. 2004. "Reference fields and methodology." In *Cultural Mediation in Language Learning and Teaching,* edited by Genievième Zarate, Aline Gohard-Radenkovic, Denise Lussier and Hermine Penz, 27–57. Kapfenberg: Council of Europe Publishing.

Hambleton, Ron K., Hariharan Swaminathan, and H. Jane Rogers. 1991. *Fundamentals of Item Response Theory.* London: Sage Publications.

Hammer, Mitchell R. 2005. "The Intercultural Conflict Style Inventory: A Conceptual Framework and Measure of Intercultural Conflict Resolution Approaches." *International Journal of Intercultural Relations* 29 (6): 675–695. 10.1016/j.ijintrel.2005.08.010

Hays, Ron D., Leo S. Morales, and Steve P. Reise. 2000. "Item Response Theory and Health Outcomes Measurement in the 21st Century." *Medical Care* 38 (9): 28–42.

Hu, Li-tze, and Peter M. Bentler. 1999. "Cutoff Criteria for Fit Indexes in Covariance Structure Analysis: Conventional Criteria versus New Alternatives." *Structural Equation Modeling: A Multidisciplinary Journal* 6 (1): 1–55. 10.1080/10705519909540118

Irishkanova, Kira, Christoph Röcklinsberg, Olga Ozolina, and Ioana Anamaria Zaharia. 2004. "Empathy as Part of Cultural Mediation." In *Cultural Mediation in Language Learning and Teaching,* edited by Geneviève Zarate, Aline Gohard-Radenkovic, Denise Lussier & Hermine Penz, 101–131. Kapfenberg: Council of Europe Publishing.

Kramsch, Claire. 1998. "The Privilege of the Intercultural Speaker." In *Language Learning in Intercultural Perspective: Approaches through Drama and Ethnography,* edited by Michael Byram and Michael Fleming, 16–31. Cambridge: Cambridge University Press.

Lussier, Denise, Réjean Auger, Monique Lebrun, and Richard Clément. 2004. *Written questionnaire. The Development of Cultural Representations.* Unpublished manuscript. Montreal: McGill University.

Lussier, Denise, Réjean Auger, Viera Urbanicová, Marcella Armengol, Paz De la Serna, and Maria Concepción De Miguel. 2004. "Representations of Other and Other Cultures in the Context of the Initial and Ongoing Training of Teachers." In *Cultural Mediation in Language Learning and Teaching,* edited by Geneviève Zarate, Aline Gohard-Radenkovic, Denise Lussier, and Hermine Penz, 181–213. Kapfenberg: Council of Europe Publishing.

Reise, Steven P., and James M. Henson. 2003. "A Discussion of Modern Versus Traditional Psychometrics as Applied to Personality Assessment Scales." *Journal of Personality Assessment* 81 (2): 93–103. 10.1207/S15327752JPA8102_01

Rubenfeld, Sara, and Richard Clément. 2007. "Intergroup Contact: The Development of an Intercultural Mediation Scale." Poster presented at the annual Canadian Psychology Association Conference, Ottawa, ON, June 2007.

Rubenfeld, Sara, Richard Clément, Jessica Vinograd, Denise Lussier, Valérie Amireault, Réjean Auger, and Monique Lebrun. 2007. "Becoming a Cultural Intermediary: A Further Social Corollary of Second-Language Learning." *Journal of Language and Social Psychology* 26 (2): 182–203. 10.1177/0261927X07300080

Samejima, Fumiko. 1969. "Estimation of Latent Ability Using a Response Pattern of Graded Scores." *Psychometrika* 34 (S1): 1–97. 10.1007/BF03372160

Samejima, Fumiko. 1972. "A General Model for Free-Response Data." *Psychometrika Monograph* 37 (18): 1–68.

Samejima, Fumiko. 1996. "Evaluation of Mathematical Models for Ordered Polychotomous Responses." *Behaviormetrika* 23 (1): 17–35. 10.2333/bhmk.23.17

Thissen, David, Wen-Hung, Chen, and Darrell, Bock. 2003. *Multilog (version 7)* [Computer software]. Lincolnwood, IL: Scientific Software International.

Wilkinson, Jane. 2020. "From Native Speaker to Intercultural Speaker and Beyond." In *The Routledge Handbook of Language and Intercultural Communication,* edited by Jane Jackson, 2nd ed., 283–298. London, New York: Routledge. 10.4324/9781003036210-22

Sara Rubenfeld and Richard Clément

Annex: Intercultural mediation scale

Instructions

After each scenario, respond to the question: "How likely are you to use the following behaviours?"
1-Not at all probable 2-Somewhat likely 3-Likely 4-Very likely 5-Extremely likely.

English scenarios

(Note French scenarios are not direct translations.)

1 (perpetrator) Someone you know brings his/her French-speaking friend to an English-speaking friend's house party. A small group of Anglophones start to insult the Francophone's accent while speaking English and you can tell that this person is offended. What would you do?

2 (perpetrator) A French-speaking person asks to join a street hockey game with you and your Anglophone friends. After playing for two minutes, the Francophone scores. Some of the Anglophones start to insult the Francophone by saying, "Francophones are a bunch of cheaters. Kick this guy out of the game!" The Francophone becomes angry and everyone starts to argue. What would you do?

3 (victim) You are at a corner store in French-speaking area of Montreal and you witness a disagreement between the cashier, who is Francophone, and a customer, who is Anglophone. The cashier is refusing to serve the customer because the customer is unable to speak French fluently. What would you do?

4 (victim) Imagine you are a guest at a wedding in Quebec City where both the bride and groom and their families are Anglophone. Part way through the evening, you notice a Francophone complaining to the band about the amount of English music they are playing. Some of the Anglophones nearby begin to get upset about this. What would you do?

Response options

(Repeated after each scenario.)

1.1 I would stop their conversation.	1 2 3 4 5
1.2 I would try to intervene to reduce the tension	1 2 3 4 5
1.3 I would clarify the argument of each person	1 2 3 4 5
1.4 I would try to make the situation less alarming.	1 2 3 4 5
1.5 I would walk away from the area	1 2 3 4 5
1.6 I would observe the disagreement from a distance.	1 2 3 4 5
1.7 I would act as though nothing unusual is happening.	1 2 3 4 5
1.8 I would wait until one person leaves to express my opinion.	1 2 3 4 5

PART VIII

Translation research and intercultural mediation

42
INTERCULTURAL MEDIATION IN TRANSLATION AND INTERPRETING STUDIES

Mustapha Taibi

Introduction

The role of a translator or interpreter is to facilitate communication between people who do not share a common language. A translator is expected to have the requisite skills and knowledge to render a written text from a source language into a target language, while an interpreter is expected to demonstrate similar skills, but orally or in sign language. The different aspects of this uncontentious bilingual nature of the work of translators and interpreters have been outlined and specified in various codes of ethics, professional protocols, and internal organization-specific workplace guidelines.

Bilingual communicative events, however, are also bicultural. Recent research has examined the types of cultural differences that may arise in different translated and interpreted settings, the communication barriers that these may engender, and the intercultural mediation required to overcome these barriers to effective communication.

A number of studies have addressed the extent to which this intercultural mediation falls within the scope of the translator or interpreter's role, particularly taking into account their participation in the bilingual and bicultural communicative event and, presumably, the likelihood that they may have bicultural competence, or at least sufficient familiarity with the relevant cultures. Classics such as Vermeer (1986), Snell-Hornby (1988) or Hatim and Mason (1990) have long established that translation and interpreting consist of mediation between cultural contexts, rather than just between language structures. These and other authors agree that translators and interpreters need to be bicultural, if not pluricultural. Hatim and Mason (1990, 223), for instance, affirm that "the translator has not only a bilingual ability but also a bi-cultural vision. Translators mediate between cultures (including ideologies, moral systems and sociopolitical structures), seeking to overcome those incompatibilities which stand in the way of transfer of meaning."

However, the nature and scope of intercultural mediation in translation and interpreting is still a thorny and controversial issue. This chapter provides a brief review of relevant literature and a discussion of the type(s) of mediation involved in translation and interpreting, and the role of translators and interpreters in this regard. Due to space limitations, the review is by no means exhaustive.

Intercultural mediation in translation and interpreting

While the focus in early translation studies was on source and target texts, it is now placed on translators as mediators: their professional identities, the clients for whom they mediate, and the social impact they have (Pym 2006). Snell-Hornby (2012, 372) argues that the future of translation

DOI: 10.4324/9781003227441-51

studies lies in "rediscovering the role of translators and translation scholars as intercultural communicators and mediators." While it is uncontroversial that language and culture are interconnected and that translation and interpreting involve mediation between texts, people, and cultural contexts, the notion of 'mediation' has been used in different senses and has therefore been problematic.

Pöchhacker (2008, 10) explains the source of the confusion by going back to the dictionary meanings of 'mediation':

- "intervention between conflicting parties or viewpoints to promote reconciliation, settlement, compromise or understanding";
- "the function or activity of an intermediate means or instrumentality of transmission";
- "intercession of one power between other powers at their invitation or with their consent to conciliate differences between them."

Pöchhacker proposes a useful distinction between three types of mediation:

1　Cultural/linguistic (intercultural relations): translation and interpreting as linguistic as well as cultural mediation, as the source text/discourse is understood in its original linguistic and cultural context and transferred (through a mediation or adaptation process) to a new language and culture.
2　Cognitive (conceptual relations): translation and interpreting involve mental processing and, therefore, a level of translator/interpreter subjectivity (i.e., impact of their personal filters: socio-cultural background, beliefs, attitudes, and so on).
3　Contractual (social relations): mediation in the sense of management of social relations and intervention to resolve conflicts and promote understanding.

While it is widely accepted that the first two categories apply to translation and interpreting, what Pöchhacker labels as 'contractual mediation' is both fuzzy and controversial. In community and business interpreting, in particular, there is often room for interpreters to coordinate participant turns, provide clarifications, and mitigate potentially disruptive or face-threatening acts (Wadensjö 1998). This brings interpreter role closer to the contractual type of mediation (Pöchhacker 2008, 14). However, contractual mediation is more closely associated with other occupations (e.g., cultural mediator, social mediator, etc.) whose main remit is conflict prevention and resolution rather than linguacultural mediation. As Katan and Taibi (2021, 29) note,

> Translators and interpreters generally 'mediate' between cultures in a figurative and implicit sense. Cultural mediators, on the other hand, mediate between people from different cultural backgrounds in a literal and contractual sense: advising, ironing out differences and avoiding and/or resolving conflicts.

As is discussed below, the role of interpreters in interactional settings may involve some interventions which blur boundaries between linguistic-cultural and cognitive mediation on the one hand and contractual mediation on the other, but it is clear that professional translators and interpreters are not social mediators or cultural advisors.

The need for intercultural mediation

Translation beyond language mediation

Literary translation is one of the areas where intercultural mediation in translation has been widely studied. To provide just one illustrative example, Bedeker and Feinauer (2006) analyze and critique the methodology of cultural transfer employed by literary translators, namely Janie Oosthuysen's Afrikaans translations of two volumes of Harry Potter. The authors reiterate that translation involves more than the transfer of word meaning, as the English and Afrikaans readerships are different, and a decision must always be made between domestication and foreignization. For instance, the source text includes culture-specific references, such as English cuisine and clothing items. "Although Afrikaans has no semantic equivalents for these terms, using the linguistic equivalents is no solution, as they are not familiar terms in South Africa" (Bedeker and Feinauer 2006, 136).

Regardless of the strategies used by literary translators or the manner in which they define their role, the meeting of two languages will inevitably give rise to an intercultural encounter and the translator therefore must take some action that goes well beyond the simple transfer of words. As Bedeker and Feinauer (2006, 139) conclude, the translator needs to have intercultural communication expertise to "apply successful translation strategies during the production of a cross-cultural communicative instrument that functions optimally in the target culture."

Another area where the need for intercultural mediation in translation has been highlighted is international business and marketing. Katan and Taibi (2021, 10) provide some clear examples where accurate translation without regard to intercultural mediation may backfire and fail to meet the requirements of the context. Product labelling for international markets is subject to different regulations and legislation as well as different cultural norms and expectations. Such cross-cultural differences are all "part of the 'something extra' a translator or interpreter will need to know" (Katan and Taibi 2021, 11). A translator in such situations will have to balance the role of language transfer with the role of intercultural mediation.

Even in academic translation, where intercultural issues are perhaps less expected, it has been shown that translators cannot do an optimal job without cultural mediation. Bennett (2013) identifies a significant imbalance between English-language academic papers and those written in other languages. She notes that not only are the writing styles disparate, but English-language academia also tends to be unaware of the intellectual traditions and writing styles of other language groups. The global dominance of English has begun to influence the style of non-English academic papers, and when these are drafted in a style at odds with the dominant English-language tradition, the question for the translator is whether their translations will be publishable without significant mediation between culture-specific academic discourses.

For example, from approximately the 17th century the plain language style started to be the norm for English scientific texts, partly due to an ideological rejection of the Catholic Church in favor of Protestantism. In some South European countries, on the other hand, the Catholic Church has fostered writing styles characterized by "verbal copiousness and complexity," "long elaborate sentences with complex subordination, (...) with figures of speech designed to create particular effects in the reader" (Bennett 2013, 98). A translator mediating such texts is therefore between a rock and a hard place: either opt for cultural representation and reflect the original style or be pragmatic and undertake stylistic adaptations to enhance publication chances.

Interpreting as interpersonal mediation

A significant body of research has likewise been conducted on the need for intercultural mediation in interpreted communicative events. The degree to which this is required varies depending on the field of discourse and the scenario in which the communicative event takes place. This section focuses on community and business interpreting, two types of interpreting that are arguably the most relevant to intercultural mediation because of the close interpersonal contact they involve.

Legal interpreting is one of the settings where interpreter role is most restricted. However, even here some level of intercultural mediation is required. Hale (2014) cites a range of communicative aspects rooted in culture that may lead to sociopragmatic failure. She defines sociopragmatic failure as relating to "misunderstandings caused by the different types of behaviour that are considered appropriate in certain settings by different languages and cultures" (Hale 2014, 323). Behaviours cited include the appropriate amount of silence in speech, turn taking, body language, pitch and volume. As it is entirely plausible that the interpreter is the only person with the necessary bicultural knowledge, the question of intercultural mediation in the interpreted setting arises yet again.

In other less regimented settings, such as healthcare, research has found that interpreters often take on active roles in terms of intercultural mediation and management of interpersonal encounters. Angelelli conducted a study of medical interpreting at California Hope, a public hospital in the United States. She found that the interpreters conducted extensive intercultural mediation in the course of their work, and would choose to "take the lead in a line of questioning," "generate specific questions," "extract the information" that the healthcare professional may wish to know and "discern the relevant pieces [of information] from the irrelevant ones" (Angelelli 2004, 129–32). This team of interpreters often felt that their overriding duty was to aid the (often vulnerable) patients, not only facilitate communication between them and healthcare professionals. Examples of interpreter interventions included interrupting a patient to refocus their speech turn, and editing and summarizing patient narratives. "When interpreters do this, they consider themselves to be bridges for the different levels of the cross-linguistic and cross-cultural encounter," Angelelli (2004, 130) explains.

One of the main reasons why community interpreters engage in this type of mediation is that there are knowledge, power, and cultural gaps between service providers and users. As Martín and Phelan (2010, 12) note in relation to health care:

> [O]ur cultural background will determine how we view health and health care, what affects our health status as well as who should deliver health services. Where to get health services and what to expect from them is also influenced by our cultural background as is how we interact with [healthcare professionals].

Some minority language speakers, such as migrants and refugees, may therefore require additional assistance in accessing healthcare and other public services. Similarly, public service providers will need intercultural mediation to understand their clients and manage their cases effectively.

Differences in cultural assumptions and power dynamics may give rise to a number of intercultural and interpersonal issues between public service providers and their clients, which complicate the interpreter's task and raise ethical dilemmas. Through interpreter narratives, Cho (2022) mentions several situations where intercultural mediation is required in medical settings. These include communication of bad news to patients, and patients' failure to respond in a way that would maximize their own well-being, as a result of cultural expectations. A patient may feel it inappropriate to question doctors, to express a lack of understanding or to request clarifications. Cho cites one medical interpreter's view:

> Sometimes, patients don't ask, when they have to. I then say why are you not asking this. It is something really important and they need to ask, so I say why are you not asking, please tell me. You should have duty of care. Especially for people who are sick.
>
> *(Cho 2022, 62–3)*

Another setting Cho covers in her book is business interpreting. She provides some examples of elaborate, off-topic communication styles used by older Korean men which, whilst fully appropriate within the realm of business in Korean culture, are inappropriate and even incomprehensible to their non-Korean business counterparts. An interpreter who is wholly faithful to the source message risks alienating the non-Korean-speaking party—clearly not the intention of the Korean speaker. Examples presented of intercultural mediation in such scenarios include the interpreter's decision to substitute the source utterance with 'generic expressions such as "nice to meet you" or "look forward to the meeting"' or to recontextualize the utterance into a form that the non-Korean visitors would find less jarring (Cho 2022, 30–1). These actions are clear instances of intercultural mediation performed well beyond the traditionally accepted scope of interpreting, with the aim of achieving pragmatic equivalence and generating the intended effect in the other party to the communicative event.

There are, of course, many other settings in which communication is facilitated by an interpreter, and invariably the question of intercultural mediation is key when there is an impediment to communication brought about by cultural differences. Katan and Taibi (2021, 23) point out that community interpreters and media interpreters "consistently intervene proactively, to ensure that communication continues smoothly across the interpersonal and cultural divides." Hlavac and Xu (2020, 53), in their discussion of the aspects of intercultural communication that arise in interpreted exchanges between Chinese and English speakers, agree that where communicative acts—including non-verbal ones—are likely to be perceived differently across cultures, it is incumbent on interpreters to communicate the intended meaning to the addressee, to avoid misunderstanding and conflict.

Whilst the following section covers views regarding the extent to which this duty is incumbent upon interpreters rather than other parties to the communicative event, it is clear that in many circumstances a total lack of intercultural mediation can lead to miscommunication or a communication breakdown.

Intercultural mediation and the role of translators and interpreters

If it is accepted that there is a need for intercultural mediation in translation and interpreting, the resultant question is: Whose responsibility is it? There appears to be a far greater divergence of opinions on who is best to fill the role of intercultural mediator than there is on whether cultural mediation is required. Also, the question appears to be more contentious in interpreting—especially in community settings—than in translation.

Translators as primary intercultural mediators

In translation there is normally less interaction with other parties than in interpreting. In some situations (e.g., executive assistant translating their supervisor's letters, or a literary translator who has direct contact with the author), there may be room for discussion and joint decision making. Otherwise, the translator is left only with their own education, professional experience, cultural knowledge, attitude towards intercultural communication, and translation brief, if any. In other words, unless there are specific author/publisher guidelines, the type and scope of intercultural mediation is largely decided by the translator. In Bedeker and Feinauer's discussion of the Afrikaans translations of *Harry Potter*, there is an assumption that the requisite intercultural mediation forms an inherent part of the translator's work. On this basis, the focus is more on "the necessity for the translator to be fully informed of the cultural markers in the source text" (2006, 137) and their competence in making these appropriately accessible to the target audience.

In the case of academic translations, Bennett (2013) argues that the requirement for mediation pits the need for extensive reformulation against preservation of the voice and identity of the original author. She notes that both options are critical, although they are at times at odds with each other. She posits that intercultural mediation is incumbent upon the translator, but underpinning this mediation is an ability to negotiate between their own ideal translation and the original author, and indeed also the other parties, such as editors and referees. The key to this strategy is quite aptly identified as educating all the parties involved in the translation on the different academic cultures underlying the two language groups, arguably more so than may be the case in other fields of translation:

> In such situations, the translator's role as mediator becomes particularly important. She needs to be able to explain to the author why certain formulations are more acceptable in English than others without seeming to subscribe unequivocally to the values encoded in them, and to show sympathy in the face of his epistemological predicament. Indeed, such situations may cause considerable distress.
>
> *(Bennett 2013, 102)*

The translator is often the only party to the process who is able to identify the need for intercultural mediation and provide it, whilst they are also likely to be the party most constrained by role perception and the paramount regard for accuracy. As Bassnett (2011, 102) affirms, the translator is "expected to go far beyond what is actually expressed and has to endeavor to second-guess the unexpressed," but this also raises questions about the extent to which this diminishes the translator's respect for the source text and the extent of leeway they may have.

However, saying that the translator is the primary intercultural mediator in translation should not blind us to the social, political and ideological context in which translation is undertaken. Under the translation brief and publisher guidelines mentioned above can lie a number of social factors and agents who may have a major impact on the type, extent and orientation of intercultural mediation through translation. Intercultural mediation is usually understood in the sense of facilitating intercultural understanding, but it can also take the form of political, religious, or cultural censorship (see e.g., Fernández and Evans 2018; McLaughlin and Muñoz-Basols 2021), or domestication as a form of power and conformity to dominant discourse (see e.g., Venuti 1998; Faiq 2016).

Between 'interpreters' and 'cultural mediators'

Angelelli's study above reveals that some medical interpreters already tend to take the lead in providing intercultural mediation as a part of their duties. Regardless of whether interpreters are qualified to take on this role, the author notes that this is indeed what is happening, whilst simultaneously acknowledging that "when [interpreters] facilitate communication, providers must be aware that they may no longer be in complete control of what is said during the medical encounter" (Angelelli 2004, 136). The interpreter's intercultural mediation thus places an additional burden on them and, at the same time, endows them with more power.

Martín and Phelan's analysis of the Irish medical system, on the other hand, draws a clear distinction between interpreters, whose role is limited to overcoming a language barrier, and cultural mediators, whose role conversely involves overcoming a cultural barrier (see cultural-linguistic vs. contractual mediation above). In Ireland, both roles exist, but they are distinct and complementary. The authors identify not just the added responsibility mentioned above that intercultural mediation would place upon an interpreter, but also the importance of professionals being qualified in the services they provide: "When interpreters move out of their role of bridging the language barrier, they are moving into a very grey area for which they are unqualified and where they may in fact cause harm" (Martín and Phelan 2010, 8).

Martín and Phelan also identify several other pitfalls of interpreters acting as cultural mediators, such as an assumption on the part of the healthcare user that an interpreter from the same cultural and linguistic background may consequently be present in order to act as an advocate. There also exists the consideration that a shared language is not synonymous with a shared culture.

The authors additionally indicate that, in some situations, it is appropriate for intercultural mediators to express their opinions. This is clearly one boundary between the roles of an intercultural mediator and an interpreter, as interpreter codes of ethics bar interpreters from voicing an opinion. As Martín and Phelan (2010, 10) note, "it is difficult to reconcile advocacy with impartiality because if impartiality is to be a central tenet of a code of ethics, it is evident that an interpreter cannot advocate for the [healthcare user]."

Cho's analysis of business interpreting involving Korean and non-Korean clients demonstrates that interpreters find intercultural mediation a natural component of their job, although they acknowledge that greater intercultural mediation is provided at the expense of message accuracy:

> [There is] a shared view of the informants that they are not mere linguistic mediators but rather active participants in communicative events … . The analysis highlights that the informants have a strong sense of responsibility for achieving communication success by actively playing agentive roles.
>
> *(Cho 2022, 21)*

This is consistent with earlier studies such as Takimoto's (2006), which showed that the participant Japanese business interpreters saw themselves as proactively involved in the intercultural communicative situations they interpreted in. They expressed opinions, advised on business protocol, provided summarized interpreting, and sought clarification on behalf of their Japanese clients. Whereas this active intercultural mediation tends to be viewed in much of the Western world as less professional and is often proscribed by interpreter codes of ethics, certain cultural contexts and interpreting settings (e.g., media or business) require more flexibility (Katan and Taibi 2021, 22–3).

Hale indicates a lack of consistency amongst surveyed court interpreters as to whether, when and how they alert courts to possible intercultural communication breakdowns. There was no consensus regarding whether interpreters believed this to be within the scope of their role or how much sway their opinions should hold. The study found that the great majority (87%) of judicial officers surveyed expected interpreters to alert them to intercultural misunderstandings. Clearly, there is cause for concern where judicial officers hold an expectation of certain behaviors on the part of interpreters and are unaware that many do not act in accordance with such expectations because they are beyond the scope of their role. Hale (2014, 330) concludes:

> This is undoubtedly a topic that raises many questions, both theoretical and logistical. Both parties—interpreters and judicial officers/tribunal members—are not certain about the best way to proceed in such situations and call for clear protocols and guidelines that they can follow.

The uncertainties surrounding intercultural mediation in interpreting are mainly due to three reasons:

1 Confusion of the different senses of mediation, as explained above, which Pöchhacker's (2008) deconstruction can resolve to a great extent. Thus, professional interpreting and the work of cultural mediators are separate and complementary occupations (Martín and Phelan 2010, 10), one offering linguistic-cultural mediation embedded in the act of interpreting, and the other offering intercultural mediation in the sense of prevention and redress of cultural conflict.
2 Lack of differentiation between interpreting settings: As Angelelli (2008, 151) points out, there tends to be a "[b]lind transfer of standards across settings," while interpreting is a situated professional practice and interpreters' role perceptions, behaviors and performance vary from one setting to another. Katan and Taibi (2021, 29) agree that "contextual factors are sometimes overlooked in the discussion of translator/interpreter leeway and intervention as a language professional with cultural knowledge."
3 Inconsistencies between professional codes of ethics and the complexity of interpreter role as demonstrated in research findings (e.g., Wadensjö 1998, Roy 2000). Research has shown that,

especially in interactional settings, interpreters draw on both linguistic and cultural skills to act as communication partners, co-constructors and facilitators, but there is still a significant gap between this reality and professional standards of practice (Angelelli 2008, 149–51).

Conclusion

Language and culture are inextricably intertwined, which makes it axiomatic that mediation between languages through translation/interpreting involves both linguistic and intercultural mediation. However, 'intercultural mediation' has been both conceptually imprecise and operationally controversial in translation and interpreting studies. Conceptually, Pöchhacker's (2008) classification of the types of mediation goes a long way towards clarifying what interpreters (and translators) may mediate. Operationally, the extent to which a translator/interpreter offers intercultural mediation depends on many factors, including the genre and task at hand, professional identity, applicable guidelines and protocols, client specifications, and self-assessment of intercultural expertise.

Although translation and interpreting share several features relating to meaning transfer, there are considerable differences between the two in terms of intercultural mediation. The most salient of these is the interactional and interpersonal nature of interpreting in contrast with the more 'static' nature of translation. Genre and setting distinctions are also necessary within both translation and interpreting to have a better understanding of the nature and scope of intercultural mediation required in each.

References

Angelelli, Claudia V. 2004. *Medical Interpreting and Cross-Cultural Communication*. Cambridge: Cambridge University Press. 10.1017/CBO9780511486616

Angelelli, Claudia V. 2008. "The Role of the Interpreter in the Healthcare Setting: A Plea for a Dialogue between Research and Practice." In Cros*sing Borders in Community Interpreting*, edited by Carmen Valero-Garcés and Anne Martin, 147–163. Amsterdam: John Benjamins. 10.1075/btl.76.08ang

Bassnett, Susan. 2011. "The Translator as Cross-cultural Mediator." in *The Oxford Handbook of Translation Studies*, edited by Kirsten Malmkjær and Kevin Windle, 94–107. Oxford: Oxford University Press. 10.1093/oxfordhb/9780199239306.013.0008

Bedeker, Laetitia, and Ilse Feinauer. 2006. "The Translator as Cultural Mediator." *Southern African Linguistics and Applied Language Studies* 24 (2): 133–141. 10.2989/16073610609486412

Bennett, Karen. 2013. "The Translator as Cultural Mediator in Research Publication." In *Supporting Research Writing. Roles and Challenges in Multilingual Settings*, edited by Valerie Matarese, 93–106. Oxford: Chandos Publishing. 10.1016/B978-1-84334-666-1.50006-0

Cho, Jinhyun. 2022. *Intercultural Communication in Interpreting: Power and Choices*. New York: Routledge. 10.4324/9781003179993

Fernández, Fruela, and Jonathan Evans eds. 2018. *The Routledge Handbook of Translation and Politics*. Abingdon: Routledge. 10.4324/9781315621289

Faiq, Said. 2016. "Through the Master Discourse of Translation." In *New Insights into Arabic Translation and Interpreting*, edited by Mustapha Taibi, 7–21. Bristol, Blue Ridge Summit: Multilingual Matters. 10.21832/9781783095254-003

Hale, Sandra. 2014. "Interpreting Culture. Dealing with Cross-Cultural Issues in Court Interpreting." *Perspectives* 22 (3): 321–331. 10.1080/0907676X.2013.827226

Hatim, Basil, and Ian Mason. 1990. *Discourse and the Translator*. Harlow: Longman.

Hlavac, Jim, and Zhichang Xu. 2020. *Chinese–English Interpreting and Intercultural Communication*. New York: Routledge. 10.4324/9781315618111

Katan, David, and Mustapha Taibi. 2021. *Translating Cultures: An Introduction for Translators, Interpreters and Mediators*. 3rd ed. London, New York: Routledge. 10.4324/9781003178170.

Martín, Mayte, and Mary Phelan. 2010. "Interpreters and Cultural Mediators—Different but Complementary Roles." *Translocations: Migration and Social Change*. http://doras.dcu.ie/16481/1/Martin_and_Phelan_Translocations.pdf

McLaughlin, Martin, and Javier Muñoz-Basols. 2021. *Ideology, Censorship and Translation*. London, New York: Routledge.

Pöchhacker, Franz. 2008. "Interpreting as Mediation." In *Crossing Borders in Community Interpreting*, edited by Carmen Valero-Garcés and Anne Martin, 76:9–26. Amsterdam: John Benjamins. 10.1075/btl.76.02poc

Pym, Anthony. 2006. "Introduction: On the Social and Cultural in Translation Studies." In *Sociocultural Aspects of Translating and Interpreting*, edited by Anthony Pym, Miriam Shlesinger, and Zuzana Jettmarová, 67:1–25. Amsterdam: John Benjamins. 10.1075/btl.67.02pym

Roy, Cynthia. 2000. *Interpreting as a Discourse Process*. Oxford: Oxford University Press.

Snell-Hornby, Mary. 1988. *Translation Studies: An Integrated Approach*. Amsterdam: John Benjamins. 10.1075/z.38

Snell-Hornby, Mary. 2012. "From the Fall of the Wall to Facebook. Translation Studies in Europe Twenty Years Later." *Perspectives* 20 (3): 365–373. 10.1080/0907676X.2012.702403

Takimoto, Masato. 2006. "Interpreters' Role Perceptions in Business Dialogue Interpreting Situations." *Monash University Linguistics Papers*, 5 (1): 47–57.

Venuti, Lawrence. 1998. *The Scandals of Translation*. London, New York: Routledge. 10.4324/9780203047873.

Vermeer, Hans. 1986. "Übersetzen als kultureller Transfer." In *Übersetzungswissenschaft—Eine Neuorientierung*, edited by Mary Snell-Hornby, 30–53. Tübingen: Francke.

Wadensjö, Cecilia. 1998. *Interpreting as Interaction*. London, New York: Longman.

43

TRANSLATION AS INTERCULTURAL MEDIATION—THE EVOLUTION OF A PARADIGM

Cinzia Spinzi

Introduction

As society becomes more globally connected, where contact with the *Other* is enhanced both physically and virtually, the ability to communicate across cultural boundaries is, effectively, a significant challenge. However, if, on the one hand, globalization reduces diversity by homogenizing discursive practices, on the other hand, it emphasizes plurality. Hence, in an increasingly transcultural world, it is perhaps unsurprising that the practice of intercultural mediation is gaining momentum, as this volume shows. Despite its being a source of cultural enrichment and creativity, cultural diversity may also be a potential source of conflict as it inevitably leads to a clash of heterogeneous value systems, each one deeply rooted in its respective society. Therefore, a greater awareness of cross-cultural differences is indispensable for mutual understanding. This *struggle* between flux and distance reinforces the importance of mediating, the essence of which "is to shape exchanges between the participating societies so that the contact will benefit those cultures, on terms consistent with their respective value systems" (Bochner 1981, 3).

Since Steiner (1975/1998, 49), translation has been positioned on the broader background of communication by many scholars and, except for David Katan (2004; 2009; 2013), the link between translation and Intercultural Communication (henceforth IC) is under-explored on "a firm linguistic basis" (House 2012, 497). Given the profound parallel shifts in both disciplines—Translation Studies (henceforth TS) and IC—it is imperative to shed light on the conceptual categories needed to interpret the processes involved. While seemingly obvious, this observation offers an exciting insight into the characteristics that make up each society and influence any discipline. This chapter aims to nudge the discussion towards the epistemological and ontological evolution of the equation of translation as intercultural mediation (henceforth IM). It starts with how it came about in both TS and IC; then, where translation encounters mediation in a more constructive direction by critically exploring its borders, strengths, and shortcomings. Furthermore, this chapter also challenges the assumption that neutrality is—or can ever be—an inherent characteristic of mediation, or indeed can be a *sine qua non* basis of any academic investigation; and that includes TS.

Interdisciplinary epistemological shifts: The birth of a paradigm

The epistemological skepticism, which started to permeate the humanities in the 1970s, had many origins: The disintegration of fixed borders, greater mobility, a rise of multiculturalism, and the

408

DOI: 10.4324/9781003227441-52

emergence of West-East differences (see Bachmann-Medick 2016). During this same period, physicist Werner Heisenberg's ground-breaking discovery also affected the epistemological foundations of scientific observation. Heisenberg's work on quantum mechanics (i.e., the relationships between subatomic particles) led to the famous conclusion that it is impossible to observe the speed and direction of a particle simultaneously. This principle of *indeterminacy* deeply informed many disciplines (Riediger 2018, 28), including that of TS, which was, at that time, still in its infancy.

Together with the anthropological turn (Bachmann-Medick 2016), the exemplary problems—in a Kuhnian sense—of these impulses were encapsulated in Hall's work (1959) and boosted the interface of disciplines from the humanities. Also crucial in this respect is the influence of Cultural Studies, which was expanding in Anglo-Saxon academia from the late 1970s; the post-positivist conception of culture revolutionized international research and challenged consolidated truths. Undoubtedly, Derrida's deconstructionism of the Western system of knowledge and his concept of 'différance' contributed to questioning traditional epistemological methods by assuming that no original truth exists, but only differences and contradictions. Moreover, the gradual shift of the researcher from the role of absolute objective observer to the more culturally relativistic role of participating agent brings with it the awareness of the scientific text as a *representation* of the individual scholar's subjective interpretation (Rudvin 2006, 24).

The cultural reorientation of translation research—the so-called *cultural turn* (Bassnett and Lefevere 1990)—dates back to the late 1980s, when the concept of translation went beyond that of automatic re-codification of texts. Dichotomous concepts such as original/copy, source/target, fidelity/freedom began to give way to new central categories, namely cultural representation, displacement, and, above all, otherness, difference, and diversity. Gradually, these notions became valued rather than criticized.

The impact of extra-textual factors on translation shattered the by-now old linguistic paradigm rigidly based on the positivist concept of equivalence between the original and target texts. Nida's (1964) change of perspective from the author-oriented slant to the receptor-oriented theory, and Newmark's focus (2001/1988) on the meaning of the text and the intention of the translator, introduced a shift in approach, resulting in the grip on the equivalence paradigm being loosened. A more profound breakthrough came with Lefevere (1992), whose concept of translation as the re-writing of an original text paved the way for translation as an act of communication. There is no doubt that the new ontological transformation of translation towards a sociological orientation, which served the needs of the ideology and poetics of a given society, called for a re-definition of the role of the translator. The translator came to be seen as a textual 'manipulator' (Lefevere 1992), a re-contextualizer and, in a broad sense, a cultural mediator (Taft 1981). If cultural context is given prominence in communication, then culture unconsciously endorses translators to act as cultural mediators (Katan 2004).

Within this vision of translation as an act of communication—intra-culturally and inter-culturally—translation entails forms of textual rewritings; this is especially apparent when addressing culture-bound terms that need to be adapted to a new cultural context. The existence of language barriers, ethnic boundaries, and a variety of textual and cultural policies cannot be ignored; translators re-create an image of the original influenced by ideology, poetics, and the expectations of the translation recipients.

All these epistemological reflection models, as said earlier, were influenced and nourished by the modern discipline of anthropology. If through Boas (1887), cultural relativism moved the focus away from the earlier sphere of colonial ethnographical investigation, Malinowski (1923) developed the notion of 'context of culture' and pointed out that in translation, implicit layers of meanings should be made explicit to be accessible to outsiders. From this perspective, and above all with Geertz's (1973) idea that human beings are caught in the web of culture while being at the same time weavers of the web's threads, culture is continuously negotiated by the people involved and is linked to the changes that they undergo and implement every day in their relationships with others. Relying on Geertz, Katan (2009) highlights that the dynamic 'look' of culture fits in well with the interculturalist development of a culture of openness since, by reflecting on their culture-bound experience, both interculturalist trainers and trainees are actively involved in the learning process. Katan's anthropological perspective of culture as a "shared model of the world, a hierarchical system of congruent and interrelated beliefs, values and strategies which can guide action and interaction, depending on cognitive context" (2009, 70) is instrumental to the understanding of the paradigm of translation as IM in that it seems to fulfill the translational purposes. Adopting Hall's iceberg model, where visible cultural aspects are above the water level and a more significant portion hidden beneath the surface, Katan (2009) distinguishes three basic levels of culture. Firstly, there is a technical level where culture is acquired through verbally explicit information. Secondly, there is a formal level linked to conversational rules—what is accepted and what is not—in social life, which is also the level most appropriately linked to the notions of *norm* and *skopos* developed in TS. Finally, there is the level of an unconscious, informal culture, which is the level of values linked to the culture and beliefs that guide cultural choices at a formal level.

Post-positivists introduced a slightly different view of culture as a vital dimension of reality's continuous transformation and construction. Translators are subjected to social and ideological pressures in order to conform to the practices established by society; culture is not so much seen as a hierarchical system divided into levels but as an integrated system through which textual meanings must be negotiated. From this perspective, the figure of the translator is no longer that of a cultural mediator but that of an agent of social change. This view, which I would argue has resulted in increased visibility of the role of the translator, has led to a distinction between *translation as mediation* and *translation as re-narration*. These epistemological changes then, which move away from an essentialist conception of culture and translation models to accommodate sociological orientation in translation and the view of culture as a process of meaning, have led translation scholars to approach their work from an intercultural communication angle.

When translation encounters intercultural mediation

Parallel shifts to those described in the previous section also concern the field of IC, which mushroomed into a discipline—or better, a prototypical discipline—due to increasing global contact on the one hand, and technological surges on the other. This ran parallel to a need to articulate phenomena such as *acculturation, culture shock, conflict management*, and *mediation* that started to emerge in academic literature (Rudvin and Spinzi 2015). These shifts may be described as moving from cross-national comparison to critical contexts of meaning-making (Hamaidia et al. 2018). For clarity, IC is considered in this chapter in its non-essentialist conceptualization as any communication-based encounter where "linguistic and/or cultural differences become relevant for processing the outcomes of interlingual communication" (ten Thije 2020, 35). For successful communication, these linguistic and cultural asymmetries, both at the verbal and written levels, require an act of mediation to be neutralized. Unlike the interpreter who constructs texts while mediating the interaction, the translator works with other people's written texts. In most cases, he/she does not receive any feedback from the author (Shäffner 2003). This means that the translator is the only intercultural mediator between the author and the reader, different from any act of intercultural communication where participants are deliberately involved (Liddicoat 2016). Mediation then is more constrained in translation than in interpreting, or in other intercultural encounters, given the presence of the two monolithic entities that do not engage with each other dialogically.

Since mediation covers numerous notions and issues within the different approaches to IC, it repeatedly surfaces, as noted by Busch and Schröder (2005) in ten Thije (2020, 36). Indeed, Translation and Intercultural Studies have a lot in common in their focus on translation and mediation; they share some of the same tools and approaches (e.g., comparative studies; second-language acquisition), which might be of mutual benefit. Relying on ten Thije's (2020, 36) insightful outline of the approaches to IC (i.e., interactive, contrastive, cultural representation, multilingualism, and transfer approaches), translation as IM is more relevant in the interactive, the contrastive, and the transfer approaches. In contrast, translation and interpreting are a means for mutual understanding in multilingual settings where English is used as a Lingua Franca.

The functionalist meaning of translation as IM is visible in the contrastive approach to IC, where mediation is necessary for solving linguistic and cultural problems. This is done through the translator's competence in locating functional equivalences whose aim is to re-create or reproduce the function of the original text in its linguaculture in the translated text. Contributions from Intercultural Studies (Hofstede 2001) have been enlightening in this regard, alongside Hall's theory of *contexting*, a meta-orientation that concerns the amount of information shared in a context of a situation and based on which communication is more text- or context-oriented. Functional equivalences are found when operating at the base of the iceberg, i.e., the informal culture, which is characterized by thinking patterns or structured filters which influence how "reality is modelled," i.e., which aspects are to be generalized, distorted, and deleted (Katan 2004, 230). This dialogue between IC and functional theories in translation has inspired a strand of specialized translation (see Manca 2012 in the field of tourism) where mediation is the *conditio sine qua non* for the transfer of cultural meanings.

The interactive approach to IC, which addresses the application of perspectivizing strategies in intercultural and mediated encounters, brings to the fore those pragmatic features which characterize a verbal encounter more than a written text. In this case, mediation entails meta-pragmatic awareness, i.e., an instantiation of a third-party perspective. In conflictual interactions, divergences and idiosyncrasies are highlighted, rather than obscured, and some linguistic and interactional features are used to signal tension ("contextualization cues" in Gumperz 1982). These features may be overt, or they may be diffuse and vary markedly across cultures. IM here starts from the awareness of cultural frames "that shape interpretation of pragmatic acts in each language, how these differ across languages, and what the consequences of these differences are for the use of these languages in intercultural communication" (McConachy and Liddicoat 2016, 17). Reflections on such issues of pragmatics, interconnected with our understanding and experience of culture, are added to the conceptualization of mediation as a brokering activity.

In the transfer approach to IC, translation and IM interface through language-learning tools to achieve intercultural competence. Byram (1997) underlines the role of interpreting and translation as specific competencies for relating both cultures to each other. However, the role of translation as IM is more visible in Katan's expansion of Bennett's Developmental Model of Intercultural Sensitivity (2004, 329–40). In this model, which foresees six steps moving from ethnocentrism to ethnor-elativism, the translator is a mediator only in the last step (e.g., integration), after reflecting on his/her ability to *decentre* from the two worldviews and a *mindshift* between them. Also, in Boylan's model (2009, 38), relevance is given to the ability "to accommodate" at the third level, where mediation is necessary to "construct shared meanings across cultural divides, through empathetic decentring and introjection." However, several excellent studies, both in IC (Davies 2012) and in the interpreting strand (Wadensjö 1998), have demonstrated that supposed neutrality is illusory given that the interpreter takes on the role of mediator/facilitator together with one of connecting different institutional practices which are a direct result of the understanding of the self.

The paradigm is undergoing an interpretative (in the hermeneutic sense) evolution. In order to become aware of one's own way of perceiving cultural differences and take ethical responsibility for translation decisions and the resulting impacts, self-reflexivity is needed. Encouraged by the concept of *Critical Cultural Awareness* (Byram 1997, 53), self-reflexivity constrains the translator/mediator to a constant reflection on its products and processes, interacting with the author and the reader.

The translator continuously moves along an interpretative parameter, focusing on the choices made by him/her as the figure at the centre of the research inquiry, embedded in a mediated dialogue between the author and the reader, the *Self* and the *Other*. The shift toward reflexivity and, hence towards a non-essentialist approach also characterizes IC, where a 'move beyond programmatic and "recipe-like" perspectives' (Dervin and Gross 2016, 6) is claimed considering that IC requires flexibility and openness.

In Western academia, the paradigm receiving investigation is undergoing an evolving process that reflects the broader shifts in other disciplines in the humanities. This can be summarized as moving from "the rationalist, unified absolutes of grand theories through the functionalist analysis of the interaction of systems, institutions and practices [...] to a more interdisciplinary interpretative/narrative approach in which a reassessment of ideas has redirected and repositioned earlier assumptions" (Rudvin 2006, 23).

Terminological indeterminacy and paradigmatic shortcomings

In the disciplinary evolution described above, some ontological and conceptual reflections are required to help us consider issues that may be, at the same time, strengths and limitations of the paradigm itself. First of all, the multi-disciplinary and multifaceted aspect of the concept of mediation can be applied to a vast array of settings (e.g., family mediation, linguistic and cultural mediation, healthcare mediation, etc.). Additionally, the parallel use of IM in the sibling discipline of Interpreting Studies has contributed to the terminological turmoil around the expression IM, reflecting the different genealogies and epistemologies following major social and political shifts in different countries. In Interpreting Studies, the term *IM* has also been controversial due to the semantic overlap with other denominations (e.g., Community Interpreter, Public Service Interpreter) boosted by increasing migration and the resulting need for inclusion and integration. In both disciplines, interpreting and translation, even though the epistemological developments have followed different trajectories, the terminological indeterminacy contributes, at least partially, to the lack of professionalization (Pöchhacker 2008). Aside from the semantic branching, the concept of IM (and even before that of *mediation*) presupposes a confrontation with the themes of tension and conflict, which we assume lie in a perceived or actual mismatch of values or expectations between two or more individuals of different cultural backgrounds. Even though a more abstract sense of mediation is embraced, the notion necessarily sets up a relationship between two parties, as shown by the word's etymology. Mediation comes from the Latin *mediatio* or *meditationis*, meaning "intervention with which an agreement is sought." Even earlier (in the late 14th century), the use of the noun *mediacioun* suggests "intervention, agency or action as a mediator or intermediary" (Lenz and Viegas 2019). Be that as it may, a problem, tension, or conflict arises. This entails more than opposites between the two parties and the in-between mediator; it requires intervention to reduce the cultural distance. In the Vygotskyan sense, every intercultural interaction presupposes linguistic and cultural misunderstandings and cognitive clashes, given that in mediated processes, the social and the individual mutually shape one another.

Put differently, IM implies a comparison of "cultural phenomena" in order "to make the strange familiar and the familiar strange" (Alred, Byram, and Fleming 2002, 19) and, inevitably, this bidirectional process of de/familiarization, with the translator filtering his/her own worldview/ideology, entails dynamism (Pöchhacker 2008, 13), transformation, and in some cases, at least in interpreting, unpredictability. In the postmodern era, mediation refers to "the extent to which translators intervene in the transfer process, feeding their own knowledge and beliefs into their processing of a text" (Hatim and Mason 1997, 147). The more the meaning is couched in context, the higher the degree of mediation will be; in other words, contextually shared communication (i.e., high-context communication cultures in Hall's model, see Katan 2016) requires the translator to

Translation as intercultural mediation

intervene to a greater extent. At this point, we encounter the pivotal tension between similarity/difference and subjectivity/objectivity, representing the limitation of the equated paradigm of translation as IM. At the same time, it is also its superior strength. It is a *Catch-22* situation (Rudvin 2006, 31) which includes both relativist and positivist perspectives to language and text and where the de-structured original text results in a new outcome through a process of subjective (cognitive, social, contractual, cultural, and linguistic in Pöchhacker 2008, 13) interpretation. Even though for Baker (2008), the problem is not in the term *mediation* but in how we understand it, she firmly rejects the neutral/objective mediation perspective best represented by functionalists. In her new epistemological framing, i.e., translation as re-narration, which relies on an interpretive hypothesis, activism comes to the fore. Chesterman overcomes the neutrality/intervention impasse by putting forward the concept of *telos*, i.e., "the personal goal of a translator in the context of a given task," as opposed to *skopos*, i.e., more immediate intentions (Baker 2008, 31–2). A *mediating* position is taken by Katan (2016, 367), who, drawing upon neuro-linguistic programming, unravels the question through the different *logical levels*. Whereas mediation aims *to improve understanding*—the more interventional model—*activism in the post-colonial sense* focuses on the *system's inequities*. Thus, two practices of intervention are possible for Katan: the first occurs at the level of language and a deeper cognitive level; the second IM practice concerns the identity and roles of the participants. Even though this might happen when dealing with community interpreting, Katan states that translators may also act as community agents "protecting or emphasizing cultural differences (foreignisation), or equally, they may decide to domesticate the text to foster communication" (2013, 87). The text's degree of intervention can tip the scales between mediation and activism. If the concept of mediation is *pushed* and strained, then translation as IM becomes "an active engagement in diversity as a meaning-making activity that involves interpreting the meaning of diverse others for oneself and for others" (Liddicoat 2016, 355).

I argue here that the limitations of the template of translation equated to IM inevitably come from the slippery word that constitutes the paradigm itself. In the sense of relating two worldviews, mediation is tenable at the formal and informal levels of culture. However, the emphasis on the hermeneutical component of the profession helps to highlight the human dimension of the translation work and recognize how translators become social actors. Since there is no such thing as a neutral communication situation of free dialogue (Spivak 1990), the translator will necessarily affect the outcome, which will, in turn, impact the target society where it will be adapted to its needs. For this reason, in the wake of Katan (2016), a new expression should be used (one viable option is 'transcreation') to avoid the risk of terminological inconsistency, which has repercussions at the professional level. Furthermore, the interface with other disciplines has both advantages and potential pitfalls. Although the interdisciplinary dialogue is mutually beneficial, the term *mediation* potentially contains an intrinsic paradox. It is excessively flexible—semantically speaking—when used in so many different settings and—linguistically speaking—when used with different pre-modifiers.

References

Alred, Geof, Michael Byram, and Mike Fleming eds. 2002. *Intercultural Experience and Education*. Bristol, Blue Ridge Summit: Multilingual Matters. 10.21832/9781853596087

Bachmann-Medick, Doris. 2016. *Cultural Turns: New Orientations in the Study of Culture*. Berlin, Boston: De Gruyter. 10.1515/9783110402988

Baker, Mona. 2008. "Ethics of Renarration: Mona Baker is interviewed by Andrew Chesterman." *Cultus* 1: 10–33.

Bassnett, Susan, and André Lefevere eds. 1990. *Translation, History, and Culture*. London; New York: Pinter.

Boas, Franz. 1887. "Response: Museums of Ethnology and Their Classification." *Science* ns-9 (228): 587–589. 10.1126/science.ns-9.228.587.b

Bochner, Stephen. 1981. "The Social Psychology of Language Mediation." In *The Mediating Person. Bridges between Cultures*, edited by Stephen Bochner. 3–36. Cambridge (MA): Schenkman.

413

Boylan, Patrick. 2009. "Cross-Cultural Accommodation through a Transformation of Consciousness." *Cultus. The Journal of Intercultural Mediation and Communication* 2: 33–48.

Busch, Dominic, and Hartmut Schröder eds. 2005. *Perspektiven interkultureller Mediation: Grundlagentexte zur kommunikationswissenschaftlichen Analyse triadischer Verständigung.* Frankfurt am Main; New York: Lang.

Byram, Michael. 1997. *Teaching and Assessing Intercultural Competence.* Clevedon; Philadelphia: Multilingual Matters.

Davies, Eirlys E. 2012. "Translation and Intercultural Communication: Bridges and Barriers." In *The Handbook of Intercultural Discourse and Communication,* edited by Christina Bratt Paulston, Scott F. Kiesling, and Elizabeth S. Rangel, 367–388. Chichester, UK: Wiley. 10.1002/9781118247273.ch18

Dervin, Fred, and Zehavit Gross. 2016. "Introduction: Towards the Simultaneity of Intercultural Competence." In *Intercultural Competence in Education,* edited by Fred Dervin and Zehavit Gross, 1–10. London: Palgrave Macmillan UK. 10.1057/978-1-137-58733-6_1

Geertz, Clifford. 1973. *The Interpretation of Cultures.* New York: Basic Books.

Gumperz, John J. 1982. *Discourse Strategies.* Cambridge University Press. 10.1017/CBO9780511611834

Hall, Edward T. 1959. *The Silent Language.* New York: Doubleday.

Hamaidia, Lena, Sarah Methven, and Jane Woodin. 2018. "Translation Spaces: Parallel Shifts in Translation and Intercultural Communication Studies and Their Significance for the International Development Field." *Translation Spaces* 7 (1): 119–142. 10.1075/ts.00007.ham

Hatim, Basil, and Ian Mason. 1997. *The Translator as Communicator.* London: Routledge. 10.4324/9780203992722

Hofstede, Geert H. 2001. *Culture's Consequences: Comparing Values, Behaviors, Institutions, and Organizations across Nations.* 2nd ed. Thousand Oaks, CA: Sage.

House, Juliane. 2012. "Translation, Interpreting and Intercultural Communication." In *The Routledge Handbook of Language and Intercultural Communication,* edited by Jane Jackson, 495–509. Abingdon, Oxon; New York: Routledge.

Katan, David. 2004. *Translating Cultures: An Introduction for Translators, Interpreters, and Mediators.* 2nd ed. Manchester, UK; Northampton, MA: St. Jerome.

Katan, David. 2009. "Translation as Intercultural Communication." In *The Routledge Companion to Translation Studies,* edited by Jeremy Munday, 74–92. London: Routledge.

Katan, David. 2013. "Intercultural Mediation." In *Handbook of Translation Studies,* edited by Yves Gambier and Luc van Doorslaer, 4:84–91. *Handbook of Translation Studies.* Amsterdam: John Benjamins. 10.1075/hts.4.int5

Katan, David. 2016. "Translation at the Cross-Roads: Time for the Transcreational Turn?" *Perspectives* 24 (3): 365–381. 10.1080/0907676X.2015.1016049

Lefevere, Andre. 1992. *Translation, Rewriting, and the Manipulation of Literary Fame.* London: Routledge. 10.4324/9781315458496

Lenz, Adriana Janice, and Moacir Fernando Viegas. 2019. "A Mediação de Conflitos Na Educação Numa Perspectiva Dialética e a Prática da Orientadora Educacional." *Revista on Line de Política e Gestão Educacional* 23 (3): 561–575. 10.22633/rpge.v23i3.12483

Liddicoat, Anthony J. 2016. "Translation as Intercultural Mediation: Setting the Scene." *Perspectives* 24 (3): 347–353. 10.1080/0907676X.2015.1125934

Malinowski, Bronislaw. 1923. "The Problem of Meaning in Primitive Languages." In *The Meaning of Meaning: A Study of the Influence of Language upon Thought and of the Science of Symbolism,* edited by Charles K. Ogden and Ivor Armstrong Richards, 451–510. London, New York: Kegan Paul, Trench, Trubner & Co.

Manca, Elena. 2012. "Translating the Language of Tourism Across Cultures: From Functionally Complete Units of Meaning to Cultural Equivalence." *Textus,* XXV (1): 51–68. 10.7370/71234

McConachy, Troy, and Anthony J. Liddicoat. 2016. "Meta-Pragmatic Awareness and Intercultural Competence: The Role of Reflection and Interpretation in Intercultural Mediation." In *Intercultural Competence in Education,* edited by Fred Dervin and Zehavit Gross, 13–30. London: Palgrave Macmillan UK. 10.1057/978-1-137-58733-6_2

Newmark, Peter. 2001. *A Textbook of Translation.* Shanghai: Shanghai Foreign Language Education Press.

Nida, Eugene. 1964. *Toward a Science of Translating.* Shanghai: Shanghai Foreign Language Education Press.

Pöchhacker, Franz. 2008. "Interpreting as Mediation." In *Crossing Borders in Community Interpreting: Definitions and Dilemmas,* edited by Carmen Valero-Garcés and Anne Martin, 76: 9–26. Amsterdam: John Benjamins. 10.1075/btl.76.02poc

Riediger, Hellmut. 2018. *Teorizzare Sulla Traduzione: Punti di Vista, Metodi e Pratica Riflessiva.* Milano: Laboratorio Weaver.

Rudvin, Mette. 2006. "The Cultural Turn in Community Interpreting. A brief analysis of epistemological developments in Community Interpreting literature in the light of paradigm changes in the humanities." In *Taking Stock: Research and Methodology in Community Interpreting, special edition of Linguistica Antverpiensia New Series (5),* edited by Erik Hertog and Bart van der Veer, 21–41. Antwerp: Hoegschool Antwerpen. 10.52034/lanstts.v5i.150

Rudvin, Mette, and Cinzia Spinzi. 2015. "Negotiating the Terminological Borders of 'Language Mediation' in English and Italian. A Discussion on the Repercussions of Terminology on the Practice, Self-Perception and Role of Language Mediators in Italy." *Lingue Culture Mediazioni—Languages Cultures Mediation (LCM Journal)*, no. 1 (2014): 1–2 (February): 57–79. 10.7358/lcm-2014-0102-spin

Shäffner, Cristina. 2003. "Translation and Intercultural Communication: Similarities and Differences". *Studies in Communication Sciences/Studi di scienze della comunicazione* 3(2): 79–107.

Spivak, Gayatri Chakravorty. 1990. *The Post-Colonial Critic. Interviews, Strategies, Dialogues.* New York: Routledge. 10.4324/9780203760048

Steiner, George. 1975 [1998]. *After Babel: Aspects of Language and Translation.* Oxford: Oxford University Press.

Taft, Ronald. 1981 "The Role and Personality of the Mediator." In *The Mediating Person: Bridges between Cultures*, edited by Stephen Bochner, 53–88. Cambridge: Schenkman.

Thije, Jan D. ten. 2020. "What Is Intercultural Communication?" In *The Cambridge Handbook of Intercultural Communication*, edited by Guido Rings and Sebastian Rasinger, 35–55. Cambridge: Cambridge University Press. 10.1017/9781108555067.004

Wadensjö, Cecilia. 1998. *Interpreting as Interaction.* London/New York: Addison Wesley Longman.

44

THE MEDIATING ROLE OF EMPATHY IN COMMUNITY INTERPRETING

Leticia Santamaría Ciordia

Introduction: Quality in interpreting

Traditionally, translation and interpreting studies focused on fidelity or "likeness to the original" (Vinay and Darbelnet 1958) in determining quality. Later, theoretical discussions overthrew fidelity and replaced it with "equivalence" as the core principle to determine quality (Nida and Taber 1982). From that moment, translators and interpreters were empowered to make decisions about whether it was necessary or not to explain, add, or omit parts of the original text/discourse in order to transfer the message and ensure communicative effectiveness.

There has been common agreement about general interpreting principles that could be applied almost to every setting. A study conducted by Kalina (2015) gathered a set of key common ethical principles: discretion, professional secrecy, careful handling of documents received, accuracy, and quality. Rodríguez and Guerrero (2002) analyzed the interpreting ethics codes of twelve countries and provided evidence that impartiality and confidentiality were the only two common principles necessary to ensure quality interpretation. The authors also placed the focus on the persistent gap between theory and practice: "Most noteworthy is the tension between the detached and uninvolved interpreter (often proffered in early textbooks) and the interpreter who actively engages in cooperative acts in a given setting" (2002, 40). Even though newer conceptualizations and wider cognitive models have been introduced over the last years, ethical abilities and moral reasoning patterns that are expected to define community interpreting still highlight detachment as the stronghold of "normative, ethical ideal" (Dean 2015, 40) for maintaining quality performance.

Nevertheless, the challenge when trying to define quality in interpreting is its dynamic nature, which makes it a notion in constant evolution that needs to be adjusted and can often only be measured through users' expectations and needs. In this sense, the multidimensional nature of community interpreting itself makes it necessary to consider adaptability and flexibility as two core principles for codes of ethics in particular settings, in order to meet quality requirements and the changing needs of the interpreter-mediated situation, alongside users' expectations.

Despite the dynamic nature of quality, which hinders measurement, and the fact that it can largely only be approached in terms of the stakeholder's accounts, some best practices for quality assessment and assurance could be suggested (Table 44.1).

Quality, while adhering to rationale standards, as an objective and subjective parameter needs to adapt to a changing reality and needs. Otherwise, quality assessment should be measured on the basis of an evolutionary but consistent approach.

416

DOI: 10.4324/9781003227441-53

Empathy in community interpreting

Table 44.1 Elements of quality assessment in community interpreting

Quality criteria in community interpreting		
Reliability	Coherence	Adjustment
Ensure accuracy	Respect the situational and cultural context	Remain attentive to standards of practice
Ensure trustworthiness	'Unpack' the implicit information and nuances of the discourse	Adapt standards to the specific needs of the situation
Remain attentive to the logic of the discourse	Be idiomatic and communicate effectively	Remain attentive to ethics and social responsibility in practice

Interpreters' positioning and roles: Normative ethics, negotiation, and boundaries

Standard ethical principles in community interpreting involve a conscious intention to take no action in order to support communicative autonomy, defined by Bancroft (2015, 362) as "the capacity of each party in an encounter to be responsible for and in control of his or her own communication." Dean (2015) focused on the role of norms as "a necessary step in the process of professionalization of a field of practice." They help define quality service and allows users to compare their own performance (what they do) with expected practice (what they are supposed to do). On the other hand, attention is drawn to the fact that, "while norms can serve to aid practitioners in ethical decisions, they can also serve to hinder ethical processes" (Dean 2015, 2).

Whereas working conditions have evolved since the profession's early stages, principles of faithfulness, impartiality and confidentiality have hardly changed while urging the interpreter "to maintain an impartial attitude during the course of his interpreting" (Boéri 2015, 36). Besides the conduit, normative role, which has been questioned over the past years, Boéry admits that scholars and professionals still "tend to perceive interpreters' involvement in the communication encounter as restricted to discourse, that is, as changing language structures and making cultural adjustments." For this author, this is "a restricted view of ethics" and a role that future generations are likely to be socialized into through training programs.

Drugan, for his part, argues that professional codes for interpreters are "advisory or educational rather than regulatory in force" (2017, 127), so they could hardly cover all the moral and ethical challenges that interpreters may encounter. As a result of that, in situations where there is or could be more than one right decision, Kalina suggests that "a set of ethical guidelines will, in the ideal case, provide criteria that enable the [interpreter] to adopt one of several possible solutions" (2015, 66). Moreover, Peleg-Baker (2014) challenges the common assumption that decision accuracy is impaired by speed of response and argues that mediation expertise can be acquired by yielding skillful automatic judgments. The author claims that the process of decision making in complex, fast-paced and dynamic conditions, such as mediation, is frequently dominated by decisions and judgments that are automatic and intuitive, especially under pressure and in uncertain environments, as is frequently the case in community interpreting.

Over time, the debate in community interpreting has moved from conduit models to a new core value that had been either ignored or neglected: mediation. From an applied and sociolinguistic point of view, interpreters are actors in sociocultural and institutional contexts and, like other players, contribute to shaping the nature of communication. This dynamic nature of interpreting settings led Leneham and Napier to suggest that many of the guiding ethical principles remain "insufficient in light of shifting requirements for interpreters in varying work contexts" (2003, 95).

Along these lines, authors such as Llewellyn-Jones and Lee (2014), Hojat (2016), and Santamaría Ciordia (2017) have supported the interpreters who are powerful agents as active co-participants and co-constructors of meaning, arguing that the supposed invisibility of the interpreter can be misread as a sign of indifference, rather than neutrality, leading to less openness and cooperation, particularly in more conversational settings and emotionally difficult contexts. Brandt (1979) even goes beyond this by claiming that it would be implausible that a person who shows neither emotional responses nor particular interests could be trusted. Likewise, Dam (2017) labels the demands of neutrality in normative assumptions about what constitutes appropriate behavior as "reductionist ideals, unfulfillable and discomforting."

Norms for interpreters and stakeholders are not necessarily the same. In this sense, Kalina (2015, 71) underlines that "it is essential that all groups should be actively involved when it comes to the definition of standards." Gerskowitch and Tribe (2021, 304) consider this "three-way relationship" as "the most helpful approach," especially in health and social care settings.

Once again, professional integrity is the principle that should regulate the interpreter's action, so as not to turn positive advocacy and the humanization of role models into an intrusive role, with the interpreter taking responsibilities that are beyond their competency, jeopardizing objectivity or projecting their values onto users. Interpreting is not merely a profession, but a social practice responding to basic communication skills. Hlavac (2017, 198) highlights how interpreting studies have undergone a social turn which has allowed "a re-appraisal of phenomena that have never been absent from mediated situations: acknowledgement of social and power relations, advocacy and even activism." In this sense, social responsibility is emerging as a concept intrinsic to many forms of linguistic and intercultural mediation and an important part of community interpreting.

Current perspectives in community interpreting suggest more flexible, context-based procedures, where best practices should rely in a meaningful way on service providers' and interpreters' judgement, flexibility and professional autonomy to avoid losing valuable opportunities for the profession to grow. In this sense, Young (1990, 104), for example, rejects the idea that morality is primarily a matter of impartiality, and even considers the ideal of impartiality "an idealist fiction," since "it is impossible to adopt an unsituated point of view."

On the other hand, the role assumed could also be a reaction to providers' expectations and rarely just a free choice of the interpreter. In part this is because the assumed role is subject to negotiation and highly determined by external factors, the stakeholders being the ones that signal the extent to which they wish to include or exclude the interpreter through linguistic and paralinguistic cues (Santamaría Ciordia 2019, 243). According to Wallace and Nebot (2019), the consideration of such specific factors would lead to different interpreting policies (either instinctive or strategic), different purposes (bureaucratic or enfranchising), and different standards of practice (traditional or innovative).

The so-called 'mythological neutrality' (Bot 2003) should therefore be considered from the point of view of the setting in which the interpreter works; for example, it may be advisable in legal settings, where impartiality is the overriding principle and authorities often demand verbatim rendering, but less so in medical or social settings, where personal involvement may be in the interest of both the patient and the care provider and communication success "can only be offered by the interpreter as he/she is truly the one communicating with the patient" (Moore 2007, 104). Indeed, interpreters need to be able to make congruous, reconcilable ethical decisions in the spectrum between neutrality and advocacy.

Empathy and emotional self-regulation

Treating a person appropriately and respectfully requires emotional and/or cognitive responses such as empathy and sensitivity to the circumstances, needs and values. Eisenberg, Fabes, and Spinrad (2007, 647) differentiate between two types of empathy, affective and cognitive. Whereas the former refers to "an emotional response that stems from another's e motional state or condition" (2007, 647), the latter recognizes empathy as "an awareness [...] of another's state or condition or consciousness." Similarly, Wispé (1986) writes of the distinction between sympathy and empathy and the need to differentiate between the purposes of each one. While the purpose of empathy is to understand the other, sympathy seeks for the other person's well-being: "empathy is a way of knowing, whereas sympathy is a way of relating" (1986, 318). Although affective distance is key to avoiding emotional overinvolvement (a sympathetic behavior), Hojat (2016, 75) argues that "cognitive overindulgence," a feature of empathy, "can always lead to a more accurate judgement."

This also reinforces Bahadir's (2012) view of empathy in interpreting not solely entailing compassion and solidarity but also including the ability to distance oneself from the interlocutors. Blumgart (1964) referred to this approach as "compassionate detachment" or "neutral empathy"; that is, an emotional appreciation of the user's feelings without becoming engulfed by them.

By the same token, Merlini and Gatti (2015, 141) conclude that "a greater perspective-taking capability is associated with more concern for the others and will less distress in the face of others' negative experience," so the more able we cognitive apprehend another person's perspective, the less self-centeredly distressed and the more other-oriented concerned we were. This cognitive dimension of empathy could therefore be understood as "a means of problem solving to complete the institutional task" (Santamaría Ciordia 2019, 261). That said, it cannot be ignored that interpreters working for public services are exposed to emotional and psychological challenges as a result of working in the front line with people who are emotionally distressed from dealing with difficult situations, often with serious legal implications. Indeed, in the 1980s it was recognized that working under stress can have some immediate and long-term effects on assisting professionals that cannot be ignored, e.g., vicarious traumatization, secondary traumatic stress, professional burnout or compassion fatigue—"the cost of caring" (Figley 1995). In a survey conducted by Crezee et al. (2013), almost 100 interpreters in refugee settings were interviewed and asked whether they felt their training had prepared them for traumatic or sensitive content. Almost half of them (48%) felt that "although training had prepared them to some extent, it was insufficient," and 67% of them recognized that "they had not had access to counselling." They also added that the need for counselling "very much depended on how the individual interpreter was able to cope" (2013, 263–4).

Within this framework, attention should be paid to general and interpreter-specific risk factors, such as a limited control over their work situation, lack of peer support, and the suppression of their own feelings while focusing on expressing others.' In this context, some organizational and individual preventive measures are needed to avert or limit the impact on interpreters. Among the organizational measures, attention could be given to some available tools that interpreters can use to evaluate stressful situations, such as the Secondary Traumatic Stress Scale (STSS), a self-report inventory designed to assess the frequency of secondary traumatic stress symptoms in professional caregivers (Ting et al. 2005), Professional Quality of Life Scale (Proqol) or the Maslach Burnout Inventory (Maslach et al. 1997), designed to assess stress in a wide range of human services professionals, based on three subscales: emotional exhaustion, depersonalization, and reduced personal accomplishment (Maslach et al. 1997). Besides that, briefing and debriefing sessions might be provided to mentally prepare for and address any issues arising from interpreting assignments, helping to ensure psychological safety (American Translators Association, ATA Code of Ethics, 2010). Crezee et al. (2013, 268) also highlight the importance of training professionals "to work with culturally and linguistically diverse clients to better equip them to work with interpreters," as well as to alert them to the benefits of briefing and debriefing.

Finally, some individual measures such as coping and self-care strategies would also be advisable, e.g., preparation for the assignment, adjusting workloads to the interpreter's capacity, sufficient breaks, maintaining positive connections with close friends and family, and accepting one's own emotional reactions. Either way, caring for interpreters can reflect well on the profession and this is reliant on raising awareness from authorities, organizations, and individuals of the professional hazards of working as an interpreter, along with recommendations to avoid/mitigate such hazards and protect interpreters' mental well-being and health.

Conclusion

In mediation, language is not just a means of expression but a strategy to access and navigate the unknown, or to help other people do so. The appreciation of the social dimensions of cross-language communication has shifted the interpreter from between to within the encounter. Successful communication means bringing together and understanding perspectives from all three co-participants co-constructing the communication together in interpreter-mediated talk and engaging professional practice while considering natural communicative instincts of those participating.

Daily practice has shown that a complex activity like community interpreting requires ongoing reconsideration of the priorities and particular nature of each setting and situation. Interpreters are leaving behind the image of an invisible conduit to become a valued co-worker. Codes of responsibility are essential for each profession, and the idea that interpreters should strive for professional detachment as a matter of principle is necessary. However, in order to be most effective in their role, interpreters should allow for sufficient 'standardized flexibility' to avoid the risk of over-intrusion, side-lining or alienating the service user, while considering the interpreter as a visible interactor guided by professionalism, cognitive empathy and social responsibility.

Further descriptive studies based on daily practice will help clarify the place of advocacy as an appropriate intervention in specific interpreter-mediated encounters. For that, misconceptions about the advocate role should be cleared up in order to properly describe and understand the rationale of this role and the sector in which it could be advisable and admissible. However, the appropriate use of advocacy in interpreted encounters requires a careful analysis and it should only be used when resolution cannot be reached through less active interventions. Along with this perspective, García Beyaert and Pons (2009) conclude that while both share the same general objective (enabling communication between providers and users), "intercultural mediators tend to intervene more in the interaction, while interpreters adopt less intrusive roles." Once again, the setting must be the key determinant in deciding the interpreting strategies, and every professional should agree to abide by the appropriate ethical challenges in each interpreting setting. Assuming that codes of practice are action guides or interpreting standards, meaningful work and a professional road map in community interpreting should be enhanced by pragmatic rules, perspective-taking capability across a spectrum wide enough to be credible, and transferable to each particular situation.

The fact that many in community interpreting are embracing empathy as a positive strategy to enhance cooperation and work efficiency requires the consideration of some immediate and long-term effects that working under emotional stress can imply. In this scenario, emphasis should be placed on developing awareness of the complexities of interpreting in sensitive settings and the importance for all parties to be well trained, prepared, and debriefed. Self-monitoring and self-assessment for interpreters and interpreters-to-be is also highly advisable, along with the recognition of potentially stressful factors and the development of coping strategies and empathy regulation skills such as perspective-taking capability and compassionate detachment.

Above all, the evolution of the conceptualization of impartiality over the years has relocated interpreting settings towards being social spaces where people intervene and collaborate in a context of trust; furthermore, it provides evidence that confidence in the interpreter's judgment and professional responsibility is essential for successful interpreting and should always consider the micro level without losing sight of the macro level.

References

ATA Code of Ethics. American Translators Association (ATA). 2010. Retrieved from https://www.atanet.org/

Bahadir, Şebnem. 2012. "Interpreting Enactments: A New Path for Interpreting Pedagogy." In *Modelling the Field of Community Interpreting: Questions of Methodology in Research and Training*, edited by Claudia Kainz, Erich Prunc and Rafael Schögler, 177–210. Berlin: LIT Verlag.

Empathy in community interpreting

Bancroft, Marjory ed. 2015. *The Community Interpreter: An International Textbook*. Columbia, Maryland: Culture & Language Press.

Blumgart, Herrman L. 1964. "Caring for the patient." *The New England Journal of Medicine* 270: 449–456. 10. 1056/NEJM196402272700906

Boéri, Julie. 2015. "Key Internal Players in the Development of the Interpreting Profession." In *The Routledge Handbook of Interpreting*, edited by Holly Mikkelson and Renée Jourdenais, 29–44. London, New York: Routledge. 10.4324/9781315745381.ch2

Bot, Hanneke. 2003. "The Myth of the Uninvolved Interpreter Interpreting in Mental Health and the Development of a Three-Person Psychology." In *The Critical Link 3*. Vol. 46, edited by Louise Brunette, Georges L. Bastin, Isabelle Hemlin, and Heather Clarke, 27–35. Amsterdam: John Benjamins Publishing Company. 10.1075/btl.46.07bot

Brandt, Richard B. 1979. *A Theory of the Good and the Right*. Oxford. New York: Clarendon Press.

Crezee, Ineke Hendrika Martine, Shirley Jülich, and Maria Hayward. 2013. "Issues for Interpreters and Professionals Working in Refugee Settings." *Journal of Applied Linguistics and Professional Practice* 8 (3): 253–273. 10.1558/japl.v8i3.253

Dam, Helle Vrønning. 2017. "Interpreter Role, Ethics and Norms." In *The Changing Role of the Interpreter*, edited by Marta Biagini, Michael S. Boyd, and Claudia Monacelli, 228–239. New York: Routledge. 10.4324/9781315621531-12

Dean, Robyn K. 2015. *Sign Language Interpreters' Ethical Discourse and Moral Reasoning Patterns*. Doctoral Dissertation. Department of Languages and Intercultural Studies. Edinburgh, UK: Heriot-Watt University. https://core.ac.uk/download/pdf/77036239.pdf

Drugan, Joanna. 2017. "Ethics and Social Responsibility in Practice: Interpreters and Translators Engaging with and Beyond the Professions." *The Translator* 23 (2): 126–142. 10.1080/13556509.2017.1281204

Eisenberg, Nancy, Richard A. Fabes, and Tracy L. Spinrad. 2007. "Prosocial Development." In *Handbook of Child Psychology*, edited by William Damon and Richard M. Lerner, 646–718. Hoboken, NJ: Wiley. 10. 1002/9780470147658.chpsy0311

Figley, Charles R. ed. 1995. *Compassion Fatigue: Coping with Secondary Traumatic Stress Disorder in Those Who Treat the Traumatized*. Brunner/Mazel. New York: Taylor & Francis Routledge.

García Beyaert, Sofia, and Jordi Serrano Pons. 2009. "Recursos Para Superar Las Barreras Lingüístico-Culturales En Los Servicios De Salud." In *Manual De Atención Al Inmigrante*, edited by Joaquín Morera Montes, Alberto Alonso Babarro, and Helena Huerga Aramburu, 53–66. Madrid, Barcelona: Ergon.

Gerskowitch, Chloe, and Rachel Tribe. 2021. "Therapists' Experience of Working with Interpreters in NHS Settings: Drawing Upon a Psychoanalytic Theoretical Framework to Contextualize the Findings of an IPA Study." *British Journal of Psychotherapy* 37 (2): 301–318. 10.1111/bjp.12630

Hlavac, Jim. 2017. "Brokers, Dual-Role Mediators and Professional Interpreters: A Discourse-Based Examination of Mediated Speech and the Roles That Linguistic Mediators Enact." *The Translator* 23 (2): 197–216. 10.1080/13556509.2017.1323071

Hojat, Mohammadreza. 2016. *Empathy in Health Professions Education and Patient Care*. Cham: Springer International Publishing. 10.1007/978-3-319-27625-0

Kalina, Sylvia. 2015. "Ethical Challenges in Different Interpreting Settings." *MonTI. Monografías De Traducción E Interpretación*, Special Issue 2: 63–86. 10.6035/MonTI.2015.ne2.2

Leneham, Marcel and Jemina Napier. 2003. "Sign Language Interpreters' Codes of Ethics: Should we Maintain the Status Quo?" *Deaf Worlds* 19 (2): 78–98.

Llewellyn-Jones, Peter, and Robert G. Lee. 2014. *Redefining the Role of the Community Interpreter: The Concept of Role-Space*. Lincoln: SLI Press.

Maslach, Christina, Susan E. Jackson and Michael P. Leiter. 1997. "The Maslach Burnout Inventory Manual." In *Evaluating Stress: A Book of Resources*, edited by Carlos P. Zalaquett and Richard J. Wood, 191–218. Palo Alto, CA: Consulting Psychologist Press.

Merlini, Raffaela and Mariadele Gatti. 2015. "Empathy in Healthcare Interpreting: Going Beyond the Notion of Role." *The Interpreters' Newsletter* 20: 139–160. http://hdl.handle.net/10077/11857

Moore, Patrick. 2007. Direct versus Indirect Speech in Community Interpreting: *Does it Really Matter?* M.A. Dissertation, University of Georgia. Retrieved from: https://getd.libs.uga.edu/pdfs/moore_patrick_200708_ma.pdf

Nida, Eugene and Charles R. Taber. 1982. *The Theory and Practice of Translation*. Leiden: E.J. Brill.

Peleg-Baker, Tzofnat. 2014. "Improving Mediators Decision Making by Becoming Cognitively Skilled: Why Systemic Reflection Is Critical for Gaining Consciousness of the Unconscious." *SSRN Electronic Journal*. 10.2139/ssrn.2443930

Rodríguez, Esther and Ángel R. Guerrero. 2002. "An International Perspective: What are Ethics for Sign Language Interpreters? A Comparative Study among Different Codes of Ethics." *Journal of Interpretation.* 2002: 49–62.

Santamaría Ciordia, Leticia. 2017. "A Conceptual and Contemporary Approach to the Evolution of Impartiality in Community Interpreting." *Jostrans, Journal of Specialised Translation* 28: 273–292.

Santamaría Ciordia, Leticia. 2019. "Identifying Points of Convergence Between Trained and 'Natural' Interpreters for Public Services." *Journal of Applied Linguistics and Professional Practice* 12 (3): 241–265. 10.1155 8/jalpp.37240

Ting, Laura, Jodi M. Jacobson, Sara Sanders, Brian E. Bride, and Donna Harrington. 2005. "The Secondary Traumatic Stress Scale (STSS)." *Journal of Human Behavior in the Social Environment* 11 (3-4): 177–194. 10.1300/J137v11n03_09

Vinay, Jean Paul and Jean Darbelnet. 1958. *Stylistique Comparée du Français et de l'Anglais: Méthode de Traduction.* Paris: Didier.

Wallace, Melisa and Esther Monzó Nebot. 2019. "Legal Translation and Interpreting in Public Services: Defining Key Issues." *Revista de Llengua I Dret, Journal of Language and Law* 71: 1–12. 10.2436/rld.i71.2019.3311

Wispé, Lauren. 1986. "The Distinction Between Sympathy and Empathy: To Call Forth a Concept, a Word Is Needed." *Journal of Personality and Social Psychology* 50 (2): 314–321. 10.1037/0022-3514.50.2.314

Young, Iris Marion. 1990. *Justice and the Politics of Difference.* Princeton: Princeton University Press.

45

EXACERBATING CULTURAL DIFFERENCES IN TRANSLATION/ INTERPRETING AS INTERCULTURAL MEDIATION

Jiayi Wang

Intercultural communication mediated by translators/interpreters (T/Is) can be ubiquitous yet invisible in today's globalised world. It ranges from the foreign movies and shows we watch to the international news we read. Since the cultural turn in translation studies, scholars have raised the idea of T/Is as cultural mediators (Bassnett 2011; Katan 2013). This notion has a growing presence in the academic and practitioner literature (Katan and Taibi 2021; Liddicoat 2016), and various terminologies have been used to describe it, including "cross-cultural mediator" (Bassnett 2011), "'mediator of cultures" (Tonkin and Frank 2010), and "cultural mediator" (Katan and Taibi 2021). However, the emergence of the established role of cultural mediators has led to confusion (Verrept 2019), as these professions tend to have a separate development trajectory and differ across countries (Miklavcic and LeBlanc 2014; Rudvin and Spinzi 2014). Thus, the current study uses *intercultural mediator* as an umbrella term to refer to the role played by T/Is in the process of translation/ interpreting as a form of intercultural mediation (IM).

Similar to conflict management research (Busch 2016), the notions of culture and IM tend to be used in an uncritical manner and are rarely questioned in the translation and interpreting literature. Conceptually, translation studies lack a cogent theory of culture as part of communication (Sun 2003), and the literature is largely based on an idealised notion of the status of T/Is as impartial intercultural mediators (Inghilleri 2005).

Nevertheless, several studies have begun to challenge the underlying assumptions (e.g., Angelelli 2004a, 2004b; Caiwen Wang 2017; Ciordia 2017; Gu and Wang 2021). Past studies on community interpreting, especially medical interpreting, have revealed some of the tensions and controversies in interpreters' IM (e.g., Brisset, Leanza, and Laforest 2013; Davitti 2013; Leanza 2005). In particular, the presence of an interpreter has been found to be more beneficial to healthcare providers than to patients (Leanza 2005) and to education providers than to migrant mothers (Davitti 2013). Issues of trust, control and power, and interpreters' roles have also been explored (Brisset, Leanza, and Laforest 2013; Ciordia 2017).

In comparison, very few studies outside of community interpreting have challenged the assumptions underlying T/Is' IM. Jiayi Wang (2017), for example, drew inspiration from the shift from culturalism to interculturality in disciplines outside of translation studies. Beyond an uncritical use of the notion of culture, interculturality examines how people use the concept of culture in their discourse and actions to justify their behaviours and thoughts, as well as those of other individuals. It

DOI: 10.4324/9781003227441-54

423

encourages critical participation in communication and ongoing reflexivity (Dervin 2016; Holliday 2018). Jiayi Wang (2017) further examined how culture was used in authentic interpreter-mediated official interactions between Chinese and American government officials and combined this with follow-up comments to highlight the complexities of the assumed role of IM. For instance, a successful IM from the American officials' perspective can be seen as a failure from the Chinese side, thereby exacerbating cultural differences.

However, there is currently a dearth of research on T/Is' failed IM, partly due to the lack of access to authentic data. The current study aims to fill this gap. The next section proposes a conceptual model of IM in translation/interpreting. This chapter then introduces the data employed to analyse the reasons why cultural differences are exacerbated in the process. Next, the main causes are presented, after which the implications of the results on the *what*, *who*, and *how* of T/Is' IM are discussed. Finally, suggestions for future research are presented.

Conceptualising IM in translation/interpreting

Katan (2013) distinguished between two levels of IM in translation: Lingual–cultural and intercultural intervention. The former focuses on a more lingual level (e.g., metaphors and culture-bound terms), whilst the latter addresses a more hidden level of meaning (e.g., communication styles and worldviews). Katan (2013) further proposed two levels of intercultural intervention in translation: A formal level focusing on differences in politeness norms, directness/indirectness, and register, etc., and a hidden informal level involving differences in values and beliefs, among others.

Katan's (2013) conceptualization presented above can be used to analyse the two levels of intercultural evaluation, namely, interpersonal sensitivities and the socio-moral order, in Spencer-Oatey's rapport management and evaluation framework (Spencer-Oatey 2008; Spencer-Oatey and Kádár 2021). The first level includes face, interactional goals, and expected rights and obligations, whilst the second level consists of social conventions and the moral values and principles that participants draw on when making judgments. Drawing on different disciplines, notably cross-cultural psychology, Spencer-Oatey's framework conceptualised affective perceptions in intercultural settings and has been widely applied to analyze intercultural encounters.

IM failure, the focus of the present study, is on affective perceptions. Thus, a conceptual model of T/Is' IM (Figure 45.1) is proposed by combining these frameworks.

Figure 45.1 depicts the proposed conceptual model of T/Is' IM, including Katan's (2013) lingual–cultural and intercultural interventions. Differences in the socio-moral order tend to be more hidden than interpersonal sensitivities (e.g., goals and face) and may trigger greater intervention. It is worth noting that the two levels are distinct yet interrelated.

Methodology

The data analyzed in the current study consisted of the following: (1) a survey of 100 experts: 50 professional T/Is, including subtitle translators and medical interpreters, and 50 experienced users of translation/interpreting service, including book publishers and TV/film producers, and (2) two follow-up focus group interviews. An open-ended survey was conducted online through email or social media, in which the respondents were asked to identify the major challenges leading to exacerbated cultural differences in translation/interpreting as a form of IM. They were also asked to share instances of such behaviors. The survey responses were analyzed to identify distinct patterns.

Next, a follow-up focus group interview was conducted with a group of five professional T/Is, including business, court, and medical interpreters; a UN translator; and a literary translator. Each of the participants had over ten years of translation experience. Another follow-up focus group interview was conducted with a group of five experienced T/I users: An editor, a TV producer, a film

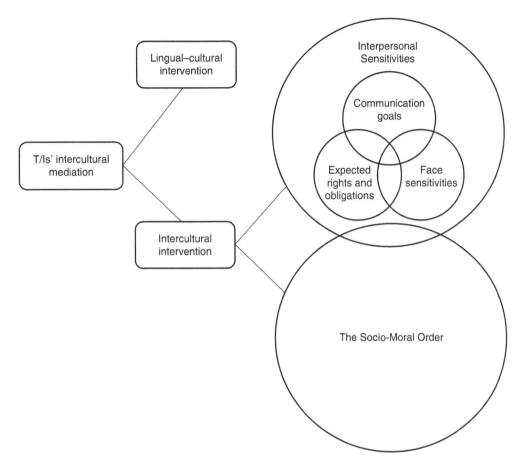

Figure 45.1 A conceptual model of T/I's intercultural mediation

producer, a solicitor, and a businessman. Each of them also had around 10 years of experience working with T/Is. Both focus groups discussed and verified the findings identified in the first phase.

Main causes of IM failure in translation/interpreting

Five main causes of IM failure were identified: Mismatched expectations, lack of power and authority (including mediational authority), cultural misunderstanding, insufficient linguistic and/or thematic knowledge, and contextual constraints, as shown in Table 45.1.

Table 45.1 Major reasons for IM failure in translation/interpreting

	Main causes	T/I practitioners (N = 50)	Users of T/Is (N = 50)
1	Mismatched expectations	36 (72%)	34 (68%)
2	Lack of power and (mediational) authority	29 (58%)	12 (24%)
3	Cultural misunderstanding	25 (50%)	26 (52%)
4	Insufficient linguistic and/or thematic knowledge	21 (42%)	27 (54%)
5	Contextual constraints	15 (30%)	39 (78%)

In Table 45.1, the initial number in each cell refers to the number of respondents who reported a reason(s) under a certain category. The percentage in brackets indicates the proportion of the total number of respondents in the particular group represented by the first number in the cell. This is followed by an examination of each category.

Mismatched expectations

The majority of our respondents (72% of the T/Is and 68% of T/I users) identified mismatched expectations as a major challenge to IM. In reality, the writer of a text and the audience of the translated text—akin to interactants in interpreting—have different or even contradictory views, as shown in the excerpt below.

Excerpt 1   The T/I's focus group interview

JANE: My professional guidelines talk about absolute impartiality, but in reality, whose culture are we orienting towards? More often, it's about managing expectations … Many legal professionals that my colleagues and I have worked with are actually against intercultural mediation in court interpreting. They expect you to be a *copy machine* of what has been said. No more, no less! However, the client would expect you to help him/her understand what is going on; they want you to bridge gaps and play a more proactive role.

MATTHEW: It's the same for all translation and interpreting activities. There is always a source and a target culture. What is the translator mediating and from whose perspective? Intercultural mediation is easier said than done.

As shown above, the respondents felt that IM in translation/interpreting is easier said than done, and that the mismatched expectations make it more challenging. The tensions they highlighted amongst professional guidelines, practitioners, and T/I clients and users support the findings of prior research (Angelelli 2004a, 2004b; Katan and Taibi 2021).

The participants also reported examples of mismatched expectations exacerbating cultural differences in translation/interpreting, including culturally loaded terms, allusions, beliefs, and attitudes, as illustrated by Excerpt 2.

Excerpt 2   *Chang, English–Chinese medical interpreter*

The migrant pregnant woman insisted that she wanted a C-section instead of a natural birth. The doctor kept telling her there was no need for this, but the patient insisted. I fully understood why she said it and why she thought so. It's a Chinese cultural myth that C-sections are safer, less painful, etc., so I intervened and explained it to the doctor. Thus, he realised the cultural difference and spent more time explaining his advice. However, the patient was unhappy with my intercultural mediation. Her expectations contradicted those of the doctor. [I believe] the interaction worsened her negative perception of UK childbirth culture.

This experience clearly demonstrates the challenges faced by T/Is when expectations are mismatched. With the best intention of bridging gaps, the interpreter may risk aggravating cultural differences.

Lack of power and (mediational) authority

Over half of the T/Is (58%) and 24% of the T/I users identified the former's lack of power and (mediational) authority as another factor exacerbating cultural differences. Unlike more established intercultural mediators (Verrept 2019), T/Is suffer from a low status with less power (Cho 2021a), and their IM role is not readily recognized. Thus, a T/I's intervention could be *frowned upon* (Lucy), *sidelined* (Charlie), *ignored* (Kyung), and *dismissed* (Lucía), as shown by Akio's experience below.

Excerpt 3   *Akio, English–Japanese business interpreter*

In Japanese, 考えておきます *(kangaete okimasu)* literally means 'I will think about it,' but it actually means 'no' in business negotiation. I was employed by an American company to interpret during their sales negotiation with a Japanese corporation. At the end, the Japanese senior manager smiled and said, 'I'll think about it.' The Americans failed to realise that they were, in fact, turned down, so I had a side conversation with them in English. However, they dismissed my explanation, saying, 'They [the Japanese] look very happy' and 'You're just a translator. You're not a negotiator.'

Akio tried to intervene when he thought the American side seemed to misunderstand the other party's reply. Specifically, when the Japanese manager said, *I'll think about it* with a seemingly happy smile, the Americans interpreted this as a positive response, but Akio did not think so. Though he tried to intervene, he was promptly dismissed by the Americans. Thus, his attempted IM failed due to the power structure implicit in the statement, "You're just a translator. You're not a negotiator." The T/I's inferior position was also echoed by other T/I users, as shown in the excerpts below.

Excerpt 4   *Kim, commissioning editor*

I work for a well-established publisher, and I must confess that translators and translation agencies have much less power than our authors and clients who have a more dominant voice.

Excerpt 5   *Muhammad, English–Arabic community interpreter and interpreter trainer*

Community interpreting literature proposes being an active advocate for the client and helping them integrate into the community, and so on, and so forth. That's hard when you don't have the power and are not a recognized intercultural mediator.

The excerpts above demonstrate T/Is' lack of power and mediational authority at work. Furthermore, as suggested by Muhammad (Excerpt 5) and Jane (Excerpt 1), academics, the profession, practitioners, and clients tend to see role boundaries differently, which is in line with the findings of prior research (Angelelli 2004a, 2004b; Katan and Taibi 2021). Given the scenarios above, it can be said that T/Is' IM has become more confusing and challenging in recent times.

Cultural misunderstanding

The third cause of IM failure is cultural misunderstanding, as identified by half of the respondents in both the T/I and the T/I user groups. One example of this is the scenario above involving the Japanese expression *I will think about it*. Indeed, the interactants may have different interpretations of the same interaction due to varying interpreting frames, which is in line with findings on interpreter-mediated intercultural communication (Wang and Spencer-Oatey 2015).

More importantly, as noted by several respondents in the current study, many cultural misunderstandings may not be cultural at all. In some cases, T/I's may falsely attribute any communication issues to cultural differences, which, in turn, may cause misunderstandings (Jiayi Wang 2017), as shown in Excerpt 6.

Excerpt 6   *The T/I users' focus group interview*

JING: It's one thing for translators to not understand the source culture and translate literally without grasping the gist, and another thing for them to claim something as a cultural difference when it's not. Both are forms of cultural misunderstanding.

BEN: Totally agree. I've seen examples of both types. The second type can be more serious … culture is used as an easy blanket explanation, which is not helpful.

JING: Yeah. I've also seen translators falsely blaming cultural differences for their translation errors. I remember someone translating 'electronic signature' as 'electronic pen signature' in an important document. When the client checked with him, he explained that it's a cultural difference, but it was actually a translation error on his part. That small error caused a lot of hassles on both sides.

This excerpt clearly illustrates T/Is' own cultural misunderstanding, as well as their false attribution of communication issues to cultural differences.

Insufficient linguistic and/or thematic knowledge

The fourth cause of exacerbated cultural differences is T/Is' insufficient linguistic and/or thematic knowledge, as identified by nearly half (42%) of the T/I group and over half (54%) of the user group. Examples of false cognates and false fluency abounded in the data.

Excerpt 7   *Louise, French–English translator/interpreter*

Translators/interpreters have to be careful of 'false friends.' Moreover, insufficient language skills may derail communication. Once, I heard an interpreter, whose French was not very proficient, literally translating 'I'm so full' as '*Je suis tellement pleine,*' but it actually means 'I'm pregnant!'

Interpreting as intercultural mediation

Excerpt 8   *Lukas, English–German translator/interpreter*

Knowing the subject and terminology is very important. You have to talk the talk. Otherwise, communication is bound to break down.

Excerpt 9   *Hui, English–Chinese translator/interpreter*

There are many terrible translations in our bilingual public signage done by inexperienced translators lacking relevant knowledge and skills … I used to work for a government project to address such mistakes in public spaces. For example, '民族园' [a theme park featuring ethnic minorities] was rendered as 'racist park.'

Contextual constraints

Finally, 78% of the respondents in the user group, especially editors, publishers, and TV/film producers, as well as 30% of our T/I respondents, identified contextual constraints as another cause of exacerbated cultural differences.

Excerpt 10   *Emma, international film producer*

The film production budget is [always] limited, and that for translation is even smaller. Deadlines are tight. Thus, it is often impossible to produce a perfect translation.

The contextual constraints (time and space) were exemplified by audio-visual translation, as described in the above excerpt, from a producer's perspective and the translator's perspective below.

Excerpt 11   *Jin, Korean–Chinese subtitle translator*

For subtitle translators, it can be quite challenging to fit our translation into a one-inch screen within a particular timeframe. Time and space constraints are a reality we have to live with. We have to think about synchronisation. We often hear negative comments about culture lost in translation, but just look at the constraints faced by translators. I watched a few viral TikTok videos bashing Netflix's *Squid Game* translation, but frankly, from a professional perspective, the English translation was not that bad. For example, the Korean language uses honorifics, and we also use kinship titles to address someone close. For example, for those older than us, we call them *oppa* (오빠, 'older brother') or *unnie* (언니, 'older sister'), etc., even though we're not kin. The English translation of *Squid Game* has dropped some of the Korean honorifics, but that's understandable because if we were translating a book, we may explain it explicitly, but in TV/film translation, the time frame and the screen space don't allow for that, so we have to compromise.

Jin highlighted the limitations they faced and argued against non-professionals' widespread criticisms of the English translation of the popular *Squid Game* series, given that certain culture-specific phenomena were dropped due to some limitations. This corroborates Cho's (2021b) evaluation of the English translation. Thus, it can be said that TV/film translators are in a constant war of words over subtitles.

Discussion

In summary, five interrelated causes of IM failure emerged from the data analysis: (1) mismatched expectations, (2) T/Is' lack of power and (mediational) authority, (3) cultural misunderstanding, (4) insufficient linguistic and/or thematic knowledge, and (5) contextual constraints. Figure 45.2 summarizes their distributions across the two groups of respondents. The black and shaded bars represent the T/I practitioners and the T/I users, respectively. The x-axis indicates the raw frequency of each category.

Clearly, both groups converged on cultural misunderstanding and mismatched expectations, but diverged on contextual constraints and lack of power and (mediational) authority. Specifically, contextual restrictions were more prominent in the user group than in the practitioner group because book publishers and film producers, for example, consider more influencing factors than the latter. In contrast, nearly twofold more people in the T/I group, compared to the user group, reported T/Is' lack of power and (mediational) authority as a main cause of IM failure because it was felt more strongly by the former than the latter.

These reasons cast light on the *what*, *who*, and *how* of IM in translation/interpreting. The findings also problematise the use of culture. Whilst it is a broad notion that what T/Is could mediate interculturally cuts across various levels of behaviours, norms, beliefs, and values, T/Is may also falsely attribute communication issues to cultural differences and use culture as a blanket explanation. Their attempts to achieve IM may also lead to othering, overgeneralization, and essentialism (Jiayi Wang 2017; Wang and Spencer-Oatey 2015). Thus, it is important to caution against the uncritical use of the notion of culture, not only amongst T/I practitioners but also amongst academics and professionals working with them.

This leads us to the *who* of IM in translation/interpreting. Who is the T/I mediating for (e.g., doctor vs. patient, TV/film producer vs. audience, police vs. suspect, the negotiating party who hires the T/I vs. the other party, etc.)? Although the findings indicate that T/I's are expected to be a neutral ally of both parties, the reality is more complex given that there are multiple ways to interpret a text or utterance within a context. Translation/interpreting is, in itself, a meaning-making process (Liddicoat 2016). At the micro level, different parties can hold divergent views of the meaning created in context, and what is perceived as a successful intercultural interaction may be viewed as a failure by others (see Spencer-Oatey and Wang 2020; Jiayi Wang 2017; Wang and

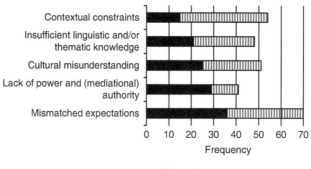

Figure 45.2 The main causes of IM failure in translation/interpreting

Spencer-Oatey 2015 for more authentic examples). At the macro level, tensions exist amongst the views of academics, the profession, practitioners, and clients (Angelelli 2004a, 2004b; Katan and Taibi 2021; Rudvin and Spinzi 2014). These contradictions may cause failed IM, and such a phenomenon requires further examination.

As for the *how* of IM in translation/interpreting, the findings contribute to a more nuanced understanding of this process. In mapping the findings onto the conceptual framework proposed in Figure 1, insufficient linguistic and/or thematic knowledge (Excerpts 7–9) and contextual constraints, such as the limitations of the screen in subtitle translation (Excerpt 11), may lead to perceived failure in lingual-cultural intervention.

As for failed intercultural intervention, mismatched expectations (Excerpts 1 and 2) and T/Is' lack of power and mediational authority (Excerpts 3–5) relate to expected rights and obligations. Excerpt 2, for example, reveals a difference in the interactional goals of the doctor and the patient, which are related to communication goals. Additionally, placing a false emphasis on culture may be viewed as a type of failed intercultural intervention (Excerpt 6), thus emphasizing the need to examine how culture is constructed and negotiated in interactions.

These conceptual and empirical insights highlight the dynamic and constructed nature of IM in translation/interpreting. The concept of culture has both stable and fluid features. Given that mediating cultures is a nuanced and contextualised process (Baker 2006; Busch 2016), both theoreticians and practitioners must challenge the assumptions underpinning the notion and practice of translation/interpreting as IM, especially its widespread uncritical use. Finally, how to promote interculturality amongst T/I scholars and practitioners, especially criticality and reflexivity, is crucial to future research.

Conclusion

Translation not only deals with words; it also enables different cultures to talk to one another. Although the notion of translation as a form of IM has become widespread in the literature, failed IM tends to be overlooked. To the best of our knowledge, this chapter is the first to systematically study how cultural differences are exacerbated during the process of translation/interpreting as a form of IM. Five main causes were identified: Mismatched expectations, T/Is' lack of power and (mediational) authority, cultural misunderstanding, insufficient linguistic and/or thematic knowledge, and contextual constraints.

Indeed, as demonstrated by the different scenarios discussed in this chapter, T/Is' IM is a complex issue involving multiple perspectives and factors. Whilst this chapter has proposed a conceptual model, empirical investigations and theorization are urgently required. Thus, in light of the current study's findings, future studies are recommended to (a) shift from essentialist, uncritical views of culture to a framework that is based on interculturality, and (b) explore how ongoing tensions amongst academics, the profession, and practitioners can be bridged. Doing so can enhance our understanding of T/Is' IM in the specific contexts in which it is applied.

References

Angelelli, Claudia V. 2004a. *Medical Interpreting and Cross-Cultural Communication*. Cambridge: Cambridge University Press. 10.1017/CBO9780511486616

Angelelli, Claudia V. 2004b. *Revisiting the Interpreter's Role: A Study of Conference, Court, and Medical Interpreters in Canada, Mexico and the United States*. Amsterdam, Philadelphia: John Benjamins.

Baker, Mona. 2006. "Contextualization in Translator- and Interpreter-Mediated Events." *Journal of Pragmatics* 38 (3): 321–337. 10.1016/j.pragma.2005.04.010

Bassnett, Susan. 2011. "The Translator as Cross-Cultural Mediator." In *The Oxford Handbook of Translation Studies*, edited by Kirsten Malmkjær and Kevin Windle. Oxford: Oxford University Press. 10.1093/oxfordhb/9780199239306.013.0008

Brisset, Camille, Yvan Leanza, and Karine Laforest. 2013. "Working with Interpreters in Health Care: A Systematic Review and Meta-ethnography of Qualitative Studies." *Patient Education and Counseling* 91 (2): 131–140. 10.1016/j.pec.2012.11.008

Busch, Dominic. 2016. "Does Conflict Mediation Research Keep Track with Cultural Theory?" *European Journal of Applied Linguistics* 4 (2): 181–206. 10.1515/eujal-2015-0037

Cho, Jinhyun. 2021a. *Intercultural Communication in Interpreting: Power and Choices.* New York: Routledge.

Cho, Jinhyun. 2021b. "Squid Game and the 'Untranslatable': The Debate Around Subtitles Explained." *The Conversation.* https://theconversation.com/squid-game-and-the-untranslatable-the-debate-around-subtitles-explained-169931

Ciordia, Leticia Santamaría. 2017. "A Conceptual and Contemporary Approach to the Evolution of Impartiality in Community Interpreting." *The Journal of Specialised Translation* 28: 273–292.

Dervin, Fred. 2016. *Interculturality in Education: A Theoretical and Methodological Toolbox.* London: Palgrave Macmillan. 10.1057/978-1-137-54544-2

Davitti, Elena. 2013. "Dialogue Interpreting as Intercultural Mediation: Interpreters' Use of Upgrading Moves in Parent–Teacher Meetings." *Interpreting* 15 (2): 168–199. 10.1075/intp.15.2.02dav

Gu, Chonglong, and Binhua Wang. 2021. "Interpreter-Mediated Discourse as a Vital Source of Meaning Potential in Intercultural Communication: The Case of the Interpreted Premier-Meets-The-Press Conferences in China." *Language and Intercultural Communication* 21 (3): 379–394. 10.1080/14708477.2021.1879107

Holliday, Adrian. 2018. "Designing a Course in Intercultural Education." *Intercultural Communication Education* 1 (1): 4–11. 10.29140/ice.v1n1.24

Inghilleri, Moira. 2005. "Mediating Zones of Uncertainty: Interpreter Agency, the Interpreting Habitus and Political Asylum Adjudication." *The Translator* 11 (1), 69–85. 10.1080/13556509.2005.10799190

Katan, David. 2013. "Intercultural Mediation." In *Handbook of Translation Studies*, Vol. 4, edited by Yves Gambier and Luc Van Doorslaer, 84–91. Amsterdam, Philadelphia: John Benjamins. 10.1075/hts.4.int5

Katan, David, and Mustapha Taibi. 2021. *Translating Cultures: An Introduction for Translators, Interpreters and Mediators* (3rd ed.). London: Routledge. 10.4324/9781003178170

Leanza, Yvan. 2005. "Roles of Community Interpreters in Pediatrics as Seen by Interpreters, Physicians and Researchers." *Interpreting* 7 (2): 167–192. 10.1075/intp.7.2.03lea

Liddicoat, Anthony J. 2016. "Translation as Intercultural Mediation: Setting the Scene." *Perspectives* 24 (3): 347–353. 10.1080/0907676X.2015.1125934

Miklavcic, Alessandra, and Marie Nathalie LeBlanc. 2014. "Culture Brokers, Clinically Applied Ethnography, and Cultural Mediation." In *Cultural Consultation. Encountering the Other in Mental Health Care*, edited by Kirmayer, Laurence J., Cécile Rousseau, and Jaswant Guzder, 115–137. New York: Springer. 10.1007/978-1-4614-7615-3_6

Rudvin, Mette, and Cinzia Spinzi. 2014. "Negotiating the Terminological Borders of 'Language Mediation' in English and Italian." *Languages Cultures Mediation* 1 (1–2): 57–79.

Spencer-Oatey, Helen. 2008. "Rapport Management: A Framework for Analysis." In *Culturally Speaking: Culture, Communication and Politeness Theory* (2nd ed.), edited by Helen Spencer-Oatey. London: Continuum.

Spencer-Oatey, Helen and Dániel Z. Kádár. 2021. *Intercultural Politeness. Managing Relations across Cultures.* Cambridge: Cambridge University Press. 10.1017/9781316810071

Spencer-Oatey, Helen and Jiayi Wang. 2020. "Establishing Professional Intercultural Relations: Chinese Perceptions of Behavioural Success in a Sino-American Exchange Visit." *Journal of Intercultural Communication Research* 49 (6): 499–519. 10.1080/17475759.2020.1788119

Sun, Yifeng. 2003. "Translating Cultural Differences." *Perspectives: Studies in Translatology*, 11 (1): 25–36. 10.1080/0907676X.2003.9961459

Tonkin, Humphrey, and Maria Esposito Frank eds. 2010. *The Translator as Mediator of Cultures.* Amsterdam; Philadelphia, PA: John Benjamins. 10.1075/wlp.3

Wang, Caiwen. 2017. "Interpreters = Cultural Mediators?" *TranslatoLogica* 1: 93–114.

Wang, Jiayi. 2017. "Mediating or Exacerbating Cultural Differences: The Role of Interpreters in Official Intercultural Interaction." In *Intercultural Communication with China*, edited by Fred Dervin and Regis Machart, 133–144. Singapore: Springer. 10.1007/978-981-10-4014-6_8

Wang, Jiayi, and Helen Spencer-Oatey. 2015. "The Gains and Losses of Face in Ongoing Intercultural Interaction: A Case Study of Chinese Participant Perspectives." *Journal of Pragmatics* 89: 50–65. 10.1016/j.pragma.2015.09.007

Verrept, Hans. 2019. *What are the Roles of Intercultural Mediators in Health Care and What is the Evidence on Their Contributions and Effectiveness in Improving Accessibility and Quality of Care for Refugees and Migrants in the WHO European Region?* Copenhagen, Denmark: WHO Regional Office for Europe. https://apps.who.int/iris/bitstream/handle/10665/327321/9789289054355-eng.pdf

PART IX

Intercultural mediation in foreign language education and the arts

46

THE INTERCULTURAL SPEAKER AS AN INTERCULTURAL MEDIATOR

Melina Porto and Manuela Wagner

Introduction

Globalized problems, such as the international health crisis due to the COVID-19 pandemic, show the need for students to learn how to cooperate across different cultures, languages, and other differences. Never has it been more important to come together and find solutions that work in diverse contexts, i.e., to engage in successful intercultural dialogue that happens locally, nationally, or internationally. Consequently, mediation, the skill to navigate different cultural and linguistic backgrounds, has become an important aspect of language education. Furthermore, dialogue among people of different social groups in increasingly plurilingual and pluricultural societies is inevitably bound up with sensitive issues and positions of power—within and between different societies—and mediation is a *sine qua non* in the task of addressing inequities and promoting social justice. This chapter provides a short introduction to the concept of mediation in language education, followed by a curricular example.

Mediation in education

The concept of mediation in language education has been influenced by different fields (e.g., Translation Studies, Mediated Discourse Studies, Linguistics). Corbett (2021) argues that the term 'mediation' currently includes different contexts and has lost "its useful specificity" (10). Liddicoat (2022) posits that mediation is under-defined and conceptualizes it either as a) problem solving, b) acting as an intermediary, or c) supporting learning. Furthermore, he raises the question about the position of mediator, i.e., whether they can truly be outside the communication they are trying to mediate, as well as who benefits from mediation. For example, different constellations of mediation include mediating for others while being inside or outside the communication as well as mediating for oneself inside the communication.

In this chapter, mediation is based on the phrase *intercultural speaker*, coined by Byram and Zarate (1996), and the concept of *intercultural communicative competence* (ICC) introduced by Byram (1997) and further developed in 2021. Someone who is interculturally communicatively competent is able to navigate languages and cultures that are different from their own whether in their own society or others. For students to develop ICC, educators foster attitudes of open-mindedness, curiosity, and tolerance of ambiguity, skills of interpreting and relating, skills of discovery and interaction, knowledge of the processes of intercultural communication and of other cultures, as well as critical

DOI: 10.4324/9781003227441-56

cultural awareness (CCA), the ability to critically analyze one's own and other people's culturally determined assumptions. CCA is a concept that contributes significantly to students' ability to help others explore and understand social groups and their cultures and societal backgrounds with which they are unfamiliar; they can mediate between people of different cultural and linguistic backgrounds.

One important implication is that language learners do not merely imitate the linguistic and cultural competence of native speakers but instead develop a distinct set of *savoirs* (i.e., the knowledge, skills, and attitudes mentioned above) that enable them to interact with interlocutors from different linguistic and cultural groups in their own society or others. Byram (1997; 2021) considers mediation one of the potential functions of being an intercultural speaker.

This notion of intercultural speaker goes further than the notion of mediator in the *Common European Reference Framework* (Council of Europe 2001), where mediation is mainly described in terms of enabling communication between parties who would be unable to understand each other without a third-party intervention of mediation.

> In both the receptive and productive modes, the written and/or oral activities of *mediation* make communication possible between persons who are unable, for whatever reason to communicate with each other directly. Translation or interpretation, a paraphrase, summary or record, provides for a third party a (re)formulation of a source text to which this third party does not have direct access. Mediation language activities, (re)processing an existing text, occupy an important place in the normal linguistic functioning of our societies.
>
> *(Council of Europe 2001, Section 2.1.3)*

Mediation does not have to involve a third party. For example, 'the language learner, like a translator, "mediates" between a text in the home or source language and that in the second or target language; and an intercultural speaker "mediates" between non-congruent world-views' (Corbett 2021, 8). Mediation also works as a process of de-centering, i.e., being able to take on a position outside of one's own 'place' (Byram 2021). In the example presented below, individuals from Argentina and Italy meet and analyze concepts from a third position that is neither one's nor the other's original position.

The *Companion Volume* (Council of Europe 2020) organizes language functions into reception, production, interaction, and mediation, further developing the concept of mediation and extending it into different contexts. Mediation is defined as follows:

> In mediation, the user/learner acts as a social agent who creates bridges and helps to construct or convey meaning, sometimes within the same language, sometimes from one language to another (cross-linguistic mediation). The focus is on the role of language in processes like creating the space and conditions for communicating and/or learning, collaborating to construct new meaning, encouraging others to construct or understand new meaning, and passing on new information in an appropriate form. The context can be social, pedagogic, cultural, linguistic or professional.
>
> *(Council of Europe 2020, 90)*

An important development in the *Companion Volume* is the inclusion of descriptor scales for mediating text, mediating concepts, mediating communication as well as for plurilingual and pluricultural repertoires.

Coste and Cavalli (2015) created a model about mediation as an important activity in education in general, as our students live in a world with increased complexity and expression of diversity, which in turn necessitates a larger repertoire of, and more nuanced, mediation skills:

The intercultural speaker

This language activity of mediation, in its transversal uses and its links with mobility, otherness and groups, is fully relevant to the democratic exercise of living and working together in society. In modern democracies, political participation presupposes a capacity for verbal mediation (62–3).

Differentiating between cognitive mediation, e.g., providing access to information, and relational mediation, i.e., building relationships with those from different backgrounds, they describe the general goal of mediation as reducing "the gap between two poles that are distant from or in tension with each other" (12). More specifically:

> To mediate is, inter alia, to reformulate, to transcode, to alter linguistically and/or semi-otically by rephrasing in the same language, by alternating languages, by switching from oral to written expression or vice versa, by changing genres, by combining text and other modes of representation, or by relying on the resources—both human and technical—present in the immediate environment (62).

Furthermore, the authors state that mediation leads to increased awareness in several areas, such as language awareness, intergroup relations and dynamics, and intercultural communication, among others.

In sum, mediation is an important aspect of intercultural communication in numerous situations and language education has a significant role to play in students' development of mediation skills. An illustration with a curricular example in higher education follows.

Example of mediation in pedagogy

The example is an online transnational project about mural art and graffiti carried out between second-year undergraduate students of English at Universidad Nacional de La Plata, Argentina and second-year bachelor's level degree students of English at Università degli Studi di Padova, Italy. There were 100 Argentinian and 75 Italian students, aged 18–22, with a B2/C1 level of English (CEFR), whose participation was voluntary.

The linguistic, intercultural, and citizenship aims included: Appreciate linguistic diversity in English, Spanish, and Italian; develop research skills; engage in intercultural dialogue with others using English as lingua franca; analyze images, texts, and practices critically; express viewpoints respectfully; develop values (respect, mutual understanding, and openness); and engage in civic participation locally and beyond.

The project had the following stages:

> In the *introduction and awareness stage*, students researched about mural art and graffiti in their own foreign language classes without interacting online yet. They strolled around their cities, La Plata, Argentina and Padova, Italy, to photograph existing murals and graffiti in their towns and create a corpus of street art in each city. They uploaded their photographs to a wiki and, using a-synchronic communication tools (chat in the wiki and email), shared their impressions.

> In the *online intercultural dialogue stage*, students met weekly in Skype in mixed nationality groups and discussed the social, cultural, and historical meanings of their corpora. They arrived at a shared and critical understanding of those forms of expression, analyzing whether they were art forms or vandalism. They designed a collaborative mural or graffiti intended to represent their group identity and positioning on the debate art or vandalism using tools such as https://www.mural.co/.

437

Finally, in the *citizenship stage*, students, in small groups, planned and implemented a civic action in their local communities. Due to restrictions at the Italian university, only the Argentinian students participated in this stage. Their civic actions included teaching a lesson on mural art and graffiti in a shelter home for poor women; drawing reverse graffiti in a local square (an environmentally friendly way of creating temporary images on walls or other surfaces by removing dirt from a surface); publishing an article in the university newspaper; creating a mural in one of their homes; and drawing a mural in collaboration with children in a state primary school in La Plata.

The data comprised photographs of street art in La Plata and Padova; chats in a wiki; recorded Skype conversations; collaboratively created murals and graffiti between Argentinian and Italian students; civic action student outcomes (newspaper articles, leaflets, photos, reverse graffiti, murals); and individually written reflection logs.

Data analysis revealed that students:

a   mediated concepts among themselves during the project and with others beyond the project,
b   used a variety of mediation strategies and activities.

The evidence of mediation is italicized in all data extracts.

Mediating concepts

The students mediated concepts among themselves during the project, decentering or taking a third position outside one's own place. This is different from mediation as a matter of being a third person between two other people (Liddicoat 2022). The Argentinian and Italian students met and analyzed concepts in this third and decentered position. For instance, describing their corpora of murals and graffiti, one group focused on the meaning of *Findus*, unknown to the Argentinian students (*I don't know*). Illustrating cognitive mediation (providing access to information) (Coste and Cavalli 2015), one Italian student offered an explanation (*there's a brand Findus*) and complemented it with multimodal support (*I'm looking for a photo, I'll give you a link*) to facilitate comprehension. In other words, consistent with Coste and Cavalli (2015), the Italian student used varied semiotic resources beyond the linguistic such as a photo and a link. She also expanded the information by adding details (*It's called 'Carletto'*). She passed on new information, encouraging her Argentinian peers to construct new meaning—two strategies mentioned by the Council of Europe (2020). Despite this focused mediation, one of the Argentinian students asked for further clarification (*Is the character of a brand?*) and used a comparison to fully understand (*Like a food brand or something like that?*).

ITAL3: It looks like the chameleon of Findus.
ITAL4: Yes.
ARG3:   *I don't know ...*
ARG4:   *Sorry.*
ITAL3: *There's a brand Findus. I don't know if you know it.*
        [pause]
ITAL3: *I'm looking for a photo* or something.
ARG4:   Yeah. It's kind of cute.
ITAL3: *It's called 'Carletto'. I'll give you a link.*
ARG4:   I think I saw it. *Let's see. Oh, it's cute.*
        [laughter]
        (...)

ARG3: *Is the character of a brand? Like a food brand or something like that?*
ITAL4: *Yes.*
ARG4: *Wow.*

(Skype conversation, Group 2)

This same group discussed one Argentinian mural about a highly sensitive theme in Argentina, the 2009 disappearance—in a period of democracy—of the adolescent Luciano Arruga under obscure circumstances in the hands of the police. The theme was particularly difficult for the Argentinian students (*his story is really sad*) because of the history with military dictatorships (the last one ending in 1983) during which people were abducted, tortured, and killed—or made to *disappear*. The following Skype conversation reveals the process of mediation of a highly sensitive concept (cognitive mediation), the disappearance of people in a democracy, which in this case ended up having the social justice aim *to know what happened* and *to remember*.

ARG4: … it says: ¿Y Luciano Arruga? Which means … It would be something like: What about Luciano Arruga? Or where is Luciano Arruga?
ITAL3: Okay.
ARG4: Like I said Luciano Arruga was a sixteen year old kid that was kidnapped and tortured by the Argentinian police.
ITAL3: Okay
ARG4: Well, his story is really sad. I like this graffiti because it reminds me every time I walk by that someone is missing.
ITAL4: Yes.
(…)
ARG4: … it reminds me every time I see this graffiti when I go to work and every time I see it, it reminds me that someone is missing and we still have to look out for him.
ITAL3 AND ITAL4: Yes
ARG4: He was just a kid who was kidnapped because he refused to work as a thief or as a robber for the police and he went missing. So his family has been looking for him since then. Yes, this one was my favorite because it's important to know what happened.
ITAL4: To remember.

(Skype conversation, Group 2)

The Argentinian students translated for their Italian peers ("Which means … It would be something like"), explained ("Luciano Arruga was a sixteen year old kid that …"), and expanded information ("he refused to work as a thief or as a robber for the police," "his family has been looking for him since then"). These are examples of mediation strategies (Council of Europe 2018; 2020), discussed in the next section.

The students also mediated concepts for third parties beyond the project. In the citizenship phase, one group of three Argentinian students travelled to Berazategui near La Plata and taught a lesson about mural art and graffiti to a group of women enrolled in a social relief governmental plan. Some of these women were mothers abandoned by their husbands, others were homeless or suffered domestic violence. Facilitating access to concepts to a vulnerable population resonates with a social justice basis for mediation (Baker 2013).

The students arranged the women and their children in groups and used two mediation activities highlighted in the *Companion Volume* (2018, 52–6, 96–9), namely group interaction and collaboration, with a particular focus on questions. The students were "creating the space and conditions for communicating and/or learning" (Council of Europe 2018, 103). In their reflection log they said: "those women were interested in the topic as they asked many questions about Banksy." These group interactions and the women's interest in and curiosity about the topic, fostered by the conditions created by the students, illustrate relational mediation, i.e., the building of relationships with those from different backgrounds (Coste and Cavalli 2015).

Another group, also mediating for third parties, designed bilingual leaflets (Spanish, English) to teach the difference between mural art and graffiti as artistic expression or as vandalism in their community. They distributed them in their university to students and teachers, and in their local community (streets, bus stops, kiosks, shops, squares) (Figure 46.1).

An example of the concept of mediation came from a group interacting with an informant, in this case a muralist.

> For this [Skype] session, we were asked to look for graffitis in our community and take pictures of the ones we liked in order to describe them on our session. For everybody's surprise, XX [name of Italian student] *met a street artist while performing this task and had the opportunity to talk to him* and take pictures of his work.
>
> *(Group description of project)*

This illustrates how an Italian student mediated a concept, the creative task of a street artist, by conveying first-hand information she gathered about street art through informal conversation with the street artist who had painted the graffiti she photographed. The Italian student acted as a third-person mediator between the artist and the Argentinian students. She also spoke with two children whom the artist had portrayed in his mural. This three-layered process (Italian student, artist, children) led to changes in perspective for everyone. The student said that "it was a very enriching experience for all of us, and it helped us to change the perspective we had about street art." In the Skype conversation, she quoted the artist, provided his interpretation of his mural, and described his creative process using his own words. This example illustrates mediation as described by Coste and Cavalli (2015): The students relied on the resources in their immediate environment (the street, mural, artist, children), combined different genres (conversation among themselves, informal interview with the artist, report of the interview in their Skype conversation), and alternated between linguistic expression (in Italian with the artist, in English among international peers) and their interpretation of semiotic means (canvas, ideograms).

> Italian student: I was with a friend and we were walking around Arcella, a part of Padua, near the train station (…) and we ask for some information to a woman, and she said that the artist was coming and we could talk to him and ask some question about his graffiti, *so we waited for the artist and when he arrived we asked about a specific canvas that we saw*, it was a stencil with two children on a bench and they had sprays in their hands and they were doing graffiti and they painted a heart with the writing "Love" and *the artist explained that the children were his children and one day the children took this bench and they put it in front of a canvas (…) there were butterflies and he said that "butterflies are a symbol of freedom" and that's all the reason why he put these butterflies* and then, in the background there were some Japanese ideograms and he said that *he loves them "cause they are very artistic, they can mean a lot of things, only one sign can mean a lot of things" and that's why he put ideograms in the background* …
>
> *(Skype conversation, Group 3)*

In summary, students negotiated the meaning of concepts in various ways in their online international groups and their own communities when they investigated murals, graffiti, and other art.

The intercultural speaker

Figure 46.1 Students mediating for third parties by distributing leaflets

Mediation strategies

The students crossed linguistic boundaries and used Spanish, Italian, and English creatively to express their ideas, foster understanding, and facilitate communication. In the *Companion Volume* (Council of Europe 2018; 2020), this process is referred to as the use of a plurilingual repertoire. For instance, one group of students planned and designed their collaborative mural and wanted to include Italian literature. They enacted several strategies, such as trying to relate to prior knowledge related to the concept and asking questions.

ITAL1: And ARG1 [name], *do you know any Italian writer?*

ARG1: *Um, I can't remember the name right now, but, um,* maybe ARG2 [name], you know it, *the author of El Gatopardo.*

ARG2: Wait, wait!

ARG1: *Oh God ...* Yeah, because *we had to read a book last year. Um ... from an Italian author* and I really, really liked it, but *I haven't read anything else by him. ButI can't remember the name!* (...)

ARG1: *Wait, wait, I'll look for it,* don't worry. *It was kind of, um, I don't really know about Italian literature* but this novel was, it was kind of boring at first, but then you get into this kind of—I mean, what matters is the beauty of how it's written, not what really happens, so ...

ITAL2: *Could you repeat the title in Spanish please?*

ARG1: *El gatopardo.*

ITAL1: *Il Gatopardo!*

ARG1: *Lampedusa.*

ITAL1: *Exactly, Lampedusa, sí.*

ARG1: *Giuseppe Tomasi di Lampedusa. Oh, say it, please, say it.*

ITAL2: *I don't know the author.*

ITAL1: *Giuseppe Tomasi di Lampedusa.*

ARG1: *Yay, that's the one!*

ITAL1: *There's a movie, too about ... and the director is a famous Italian director.*

ARG1: *Really?*

(Skype conversation, Group 1)

They lacked prior knowledge ("I don't really know about Italian literature," "I don't know the author," 'really?') but nonetheless attempted to make connections with prior experiences ("we had to read a book last year. Um ... from an Italian author") which is a mediation strategy to explain a new concept.

Sometimes the students did not quite show a competence associated with a descriptor but indicated that they might be developing the necessary skills. For example, making the comparison to a famous Italian movie, the student approached the CEFR descriptor *Can explain a new concept or procedure by comparing and contrasting it to one that people are already familiar with.*

Using Spanish, English, and Italian, translation, acknowledged as an important mediation strategy in the CEFR and the *Companion Volume*, was a useful mediation strategy for the group ("Could you repeat the title in Spanish please?", "Oh, say it, please, say it" [in Italian]). The process was demanding in time and effort ("Wait, wait!", "Oh God," "But I can't remember the name!", "Wait, wait, I'll look for it," "It was kind of, um ..."). The use of repetition was also pervasive ("El gatopardo," "Il Gatopardo!", "Lampedusa," "Exactly, Lampedusa," and "Giuseppe Tomasi di Lampedusa" repeated twice). The outcome of this mediation process was an A-ha moment, or revelation ("that's the one!") and the exclamation *Yay* is an indication that understanding had finally occurred.

All students explained, clarified, and paraphrased information, indicating that the adaptation and modification of language was another prevalent mediation strategy (Council of Europe 2001; 2020;

The intercultural speaker

Coste and Cavalli 2015). For instance, in the creation of their collaborative mural, another group of students used explanation ("the tittle is *A Stuffed Cake* by Blue"); paraphrasing ("what I meant is"); description ("it looks like a cake", "is quite"); comparison and contrast ("seems to be like ...," "it can seem beautiful ... but ... behind it this is just ...," "like, like ..."); and clarification ("seems like a cake, but this is a cake"). Consistent with Coste and Cavalli (2015), who point out the benefits of mediation in terms of awareness in several respects, in this example one of the outcomes of these mediation strategies was increased language awareness, in particular concerning the use of specific lexical items to facilitate understanding (e.g., *trash*). The students spent considerable time finding specific words and expressions to express their meanings ("I can't find the word", *trash*) and used Spanish ("no me sale la palabra") and Italian when needed. Expressions indicating hesitation prevailed (*ahh, mmm, oh, oh!, eh?*) and this is evidence of the difficulty posed by mediation. The students were working hard in their mediation trying to find the wording in their translation that would help in the process of meaning-making.

ITAL1: For example, *what I meant* for *ahh* ... this is a graffiti for ... *ahh* ... *mmm* ... of a Blue, that I told last time
(...)
ARG1: I like it, I like *it looks like a cake.*
[laughter]
ITAL1: *Seems like a cake, but this is a cake, the tittle is 'A Stuffed Cake' by Blue.*
[laughter]
ITAL1: *But, of course* there is the ... *mmm* ... the shit in the ... under the ground, *because* outside *it can seem beautiful*, it can seem beautiful and ahm... nature ...
[laughter]
ITAL1: *But the* ... *ahh* ... *mmm* ... behind it this is just *ahh*... shit ...*I can't find the word but you understand the meaning of the* ... *the graffiti is a* ...
ARG1: Yes.
ITAL1: *Is quite* ... *mmm* ...
ARG2: *Inside the cake, seems to be like a* ... *mmm no me sale la palabra.*
ARG1: Yeah *like* ...
ARG2: *Like, like* ... *trash?*
ARG1: *Ahh* ...
ITAL1: *Yeah.*
ARG2: *Ahh* ... ok.
ARG1: Yes.
ITAL2: *But* ... *I have, I have a problem because I don't know what graffiti should*...
ARG1: *Oh!*
ITAL2: *Oh* ... *Alice?*
ITAL1: *Eh?*

[They speak in Italian] (Skype conversation, Group 4)

In sum, the students deployed several mediation strategies identified in the literature such as translation, paraphrase, rephrase, alternation of languages, and alternation and combination of modes of representation, for instance linguistic, semiotic, and contextual, including resources present in the immediate environment. These strategies in turn fostered, and were supported by, the necessary conditions for communication and learning such as collaboration and willingness to construct and understand new meaning and help others do the same. There is also some evidence that students showed beginning awareness of the skills and strategies of mediation.

Conclusion

Mediation is a crucial skill as it enables students to negotiate meaning and helps others make meaning when they find themselves in situations in which they communicate with people from different backgrounds. There are pedagogical approaches that facilitate the thoughtful and intentional planning of curricula that foster students' plurilingual and pluricultural knowledge, skills, and attitudes needed to make progress in mediating concepts, texts, and communication. Successful mediation requires students to draw on all their linguistic, cultural, and semiotic resources that in turn can support their ability to fully appreciate linguistic and cultural diversity. This does not only have an impact on students' ability to communicate and collaboratively solve problems with those whose backgrounds differ from their own, but also has the potential for educators to address justice, equity, and inclusion in education. For example, mediation skills can and should help both students from dominant as well as minoritized backgrounds, and develop an understanding of and appreciation for linguistic and cultural diversity. In the example the Argentinian students cognitively mediated new content for vulnerable women locally, content that these women would not have accessed otherwise, contributing to inclusion. They also used mediation in reference to sensitive issues, such as the disappearance of people in a democracy, contributing to raising awareness among their Italian peers about human rights abuse in the local context.

Including the pedagogical aim of mediation often means providing opportunities for students to engage with those from a different background. In the example shown here, this involved an international collaboration between students from Argentina and Italy. Such goals can also be achieved by asking students to interact with partners within their own communities but from different linguistic and cultural backgrounds.

Finally, as a way forward, the students were becoming aware of the dimensions of the skills of mediation. It would be important to investigate how such awareness develops and what role the explicit analysis of the skills has. Is a good mediator just able to use the skills of mediation or should they also be conscious of them, for instance by being able to decide which ones are most appropriate in any given situation? What is the role of language teaching in this respect?

References

Baker, Mona. 2013. "Translation as an Alternative Space for Political Action." *Social Movement Studies* 12 (1): 23–47. 10.1080/14742837.2012.685624

Byram, Michael. 1997. *Teaching and Assessing Intercultural Communicative Competence*. Clevedon, Philadelphia: Multilingual Matters.

Byram, Michael. 2021. *Teaching and Assessing Intercultural Communicative Competence: Revisited*. Bristol, UK: Multilingual Matters. 10.21832/9781800410251

Byram, Michael, and Geneviève Zarate. 1996. "Defining and Assessing Intercultural Competence: Some Principles and Proposals for the European Context." *Language Teaching* 29 (4): 239–243. 10.1017/S0261444 800008557

Corbett, John. 2021. "Revisiting Mediation: Implications for Intercultural Language Education." *Language and Intercultural Communication* 21 (1): 8–23. 10.1080/14708477.2020.1833897

Coste, Daniel, and Marisa Cavalli. 2015. *Education, Mobility, Otherness. The Mediation Functions of Schools*. Council of Europe, Language Policy Unit, DGII - Directorate General of Democracy. https://rm.coe.int/ education-mobility-otherness-the-mediation-functions-of-schools/16807367ee

Council of Europe. 2001. *Common European Framework of Reference for Languages: Learning, Teaching, Assessment*. Cambridge: Cambridge Univ. Press. https://www.coe.int/lang-cefr

Council of Europe. 2018. *Common European Framework of Reference for Languages: Learning, Teaching, Assessment. Companion Volume with New Descriptors*. Strasbourg: Council of Europe. https://www.coe.int/lang-cefr

Council of Europe. 2020. *Common European Framework of Reference for Languages: Learning, teaching, assessment—Companion Volume*. Strasbourg: Council of Europe. https://www.coe.int/lang-cefr

Liddicoat, Tony. 2022. "Intercultural Mediation in Language Teaching and Learning." In *Intercultural Learning in Language Education and beyond: Evolving Concepts, Perspectives and Practices*, edited by Troy McConachy, Irina Golubeva, and Manuela Wagner, 41–58. Bristol, Jackson: Multilingual Matters.

47
INTERCULTURAL MEDIATION IN CONTEXTS OF TRANSLANGUAGING

Keiko Tsuchiya

Introduction

Increasing mobility of population beyond national borders has been a notable phenomenon in the *super-diverse* society (Vertovec 2007). This creates a space where plurilinguals with diverse lingua-cultural backgrounds encounter and interact, using multiple languages available to them in their daily lives. In other words, plurilinguals *translanguage* to perform and co-construct their complex multicultural identities while engaging in meaning making practice in interaction. The term *translanguaging* was originated in the Welsh-English bilingual education in the 1980s (Lewis, Jones, and Baker 2012). It denotes two concepts: One is "the complex language practices of plurilingual individuals" and another "the pedagogical approaches that use those complex practices" (García and Wei 2014, 20). In the model of translanguaging in dynamic bilingualism, multiple languages are not considered as separate entities. Rather, plurilingual individuals draw on functions necessary at a moment of interaction from their wholistic linguistic repertoire. Translanguaging theory creates ripples on bi/multilingual education and its research, being perceived both as potentials and fears (García and Lin 2017; Kubota 2016). Three research areas of translanguaging were identified (Adapted from Lewis, Jones, and Baker 2012, 650; Cenoz 2017):

- Classroom translanguaging: Teacher-directed translanguaging (Llinares, Morton, and Whittaker 2012; Nikula and Moore 2019), learner-direct translanguaging (Espinosa, Herrera, and Montoya Gaudreau 2016; Seltzer, Collins, and Angeles 2016),
- Universal translanguaging: Translanguaging space (Wei 2011), translanguaging performance (Lin, Wu, and Lemke 2020),
- Neurolinguistic translanguaging: Bilinguals' brain activities in translanguaging (Antón et al. 2016).

In CLIL (content- and language-integrated learning) classrooms (Coyle 2007) classes, for example, teachers use translanguaging to help enhance learners' comprehension (Llinares, Morton, and Whittaker 2012; Nikula and Moore 2019). Learners translanguage to understand contents (Espinosa, Herrera, and Montoya Gaudreau 2016) and express their feelings (Seltzer, Collins, and Angeles 2016) (classroom translanguaging). Neurologists are also intrigued by the translanguaging theory and have investigated bi/plurilinguals' brain activities. Results from the experiments of bilinguals' cognitive efforts when accessing single and mixed codes contradict the myth of the monolingual approach in language education (Antón et al. 2016) (neurolinguistic translanguaging). These

DOI: 10.4324/9781003227441-57

445

research themes are salient, but the focus of this chapter is on the second, universal translanguaging, looking at the dynamic, symbolic, and wholistic use of plurilingual individuals' linguistic repertoire in intercultural encounters at work in Southeast Asia.

Translingual practice is another theoretical concept in multilingual practice proposed by Canagarajah (2012). In translingual practice, plurilinguals' orientation towards "language systems and semiotic resources" is dynamic, and "mobile codes can freely merge to take on significant meaning and new indexicalities" (11). Thus, transcultural practice centralizes interactants' meaning-making in interaction and performing multilingual/cultural identities in a given context. This chimes with redesigned translanguaging theory in Pennycook (2017). Through an ethnographic observation of interactions at a Bangladeshi-run shop in Australia, which involved English, Bangla, and Arabic, Pennycook redefined translanguaging as practices that attend "not only to the borders between languages but also to the borders between semiotic modes" (270), such as "products, smells, languages, layout" (272) at the shop where the interaction took place.

Translanguaging practices sometimes co-occur in or with the practice of *mediation*. In other words, translanguaging could incorporate *mediation*. Drawing on the notions of *speaking of another* in Schiffrin (1993) and *animator* in Goffman (1981), Hynninen (2011, 966) defined mediation as "a form of speaking for another, where a co-participant starts rephrasing another participant's turn that was addressed to a third party" through a conversation analysis of classroom interactions between learners and a teacher in *English as a lingua franca* (ELF, Seidlhofer 2011). Hynninen identified the following sequence of mediation (2011, 974):

1   Trouble-source turn by A,
2   (other-initiation of repair by B),
3   Rephrasing of A's turn by C, i.e., mediation,
4   Reaction from B,
5   (evaluation and/or elaboration of B's turn by C).

In the ELF interaction between Students A and B in a classroom, there is a trouble source in A's turn. B might (or might not) attend the trouble by themselves, initiating repair, which means "efforts to deal with trouble-sources or repairables—marked off as distinct within the ongoing talk" (Schegloff 2007, 101; Sacks, Schegloff, and Jefferson 1974). Teacher C then mediates between Students A and B by rephrasing A's utterance for B. This is followed by Student B's response sometimes with Teacher C's elaboration of B's utterance.

In reference to Hynninen's (2011) study, this chapter reconsiders the process of mediation in a translanguaging space outside of a classroom, concerning interactants' *epistemic authority* and *framing*. Epistemics in interaction involves "knowledge claims that interactants assert, contest and defend in and through turns-at-talk" (Heritage 2013b, 370). Heritage distinguishes *epistemic status* from *epistemic stance*: The former refers to relatively static knowledge interactants possess while the latter is "the moment-by-moment expression of the social relationships with an epistemic domain which is managed through design of turns at talk" (Heritage 2013a, 553). In the excerpt below, for instance, Jenny (Jen) is praising Vera's (Ver) family while indexing her epistemic stance (see Appendix 1 for the transcription conventions) (Heritage 2013b, 381):

```
1   Jen:          Mm [I: bet they proud o-f the fam'ly. =
2   Ver:          [Ye:s.
3   Jen: →        =They're [luvly family now ar'n't [they
4   Ver: →        [°Mm:. °      [They are: ye[s.
5   Jen:                                      [eeYe[s::
```

| 6 | Ver: | [Yes. |
| 7 | Jen: | Mm:: <u>All</u> they need now is a <u>little</u> girl <u>t</u>ih complete i:t. |

(Heritage 2013b, 381)

Jenny starts the activity of complimenting Vera's family in line 1, downgrading her epistemic stance in line 3 by using a tag question. Responding to Jenny's compliment, Vera claims her epistemic primacy of her family, confirming Jenny's compliment in line 4. Interactants, thus, assert their epistemic stance, upgrading or downgrading their epistemic authority in interactions.

In addition to their indexicality of epistemic stance, this chapter discusses how translanguagers *frame* the activity of mediation in a multiculturally embedded interaction. On the basis of Bateson (1972 [2000]), Goffman (1974) conceptualized the notion of frame:

> I assume that definitions of a situation are built up in accordance with principles of organization which govern events—at least social ones—and our subjective involvement in them; frame is the word I use to refer to such of these basic elements as I am able to identify.
>
> *(Goffman 1974, 10–11)*

Goffman elaborates the concept and established frame analysis, adding detail descriptions of *keys*: "the set of conventions by which a given activity, one already meaningful in terms of some primary framework, is transformed into something patterned on this activity but seen by the participant to be something quite else" (43–4). One of such *keying* processes is *regrounding*, which requires "the performance of an activity more or less openly for reasons or motives felt to be radically different from those that govern ordinary actors" (74), exemplifying the concept with describing Princess Margaret's charity at a church bazaar where she was selling stockings. It was framed as selling-buying at a bazaar, but the participants were well aware of the double discourses with the presence of the princess. Multiple frames are interweaved in regrounding.

Frames and regrounding in mediation practice in translanguaging contexts are analyzed and discussed in this chapter, looking at interactions among business persons with different linguacultural backgrounds. The data were extracted from a miniature corpus of the author, which stores three recordings of Business ELF (BELF) casual lunch meetings the author collected at a branch of a Japanese trading company in Southeast Asia. Two features in mediation observed in the BELF interactions are highlighted here:

1. epistemics and interpersonal behaviors of a mediator and a recipient in mediation in a translanguaging space,
2. the recipient's reflection of mediating behaviors with translanguaging.

The next sections elucidate these themes one by one with two case studies from Asian BELF interactions, where plurilinguals mediate and translanguage each other. Through the practices, the participants address transactional and interpersonal levels of interaction, indexing their multicultural identities and reflecting their own or others' behaviors.

Epistemics and interpersonal behaviors in mediation in a translanguaging space

The first case study, which I shall call the *Fuqing* case, is shown in Extract 1. The conversation involved four participants, Ray, a Chinese worker who grew up in Japan and claimed his first language (L1) is Japanese, second language (L2) English, and third one (L3) Chinese; Tina, a

Singaporean worker whose L1 is English and L2 Chinese; Gina, a Malaysian worker who has worked for a Japanese company for long so she is fluent in Japanese (her L3) together with Chinese (L1) and English (L2); and Keiko is the author, whose L1 is Japanese and L2 English. All names are pseudonyms except the author's. The annotation conventions in the Cambridge and Nottingham Corpus of Discourse in English (CANCODE) (Adolphs 2006) were applied to the transcriptions (see Appendix 2 for the transcription conventions). Chinese words are written in italics and Japanese in bold in the transcripts. Before this extract, Ray was talking about his parents' visit from mainland China to the country where the branch was based. Ray shared a story about his experience at a local Chinese restaurant, where he had dinner with his parents. At that time, Ray was surprised with the fact that their parents did not understand the restaurant staff's language although they both spoke Chinese and found that the restaurant staff were conversing in *Fuqing*, which is a dialect in China. Then, he asked his Chinese-speaking colleagues, Gina and Tina, in the lunch meeting whether they could speak *Fuqing* (line 1).

Extract 1   The case *Fuqing* (Tsuchiya 2020, 267)

1	Ray	can you speak the Cantonese or *Fuqing* language?
2	Tina	yeah.
3	Ray	at home?
4 →	Gina	if you have elder because=
5	Ray	you can?
6	Gina	er for me I I understand+
7	Ray	understand?
8	Gina	+but I don't speak.
9	Ray	oh:
10	Gina	I understand=
11 →	Tina	but for me if I am <\$G?> I speak <\$G?> then maybe sometimes *Hokkien* <\$G?> because we have elderly at home.
12	Keiko	*Hokkien* language.
13	Ray	*Hokkien Hokkien* language.
14	Tina	er *Hokkien Hokkien* H-O-K-K-I-E-N.
15	Ray	Hokkien.
16 →	Gina	*Fuqing*. [Mediation]
17 →	Ray	*Fuqing* **desho**. [Translanguaging]
		<\$E> the copula and particle **de-sho** in Japanese means 'isn't it' in English. </\$E>
		Hokkien **men** ah *Hokkien mien* **da** *Hokkien* **men**.
		<\$E> The Japanese word **men** and the Chinese one *mien* Both mean 'noodle' in English. The Japanese word **da** is a copula. </\$E>
		<\$E> laugh </\$E>
18	Gina	*Hokkien mien* <\$E> laugh </\$E>

Gina answered she could understand the dialect, but she could not speak it in lines 6 to 10. Then, Tina said she sometimes spoke it in line 11. When she said so, Tina used the term *Hokkien*, which is a variety of *Fuqing* dialect. Keiko and Ray repeated the word in lines 12 and 13, which were taken as *repair initiation* (Schegloff, Jefferson, and Sacks 1977) to ask for clarification of the term by Tina. Tina

Intercultural mediation in translanguaging

then in line 14 repeated the word and spelled it out for us, which is *self-repair* to increase explicitness as described as a feature in ELF clarification strategies in Kaur (2011). Ray acknowledged in line 15 and Gina uttered *Fuqing* to mediate Tina and Ray. In a response to Gina's mediation, Ray uttered *Fuqing* and translanguaged by attaching a Japanese sentence final particle *desho*. This particle is an equivalent to a tag question, *isn't it*, in English.

In the case *Fuqing*, multiple discourses were enacted. The interactants tried to enhance "mutual intelligibility and communicative efficiency," and at the same time constitute and assert "their [ELF users] multilingual identities" (Seidlhofer 2011, 97–9). The former (intelligibility and efficiency in intercultural ELF interactions) is closely related to *interactional strategies*, which are part of *performative competence* of translinguals in Canagarajah (2012): "they [translinguals] depend on practices that are adaptive, reciprocal, and dynamic to co-construct meaning" (175). This feature of performativity was observed in Tina's use of repetitions for clarity and Gina's mediation to facilitate between Ray and Tina in the case *Fuqing*. The latter (plurilingual's constitution and assertion of their multi-layered socio-cultural identities) is also performative an interpersonal, which is called *envoicing* strategies in Canagarajah (2012): "their [translinguals'] negotiatory effectiveness is explained by their ability to start from their social positioning" (175). One such example observed in the case *Fuqing* is Ray's translanguaging in line 17, '*Fuqing desho*,' which emerged to express his multiple cultural identities who belong to both Japanese and Chinese cultures. Both languages are shared with Gina.

Negotiation of their epistemic primary between Gina and Ray was also noticeable in the case *Fuqing*. With the mediation practice in line 16, Gina claimed her epistemic primacy over the recipient, Ray, uttering '*Fuqing*' to tell him that Hokkien is a Fuqing dialect, showing her knowledge of the dialect. Ray first acknowledged the mediation by Gina with translanguaging in Chinese and Japanese, hedging with the tag-question in 17, '*Fuqing desho*' ('*Fuqing*, isn't it?'). Then he immediately upgraded his epistemic stance by sharing his knowledge related to the dialect, '*Hokkien men*,' with which he referred to an instant noodle imitating a hot noodle dish from Fuqing province. Here, he translanguaged again in Chinese and Japanese while repeating the word in a joking tone. The next section looks at mediation and translanguaging as a reflexive practice.

Reflecting mediating behaviors with translanguaging

Plurilinguals' reflexive practice was observed in the second case study in Extract 2, which here is termed the *Prawn* case. The conversation was extracted from the same small BELF corpus of the author, but a different lunch meeting session from the case *Fuqing*. The conversation in Extract 2 was held at a restaurant nearby their office, and six interactants with four nationalities were involved: Ben (Indonesian), Gina (Malaysian), Sarah and Chris (Singaporeans), and Tanaka and Keiko (Japanese). Tanaka is an old friend of the author and he was in a managemental position in the company. Tanaka organized the recording sessions for the research and took the role of a host in the lunch meeting. Tanaka and the colleagues at the table knew Ben could not eat pork, so Tanaka was careful when he ordered dishes. In Extract 2, Ben asked whether the dish in front of Sarah was stir-fry with tofu and seafood, not pork, to make sure before he ate in line 1.

Extract 2   The case *Prawn*

1	Ben	is it tofu and seafood?
2	Sarah	<$G?> prawn inside.
		<$E> prawn sounds like [pɔː] with weak /r/ and /n/ sounds </$E>
3	Ben	ah pork.
4	Sarah	this is prawn. <$E> again, prawn sounds like [pɔː] </$E>

5	Tanaka	ah! really?
6	Ben	okay
7	Tanaka	everything is pork.
8 →	Chris	eh? prawn!
9	Ben	ah prawn!
10	Tanaka	okay.
11	Ben	I think=
12	Sarah	prawn. <$E> with a soft voice </$E>
13 →	Ben	one inside the ocean
14	Tanaka	okay okay.
15 →	Ben	no no no right I'm asking
16	Gina	one in the ocean. <$E> laugh </$E>
17	Ben	it's okay it's okay it's okay.
18	All	<$E> laugh </$E>
19	Chris	it's prawn. I got it. <$E> laugh </$E>
20 →	Tanaka	pra:wn. <$E> with an emphasis with the /r/ sound and a louder voice like an actor </$E>
21	Gina	Tanaka **san**. <$E> laugh </$E> <$E> **san** in Japanese is an equivalent to 'Mr.' in English. </$E>
22	All	<$E> laugh </$E>
23 →	Tanaka	good material.
24	Keiko	<$E> laugh </$E> Yes.
25	All	<$E> laugh </$E>
26	Gina	prawn. <$E> laugh </$E>
27	Ben	specifically mention it's in the ocean. <$E> laugh </$E>
28	All	<$E> laugh </$E>
29	Tanaka	so you can have this, right?
30	Ben	yeah. I guess.

Sarah answered to Ben in line 2, saying 'prawn inside,' but the word *prawn* sounded like [pɔ:] with weak /r/ and /n/ sounds in the utterance. So Ben thought Sarah said pork and uttered 'ah pork' in line 3. Sarah said it again with the same pronunciation, 'this is prawn' in line 4. Tanaka was listening to the conversation and said 'ah! really?' in line 5, and 'everything is pork' in line 7. Then, Chris realized the trouble source in Sarah's utterances and mediated in line 8, saying 'eh? prawn!', and Ben realized Sarah said prawn not pork, uttering 'ah prawn!' in line 9. Sarah repeated the word with a soft voice in line 12 and Ben added a clarification 'one inside the ocean' in line 13. Soon after Ben said so, he framed his utterance as a question, explicitly saying, 'no no no right I'm asking,' to save Sarah's positive face (Brown, Levinson, and Gumperz 2018) by showing that he was not correcting or blaming her. Gina started teasing Ben in line 16 by repeating his previous utterance 'one in the ocean' with laugher. Chris showed his understanding of Sarah's pronunciation, uttering 'it's prawn. I got it' in line 19. Tanaka then joined the teasing exaggerated the pronunciation and said, 'pra:wn' with an emphasis on the /r/ sound and a louder voice as if he was acting in line 20, translanguaging from his English to English of native speakers. Soon after Gina uttered 'Tanaka-san (Mr. Tanaka)' in a somewhat remonstrating tone in line 21, which was followed by laugher by everyone. Tanaka continued the teasing and framed the incident in the discourse of contributing to the author's BELF research, saying 'good material' in line 23 to Keiko since she explained the recordings were used to analyze practices of BELF to improve English education in Japan before the session. Keiko responded to him with 'yes' in line 24 with laughter, going

Intercultural mediation in translanguaging

with the teasing, and Ben also joined the teasing, adding 'specifically mention it's in the ocean' with laugher in line 27 (see Chapter 4 in Hutchby and Wooffitt 2008 for sequence patterns of teasing). After the laughter in line 28, Tanaka went back to the original topic, which was Ben's inquiry about the ingredients of the dish, and asked 'so you can have this, right?' in line 29, to which Ben answered 'yeah' in the next turn, closing the episode.

How to deal with deviant linguistic behaviors in BELF was focused in Firth (1996), who recognized BELF users' discursive practice of *making it normal* and *letting it pass*. However, whether interactants let it pass or do not let it pass depends on the contexts (see the practice of not letting it pass in Tsuchiya and Handford 2014). In the case *Prawn*, the participants did not let pass Sarah's deviant pronunciation and co-operated for the activity of mediation and clarification since the issue they were dealing with was critical. Their awareness of what they themselves are doing to enhance intelligibility in an interaction are also observable in the extract: Ben's framing of his other-repair as an inquiry to save Sarah's face, Tanaka's monitoring the conversation between Sarah and Ben, explicitly raising the trouble source (the deviant pronunciation) by translanguaging to English of native speakers while saving the speaker's (and their own) face through the activity of teasing. By so doing, Tanaka regrounded the mediation as their contribution to the author's research (lines 20–8). Similarly, in the previous case, Ray's repetition of the word '*Hokkien mien*' could also be seen as a regrounding, showing his acknowledgment of the mediation while transforming himself from a mediatee to a knower. Thus, this involves mediatee's evaluation of mediation, and the practice is reflexive. This chapter ends with a discussion on this reflexive practice in the following concluding section.

Concluding remarks—Mediation and translanguaging as a reflexive practice

With a review on definitions and various research themes in translanguaging and some related concepts, i.e., translingual practice, epistemic stance, frame, and regrounding, this chapter looked at the multi-faceted practice of mediation with translanguaging, drawing on case studies of such practices observed in BELF casual meetings in Southeast Asia. In reference to Hynninen (2011), the phases in mediation are redefined with translanguaging:

1   mediator's recognition of recipient's (possible) non-understanding,
2   mediator's rephrasing (with translanguaging),
3   recipient's acknowledgement,
4   recipient's evaluation of the mediation act (with translanguaging).

As illustrated in Figure 47.1, first a hearer (mediator) who is listening to an interaction between a speaker and a recipient recognizes the recipient's (possible) non-understanding or misunderstanding of the speaker's previous utterance (*recognition*) and rephrases it with (or without) translanguaging (*mediation*) to enhance the recipient's understanding. This is followed by the recipient's acknowledgment when meaning-making has been successfully achieved (*acknowledgment*). If not, the process of the mediator's rephrasing or/and the speaker's repair actions are iterated. After establishing mutual understanding, the recipient evaluates the mediation act, claiming their epistemic authority on some occasions (*evaluation*).

In this process of mediation, four aspects in mediation with translanguaging are involved:

- Transactional practice: co-constructing meanings with multiple semiotic resources, cf. interactional strategies (Canagarajah 2012),
- Interpersonal practice: co-establishing interpersonal relationship and multicultural identities, cf. envoicing strategies (Canagarajah 2012),
- Epistemic practice: Mediator and Recipient's claiming epistemic authority,
- Reflexive practice: Recipient's reflection and evaluation of mediation practice.

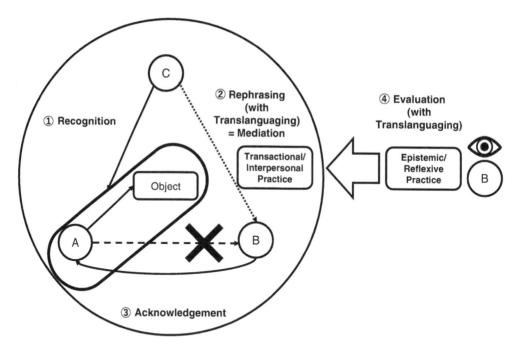

Figure 47.1 Phases and practices of mediation with translanguaging

In mediation with translanguaging, plurilinguals are engaged in meaning making activity (*transactional practice*) while saving their interactants' face, sharing their multicultural identities with them (*interpersonal practice*). Simultaneously, mediators (and also mediatees) assert their epistemic primacy and authority, showing their knowledge about the topic and their understanding of the speaker's utterance (*epistemic practice*). While being mediated, recipient mediatees reflect the practice and evaluate the mediation, regrounding a primary framework of mediation (*reflexive practice*).

Although interactants' behaviors in mediation in a translanguaging space were captured only as linguistic data in the extracts in this chapter, further research of plurilinguals' use of metalinguistic and multimodal resources in mediation and translanguaging in intercultural encounters would benefit in understanding the complex and multi-layered activity of mediation in intercultural communication.

References

Adolphs, Svenja. 2006. *Introducing Electronic Text Analysis*. London: Routledge.
Antón, Eneko, Guillaume Thierry, Alexander Goborov, Jon Anasagasti, and Jon Andoni Duñabeitia. 2016. "Testing Bilingual Educational Methods: A Plea to End the Language-Mixing Taboo." *Language Learning* 66 (S2): 29–50. 10.1111/lang.12173
Bateson, Gregory. 1972 [2000]. *Steps to an Ecology of Mind*. Chicago: The University of Chicago Press.
Brown, Penelope, Stephen C. Levinson, and John J. Gumperz. 2018. *Politeness*. Cambridge: Cambridge University Press.
Canagarajah, Suresh. 2012. *Translingual Practice*. London: Routledge.
Cenoz, Jasone. 2017. "Translanguaging in School Contexts: International Perspectives." *Journal of Language Identity and Education* 16 (4): 193–198. 10.1080/15348458.2017.1327816
Coyle, Do. 2007. "Content and Language Integrated Learning: Towards a Connected Research Agenda for CLIL Pedagogies." *International Journal of Bilingual Education and Bilingualism* 10 (5): 543–562. 10.2167/beb459.0

Espinosa, Cecilia M., Luz Yadira Herrera, and Claudia Montoya Gaudreau. 2016. "Reclaiming Bilingualism: Translanguaging in a Science Class." *In García and Kleyn* 2016: 160–177.

Firth, Alan. 1996. "The Discursive Accomplishment of Normality: On 'Lingua Franca' English and Conversation Analysis." *Journal of Pragmatics* 26 (2): 237–259. 10.1016/0378-2166(96)00014-8

García, Ofelia, and Angel M. Y. Lin. 2017. "Translanguaging in Bilingual Education." In *Bilingual and Multilingual Education*, edited by Ofelia García, Angel M. Y. Lin, and Stephen May, 117–130. Springer. 10.1 007/978-3-319-02258-1_9

García, Ofelia, and Li Wei. 2014. *Translanguaging*. London: Palgrave Macmillan UK.

Goffman, Erving. 1974. *Frame Analysis*. London: Harper and Row.

Goffman, Erving. 1981. *Forms of Talk*. Philadelphia, PA: University of Pennsylvania.

Hepburn, Alexa, and Galina B. Bolden. 2013. "The Conversation Analytic Approach to Transcription." In *The Handbook of Conversation Analysis*, edited by Jack Sidnell and Tanya Stivers, 57–76. Chichester: Blackwell.

Heritage, John. 2013a. "Action Formation and Its Epistemic (And Other) Backgrounds." *Discourse Studies* 15 (5): 551–578. 10.1177/1461445613501449

Heritage, John. 2013b. "Epistemics in Conversation." In *The Handbook of Conversation Analysis*, edited by Jack Sidnell and Tanya Stivers, 370–394. Chichester: Blackwell.

Hutchby, Ian, and Robin Wooffitt. 2008. *Conversation Analysis*. Cambridge: Polity Press.

Hynninen, Niina. 2011. "The Practice of 'Mediation' in English as a Lingua Franca Interaction." *Journal of Pragmatics* 43 (4): 965–977. 10.1016/j.pragma.2010.07.034

Kaur, Jagdish. 2011. "Raising Explicitness Through Self-Repair in English as a Lingua Franca." *Journal of Pragmatics* 43 (11): 2704–2715. 10.1016/j.pragma.2011.04.012

Kubota, Ryuko. 2016. "The Multi/Plural Turn, Postcolonial Theory, and Neoliberal Multiculturalism: Complicities and Implications for Applied Linguistics." *Applied Linguistics* 37 (4): 474–494. 10.1093/applin/amu045

Lewis, Gwyn, Bryn Jones, and Colin Baker. 2012. "Translanguaging: Origins and Development from School to Street and Beyond." *Educational Research and Evaluation* 18 (7): 641–654. 10.1080/13803611.2012.718488

Lin, Angel M. Y., Yanming Wu, and Jay L. Lemke. 2020. "'It Takes a Village to Research a Village': Conversations Between Angel Lin and Jay Lemke on Contemporary Issues in Translanguaging." In *Critical Plurilingual Pedagogies: Struggling Toward Equity Rather Than Equality*, edited by Sunny M. C. Lau and Saskia van Viegen, 47–74. Cham, CH: Springer.

Llinares, Ana, Tom Morton, and Rachel Whittaker. 2012. *The Roles of Language in CLIL*. Cambridge: Cambridge Univ. Press.

Nikula, Tarja, and Pat Moore. 2019. "Exploring Translanguaging in CLIL." *International Journal of Bilingual Education and Bilingualism* 22 (2): 237–249. 10.1080/13670050.2016.1254151

Pennycook, Alastair. 2017. "Translanguaging and Semiotic Assemblages." *International Journal of Multilingualism* 14 (3): 269–282. 10.1080/14790718.2017.1315810

Sacks, Harvey, Emanuel A. Schegloff, and Gail Jefferson. 1974. "A Simplest Systematics for the Organization of Turn-Taking for Conversation." *Language* 50 (4): 696–735. 10.2307/412243

Schegloff, Emanuel A. 2007. *Sequence Organization in Interaction*. Cambridge: Cambridge University Press.

Schegloff, Emanuel A., Gail Jefferson, and Harvey Sacks. 1977. "The Preference for Self-Correction in the Organization of Repair in Conversation." *Language* 53 (2): 361–382. 10.2307/413107

Schiffrin, Deborah. 1993. "'Speaking for Another' in Sociolinguistic Interviews: Alignments, Identities, and Frames." In *Framing in Discourse*, edited by Deborah Tannen, 231–259. Oxford: Oxford University Press.

Seidlhofer, Barbara. 2011. *Understanding English as a Lingua Franca*. Oxford: Oxford University Press.

Seltzer, Kate, Brian A. Collins, and Katrina Mae Angeles. 2016. "Navigating Turbulent Waters: Translanguaging to Support Academic and Socioemotional Well-Being." In *Translanguaging with Multilingual Students: Learning from Classroom Moments*, edited by Ofelia García and Tatyana Kleyn, 140–159. London: Routledge.

Tsuchiya, Keiko. 2020. "Mediation and Translanguaging in a BELF Casual Meeting." In *English as a Lingua Franca in Japan: Towards Multilingual Practices*, edited by Mayu Konakahra and Keiko Tsuchiya, 255–278. Basingstoke: Palgrave. 10.1007/978-3-030-33288-4_12

Tsuchiya, Keiko, and Michael Handford. 2014. "A Corpus-Driven Analysis of Repair in a Professional ELF Meeting: Not 'Letting It Pass'." *Journal of Pragmatics* 64: 117–131. 10.1016/j.pragma.2014.02.004

Vertovec, Steven. 2007. "Super-Diversity and Its Implications." *Ethnic and Racial Studies* 30 (6): 1024–1054. 10.1080/01419870701599465

Wei, Li. 2011. "Moment Analysis and Translanguaging Space: Discursive Construction of Identities by Multilingual Chinese Youth in Britain." *Journal of Pragmatics* 43 (5): 1222–1235. 10.1016/j.pragma.2010.07.035

Keiko Tsuchiya

Appendix 1

Symbol	Explanation
Word	Underlining indicates emphasis.
[ ]	Square brackets indicate overlapping talk.
:	Colons indicate prolonged sound.
=	Equal signs represent latching, which is a transition from a turn to another without a pause.

(Adapted from: Hepburn and Bolden 2013).

Appendix 2

Symbol	Explanation
<$G?>	Underlining indicates emphasis.
=	Unfinished sentences.
+	When an utterance is interrupted by another speaker, this is indicated by using a + sign at the end of interrupted utterance and at the point where the speaker resumes his or her utterance.
<$E> ... </$E>	Extralinguistic information, which includes laughter, coughs and transcribers' comments.

(Adapted from: Adolphs, 2006).

48
CHILDREN AS INTERCULTURAL MEDIATORS

Zhiyan Guo

Introduction

In this chapter, intercultural mediation will be explored in a different arena, with children taking the major role in their immigrant families. International mobility has seen an increasing number of children in the world exposed to more than one language and possibly many forms of that language in their upbringing. Entering a new society, parents and children in immigrant families acculturate themselves at very different rates in various aspects of life. Immersing themselves in the host culture through access to education and interaction with peers, children tend to gain proficiency in the mainstream language and adapt to the culture much more quickly than their parents. Despite a large immigrant population in many countries, professional translation and interpretation services seem to be neither supplied sufficiently nor readily available, and so parents needed to resort to children for help in most cases. Children as intercultural mediators become necessary, normal, commonplace, and even essential in everyday literacy practice and family life in immigrant households (e.g., Orellana 2009). Between their family's heritage culture and the new society, children mediate from a very young age to adolescent and emerging adulthood. Instances of them as mediators can be found in various forms, from a 3-year-old describing the TV program to his Italian-speaking parents at home (Harris 1977) to teenage children translating institutional documents and interpreting at formal or informal occasions for their parents (e.g., Hall and Sham 2007; McQuillan and Tse 1995; Orellana 2009).

In the last two decades, child intercultural mediation (CIM) has been studied in multiple countries. Although a larger amount of research on language brokering has been conducted among immigrants with Latino backgrounds in the United States (e.g., Tse 1995; Phoenix and Orellana 2021), an increasing number of studies have been carried out among ethnically diverse immigrant communities in other countries such as the United Kingdom (e.g., Hall 2004), Canada (e.g., Hua and Costigan 2012), Italy (e.g., Antonini 2016), Germany (e.g., Titzmann 2012), Spain (e.g., Pena-Díaz 2019), Australia (e.g., Tomasi and Narchal 2020), and Sweden (e.g., Gustafsson 2021). Despite normal activities that occur in many migrant households and communities, children as intercultural mediators tend to be relegated to outside the classroom in most countries (Alvarez 2017). It is of necessity to study child intercultural mediation as a distinct area. This chapter will define CIM, summarize the emerging debates and issues in the existing literature, and point out future directions for research.

DOI: 10.4324/9781003227441-58

Defining child intercultural mediation (CIM)

Defining CIM should start with the concept of "natural translation" initiated by Harris (1977) and Harris and Sherwood (1978). This references a kind of translation "done by bilinguals in everyday circumstances and without special training" (Harris 1977–99). These papers can be recognized as the first serious examination of child language brokering (Hall and Guo 2012), one form of CIM depicting the phenomenon of children mediating between a parent and a different language user in a new country. It was neglected by the research community until Shannon (1990), who published the first transcript of a language brokering event from the Hispanic community in California. Yet the term of *language brokering* was only first used in McQuillan and Tse's (1995) study to portray adolescents in the family translating between English and their heritage language for their parents whose English was limited, on the basis of their memories of the experiences. Although more existing studies are centered on this type of language-only mediation, children's mediation for their parents exist in all families—between local and national cultures or between main and subcultures— irrespective of their parents' prior knowledge of the mainstream language (see Guo 2014). It is children who are "effectively facilitating communication between two linguistically and culturally different parties" (Bauer 2013, 205).

Amongst the burgeoning interdisciplinary literature, researchers have encapsulated CIM as a continuum with explicit and implicit mediation at each end—the former being language brokering as an anchor, and the latter being cultural brokering as a foundation. Their characteristics are elaborated in Hall and Guo (2012). There are studies also using cultural brokering to explore how children mediate both linguistically and culturally between family members and individuals from the mainstream society (Jones and Trickett 2005). Nevertheless, language brokers always have to process cultural information—e.g., beliefs, values, and norms, along with language—in their mediation. Kam and Lazarevic (2014) listed the terms of procedural brokering and media brokering that may apply to knowledge gaps between generations and sub-cultural groups in both immigrant families, and all families with children. Napier (2021) studied in depth child mediation between spoken and sign language brokering. For the purpose of this chapter, *CIM* is used as an umbrella term covering all types of brokering in immigrant families, even though child language brokering (CLB) is the more widely documented type. In the following sections, the main issues from existing literature will be briefly discussed.

Translanguaging in CIM

Translanguaging is

> the act performed by bilinguals of accessing different linguistic features or various modes of what are described as autonomous languages, in order to maximize communicative potential ... centered, not on languages as has often been the case, but on the practices of bilinguals that are readily observable in order to make sense of their multilingual worlds.
>
> *(Garcia 2009, 140)*

This provides a fresh stance to perceive bilingualism not as two single linguistic systems, but as one whole set of repertoires that any bilingual uses automatically in meaning-making in any situation—for others or for themselves.

CIM can be perceived as occurring within multilingual and multicultural contact zones (Crafter and Iqbal 2020), rather than isolating language brokering as just involving code-switching from one language to another. Language brokers pool and leverage full repertoire of knowledge and skills they have acquired in their bilingual and bicultural experiences in both countries. They deploy linguistic resources and modalities to negotiate meaning and achieve a shared understanding in their interactions. They constantly judge and juggle different ways of separating or integrating two linguistic and cultural systems and social norms—with or without their own awareness. Their ability to self-regulate their linguistic and cultural selection according to social conventions in different settings can also be invisible to others (Orellana and Garcia 2014). CLB can be viewed as a form of translanguaging, as children do not only use their languages together crossing linguistic borders, but also understand and negotiate the emotional tone of what is being said, while learning about how they and their parents and family are socially positioned in the mainstream society. They constantly create and negotiate translanguaging spaces where they bring together social, linguistic and cultural repertoire, rather than just translating and using two separate language systems with clear-cut boundaries (Li 2011; Phoenix and Orellana 2021). Child mediators start with being bilingual but goes far beyond it.

Among the few studies examining what happens during brokering, Reynolds and Orellana (2014) linked language mediation with translanguaging practice. They recognize CLB's simultaneous identities and consider various forms of translanguaging in the role-playing of scenarios such as reading and translating the post, answering a phone call from a medical service, or purchasing products at a shop. Analyzing the transcripts of audio-recorded interpreter-mediated interaction based on improvised and rehearsed skits, they examined the relationship between language brokering and other bilingual communicative practices such as switching between codes and modalities. CLB was viewed within a larger repertoire of multivocalic practices (Reynolds and Orellana 2014). At teacher-parent conferences, child language brokers transferred seamlessly across language barriers and social norms embedded in the mainstream educational institutions (e.g., García-Sánchez, Orellana, and Hopkins 2011). Though languages tend to be normalized and recognized as separate in classrooms, in bilingual and bicultural children's minds, separation, combination or integration seems to be automated in the mediating process, in accordance with social conventions in different settings. In CIM there are translanguaging moments reflecting "the dynamic practices of individuals in bilingual contexts" (Alvarez 2014, 326). They open up spaces for children to deploy their entire linguistic repertoire and intercultural resources, even when they are using one linguistic form, English as opposed to their heritage language. Seeing child mediation through a translanguaging lens, researchers can break out of a monolingual mentality and go beyond seeing different languages as separate bodies of knowledge (Orellana and Garcia 2014), but understand how knowledge can be transmitted and constructed in a dialogic process, to which the next section turns.

CIM as a dialogic process

From a sociocultural perspective, CIM or CLB activities with parents can be seen as a joint endeavor in which scaffolding takes place. The notion usually refers to the provision of adult or more competent help within the child's (less experienced) zone of proximal development (ZPD). It can also be understood as a collaboration in which more experienced adults or teachers build for children or learners in any educational setting. Bilingual child language brokers are positioned between at least two parties in many mediating events. However, the majority of extant literature has singled out CLB as one particular kind of communication where children single-handedly manage the complex tripod interaction. This way of taking brokering as single activities solely conducted by children may not offer a full picture of intercultural mediation.

A few studies extend into a broadened perspective to view child mediation as a bilingual, dialogical, and cross-generational exchanges in an intercultural contact zone (Crafter and Iqbal 2020). These are a shift in focus from individuals to contextual dynamics. This transfers the perspective from an individual child to the child-in-cultural context to understand the moment-to-moment unfolding of immigrant family brokering, as proposed by Eksner and Orellana (2012), who argue that CIM can challenge the theoretical framework of expert-novice relationships in the way that knowledge is located between the brokering child and the parent-interlocutor. Rather than forming a one-way route of the child being the active broker and the parent the passive recipient, both participants act as collaborators to work through mediation together, with expertise, experiences, and skills not clearly assigned to one party, but in constant shift between the two.

Crafter and Iqbal (2020) offers a sociocultural understanding of CLB and CIM, conceptualizing them as situated practice (Vygotsky 1978). This involves all participants sharing and negotiating information while developing new skills and identities (Orellana 2009), with knowledge and competence distributed among participants in sociocultural contexts—favorable or hostile (Crafter and Iqbal 2020, 2021). Guo (2014) illustrated that scaffolding was set up by Ming, the daughter, as more knowledgeable partner in describing terminology and rules in football, shifting the concept of the ZPD because the learner here was an adult, the mother. These instances argued against the conventional model that only adults can be a more experienced participant in a shared activity with a child; rather, all participants collaborate towards their communal goal. Child intercultural mediation or language brokering becomes jointly constructed occasions where children and parents scaffold each other by pooling their linguistic, cultural, cognitive, and social skills. While child language brokers used complex linguistic, cognitive, and metacognitive strategies to translate and interpret (Eksner and Orellana 2012), they also draw on their parents' diverse contextual and social knowledge to accomplish their mediation.

The stance of a dialogic, socially situated, and distributed cognition of child intercultural mediation (Cole 1996; Engestrom, Miettinen, and Punamaeki 1999) also highlights that scaffolding can be reciprocal. Thus, in CIM, both scaffolds and the ZPDs of the participants are dynamically shifting (Eksner and Orellana 2012), with domains of learning varying and the roles of 'expert' and 'novice' flowing back and forth between children and parents (Eksner and Orellana 2012). Children take the lead in language brokering for their parents, but they mutually support each other's social learning; their linguistic and metalinguistic knowledge and metacognitive skills in their first and second languages are acquired in collaboration.

Power dynamics in CIM

Child mediators are faced with different audiences and are under different dynamics of power relations (Alvarez 2017). The impact of CLB on the family dynamics can be demonstrated in various ways. Early studies argued that language brokers affect the contents of the message they convey, and impact on parents' perceptions (McQuillan and Tse 1995). In the flow of conversation in language brokering, the child "spokesperson for the family" (Weisskirch 2007, 546) may be unable to consult their parents during decision making, during which process their parents' authority may have been suppressed. Contrastingly in non-immigrant families, a 'normative' childhood may more often assign the decision-making roles to parents (Titzmann 2012). This increased responsibility by child language brokers has been linked to a concept of parentification (Puig 2002; Oznobishin and Kurman 2009), adultification (Suárez-Orozco and Suárez-Orozco, 2001), role reversal, surrogate parents, or role-re-distribution (Pedersen and Revenson 2005). Thus, children take on responsibilities originally associated with adults in the conventional family system or hierarchy (Titzmann 2012), and parents depend on their children for more practical and emotional support (Jurkovic 2014) than they would in the non-immigrant contexts. These concepts, however, can undergo further scrutiny.

Earlier researchers recounted that child language brokers take on a wide range of translation and interpretation tasks including at doctor's offices, banks, and pharmacies; during credit card applications; shopping transactions; describing movies and television shows; and even explaining their own or their siblings' school report to their parents. These do not just "require considerable linguistic, arithmetic, and social-cultural dexterity" (Dorner, Orellana, and Li-Grining 2007, 452), they also contribute to parents' understanding of governments, institutions, and education in the mainstream society as the children offer advice and analysis of situations in these settings according to their bilingual and bi-cultural understanding. In assuming this adult-like authority and responsibility in creating meanings in formal settings language brokers were pushed to grow up to understand the meanings and consequences of these official texts (Alvarez 2017). Given the responsibilities children were given and emotional and practical benefits families gained, CIM can be conceptualized as work, though no child mediators were ever paid monetarily. Crafter and Iqbal (2020) perceive CLB as a space of cultural mediation where 'adultlike' work children undertake in complex cultural contact zone, because their spheres of experiences may exceed the widely held expectations of a normal childhood in a Western society (see more discussion on child mediation as work in Crafter and Iqbal 2021).

While power dynamics continue to be a focus of much discussion in the field, it is clear that CIM does redistribute some intergenerational authority between parents and children (Alvarez 2017). Depending on specific contexts, such a perspective as reversed roles could be seen as accelerating children's independence, transcending the 'normal' childhood developmental stages. However, the responsibilities faced by children in these 'adultified' roles actually carry even more stake for families in situations where children mediate between their family and another adult in a position of authority at the mainstream society. Yet the relationship dynamics in immigrant families are more complicated than a simple role-reversal (Eksner and Orellana 2012). Proponents of the 'parentified child' debate within CLB may not have accounted for the nuances in language brokering activities. This perspective could be misguided as children socialize their parents in the same way as their parents would do with them in non-immigrant contexts. Children in Alvarez (2017) described their language brokering as their family obligation, nothing more than helping out in and outside the home. With the strength of language brokering, children leverage for the overall well-being of family in the new society while extending their own biliteracy and biculturality (Orellana 2009). The resulting mutual benefit may not lead to a complete role reversal or a dynamic overturn (Alvarez 2017), but their help contributing to the good of the family which can be reframed in the same way as other 'non-normative' childhood experiences, e.g., in family care practice and other caring responsibilities to adults at home (Crafter and Iqbal 2021). Children are agentive with weakened parental authority and temporary repositioning between children and adults. But children may not wield consistent control over adults or their parents. Despite traditional generational boundaries were shifted or even erased in cases of CLB, children are not always 'left alone' but still supported by parents.

Effects and outcomes of CIM

Research has found different outcomes and effects in various CIM and CLB experiences in different settings on all parties in terms of emotional, attitudinal, cognitive, and academic performance, and psychological well-being.

Positive outcomes

Positive outcomes include improvement in bilingual development, cognitive skills, communication skills, and academic performance, as well as positive emotions including increase in confidence, self-efficacy, empathy, sense of belonging, and prosocial development (Weisskirch 2007). Language brokering children may grow cognitively more advanced than non-brokering bilinguals (Orellana 2009). Not just do they enhance their cognitive skills such as a metalinguistic awareness of parts of speech and grammar structures, different accents, and registers of voices (Rianey, Flores-Lamb and Gjorgieva 2017), they also develop their language switching abilities sooner than non-brokering peers. Previous studies on language brokering revealed a series of strategies youth language brokers developed in the two languages and biliteracies (Orellana and Reynolds 2008). Language brokers brought to their classroom cultural, intercultural, and linguistic strengths developed in their daily mediation work between parents and mainstream society. This promoted academic development, as Dorner, Orellana, and Li-Grining (2007) demonstrated that higher-level language brokering can be linked to better scores in reading tests.

Most children, through mediation, gain social benefits in understanding different values, norms, social conditions, and self-concepts (Garcia-Sanchez, Orellana and Hopkins 2011). In helping their parents, they generated sympathy for their parents' hardships and developed a stronger sense of family responsibility, belonging, obligation, and familial interdependence (Jones and Trickett 2005). These positively affected their feelings towards CLB, further supporting their families (Hall and Sham 2007). Similarly, through CLB, children have opportunities to develop empathy for other people (Guan, Greenfield, and Orellana 2014). This affective development tends to have positive impacts on children's psychological well-being, self-efficacy and interpersonal skills.

Negative outcomes

Negative outcomes include negative emotions and feelings such as stress, burdens, and depression that may be associated with poor parenting relationships caused by cultural mediation. As a possible source of family conflict and strain, CLB can be tedious and embarrassing (Jones and Trickett 2005) and negatively impact family relations (Morales and Hanson 2005), psychological and social well-being (Weisskirch 2007), and children's identity development (Orellana 2009). Other studies explored how the frequency and the nature of CLB can negatively affect mental health, risk factors, and behaviors of individuals (Kam 2011).

Although positive and negative outcomes and effects were listed separately above, almost all previous studies reported mixed feelings during language brokering. More detailed reviews of the effects of language brokering on children can be found in Shen, Tilton, and Kim (2017).

Future directions

In researching CIM itself, there is a promising increase of studies carried out on children themselves in language brokering. Despite this, more research is needed on the continuity and change of CIM over time, the differences at various stages of language brokering in children's life journey, and the possible consequences and developmental implications. Longitudinal studies are still needed to examine the process of language brokering and its impact upon the life of children and the family. Ethnographic studies could explore more real-time language brokering as it unfolds in families and communities; more naturally occurring data need to be captured to reveal more characteristics of CIM in action and its effect on family's adaption to the new country. More studies can be conducted on a wider range of ethnic groups in different countries. These will illuminate similarities and differences in language brokering experiences among various linguistic and ethnic groups internationally, as language brokering should be treated beyond a singular phenomenon common to all ethnic groups of immigrants.

In examining CIM, parties other than children themselves could be more widely considered. This includes parents and family members, and other adults in a triadic interaction. This can examine: roles each party plays, relationship dynamics, community features, parental perspectives, teachers' view of language brokering, gender roles, parents' stages of development, and language proficiency. More measurement methods could help determine frequency and outcomes, as well as more accurately assess language brokering.

A theoretical model of CIM could incorporate asset-based and strength-based perspectives to reify deficit-based perspectives (Weisskirch 2017) that view child mediation as a form of 'giftedness' (Valdés 2003) ethnic minority children bring to the new society. Importantly, CIM can be a tool to increase involvement and interest in language learning, preventing language loss, and promoting language sustainability. Even though children are conventionally seen to have a 'lower status' in relation to adults, it is clear that children as intercultural mediators be given more power and responsibility than their non-brokering peers. Even if their authority and expertise are not often recognized in school, it is routinely called upon outside it. In both arenas children's agency should not be ignored but promoted more widely (Orellana and Garcia 2014).

Conclusion

This chapter explored CIM from its definition, key research findings, and future directions. While the effects and outcomes of child language brokering are the most commonly researched areas, recent scholarly attention has been drawn to viewing CIM as a translanguaging, and socially situated and distributed dialogic process in the dyadic and triadic interaction, within which the power relationships are shifting and dynamic. The research done so far demonstrates the benefits of CIM to children, their parents and families, and to public institutions such as schools, medical services, and welfare departments. As an acculturative strategy for individuals, and the easiest resources available for immigrant families in most countries, CIM offers an extra channel for gaining insight into how to integrate immigrants into host societies. More policies and strategies are needed to cope with the cultural and linguistic diversity and changes led by increasing international mobility.

References

Alvarez, Steven. 2014. "Translanguaging Tareas: Emergent Bilingual Youth Language Brokering Homework in Immigrant Families." *Language Arts* 91 (5): 326–339.

Alvarez, Steven. 2017. "Brokering Literacies: Child Language Brokering in Mexican Immigrant Families." *Community Literacy Journal* 11 (2): 1–15. 10.1353/clj.2017.0000

Antonini, Rachele. 2016. "Caught in the Middle: Child Language Brokering as a Form of Unrecognised Language Service." *Journal of Multilingual and Multicultural Development* 37 (7): 710–725. 10.1080/01434632. 2015.1127931

Bauer, Elaine. 2013. "Reconstructing Moral Identities in Memories of Childhood Language Brokering Experiences." *International Migration* 51 (5): 205–218. 10.1111/imig.12030

Cole, Michael. 1996. *Cultural Psychology. A Once and Future Discipline*. Cambridge, MA: Belknap Harvard.

Crafter, Sarah, and Humera Iqbal. 2020. "The Contact Zone and Dialogical Positionalities in 'Non-Normative' Childhoods: How Children Who Language Broker Manage Conflict." *Review of General Psychology* 24 (1): 31–42. 10.1177/1089268019896354

Crafter, Sarah, and Humera Iqbal. 2021. "Child Language Brokering as a Family Care Practice: Reframing the 'Parentified Child' Debate." *Children & Society* July, chso.12485. 10.1111/chso.12485

Dorner, Lisa M., Marjorie Faulstich Orellana, and Christine P. Li-Grining. 2007. "'I Helped My Mom,' and It Helped Me: Translating the Skills of Language Brokers into Improved Standardized Test Scores." *American Journal of Education* 113 (3): 451–478. 10.1086/512740

Engeström, Yrjö, Reijo Miettinen, and Raija-Leena Punamäki-Gitai eds. 1999. *Perspectives on Activity Theory. Learning in Doing*. Cambridge; New York: Cambridge University Press.

Eksner, H. Julia, and Marjorie Faulstich Orellana. 2012. "Shifting in the Zone: Latina/o Child Language Brokers and the Co-Construction of Knowledge: Child Language Brokers and Knowledge Construction." *Ethos* 40 (2): 196–220. 10.1111/j.1548-1352.2012.01246.x

García, Ofelia. 2009. "Education, Multilingualism and Translanguaging in the 21st Century." In *Social Justice through Multilingual Education*, edited by Mohanty, Ajit, Minati Panda, Robert Phillipson and Tove Skutnabb-Kangas, 140–158. Bristol: Multilingual Matters.

García–Sánchez, Inmaculada M., Marjorie Faulstich Orellana, and Megan Hopkins. 2011. "Facilitating Intercultural Communication in Parent–Teacher Conferences: Lessons from Child Translators." *Multicultural Perspectives* 13 (3): 148–154. 10.1080/15210960.2011.594387

Guan, Shu-Sha A., Patricia M. Greenfield, and Marjorie F. Orellana. 2014. "Translating into Understanding: Language Brokering and Prosocial Development in Emerging Adults from Immigrant Families." *Journal of Adolescent Research* 29 (3): 331–355. 10.1177/0743558413520223

Guo, Zhiyan. 2014. *Young Children as Intercultural Mediators: Mandarin-Speaking Chinese Families in Britain.* Bristol; Buffalo: Multilingual Matters.

Gustafsson, Kristina. 2021. "Child Language Brokering in Swedish Welfare Institutions: A Matter of Structural Complicity?" In *Translating Asymmetry—Rewriting Power,* edited by Ovidi Carbonell i Cortés and Esther Monzó-Nebot, 157:125–144. Amsterdam: John Benjamins. 10.1075/btl.157.06gus

Harris, Brian. 1977, "The Importance of Natural Translation", *Working Papers on Bilingualism* 12: 96–144.

Harris, Brian, and Bianca Sherwood. 1978. "Translating as an Innate Skill." In *Language Interpretation and Communication,* edited by Gerver, David and H. Wallace Sinaiko, 155–170. New York: Plenum Press.

Hall, Nigel. 2004. "The Child in the Middle: Agency and Diplomacy in Language Brokering Events." In *Claims, Changes and Challenges in Translation Studies,* edited by Gyde Hansen, Kirsten Malmkjaer, and Daniel Gile, 285–296. Amsterdam: John Benjamins. 10.1075/btl.50.24hal

Hall, Nigel, and Zhiyan Guo. 2012. "Child Language and Cultural Brokering" In *Interpreting Brian Harris: Recent Developments in Translatology,* edited by Ivars, Amparo Jiménez and Jesús Blasco Mayor, 51–76. Bern, Switzerland: Peter Lang.

Hall, Nigel, and Sylvia Sham. 2007. "Language Brokering as Young People's Work: Evidence from Chinese Adolescents in England." *Language and Education* 21 (1): 16–30. 10.2167/le645.0

Hua, Josephine M., and Catherine L. Costigan. 2012. "The Familial Context of Adolescent Language Brokering Within Immigrant Chinese Families in Canada." *Journal of Youth and Adolescence* 41 (7): 894–906. 10.1007/s10964-011-9682-2

Jones, Curtis J., and Edison J. Trickett. 2005. "Immigrant Adolescents Behaving as Culture Brokers: A Study of Families From the Former Soviet Union." *The Journal of Social Psychology* 145 (4): 405–428. 10.3200/SOCP.145.4.405-428

Jurkovic, Gregor. 2014. *Lost Childhoods: The Plight of the Parentified Child.* New York: Routledge.

Kam, Jennifer A. 2011. "The Effects of Language Brokering Frequency and Feelings on Mexican-Heritage Youth's Mental Health and Risky Behaviors." *Journal of Communication* 61 (3): 455–475. 10.1111/j.1460-2466.2011.01552.x

Kam, Jennifer A., and Vanja Lazarevic. 2014. "Communicating for One's Family: An Interdisciplinary Review of Language and Cultural Brokering in Immigrant Families." *Annals of the International Communication Association* 38 (1): 3–37. 10.1080/23808985.2014.11679157

Li, Wei. 2011. "Moment Analysis and Translanguaging Space: Discursive Construction of Identities by Multilingual Chinese Youth in Britain." *Journal of Pragmatics* 43 (5): 1222–1235. 10.1016/j.pragma.2010.07.035

McQuillan, Jeff, and Lucy Tse. 1995. "Child Language Brokering in Linguistic Minority Communities: Effects on Cultural Interaction, Cognition, and Literacy." *Language and Education* 9 (3): 195–215. 10.1080/09500789509541413

Morales, Alejandro, and William E. Hanson. 2005. "Language Brokering: An Integrative Review of the Literature." *Hispanic Journal of Behavioral Sciences* 27 (4): 471–503. 10.1177/0739986305281333

Napier, Jemina. 2021. *Sign Language Brokering in Deaf-Hearing Families.* Cham, Switzerland: Palgrave Macmillan.

Orellana, Marjorie Faulstich. 2009. *Translating Childhoods: Immigrant Youth, Language, and Culture.* New Brunswick: Rutgers University Press.

Orellana, Marjorie Faulstich, and Ofelia García. 2014. "Language Brokering and Translanguaging in School". *Language Arts* 91 (5): 386–392.

Orellana, Marjorie Faulstich, and Jennifer F. Reynolds. 2008. "Cultural Modeling: Leveraging Bilingual Skills for School Paraphrasing Tasks." *Reading Research Quarterly* 43 (1): 48–65. 10.1598/RRQ.43.1.4

Oznobishin, Olga, and Jenny Kurman. 2009. "Parent–Child Role Reversal and Psychological Adjustment among Immigrant Youth in Israel." *Journal of Family Psychology* 23 (3): 405–415. 10.1037/a0015811

Pena-Díaz, Carmen. 2019. "Child Language Brokering: Challenges in Spanish Intercultural Education." *Intercultural Education* 30 (4): 368–382. 10.1080/14675986.2018.1540107

Pedersen, Sara, and Tracey A. Revenson. 2005. "Parental Illness, Family Functioning, and Adolescent Well-Being: A Family Ecology Framework to Guide Research." *Journal of Family Psychology* 19 (3): 404–419. 10.1037/0893-3200.19.3.404

Phoenix, Ann, and Marjorie Faulstich Orellana. 2021. "Adult Narratives of Childhood Language Brokering: Learning What It Means to Be Bilingual." *Children & Society* May, chso. 12462. 10.1111/chso.12462

Puig, Maria Elena. 2002. "The Adultification of Refugee Children: Implications for Cross-Cultural Social Work Practice." *Journal of Human Behavior in the Social Environment* 5 (3–4): 85–95. 10.1300/J137v05n03_05

Rainey, Vanessa R., Valerie C. Flores-Lamb, and Eva Gjorgieva. 2017. "Cognitive, Socioemotional, and Developmental Neuroscience Perspectives on Language Brokering." In *Language Brokering in Immigrant Families,* edited by Robert S. Weisskirch, 205–223. New York: Routledge. 10.4324/9781315644714-11

Reynolds, Jennifer F., and Marjorie Faulstich Orellana. 2014. "Translanguaging within Enactments of Quotidian Interpreter-Mediated Interactions." *Journal of Linguistic Anthropology* 24 (3): 315–338. 10.1111/jola.12057

Shannon, Sheila M. 1990. "English in the Barrio: The Quality of Contact among Immigrant Children." *Hispanic Journal of Behavioral Sciences* 12 (3): 256–276. 10.1177/07399863900123002

Shen, Yishan, Kelsey E. Tilton, and Su Yeong Kim. 2017. "Outcomes of Language Brokering, Mediators, and Moderators." In *Language Brokering in Immigrant Families*, edited by Robert S. Weisskirch, 47–71. New York: Routledge. 10.4324/9781315644714-4

Suárez-Orozco, Carola, & Suárez-Orozco, Marcelo. M. 2001. *Children of Immigration.* Cambridge, MA: Harvard University Press.

Tse, Lucy. 1995. "Language Brokering among Latino Adolescents: Prevalence, Attitudes, and School Performance." *Hispanic Journal of Behavioral Sciences* 17 (2): 180–193. 10.1177/07399863950172003

Titzmann, Peter F. 2012. "Growing Up Too Soon? Parentification among Immigrant and Native Adolescents in Germany." *Journal of Youth and Adolescence* 41 (7): 880–893. 10.1007/s10964-011-9711-1

Tomasi, Ana-marija, and Renu Narchal. 2020. "Experiences and Psychological Well-Being of Language Brokers in Australia: A Mixed Methods Approach." *Australian Psychologist* 55 (4): 397–409. 10.1111/ap.12443

Valdés, Guadalupe. 2003. *Expanding Definitions of Giftedness: The Case of Young Interpreters from Immigrant Communities.* New York: Routledge.

Vygotsky, Lev S. 1978. *Mind in Society: The Development of Higher Psychological Processes.* Cambridge, MA: Harvard University Press.

Weisskirch, Robert S. 2007. "Feelings about Language Brokering and Family Relations Among Mexican American Early Adolescents." *The Journal of Early Adolescence* 27 (4): 545–561. 10.1177/0272431607302935

Weisskirch, Robert S. 2017. "Future Directions for Language Brokering Research." In *Language Brokering in Immigrant Families*, edited by Robert S. Weisskirch, 294–305. New York: Routledge. 10.4324/9781315644714-15

49

INTERCULTURAL MEDIATION IN THE WORLD LANGUAGE CLASSROOM

Christelle Palpacuer Lee

Introduction

Language education is a dynamic field that is informed by several disciplines and traditions with an interest in language, culture, and learning. A wide range of methodological orientations and conceptual tools are now available for language educators to creatively address and shape the practices of language teaching and learning. In the context of globalization, teaching world languages has become increasingly complex. Language educators are grappling with ways to honor and operationalize the linguistic and cultural diversity of today's language classrooms, the hybridity of language practices, as well as the goals of world language education. For several decades now, language education has focused on equipping global citizens with the skills, dispositions, knowledge, and competencies they need to live, work, and engage with an increasingly diverse and plurilingual world. Intercultural mediation represents a cornerstone of language education's responses to these challenges and possibilities for the 21st-century language classroom. This chapter describes and interrogates the notion of intercultural mediation for the world language classroom. It focuses largely on research conducted in European and North American contexts, paying attention to the contributions of scholars, educators, and advocates advancing a view of intercultural mediation as a construct to inform socially and culturally responsive praxis, as well as democratic engagement in a plurilingual world.

Territories, frontiers, and early explorations

The term *intercultural mediation* first appeared in the language education literature in the 1990s. It was primarily associated with the notion of conflict resolution and with the management of cultural differences. As such, intercultural mediation was bound to an awareness of cultural differences, and to the accumulation of knowledge about other cultures, in order to "develop the ability to handle cross-cultural problems which result from those [cultural] differences" (Meyer 1991, 137). In the world language curricula, materials, and classroom activities, culture was treated separately from language. In the United States, instruction targeted four main domains of language learning: Reading, writing, speaking, and listening. Culture represented a fifth domain, separate from the other four language activities (Damen 1987). When students engaged with culture, it was generally through comparative activities between their own and an idealized target culture. This engagement was directed towards an understanding of the practices and perspectives of culturally different

464

DOI: 10.4324/9781003227441-59

speakers. In this sense, intercultural mediation was not yet intercultural, but rather cross-cultural. Before—and sometimes long after—the advent of communicative methods for language education, which focused on the use of the target language and not just on the knowledge about the foreign language, intercultural mediation was limited to an awareness of cultural differences and to transactional practices.

Much of the scholarship and literature on language education at the time was devoted to challenging and expanding these views on the place of culture in the language classroom (Risager 1991; Kramsch 1993). To advance forward, language educators needed to simultaneously expand upon the definition of culture and to integrate language and culture in world language instruction, curricula and policies (Kramsch 1993). In the language classroom, a first step was to attempt to move past essentialized and reductionist approaches to culture in the language classroom, which could be counterproductive and lead to the reinforcement of stereotypes (Risager 2006). Another avenue taken by educators and applied linguists was to challenge and to reformulate the distinctions and hierarchies that characterized the discourses of world language pedagogy. For instance, Claire Kramsch (1997) critically examined the distinction between native and non-native speaker instantiated in the structures, curricula, and practices of world language education. In a subsequent publication, she resolved this distinction by instead using the term *intercultural speaker* to refer to language learners (Kramsch 1999).

Despite an overall compartmentalized approach to world language learning, there were efforts at bringing culture-in-language teaching to the classroom, which would bear fruition in moving the profession forward. An emphasis on mutual understanding and problem-solving practices between speakers of different languages-cultures is still inscribed in educational and instructional discourses concerning intercultural language pedagogy for the world language classroom (Dasli 2011; Kohler 2015). However, the educational landscape has changed significantly, and the role and function of intercultural mediation have further expanded beyond the management of conflict and misunderstanding.

The exploration of the interstices

Since the publication of Michael Byram's (1997) ground-breaking model for the development and assessment of intercultural communicative competence in language education, the interpretation of intercultural mediation has both shifted and expanded. In the subsequent literature on language education, intercultural mediation has been closely associated with intercultural competence for the world language classroom (Buttjes and Byram 1991; Byram 2002; Zarate et al. 2004; Liddicoat and Scarino 2013). In deploying intercultural competence, language learners expand upon their ability "to see relationships between different cultures—both internal and external to a society—and to mediate, that is interpret each in terms of the other, either for themselves or for other people" (Byram 2000, 10). There are two important points about intercultural mediation in this view of intercultural competence: First, intercultural mediation is framed in terms of interpretive practices. In other words, intercultural mediation is an interpretive process that provides access to other languages-cultures and other viewpoints. In turn, learners' own familiar worldviews and perspectives are also mediated through these different perspectives. In that, intercultural mediation is a reflexive and critical process (Byram 2000, 2021; Kramsch 1993). The conditions and contexts for mediation are examined in the classroom, and in other spheres of learning, so as to maximize opportunities to critically investigate encounters with alterity, with the self, and with subjectivity. In turn, these activities prompt interpretations, critical reflection, as well as communication (Kearney 2016). Second, mediation for intercultural competence is not necessarily bound by national–cultural frames; it can also be intra–cultural. This second point brings attention to the reflexivity of mediation practices and processes in the intercultural language classroom. Mediation takes place in a movement from self to others, and from others to self (Liddicoat 2014). In turn, learning languages and cultures is not just a cognitive process, it is also a process of socialization into various communities of speakers.

More broadly, intercultural mediation refers to the ability to see oneself and others through different lenses, to navigate zones of contact between different languages and cultures, and to develop a shared understanding of cultural products, practices, and perspectives (Kramsch 1993; Liddicoat and Scarino 2013; Pratt 1991; Zarate et al. 2004). Mediation for intercultural competence does not only aim at resolving misunderstandings or communication problems between speakers of different languages-cultures, but also strives to build the necessary competences to engage in mediation activities with others. Such activities propose to explain cultural practices and worldviews through comparison, dialogue, and the negotiation of meaning across cultural perspectives. Intercultural mediation is thus "an active engagement in diversity as a meaning-making activity that involves interpreting the meaning of diverse others for oneself and for others" (Liddicoat and Scarino 2013, 54). This view of intercultural mediation highlights the subjective and dialogic nature of interpretive practices, competences, and dispositions necessary for learners to act as mediators and as speakers of culture (Kramsch 1993; Liddicoat and Scarino 2013). In these roles, language learners develop the capacity to understand multiple perspectives as well as their own (Kramsch 1999; Abdallah-Pretceille 2003; Byram et al. 2002). Across pedagogical discourses, intercultural mediation practices in the world language classroom are viewed in terms of interpretation and of action (Liddicoat and Scarino 2013).

A view of intercultural mediation as interpretive practice is not always explicit on the political and ideological dimensions of intercultural mediation in the language classroom. Michael Byram (1997) evokes the possibility of "conflict in perspectives, not only harmonious communication" (101) in this process. However, there are other possible tensions that can emerge in intercultural mediation, in relation to the negotiation of subjectivity, agency, identity, power dynamics, and membership. In intercultural encounters, the negotiation, "[e]valuation and comparison of one another [cultural identities] does not happen in opposite-directional parallel lines" (Guilherme 2002, 153), but instead in a space where power and "ideological perspectives from both sides collide" (153). Language education is developing an action-oriented educational agenda to address the critical and political engagement with linguistic and cultural diversity in intercultural mediation, and with equity and justice (Canagarajah 2014; Guilherme 2002; Phipps 2019). And, transformative and critical pedagogies that orient towards collective social action take into account the tensions associated with learning and mediation in often asymmetrical relationships of power. In her critique of the limitations of the intercultural communicative competence model, Claire Kramsch (2006) introduces the notion of symbolic competence as a way to attend to the interplays of language, culture, and power in educational discourses and classroom practices.

Another limitation is that the role of language might often be overlooked in intercultural mediation practices in the classroom (Dervin 2011; Dervin and Liddicoat 2013). Anthony Liddicoat (2014) argues that

> a view of language simply as a tool for intercultural mediation misses the reality that language is itself a site of intercultural mediation in that it is shaped by the cultures within which it is used and is a constituent part (262).

This proposal to revisit the role of language in intercultural mediation practices from a discourse perspective has opened additional possibilities for the world language classroom (Liddicoat, this volume; Kramsch 2006; 2014; 2020). Such new possibilities amplify the understandings and interpretations of intercultural mediation, and take place in the larger context of a movement towards paradigm shifts in language education.

The world language classroom

Expanded views on mediation

In a transforming language education landscape, the multi-faceted and 'nomadic' (Lenoir 1996) notion of mediation for intercultural language education has received increased attention from scholars, policy-makers, and practitioners. Lev Vygotsky's sociocultural theory of mind (Vygotsky and Cole 1978) has had a significant influence on the conceptualizations and understandings of mediation in language education (Lantolf 2000). One of Vygotsky's (Vygotsky and Cole 1978) most important contributions is to advance that all human activities—including learning—take place in cultural contexts and through cultural activity, and are mediated by material or symbolic tools and by other people. This claim positions mediation as a complex social and cognitive process through which people engage with, act upon, and transform the world and the tools at their disposal. This has far-reaching implications for pedagogy. First, learning is conceived as a social and cognitive activity, whereby new knowledge, mediated by material or symbolic artifacts and by others, is appropriated and integrated into cognitive and social activities. Second, language is one of the most powerful symbolic tools at our disposal to mediate social and cognitive activities. In the world language classroom, language is simultaneously the object of learning (the new language-culture), a tool for learning (using language as one of the resources for learning), and a site for learning ("shaped by the cultures within which it is used and is a constituent part,") (Liddicoat 2014, 262).

This view of mediation in world language education is best illustrated by the 2020 *Common European Framework of Reference for Languages—Companion Volume* (CEFR—CV) published by the Council of Europe as an update to the 2001 *Common European Framework of Reference for Languages* (CEFR) (Council of Europe 2001). For Enrica Piccardo (2018), who contributed to the development of the descriptors related to mediation practices in the 2020 CEFR—CV, mediation has emerged as a promising conceptual tool that can function as a lens through which scholars and educators can re–envision the scope and goals of world language education, and guide the development of policies, pedagogies, as well as instructional resources that support the work of educators and plurilingual students in 21st-century classrooms (Piccardo 2018).

The CEFR—CV inscribes mediation within a constellation of adjacent notions and constructs framed by post-structuralist and sociocultural perspectives on language, culture and learning:

> In mediation, the user/learner acts as a social agent who creates bridges and helps to construct and convey meaning, sometimes within the same language, sometimes from one language to another ... The focus is on the role of language in processes like creating the space and conditions for communicating and/or learning, collaborating to construct new meaning, encouraging others to construct or understand new meaning, and passing on new information in an appropriate form.
>
> *(Council of Europe 2020, 90)*

This statement about mediation emphasizes meaning and meaning-making practices. Mediation in the language classroom involves the co-construction and communication of meaning across languages and cultures, and within languages and cultures. Mediation is thus a cross-linguistic and cross-cultural process centered around meaning-making practices, but it is also intra-cultural and interpersonal. In the world language classroom, the main function of mediation is to *create bridges* across social actors, as agents, and across contexts through language. In that sense, mediation is transformative: Change can occur along cognitive, social and cultural dimensions. Mediation is also action-oriented as learners co-construct new meanings, but also as they reformulate, creatively adapt, and amplify their meaning-making practices in the world language classroom.

In this expanded view, intercultural mediation takes on additional dimensions beyond communication across languages-cultures to reach a mutual understanding. Mediation for pluricultural

Christelle Palpacuer Lee

and plurilingual competence could thus be interpreted as the situated and transformative practices and activities through which plurilingual speakers negotiate, challenge, reformulate, and co-create meaning across sites of practice, and engage in social action through language. This extended view of mediation, within a plurilingual paradigm, aligns closely with recent advances in applied linguistics and language education (Blyth 2019; Kearney 2016). Post-structural perspectives on language and culture embrace complexity (Larsen-Freeman and Cameron 2008), ecological and discursive frames (Lier 2004; Kramsch 2002, 2020), and Vygotsky's theory of mind (Lantolf 2000). Such dynamic, meaning-based views of language and culture both destabilize and amplify the objects of study in language education (Kearney 2016). In turn, it also impacts practices in language classrooms.

Future directions

Rapid and exponential changes in our ways of being, learning, and living together in a global, diverse, and interconnected world have destabilized and fundamentally transformed the contexts, practices, and the conditions for language learning and teaching (Kramsch 2014). The ideological, educational, and pedagogical dimensions of language education are shifting and expanding. This movement toward change is inviting reformulations, critical investigations, and conceptual shifts across discourses and educational contexts in language education, as well as the possibilities for instruction (Dervin and Simpson 2021; Dervin and Gross 2016; Kearney 2019; Phipps and Levine 2010; Piccardo and North 2019). New visions for language education are taking shape, aligned with and reflecting, superdiversity (Vertovec 2011), multiple identities (Norton 2013), hybridities (Canagarajah 2014; 2016), and multilingualism (Blommaert 2010). The notion of plurilingualism has emerged in policy as a response to this changing landscape, expanding the terrain, interpretations, and practices associated with intercultural mediation.

The term plurilingualism was first used in language education policy in the 2001 version of the *Common European Framework of Reference* (henceforth, CEFR) (Council of Europe 2001; Coste, Moore and Zarate 2009) as an overarching construct for language education. In contrast with multiculturalism, viewed as the accumulation or juxtaposition of diverse languages-cultures, as well as an advocacy and critical tool to challenge monolingual ideologies, the notion of plurilingualism emphasizes "the interrelation and interconnection of languages—particularly but not exclusively at the level of the individual—in relation to the dynamic nature of language acquisition" (Piccardo 2018, 213). In turn, this relational view of linguistic diversity further expands the scope of language learning first "horizontally, toward the use of multiple languages" (Piccardo and Puozzo 2015, 319), acknowledging the variety of linguistic repertoires speakers bring to the classroom; and second, "vertically, toward valuing even the most partial knowledge of a language" (ibid), and thus broadening the notion of competence (Piccardo and North 2019). A plurilingual frame also emphasizes the sets of relations between language and culture, where "[l]anguage is not only a major aspect of culture, but also a means of access to cultural manifestations" (CEFR 2001, 6). Cultural competence, then is reformulated and extended as the dynamic interrelationships between the plural and dynamic linguistic and cultural repertoires speakers, as agents, have access to. Plurilingualism is an overarching frame that has the potential to transform the ideological contexts and discourses in language education (Piccardo, North and Goodier 2019). In turn, this frame can further expand the processes and practices of intercultural mediation, addressing and amplifying the hybrid, multiple, situated, and dynamic practices of plurilingual speakers.

Conclusion

Language education is increasingly centering practices that orient towards action. Emerging pedagogies for the world language classrooms engage with expanded views on language, culture,

The world language classroom

and learning that embrace the complex, fluid, dynamic, and situated nature of language, culture, and self in multi/plurilingual and global settings. In this changing educational landscape, the understandings and functions of intercultural mediation expand beyond a single focus on communication and mutual understanding. Intercultural mediation is also interpreted as situated and transformative practices and activities through which plurilingual speakers negotiate, challenge, reformulate, and co-create meaning; and engage in social action through language. Intercultural mediation is a dynamic and intercultural notion that reflects conceptual reformulations as well as tensions in language education, and opens creative as well as innovative avenues for world language classroom practices.

References

Abdallah-Pretceille, Martine. 2003. *Former et éduquer en contexte hétérogène*. Paris: Economica.

Blommaert, Jan. 2010. *The Sociolinguistics of Globalization*. Cambridge: Cambridge University Press. 10.1017/CBO9780511845307

Blyth, Carl. 2019. "Designing Foreign Language Curricula and Pedagogy in Terms of Meaning-Making: The Application of Languaculture and Designs of Meaning." In *AAUSC 2019 Volume—Issues in Language Program Direction: Pathways to Paradigm Change: Critical Examinations of Prevailing Discourses and Ideologies in Second Language Education*, edited by Beatrice Dupuy and Kristen Michelson, 153–175. Boston, MA: Cengage. http://hdl.handle.net/10125/69796

Buttjes, Dieter and Michael Byram eds. 1991. *Mediating Languages and Cultures: Towards an Intercultural Theory of Foreign Language Education*. Clevedon, UK: Multilingual Matters.

Byram, Michael. 1997. *Teaching and Assessing Intercultural Communicative Competence*. Clevedon, PA: Multilingual Matters.

Byram, Michael. 2000. "Assessing Intercultural Competence in Language Teaching." *Sprogforum*, 18 (6): 8–13.

Byram, Michael. 2002. "On Being 'Bicultural' and 'Intercultural.'" In *Intercultural Experience and Education*, edited by Geof Alred, Michael Byram, and Mike Fleming, 50–66. Bristol, Blue Ridge Summit: Multilingual Matters. 10.21832/9781853596087-007

Byram, Michael. 2021. *Teaching and Assessing Intercultural Communicative Competence: Revisited*. Bristol, Blue Ridge Summit: Multilingual Matters. 10.21832/9781800410251

Byram, Michael, Bella Gribkova, and Hugh Starkey. 2002. *Developing the intercultural dimension in language teaching: A practical introduction for teachers*. Strasbourg: Council of Europe.

Canagarajah, Suresh. 2014. "Theorizing a Competence for Translingual Practice at the Contact Zone." In *The Multilingual Turn: Implications for SLA, TESOL and Bilingual Education*, edited by Stephen May, 78–102. New York; London: Routledge.

Canagarajah, Suresh. 2016. "Crossing Borders, Addressing Diversity." Language Teaching 49 (3): 438–454. 10.1017/S0261444816000069

Coste, Daniel, Danièle Moore, and Geneviève Zarate. 2009. *Plurilingual and Pluricultural Competence*. Strasbourg: Council of Europe Publishing. https://rm.coe.int/168069d29b

Council of Europe. 2001. *Common European Framework of Reference for Languages: Learning, Teaching, Assessment*. Strasbourg: Council of Europe Publishing. https://www.coe.int/lang-cefr

Council of Europe. 2020. *Common European Framework of Reference for Languages: Learning, Teaching, Assessment—Companion Volume*. Strasbourg: Council of Europe Publishing. https://www.coe.int/lang-cefr

Damen, Louise. 1987. *Culture Learning: The Fifth Dimension in the Language Classroom*. Reading, MA: Addison-Wesley.

Dasli, Maria. 2011. "Reviving the 'Moments': From Cultural Awareness and Cross-cultural Mediation to Critical Intercultural Language Pedagogy." *Pedagogy, Culture & Society* 19 (1): 21–39. 10.1080/14681366.2011.527118

Dervin, Fred. 2011. "A Plea for Change in Research on Intercultural Discourses: A 'Liquid' Approach to the Study of the Acculturation of Chinese Students." *Journal of Multicultural Discourses* 6 (1): 37–52. 10.1080/17447143.2010.532218

Dervin, Fred and Anthony J. Liddicoat. 2013. "Introduction: Linguistics for Intercultural Education." In *Language Learning & Language Teaching*, edited by Fred Dervin and Anthony J. Liddicoat, 33: 1–25. Amsterdam: John Benjamins. 10.1075/lllt.33.01der

Dervin, Fred and Zehavit Gross eds. 2016. *Intercultural Competence in Education*. London: Palgrave Macmillan. 10.1057/978-1-137-58733-6

Dervin, Fred, and Ashley Simpson. 2021. *Interculturality and the Political within Education*. London: Routledge. 10.4324/9780429471155

Guilherme, Maria Manuela. 2002. *Critical Citizens for an Intercultural World: Foreign Language Education as Cultural Politics*. Clevedon, UK: Multilingual Matters. 10.21832/9781853596117

Kearney, Erin. 2016. *Intercultural Learning in Modern Language Education: Expanding Meaning-Making Potentials*. Bristol, UK; Buffalo: Multilingual Matters.

Kearney, Erin. 2019. Developing Interculturality in Modern Language Education: A Professional Vision Perspective on Current Practices and Future Directions. Talk given at the 2019 MLA Convention, Chicago.

Kohler, Michelle. 2015. *Teachers as Mediators in the Foreign Language Classroom*. Bristol, UK; Buffalo: Multilingual Matters.

Kramsch, Claire. 1993. *Context and Culture in Language Teaching*. Oxford, UK: Oxford University Press.

Kramsch, Claire. 1997. "Guest Column: The Privilege of the Nonnative Speaker." *PMLA* 112 (3): 359–369.

Kramsch, Claire. 1999. "The Privilege of the Intercultural Speaker". In *Language Learning in Intercultural Perspective: Approaches Through Drama and Ethnography*, edited by Michael Byram and Michael Fleming, 16–31. Cambridge: Cambridge University Press.

Kramsch, Claire J. ed. 2002. *Language Acquisition and Language Socialization: Ecological Perspectives*. London; New York: Continuum.

Kramsch, Claire. 2006. "From Communicative Competence to Symbolic Competence." *The Modern Language Journal* 90 (2): 249–252. 10.1111/j.1540-4781.2006.00395_3.x

Kramsch, Claire. 2014. "Teaching Foreign Languages in an Era of Globalization: Introduction: Teaching Foreign Languages." *The Modern Language Journal* 98 (1): 296–311. 10.1111/j.1540-4781.2014.12057.x

Kramsch, Claire. 2020. *Language as Symbolic Power*. Cambridge: Cambridge University Press. 10.1017/97811 08869386

Lantolf, James P. ed. 2000. *Sociocultural Theory and Second Language Learning*. Oxford: Oxford University Press.

Larsen-Freeman, Diane and Lynne Cameron. 2008. *Complex Systems and Applied Linguistics*. Oxford: Oxford University Press.

Lenoir, Yves. 1996. *Médiation cognitive et médiation didactique*. In *Le didactique au–delà des didactiques. Débats autour de concepts fédérateurs*, edited by Claude Raisky and Michel Caillot, 223–251. Bruxelles: De Boeck Université.

Liddicoat, Anthony J. 2014. "Pragmatics and Intercultural Mediation in Intercultural Language Learning." *Intercultural Pragmatics* 11 (2). 10.1515/ip-2014-0011

Liddicoat, Anthony and Angela Scarino. 2013. *Intercultural Language Teaching and Learning*. Hoboken, NJ: Wiley-Blackwell.

Lier, Leo van ed. 2004. *The Ecology and Semiotics of Language Learning: A Sociocultural Perspective*. Dordrecht: Springer Netherlands. 10.1007/1-4020-7912-5

Meyer, Meinert. 1991. "Developing Transcultural Competence: Case Studies in Advanced Language Learners." In *Mediating Languages and Cultures: Towards an Intercultural Theory of Foreign Language Education*, edited by Dieter Buttjes and Michael Byram, 136–158. Clevedon, Avon, UK; Philadelphia: Multilingual Matters.

Norton, Bonny. 2013. *Identity and Language Learning: Extending the Conversation*. Bristol, Blue Ridge Summit: Multilingual Matters. 10.21832/9781783090563

Phipps, Alison. 2019. *Decolonising Multilingualism: Struggles to Decreate*. Bristol, Blue Ridge Summit: Multilingual Matters. 10.21832/9781788924061

Phipps, Alison, and Glenn S. Levine. 2010. "What Is Language Pedagogy For?" In *Critical and Intercultural Theory and Language Pedagogy*, edited by Glenn S. Levine and Alison Phipps, 1–1. Boston, MA: Heinle Cengage Learning. http://www.slrpjournal.org/item/262

Piccardo, Enrica. 2018. "Plurilingualism: Vision, Conceptualization, and Practices." In *Handbook of Research and Practice in Heritage Language Education*, edited by Peter Pericles Trifonas and Themistoklis Aravossitas, 207–225. Cham: Springer International Publishing. 10.1007/978-3-319-44694-3_47

Piccardo, Enrica, and Isabelle C. Puozzo. 2015. "From Second Language Pedagogy to the Pedagogy of 'Plurilingualism': A Possible Paradigm Shift?" / "De la didactique des langues à la didactique du plurilinguisme: un changement de paradigme possible?" *The Canadian Modern Language Review/La Revue Canadienne des Langues Vivantes* 71 (4): 317–323. 10.3138/cmlr.71.4.324

Piccardo, Enrica and Brian North. 2019. *The Action-Oriented Approach: A Dynamic Vision of Language Education*. Bristol, UK: Multilingual Matters. 10.21832/9781788924351

Piccardo, Enrica, Brian North, and Tom Goodier. 2019. "Broadening the Scope of Language Education: Mediation, Plurilingualism, and Collaborative Learning: The CEFR Companion Volume." *Journal of E-Learning and Knowledge Society* 15 (1): 17–36. 10.20368/1971-8829/1612

Pratt, Mary Louise. 1991. "Arts of the Contact Zone." *Profession* 1991: 33–40.

Risager, Karen. 1991. "Cultural References in European Foreign Language Textbooks: An Evaluation of Recent Tendencies." In *Mediating Languages and Cultures: Towards an Intercultural Theory of Foreign Language Education*, edited by Dieter Buttjes and Michael Byram, 181–192. Clevedon, Avon, UK; Philadelphia: Multilingual Matters.

Risager, Karen. 2006. *Language and Culture: Global Flows and Local Complexity*. Clevedon, UK: Multilingual Matters. 10.21832/9781853598609

Vertovec, Steven ed. 2011. *Anthropology of Migration and Multiculturalism: New Directions*. London: Routledge.

Vygotsky, Lev Semenovich, and Michael Cole. 1978. *Mind in Society: The Development of Higher Psychological Processes*. Cambridge: Harvard University Press.

Zarate, Geneviève, Aline Gohard-Radenkovic, Denise Lussier, and Hermine Penz. 2004. *Médiation culturelle et didactique des langues*. Kapfenberg: Council of Europe Publishing.

INDEX

Aakhus 240, 243
Abdul Cader, Akram 172–79
abjection 89
absolution 45–46
abstract sense of mediation 412
Abu Nimer, Mohammed 111–18
accent 333, 336, 459
acceptability, contextual 100
access; to justice 4, 27, 32, 56, 271, 282, 286; to
    services 332
accessibility 51, 105–6, 109, 167, 332
accommodating 114, 188, 278, 332–33
accountability 33, 35, 38, 55, 82, 98, 107,
    141–42, 343
acculturation 410
achievement 30, 36, 165, 210, 225, 321, 379–80
acknowledgement 45, 216, 323, 418, 451
actions 325; rational choice 314, 317
active listening 37, 60, 183
activism 418
activities, cultural 85–86, 89, 467
adaptability, defined intercultural 216
adaptive mediation 100
adjudication 27, 33, 68, 121, 192, 270–71
adjustment 372; to new cultures 371
administrative frameworks for dispute resolution 28
ADR (Alternative Dispute Resolution) 4, 12–14, 27,
    46, 98, 121–22, 153, 159–60, 189, 193–95, 265,
    268, 276, 278, 285–86
adversaries 37, 108, 120–22, 298
advocacy 119, 122–23, 289, 404, 418, 420, 468
Africa/African 27, 32–34, 37, 119, 155, 173, 190, 268
African American 52, 54, 57, 150, 175
African Union 97, 113
Agamben, Giorgio 310
Agar, Michael 145, 230, 235, 302, 305
age 13, 60, 104, 108–9, 131, 158, 183, 205, 220, 222,
    242, 281, 298, 316–17, 340, 360, 364

agency 37, 47, 52, 87, 114, 116–17, 130–32, 203–5,
    223, 234, 289, 321–26, 412, 461, 466
agent 61, 114, 206, 224, 409–10, 436, 467
agentive 145–46, 206, 405, 459
aggression 91, 120, 164, 192–93, 193, 195, 230,
    232–34, 297
aggressive/aggressiveness 150, 164, 192–93, 222, 278,
    293, 296–98
agonism 100
AI 107
Alexander, Nadja 26–27, 34, 47
Allen, Susan H. 128–35
alliances 316, 318
Allport 294, 369
alterity 204, 209, 465
Alternative Dispute Resolution 4, 13–14, 27, 33, 121,
    189, 265, 270, 276, 285, 340
alternatives 33, 121, 226, 266, 271, 349
ambiguity 60, 80, 96, 125, 181, 184, 254, 256,
    310–11, 435
American Bar Association 52, 159
Americanization 26
amnesty 39
analysis 44–45, 247, 331, 341–42, 358, 446
Anderson, Dorcas Quek 67–76
and peace studies 284–86
anger 150, 221
Anglophone group 389–92
Antaki, Nabil H. 27–28
anthropological 8, 24, 95–96, 98, 265–66, 268,
    270–71, 275–76, 282, 284–86, 313, 409–10;
    approach 276, 282
anthropologists 25, 53, 181, 190, 267, 269, 275, 277,
    295; legal 266, 268, 270, 286
anthropology 1, 4, 7, 12, 14, 31, 164, 191–92,
    265–71, 266, 275–76, 278, 284–87, 293, 302, 310,
    409; of conflict 164; of law 266, 270
anti-law ideology 270

Index

anxiety 149–50, 296
apologies 39, 79, 141, 372
Appiah, Kwame Anthony 28
applied linguistics 205–6, 468
approaches; formulaic 140; indigenous 130; individual 278, 388; monolingual 445; redefining 183; reductionist 465; theoretical 216, 317
approachment 105, 107–9
appropriation 205–6
arbiter 279
architectonic 146, 149–50; text 146, 149–50
archival research 266
Argentina 34, 436–37, 439, 444
Argentinian students 438–40
argument 25, 27–28, 32, 99, 146, 165, 186, 195, 204–5, 220–22, 265–66, 271, 296–98, 305, 334, 343, 384
argumentation 165, 240, 378; styles 240
Aristotle 130, 164
arts 5, 59, 61, 131, 180, 186, 433, 437, 440
ascription 30, 340, 362–64
Asian American 56
Asian Americans 56
Asian cultures 56
Asmussen, Ida Helene 43–50
assault 80, 164
assertiveness 106, 278
assimilation 32, 166–68
Association for Conflict Resolution 56
asymmetrical 208, 316–17, 466
asymmetric conflicts 119, 125
ATA (American Translators Association) 419
attentive listening 77
attitude 5, 10, 56, 59–61, 63, 89, 96, 114, 164–65, 169, 181–82, 184, 191, 201–2, 210, 216, 220, 226, 233, 240, 246, 269, 281, 294, 296–97, 301, 305–6, 331, 336, 342, 372, 400, 403, 417, 426, 435–36
attitudinal 30, 459
Augsburger, David 23–26, 141, 189, 192–94, 275, 278–79
Australia 34, 46, 166, 240, 318, 351, 446, 455
autonomy 27, 37, 90, 166, 168, 323
avatars 72
avoiding 113, 195, 278, 296, 323–25, 379–81, 383–84, 400, 419
Avruch, Kevin 3–4, 7, 12, 23, 25–26, 30, 32, 35, 53, 55–56, 67–68, 98, 112, 130, 189, 241, 250, 268–69, 275, 277–79, 282, 285–86, 289, 322
awareness 4, 6, 11–12, 28, 51, 54–57, 60, 67, 73, 86, 115, 122, 124–25, 132–33, 140, 145, 156, 165–66, 169, 183–84, 210, 216, 237, 239, 255, 272, 281, 289, 341, 349, 353–54, 370–71, 408–9, 411, 418–20, 436–37, 443, 451, 457, 459, 464–65; training 156

Bachmann-Medick, Doris 8, 409
baggage 238
Bangladesh 446

Banksy 440
Baraldi, Claudio 320–28
Bargiela-Chiappini, Francesca 238–39
barriers 52, 57, 60, 114, 146, 149, 155, 158, 161–62, 163, 165, 167, 173, 221, 223, 285, 332–33, 399, 409, 457
Bateson, Gregory 62, 447
baths, historic 146–49, 151
Baumann, Gerd 229–30, 232
Bauman, Zygmunt 163, 311, 314, 317
becharaa 280
behavior/behavioral 3, 14, 38, 43, 46, 61–63, 70–73, 79–80, 85, 88–89, 121, 141, 160, 166–68, 172–73, 176–78, 182, 191–92, 211, 217, 221, 232, 237–38, 256, 267–68, 270–71, 281, 293, 298, 306, 317, 322, 344, 350, 358–59, 364, 369–74, 379, 391, 393, 418–19; cohesive 359; conflict-related 358; dominant 324, 379; mediational 388–89; non-discriminatory 391; non-verbal 372
Belgium 34, 46, 304
belief 30, 39, 56, 82, 95, 115, 138, 172, 190, 269, 278; systems 30, 95, 115, 190
Bennett, Janet 255, 258, 401, 403, 411
Bennett, Milton 255
Bercovitch, Jacob 8, 96, 165, 275, 280–81, 373
Berger, Peter 47, 313
Berry, John 222–23, 225–27, 238–39
Bhabha, Homi 10, 202–6, 208, 229, 310
bias 35, 56, 78, 82, 114–16, 120, 156, 183–84, 188, 289, 294, 335, 343, 346–47; implicit 159, 161, 176
Bible 32
binary model 310–11, 317–18
biology 164
biopower 151
Björkqvist, Kaj 7
Black people 155, 337
Black, Peter 7, 30, 35, 322
Blommaert, Jan 145, 468
Boas, Franz 7, 409
Bochner, Stephen 8, 408
body language 73, 106, 370, 372, 402
Bolten, Jürgen 8, 61
Bond, Greg 23–29
borders 304, 317, 408, 446
Bourdieu, Pierre 47, 86, 89–90, 230
brainstorming 37, 279
Bramsen, Isabel 104–10
Brazil 34, 57, 344
bridge 8, 81, 99, 146, 168, 173, 220–27, 334, 387, 426; metaphor 220–26, 220–27
bridging 99, 167, 222, 224, 226, 301, 303, 334, 340, 404
Brigg, Morgan 27, 226, 239–40, 285
British Columbia 68, 284
Bröckling, Ulrich 310–19
broker/brokering 173, 456
Brownlie, Siobhan 340–48
Brown, Penelope 9, 450

473

Index

brutal 78, 139
Buddhist 114, 138
building consensus 119, 123
Busch, Dominic 1–19, 245–52
Bushmen community methods of conflict
 resolution 191
Bush, Robert A. 9, 12, 26, 32–33, 47, 121, 123,
 245, 324
business 30–32, 36, 39, 97, 104, 131, 145, 155,
 157–58, 165, 245, 255, 257, 342, 362–63, 374,
 400–402, 405, 424, 427, 447; mediation 245
business English as a lingua franca (BELF) 447,
 449–51
Buzzanell, Patrice M. 253–61
Byram, Michael 7, 207, 210, 215–16, 303, 305, 387,
 393, 411–12, 435–36, 465–66

Cai, Deborah A. 292–300
Canada 34, 46, 166, 192, 284, 388, 394, 431, 455
capitalist culture 30
Caplow, Theodore 314–18
care 129, 167, 225–26, 321, 323, 402, 404–5,
 412, 423
career 1, 52, 155, 157–58, 256
Cartesian Dualism 210–11
case studies 5, 7–8, 27, 63, 82, 168, 189, 223, 275,
 280–81, 447, 449, 451
Casmir, Fred 257
categories 340, 342–43, 346, 359–60, 362
Catholic 45, 335, 401
CEDR 32
Centre 97, 168
chairperson 279
Charkoudian, Lorig 35, 119, 121
Chené, Roberto 53, 113
Cheyenne 267
Chicago School 45
child intercultural mediation. *See* CIM
child language brokering. *See* CLB
children 36, 39, 61, 131, 149, 165, 185–86, 193, 250,
 297, 302, 315, 321, 343, 346, 438–40, 455–61;
 language brokers 457–58; mediating 456
Chile 34, 351
China/Chinese 3, 27, 34, 56, 71–72, 97, 138, 140,
 249–50, 277, 281, 294, 298, 316, 342, 403, 424,
 426, 429, 447–49; cultures 281, 449
choices, cultural 410
Cho, Minji 136–44
Christian 24, 26, 45–46, 115–17, 123
Christmas Eve 46
church 45, 401, 447
CIM (child intercultural mediation) 455–60
citizen initiative mediation 151
citizenship 207, 437–39
civil cases 34
Civil Resolution Tribunal 68
civil rights movement 52
clash of cultures 31

CLB (child language brokering) 456–60
Clément, Richard 387–96
CLIL (content and language integrated learning) 445
Cloke, Kenneth 180–88
CMC. *See* computer-mediated communication
coalition 314–18
CoBrA 318
co-constructing meanings 225, 451
coercion 38, 97, 311
coexistence 1, 7, 39, 100, 164, 166, 193, 240,
 369, 373
cognition 98, 148, 210, 220, 240, 342, 370–71, 458
cognitive 59–60, 63, 121, 149, 151, 207, 210,
 220–21, 242, 256–58, 342, 350, 370–71, 374, 400,
 410, 412–13, 416; disorder 149; linguistics 220;
 mediation 400, 437–39; overindulgence 419
cognitivist 207
cohesion 146, 181, 226
Cold War 11, 31, 189, 193, 316
collaborating 57, 181, 224, 278, 383, 436, 467
collective memory 136–38, 140, 146–47
collectivism 71, 191, 238, 293, 379, 384
collectivists 3, 32, 69, 71–72, 139–40, 190–91, 194,
 302, 373, 379–80; cultures 32, 191, 373
Collins, Haynes 145–52
colonialism 27, 34, 114, 139, 195, 232, 268, 302, 306
commonalities 8, 379
Common European Framework of Reference 7, 220,
 224, 387, 467–68
common ground 109, 220, 279, 361
communication 1, 5–6, 26, 28, 31–32, 36–37, 59–60,
 62–63, 67–73, 87, 89, 98, 106, 108, 116, 128, 140,
 163–67, 181, 184–85, 194, 201–8, 210–17, 220,
 222–25, 237–42, 253–56, 258, 281, 285, 292–98,
 301–6, 315, 320–25, 331, 341, 344, 346, 349–51,
 354, 369, 373–74, 378, 380, 387, 399, 401–5,
 408–13, 417–18, 420, 423–25, 428–31; norms
 297, 369; patterns 31; processes 70, 87, 116, 211,
 213, 293, 321–23, 325; systems 320–21, 323–25
Communication as Design (CaD) 253
communicative action 88
communicative event 321, 353, 399, 401, 403, 405
communitarian 11–12, 28
community; mediation 37, 51–53, 56, 192, 245;
 mediation centers 52–56; policing 81–82
comparative 7–8, 190, 275, 277, 279, 349, 411, 464
comparisons 277
compassionate detachment 419–20
compassion fatigue 419
competence 60–62, 210–11, 216, 250, 254–55, 333,
 369–70, 373–74, 387, 403, 442, 458, 468
competency approach 51, 53–54
competing 120, 181, 278, 287–89, 315–16, 362
competition 30, 97, 141, 163, 182, 288
complaints 79–80, 82, 151, 333, 360; systems 82
complexity 1, 61–63, 70, 86, 97, 100, 124, 130–31,
 159, 182, 241–42, 254, 281, 313, 373, 401, 405,
 436, 468

474

Index

compromising 33, 38, 106, 151, 165, 177, 185, 226, 267, 271, 278, 289, 333, 379–84, 400
computer-mediated communication (CMC) 68–70
concept of action 86–87
conceptualization 67, 69, 204, 214–15, 220–21, 223–24, 226, 370, 372, 411, 416, 458
conciliatory 34
conditions; natural 164, 177; necessary 443
Condon, John 5
conduit 223–25, 417, 420
conferencing 46, 68, 71–73
confession 45–46, 312
confidentiality 27, 36, 105–6, 109, 158, 161, 185, 416–17
Confirmatory Factor Analysis (CFAs) 389
conflict; cultures 25, 180, 183, 187; management styles 56, 372–74; management, triadic 13, 77; mediation 1, 23–24, 61, 137, 275–78, 281–82, 321, 340, 378; myths 24; in non-Western societies 192; parties 59–63, 80, 87–88, 95–98, 105–6, 109, 132, 137, 253, 279; partners 62, 77, 80, 82; perceptions 285; resolution and peacebuilding theory 112, 114; resolution skills 181–82, 184; s in cross-cultural situations 194
Conflict Resolution Quarterly 239
confrontation 27, 56, 73, 90, 124–25, 149, 164, 167, 192, 254, 316, 350, 412
congruence 168, 359
connectedness 28, 130, 279
conscience 46
consciousness 125, 129, 132–33, 187, 208, 214, 297, 313, 319
consensus 69, 90, 97, 100, 119, 121, 123, 155, 181–82, 186, 188, 192, 216, 226–28, 278–80, 405
construction 10, 13, 36, 44–45, 61–62, 87, 89–90, 120–21, 189, 204, 207, 225, 232, 247, 284, 306, 312, 316, 321–22, 324–26, 341, 347, 350, 359, 387, 410, 467
constructionist 44, 202
constructivist 9, 12, 68, 86, 230, 241, 247
content analysis 239
contexting 411
contexts 6, 9, 23, 25, 28, 31–33, 35, 43–44, 47, 54, 57, 60–63, 68–69, 71–73, 77–78, 80–82, 87–90, 96–98, 107–9, 114, 116–17, 119–25, 128–33, 146, 156, 159, 168, 181–83, 191–92, 194, 205–6, 224, 239–42, 246, 250–51, 253, 256, 266, 268, 270–71, 275–76, 279–81, 285–86, 288, 292, 298, 301, 305–6, 314, 322–23, 331–33, 335, 340, 342, 347, 349–51, 353–54, 358, 364, 371–74, 378, 387–88, 400–401, 404, 409–13, 418–20, 430, 436, 446, 457, 464, 466; diverse 60, 285, 435; global 129, 205; ideological 404, 468; institutional 417; international 35, 88, 111; political 268, 270–71, 278
contextual constraints 354, 425, 429–30
contextualization cues 411
contrastive approach 301, 303, 411

conventional childhood 168, 248, 459
conventions 145, 151, 212–13, 333, 371, 447
conversation 10, 14, 39, 44–45, 53–54, 73, 88, 107–8, 116, 133, 150, 183–84, 186, 201, 208, 222, 224–25, 232, 247, 254–55, 296–97, 301, 305, 322, 331–34, 336, 341–42, 358, 396, 410, 418, 427, 438–40, 442–43, 446–48, 449–51, 458; analysis 44–45, 331, 341–42, 446
convivial 146
conviviality 146, 151
cooperativeness 278
coordination 98, 108–9, 132, 322, 331
cop culture 78
coping 79, 120, 123, 150, 168, 277, 419–20
Corbett, John 220–28
cosmopolitan 13, 31–32, 229, 312
Costa Rica 34
counselling 303, 419
court based mediation 358, 360, 364
Covid-19 104, 109, 119, 145, 160, 435
COVID, mediation during 104–10
Crawshaw, Robert 206
creating the third force 191, 193, 195
credentials 158, 160
credibility 78, 97, 345, 362
CREK 68
crime 45, 77–78, 82, 185, 266, 297, 314
crisis diplomacy 96–97
criticality 207, 431
critics 80, 257, 267, 271, 289
cross-cultural 3, 5, 7–8, 12, 23, 28, 31, 39, 51, 54, 139, 181, 183–84, 186, 189, 194, 202, 205, 223, 237–38, 241, 255, 275, 277, 279–82, 293, 372, 374–75, 401–2, 408, 423, 464–65, 467; communication 5, 223
CTT (Classical Test Theory) 389
cues-filtered-out theories 70
cultural anthropology 1, 7, 12, 266, 310
cultural awareness 411
cultural brokering 456
cultural competence 54–55, 436, 468
cultural competency 32, 51, 54–54, 281
Cultural Competency Certification 32
cultural contexts 59–60, 63, 266, 275, 332–33, 369, 372, 374, 399–400, 405, 409
cultural diversity 52, 54, 114, 182, 202, 211, 224, 324–25, 369–73, 464, 466
cultural humility 51, 53–56
cultural identities 4, 35, 113, 120, 166–67, 302, 306, 322, 325, 340–41, 359
cultural intelligence 183, 369–71, 373, 378
culturality 3, 5–6, 87
culturally 5, 23, 25–27, 32–33, 36–38, 48, 51–56, 61, 63, 72–73, 88–89, 91, 96, 106, 166–67, 181, 183–84, 186, 188, 205, 237, 240–42, 256, 278, 281, 288, 322, 325, 340, 350, 354, 359, 369–71, 374–75, 379, 409, 419, 426, 436, 456, 464
cultural misunderstanding 51, 412, 425, 428, 430

475

Index

cultural norms 31, 111, 174–75, 183, 194, 213, 216, 297, 304, 373–74, 401
cultural value orientations 378, 381, 383–84
cultural values 275, 277, 280, 293, 298, 350, 359, 371, 374, 378, 383–84
cultural violence 285, 288–89
culture and religion 111–13
cultures 25, 180, 183, 186, 190; -general 238–39; -specific 2, 59–61, 63, 166–67, 239, 249, 401, 430
cultures, non-Western 189–90, 226, 239–40
curatorial text 146, 148–50
curricula 465

Danish 46, 318
Davidheiser, Mark 190, 241–42, 279, 281–82, 285–86, 289
Dayton Accords 37
debriefing 419
decentring 14, 234, 411, 436
decision-making 24, 271, 285, 317, 370, 372–73, 458
decoloniality 230, 232, 235
deductive conception of intercultural mediation 3, 11
de-escalation 78, 276
defensive design 148
delegitimization 125
democracy 34, 163, 207, 231, 439
democratic 77, 82, 119, 182, 258, 437, 464
Dervin, Fred 6, 146, 301–2, 322, 412, 424, 466, 468
descendants 98, 123
design 73, 81, 115–17, 145, 148, 186, 188, 242, 247, 253–54, 256–58, 280, 341, 446; processes 253–54, 256–58
desired outcome 35, 39
Desivilya Syna, Helena 119–27
d'Estrée, Tamra Pearson 7, 13, 129–30, 285
development; affective 460; bilingual 459; epistemological 412; incremental 131–32
Developmental Model of Intercultural Sensitivity 255, 411
deviant behavior 267
diagram 278
dialect 448–49
dialogue 33, 37, 39, 61, 77, 79, 81–82, 90, 96, 99–100, 105–7, 109, 116, 128, 132, 150, 152, 167, 173, 182–84, 188, 191, 226, 234, 248, 256–57, 265, 269, 271, 321–22, 354, 411–13, 435, 437, 466
diaspora 106, 314
difference 3–4, 7, 13, 23–28, 32, 34, 51, 54, 60, 62, 67, 69, 71–72, 88, 96, 99, 101, 111–14, 114, 122, 130, 136, 139, 141, 151, 166, 172, 175, 183, 202–4, 203, 208, 210, 215, 229, 237, 240, 242, 246, 250, 254–58, 280–82, 282, 293, 296, 298, 302, 306, 310, 322, 331–37, 340, 351, 359, 361, 369–71, 373, 375, 378, 387, 399, 401, 403, 408–9, 412–13, 424, 426–30, 428, 431, 440, 464–65; significant 99, 138; worldview 287
digital diplomacy 104

digital technologies in diplomacy 108
dimensionality 389, 391
dimensions 67, 72, 239, 242, 249, 306, 378–79, 381, 467; cultural-sensitive 238; pedagogical 468; political 113; pre-reflexive 86; transcultural 239
Dingwall, Robert 39, 245, 311
diplomacy 31, 37, 96–98, 104–8, 105, 108, 111, 128–29, 131, 280
diplomats 33, 36, 97, 117
directive 34, 37, 182, 279–81, 293, 333
director 53, 442
discourse 9–12, 14, 27–28, 86, 90, 116, 137, 172, 193, 201–2, 204–7, 222–23, 235, 247, 250, 276, 303, 340–43, 347, 400–401, 404, 416–17, 423, 450, 466; analysis 11
discrimination 78, 80, 82, 90–91, 99, 125, 150–51, 166–68, 183, 255, 302, 306, 332, 337, 369, 388, 391
discursive 1, 204, 256, 288, 340, 342–43, 408, 451, 468
discussion 4, 9–10, 25, 107, 115–16, 124–25, 132, 165, 216, 221, 225, 234, 241, 248, 253, 297–98, 304, 334–37, 340, 352, 381, 391, 399, 403, 405, 408, 430, 451, 459
disempowerment 114
disharmony 164
disparities in power 268, 271
disputants 28, 30, 67–71, 73, 161, 174–78, 194, 237, 240–42, 271–72, 280–81, 333, 358–59, 361, 363–64, 373
distributed cognition 458
distrust 71–73, 82, 310
diverse 13, 28, 32, 51–52, 54, 60, 68, 96, 112, 114, 119–24, 146, 155, 159–61, 182, 184, 188, 190, 253, 255, 258, 277, 285–86, 306, 324–25, 354, 369, 371, 374, 413, 419, 435, 445, 455, 458, 464, 466, 468
diversity 27, 54, 114, 182, 202, 205, 224, 234, 281–82, 324–25, 369–73, 408, 464, 466
divided societies 119–21
divorce 36, 121, 189, 193, 281, 331, 335, 340, 343, 346
doing citizenship 207, 437–39
Doyle, Martha 136–44
Druckman, Daniel 3, 131
Durkheim, Emile 266–67, 293
dyad 2, 87, 313, 317
dyadic 1, 10, 87, 269–70, 313, 316

Earley, P. Christopher 183, 370, 372, 374
Eastern Europe 189, 296
ebay 67
Eddington, Sean 253–62
educators 168, 195, 276, 435, 464–65, 467
edusemiotics 210–11, 213–16
Edwards, Derek 137, 342–45
effectiveness of mediation 362
effects and outcomes of child language brokering 461

ego 313
elite 87, 97, 121, 190, 296
e-mail 70, 424, 437
embodied 23, 47, 133, 145, 221, 257, 311
emergency telephone calls 332
emic, constructivist 242
emoticons 71–72
emotional expression 63, 182, 295, 381
emotional intelligence 63, 158, 370, 378–83
emotional reactions 180, 419
emotions 3, 8, 25, 37, 46, 61, 63, 72–73, 88–89, 91,
    120, 138, 185, 240, 257, 280, 321, 342, 375,
    379–81, 384, 459–60
Empathic Design 253
empathy 33, 39, 46, 61, 63, 148, 168–69, 183–84,
    188, 223, 225, 254, 256–58, 290, 416, 418–19,
    418–20, 459–60
empowerment 112–13, 112–14, 117, 123, 253, 258,
    269, 289, 322–25
End of History 31
engagement 119, 122, 137, 147; constructive 128,
    133; direct 125
English as a lingua franca (ELF) 446
English of native speakers 450–51
Enlightenment 9, 220
énoncé 203
entitlement 47, 270, 343, 345
enunciation 203–4
enunciator 279
environment 30, 54, 145, 150, 180–81, 187, 211,
    286–87, 369–70, 417
environmental conflicts 284–86, 285–86
envoicing 449, 451
epistemic practice 451–52
Epistemics 446–47
epistemic stance 446–47, 449, 451
epistemic status 446
epistemology 195, 201–2, 322
equity 38, 114, 255, 282, 322–23, 346, 466
escalation 51, 122, 128, 269
essence 43, 125, 258, 313, 322, 408
essentializing 14
ethical processes 417
ethnic 24, 32, 36, 52–53, 61, 79, 82, 98, 114, 116,
    119–20, 163, 166, 175, 202, 205, 241–42, 276,
    281–82, 284, 294, 297–98, 312, 332, 336–37, 409,
    429, 460
ethnicity 30, 35–36, 39, 52, 158, 220, 222, 276, 281,
    306, 331, 334, 340–42, 342, 359
ethnic minorities 52, 82, 116, 119, 429
ethnocentric 6, 27, 32, 163, 165, 203, 255, 324
ethnocentrism 255, 325, 411
ethnographic 7, 13, 25, 60, 147, 149, 230, 238, 246,
    275–76, 279–81, 284–90, 304, 446, 460
ethnographic methods 238, 284
ethnography 230, 232, 266, 285, 287, 289; of
    conflict 287

ethnology 1
ethnomethodological 247, 331, 341–42
ethnomethodology 247, 331, 341–42
ethnorelativism 255, 411
ethology 164
ethos 46, 61, 146
etic 3, 13, 68, 237–39, 241–42
etiquette 36, 145, 150
Eurocentric 111, 117
Europe 7, 32, 61, 80–81, 116, 119, 167–68, 175, 189,
    206, 224, 245–48, 250, 296, 304, 350, 387, 436,
    438–40, 442, 467–68
European 7, 33–34, 82, 113, 123, 139–40, 163, 167,
    204, 206, 220, 224, 234, 245, 247, 292, 294, 302,
    304, 387, 401, 436
evidence 25, 36, 38, 77, 80, 134, 174, 176–77,
    221–22, 226, 234–35, 297, 341–42, 378, 416, 420,
    438, 443
exclusion 89, 112, 120, 124–25, 148, 151,
    311–12, 343
expatriates 173
expertise, self-proclaimed cultural 54
explicit knowledge 88
eyes 45, 78, 86, 137, 141, 293

face theory 23, 28
face-to-face 43–45, 67–68, 70–72, 104, 106, 108–9,
    181, 294, 302–3; meetings 43–44, 104, 108–9
facework 9
facilitative model of mediation 26
facilitator 37, 46, 108, 124–25, 129, 132, 223, 248,
    287, 406, 411
failed mediation 145–46, 146, 150
Fairclough, Norman 47, 233
fairness 176, 241
faith 97, 112–16, 112–17, 172, 177, 241, 340
familiar diversity 85, 88
family; conflicts 77, 460; literacy practices 455;
    mediation 28, 164, 168, 192, 245, 334, 336, 340,
    343, 412
Fantini, Alvino 5, 387–88
fear 52, 78–80, 106, 142, 181, 184, 276, 281, 304
feminism 232–33
fieldwork 202
figures of the third 313
Fink, Edward L. 292–300
First Nations 284, 287–88
Fisher, Roger 3, 8, 12, 23–27, 32, 43, 54, 56, 97,
    128–29
Fitzpatrick, Brenda J. 284–91
fluidity 163, 207, 280, 364
focus; group interview 424, 428; on interests 23, 32,
    193; on problems 11, 24–25, 62
focus groups 124, 425; interview 424, 426, 428
Folger, Joseph 9, 12, 26, 32–33, 47, 121, 123,
    245, 324
folk tales 24

Index

foreignization 401
foreign language; education 433; learning 387; teaching 1, 6
forgive 177–78, 188, 240
forgiveness 24, 39, 45
formulations 325, 341–43, 404
forum shopping 132, 271
fostering diversity in mediation 156
Foucault, Michel 45–46, 86, 120, 125, 151, 206
fourth party 68–70, 72; culture 68–70, 73
fourth-party culture 68–70, 73; on intercultural communication 69; on mediation 70
frame/framing 10, 44–47, 97, 116, 120–21, 132, 183, 190, 221–22, 225, 227, 242, 257, 277, 286, 325, 411, 413, 446, 451, 465; analysis 44, 447
framework, conceptual 55
France 34, 150, 231, 233
Franco, Emilian 245–52
frequency of child language brokering 456
Friedman, Gary J. 10, 33, 121–22
Fromm, Erich 164
Fry, Douglas 7, 190, 192, 195, 275, 277–78, 280, 449
Fukuyama, Francis 11, 31

Galtung, Johan 128, 164, 169, 288
Gambia/Gambian 190, 281
games 231, 314–18
game-theoretical studies 3, 316
game theory 25, 314
Gamson, William A. 314
Garcia, Angela Cora 331–39
Garfinkel, Harold 331
Geertz, Clifford 7, 61, 207, 277, 409–10
gender 23, 30, 35–36, 39, 60, 79, 89–90, 112, 115, 149, 158, 180, 205, 220, 222, 232–34, 241–42, 247, 281–82, 302, 306, 316, 334, 340–41, 345, 360, 364, 460; studies 247, 302
generations 33, 36, 138–39, 267, 277, 417, 456
geopolitics 105
German/Germany 6, 8, 33–34, 71, 81–82, 86–88, 90, 96–98, 168, 247, 293, 304–5, 318, 334, 429, 455
gesture 334
Getting to yes 3, 12, 23, 27, 32, 98
Giljohann, Stefanie 77–84
Girard, René 310
Glasl, Friedrich 269–70
globalization 13, 26, 164–65, 168, 173, 178, 229, 306, 369, 408, 464
Global North 195, 204
Global South 189, 195
Goffman, Erving 9, 43–45, 47–48, 149, 446–47
Golbert, Rebecca 275–83
Gonțalves, Gabriela 369–37
gossip 276
graffiti 437–40, 443
grammar 234; of culture 234
grand narrative 233–34
gravitas 109

Greatbatch, David 39, 245, 331
Great Power politics 105
Grenoble 150–51
ground, common 109, 220, 279, 361
groups; dominant 121, 190, 240; identities 53, 136, 286, 437; interactions 439–40; marginalized 5, 78; national 241, 285; participant 388; religious 32, 97, 113; social 30, 61, 122, 137–38, 163, 281, 322, 435–36; sub-cultural 456
Gudykunst, William 238–39
guidance 98, 107, 173, 225
Guilherme, Manuela 6, 466
Guilt 77
Gulliver, Philip 8, 267, 271, 285
Gumperz, John 302–3, 323, 325, 411, 450
Gunkel, Marjaana 378–86
Guo, Zhiyan 455–63

habituation 215–16
Hagemann, Anine 104–10
Hall, Edward T. 26, 28, 31, 67, 139, 181–82, 293, 306, 361, 369, 373–74
handling styles 378–81, 383–84
harm 39, 115, 131, 137, 141–42, 194, 269, 288, 404
harmony 10, 12, 28, 32–33, 56, 124–25, 140, 164, 191, 256, 280, 286, 298, 387
Harris, Marvin 237, 455–56
Hartmann-Piraudeau, Andrea 245–52
Harvard 26, 98, 269; rational choice model 269
Haudenosaunee 139
healthcare 129, 165, 167–68, 220, 402; system 167, 225, 323
hegemonic 27, 203–4, 208
hegemony 27, 87, 91, 289
Heisterkamp, Brian L. 358–65
Heritage 232, 288, 321, 325, 331, 446–47, 455–57
Heritage, John 321, 325, 331, 446–47
Herlyn, Menno-Arend 8
hermeneutic 43, 130, 203, 354, 411
Herrmann, Margaret 3
heterocentration 164
high and low context cultures 71
high-context culture 57, 71
Himmelstein, Jack 10, 33
historical baths 146
historical experiences 28, 111
historical meanings 437
history 7, 27, 31, 78, 80, 111, 132, 137–41, 147, 150, 156, 162, 176, 178, 195, 221–22, 265, 268, 276, 280, 286, 288, 292–93, 296, 344, 388, 439; oral 147
Hobbes, Thomas 164
Hofstede, Geert 31, 56, 67, 139, 249, 293, 302, 306, 369, 379–81, 411
holistic 1, 62, 133, 139–40, 266, 270, 277, 284, 286
Holliday, Adrian 5–6, 9, 229–36, 322, 359, 424
Holper, Anne 95–103
homogeneous 32, 52–54, 56, 166, 229

478

Index

homo sacer 310
honesty 69, 166, 184, 362, 374
Hong Kong 34
Hopi tribe 139
horticultural Jews 311
hostile architecture 148
hostility 51, 148, 225, 294
House, Juliane 8
human agency 258
Human-Centered Design (HCD) 253, 256, 258
humanities 55, 115, 298, 301, 408–9, 412
humanization 418
human rights 7, 34, 95, 99, 122, 129, 268
humility 51, 54–57, 115, 169, 255, 298
Hungary 247
Huntington, Samuel 11, 31
hybridity 108–9, 130–31, 206, 229, 323; cultural 13;
  natural 229
hybrid peace mediation 104–5, 107, 109
hyperpersonal 70

IBM 31, 293
iceberg 410–11
icebreaker 109
identity/identification 4, 9, 13, 27, 30, 32, 35, 43–48,
  53–56, 62, 68, 71, 79, 89, 91, 95–96, 99–100,
  112–17, 120–23, 125, 136, 138, 145, 147, 158,
  164, 166–68, 182–83, 185, 187, 193, 203–4,
  206–7, 225–26, 232, 235, 241–42, 245, 253,
  255–56, 258, 276, 279, 281–82, 284, 286, 288–89,
  302, 306, 311–12, 320, 322, 324–26, 331, 335–36,
  340–42, 350, 354, 358–64, 369, 399, 403, 406,
  413, 437, 445–47, 449, 451–52, 452, 457–58, 460,
  466, 468
identity theory to conflict resolution 27
ideology 6, 9, 12, 26, 28, 33, 61, 89, 204–6, 212,
  222–26, 251, 270, 286, 304, 350, 399, 401, 404,
  409–10, 412, 466, 468
IDI (Intercultural Development Inventory) 255
ignorance 6, 26, 176–77, 210
immigrant families 455–56, 456, 458–59, 461
immigration 11, 34, 39, 119, 165–66, 178, 294
impartial 25, 27, 79, 81, 121–22, 129, 159, 165, 174,
  279, 313, 405, 416–18, 420, 423, 426
impartiality 27, 81, 122, 159, 405, 416–18
imperialist 27
implicit child cultural mediation 456
imports 11, 113
IMS (Intercultural Mediation Scale) 388, 391
inclusion 38, 68, 104, 108–9, 112, 114, 126, 151,
  155–56, 159, 167, 255, 258–59, 311–12, 381, 388,
  412, 436, 444
inclusive 37, 51–52, 54–55, 57, 114, 122, 145–52,
  155–62, 182, 216, 248, 255, 304
inclusivity 95, 146, 148, 151, 248
indeterminacy 409, 412–13
Indian 71, 139, 202
indifference 163, 418

indigenous 24, 26, 28, 34, 37, 39, 130, 139, 189–96,
  206, 268, 276, 284–85, 287; communities 139,
  190, 192–96, 287; conflict management strategies
  191, 193, 195; conflict resolution 190; cultures 24,
  195; processes of peacemaking 192–95; processes
  of peace-making 190, 192–96; process of
  peacemaking 190
individualism 27, 31, 69, 71, 91, 163, 191, 238, 293,
  379–80
individualist/individualistic 26–28, 69, 139–40, 181,
  190–91, 193, 302, 373, 380; cultures 190–91
inductive 3, 11
inequality 90, 123, 321, 332, 337, 380, 384
inferences 341, 343, 345–46; causal 343
informal mediation 12, 80–81
informants 105–6, 405, 440
initiative 156, 161, 223
injunctive norms 350, 353
inoculation 343, 346
insider 95, 115, 129, 185, 233, 237–38, 279–81
insider-partial 129, 279–81
instant messaging 71
institutional procedures 332–33, 332–33
institutional roles 120, 205
institutions, educational 119, 121–22, 157, 205, 457
insults 297
integration 116, 136, 173, 216, 268, 270, 284–85,
  412, 457
intelligence 63, 158, 183, 369–70, 370, 378–8
interaction(s) 1, 5, 10, 14, 43–45, 47–48, 62, 68,
  70–73, 78–79, 81, 87, 90–91, 95–96, 105–7, 109,
  111, 119, 121, 128–29, 136, 145–46, 149, 151,
  161, 167, 172, 180, 194, 208, 211, 216, 225, 237,
  239–42, 253–54, 257, 268, 272, 277, 282, 286,
  292, 302–3, 306, 313–14, 316, 318, 320, 322–26,
  331, 333–38, 341–43, 347, 349–55, 359, 370–74,
  379, 387, 403, 410–12, 420, 424, 426, 428,
  430–31, 435–36, 439–40, 445–47, 449, 451, 455,
  457, 460–61; conflictual 411; doctor-patient 323,
  333; dyadic 1, 10; face-to-face 68, 70, 72, 302–3;
  in-person 71, 161; triadic 81, 87, 460
interactional 9, 242, 255, 297, 322–23, 331–33,
  340–42, 364, 400, 406, 411, 424, 431, 449, 451
interactionist 45, 47
interactive peacemaking 128–31, 128–34
intercorrelations 390
intercultural 1–14, 24–25, 30, 32–35, 37, 39, 43–44,
  48, 51–57, 59–64, 67–74, 77–83, 85–91, 95–101,
  115–16, 119, 122, 126, 129, 132–33, 136–42,
  145–52, 163–69, 172–78, 184, 201–8, 210–17,
  220–27, 229–35, 237, 240, 242–43, 245–47,
  249–51, 253–59, 281–82, 285, 289–90, 293,
  301–7, 320–26, 331–38, 340–42, 346–47, 349–55,
  359–64, 369–75, 378–85, 387–94, 399–406,
  408–13, 418, 420, 423–31, 435–52, 455–61,
  464–69; adaptation 324, 326; communicative
  competence 61, 224–25, 388, 435, 465–66;
  competence 5, 11, 60–61, 168, 207, 210–11, 211,

479

Index

237, 254–55, 301–7, 373, 387, 393, 411, 465–66; conflicts 30, 62, 79–80, 82, 230, 253–56, 369, 378, 387–89, 391–92; disputes 14, 35, 37, 67, 175, 177–78, 373–75; education 33, 167, 305–6; learning 210–11, 213–16; misunderstandings 8, 80, 99–100, 405; negotiation 34, 374–75; pragmatics 349–51, 359; social infrastructure 151–52; space 145, 147, 149, 151; speaker 7, 387, 435–44, 465; studies 168, 202–3, 203, 206–7, 207, 410–11, 411; training 32, 59, 165, 306

intercultural communication competence (ICC) 211, 213–16, 435

Intercultural Conflict Management 253–59

interculturalism 206

interculturality 2, 5–6, 9–11, 67–74, 95–101, 146, 204, 207, 245–46, 250, 305, 340–42, 346–47, 359–64, 378, 423, 431

intercultural mediation 1–14, 25, 34–35, 37, 39, 44, 48, 51–57, 59–64, 67–69, 74, 77–83, 85–91, 95, 119, 126, 136–42, 163–69, 172–78, 201–8, 211, 220–27, 229–35, 237, 240, 242–43, 245, 247, 250–51, 253–58, 281–82, 285, 289–90, 301–7, 320–26, 331–38, 340, 347, 349–55, 359, 369–75, 378–85, 387–94, 396, 399–406, 408–13, 418, 423–31, 445–52, 455–58, 464–69

Intercultural Mediation Scale 388, 396

intercultural mediation scale 388

interdisciplinary 1–14, 169, 301, 408–10, 412–13, 456

interest-based 43–44, 99, 121–23, 182–83

interest-based mediation 122–23

interest groups 30, 105

interests 5, 23–28, 32, 39, 43–44, 46–47, 52, 97–100, 120–21, 128, 151, 164–65, 182–83, 190–91, 193, 203, 208, 253–54, 258, 265, 268, 271, 279–82, 285, 288, 292, 314, 364, 371, 418

interests-based mediation 27

interethnic 4–5, 61, 242

interfaith 112, 114, 116, 172

interfaith engagement 112, 114, 116

intergroup conflict 119–20, 137, 189, 332, 337, 387–94

intergroup relations 122–23, 126, 369, 437

intermediary 24, 207, 284, 351, 412, 435

international 4, 6–8, 14, 28, 31–39, 61, 63, 67, 88, 95–97, 104–5, 107–9, 111, 114, 116, 145, 158, 165, 208, 221, 246, 250, 275–76, 279–82, 292, 305, 318, 321, 378–79, 401, 409, 423, 429, 435, 440, 444, 455, 461; mediation 32, 35, 67, 104, 109, 275, 280–82

International Mediation Institute 32, 35

international peace mediation 28, 104–5, 105

interpersonal intelligence 370

interpersonal practice 451–52

interpersonal relationships 254, 293, 313

interpretation 1–2, 10, 44, 54, 61–63, 85–86, 89, 98,

113, 137, 146, 172–73, 203–6, 211, 213–16, 224, 230, 234–35, 238, 241, 245, 257, 266, 277, 296, 306, 323, 349–52, 354–55, 370, 409, 411, 413, 416, 428, 436, 440, 455, 458, 465–66, 468

interpreter 173, 212–13, 223–25, 245, 303–4, 306, 332, 351, 354, 399–406, 410–12, 416–20, 423–24, 426–29, 457

interpreting 167–69, 216, 223, 225, 350, 353–54, 373, 399–406, 410–13, 416–20, 423–31, 435, 455, 466

interpretive 9, 12, 242, 277, 352, 413, 465–66

interpretivist 202

interracial 242

interreligious peacebuilding 114–16

intersectionality 136

intersubjectivity 146, 230, 313

intervention 1, 10–11, 34, 59, 73, 88, 98, 111, 114–17, 120–25, 140, 149–51, 155, 159, 163, 166, 168, 201, 203, 208, 222, 276, 278, 286, 311, 324, 335–37, 351, 354, 369, 373, 388, 391, 393, 400, 403, 405, 412–13, 420, 424, 426–27, 431, 436

interviews 45, 134, 186, 223, 238, 242, 246–47, 256, 266, 287, 295, 341, 424

Intifada 136

intimidating 78

intractable 39, 186, 255–57; conflict 256–57

intrinsic motivation 371

Iran 37, 88

Ireland 34, 36, 46, 247, 404

Iroquois 139

irreconcilable 100, 201, 220, 278

Islamic/Islam 31–32, 114, 116, 172–78, 190, 195; beliefs 172–74; forms of intercultural mediation 172–73, 175, 177; law 174, 176–77; mediation 173–74, 176; mediation in 175; mediator 175–77; perspective 172–73, 175; principles 172–73, 175; understanding of mediation 174

Israel 34, 111, 115, 120, 123–24, 136, 178, 226, 239–40

Israeli/Palestinian conflict 136

ISRP (Integrated Subject Research Pool) 389

Italy 5, 34, 165, 168, 318, 436–37, 444, 455

Item Response Theory (IRT) 391

Jacobs, Scott 53, 240, 245, 331

Japanese/Japan 27, 34, 56, 71, 342, 352–53, 353, 405, 427–28, 440, 447–50; cultures 31, 56

Jewish 82, 111, 117, 120, 123–25, 295–98, 312, 314

Johnson, Marvin E. 155–62

Jones, Tricia 3, 220, 229, 233, 358, 417, 445, 456, 460

Jorn, Asger 318

Judgement Day 45

judges 33–34

justice 4, 25, 27, 32–34, 38–39, 46, 52, 56–57, 61, 77, 98, 120–21, 143, 159–60, 166, 174, 176–77, 180,

188, 193, 238, 241, 248, 254–55, 257–59, 271, 281–82, 286, 288–89, 435, 439, 444, 466
justice-oriented design approaches 257–58

karma 138
Katan, David 173, 351, 400–401, 403, 405, 408–13, 423–24, 426, 428, 431
keying 447
Kluckhohn, Clyde 53, 96, 293
knowledge 26, 28, 32, 35, 54–56, 59–61, 77–81, 85–86, 88–91, 98, 107, 112, 124, 129–34, 137, 140, 159, 166, 169, 176, 193–95, 201, 204–5, 210–11, 213, 216, 233–34, 238, 242, 246, 248–50, 253, 256, 265–66, 270, 276, 279, 284–85, 288, 297, 299, 301, 303–6, 310, 321, 325, 331, 333, 335, 338, 341, 343, 359, 369, 371, 374–75, 387, 399, 402–3, 405, 409, 412, 425, 428–31, 435–36, 442, 444, 446, 449, 452, 456–58, 464–65, 467–68; intercultural 303, 305; personal 193, 325; practical 130, 371; tacit 88; theoretical 60, 371
Korea 56, 71, 332, 402, 405, 429
Korean culture 428
Korean speakers 358, 428
Kramsch, Claire 6, 204–8, 234, 303, 322, 354, 387, 465–66, 468
Kressel, Kenneth 4, 119, 121, 123, 239
Kriegel-Schmidt, Katharina 85–92
Kroeber, Alfred Louis 53, 96
Kuhn, Thomas 132

Lakoff, George 220–21
Landeskunde 204
language(s) 1–2, 6–10, 12, 14, 24, 30, 32–37, 53, 57, 60–61, 73, 79, 81, 86, 90, 105–7, 114, 158, 163, 165–68, 173, 175, 178, 181–82, 184, 190, 203–7, 211–12, 220, 224–26, 229, 248, 253, 282, 285–86, 288, 293, 301–6, 311, 321, 323–24, 331–34, 337, 340–41, 345, 347, 349–50, 353–55, 369–70, 373–74, 387–89, 393, 399–406, 409, 411, 413, 417, 420, 428–29, 435–37, 442–49, 455–61, 464–69; acquisition 468; awareness 437, 443; brokering 455–61; classroom 464–69; difference 305, 331–32; education 14, 207, 220, 387, 435, 437, 445, 464–69; first 349, 447; functions 354, 436; heritage 456–57; mainstream 455–56; mediation 86, 321, 400–401, 457; native 173, 334; proficiency 333, 460; second 447, 458; skills 61, 158; translations 37, 253
Latino 52, 54, 187, 455
Latour, Bruno 47
laugher 450–51
laughter 438, 443, 450–51
lawless 267
law school 26, 157, 159
lawyer 24, 33, 36, 39, 52–53, 160, 165, 226, 270
lay mediators 33
leader 28, 30, 57, 97, 105, 109, 111–12, 114, 117,

124–25, 174–76, 189, 192, 194, 279, 384; tribal 174, 176
leadership 45, 82, 97, 129, 161, 192, 194
learner 7, 204–7, 211, 224–26, 352, 436, 445–46, 457–58, 465–67
learning processes 210–11, 369, 410
Lebanon 190
LeBaron, Michelle 4, 12–13, 35, 48, 322, 325–26
Lederach, John Paul 8, 10, 23, 26, 112, 129, 140–41, 189, 194, 275, 278–79, 281, 285, 288
legal anthropological research 265–66, 268, 270–71
legal anthropology 4, 265–72, 275, 278, 285–86
legal cultures 8, 33–34
legal pluralism 268
legal profession 26, 159
legal research 265, 270
legal system 33–34, 195, 250, 266, 276, 282, 285, 371
legal translators 401
level of self-disclosure in online communication 71
Levinas 10, 164, 204
Levinson, Stephen C. 9, 450
LGBTQ+ 30
liberal peace semiotic 95, 100
liberation 45–46, 82
Liddicoat, Anthony J. 349–57
likelihood of intercultural conflicts 369
line 1, 24, 45–47, 57, 71, 77, 80, 86, 96, 190, 195, 210, 213, 266–67, 270, 287, 289, 334–35, 337, 360–62, 374, 391, 402, 419, 428, 447–51
linguaculture 411
lingua franca 33, 411, 437, 446
linguistic diversity 2, 302, 437, 468
liquid 6
liquidity 163
Lisbon Municipal Police 81
listener responses 333
listening sessions 56
litigation 34, 189, 265, 267, 343
lived experiences 112, 137, 150, 257–58
local knowledge 112, 129
lockdown 104, 108–9
logic 46, 81, 114, 311–12, 417
long-term relationships 138–39, 381
Loop of Understanding 10
low-context culture 71
Luckmann, Thomas 47, 313

MacDonald, Malcolm N. 201–9
Machiavelli 164
Madagascar 138
Malagasy 138
Malaysia 280, 448–49
Malinowski, Bronislaw 266–67, 409
management 4, 8, 13, 28, 56, 60–61, 82, 91, 119, 121, 164–65, 167, 191–92, 195, 239–41, 250, 254–55, 258, 276–78, 280, 359, 372–74, 410, 423; styles 56, 374

Index

managers 187, 305, 358, 362–63, 375, 384, 427
mandatory 32, 34, 193–94, 271–72
mandatory mediation 271
mapping 149, 187, 354
marginalization 125, 150, 155, 166, 195, 242
marginalized 5, 51–54, 56–57, 78, 114, 122, 289, 324
masculinity 380, 382–84
masculinity/femininity 31, 379
MASEM (meta-analytic structural equation modeling) 381, 383–84
Maslach Burnout Inventory 419
material 5, 25, 27, 47, 57, 63–64, 97, 146, 190, 201–3, 207, 212, 231–32, 234, 254, 256, 258, 269, 286, 311, 450, 464, 467
mathematical theory 293, 315
Mayer, Claude-Hélçène 59–66
MCA. *See* Membership Categorization Analysis
meaning; and meaning-making practices 467; and symbols of culture 204
meaning-making 61, 95, 112–13, 117, 225, 254, 349–50, 353–55, 410, 413, 443, 446, 451, 456, 466–67
media; coverage 78; richness 70–72; richness theory 70–71; social 107–8, 161, 424
mediacioun 412
Mediated Discourse Studies 435
mediate/mediated 34, 38, 53, 59, 61, 68–70, 96, 98, 108, 111, 113, 117, 140, 157–60, 174–78, 184, 186, 205–7, 265, 271, 279, 286, 298, 321–23, 325–26, 337, 349, 375, 387–88, 391, 399–400, 406, 411–12, 416, 418, 420, 423–24, 428, 430, 435–40, 444, 447, 449–50, 452, 455–57, 459, 465, 467
mediating role of empathy 416
mediation 1–2, 13–14, 23–24, 37, 51–57, 60–61, 63, 95, 137, 157, 189, 192, 194, 239–40, 245, 276–78, 281–82, 321, 331, 333, 340, 347, 378; activities 96–97, 266, 439, 466; advanced 60; and arbitration 160, 280; classical 82; cognitive 400, 437–39; contractual 400, 404; cross-linguistic 224, 436; deep-rooted structures and policies 156; dialogic 322–24; facilitative 240, 333; institutionalized 97; interest-based 122–23; mandatory 271; model 32, 47, 111, 173, 240, 275–76, 278–79, 282, 384; and negotiation 25, 72; online 32, 68, 73, 108; for others 351; partial 384; political 11, 96–97; practices 4, 9, 56, 59, 245, 250, 276, 279, 447, 449, 451, 465, 467; principles 87, 245; process 31–33, 60, 67–69, 80, 85–86, 88–90, 98–100, 107–8, 114, 116, 137–38, 193, 220–21, 279–82, 331–33, 358–59, 373–74; relational 437, 440; for self 352; sessions 43–44, 46–47, 157–58, 240, 242, 331–33, 335–36, 340–41, 343–46, 358, 360, 363; strategies 224, 239, 248–49, 438–39, 442–43; subjects 88–90; teams 108, 115; theory 43, 63
mediator; neutrality 241; notions of culture 245, 247, 249; roles 36–37, 279; strategies 30–39
medical interpreters 223, 402, 404, 424, 426

meditationis 412
meetings; individual 124; informational 34; initial 343; joint 124–25
membership 31–32, 91, 146, 220, 247, 254, 322, 331, 334–36, 340–47, 359, 364, 466; categorization analysis 247, 340–47; category 146, 247, 334, 340–47
Membership Categorization Analysis (MCA) 247, 340–41, 343, 346
memory 136–41, 146–47, 192, 297, 342, 456; conflicting 138
Menkel-Meadow, Carrie 30–42
Mennonite 26
mental maps 370
Merry, Sally Engle 266, 268–72, 275–76, 286–87
Mestrovich Seay, Aliah 253–62
meta-analyses 381, 384; bivariate 381, 384; variate 381
meta-analytic procedures 381
meta-analytic structural equation modeling. *See* MASEM
metacognition 370
metacognitive 370–74, 458
meta-cognitive process 149
metacultural 166
metaculture 25
metaphor 6, 8, 10, 44, 69, 140, 204, 207, 220–27, 292
metapragmatic awareness 353–55
meta-pragmatic awareness 349, 411
methodological nationalism 229
Mexico 34, 53, 139
micro-aggression 230, 232–33; awareness 156
micro inequities 156
Middle Eastern 32, 124
migration 5, 7, 11, 78–79, 81, 163, 168, 196, 304, 412
Mills, C. Wright 234, 314
mindshift 411
minorities 10, 31, 52–54, 61, 78–83, 91, 116, 119, 123–25, 155, 166, 205, 240, 289, 324, 332, 388, 393, 402, 429, 460
misunderstanding 8–9, 11, 30, 51, 80, 89, 99–100, 109, 164, 216, 225, 256, 298–99, 306, 332–33, 337, 378, 402–3, 405, 412, 425, 428, 430–31, 451, 465–66
mode instrument 278
models; alternative 148; classic 193; cognitive 416; compositional 216; ground-breaking 465; hybrid 108–9, 173; of mediation 109; mental 373; pyramid 269; theoretical 460; therapeutic 240
modernist 201
modernity 311–12, 317
momentum 18, 108, 110
Monk, Gerald 4, 9, 12, 47–48, 121, 123, 321, 324–25
monochronic 139
moral reasoning advocacy 416
Moroccan Arabs 138
Moscati, Maria 8

482

Index

motivation 34, 61, 115–16, 129, 149, 286, 306, 343, 370–72, 374, 379

MTT (Modern Test Theory) 389, 391

Müller-Jacquier, Bernd 8, 89, 306

multicultural backgrounds 78–80, 82

multiculturalism 13, 166, 178, 202–3, 206, 268, 369, 408–9

multiculturality 373

multi-ethnic 61, 163

multilingual/multilingualism 205, 302–6, 411, 445–46, 456, 468

mural art 437–40

murals 437–40, 443

museum 146

Muslim 27, 111, 114–17, 123, 172–78

Myanmar 109

Nader, Laura 12, 265–68, 275, 282, 285–86

NAFCM (National Association for Community Mediation) 52–53

narrative; analysis 358; history 27; mediation 9, 12, 43, 47–48, 121, 123, 324; therapy 47

National Association for Community Mediation (NAFCM) 52–53

National Conference on Peacemaking and Conflict Resolution 53

nationalism 229

nationality 30, 35–36, 146, 151, 220, 223, 225, 332, 334, 340–41, 359, 437, 449

nation-states 145–46, 229, 232, 311

native/nonnative speakers 205, 306, 332–33, 349–50, 436, 450–51, 465

natural translation 456

Navaho 240

needs satisfaction 26

negotiation; order 149–50; reality 121, 125; theory 3, 23–24, 26–27, 43, 189

neighbors 1, 77, 97, 119, 121, 148, 150, 157, 205, 294, 306, 331, 360

neoliberalism 163

Netflix 429

the Netherlands 34, 247, 271, 297, 304–5

Neuro Linguistic Programming 413

neuroscience 220

neutral empathy 419

neutrality 13, 25, 47, 77, 80, 111, 122–23, 159, 240–41, 245, 287, 331, 335, 408, 411, 418

New Testament 45, 293

Nicaragua 34

Nigerian 333

9/11, 31

noise disturbance 77

non-binary 30

non-fiction 229–30, 234–35

non-native speaker 332–33, 350, 465

non-negotiables 96, 99, 204

nonverbal 61, 89, 372, 374, 403; behaviors 114, 210, 293; cues 67, 70–73

nonviolence 97, 190, 193, 280

normative principles 44

norms 2, 25, 27, 30–32, 36, 48, 56–57, 62, 68, 73, 78, 91, 97–98, 111, 114, 139–41, 149, 156, 161, 166, 191–94, 205, 212, 216, 229–30, 245, 247, 267, 297, 304, 306; injunctive 350, 353; pragmatic 350, 353

North America 26, 189, 193, 206, 241, 279

North American 138, 140, 169, 193, 206, 245, 275–76, 279, 285, 464

Norway 33, 44, 46, 97, 241

Norwegian 33–34, 46, 241, 333

nurse 54, 186, 295

object of culture 3

observation 45, 86, 89, 130, 132, 146, 162, 191–92, 201, 204, 229–30, 233, 238, 246, 251, 268, 284, 290, 295–96, 315, 324, 331, 446; direct 229, 331

observer 1, 62, 130, 184, 237, 279, 285, 310, 409

ODR (Online Dispute Resolution) 67–74, 160, 189, 193–94

offender 39, 44–45, 192–93

officers, judicial 33, 405

offline 73

of honor 297–98

ombudsman 79, 82

ombudsperson 79, 82

online; communication 69–72, 104; dispute resolution 67–74, 160; mediation 32, 68, 73, 108

ontology 27, 119, 201–2, 286, 312, 408–9, 412

open access 134

open-mindedness 435

operational intercultural mediation space of mutual understanding 61

operation, logical 214–15

opponents 107, 240, 287–88, 313–14, 318, 373

oppositions 113, 238, 318; binary 311

oppression, institutional 121

order; cultural 60; moral 350; socio-moral 424–25

Organization for Security and Co-operation in Europe. *See* OSCE

organizations; faith-based 112; informal 305; interactional 331, 333; private 33; social 331, 350; third-party 109; women's 98

Orientalism 233

orientation of intercultural mediation 404

Original Dispute Resolution 189

OSCE (Organization for Security and Co-operation in Europe) 80, 97

Oslo Accords 33, 37

ostracism 276

othering 91, 99, 151, 233–34, 430

otherness 6, 8, 32, 203, 409, 437

outcomes; anticipated 123, 265; collaborative 186; of learning 210; mediated 38

out-groups 226, 294

outsiders 115, 129, 182, 185, 192, 237, 279, 409; accounts of culture 238; mediator 279–80

483

Index

overrepresentation 78

pain 54, 181, 295–96, 298
Palestinians 124, 136, 190
Palpacuer Lee, Christelle 464–71
pandemics 53, 69, 108–9, 133, 145, 161, 435;
   mediation during 104–10
paradigms 1–3, 6, 9, 12, 68, 95, 99, 194–95, 267–68,
   270, 359, 408–13, 466, 468; cognitivist 207; shifts
   1, 12, 28, 189, 194–95, 466; social
   psychological 207
Paraguay 34
parallelism of interests 314
paraphrasing 10, 26, 60, 443
pardon 178
parentified child 459
Parsons, Ruth 7, 13, 129–30, 285
participant observation 266, 284, 287
particularism 277
parties; aggrieved 46, 192; conflicted 183; political 30,
   97, 115, 315; religious 111, 113; warring 96, 226
passionate attachment 89
the past 9, 12, 59, 113, 136–42, 147, 211, 215–17,
   224, 231, 301, 347, 417
past experience 161, 215–16
pastoral care 24
patient 54, 224, 295, 325, 333, 402, 418, 426, 430
Paypal 67
peace; diplomacy 104–8; making 24, 189–90,
   192–93, 195; mediations 28, 95–101, 104–5,
   107–8, 110; negotiations 107
peacebuilding 10, 26, 100, 112–17, 127, 173,
   195, 275
peaceful 39, 59, 77, 100, 136, 166, 170, 192–93, 373
peacemakers 31, 129–30, 189, 192, 194
peacemaking 53, 98, 100, 104, 128–34, 190–96, 279,
   281; in cross-cultural situations 194; in peaceful
   cultures 190; practice 129, 131, 133; processes
   192–93, 195
peace mediation processes 97, 99, 104–10; complex
   99; concrete 100; international 104
pedagogical 205–7, 445, 468
pedagogy 6, 12, 207, 437–38, 465; intercultural
   language 465
Peirce, Charles S. 130, 210–11, 213–15, 310
people-centered 129–34
People of Color 52–53, 159
perceptions; differing 67, 137; negative 71, 426;
   subjective 137, 205
performance 44, 163, 210, 369, 372, 379, 416–17,
   447, 459
perpetrator 45–46, 78, 137, 378, 389–94, 396
personality 7, 23, 164, 182, 187, 231, 287, 343, 372
perspectives; competing 287; critical 121–23, 245;
   cross-cultural time 139; cultural-theoretical 86;
   external 245; model 86–90; new 43, 131–33, 256
perspectivity 85–87
perspectivizing 304, 311

phase model 10–11, 23
phases of dispute processes 269
phenomenological 43
the Philippines 108, 240
physical confrontation 149
physical space 36, 67, 106, 145, 151
physician 54
Pike, Kenneth 237–38
place 4, 9, 13, 46, 54–56, 87, 109, 114, 116, 119, 132,
   139, 146, 151, 156, 164, 166, 174, 177, 181, 183,
   186, 201–10, 215–16, 233, 271, 278, 280,
   284, 304
Plato 164
pluralistic 114, 164, 167, 182, 258, 268, 271, 282
pluricultural 224, 435–36, 444, 467
plurilingual 224, 435, 442, 444–45, 448–49, 464,
   467–68
plurilingualism 468
plurilinguals 435–36, 445–47
pointillist time 163
police 52, 77–82, 177, 430, 439; brutality 52; officer
   77–81; stations 79, 82
politeness 9, 71, 304, 397, 424
political dimensions of culture 111
political science 1, 8, 13, 98, 117, 285
politics 13, 27–28, 31, 48, 95–98, 105, 113–14,
   321, 378
Pollock, David 207
polychronic 139
Popeye Problem 32
Popova, Julia 32, 61
popular culture 2, 205
Portera, Agostino 163–71
Porto, Melina 435–44
position/positioning 5, 8, 26, 28, 44–46, 60–61, 106,
   109, 206, 208, 225, 227, 230, 237, 241, 254, 256,
   287, 304, 306, 312, 314, 316, 321, 325, 341,
   343–44, 427, 436–38, 449, 459
positions; cultural 222, 335; expressed 334, 336;
   mediator's 46
postcolonial 24, 26–28, 202, 204, 229, 231, 302, 306,
   310, 413
postmodernity 311–12, 317
postmodern/postmodernity 27, 302, 310–12,
   317–18, 412
post-positivist 409–10
post-structuralism 47
poststructuralist 86, 201, 207, 467
potential for conflict 106, 145, 149
Potter, Jonathan 342–46, 401, 403
poverty 166–67
power; analysis 113, 116; asymmetries 80, 121–22,
   122, 124, 289; asymmetry sensitivity (PAS) 124;
   disparities 90–91; distance 31, 242, 249, 379–80,
   382–84; imbalances 6, 36, 54–56, 119–26, 248,
   271; relationship 461
practice 2, 4, 9, 11, 13, 23, 25–26, 28, 33, 43, 45–48,
   51, 57, 59–60, 63–64, 72–73, 82, 89, 108–9, 112,

484

Index

114, 124, 129–34, 140, 145–46, 156–57, 160, 174–75, 189–91, 205, 208, 210, 213, 220, 234, 241, 245, 250–51, 257, 266–67, 271–72, 275–76, 278–79, 282, 284–86, 303, 305, 312, 340, 350, 405–6, 408, 413, 416–18, 420, 431, 445–47, 449, 451–52, 455, 457–59, 466, 468; best 129, 416, 418; dynamic 457, 468; family care 459; institutional 276, 411; interactional 340; local 240; multi-faceted 451; reflective 130, 133; transformative 468
pragmatic(s) 8, 23, 32, 33, 39, 100, 253, 265, 302, 331, 349–355, 359, 401, 403, 411, 420
pragmatic norms 350, 353
prejudice(s) 35, 78, 81, 165–66, 183–84, 188, 195, 233–35, 294, 336–37, 342, 369
pre-mediation 36, 146, 148–49, 148–50, 242
prescriptives 26, 194, 245–46, 285; mediation 245
presuppositions 323–25
pretextual 30
prevalence of mediation 278, 280
prevention 79, 82, 180–81, 186, 241, 276, 400, 405
principled negotiation model 23
principles of mediation 23, 26, 121, 245
privatization of justice 39
privilege 36–37, 238, 257
problem-solving; approach in mediation 25; orientation 26; style 374; workshop 25
professional autonomy 418
professional burnout 419
professionalization 412, 417
Professional Quality of Life Scale 419
projections 44, 172, 312, 332
prompter 279
proposition 175, 203, 226
prosocial development 459
protagonists 3, 122–23, 125, 168
Protestant 45, 231, 295
prototypes 253, 256–57
protracted intergroup conflict 119–20
protracted political conflict 119–20, 125
proverbs 24, 141
proxemics 145, 149
Pruitt, Dean G. 4, 121
psycholinguistics 220
psychological concepts 342, 378
psychological safety 419
psychology 1, 8, 14, 31, 44–45, 99, 164, 167, 202, 256, 269, 285, 293–94, 294, 316–17, 340–47, 378–85, 388–89, 424
psychotherapy 164
public order 77
public spaces 145, 148, 150–51, 429
punishment 77, 193–94
Pyatovskaya, Evgeniya 253–62
pyramid models 269

qualitative 1, 44, 120, 168, 286, 381
quality assessment 416–17

quantitative 120, 239, 246, 316, 381
Quek Anderson, Dorcas 67–76
questionnaire 241, 294, 298, 341, 388, 393
questions; asking 37, 186, 248, 442; complex 59; fundamental 69, 276; intercultural 98; interview 242
Qur'an 172–77, 172–77

race 13, 30, 35–36, 39, 52, 90, 112, 115, 142, 155, 158–59, 220, 222, 282, 294, 306, 331, 334–36
racial awareness 156
racial discrimination 82, 337
racial/ethnic group 336
racial prejudice 336–37
racial profiling 79, 82
racial stereotypes 336–37
racism 39, 79–80, 82, 91, 99, 155, 195, 203, 229–30, 233, 302, 306, 311, 332, 337
racist 233–34, 294, 336
Radcliffe-Brown, Alfred Reginald 267
rapprochement 9, 105, 359
rational choice 3, 25, 27, 101, 269, 271, 314, 317–18
rational individualism 27
rationality 3, 32, 101, 220, 240
reality, cultural 229, 275
reciprocity 31, 61, 85, 266
recognition 9, 32, 96, 99–100, 123, 146, 204, 253, 278, 289, 324–25, 354, 369, 373, 420, 451
reconciliation 35, 39, 46, 117, 128, 174–75, 180, 186, 193–94, 201, 220, 222–23, 227, 256, 280–81, 400
recontextualization 205–7, 403
reflection 10, 12, 23, 28, 44, 55, 60, 62, 85–86, 125, 138, 164, 167, 176, 210, 226, 231, 254, 301, 305–6, 311–12, 316, 324, 342, 354, 409, 411–12, 438, 440, 447, 451, 465
reflexive 227, 312, 322, 354, 465; coordination 321, 323, 325–26; practice 449, 451–52
reflexivity 9, 115, 253, 286, 321–22, 411–12, 424, 431, 465
reformulations 10, 332–33, 403, 468–69
reframing 183, 221, 227, 257, 325
regret 45
regrounding 447, 451–52
relationship dynamics 459–60
relativism 166–67, 216, 284–85, 409
relevance of culture 100, 250, 280
relevance of interculturality 99, 359
reliability 176–77, 315, 381
religion 30, 36, 61, 111–17, 131, 151, 166, 172–73, 175, 177, 190, 222–23, 268, 280–82, 331, 334–36
religious differences 112, 115, 280, 335
remorse 45
Renaissance 220
renegotiation 163, 278
repair 148, 192–94, 321, 323, 332–33, 337, 341, 446, 451
repair of misunderstandings 333
rephrasing 437, 446

485

Index

representation 52, 230, 303, 354, 401, 409, 411, 437, 443
representative bureaucracy theory 80
research 1–6, 8–14, 28, 43–45, 48, 53, 56, 59, 63, 67–69, 71–72, 78, 86, 89–90, 98, 106, 119–20, 122, 124, 126, 129–34, 136–38, 146, 161, 165, 168, 174, 191, 193, 196, 210, 213, 215, 222, 230, 238–42, 245–47, 250, 265–71, 280, 283–87, 289–90, 292–99, 302–4, 306, 314, 316, 324–25, 331–38, 350, 355, 369–70, 375, 378–85, 393, 399, 401–2, 405, 409, 412, 423–24, 426, 428, 431, 437, 445–46, 449–52, 455–56, 459–61, 464
resistance 46, 116, 180, 232, 239, 268, 342
resolution 1–5, 7–8, 10–11, 13, 23–28, 31–35, 37–39, 43, 46, 52–54, 56, 67–68, 78–82, 96, 98, 109, 111–17, 115, 121, 128–34, 136–37, 159–60, 165, 167, 173, 180–84, 182, 189–95, 220–22, 237, 239–40, 240, 265–66, 268–70, 275–77, 278, 280–82, 284–87, 289, 322, 340, 360, 369, 378, 384, 388, 464
resolution systems 33, 35, 67, 276
respect 8, 24, 35, 56, 61, 63, 77, 79–82, 91, 99, 120, 126, 130–32, 139, 145, 159–60, 166, 168–69, 185, 190–91, 193, 195, 204, 211, 216, 238, 240–41, 249, 290, 297, 304, 324–25, 343, 358, 374, 388, 404, 409, 443–44
responsibility 7, 10, 38, 46, 80, 108, 124, 141, 161, 165, 169, 193–94, 287, 342–43, 347, 361, 379, 403–5, 411, 418, 420, 458–61
restorative justice 34, 38, 46, 160, 180
rich point 145, 302, 305
rights 89, 151, 166, 183–84, 248, 270, 288, 425
risk factors 167, 419, 460
role 1, 3–4, 6–9, 14, 23, 37, 44–45, 47–48, 51, 53, 60–61, 63, 78, 90, 97–98, 106, 108–9, 111–13, 115–16, 120, 124–25, 130–31, 136–42, 157–59, 161, 165, 167–68, 173, 175–76, 178, 182–84, 191–93, 195, 202, 205, 207, 213–16, 221, 223–27, 232, 234, 239–40, 245–46, 251, 270–71, 276–77, 279–80, 282, 284, 286–87, 289, 296–97, 305–6, 315, 320, 323, 331–33, 338, 342–43, 347, 350–51, 355, 360, 364, 370, 374–75, 378, 380, 389, 393, 399–405, 409–11, 413, 416–20, 423–24, 426–28, 436–37, 444, 449, 455, 458, 460, 465–67; of language 224, 436, 466–67; of learning 213, 216; redistribution 459; reversal 458–59; of selected cultural value orientations 378; of translators and interpreters 399, 403
room 46
Rubenfeld, Sara 387–96
Russia 32–34, 61, 239, 296, 304
Rutherford, Jonathan 202

safety 77–78, 142, 419
Salacuse, Jeswald W. 3
Salmon, Elizabeth D. 369, 373–74
sanctions 80, 98, 266–67
sans-papiers 312

Santamaría Ciordia, Leticia 416
savoirs 436
scale validation
scapegoat 310
Schegloff, Emanuel A. 331–34, 341, 446, 448
schema 25, 35, 270, 342
Schlägel, Christopher 378–86
Scimecca, Joseph 7, 189
script 46, 184–85, 230, 343
Secondary Traumatic Stress Scale (STSS) 419
secondary victimization 79
second language; learning 387
second-language 387, 393, 447, 458
sector 165
secular 111–14, 116–17, 123
security 72, 77, 83, 98, 115, 285
Seidel, Timothy 111–18
self 43–48, 60, 86, 88, 133, 146, 169, 184, 191, 204, 216, 223, 227, 239, 312, 350–53, 359–60, 364, 384, 411–12, 465–66, 469
self-assessment 35
self-care strategies 419
self-concepts in interaction 350
self-determination 33, 38, 159
self-disclosure 24, 69–73, 194
self-efficacy 371, 459–60, 460
self-identity 43–44, 46–47; contextual 43–44, 46
self-reflexivity 115–16, 411
self-regulation 149–50, 418–19
semiosis 201, 205, 211–16; process 211–12, 214
semiotics 6, 96, 201, 203–4, 206, 210–12, 214, 216, 438, 440, 443–44, 446, 451
sensitivity 32, 124–25, 269, 321–22, 325, 418, 425
Serres, Michel 310
session 46, 107, 156, 184, 239, 331–32, 334–37, 360, 440, 450
Seventh Generation Principle 139
shared meanings 5, 123, 411
shared space 106, 146
Shari'ah 175
Shen, Juming 210–19
shepherd 45
Shetland Islands 44
shifting dynamics 132, 458, 461
shock 8, 374, 410
shuttle diplomacy 37, 107, 129
signatures 151; electronic 428
signification 204, 211
significatory 203
signify 146, 206–7
signs 73, 149, 203–4, 211–13, 250
silencing 56, 91, 125
silent language 181–82, 184, 293, 374
Simmel, Georg 7, 293, 298, 310, 312–17
sin 45–46
sincerity 175–76, 178, 374
Singapore 13, 34, 74
singularization 90

SIP (social information processing) 70–72
Site C Clean Energy Project 284
skills 35, 51, 53, 55–56, 59–63, 67, 79, 98, 114, 117,
    129, 157–58, 165, 169, 181–84, 205, 210, 216,
    233, 242, 255–56, 258, 271, 301, 303, 305–6, 321,
    334, 370, 374, 399, 406, 418, 420, 428–29,
    435–37, 442–44, 456, 458–60, 464; cognitive 242,
    459; communicative 62
skopos 410, 413
Skype 437–40
Skype conversation 439–40, 442–43
small culture(s) 229, 234, 322–326, 359, 364
Smolyaninova, Olga 32, 61
social 1–3, 5–8, 10, 12, 26–27, 30–34, 36, 43–45,
    47–48, 53, 56, 60, 62, 73, 78, 85–86, 89–90, 96,
    98–100, 105–6, 112–13, 115–17, 122, 124–25,
    133, 136, 138, 140, 145, 149, 155, 160, 163,
    167–68, 180–81, 188–89, 192, 194–95, 201, 204,
    206–7, 224, 226, 230, 232–33, 239–40, 242, 246,
    254, 256, 265–67, 269, 272, 275, 277–78, 280–81,
    285–86, 292–94, 297, 301, 306, 313–16, 318,
    321–22, 333, 338, 342, 344, 349–50, 359, 369,
    372–74, 384, 387, 393, 399–400, 404, 410,
    412–13, 418, 436–37, 446–47, 457–58, 460,
    466–69; advocacy 119, 123; category 220; class
    205, 222, 271, 282, 345; collective 137;
    infrastructure 146, 150–52; intelligence 370; justice
    61, 120–21, 159, 241, 248, 255, 258, 435, 439;
    media 107–8, 161, 424; order 111, 193, 268, 270,
    312, 331; presence 70–72; presence theory 70;
    space 146, 148, 371, 420; structure 156, 191, 202,
    276, 288, 310, 317, 323
social action 393, 468
social behaviors 180, 191, 270
social change 195, 321, 410
social conflict 10, 121–22, 125, 192, 293–94
social identity model of deindividuation effects
    (SIDE) 71
social information processing theory (SIP) 70–72
social institutions 155, 282, 313
socialization 310, 372, 466
social justice 120–21, 241, 255, 258, 435, 439
social psychology 99, 202, 269, 285, 316
social relations 98, 150, 168, 313, 400
social responsibility 417–18
social spaces 146, 371
social structures 191, 202, 276, 310, 317, 323
social systems 32, 62
social theory 12, 27
sociation 312–14
societies 2–4, 7, 11, 28, 34, 39, 61, 77–78, 86, 88, 96,
    101, 108, 111, 119, 121–22, 136, 139–40, 164–65,
    172–73, 178, 180, 182, 189–90, 192–93, 195,
    202–3, 206, 208, 224, 254, 257, 266–68, 270,
    275–78, 285, 293, 298, 379–80, 408, 435–36, 461;
    collective 139–40; industrialized 165, 190;
    mainstream 456–57, 459–60; new 455, 459–60;

pluricultural 435; traditional 190, 192, 195,
    267–68, 278
sociocultural perspectives 457, 467
sociologist 25–26, 31, 34, 86, 88, 266, 292–94, 311
sociology 85–87, 164, 167, 310, 312, 316
Solomon 32, 292
solutions; virtual 104, 108; win-win 269, 380
Somalia 109
Sousa, Cβtia 369–77
space 10, 36, 46, 61, 63, 67, 74, 87–88, 90, 100, 106,
    108–9, 113–15, 117, 121–23, 125–26, 132–33,
    140, 145–52, 159, 161, 163, 181, 187, 195, 201,
    205, 207, 234, 254–56, 314, 324, 326, 371, 399,
    420, 429, 436, 439, 445–47, 452, 457, 459, 466;
    cultural 88; of cultural mediation 459; diverse 114,
    146; historic 151; interactive 132, 146; operational
    intercultural mediation 61; safe 63, 106; shared
    106, 146; virtual 106, 109, 145, 207
Spain 34, 247, 455
Spaniards 138
spatial 59, 145–46, 149, 206–7, 221, 223, 225–27,
    304; analysis 146
spatialization 205–6
Spencer-Oatey, Helen 306, 322, 350, 424, 428,
    430–31
Spinzi, Cinzia Giacinta 408–15
spontaneous intercultural lay mediation 12
Squid Game 429–30
stakeholder 36, 107, 115, 122, 126, 254, 265, 270,
    280, 416, 418
standards 63, 161, 168, 240, 304, 406, 416, 418, 420
state 14, 59–60, 78, 81, 105, 109, 111–13, 155–56,
    158–59, 164, 185, 189–90, 195–96, 202, 204–7,
    229, 266, 268, 275–76, 278, 280–82, 295–96, 304,
    311, 317, 334, 364, 373, 418, 437–38
stereotypes 51, 78, 165–66, 184–86, 232–34, 297,
    324, 332, 336–37, 345, 360, 363–64, 369, 465;
    biased 78
stigmatization 165, 168
Stokoe, Elizabeth 336, 341, 343, 345
stories, constructive 358
storyboarding 37
storytelling 78, 193, 246, 358–64; in mediation
    358–59, 361, 363
street art 437–38, 440
street artist 440
stress 420
structural coupling 323
structural functionalism 267
structural violence 241–42, 288–90
structure 13, 52, 60, 80, 82, 91, 113, 116, 122, 125,
    128, 136, 146, 148–49, 155–56, 161–62, 167–68,
    180, 191, 194–95, 202, 204, 221–22, 225, 227,
    238, 251, 272, 278–79, 288–89, 293, 305, 310,
    313, 317, 321–23, 332, 343, 347, 358, 399, 417,
    427, 459, 465; of mediation 86, 240
STSS (Secondary Traumatic Stress Scale) 419

Index

subaltern 204, 206
subcultures 371, 456
subject(s) 5, 8, 13, 35, 61, 85, 87–89, 105, 137, 190, 192–195, 201, 203–205, 207, 253, 271, 284, 332, 401, 418, 429
subjectification 207
subjective 78, 91, 120, 137–38, 169, 205, 246–47, 270, 317, 374, 409, 413, 416, 447, 466
subjectivity 89, 137–38, 141, 204, 275, 465–66
subjectivizing agency 87
Sulaha 190
Sulh 174
Sunnah 172, 175–76
superdiversity 468
surveillance 106, 149
survey 2, 31, 107, 238, 241, 246, 256, 405, 419, 424
sustainability 81, 117, 139, 253, 461
Svensson, Isaak 97, 108
Swedish 46, 332
swimming pool 146–49, 151
Switzerland 34, 96–97, 304
symbol(s) 26, 112, 181, 187, 204, 205, 207, 212, 277, 323, 454
symbolic 100, 113, 201–2, 206–8, 286, 288, 446, 467; competence 204–5, 354, 466; mediation 207; violence 230
symbolism 109–10
sympathy 89, 404, 419, 460
Syria 105
system(s) 25–26, 31, 33–35, 39, 52, 56, 60–62, 67–74, 80, 82–83, 95, 99–101, 115–16, 130, 160, 167, 174, 180, 189–90, 192, 195–96, 202, 205–7, 212, 223, 225–26, 237–38, 241, 250, 253–55, 266, 276–77, 280–82, 285, 310–13, 315, 320–26, 333, 351, 371, 399, 404, 408–10, 412, 456–58
systemic thinking 62–63

tacit knowledge 88–89
Taibi, Mustapha 399–407
talking cure 33–34
Taoist 138
Taras, Vas 378–86
teachers 7, 34, 61, 90, 163, 165, 168, 206, 375, 440, 445, 457, 460
teams 249, 257, 304, 318, 381, 402
teasing 450–51
technique 4, 10, 26, 33–35, 37, 39, 46, 60, 63, 87, 90, 165, 183–84, 237, 239–41, 245, 247, 269, 285–86, 331–33, 335–36
technological tools 68–70, 72
technology 38, 68–69, 72, 74, 105–7, 160–61, 288
Tel Aviv 136
telos 413
temporal orientation 138–42
ten Thije, Jan D. 301–9
thematic knowledge 425, 428, 430
theoreticians 7
theory building 7, 12

therapeutic 46, 286; model of mediation 240
thinking 51, 60–61, 169, 207, 370
thirdness 6, 201–8
third party 8, 24–25, 27, 33, 35, 37, 39, 57, 59, 68, 97, 105–6, 109–11, 114–17, 120–25, 192, 194, 223, 237, 249, 269, 277–81, 310–13, 316, 318, 340, 351, 387–88, 411, 436; intervention 59, 114–15, 120–23, 125, 278, 436; involvement 119–25, 279; mediators 105, 192, 223, 279; neutral 33; ostracized 311–12, 314
third person 6, 12, 173–74, 373, 438
third space 10, 201–8, 229, 310
Thomas, Marc-Simon 265–74
three-sided football 317–18
TikTok 207, 429
time 2–3, 8–11, 13, 23–26, 33–35, 37–38, 44, 53–54, 59, 67–73, 77, 87, 95–96, 104, 107–8, 110, 116, 131–32, 136, 138–39, 142, 147, 149–51, 157, 161, 163, 165–66, 174, 176, 181, 184, 186–87, 189–90, 194, 204–5, 208, 221, 223, 230, 234–35, 239, 241, 248–50, 254, 257, 268, 275–77, 281, 284–87, 289, 292, 294, 304, 306, 313, 316, 318, 322, 332–33, 343, 353, 374, 384, 391, 403–4, 409, 412–13, 417, 426, 428–29, 439, 442–43, 448–49, 460, 465
Ting-Toomey, Stella 8–9, 23, 32, 36, 59, 69, 71, 254, 322, 378
Tint, Barbara 136–44
togetherness 107, 148
tolerance of ambiguity 435
toolbox 140
track one 105, 109, 131
track three 105
track two 105, 108–9, 131
tradition 2, 4, 7, 14, 27, 37, 54, 98, 114, 117, 139, 169, 172, 178, 181, 192–94, 203, 210, 238–39, 266, 277, 350, 401, 464
traditions; cultural 54, 172
trainers 26, 63, 194
training 7, 26, 28, 30, 32–35, 38, 54, 59–64, 68, 80–81, 86, 88, 97–98, 117, 156–57, 161, 165, 194, 224, 230, 233, 245–46, 279, 285, 303, 305–6, 322, 360, 384–85, 417, 419; programs 157, 224, 417; special 80, 456
transactional practice 451–52, 465
transcendence in conflict cultures 183
transcreation 413
transcultural 61, 63, 166, 173, 239, 408, 446
transfer approach 303, 305, 411
transformation, humane 256
transformative 4, 9, 14, 33, 36, 112, 121, 123, 188, 255, 269, 325, 466–69; mediation 9, 123, 324; relaying 321, 325
transforming 11, 122, 180–88, 323, 451, 467
transitional space 133
translanguage 445, 447, 449
translanguaging 445–47, 445–52, 456–57, 456–57, 461; moment 457; neurolinguistic 445
translation 4, 6, 14, 37, 61, 88, 168, 220, 224, 226,

241, 245, 253, 284–90, 303, 332, 378, 396, 399–406, 408–13, 416, 423–31, 436, 442–43, 445, 456, 458; studies 1, 6, 220, 399, 408, 423, 435
translator 5–6, 34, 36, 167, 332, 351, 399–401, 403–6, 409–13, 416, 423–24, 426–30, 436
translingual practice 446, 451
transparency 33, 311
triad 1–2, 6, 87, 310, 312–13, 315–17
triadic 1, 6, 11, 13, 68, 77–83, 87, 210–17, 269–70, 310, 313–14, 316–18, 460–61
triadology 310–18
triadomania 310
trial 269–70
triolectics 318
trust 36, 56–57, 67, 70–72, 78, 80–83, 104, 107, 122, 125, 129, 132, 155, 168, 279, 317, 362, 372, 420, 423
trustworthiness 176
Truth and Reconciliation Commission 35
Tsuchiya, Keiko 445–54
Turkish 61, 81, 175, 297, 332
turn 409, 423; taking 241, 332–33, 342, 402
Tuso, Hamdesa 189–97

the UK 32, 34, 149
Ukrainian peace discourses 99
UN 97–98, 104–5, 107–9, 114, 128, 424
unacknowledged polysemy 351
unbiased 25, 35, 178, 255, 288
uncertainty avoidance 31, 379–84, 379–84
uncompensated work 157, 161
underrepresented 54–57, 80
understanding 1–2, 4, 6, 8–10, 12–13, 26, 32–33, 36–39, 43–44, 47, 53–54, 56, 61–62, 69, 71, 77, 80–81, 88, 95–96, 99–100, 104–9, 111–15, 121–22, 128–29, 131, 136–41, 145, 148, 156, 158–60, 163–64, 166–68, 172–77, 183, 186, 190, 201, 203, 210–11, 213–14, 220–21, 223–24, 227, 237–40, 242–43, 247, 253–58, 265–66, 268, 270, 276–77, 282, 284–87, 289, 294–96, 304–6, 314, 316, 320–26, 331, 333–34, 337–38, 347, 349–54, 358–60, 369–70, 373–74, 378, 387, 393, 400, 402, 404, 406, 408, 410–11, 413, 420, 431, 437, 442–44, 450–52, 457–60, 464–67, 469; common 164, 190, 351; of culture 4, 96, 247; empathic 223; hegemonic 203; in-depth 107, 109; of intercultural mediation 95, 201, 321, 323, 325; intersubjective 333, 337; microanalytical 276; power 112, 115; shared 96, 211, 333, 359, 373, 457, 466; sustainable 77; traditional 270
United Kingdom 146–47, 455
United Nations 97–98, 107, 113
United States 3–4, 26, 34, 39, 51–53, 56, 71, 97, 119, 139, 150, 155, 157, 165, 189, 193–94, 194, 241, 246, 255, 265, 268, 279, 281, 285, 292, 294–95, 295, 360, 402, 455, 464
universal credentials 157

universalism 166–67, 277, 322, 325–26; of mediation 322
universality 23, 32, 98
universal problem solving 184
unobtrusive mediation 149
unsolvable 379
unstoried experiences 324
urban locality, changing 148
Ury, William 3, 8, 12, 23–27, 32, 43, 142, 191–93, 195, 234, 322
Useem, John 206–7
Useem, Ruth 202
use of culture 98, 430

values 3–5, 24, 27–28, 31, 38, 48, 53, 56–57, 60, 62, 64, 68, 72, 78, 82, 89–90, 95–96, 98, 100, 111, 116, 122, 125, 137–39, 151, 156, 158–59, 161, 163, 166, 178, 180, 182–85, 188, 191–93, 195, 201–3, 207, 215, 233–34, 237, 239–40, 242, 255, 258, 275, 277–78, 280, 282, 284–86, 288, 293–94, 298, 324, 331, 334, 338, 350, 353, 358–59, 364, 369, 371, 373–75, 378–85, 389, 391, 404, 408–10, 412, 417–18, 420, 424, 430, 437, 456, 460; of anthropology 285; basic 31; civic 207; clashes 95; conflicts 3; equal 90; human 62; judgments 350; moral 424; non-negotiable 96, 99; orientations 378, 381, 383–84; religious 334; sacred 96; significant 215; symbolic 100; systems 31, 56; universal 293
vandalism 437, 440
variation 7, 13, 68, 73, 112, 276, 280
variations; cross-cultural 280; intragroup 241, 281
Vasilyeva, Alena L. 237–44
veridical 30
verification 176, 371
victim(s) 45, 46, 78, 90, 141, 185, 234, 297, 314, 388–394, 396
victimhood 141
victim offender mediation (VOM) 44
victim scenarios 388–89, 391, 393
Victim Services 53
videoconferencing 68, 71–73
Viet Nam Paris Agreement 37
violence 30, 39, 79, 91, 96–97, 99, 112, 120, 128, 136, 150, 165, 190–92, 191–92, 195–96, 222–23, 223, 226, 230, 241, 285–90, 297–98, 298, 310–12, 310–12, 344, 439; domestic 439; physical 79, 344; self-perpetuating 97; structural 241–42, 288–89; symbolic 230
violent conflicts 96–98, 226
virtual diplomacy 105–6
virtualization 104, 106, 108–9
virtualizing meetings 105
virtual mediation 105, 107–8, 110, 160
virtual meetings 105–10
visions 1–14, 164, 287, 399, 409, 468
visitor text 146, 150–51

Index

vocal expression 296
Vogt, Catharina 77–84
Volpe, Maria R. 155–62
volunteerism 157
volunteers 33, 53, 147, 157, 240, 246, 254, 360; mediators 53, 157, 360; work 157
Vygotskyan 220, 412, 467–68
Vygotsky, Lev S. 220, 412, 458, 467–68

Wadensjö, Cecilia 400, 405, 411
Wagner, Manuela 435–44
Wallensteen, Peter 108
Wall, James A. 3, 31, 59, 119, 121, 123, 239–40, 379
Wang, Jiayi 423–32
Watson-Gegeo, Karen Ann 7
web of culture 409
welfare 146, 295–96, 461
Weltanschauung 163, 166
the West 28, 189, 193–94, 232–35
West as steward discourse 235
Western 1–4, 7, 11, 13–14, 23–29, 31, 33, 36–37, 39, 56, 63, 68, 117, 119, 130, 140, 142, 164, 172–73, 190, 192–95, 229, 232–34, 239–40, 245, 268, 271, 292–93, 405, 409, 412, 459; cultures 239–40; model 13, 26–28; societies 2, 11, 192, 293, 459; values 24, 193, 240
White, Geoffrey M. 7
Williams, Raymond 53, 70
Winslade, John 9, 12, 43, 47–48, 121, 123, 321, 324–25
win-win 78, 193, 265, 269, 271, 379–80
wisatah 174
wisdom 24, 158, 176–77
witnessing 45, 163, 389
women 105–6, 149–50, 185, 221, 231–32, 234, 267, 281, 345, 438–40

work, cultural 324
workgroups 384
working class 30, 296
workmanship 139
workplaces 36, 51, 119, 122, 257; setting 230
workshops 56, 81, 116; on cultural humility 56
world; modern 173, 311; plurilingual 464; transcultural 408
world language; classroom 464–69; education 464–65, 467; learning 465
worldview; 13 45, 61, 68, 96, 113, 140, 194, 195, 220, 237, 240–242, 249, 251, 255, 258, 278, 281, 282, 286–290, 411–413, 424, 465, 466; analysis 286, 288–89; competing 288–89; conflict 286–87; conflicting 286; dominant 288; indigenous 195; translation 284–90
worldview analysis 286, 288–89; and translation 286, 289
worship 172, 175

Yemen 105, 107–8
Yokotsuka, Shino 51–58
young children 131
young people of Italian origin 168
youth, use of digital tools 109

Zartman, William 11, 174, 190, 285
Zborowski framework 296
Zhou, Ying 210–19
Zhu, Hua 12, 238–39, 301, 306, 340–42, 346–47, 359, 363
zones; comfort 159; complex cultural contact 459; multicultural contact 456
Zoom 68, 72, 133; mediation 68, 72, 133